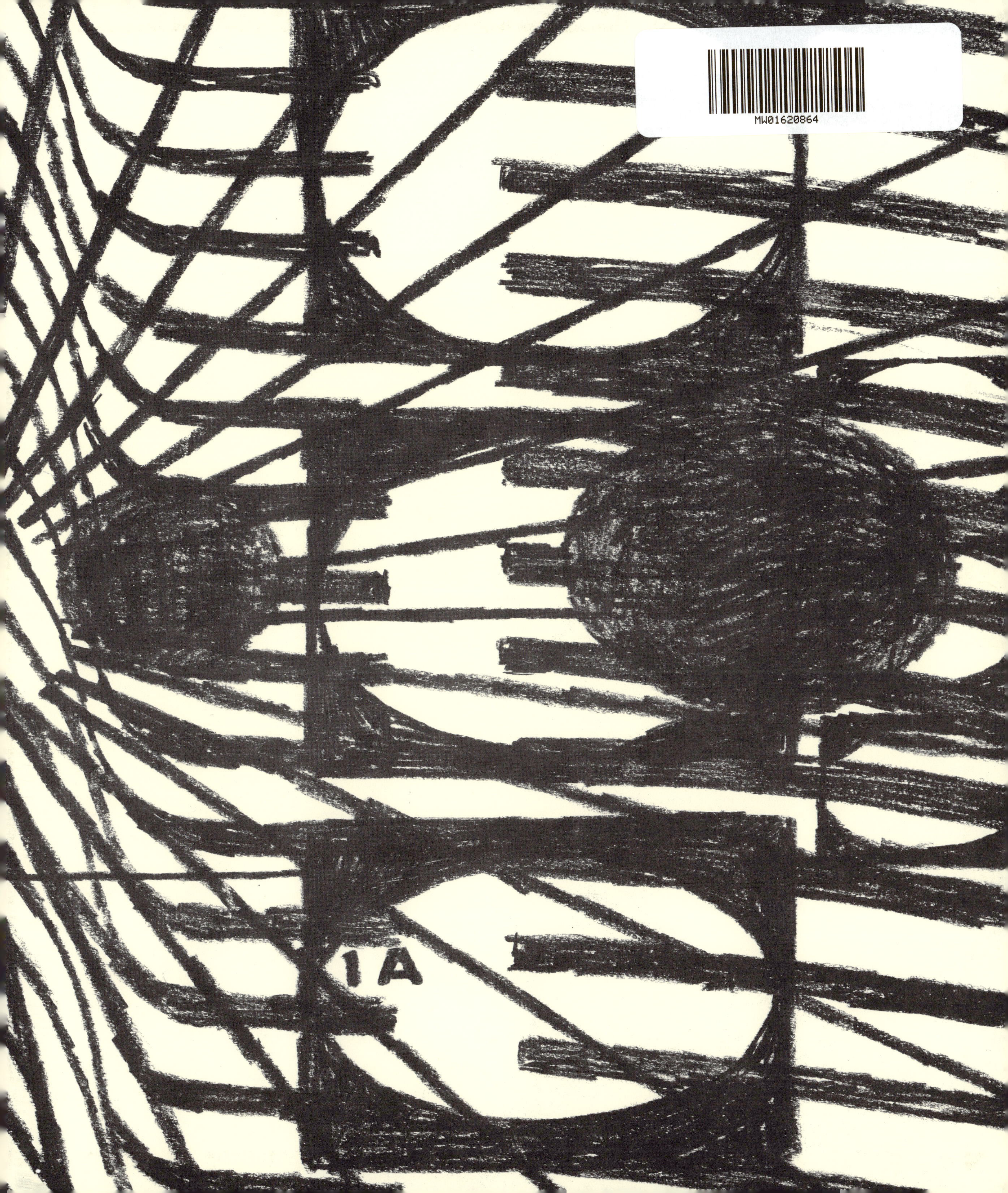
1A

Terry Winters
Paintings, Drawings, Prints
1994–2004

Terry Winters
Paintings, Drawings, Prints
1994–2004

Edited by
Adam D. Weinberg

Essays by
Richard Shiff
Rachel Teagle
Adam D. Weinberg

Published by
Yale University Press
New Haven and London
in association with the
Addison Gallery of American Art
Phillips Academy
Andover, Massachusetts

Terry Winters Paintings, Drawings, Prints 1994–2004
Organized by the Addison Gallery of American Art, Phillips Academy, Andover, Massachusetts

This exhibition and publication have been funded in part through generous donations from the Bertha and Isaac Liberman Foundation, The Fifth Floor Foundation, and the Harriet Ames Charitable Trust.

EXHIBITION DATES
Addison Gallery of American Art, Phillips Academy, Andover, Massachusetts
18 September 2004–2 January 2005

Museum of Contemporary Art San Diego, Downtown, San Diego, California
23 January–17 April 2005

Contemporary Arts Museum, Houston, Texas
30 April–10 July 2005

Published by Yale University Press in association with the Addison Gallery of American Art, Phillips Academy

Addison Gallery of American Art
Phillips Academy
180 Main Street
Andover, Massachusetts 01810
www.addisongallery.org

Yale University Press
302 Temple Street
P.O. Box 209040
New Haven, Connecticut 06520
www.yalebooks.com

Cover: Terry Winters, *Untitled*, 2004, graphite on paper, 22 3/8 x 30 1/8 in. (56.8 x 76.5 cm)
Endsheets: Terry Winters, *Untitled*, 2004, graphite on paper, 22 3/8 x 30 1/8 in. in. (56.8 x 76.5 cm)
Page 6: Terry Winters, *Rates of Change*, 2004, graphite on paper, 12 x 9 in. (30.5 x 22.9 cm)
All: Collection of the artist

Library of Congress Cataloging-in-Publication Data

Shiff, Richard.
Terry Winters : paintings, drawings, prints 1994/2004 / Richard Shiff, Rachel Teagle, Adam D. Weinberg ; edited by Adam D. Weinberg.
p. cm.
Catalog of an exhibition held at the Addison Gallery of American Art, Andover, Mass., at the Museum of Contemporary Art, San Diego, and at the Contemporary Arts Museum, Houston, Texas.
Includes bibliographical references and index.
ISBN 0-300-10456-1 (Yale) -- ISBN 1-879886-54-57 (Addison)
1. Winters, Terry--Exhibitions. I. Winters, Terry. II. Teagle, Rachel. III. Weinberg, Adam D. IV. Addison Gallery of American Art. V. Museum of Contemporary Art, San Diego. VI. Contemporary Arts Museum. VII. Title.

N6537.W5678A4 2004
760'.092--dc22
2004007719

ISBN: 0–300–10456–1 (Yale)
ISBN: 1–879886–54–57 (Addison)

Editor: Joseph N. Newland, Q.E.D.
Designer: 2x4, New York City
Printed and bound in China

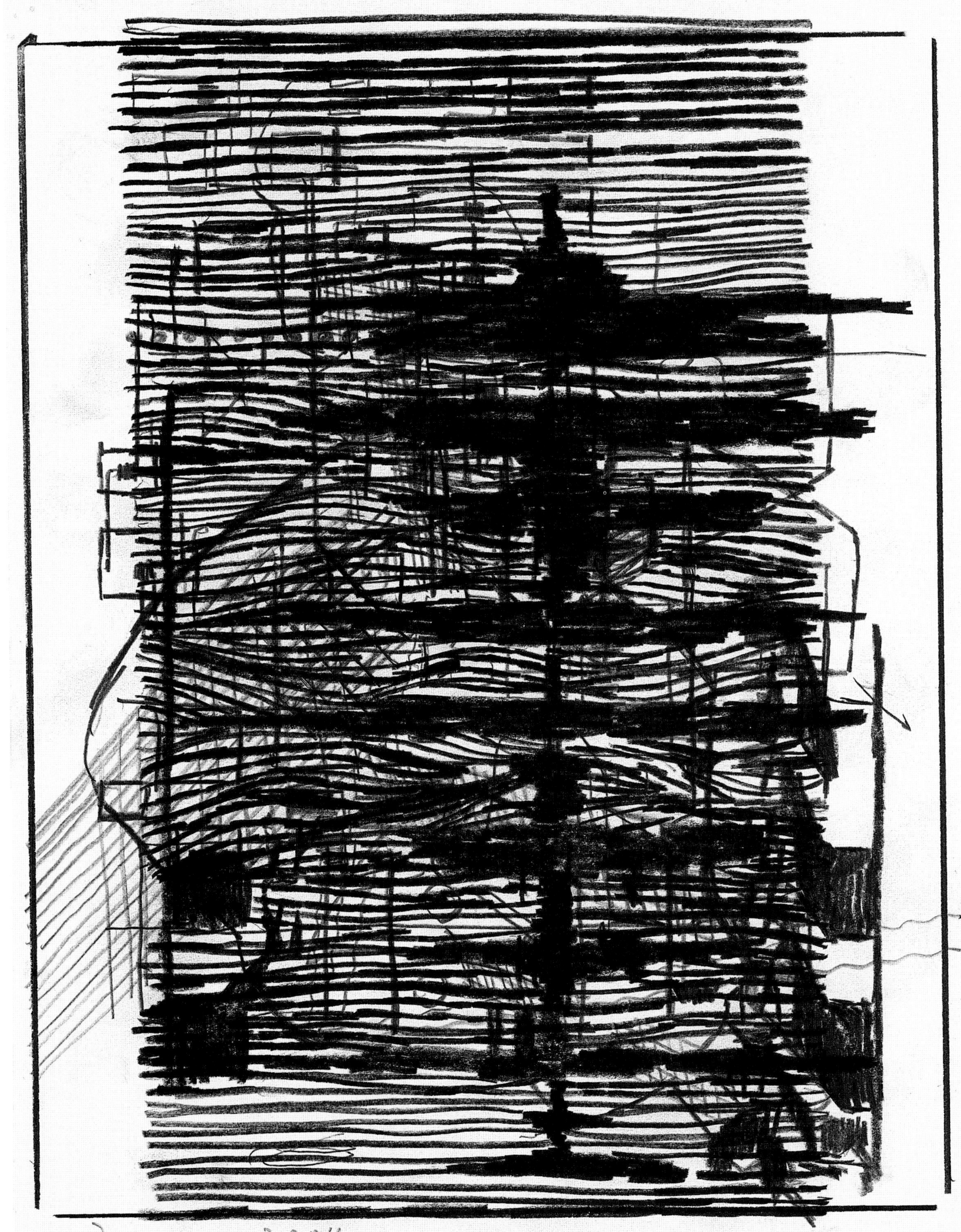
2004

FOREWORD

Terry Winters Paintings, Drawings, Prints 1994–2004 is the fortunate result of the fertile synergy of Adam Weinberg's enthusiasm and perseverance and Terry Winters's engagement and dedication. It has been a delight for me to witness this outstanding publication and accompanying exhibition come into being in Weinberg's and Winters's capable hands. As Interim Director at the Addison Gallery, I acknowledge not only the debt we owe to artist and curator but also join the exhibition curator in offering grateful thanks to all those on the Addison staff who have toiled to bring this project to a happy completion. At the Addison, Curatorial Associate Juliann McDonough and Charles H. Sawyer Curatorial Fellow Emily Shubert, as well as former Administrative Assistant Jenna Signore, ably juggled the myriad details necessary to produce both the catalogue and the exhibition. Leslie Maloney, Chief Preparator, and Denise Johnson, Registrar, also have been critical contributors, the former with exhibition design, and the latter with assembling loans and preparing the tour of the exhibition.

The Addison offers special thanks to the many lenders to the traveling exhibition. They have been remarkably generous despite the fact that lending has left large spaces on their walls both literally and metaphorically. We hope the pleasure of experiencing this extraordinary exhibition and the knowledge of how important their contribution has been for this project will sustain them. We are also grateful to funders whose commitment to Terry Winters's vision and to this exhibition has been longstanding. Steven and Ann Ames are lovers of painting who understand that supporting a painter's work at midcareer benefits both the artist and the public at large. When asked for help, they immediately and generously committed major support to the exhibition and catalogue. Jeffrey Klein, representing the Louis and Bessie Adler Foundation, Inc., has considered this to be an important project from the beginning. We deeply appreciate the generosity and vote of confidence that his support and that of the Adler Foundation represent. We also are honored by Wynn Kramarsky's encouragement and interest in the Addison's efforts and offer special thanks for his support of this exhibition.

Susan C. Faxon
Interim Director and Curator of Art Before 1950

ACKNOWLEDGMENTS

When I became director of the Addison Gallery in 1999, one of the first exhibitions I sought to curate was of Terry Winters's work. Winters was intrigued and enthusiastic about the idea. I suggested working collaboratively with him to organize an exhibition that would provide an overview of his art since his midcareer survey of 1991–92 organized by the Whitney Museum. Although there have been numerous exhibitions that focused on different bodies of work both in the United States and abroad, there has not been an exhibition that revealed the larger trajectory of his output in all media and the unique way in which his paintings, drawings, prints, and books feed one another. Over the course of the last few years, Winters and I have discussed, argued about, and refined the selection of works, the sections of the exhibition, and, most importantly, the starting point of the exhibition. While the curatorial process has been a dialogue with the artist, the structure, conception, and final selection were mine. Yet I know that the exhibition has been greatly enhanced by our dialectic. Winters has been a most generous partner in this process, always allowing one more studio visit to reconsider a work or an idea. I feel fortunate not only to have had such an intimate and prolonged exposure to the work but also to have benefited from the artist's insights about art in general. I am deeply grateful for his support, patience, and friendship. This exhibition is a fitting culmination to my tenure as director at the Addison Gallery.

There is a small group of individuals, the Winters SWAT team, who have assiduously and tirelessly worked to assure that we left no stone unturned, no detail unattended to. First of all, we offer our great appreciation to Hendel Teicher, who has encouraged and supported this project from its inception. Winters's stalwart assistants, Hillary Harp, Jack Warren, and, especially, Jen Nelson, prepared endless checklists, tracked down images, researched, and undertook many critical tasks hidden from public view. The exhibition could not have occurred had it not been for the efforts and advice of Matthew Marks and Jill Sussman, Director, of the Matthew Marks Gallery, in New York. Throughout this long process they provided easy access to work and assisted with key loans. Sabrina Buell, also of the gallery, helped with numerous organizational details. I am also indebted to Barbara Krakow, of Barbara Krakow Gallery in Boston, whose early enthusiasm for this exhibition and long-term support of Winters's work encouraged me in my efforts to pursue this project.

To Richard Shiff and Rachel Teagle, coauthors on this volume, I am deeply appreciative both for their insightful texts that taught me things about Winters's work—which I thought I knew so well—and also for the conversations that helped inform the shape and direction of the exhibition itself. It is rare that a group of authors have the opportunity to work collaboratively with an artist to shape a book conceptually. The visual form of the book is due to the outstanding talents of Susan Sellers of 2x4, whose sensitivity toward and understanding of the artist's work is profound, and who was assisted by Jiminie Ha. Editor Joseph N. Newland of Q.E.D. once again lent his well-honed editorial insights to the process. Yale University Press and their Art and Architecture Publisher Patricia J. Fidler are exemplary new publishing partners.

I would like to express my gratitude to Susan Faxon for her partnership during my years at the Addison and most recently for guiding this exhibition to fruition. To the staff at the Addison, whose professionalism, attention to detail, and love of working with artists is second to none, I am so grateful. I would also like to offer heartfelt thanks to Steven and Ann Ames for their early and enthusiastic support of this exhibition. And, I convey my appreciation to Jeffrey Klein, representing the Louis and Bessie Adler Foundation, Inc., who has long been a fan of Terry Winters's art.

In the end, every exhibition is an act of faith. I am deeply grateful to everyone—staff, lenders, dealers, and funders—for their faith in me, and especially to Terry Winters.

Adam D. Weinberg
Guest Curator
The Mary Stripp and R. Crosby Kemper Director,
Addison Gallery of American Art, 1999–2003

ADAM D. WEINBERG

Introduction

All systems for defining models are in a sense equal.
Félix Guattari

Terry Winters came of age at the height of Minimalism, post-Minimalism, and Process art of the late 1960s and '70s. His art, particularly before 1990, bears many of the concerns of late modernism. Winters's work of the last decade reveals an artist who has woven these disparate strains of idea, object, and physical process into the primary logic of his art. His aesthetic embraces multiplicity and simultaneity, and addresses overlapping systems and the slippage between them. Functioning as direct records of personal expression, they are also fully constructed metaobjects, self-critiquing images of phenomena or events based on intuitive systemic thinking. In his work of the 1970s and '80s Winters undertook an investigation of the structures of natural forms. This engagement later extended to a preoccupation with process as manifested in architecture, cognitive science, and information technology. For Winters, abstract art became a vehicle not for "reproducing or inventing form but for harnessing forces." By utilizing expressive means, "data becomes pictorial and spatial"; information and process are the image.

This exhibition presents a decade of Winters's interdependent work, encompassing paintings, drawings, prints, and artist books. It reveals the ways in which the artist creates sets and subsets of distinctive works that interact with bodies of previous and other current work. Topological and coextensive, these aggregate bodies of works constitute a world apprehended from diverse, yet connected, viewpoints.

Winters's art couples theoretical and speculative approaches with the physical experience of mark-making. Each work involves a sensuous materiality of surface combined with cognitive schemata that appeal to the intellect. His art contains an astounding array of forms: sinuous, undulating, halting, fluid, and crisp. The surfaces range from delicate rivulets—skeins and pools of ink on various papers—to tangled and thickly impastoed layers of oil on linen. His color sense is equally varied, from subtle shifts in monochrome to chromatic "chords" of both complementary and discordant hues that generate fresh visual harmonics. For Winters, "Painting is a way of thinking. Ideas are created through the manipulation of materials and images—new assemblages of sensations are constructed. Intuition is a method, indeterminate but exacting."

The diversity of Winters's images reflects his working methods. Since the early 1980s he has used printmaking, drawing, and painting in equal measure, often in the same period or phase. Sometimes prints lead into drawings or vice versa, and either might lead to paintings, which in turn often lead back to works on paper. This interlocking relationship of media parallels the complexity of the bodies of works themselves. The prints and drawings are often produced in series, with the number in a given suite ranging from three to one hundred images. There are also numerous large-scale, mixed-media works on paper that blur the distinction between drawing and painting. The paintings exhibit a density and physicality that echoes and builds upon the works on paper.

This exhibition presents seven groupings: Foundations and Systems 1994; Computation of Chains 1995–1998; Graphic Primitives 1998; Location Plan 1999; Set Diagram 2000–2002; Meshworks 1999–2002; and Turbulence Skins 2002–2004. Although the titles of these groups are taken from specific series, they also embrace larger thematic concerns. And, while works in a given series share certain visual and conceptual characteristics, as one might expect, ideas often migrate and inflect those of another.

FOUNDATIONS AND SYSTEMS 1994

In 1992, upon completion of his midcareer survey at the Whitney Museum, Winters began an intense period of production and made more than a dozen major cycles of drawings over a two-year period. Expanding his investigations into generative forms, the artist considered his own working methods to be intricately connected to these processes. This shift revealed itself as a move from more or less discrete object-forms to a newfound immersion in form as field. In drawings that seem to metamorphose before our eyes, the subjects are not so much represented as they are the capturing of multiple forces in the act of becoming.

In 1994–95 Winters produced a cycle of fifty drawings (plus title page) called *Foundations and Systems*. As the title suggests, they offer a platform and structure from which to build. The soft, small-scale, graphite drawings of this series in effect represent a humble manifesto, which in the words of Michael Semff "affirm the objectification of a condition." In 1994 Winters also produced *Tenon's Capsule 1–6*, a tour-de-force series of large-scale works on paper that reveal the new complexity of his art "packed" into six interrelated yet self-contained pieces. Given the boldness of these objects, one is tempted to suggest that they are the culmination of the Foundations and Systems. In fact, they are simultaneous expressions of emancipation in which the intensity of saturated whites and blacks in four media—charcoal, graphite, ink, and acrylic—create multiple surface textures that are at once inchoate trajectories and fully realized forms. The *Tenon's Capsule* works serve as a keynote for the exhibition.

COMPUTATION OF CHAINS 1995–1998

In 1995 Winters embarked on an expansive 125-image series of ink drawings just over eight by eleven inches each, which he "composed from different sources—architectural renderings, medical photographs, and computer graphics." The *Computation of Chains* drawings and subsequent paintings such as *Computational Architecture*, 1995, and *Image Location*, 1997, provide an explosion of information—great pulsating blasts of schematic data. While the *Foundations and Systems* drawings generally retain an emotional interiority and sense of enclosure, in the *Computation* series the field becomes a "screen" on which layer upon layer of grid-like energies reverberate outward, edge to edge. The colors of the paintings tend toward primary hues of striking brilliance when compared with the earth tones of Winters's earlier work. In large vertical drawings such as *Scene Generation*, 1997, *Connected Slice*, 1996, and *Multi-Form Visualization*, 1996, networks of lines and submerged structures build upward and suggest the architectonic. Furthermore, each projects a different spatial model: the first a brilliant, allover layered structure; the second an embedded interior/exterior chamber; and the third a multipartite armature. The building of strata further evolved in the intaglio prints *Set of Ten* that are part of the artist book *Perfection, Way, Origin*, 2001, which includes a text by the literary critic Jean Starobinski in a convergence of language and image. Each print is broken into a tripartite structure, which causes them to be read concurrently as vertical and horizontal works and—seen as a group—shifting, animated cells.

GRAPHIC PRIMITIVES 1998

Graphic Primitives consists of nine black-and-white wood cuts that parallel a series of nine paintings of the same name. Lineal descendants of the *Computation of Chains* drawings, the *Graphic Primitives* tend toward containment within their cellular units rather than expansion into an allover field. Resembling circuits rather than networks, the movement is localized, not dispersed. The woodblocks for the *Graphic Primitives* prints were incised by laser using information entered and manipulated by the artist in a computer graphics program. The regularity of the line standardized these remote-controlled images even as the forms themselves were generated gesturally. As John Rajchman wrote, the *Graphic Primitives* prints and the subsequent paintings reflect "the interferences of painting with computer-generated images, rather as if our brains had moved into a space that no longer belongs to either." These hybrid images conjoin the natural and the synthetic, variously recalling urban grids, insect wings, circuit boards, spiderwebs, and radar screens. Winters's interest is in diagramming the new mental spaces created through the merging of technological, architectural, and biological forms.

While suggesting similar sources, paintings such as the *Graphic Primitives* have a density, expressiveness, and chromatic richness that expand one's reading of the prints. A bifurcation of the image exposed in the *Graphic Primitives* is especially pronounced in related oils such as *Color and Information*, 1998. This fissure, a visual analogue to the cerebral hemispheres, not only represents a challenge to a unified perspective but also, implicitly, to the notion of the unity of knowledge. A critical work of this period, *Gray-Scale Image*, 1998, plays off the tonalities of the prints while exploiting the processes of painting. The unity of this work is purposely undermined through the disassembling and dissolving of the form into individual molten units.

LOCATION PLAN 1999

Winters's *Location Plan* works derive from a commission for the Trisha Brown Dance Company for which the artist conceived the visual presentation and designed the costumes. Begun in 1999 with *Five Part Weather Invention*, the commission grew into *El Trilogy*, 1999–2001, a total of three choreographic sections and two solo interludes. The stark black-and-white lattices, arcs, and scripts of the drawing *Linking Graphics, 1*, were translated into a theater-scale backdrop for the first section. The dancers move in front of and in relation to the image, which at times serves as a counterpoint to the mostly bright-colored costumes in yellow, red, and cyan, and gray. The costumes are also linked to a color bar and gray scale reproduced at the top of the backdrop. At other times the lighting renders the dancers' silhouettes as if moving elements of the drawing itself.

The thirty ink-on-vellum *Location Plan* drawings are themselves "maps" of transitional states. As a result, these images appear to be "instants" in flux, and each drawing in the series modifies the terms of every other drawing. The optically energizing, horizontal bands that dominate these works resemble magnifications of the linear units that constitute electronically transmitted visual data. For the third section of *El Trilogy*, Winters created a backdrop using a grid (four images by six images) of selected *Location Plan* drawings. The dancers—themselves moving, linear units—parallel the individual cells of the drawings. As Winters has said, "From the spectacular to the vernacular, Trisha Brown has mapped a complexity of sensations through the use of open-ended narrations. Her story lines trace emotional states far from equilibrium yet somehow perfectly balanced." The oils of this group, such as *Blue Diagram* and *Graph of Curves*, both 1999, retain the oscillating energies of the drawings while reaching a state of repose. Among the drawings, shifts occur as much from image to image as within each image itself. In the oils, fluctuations and permutations emanate from layers, lines, and accretions of pigment.

SET DIAGRAM 2000–2002

Set Diagram, a group of one hundred paintings, each measuring one yard by one meter, refers to a technical term used for visual representations of two or more sets of information. Within Winters's larger oeuvre, these oils function as drawings—works small enough for ideas to be generated and executed relatively rapidly. Winters began with the premise that each canvas in this extended series was a singular object with its own rules, not a part of a unified set with related imagery. Composed of a wide range of structures, elements, and colors they are individual painted diagrams that collectively define a mutable pictorial space. Conceived as building blocks to be assembled in variable configurations, *Set Diagram* creates a community of works, in effect a social space. Sixty of these paintings were initially exhibited in a site-specific gallery installation designed with the Dutch architect Rem Koolhaas. Dynamically distributed across one long wall, paintings hung singly and in groups, from floor to ceiling, and even on the ceiling. With a desire to fashion an environment of painted forms, Winters took his cue from early twentieth-century abstraction, Russian Constructivism, and Dutch de Stijl as well as the architectural aspirations of later modernists such as Frederick Kiesler and Ray and Charles Eames.

MESHWORKS 1999–2002

While the *Set Diagram* canvases literally construct a space, the twenty large-scale graphite drawings of the Meshworks series each describe a space through whorls and waves of parallel lines that bend and coil. Compared with the *Set Diagram* paintings, this body of work constitutes a more focused investigation in which the complex spaces described are "suggestive of the interconnected geographies of computer networks as well as the synaptic connections of brain space." The overlaying of twisting spirals on a ground of parallel lines implies graphing and measurement, while the torqued forms suggest computer modeling of "real" phenomena in a virtual realm where time and space become indistinguishable. The idea of modeling, first introduced in his 1994 print series *Models for Synthetic Pictures*, has increasingly become a preoccupation of Winters's work. In addition to the large drawings and two monumental prints, this section includes several large-scale oils, among them *Functions, Vectors, and Speeds*, 2001, and *Luminance*, 2002, which both bristle with the energies of layers and linear meshes.

TURBULENCE SKINS 2002–2004

In 2002 Winters made a series of modestly scaled, fourteen-by-eleven-inch graphite on vellum drawings, which most recently have become the basis for a set of prints with text by Ben Marcus. The *Turbulence Skins* drawings, which all told number forty-two are, according to the artist, about "mapping changes in intensity." These drawings seem to describe unperceivable phenomena in space. They are records of unpredictability and open-endedness, as if an incident were in the process of coalescing or dissipating. When one considers the definition of turbulence as "irregular atmospheric phenomena," the drawings are aptly titled. In some, one is particularly struck by the placement of the forms on the sheet—in number 22, for example, the image seems to be shifting in or out of view as if on a screen—while others, such as number 32, seem to offer a partial (read "less than optimum") view. Drawings such as this refer to what is unseeable, to the ineffable.

Shortly after the *Turbulence Skins* drawings, the artist produced seven mammoth vertical *Boundary Layers* drawings. These tend to complicate matters through superimposition, stacking, and hybridization of seemingly conflicting visual languages. They stress multiplicity and disjunction. Despite their heterogeneity, the *Boundary Layers* somehow, miraculously, reach a state of détente. This sensibility is most fully explored in the *Standardgraph* paintings. Going well beyond the decades-old modernist struggle between two- and three-dimensional representation, works such as *Standardgraph/3*, 2003, appear to have zones that one sees and senses—creating what seems to be irreconcilable spatial warps. Rifts, fissures, and dislocations undermine the ground of the painting and the viewer's ground. Throughout Winters's work, the role and use of drawing has been a complicated one. In recent years, particularly in *Set Diagram*, he has tested the idea of making paintings function more like drawings—using a standard, small-scale format, producing them more rapidly, and allowing each one to dictate its own terms. Contemporary painting is sometimes thought of as an amalgamation of mark-making and a set of ideas where each work in a series builds on a previous one until a conception has reached a certain degree of resolution. This is a strategy Winters continues to pursue in the *Standardgraphs*. But, what if one were to treat large-scale paintings not as a series but as unique creations where each one is a complete, independent, visual idea yet linked to a larger conceptual constellation where multiple strategies are simultaneously in operation? In Winters's recent canvases such as *Untitled (Red)*, *Untitled (Violet)*, *Untitled*, and *Scale*, all of 2003, we seem to discover that he has reached an intersection with two (at least) different strategies at play. What happens when these disparate systems play themselves out over the entire body of his work? As with all of Terry Winters's art, process will lead to revelation—over time.

RICHARD SHIFF

Manual Imagination

At each instant, our present infinitely contracts our past.... What, in fact, is a sensation? It is the operation of contracting trillions of vibrations onto a receptive surface. Quality emerges from this, quality that is nothing other than contracted quantity.... There is a correlation between life and matter, between expansion [material quantity] and contraction [living quality].
Gilles Deleuze[1]

Something is being described through the work itself, through a kind of manual imagination. There are people who can make theoretical constructions.... But I'm painting pictures.... I can't step outside that process and construct an objective account of the pictures.... The paintings are ... projections, they take me places.
Terry Winters[2]

By projection, an artist gets from here to there and beyond, somewhere. "Paintings take me places," Terry Winters says, pondering the passive consequence of his active creativity. Projection, whether mechanically with a lens or imaginatively with a picture, expands contracted sensation in the form of an image, in time as much as in space, giving sensation a sense of direction.[3] Where projective painting actually leads is not something Winters believes he fully controls. Despite his expertise, his application of "manual imagination" is more bodily intuition than technical know-how. He looks to his art for "a visualization or actualization of the virtual... an expanded picture of the unconscious."[4] This notion of a pictorial unconscious has its complications: on the one hand, painting offers access to the unconscious, an exposure; on the other hand, it brings material extension to whatever area of the unconscious it enters. What is exposed does not remain untouched, unaltered. Painting invents the unconscious, finding it and making it in a single movement.[5]

Winters frequently refers to expansion, extension, projection, multiple dimensions, the virtual, the actual; and he seems ambivalent concerning the use of active or passive voice to describe an artist's experience, as if painting could never secure this distinction.[6] He is too consistent about all of this for it to be dismissed as quirky. Recently, his predilections may have received a boost in motivation. In the mid-1990s he discovered the philosophical writings of Gilles Deleuze, which had the uncanny effect of showing him virtual realities and imaginative places he had already visited.[7] If Winters's painting was picturing the unconscious, then Deleuze was writing it. Until his death in 1995, he was prominent among those intellectual explorers who "make theoretical constructions"—an alternative means of projection that affords entry into the same places artists go. Deleuze's discursive prose fails to terminate in the structured understanding that philosophical argument ordinarily aims to establish. To Winters, this was no shortcoming. He never expected to receive from Deleuze or any other writer a definitive, "objective account" of the experience of painting. Instead, when reading Deleuze, he recognized a painter-to-writer affinity, confirmed by the sense of an artist-to-artist bond.

INFLECT

Deleuzean theory turns from vertical, "arborescent" hierarchies of value to move within a horizontal, "rhizomatic" system of multidirectional exchange: "The rhizome connects any point to any other point.... A rhizome has no beginning or end; it is always in the middle."[8] Many roots turning every which way are better than one privileged, radical source, Deleuze argued, expressing an ideological orientation hardly unusual among intellectuals of his generation. Yet, to attribute a particular orientation to Deleuze runs counter to his attitude. He would prefer to speak of an "assemblage" of ideas by multiple links and overlaps, a pattern of thought by no means as orderly as an ideology, a politics, or a science.[9] To put it another way, his theory itself had a rhizomatic inflection. Perhaps this was only a bias, a bent, an inclination.

Theories, forms, thoughts, and sensations, all in communication (like people in conversation), inflect one another. The verb *inflect* signifies a movement—a turn, bend, or curve—that can be either a transitive or an intransitive action. Drawings have inflection, just as verbal statements do. An inflected line may seem to turn of its own accord, assuming its particular nature (intransitive inflection). Or it may appear to turn because of the effect of other lines in its vicinity, or because of some other feature of the context or medium (transitive inflection).

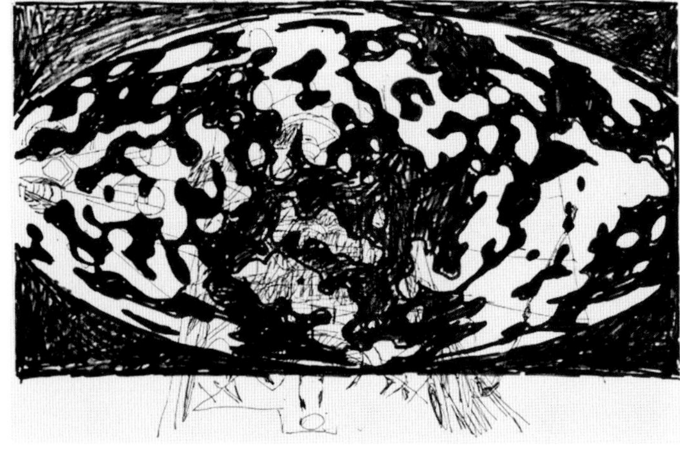

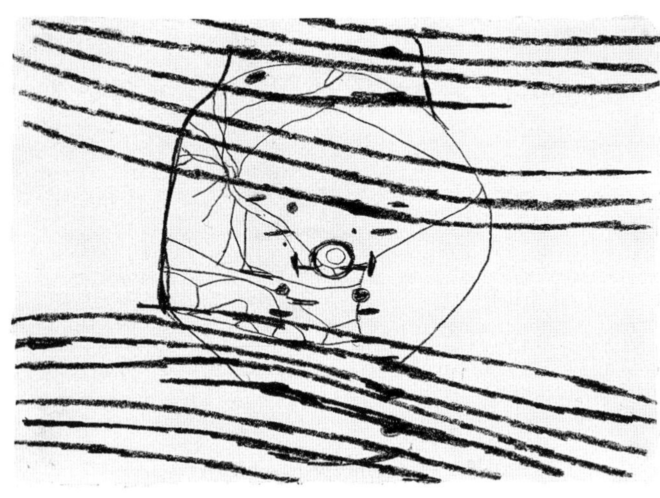

When a draftsman's strokes follow upon each other, bending to a collective rhythm as in the conventional representation of a wave, they may acquire this second sense of inflected movement. But with pattern or rhythm, we never know whether one line induces the next into the sequence, or, to the contrary, each is an independent iteration, revealing its character, which by a coincidence of influences takes a form closely resembling that of the neighboring lines. Winters is fascinated by diagrammatic lines that build into patterns, as in *Meshworks, 10*, 2000 (p. 116), or evolve into more complicated graphic motifs, as in *Location Plan, #28*, 1999. Such lines seem to join planar extension to volumetric dimension and lead the artist to the edge of his controlling and his being controlled. Winters inflects his line, but the nature of his drawing instrument and the character of his evolving surface of lines lends to that movement a different inflection—inflection upon inflection, active and passive, directions taken but not definitively.

Winters's line is a test of Deleuzean theory. This is not an idle observation. The conjecture is worth pursuing not only because of Winters's enthusiasm for Deleuze, but also because the painter has been involved with projects that link bodies of writing to graphic images. In these instances, text has not been used to explain image, nor has image been used to illustrate text; if so, we would be dealing with a condition of intellectual re-flection rather than with a more physical and emotional in-flection. Winters provided both image and text for two of his recent book projects, *Ocular Proofs*, 1995, and *Intersections and Animations*, 1999. He gleaned his textual material from notebooks recording his thoughts along with fragments of others' writings. For a third project, *Perfection, Way, Origin*, 2001, he collaborated with the literary scholar Jean Starobinski. The title of Starobinski's text made Winters "cringe a little" because his art is never so complete as to be perfected; and, although many of his images may have sources (for example, in medical illustration or computer graphics), they grow away from such origins rather than toward them.[10] Neither origin nor end is Winters's concern. Instead, he paints the rhizomatic middle term, the "way"—and painting in turn takes him places. Starobinski states that "every work ... is only a way.... It has no power to be

Terry Winters
Location Plan, #28, 1999
From a series of 30 drawings
Ink on vellum
11 1/2 x 16 3/8 in. (29.2 x 41.6 cm)
The Judith Rothschild Foundation, New York

Terry Winters
Crystal Lattice, 1994
Graphite on paper
10 7/8 x 14 3/4 in. (27.6 x 37.5 cm)
Private collection, courtesy of Galerie Fred Jahn, Munich

more than this movement."[11] Ways and movements are inflections of alternative ways and movements.

One of the Deleuzean ways that especially impressed Winters was the form of *A Thousand Plateaus*, which the philosopher co-authored with psychoanalyst Félix Guattari. They called the separate sections of their book "plateaus" rather than chapters, to suggest not only boundlessness but also the possibility of reading the sections in any sequence. They intended their book to lack "culmination and termination points, [for] a plateau is always in the middle, not at the beginning or the end ... plateaus that communicate with one another across microfissures, as in a brain."[12] Here, writing was mimicking living thought, rather than stabilizing a process of thought by imposing an order, which would be alien to a mind's meanders. Plateaus operate like the tissues of a brain or the layered renderings of a drafting process. Having shifted to one layer, the imaging process can move back again. Plateaus move thought along, complicating it like the successive screens of computer imaging or—more germane to the case of Winters—like the coats of paint and traces of graphite that record every moment of an artist's effort: "keep moving, even in place, never stop moving," write Deleuze and Guattari.[13] Plateaus are layers touching and inflecting other layers, limitlessly, just as the thinly drawn lines within *Location Plan, #28* interact with the thickened globular forms, the two incompatible configurations becoming at once obscured, opened, and energized. Because a plateau has neither privileged direction nor fixed order, no process assumes a satisfying end on its plane. A plateau keeps going; it gets somewhere, yet never to climax.[14]

To write plateaus (chapters without resolution) is to apply a theory, the Deleuze-Guattari theory. To cement their theory, the authors allowed an exception to it. They committed *A Thousand Plateaus* to a relatively conventional conclusion, "which," they advise, "should be read at the end."[15] In Winters's terms, any theory amounts to a "product of cognition," the kind of directed thinking that sets "boundaries" one would do better to be without. Certain features of *A Thousand Plateaus* do suggest that it results in a boundary statement: not only its summarizing conclusion, but also its numerous references to sources. It displays its citational credentials and argues with the authorities just like an academic text.[16] Before Winters became seriously involved with Deleuzean formulations, he had warned that a living world can have no firm ground in reference and no finite summation, because it has no real boundaries.[17] Neither does a plateau, Deleuze might have replied. A plateau leads everywhere. A summation of plateaus is not a total, nor an end or resolution, but a continuing, nonlinear series. The limitation that Deleuze's theory sets to thought can only be a no-boundary condition, a boundary permeable in its entirety.[18] The philosopher's conception parallels his notion that sensation is a contraction of lifeless physical matter, potentially encompassing everything, but (because living and therefore evolving) never in stable form. Deleuze's writing anchors thought and feeling no more securely than Winters's painting, which explodes living sensation into multiple layers of physical substance. Multiplicity is the painter's way. "Theories can be constricting," Winters warns, "and I want my paintings to remain open."[19] Deleuzean theory is the one he welcomes, an anti-theory with no effective closure.

SUBLIME

Winters has never shied away from showing signs of the effort he expends and the ambivalence he feels at every moment as he develops a canvas. The cause of ambivalence is experimentation: any given mark may succeed; any given mark may fail. One of his characteristic types of line, slightly jagged and seeming to retrace itself as it goes along—as in the arcing, horizontal bands of *Crystal Lattice*, 1994—manifests this double inclination, now forward, now backward, to the left, to the right, every way. Winters's line extends time as well as space, moving quickly and slowly at once. Its forms lead to others of related kinds, to relations not otherwise manifest. Life has its vicissitudes; our thoughts and emotions wander. And so must art.

By his own account, Winters attempts to make his marks as directly as possible, and often as speedily as possible. He wanders with determination. This is especially true of certain series that employ a fixed format of relatively modest dimensions, such as the 125 drawings titled

Computation of Chains, 1995/96, and the 100 paintings titled *Set Diagram*, 2000–2002. Each work in the latter series spans one meter by one yard, dimensions Winters selected because of their straightforward acceptance as culturally sanctioned and entirely conventional (that is, uninflected by personal choice).[20] Straightforwardness and dispatch nevertheless cannot guarantee direct results. Any contrary indication leading Winters to re-assess how a particular drawing or painting is developing is likely to end in half-obscured traces. Commitment to directness and speed prevents the artist from removing the record of his creative actions, however tentative they may be. But this practice has more than the liberating character of speed and the economy of expediency behind it. In the predominantly blue painting *Untitled* of 2003 (pp. 156–57), an underlying pattern of pink (or pink and blue) remains exposed. We have no immediate evidence that this exposure is anything other than innocent and unmotivated. The alternative is to regard this remnant of past moments in a chain of sensation as consciously displayed or unconsciously suppressed. Either of the latter responses would harness Winters's art to existing interpretive discourses of personal expression and set limits to his "projection"—where his art can go and the places it can take him, as well as us.[21] The effect of pictorial conflict or anomaly (the pink intrusion) is most evident toward the top edge of *Untitled*. Winters often works by layering one pattern of marks over another, without modifying the materiality of the initial layer, which might otherwise be done by scraping it down or smoothing it over. When Winters occludes a pattern of marks by simple superposition, the paradoxical result can be that they become all the more manifest, if only (as often happens) as a kind of embossing, a set of ridges and bumps that inflect the color and form of the uppermost layer, perhaps to appear at cross purposes with the image that finally emerges.

What finally emerges? Or rather, what finally emerges when we resist the typical interpretive ploy of exclusion, of referring to a picture as revealing something (its presumed subject) and suppressing most everything else, of promoting a position and refusing others? Consider *Parallel Rendering 1*, 1996 (p. 47). There curving strokes sometimes end abruptly as they intersect with other bars of color, yet they continue visually as an embossed ghost of a former presence. In another painter's work such an effect might detract from the primary pictorial theme, but for Winters it serves to remove a sense of dominance or singleness of purpose and to raise the level of sensory tension. The "pattern" in *Parallel Rendering 1* is decidedly hard to define, not an unusual condition of Winters's art. His designs are incompossibles. They move simultaneously in several directions, having multiple senses that make no (one) sense.[22] *Parallel Rendering 1* forms a grid, a mesh, a weave, a set of angles, a set of curves, a spiral, an ellipse and a rectangle, all in a glance. It is thick and thin, dense and airy. When one visual or tactile direction in the work becomes dominant, another intervenes, whether as opposition or merely as modification. Some of the shifts affect our spatial sense; some affect our temporal sense. Each of the many elements of pattern that constitute the one unruly diagram of Winters's painting is a sensory force that impacts on all others. By actively interfering and leaving traces of conflict (the ridges and bumps of a Winters oil painting), each element becomes as much like the others as it can be. The very fact of the material interference and physical contiguity causes all conceivable resemblance to become evident. Rectangles begin to circle, and the curving line goes straight. Yet this happens with every element retaining its material specificity. Interference—over which Winters might claim an unintended mastery—is that tenuous moment at which sameness and difference are equally evident as relational values, as mutual inflection.

Most often, interference in painting occurs when the general motifs and their constituent marks become independently apparent. Here Deleuze's term, and Winters's as well, is "asignifying." Asignifying marks are too assertive to be subordinate to a representational theme or any schematic figuration; they form a material abstraction that no abstract concept or referential sign can encompass.[23] At moments of interference, a viewer recognizes internal forces of change and conflict within the image.[24] At the right of *Untitled*, horizontal, smeary strokes fold white into blue to form a zone of coarse streaking. At the left, a more organized pattern of alternating blue and white bands, horizontals that slope

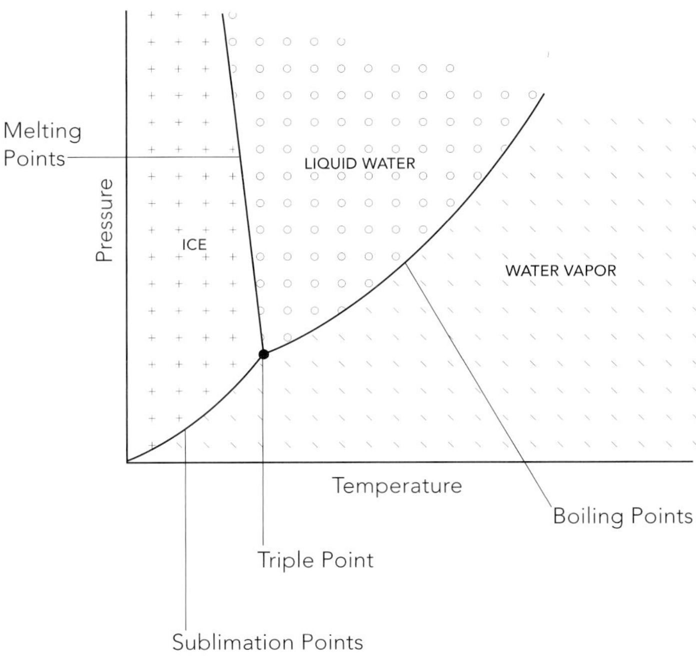

Phase diagram for water

downward to the right, "expose" or "reveal" (the connotations differ) the traces of blue-and-pink pattern beneath them, a level of order that would seem to have been "suppressed" by the smears of paint at the opposite side. *Expose*, *reveal*, and *suppress* are terms that ambiguate empirical understanding and psychic fantasy. They are the interpreter's desperate metaphors, offered to motivate and complete a "pictorial narrative" that has more to do with the felt intensity of experiential time than with telling a repeatable story in abstract time.[25] Without failing to create an image that appears whole as a picture, Winters has left *Untitled* moving in many moods, senses, and directions.[26] If there is a pattern to his work—whether psychological, biological, or logical—it is a pattern that completes itself only in changing.

Among the various graphic systems and mappings that have fascinated Winters are phase diagrams, which relate the solid, liquid, and gaseous states or phases of a chemical compound to environmental temperature and pressure. The phase diagram for water, for instance, shows those combinations of temperature and pressure at which solid ice becomes vaporous without passing through a liquid form. (The technical term for this phenomenon is *sublimation*; for water, it happens only at abnormally low atmospheric pressure, though within a familiar range of temperature.) Each phase diagram has a "triple point" where a certain combination of temperature and pressure causes all three states of the same substance to be present simultaneously. The triple point is a counter-intuitive "fact" of nature, unstable even in concept, and its presence is unlikely to be observed empirically without utter confusion. Perhaps it should be called a multiple-singular event, that is, an incompossibility. Imagine passing through a maze of ice, water, and vapor, with the one elemental substance shifting in every way between its phases of solid, liquid, and gas; a vaporous opening might suddenly become a solid wall (here the technical term is *deposition*, a gas becoming a solid). The linear form of a phase diagram indicates, nevertheless, that the triple point is very real, whether or not a person ever experiences it outside of its diagrammatic image. It exists as a figure, an abstraction, a set of coordinates, a thought. Once the phases of matter begin to acquire their graphic form, based on whatever empirical information can be gathered, it becomes evident that the three phase-transition boundary lines (solid/gas, solid/liquid, liquid/gas) must connect at some point. This is the triple point, a truth of rendering.[27]

Winters works at the "triple point" of pictorialism, at the point of maximum dedifferentiation and interference. His graphic forms occupy the counterintuitive join of conflicting phases and forces, an area of the greatest intensity and instability. How does the triple point play out in a particular work? The 1996 drawing *Animation* is a mazelike network of charcoal, graphite, and oil (p. 63); a circular motif dominates and paradoxically converts into a rectilinear grid. (In the language of phase transitions, the circularity "sublimes" into the grid.) If there is a "circle," its actualization is not quite established; implied by thick curving lines, it is nowhere completed. In fact, its curve becomes indistinguishable from a wave phase. The transitional wave within *Animation* consists of clusters of undulating curves, which, because they bend a little too abruptly here and there, appear to curve themselves into angles. Winters's line has induced curves to inflect angles, and angles to inflect curves. (Here, *inflect* is both transitive and intransitive.) Now imagine that the circle implied by the broadest of the dark marks in *Animation* is a "solid." The less heavy, wavy lines become its "liquid" phase, while the more slender, diffuse lines of the grid or mesh constitute an enveloping "gas." Although grossly metaphorical, this description respects the transitional, plateaulike multiplicity of Winters's forms. His environmental magic trick is to have suspended these phases or forms in their state of becoming-each-other, that is, at what could be called their triple point, their point of maximum mutual interference. At the triple point a round circle inflects to become a curving yet angled wave (it "melts"); but it also, just as directly, becomes a rectilinear grid (it "sublimes"). These transformations are not contradictory, but Deleuzean—"unconscious" contractions and expansions of graphic form that correspond to sensations at the very edge of consciousness. Winters further complicated matters by adding strokes of yellow, which reinforce some lines to the exclusion of others. The yellow pulls those lines illusionistically forward, affecting the implied spatial level at which any given line or segment of pattern may lie. He left *Animation* so very animated that familiar senses of pictorial order and disorder, construction and chaos, cannot hold.

SENSE

Given time to inspect *Untitled*, *Parallel Rendering 1*, and *Animation* (to peel them back, as it were, spatially and temporally), we might determine that the physical layers of color and the textured strokes that structure these works assume a precise sequence from bottom to top, from then to now. None of the works, however, developed its present appearance as the result of hierarchical ordering. The logic of sequence, the obliteration of the past by the present, has no power over Winters's art. None of his layers of effort tolerates being subordinated to any other effort. The layers, sets of marks, and phases of each of his paintings fold into a single sensation to generate an image as if from inside itself. Questions of origin, source, and external reference become academic; they fail to bear on the sensory, the emotional, and even the intellectual import of Winters's work.[28] To sense the work is to stay within it, just as the artist did in making it. Like certain plastics and fabrics, and also the human brain, a painting can have its own material memory. The present of the work "infinitely contracts [its] past"; its living quality "is nothing other than contracted quantity" (this is Deleuze thinking back to Bergson, not forward to Winters).[29]

Accordingly, Winters frequently recalls a layer from the tactile bottom to the visual top of a painting; he accomplishes this by direct, physical action, scraping or scratching down to the fundament. The dominant formal motif of *Scale*, 2003 (pp. 148–49), is a product of this technique. Another example is *Set Diagram 69*, 2001 (p. 105), where broad planes of yellow, having been obliterated by layers of gray (various combinations of black and white), reappear as yellow lines incised into the thick skin of gray paint. Winters's incisions and scrapings create the figure of a spoked wheel, visually superimposed over a ground of two sets of horizontal bars. The horizontals are themselves out of sync: an upper set drops slightly downward to the left; a lower set drops slightly downward to the right. Nothing indicates that this "background" variation has an external reference, despite the "foreground" wheel. The variation may simply have resulted from the directness and speed of the artist's paint application. Winters has no theory to guide such actions on the plateau of his canvas or paper surfaces. In fact, no theory is needed, for his actions are their own guide. The painter expands the sensation contracted within him, working it out in pigment as the pigment moves, perhaps to contract sensation once again in its altered state. Painting breathes: expansion, contraction, expansion, contraction.

Winters's painted images are free to be decisive but also free to drift. Often they drift from one medium into another, as if the transfer of medium (say from painting to etching, or even small-format drawing to large-format drawing) were analogous to layering within a single work. With drift, direction can shift back and forth, ever inflected. Winters's *Computation of Chains* series, begun 1995, and the related imagery of *Graphic Primitives*, 1998, exist as drawings, paintings, etchings, computer prints, and woodcuts. He has taken hand-rendered images and processed them through a computer algorithm: "I wanted to see what this sort of naked complexity would look like, where there was an evenness to a line, without the benefit of inflection." And then he has returned the seemingly neutralized, digital picture to hand-work, "back to a physical density."[30] Yet "naked complexity" is itself a gradient of inflection on an ever-evolving continuum of graphic form. In recognition of a multiplicity of phases of the "naked," Winters has included among his drawing instruments ball-point, roller-ball, and felt-tip pens.[31] These devices generate lines far removed from the aesthetics of traditional steel-point, pen-and-ink inflection, yet still record turns of the wrist and variations in applied pressure. Deleuze, too, drifted—topic to topic, plateau to plateau. His philosophical subjects ranged from the "logic of sense" or perceived meaning (master of non-sense, Lewis Carroll) to the "logic of sensation" or perceived feeling (master of paint, Francis Bacon). Well before Winters was aware of Deleuze, the writer had developed his own version of a "manual" imagination, spurred by Bacon's example. The manual aspect of painting brings about a "veritable insubordination of the hand," Deleuze stated in 1981. "The painting remains a visual reality, but what is imposed on sight is a space without form and a movement without rest."[32] Winters's sense of manual restlessness derives not from Bacon's dissolution of representation and abstraction but from the analogous activity of Willem de Kooning. Testing out models of professionalism during his early years as an artist, Winters was impressed by photographs of de Kooning in his studio, dressed like a workman, a house painter.[33] De Kooning was a connoisseur of paint, its physical substance, not its finished, textbook style. He surrounded himself with the material traces of his creative imagination, a new stylistic sense or direction. His style sedimented in the many papers he would use to imprint or "pull" the record of an image in process, as if to keep layers of sensation available for material use in any conceivable sequence. De Kooning's hand appeared to lead him into disorder as much as into order. Through the signs of this ingenuity, Winters understood from the beginning of his career that art could never diverge from craft: it evolved through a medium and the skillfully inventive, even playful, use of materials and tools. The risks associated with artistic practice developed not only from the resolve to follow one's imagination, but also from the fact that no amount of experience would prevent the materials and tools from continuing to assert their independent will. If, by Deleuzean logic, conscious sensation is contracted matter, then materials have at least a touch of consciousness. "I've created the image," Winters reports, "but at the same time, I'm not in total control. My approach is to build a series of improvisational responses, a set of operating procedures... a practice."[34]

In fact, de Kooning's fame related both to his phenomenal manual control and to practices that would cause his skilled hand to slip as it met material resistance. He intuited that materials are never to be mastered, but rather to be engaged. During the 1960s, he sometimes drew the human figure while keeping his eyes closed, having manual imagination alone to guide him: "I feel my hand slip across the paper. I have an image in mind but the results surprise me. I always learn something new from this experience.... When I am slipping, I say, 'Hey, this is very interesting.'"[35] De Kooning was being

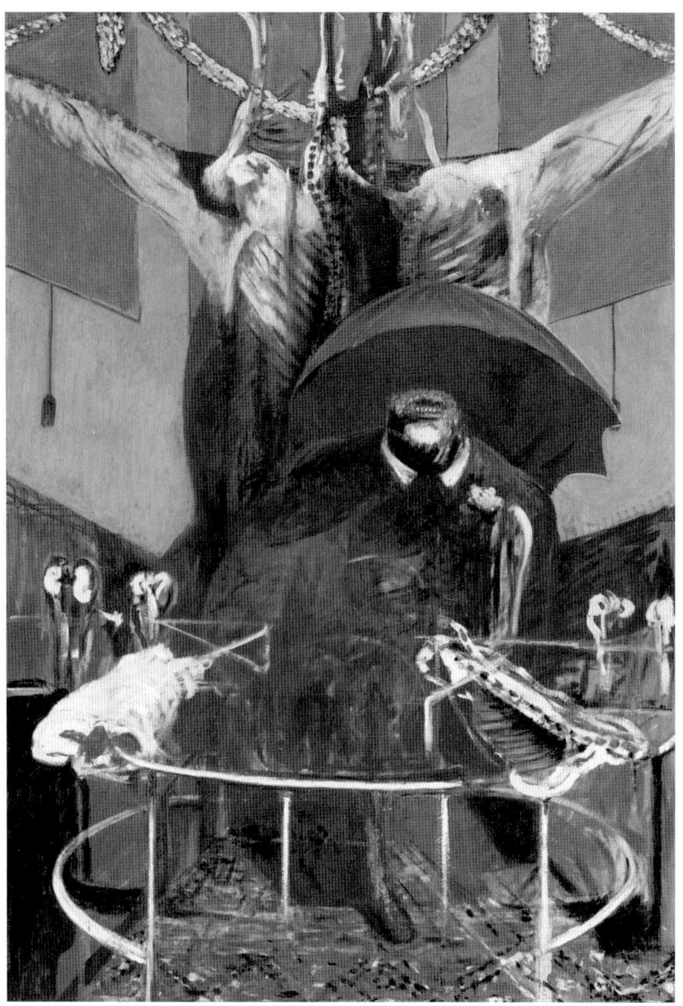

Francis Bacon (United Kingdom, 1909–92)
Painting, 1946
Oil and tempera on canvas
48 7/16 x 41 1/2 in. (123 x 105.5 cm)
The Museum of Modern Art, New York

taken somewhere—by his materials and by himself. From outside the process, Deleuze similarly referred to a painter's hand as insubordinate. As if forced by material conditions to slip, it generated a "diagram-accident ... scrambl[ing] the intentional figurative form."[36] Deleuze's example, of course, was not de Kooning but Bacon. The works of both artists demonstrate how deeply a painter's hand extends into the process of thought, as the thinking and sensing body becomes one with the gesture of its appendage, controlled or not. The body must think what the hand shows it ("painting ... takes me places"). But it also seems to a great extent that whatever the hand accomplishes must have been willed. Artistic hands are not spastic. Would the willing be conscious or unconscious? De Kooning insisted that his results surprised him. His paintings of the 1970s, which Winters especially admires, bring disparate layers to a single surface, exposing disjunctive moments within the painter's process. We might consider these enfolded, dissociated surfaces as plateaus of the unconscious. The eruption of pink within the blue of Winters's own *Untitled* of 2003 recalls the de Kooning effect. Winters remains the one who painted this anomalous element, while the prevailing order too is his. Everything that slips into the picture is his, by conscious or unconscious design, conscious or unconscious accident. Yet the sense slips away. Otherwise there would be little need to keep painting; any single work would immediately tell all.

The cause of Winters's attraction to Deleuze extends beyond the philosopher's concern for painting and his independent way of theorizing the manual. Deleuze as a writer manifests a certain insubordination, just as Bacon (or de Kooning, or Winters) does as a painter. Winters states that the multiple, indeterminate form of Deleuze's argumentation is what he initially found so appealing. In addition, Deleuze had a penchant for thinking planometrically: conceiving differences in terms of lines, spaces, diagrams, and visual figures. As much as he advocated disarticulation, he often set his layers of conceptual abstraction into metric Euclidean order—for example, associating one notion with surface, a related one with angle, still another with point.[37] Ultimately, however, this characterization of Deleuze's structure of thought loses its appropriateness; for when he diagrams, he is more

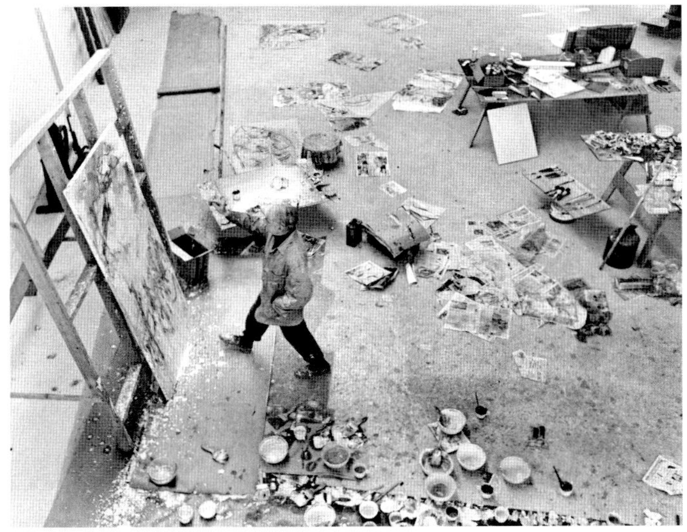

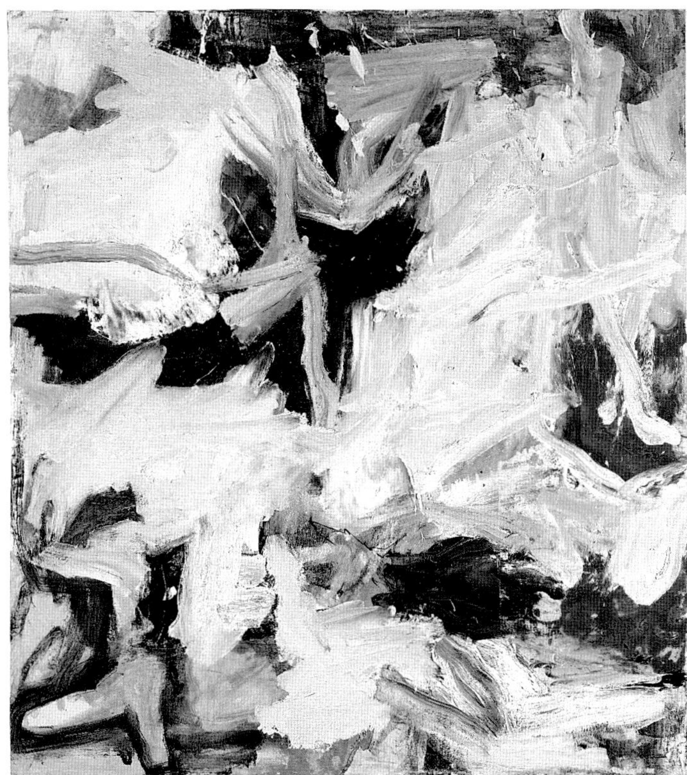

Hans Namuth (Germany 1915–90 United States)
Willem de Kooning, 1968
Gelatin silver print
Center for Creative Photography,
The University of Arizona

Willem de Kooning (Netherlands 1904–97 United States)
Untitled IV, 1977
Oil on canvas
80 x 70 in. (203.2 x 177.8 cm)
The Menil Collection, Houston,
gift of Adelaide de Menil Carpenter

the adventurous topologist than the steady geometer. Topological configurations can be twisted, stretched, and compressed into new shapes; and yet the surface properties that the science of topology recognizes as crucial may remain unaffected. To the measuring eye of the geometer, the same configurations will have fundamentally changed. When the circle becomes the wave and the grid, and when the grid becomes the wave and the circle—all on the single pictorial surface of Winters's *Animation*—the geometry of the drawing has attained topological flexibility. On the metric scale, it registers as decidedly nonmetric, that is, not subject to ordinary rules of measure.[38] Deleuze, who died the year before *Animation* was created, would have taken strong interest.

Planometric: What might this term indicate, were we to think freely on the nonmetric plateau of Deleuze-becoming-Winters and Winters-becoming-Deleuze? The notion may at first seem anti-Deleuzean. Planometric: extending one's thought on a plane. Planometric: marking out a measured direction on the plane. Yet, things planometric also meander; their direction cannot be specified. The planometric artist is free to zigzag, just as free to go straight; free to use an inflected line (like Winters in his drawings), just as free to disinflect through a computer algorithm (like Winters in others of his drawings). In English, the prefix *plano* has a double derivation and a double meaning. From its root in Greek, it signifies a wandering movement; from its root in Latin, it signifies the quality of being a surface, of having planarity.[39] The Deleuzean theory of the plateau is planometric in both senses, and so is Winters's practice. Both writer and painter comprehend life and thought as a complex graphic order, and both encourage wandering. (Deleuze refers to nomadism and "nomad art."[40]) For the wanderer to remain at the surface will be sufficient. Deleuze suggests that a planar surface is material depth infinitely extended in the horizontal dimension; surfaces therefore level all pretenses to hierarchical profundity.[41] Winters is enough of a traditionalist to figure images of depth on paper and canvas, as if to reveal a potential of the surface, any surface, that would otherwise remain inapparent. To his eye, all surfaces encompass depth. The skewed rhomboids and meshlike forms of *Scale* imply depth without entering it definitively, either by illusionistic perspective or by physical incision. Yet, inscribed lines constitute the dominant graphic figure. *Scale* straddles the several conceptualized categories and boundary conditions that Winters is exploring.

Accordingly, Winters's interest in the flat has never prevented him from rendering the twist of a volume in space. *Turbulence Skins/12*, 2002 (p. 143), a very dense image, as well as the less dense *Turbulence Skins/35*, 2002 (p. 145), are linear structures that look as if they might be describing ribbed, partially flattened spheres, cylinders, or cams. It is a type of form to which Winters seems inclined. The lines may correspond to structural members of an actual physical object, but more likely they trace the kinds of diagrammatic forces seen also in *Scale*. "My approach is diagrammatic," the artist announces; "each image becomes a superposition of maps."[42] Like phase diagrams, maps interpolate and extrapolate as much as they graph what has already been experienced. Lines project conditions that might exist, either as something unknown or as a variant of something known. Painting and drawing live in this curious state of becoming—becoming apparent and inapparent at once: "As recording instrument [tracking the known] and experimental device [projecting the unknown], drawing can make things 'unhidden.'" Once unhidden, virtualities come into view. They are to be sensed, but perhaps not distinctly. "Invent, test and play," Winters says.[43] Slip a bit, advised de Kooning.

Like Deleuze, Winters is willing to overturn long-standing intellectual habits. He takes comfort in proceeding by testing and playing, without being compelled to articulate a definite goal. Asked about his sustained interest in Deleuze's writings, he implies that this is conceptual material he would never presume to have mastered, something to be tested out like a graphic tool. He reads Deleuze sympathetically, but "no," he says only half facetiously, "I don't think it makes sense to me."[44] Deleuzean theory holds thinking so close to the limits of sense that it resembles drawing and painting, ever unresolved, never reaching climax. Pursuing thoughts about surfaces, Deleuze writes that "everything happens at the border," the edge of where you are.[45] When Winters pages through Deleuze, he recognizes in turn that an argument extended through the medium of words contracts into a sensation like a unified image emerging from the extended lines and colors of a picture: "Drawing is the prototype—the first time the image is seen.... Signs are generated to be felt and sensed."[46] Configured signs contract or encompass the levels of experience that both Winters's drawings and Deleuze's texts also expand. It is in this context that Winters speculates about art and the unconscious. As we know, he wonders whether a drawing or painting might best be regarded "as a visualization or actualization of the virtual ... an expanded picture of the unconscious." Art renders the unconscious unhidden, always for the first time. It invents (finds and makes, makes and finds).

Anyone who has drawn a line realizes from the experience how immediate it is. You follow along with the line as much as you lead it to where you want it to go—or think you want yourself to go. Are you extending the line? Or does it extend you? Perhaps it contracts you, draws your attention down to a point, the point of the stylus that draws the line. There may be no purpose to theorizing the sensation of line that everyone already feels with intimacy. But what can Winters's line be drawing when it extends beyond the closed volume that the image in *Turbulence Skins/35* approximates—when radial forms violate the outer ring, or when the line of circumference doubles itself at the bottom edge of the figure? Does the "extra" line of this doubling amount to a corrective measure? Or does it signify an additional structural member of the form, which, in fact, features internal repetition? Given the flow of the medium, can such a drawn volume actually ever be "closed," complete in itself, adequately drawn, or sufficiently corrected? It seems that the aesthetic charge of an image becomes strongest (unhidden?) precisely where the hand loses control or acts willfully, when it senses its situation and responds to it, becoming self-conscious about the evolving process of drawing. This is the point at which any hesitation, any brief moment of reflection, raises a counterflow of undecidable questions. It is where Deleuze's manual insubor-dination and Winters's manual imagination enter the picture. Winters says, "I can't step outside [the painting] process and construct an objective account." Nor can we. To make conscious sense of drawing and painting, to keep sense moving, the painter simply continues to paint. A wary critic but savvy viewer joins the line.

SWITCH

... induce spontaneous phenomena ... make something happen ...

Terry Winters[47]

Sense, understanding, is not the resolution of thought but its direction. Like a line, thought moves; this is its nature. To grasp a present situation, we need no more than sense that things are coming and that they are going. Living does not require a fixed image of the totality of its conditions; and, in any case, such an image would amount to a false picture of stability in an individual's state of being. "You arbitrarily define the present as that which is," Henri Bergson wrote in a passage Deleuze cites, "whereas the present is simply what becomes, whatever is in the process of being made."[48] In the same spirit, Winters replies extemporaneously when asked why he works as he does, and what it all might mean for his feeling of life:

Living in the present is always a sense [of] becoming.... The paintings have been less and less about some very fixed notion of identity.... The work is really about contingencies and the pragmatics of making things, and making do with things that are in the world. The application is towards a very practical, pragmatic, daily thinking.... [To] make things and become.[49]

The meaning, the sense, the direction that phenomena acquire, is the sense of becoming. An artist starts somewhere (many places) and causes "that which is" to come alive, to become. As Winters has said, "Paintings are projections. They take me places" (many places). He makes "something happen" by a process he calls "pragmatic negotiations."[50] In his more colloquial moments, he simply refers to "making do" with the given conditions, both psychic and material. Does he also "induce spontaneous phenomena"? Why do both kinds of phrasing occur to Winters as he thinks about the sense of painting and drawing? The same question arises from thinking about thinking. Is it, in fact, proper to speak of notions of causality and spontaneity as *occurring* to Winters, as if he actively thought them? Or do these thoughts *happen* to him, as if he were instead their directed object, not their directing subject? Winters states that he makes his abstract paintings in order to "build something real." But the sensory reality that shows itself through painting is never something Winters knew in another material existence. Nor is it a form of his preexisting fantasy world. Then where was it, and where is it? Does it come out of nowhere? Like a triple point, it occupies many places: here, there, and neither here nor there.

Recently Winters made two graphite drawings that feature the inscription "ENTER" within a motif of concentric circles: *Sketchbook Pages #29*, 2001, and *Sketchbook Pages III, #6*, 2002, to which the central buttonlike form of the oil painting *Untitled (Red)*, 2003 (p. 151), may bear some relation. In the two drawings, the set of diminishing circles connotes a change in scale, dimension, or level; and within the central circle, the height of the lettering decreases slightly from the midpoint to both left and right, as if the represented surface were convex. Winters states that he was thinking of "pushing a button to enter some kind of other space." These images may be approaching as explicit a theory as the artist allows. His circles become a suggestive vortex leading to a higher or deeper level, while the convex button, the projective means of entry, beckons to be touched. *Sketchbook Pages III, #6* shows the button at two different positions, as if switching. It is a push-push switch: push for "enter"; push again for "exit." Winters's "other space," entered with a push, may well be the unconscious, contracting and expanding like a present and a past, passing freely between different phases of time and space.

By manual action, a button can activate a phase transition; and by manual imagination, the graphic drawing of a button can do the same. Given our culture's industrial past—contracted within our postindustrial present—button-pushing is a powerful metaphor for an immediate change in conditions, both physical and emotional. At the push or pull of a toggle, dial, knob, or button, we routinely switch on a source of illumination, heating, or cooling. We operate a control panel of buttons and switches to set any number of processes in motion. When everything is working, we worry vaguely over someone pushing a nuclear or WMD button. Children of recent generations encountered the power of buttons

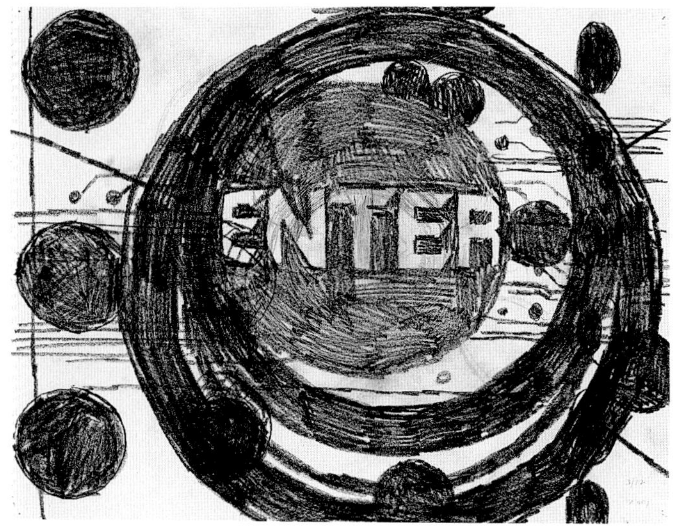

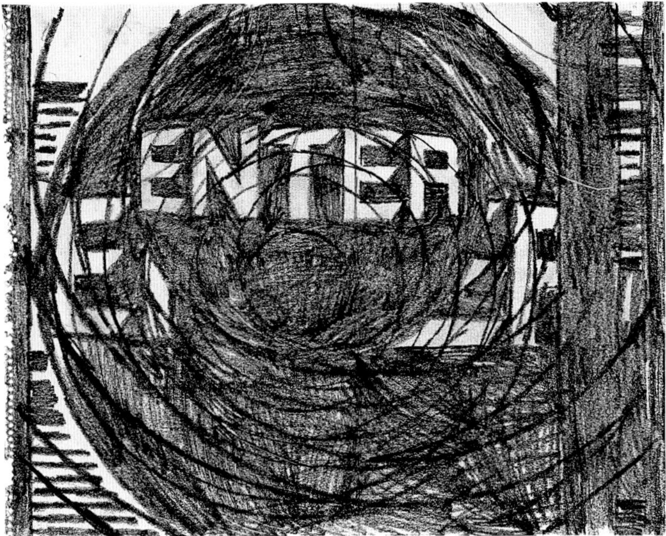

Terry Winters
Sketchbook Pages #29, 2001
Graphite on paper
14 x 18 in. (35.6 x 45.7 cm)
Collection of the artist

Terry Winters
Sketchbook Pages III, #6, 2002
Graphite on paper
14 5/8 x 18 1/8 in. (37.1 x 46 cm)
Courtesy of Matthew Marks Gallery, New York

and switches as a basic feature of the typical industrialized home: "Don't ever touch that," a parent warns. Like others, Winters grew up understanding that the miraculous binary operation of switches corresponds to the manual physicality of pushing and pulling, turning and rotating, flipping and flicking. Any child can do it. A variant of the device that turns on the lights now operates our advanced information systems. It has been miniaturized, too tiny for unmediated hands to control.

At some point in recent technological history, electro-mechanical and electronic switches became more familiar than purely mechanical ones. On the near side of this transition, the single-button, push-push type (like Winters's "ENTER," as opposed to the push-pull type) comes into its own. Touching the push-push button simply activates whatever procedure negates the previous one or is programmed to follow it in a predetermined sequence. With push-push, neither mechanical nor spatial orientation differentiates "on" from "off." As with phase transition, no stable barrier need be crossed in moving from one state ("on") to the alternative ("off"); the two states just follow each other, as if arbitrarily. At the phase boundary where ice sublimes into vapor, vapor is equally likely to depose into ice. This, at least, is how it will seem to the human observer, unable to sense any prevailing direction—if there should be one—in minute shifts in temperature and pressure. Instead of push-push, some single-button switches are more properly called engage-release or push-to-make; they have distinguishable "in" and "out" positions that correspond to "on" and "off" but require constant application to activate ("Shift" and "Ctrl" and "[Apple]" on a computer keyboard). Other engage-release switches move only to alter whatever function they control and have been designed to resume their initial state immediately ("Num Lock"). Still others of the single-button type are activated by the mere contact of touch and do not move at all.

Push-push and engage-release switches have no origin, ground, orientation, or perfected end. They only facilitate. Each is a way. They establish nothing but the difference that engagement or connection makes. The switch itself, as well as its operation, signifies "change" rather than any specific change. It may not indicate what it does, but it does do something. It projects you somewhere. And this is what Winters intended his "ENTER" to do, along with his other abstractions and diagrammatic signs. Consider the somewhat amorphous ellipsoids distributed across Winters's painting *Standardgraph/4*, 2003 (pp. 140–41). Call them "amorphoids"—shapes that lose form while gaining it and gain form while losing it. Each amorphoid is a microcosmic variant of the dynamic motif of *Animation*: a form that is becoming-circle, becoming-wave, and becoming-grid simultaneously. An environment of circles, waves, and grids in *Standardgraph/4* induces these transitions, these becomings, which were already immanent in the amorphoids. A few months before working on his *Standardgraph* series, Winters wrote: "Emergent becomings are produced according to immanent and transformable conditions."[51]

If the push-push switch removes definitive direction from the experience of change, another type of electromechanical device, the heat-sensitive or thermal switch, creates the conditions for a phase transition in the body's intervening sensory system. For anyone accustomed to associating switches with touch, pressure, and the focused exercise of a certain small amount of force (linked in turn to every past experience of weight, momentum, resistance, and gravity), heat-sensitive operations mystify because they require no pressure, only contact. They depend on a passive factor involved in every human touch: body temperature. Usually functionally inactive in the external world, body temperature hides from self-sensation. People are unlikely to be aware that they are operating heat-sensitive switches until the finger's "touch" abandons them. If a person presses an elevator button with gloved hands on an unusually cold day, the chilled gloves can prevent the body's warmth from reaching the surface. This application of touch fails to convey heat sufficient to register, and a temperature-activated switch does not perform. Such an experience causes a person to feel suddenly without substance, incapable of leaving a physical trace. Under this condition, the switch dematerializes the living experience of touch, as if sensation could no longer contract matter to a body's finger point ("Sensation... contract[s] trillions of vibrations onto a receptive surface," Deleuze wrote). Seeming to lack all weight, pressure, and presence, the hand no longer inflects. Like pushing a pen with no ink, or pulling a brush with no paint, applying more force to the temperature-activated button accomplishes nothing. "Painting is a circuit, a feedback loop," Winters says.[52] The moment of art comes to this performance of switching when the informational feedback to the body itself switches. Frustration with an elevator button brings the realization that some other "phase" of bodily function is being solicited. Here, insubordination in the material world has put a challenge to manual imagination. A proper reaction is to reorient one's personal phase diagram so that passive temperature now dominates active pressure.

Winters knows that the cultural and technological environment inflects a conscious body in unfamiliar, often hidden ways. This is the problem his art addresses. He is committed to leaving an open physical trace in his painting—scratched lines, worn colors, layers of ridges and bumps—but never assumes that the telling signs of a body's experience are restricted to its self-assuring, habitual mannerisms. There are innumerable modes of touching and of being touched, and each can be a "way" (in the Starobinski/Winters sense) of getting somewhere. Winters has avoided developing a personal mythology and has never cultivated an exclusive, autographic mark.[53] Something grander than personality is at stake for him: the continuum or "correlation between life and matter" (Deleuze).[54] He wants to know what of life can be sensed through a stylus and graphite, or through a brush and oil paint, as well as through a computer algorithm—what classes of information the various material markings and physical operations register as meaningful evidence. Like a phase diagram, his plateau-pictures convert unsensed information into something "unhidden" (Winters's word).[55] Why "unhidden"? Like an "actualization of the virtual" (Winters again, but Deleuze too), a thing unhidden occupies a phase of matter different from the same thing hidden. It is not that we see something previously unseen, a revelation, but rather that something shows itself in a different way and form. Once manifest, the unhidden thing still changes: all elements of reality are linked even as they differentiate, and collectively they continue to evolve.[56] Inflecting, subliming, sensing, switching, evolving: Winters's pictorial unconscious may not have become unhidden, but unhiding.

NOTES

1. Gilles Deleuze, *Bergsonism*, trans. Hugh Tomlinson and Barbara Habberjam (New York: Zone Books, 1988 [1966]), 74, 103. Deleuze's statement refers to Henri Bergson, *Matière et mémoire* (Paris: Presses universitaires de France, 1968 [1896]), 166–69. It has the advantage of eliminating the conceptual barrier between what is human (consciousness) and what is nonhuman (materiality) so that situations can be described without giving preference to either. Living consciousness and dead matter exist on a continuum, and each can be all-encompassing. This disarticulation of the traditional difference (human/nonhuman or, more generally, animate/inanimate) has been attractive to those interested in hybrid forms such as cyborgs, robots, and intelligent machines. There has been far more attention given to machines becoming intelligent than to people becoming unintelligent, which may be the more pressing social issue. See also Gilles Deleuze, *Francis Bacon: The Logic of Sensation*, trans. Daniel W. Smith (London: Continuum, 2003 [1981]), 45: "Sensation is vibration.... The body is completely living, and yet nonorganic." Or Gilles Deleuze and Félix Guattari, *A Thousand Plateaus: Capitalism and Schizophrenia*, trans. Brian Massumi (Minneapolis: University of Minnesota Press, 1987 [1980]), 503: "The organism is that which life sets against itself in order to limit itself, and there is a life all the more intense, all the more powerful for being anorganic." Instead he emphasizes the expansion of unconscious territory—unoccupied, unpossessed, an unconscious neither individual nor collective. His art opens things hidden so that they transform into things "unhidden" (as discussed below). What is important is the change itself, which preserves both hidden and unhidden potentials. Winters's "unconscious" does share a feature with its Freudian counterpart: its "content" is likely to emerge as conscious experience in a dissociated manner—manifested as multiplicitous sense, every which way.

2. Terry Winters, "Conversation with Adam Fuss," in *Terry Winters: Computation of Chains* (New York: Matthew Marks Gallery, 1997), 9, 14.

3. Coincidentally, *projection* belongs to the technical language of set diagrams, which graph relations of inclusion and exclusion between sets of properties. Set diagrams and projections give logical abstractions a material face. Between 2000 and 2002, Winters created a series of paintings titled *Set Diagram*, often using forms that resemble those of set projections (interlocking circles, ellipses, and other, more complex curvilinear figures).

4. This and other statements, opinions, and recollections attributed to Winters, when given no specific source, derive from a series of conversations with the author between June and December 2003. Winters also states: "Painting can make unconscious patterns visible.... The animation develops, and somewhere along the way a connection is made between me and the formal configurations of the work" ("Conversation with Adam Fuss," 19). Compare remarks by Jasper Johns, an artist Winters admires: "[A painter] just paints paintings without a conscious reason.... Your thought takes a certain form and you have to follow it" (Jasper Johns, statement to *Newsweek* [published 31 March 1958], interview by Amei Wallach [22 February 1991], in Kirk Varnedoe, ed., *Jasper Johns: Writings, Sketchbook Notes, Interviews* [New York: Museum of Modern Art, 1996], 81, 261). Winters's material, pictorial "unconscious" has little, if any, direct link to classical psychoanalysis, whether Freudian or Jungian.

5. Compare Deleuze's understanding of Bergson's "creative evolution": "There is here no longer any coexisting whole; there are merely lines of actualization, *some successive, others simultaneous*, but each representing an actualization of the whole in one direction.... They only actualize by inventing" (Deleuze, *Bergsonism*, 100–101 [emphasis in original]). Winters's interest in biological forms and the evolution of life, overtly expressed in his imagery of the 1980s, could be investigated through this Deleuzean inflection of Bergsonism. The present essay deals instead with the artist's related but differently directed concerns of the past decade.

6. On the question of voice, note Winters's frequent use of passive and impersonal voice in the notebook statements that constitute the text for his book *Ocular Proofs* (New York: Grenfell Press, 1995). This may be a rhetorical ploy, a device to remove any effect of authorship or origin: "uneven tensor fields are produced by simulations...interaction is used in real time."

7. "A friend gave me a copy of *The Fold* [Gilles Deleuze, *The Fold: Leibniz and the Baroque*, trans. Tom Conley (Minneapolis: University of Minnesota Press, 1993 [1988])] sometime in the mid-nineties. That's when I started to pay attention. Subsequently, I've pretty much looked over all [of Deleuze's] work." Winters suspects that he had previously noticed selections from Deleuze's writing included in anthologies such as *Incorporations* (ed. Jonathan Crary and Sanford Kwinter [New York: Zone, 1992]), without realizing that these texts might relate to his art. In 2003 he added *Francis Bacon: The Logic of Sensation* to the number of Deleuze's works he had read, but in no case was he seeking particular justification for his own practice. He simply finds Deleuzean thought congenial. Deleuzean interpretations of Winters's art have been developed in Enrique Juncosa, "Thought as Image," *Terry Winters* (Valencia: IVAM; London: Whitechapel Art Gallery, 1998), 11–22; John Rajchman, "Painting in the Brain-City," *Terry Winters: Graphic Primitives* (New York: Matthew Marks Gallery, 1999), 7–15; and Harry Cooper, "Drawing and Writing with TW," in Michael Semff, ed., *Terry Winters Zeichnungen/Drawings* (Munich: Staatliche Graphische Sammlung, 2003), 12–27, 44–45. See also Nan Rosenthal, "Painting What We Can't See," *Terry Winters: Printed Works* (New York: Metropolitan Museum of Art, 2001), 28–29.

8. Deleuze and Guattari, *A Thousand Plateaus*, 21, 25.

9. Deleuze and Guattari, *A Thousand Plateaus*, 22–23.

10. On Winters's thoughts about *Perfection, Way, Origin*, see Nancy Princenthal, "Perfect Like a Hedgehog: The Printed Works of Terry Winters," *Art on Paper* 6 (September–October 2001): 50.

11. Jean Starobinski, "Perfection, Way, Origin," trans. Richard Pevear, in Terry Winters, *Perfection, Way, Origin* (West Islip, N.Y.: Universal Limited Art Editions, 2002), n.p. Starobinski eventually argues that perfection, way, and origin "are names of three temporal places" which become one, having been kept separate only by our habits of thought.

12. Deleuze and Guattari, *A Thousand Plateaus*, 21–22 (order of phrases altered).

13. Deleuze and Guattari, *A Thousand Plateaus*, 159.

14. Adopting the term *plateau*, Deleuze and Guattari (*A Thousand Plateaus*, 22, 158) cite its use by Gregory Bateson, who referred to the Balinese "method of dealing with quarrels" as "the substitution of a plateau for a climax" (Gregory Bateson, *Steps to an Ecology of Mind* [New York: Random House, 1972], 113).

15. Deleuze and Guattari, *A Thousand Plateaus*, xx.

16. This feature becomes the foundation for a critique of Deleuze and Guattari in Christopher L. Miller, "The Postidentitarian Predicament in the Footnotes of *A Thousand Plateaus*: Nomadology, Anthropology, and Authority," *Diacritics* 23 (Fall 1993): 6–35.

17.Terry Winters, in Clifford S. Ackley, "Terry Winters and Cliff Ackley: A Conversation," *Art New England* 14 (June–July 1993): 31.

18. Starobinski objects: "One recent critical exaggeration wants to see only nomadic apparitions [an allusion to Deleuzean terminology], or an infinite text with no edge or outside" ("Perfection, Way, Origin," n.p.).

19. Winters, "Conversation with Adam Fuss," 9.

20. In 1977 Winters worked in New Mexico installing Walter de Maria's environmental sculpture *The Lightning Field*, which measures one mile by one kilometer. Winters's predilection for neutral, standard sizes may be related to his experience with de Maria's art.

21. Deleuze would identify these limitations with "signifiance" and "subjectification," the customary analysis of art and individual human expression by way of semiotics and psychoanalysis; see Deleuze and Guattari, *A Thousand Plateaus*, 111–48.

22. On incompossibility ("a movement without displacement...internal discordance"), see Maurice Merleau-Ponty, "Eye and Mind" (1961), in *The Primacy of Perception*, ed. James M. Edie, trans. Carleton Dallery (Evanston: Northwestern University Press, 1964), 184–85; and Deleuze, *The Fold*, 59, 80–82, 150 n.1.

23. Compare Deleuze, *Francis Bacon*, 1–7, 99–102.

24. Compare Gilles Deleuze and Félix Guattari, *What Is Philosophy?*, trans. Hugh Tomlinson and Graham Burchell (New York: Columbia University Press, 1994 [1991]), 216–18. On aspects of interference, see Richard Shiff, "Cézanne's Blur, Approximating Cézanne," in Richard Thomson, ed., *Framing France: Essays on the Representation of Landscape in France, 1870–1914* (Manchester, U.K.: Manchester University Press, 1998), 59–80; "Realism of Low Resolution: Digitisation and Modern Painting," in Terry Smith, ed., *Impossible Presence: Surface and Screen in the Photogenic Era* (Chicago: University of Chicago Press, 2001), 124–56; "Puppet and Test Pattern: Mechanicity and Materiality in Modern Pictorial Representation," in Bruce Clarke and Linda Dalrymple Henderson, eds., *From Energy to Information: Representation in Science and Technology, Art, and Literature* (Stanford: Stanford University Press, 2002), 327–50, 420–26.

25. The phrase "pictorial narrative" is Winters's ("Conversation with Adam Fuss," 9). On the subject of time (Aion and Chronos), see Gilles Deleuze, *The Logic of Sense*, trans. Mark Lester, ed. Constantin V. Boundas (New York: Columbia University Press, 1990 [1969]), 162–68.

26. A floating fragment of an arrow or winglike motif, seen on the right side of *Untitled*, complicates its relation to the left side, which has an extended (more anchored? more definitive?) version of the same motif.

27. The fourth phase of matter, plasma (super-high-energy gas), does not enter into an ordinary phase diagram. It lies still further outside that part of the physical world accessible to direct sensation. I thank Stephen Coombes, University of Nottingham, and James Lawrence, The University of Texas at Austin, for information on phase diagrams.

28. This is not to deny that sources exist and that Winters keeps them in mind: "Each drawing [of the *Computation of Chains* series] is a synthesis, an image composed from different sources—architectural renderings, medical photographs, computer graphics—as well as from direct observation" (Winters, "Conversation with Adam Fuss," 16). Because most of Winters's source material is already in a planar, pictorial form, he speaks of his images as having an "isomorphic relationship...rather than a representational relationship to the world.... They were made from the same stuff, and formed by the same processes" (Terry Winters, interview by Nan Rosenthal, 2001, unedited transcript [order of phrases altered], courtesy Nan Rosenthal, Terry Winters, and The Metropolitan Museum of Art).

29. See note 1.

30. Winters, interview by Nan Rosenthal, 2001, unedited transcript.

31. Examples are the drawings for Winters's book *Intersections and Animations* (New York: Dome Editions, 1999).

32. Deleuze, *Francis Bacon*, 155.

33.Concerning de Kooning, see also Terry Winters, symposium statement, 12 October 2002, in *Terry Winters Zeichnungen/Drawings*, 11.

34. Winters, "Conversation with Adam Fuss," 7.

35. Willem de Kooning, interview by Sam Hunter, "De Kooning: Je dessine les yeux fermés," *Galerie Jardin des Arts* 152 (November 1975): 69; audiotaped statement, interview by Michael C. Sonnabend

and Kenneth Snelson, summer 1959, typescript, Willem de Kooning Foundation, New York (prepared for the film *Sketchbook No. 1: Three Americans—Willem de Kooning, Buckminster Fuller, Igor Stravinsky*, directed by Robert Snyder, written by Michael C. Sonnabend, distributed by Time Inc., 1960).

36. Deleuze, *Francis Bacon*, 157.

37. Deleuze and Guattari, *A Thousand Plateaus*, 159.

38. On metric and nonmetric in geometry, see Manuel DeLanda, *Intensive Science & Virtual Philosophy* (London: Continuum, 2002), 24–26.

39. Deleuze uses the term *planomenon* encompassing both of these senses (for example, Deleuze and Guattari, *A Thousand Plateaus*, 506).

40. "There exists a nomadic absolute, as a local integration moving from part to part and constituting smooth [nonhierarchical, dedifferentiated] space in an infinite succession of linkages and changes in direction" (Deleuze and Guattari, *A Thousand Plateaus*, 494).

41. "As one advances in the story [of Lewis Carroll's *Alice*], the digging and hiding gives way to a lateral sliding from right to left and left to right. The animals below ground become secondary, giving way to *card figures* which have no thickness. One could say that the old depth having been spread out became width" (Deleuze, *The Logic of Sense*, 9 [emphasis in original]).

42. Winters, symposium statement, 11.

43. Ibid.

44. Terry Winters, in public conversation with Richard Shiff, The Metropolitan Museum of Art, New York, 9 September 2001, videotape (courtesy The Metropolitan Museum of Art and Terry Winters). Deleuze (especially with co-author Guattari) employs a polemical, even self-indulgent style, and there may be good reason to notice that sense is being lost. This leaves a critical reader in a bind; see, for example, René Girard, "Delirium as System" (review of Deleuze and Guattari's *L'Anti-Oedipe* [*Anti-Oedipus: Capitalism and Schizophrenia*], 1972), *"To Double Business Bound": Essays on Literature, Mimesis, and Anthropology* (Baltimore: The Johns Hopkins University Press, 1978), 99–100.

45. Deleuze, *The Logic of Sense*, 9.

46. Winters, symposium statement, 11.

47. Winters, *Intersections and Animations*, n.p. (sections 5 and 49).

48. Bergson, *Matière et mémoire*, 166 (my translation). I have expanded Bergson's reflexive verb *se fait* into the synonymous English terms *become* and *be made*.

49. Winters, in conversation with Shiff, videotape.

50. "Pragmatic" is a common notion, but also has a specifically Deleuzean connotation of operating under conditions of the most open "becomings and multiplicities" (Deleuze and Guattari, *A Thousand Plateaus*, 251).

51. Winters, symposium statement, 11.

52. Winters, "Conversation with Adam Fuss," 19.

53. Referring to Winters's work of the 1980s, Lisa Phillips contrasts him to the early Abstract Expressionists: "[He] uses generic, diagrammatic forms, drawn from preexisting sources [which] have the familiarity of what Johns called 'things the mind already knows'" (Lisa Phillips, "The Self Similar," *Terry Winters* [New York: Whitney Museum of American Art, 1991], 18–19).

54. See note 1.

55. Winters, symposium statement, 11. Winters recalls no particularly clear motivation for selecting this word: "'Unhidden' seemed to more accurately convey the open-ended process of image-making. It just seemed more pragmatic than saying something was 'revealed.'...Hidden/unhidden could also suggest the implicate/explicate orders of nature described by [physicist] David Bohm." Winters refers here to David Bohm, *Wholeness and the Implicate Order* (London: Routledge, 2002 [1980]). In addition, one thinks of the philosophical notion of "unconcealment" (the usual translation for Martin Heidegger's German term *Unverborgenheit*), but Winters reports that this particular reference has only now become unhidden.

56. See note 5.

FOUNDATIONS AND SYSTEMS

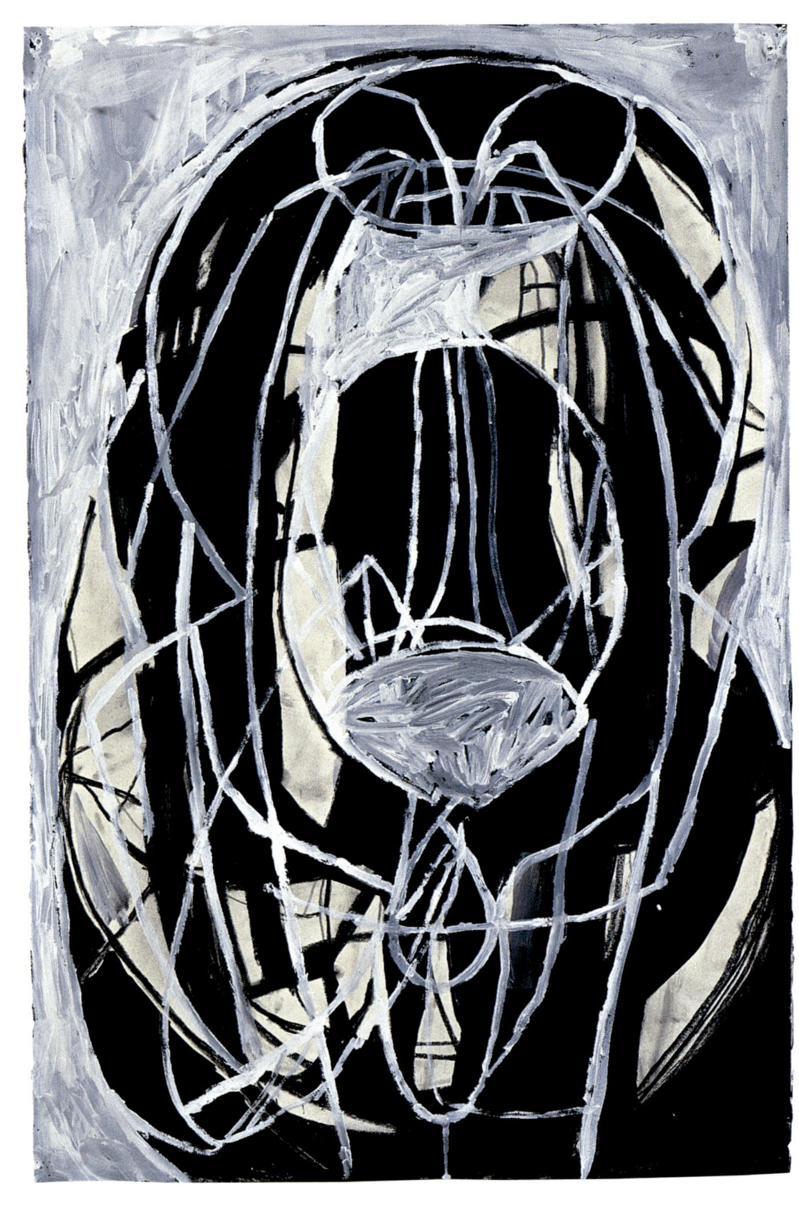

Tenon's Capsule 1, 1994
Charcoal, graphite, ink, and acrylic on paper
40 x 26 1/16 in. (101.6 x 66.2 cm)
Private collection

Tenon's Capsule 2, 1994
Charcoal, graphite, ink, and acrylic on paper
40 3/16 x 26 1/4 in. (102.1 x 66.7 cm)
Collection of Harry W. and Mary Margaret Anderson

Tenon's Capsule 3, 1994
Charcoal, graphite, ink, and acrylic on paper
41 5/8 x 29 3/4 in. (105.7 x 75.6 cm)
Collection of Robert and Jane Meyerhoff, Phoenix, Maryland

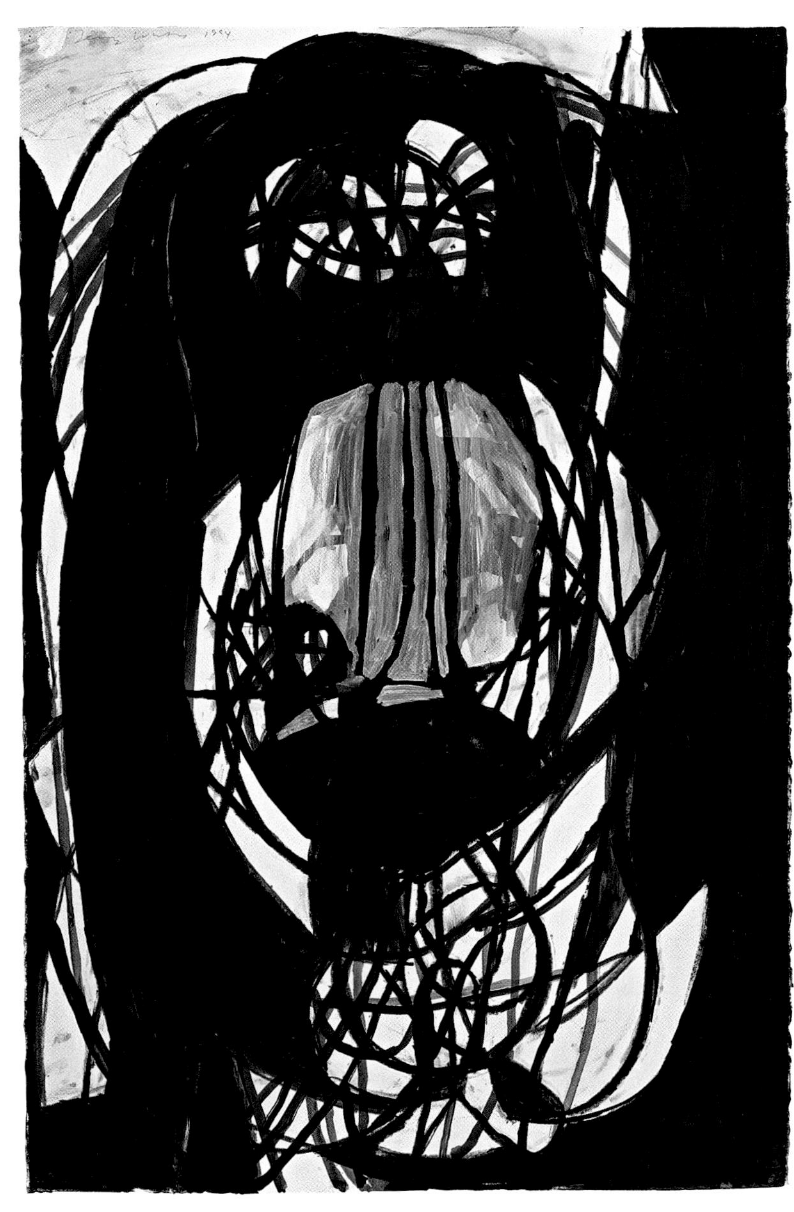
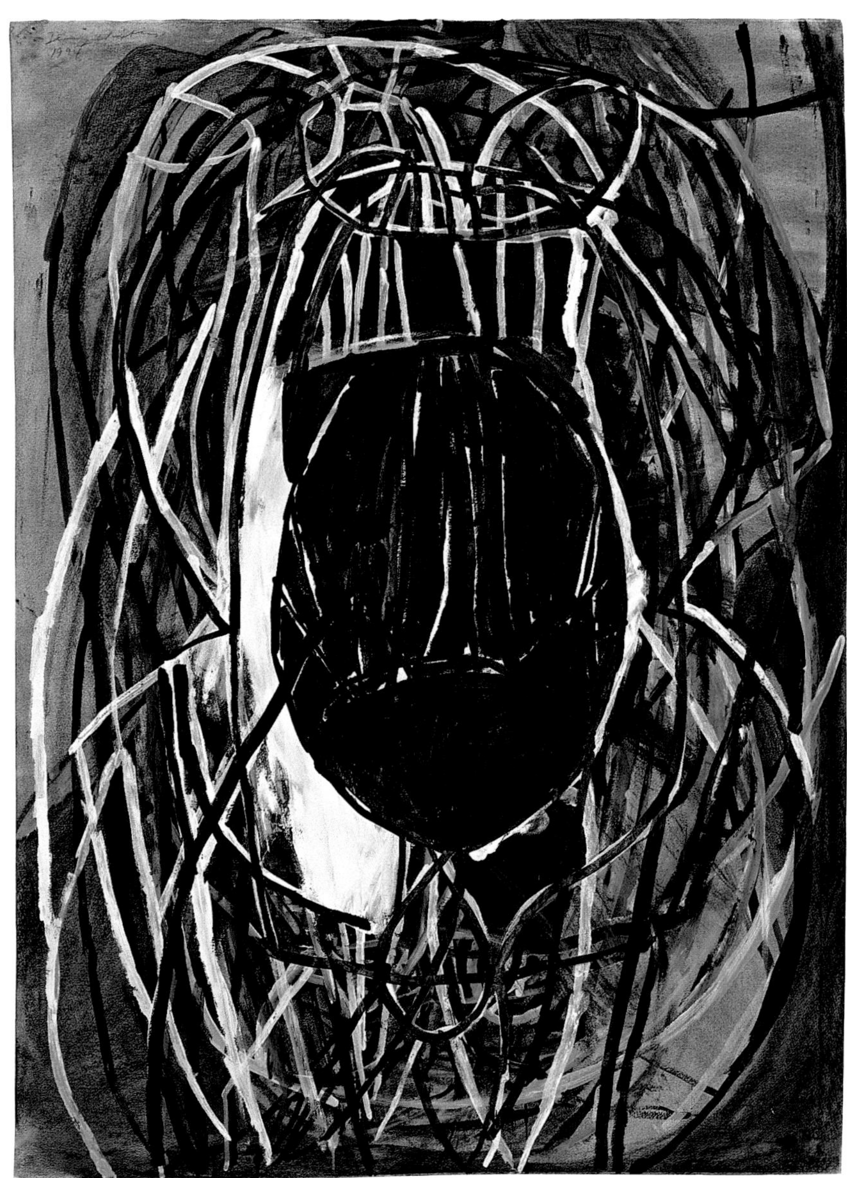

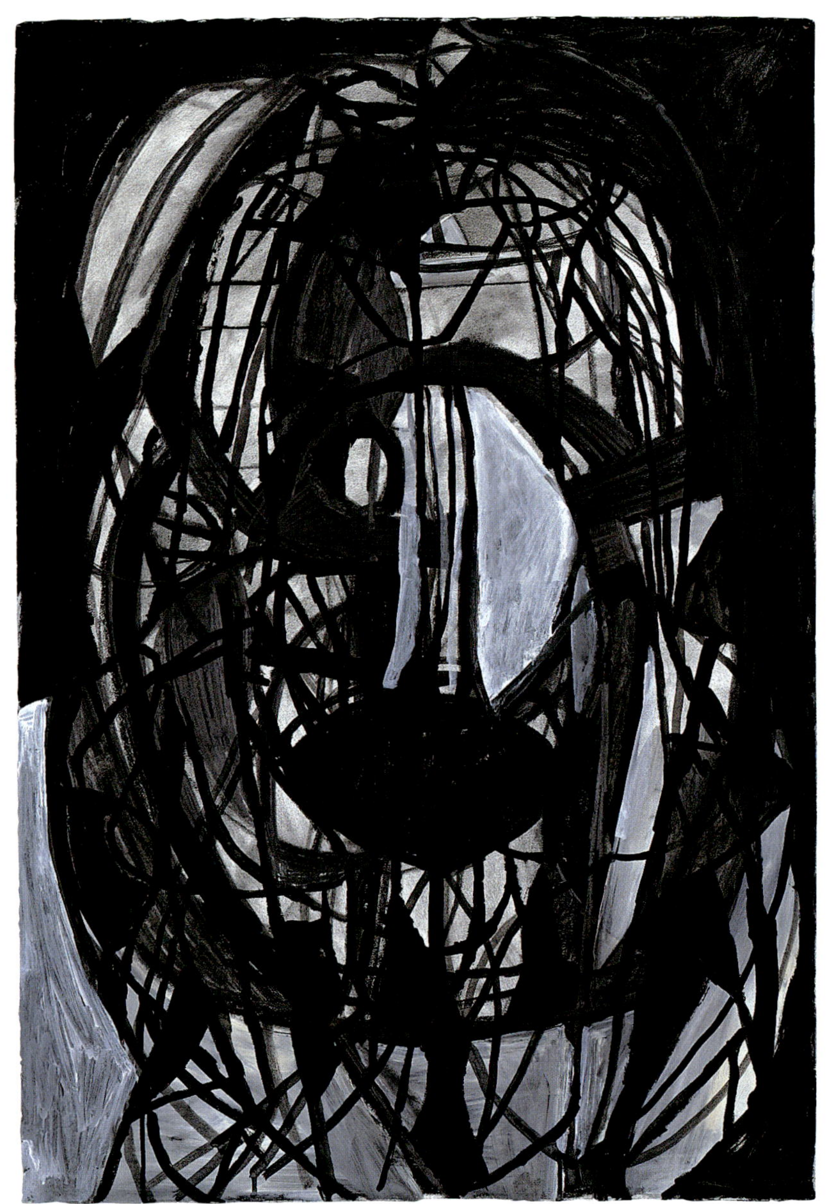

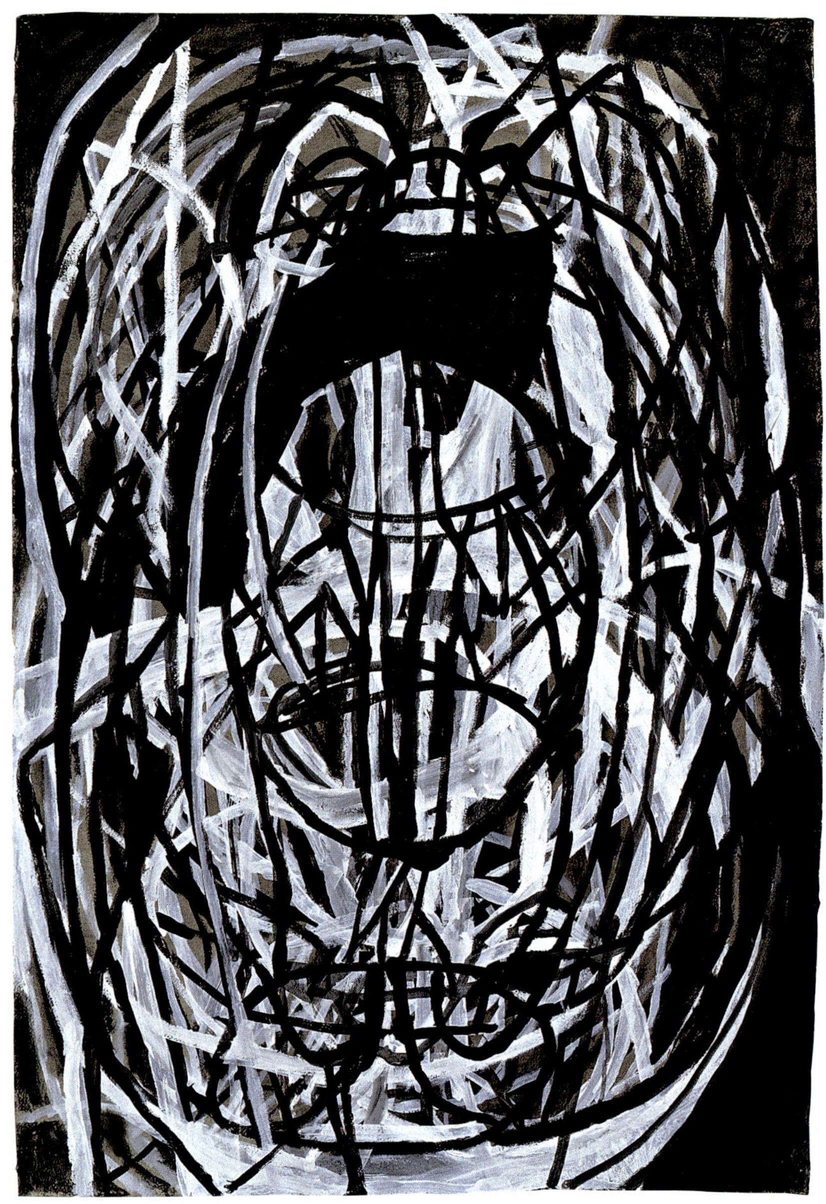

Tenon's Capsule 4, 1994
Charcoal, graphite, ink, and acrylic on paper
41 7/8 x 28 in. (106.4 x 71.1 cm)
Collection of Harry W. and Mary Margaret Anderson

Tenon's Capsule 5, 1994
Charcoal, graphite, ink, and acrylic on paper
40 x 27 1/8 in. (101.6 x 68.9 cm)
Private collection, New York

Tenon's Capsule 6, 1994
Charcoal, graphite, ink, and acrylic on paper
40 3/8 x 25 5/8 in. (102.6 x 65.1 cm)
Collection of Harry W. and Mary Margaret Anderson

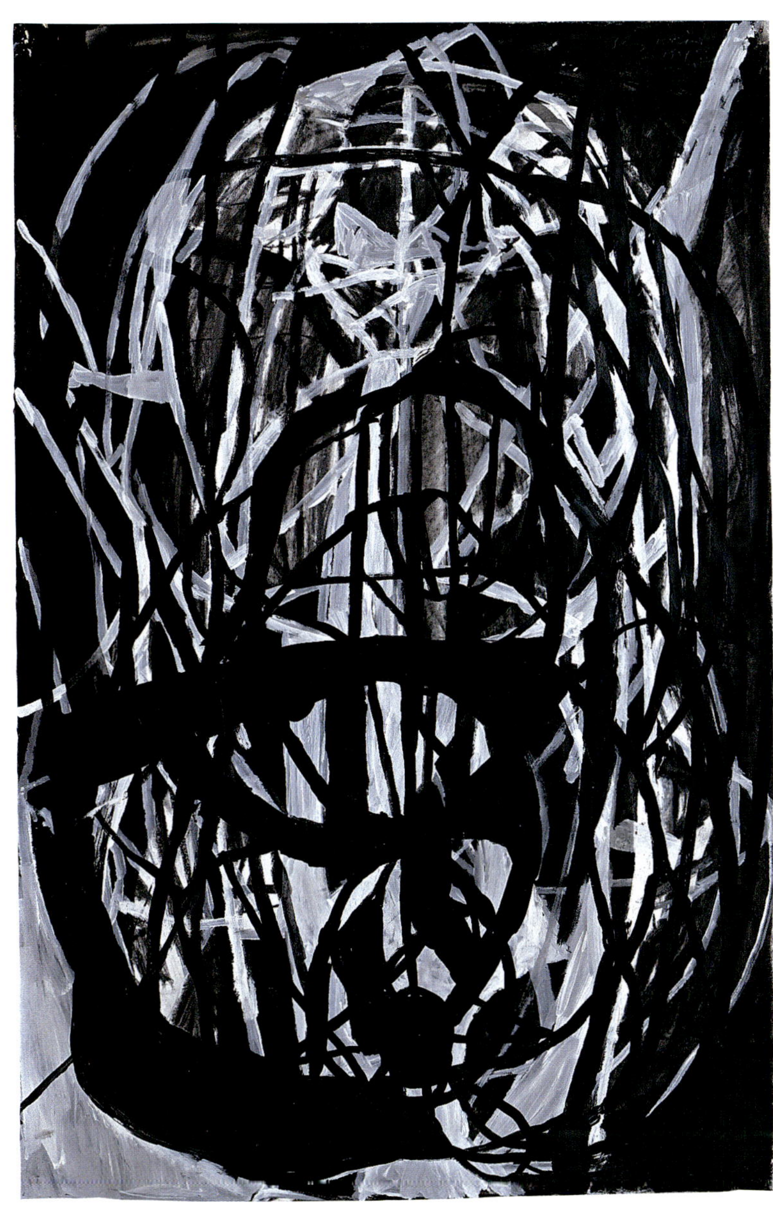

COMPUTATION OF CHAINS

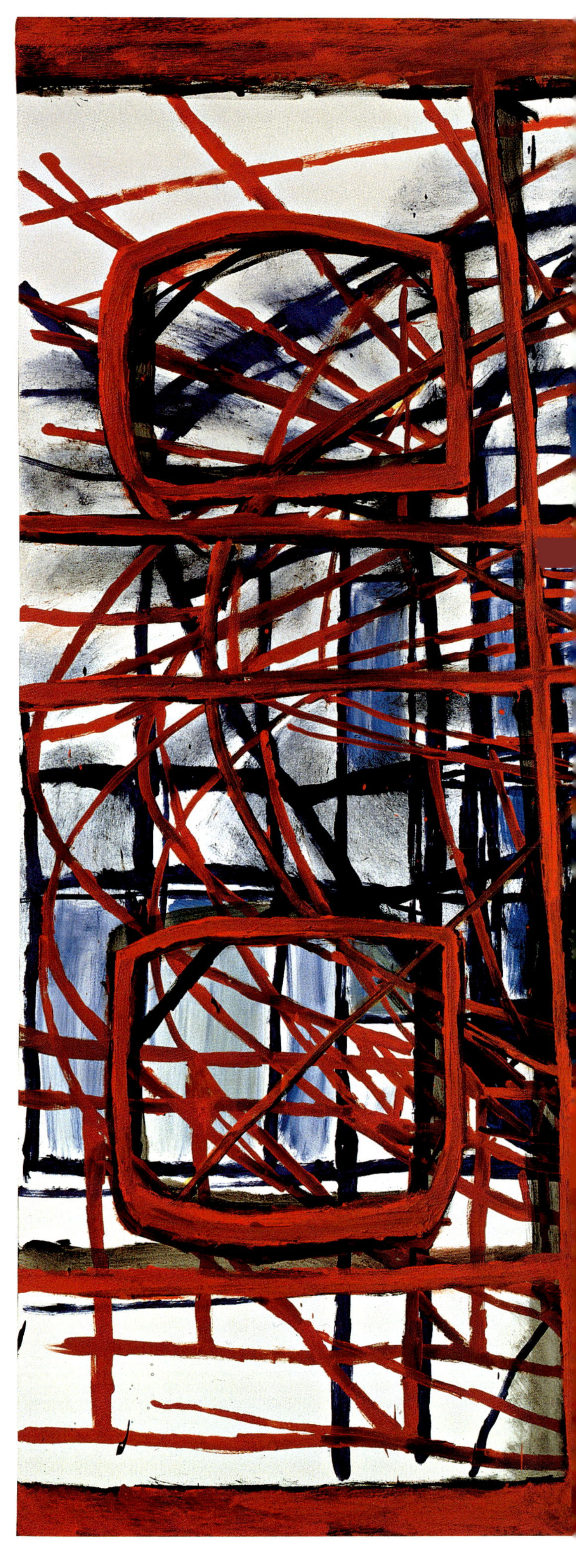

Computational Architecture, 1995
Oil and alkyd resin on linen
92 1/4 x 118 1/4 in. (234.3 x 300.4 cm)
Collection of the artist

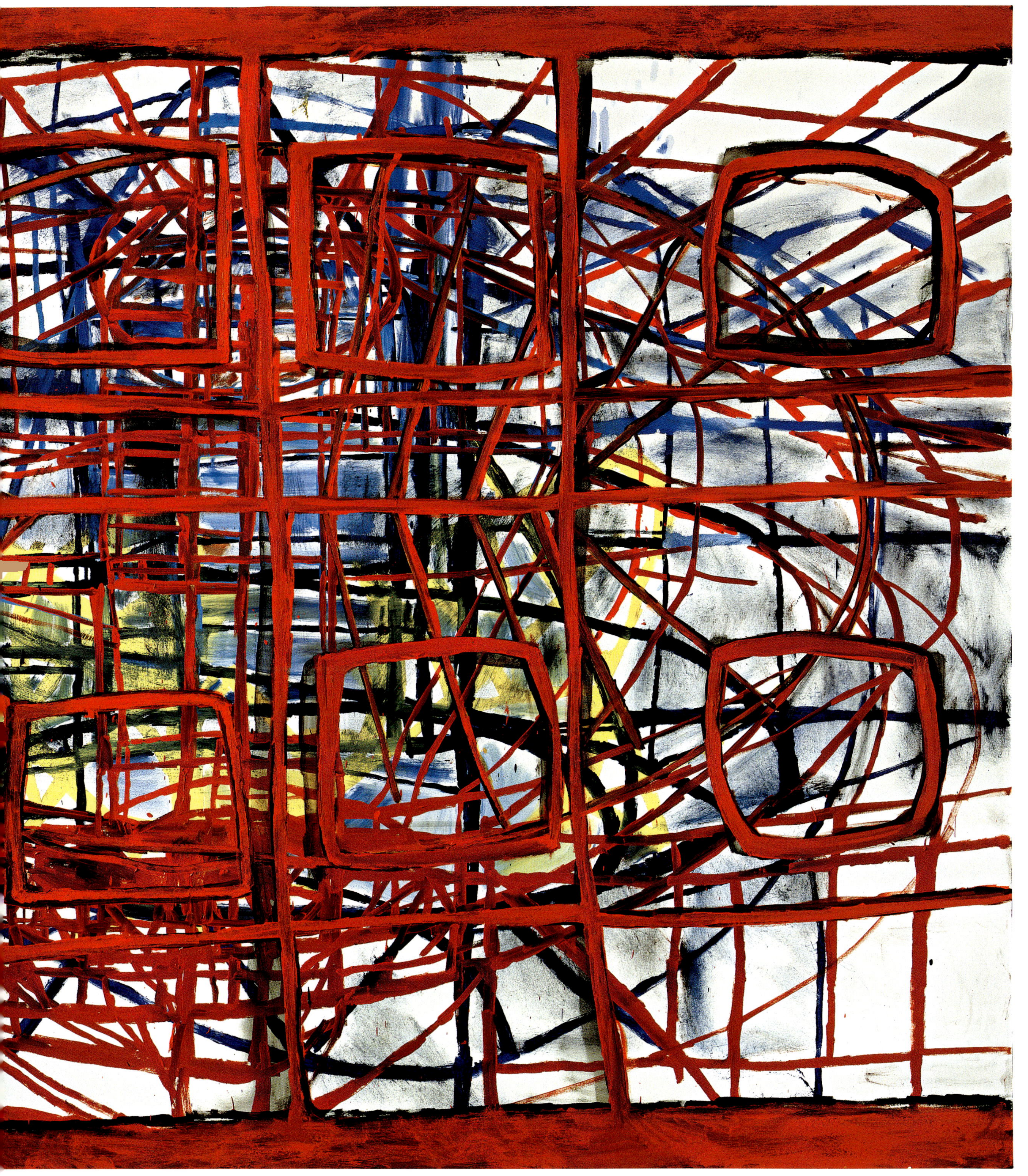

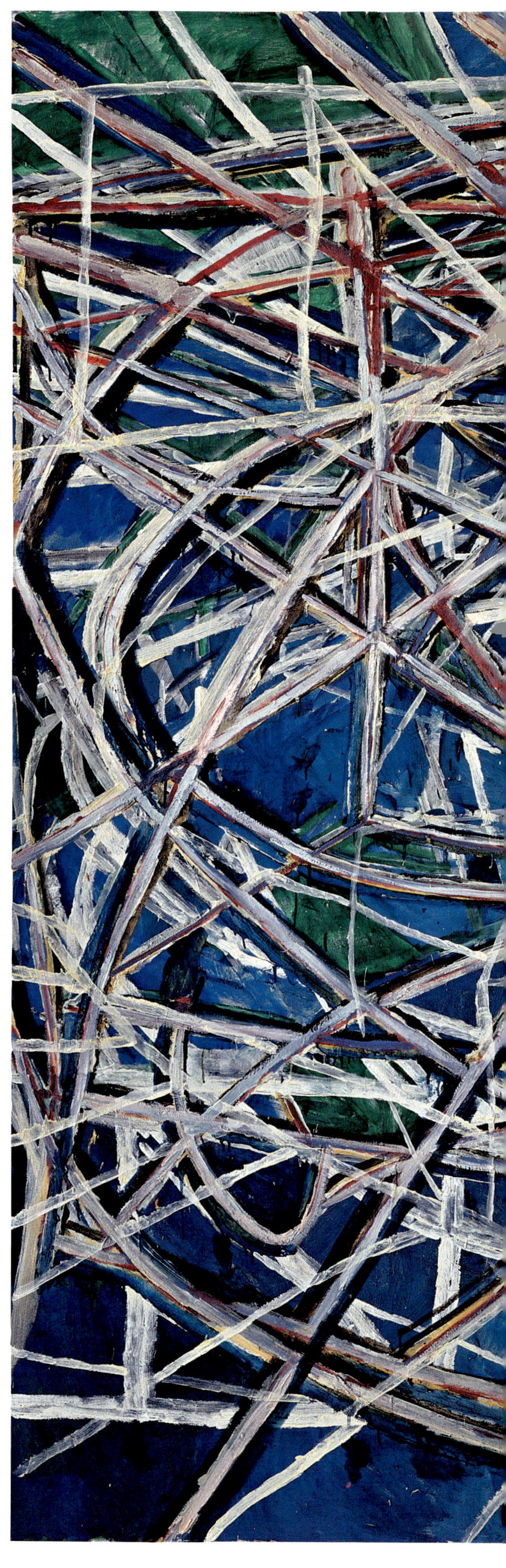

Image Location, 1997
Oil, alkyd resin, mica, and graphite on linen
96 x 120 in. (243.8 x 304.8 cm)
The UBS Art Collection

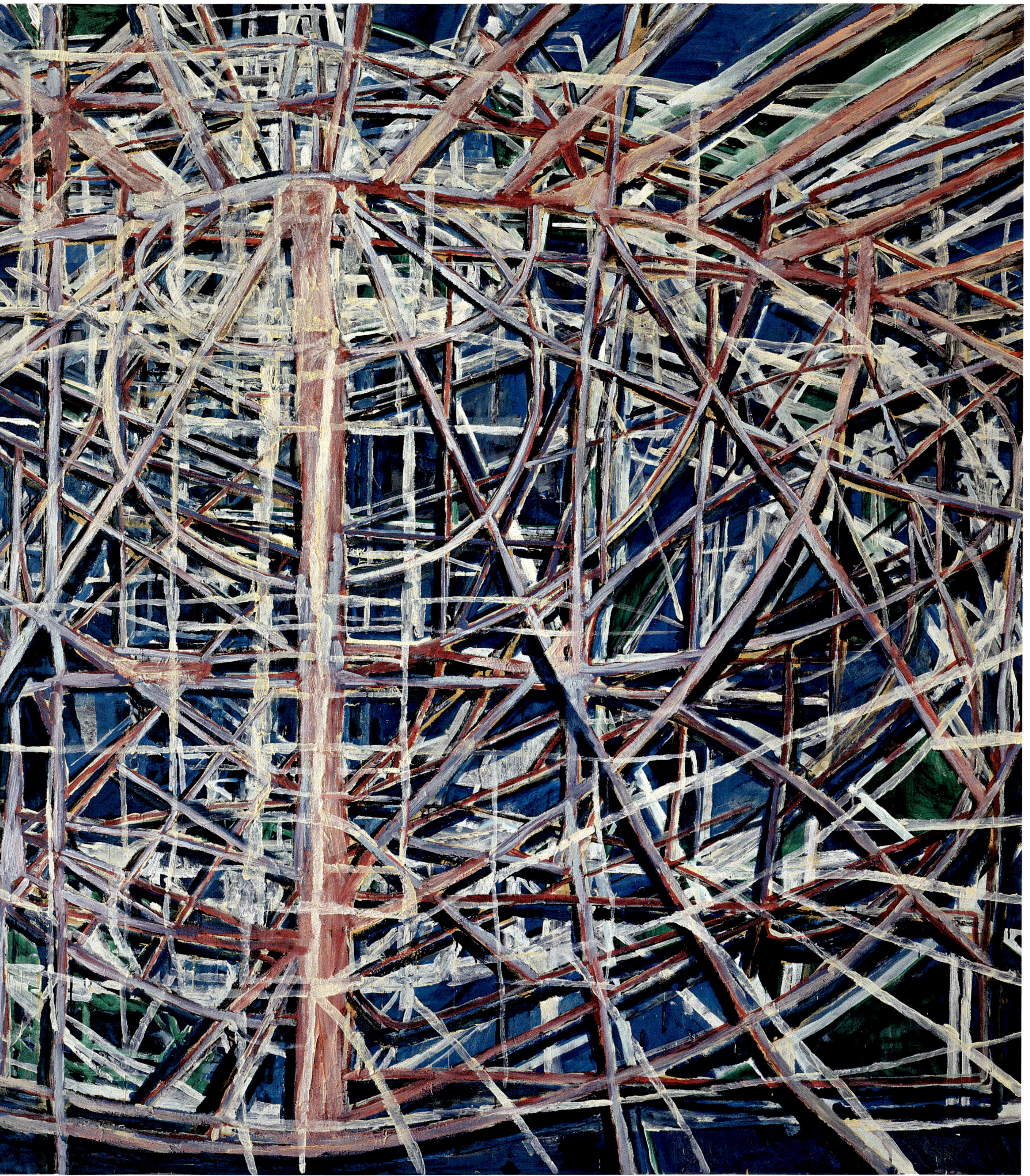

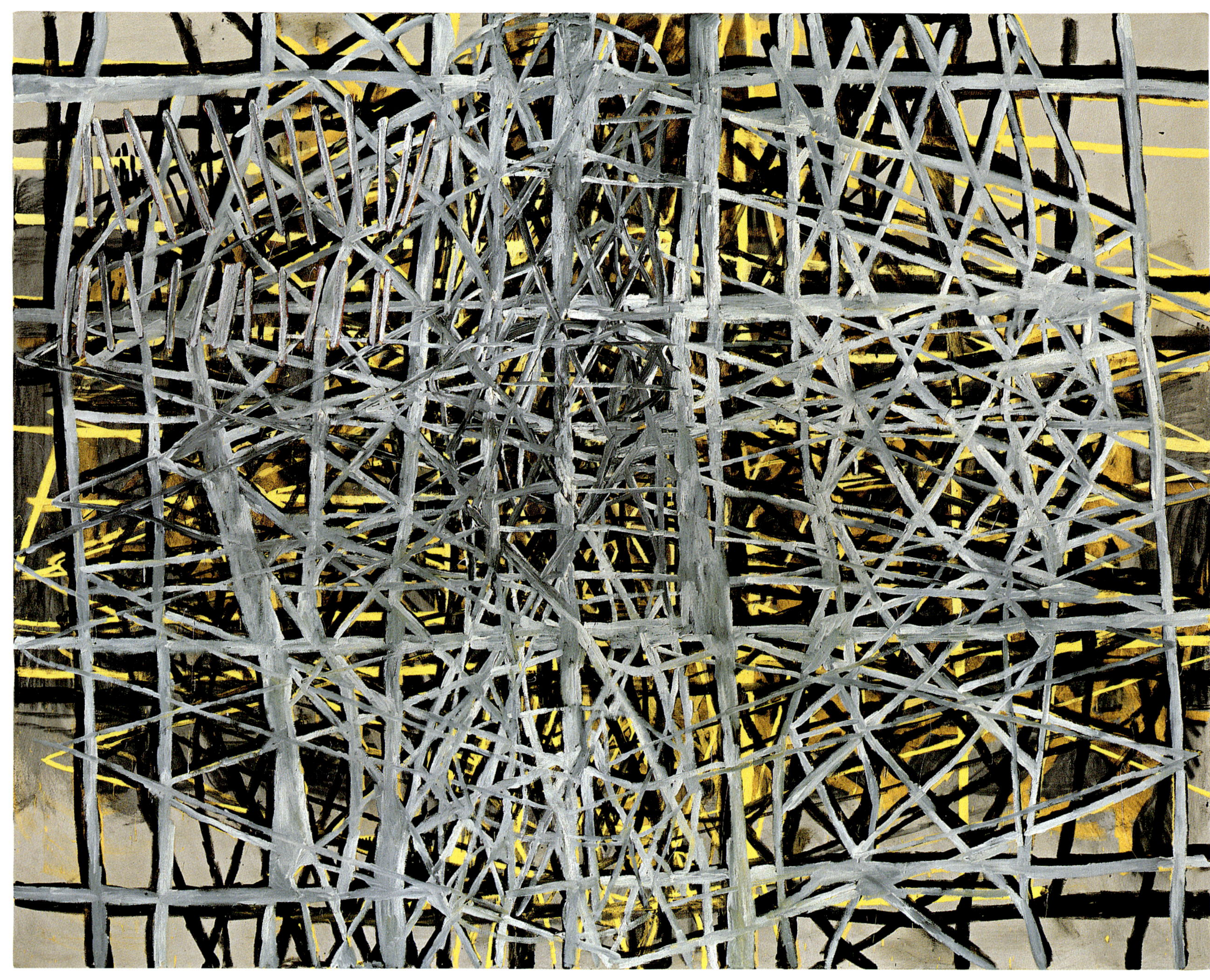

Parallel Rendering 2, 1996
Oil and alkyd resin on linen
96 x 120 in. (243.8 x 304.8 cm)
Tate, gift of The American Fund

Parallel Rendering 1, 1996
Oil and alkyd resin on linen
74 x 98 in. (188 x 248.9 cm)
Private collection

Parallel Rendering 3, 1996
Oil on linen
61 x 81 in. (154.9 x 205.7 cm)
Private collection, courtesy of Galerie Max Hetzler, Berlin

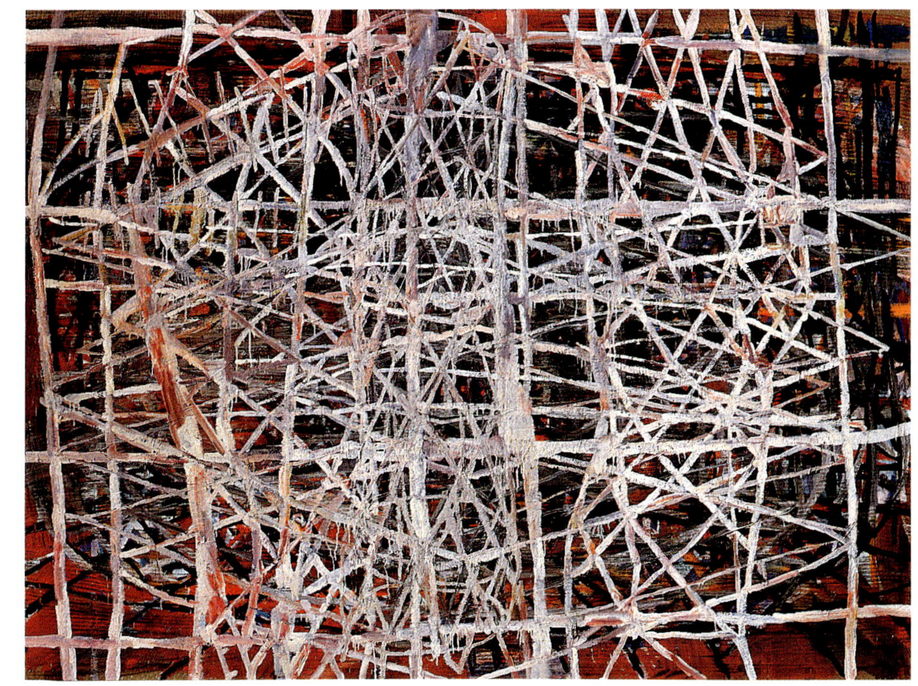

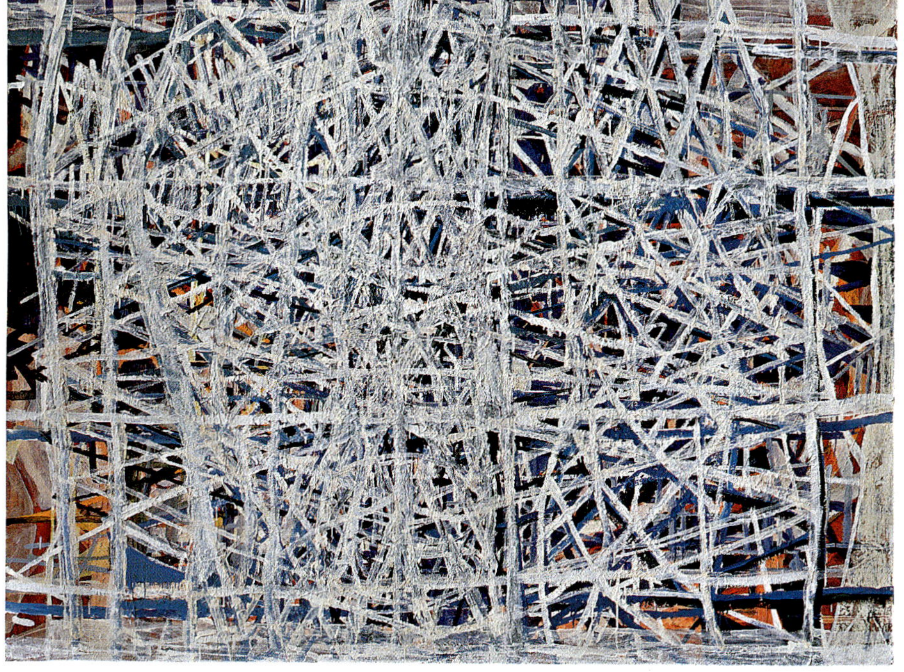

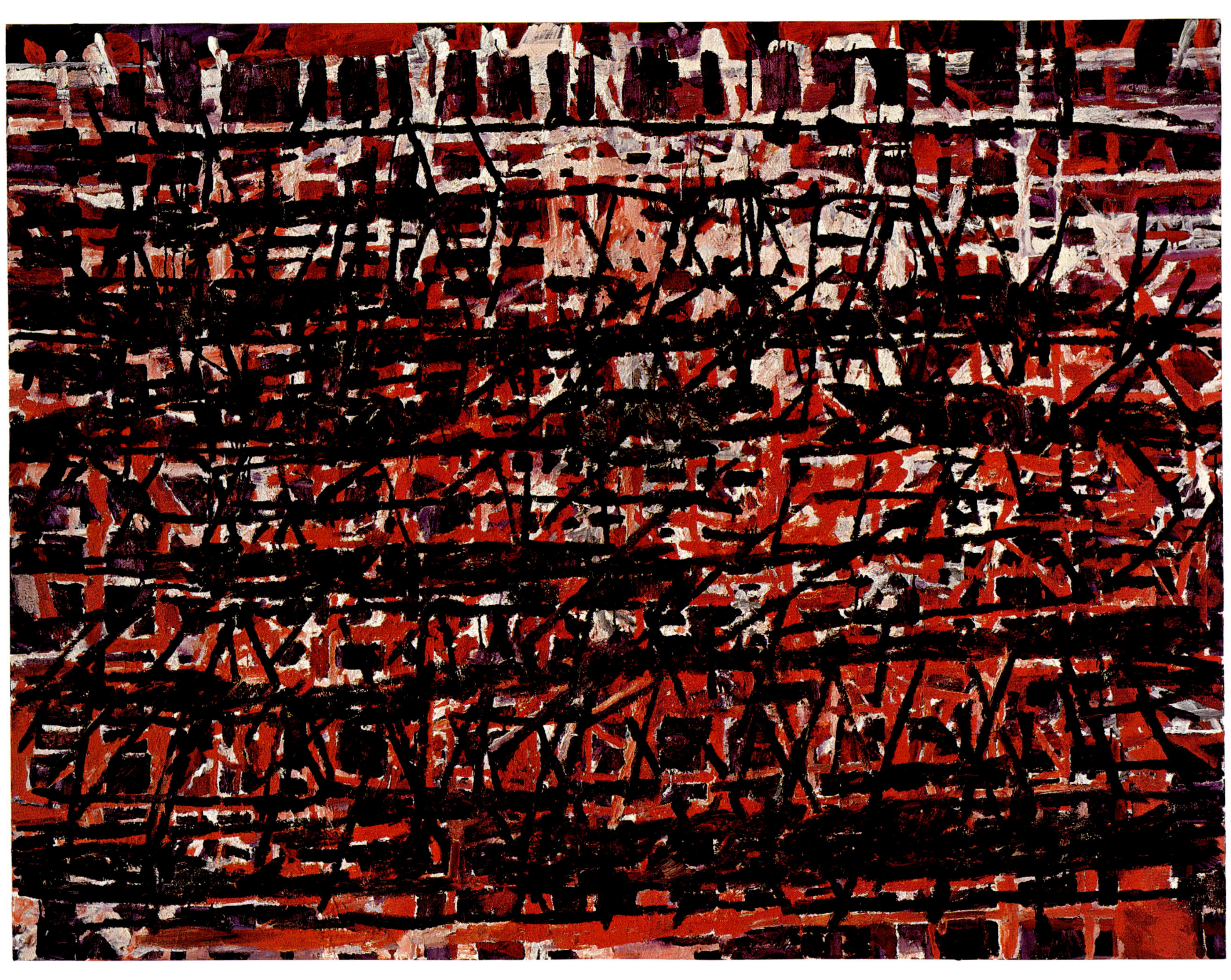

The Effects of Changing, 1997
Oil on linen
68 x 88 in. (172.7 x 223.5 cm)
Collection of the artist

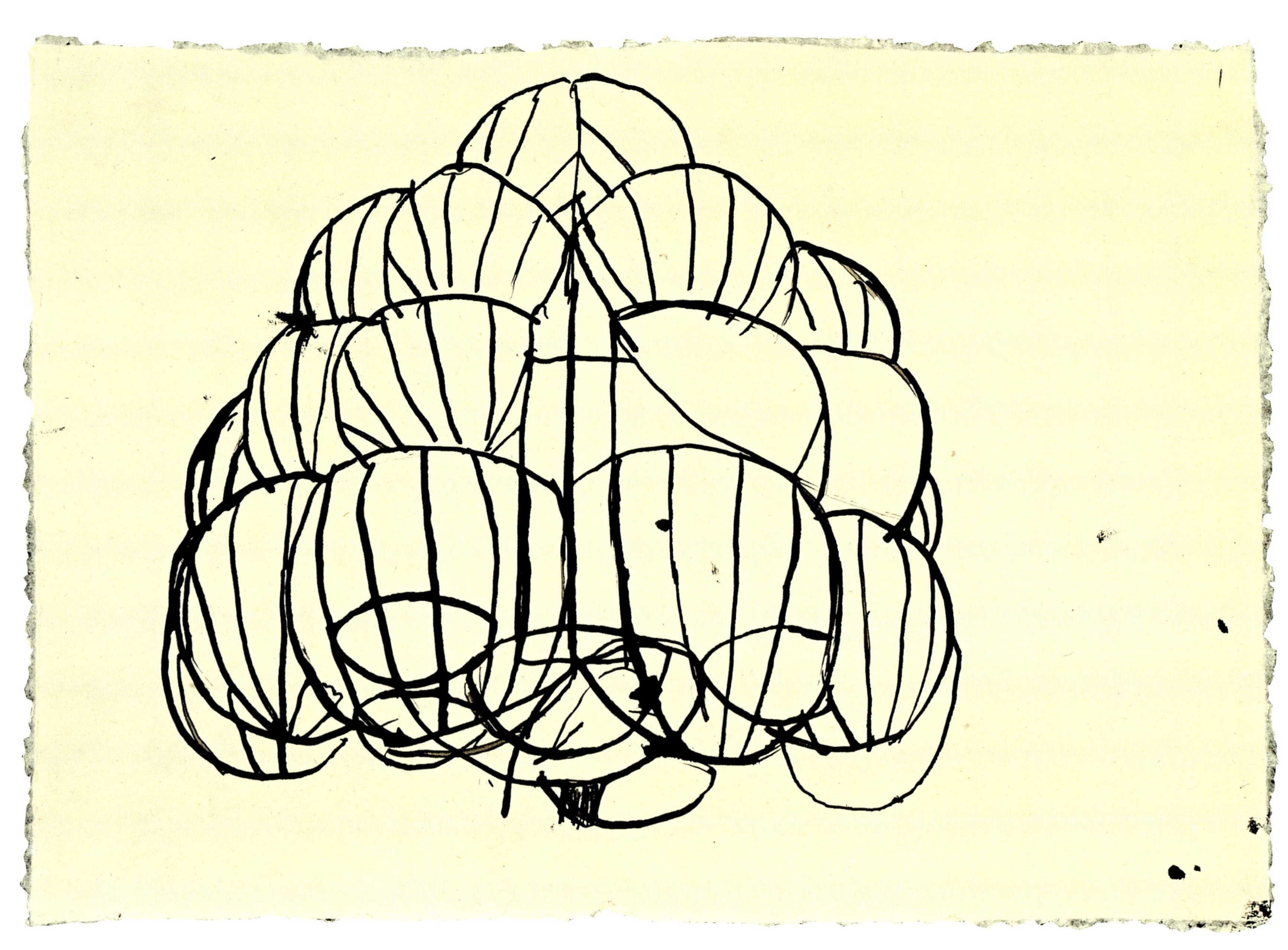

Pages 50–53:
Computation of Chains, 1995/96
From a series of 125 drawings plus title page
Ink on paper
Each, 8 1/8 x 11 1/2 in. (20.6 x 29.2 cm) (slightly irregular)
Collection of the artist

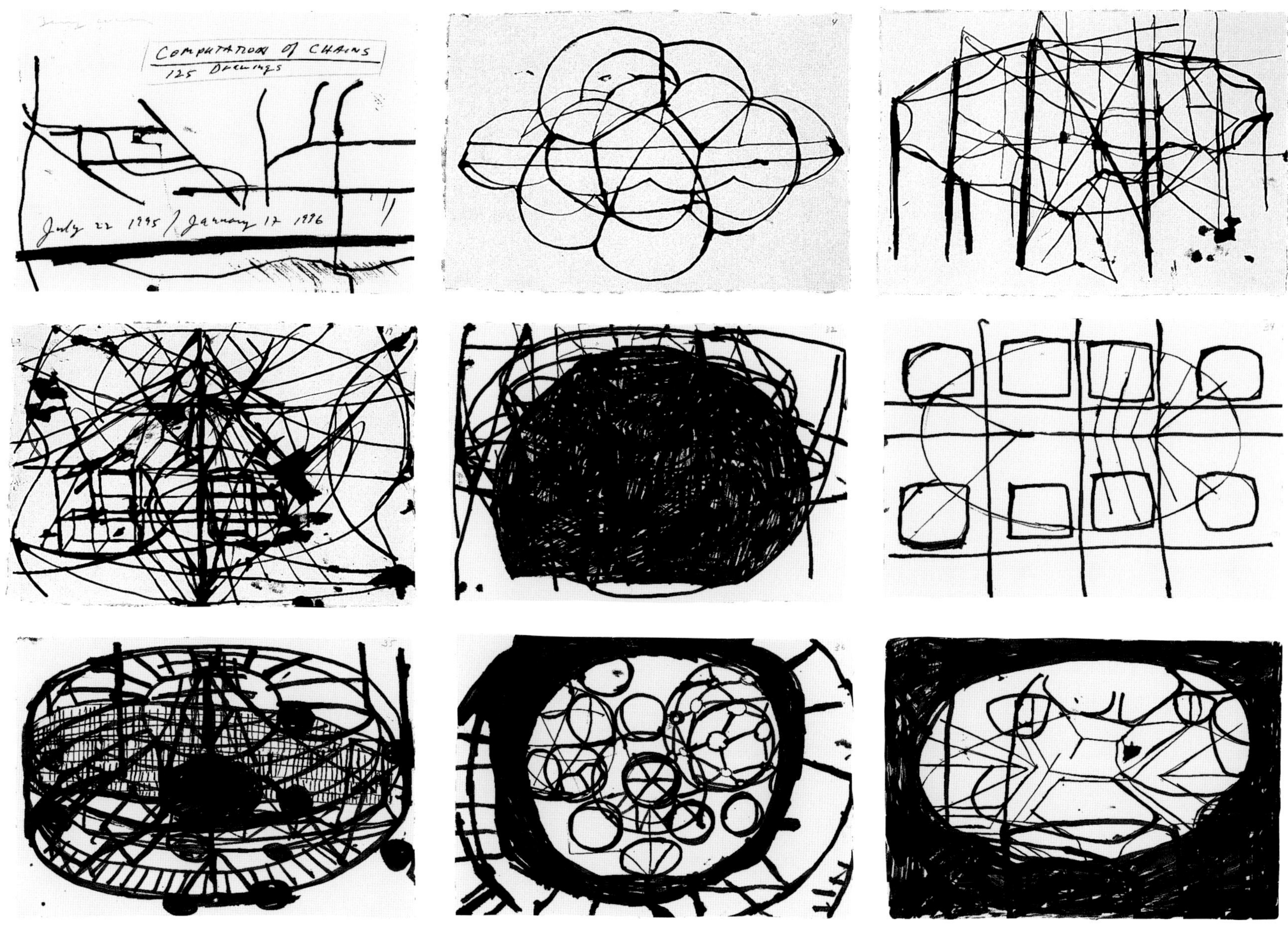
COMPUTATION OF CHAINS
125 Drawings
July 22 1995 / January 17 1996

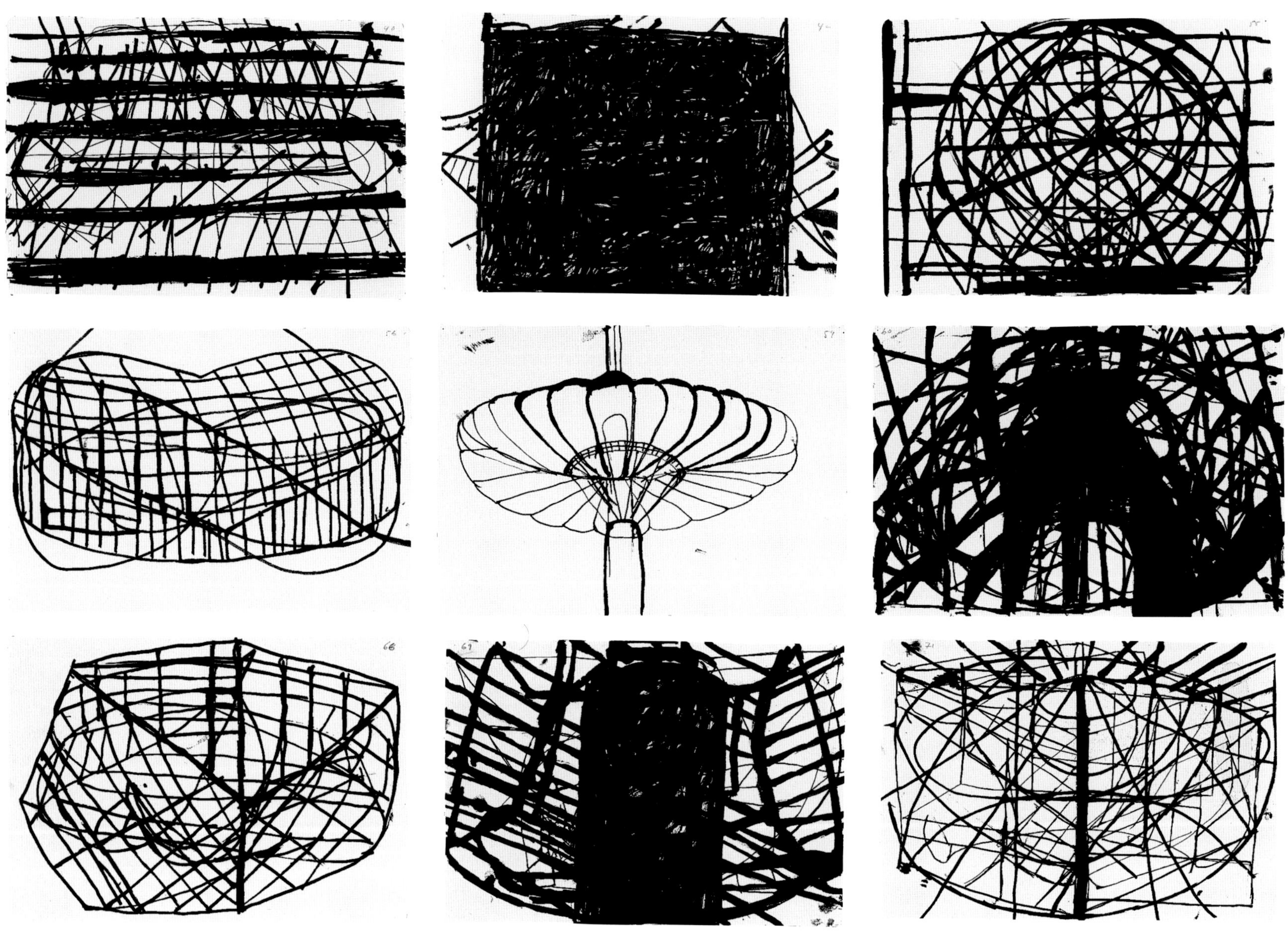

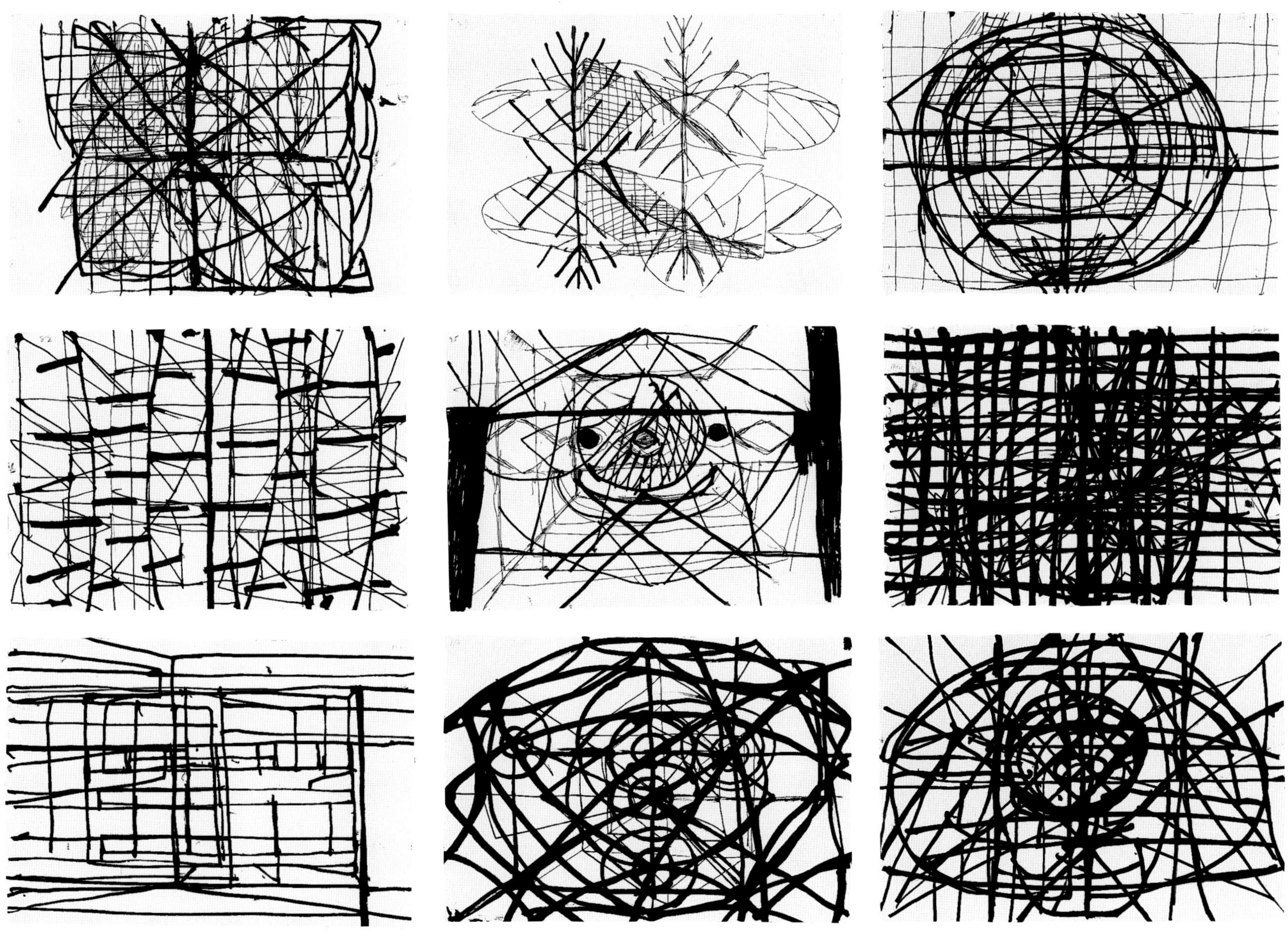

Systems Diagram, 1996
Etching, soft-ground etching, and sugar-lift aquatint on paper
42 x 50 in. (106.7 x 127 cm)
Private collection, New York

Pages 56–57:
Perfection, Way, Origin, 2001
Bound book containing a translated text by Jean Starobinski and 28 etchings by Terry Winters, issued with the *Set of Ten* portfolio of intaglio prints and a bound copy of the original French text, all in an aluminum box
Book, closed, 18 7/8 x 15 x 2 in. (47.6 x 38.1 x 5.1 cm)
Courtesy of Universal Limited Art Editions (ULAE)

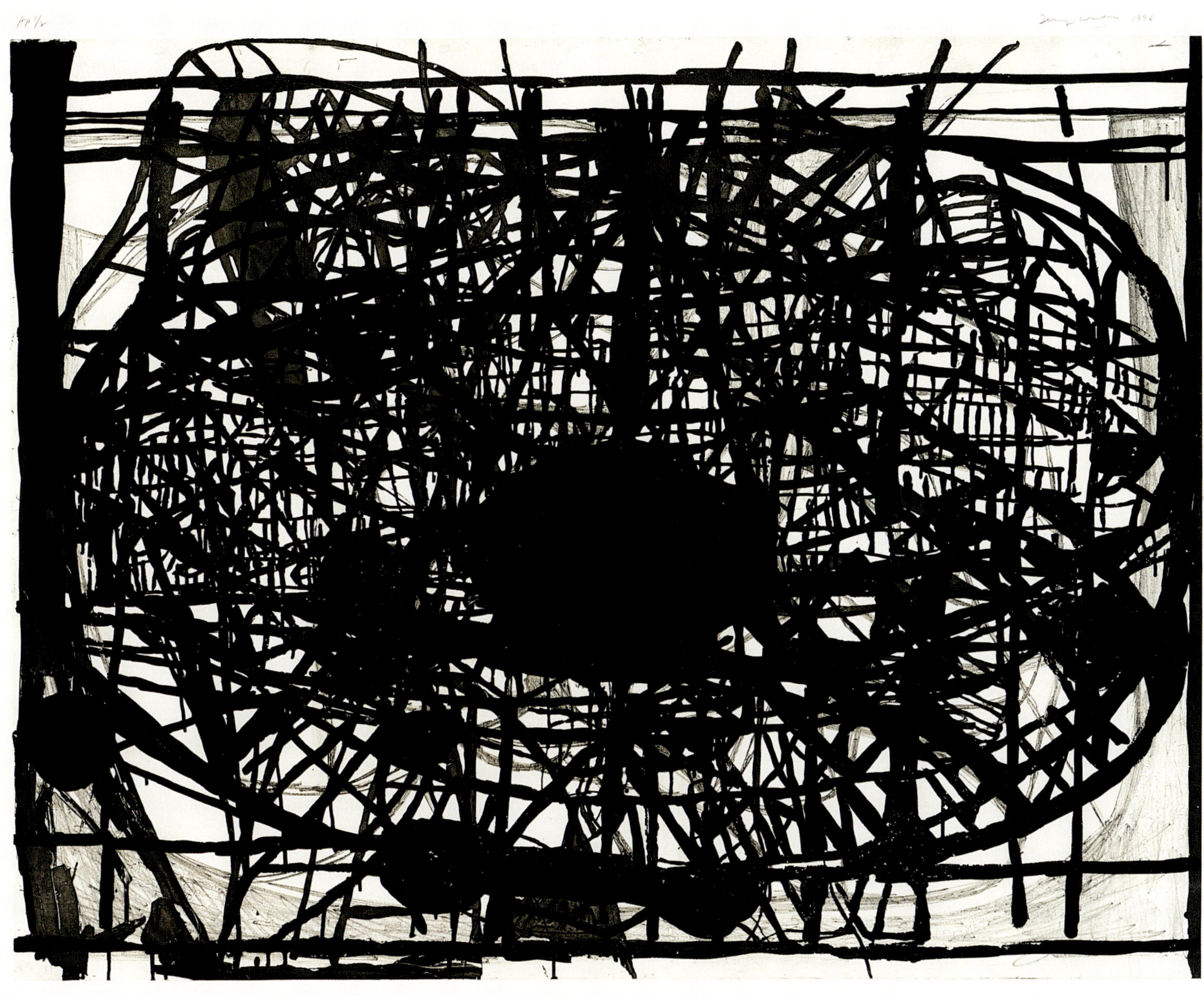

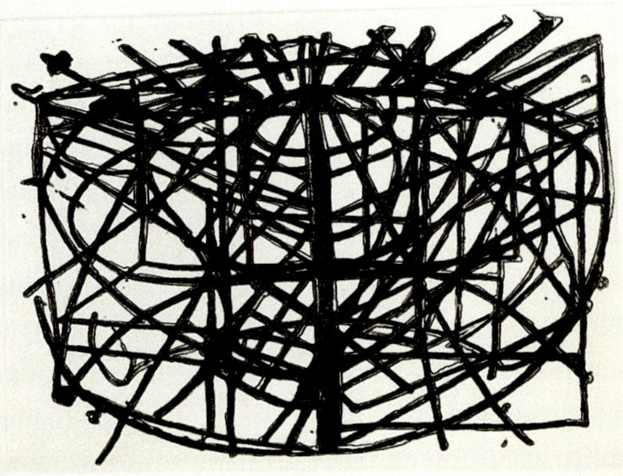

The Instant of Dissolution

The loss of the preeminence of the Work and the importance given to preparatory states are therefore correlative phenomena: the one entails the other. Today we like to see a series of different moments succeed one another, an adventurous journey in which each stage equals the preceding stage in legitimacy, so much so that in the end these different moments become indifferent. We have lost confidence in the durable compactness of a work, and we no longer accord it more than a tenuous present, between a past and a future that are still more tenuous, or simply guessed at. The prior moments are sometimes accessible to our objective knowledge. At other times, if documents relative to the prior states are lacking, we imagine them, we try to reconstitute them, starting from the characteristics of the work itself, from its contradictions, from its irregularities, from what seems missing in its homogeneity. Whether through reliance on documents or by means of conjecture, we go back to a childhood, to early dreams, to foretexts that are stammerings. And we cannot resolve on attributing a "definitive state" to the whole undertaking: a closer examination reveals it to us as unstable and fragile. We feel ourselves drawn into following through the later states, where the object produced is transformed and deformed. It has undergone cuttings, rewritings, alterations, arbitrary restorations, reinterpretations, sacralizations and desecrations, the wear and tear of celebrity, thumbings of the nose (a mustache on the Mona Lisa)—and it is sometimes given over to a strange decomposition.

Distending and fragmenting the moment of the work is only one aspect of our theoretical and practical behavior toward the work of art. We are still granting it a temporality of its own. We are still allowing for a succession of provisional totalities. A more radical attitude consists in withdrawing all temporal support from them, that is, in willing them to be as ephemeral, as perishable as possible, in attributing to them no more than the time of a gesture, in closing this gesture again over the very body of the artist. Some contemporary works disavow the condition of being a work. They labor for their own undoing, which demands of the "artist"—a usurped name, perhaps

I

Of Perfection

Every work is on the way to the Work.

This thought accompanied poets and artists for a long time. The concern for perfection directed the desire of those who aspired to the victors' garland. Perfection was what they did not possess but were charged with attaining and adding to the world. For some it was what made the beauty of the world more complete. They had no right to be satisfied before they reached it. They wanted to be supreme, or nothing. This thought has been perpetuated in various guises over the centuries: we still recognize it in the plan for works of world form, which was pondered during the century now coming to an end.

Perfection is taken to have been the ideal of classicism. It was Romantic thought, above all, that attributed this ideal to classicism, in order to criticize it or regret its passing. In fact, the majority of Romantic artists remained attached to the ideal of perfection. They even conferred a transcendent ideality upon it. They sometimes attributed to it the contradictory qualities of wholeness and limitlessness. At the turn of the nineteenth century, in the exalted prose of his *General Draft*, the great German poet Novalis wrote:

> *No perfection is expressed in isolation; the perfect object expresses at the same time a whole related world. That is why the veil of the virgin flutters around what is perfect of any kind—a veil which the lightest contact dissolves into a magic perfume that becomes the cloudy chariot of the seer. It is not only antiquity that we see. It is at the same time the sky, the spyglass, and the fixed star—and thus the authentic revelation of a higher world. Let it not be too rigidly believed that*

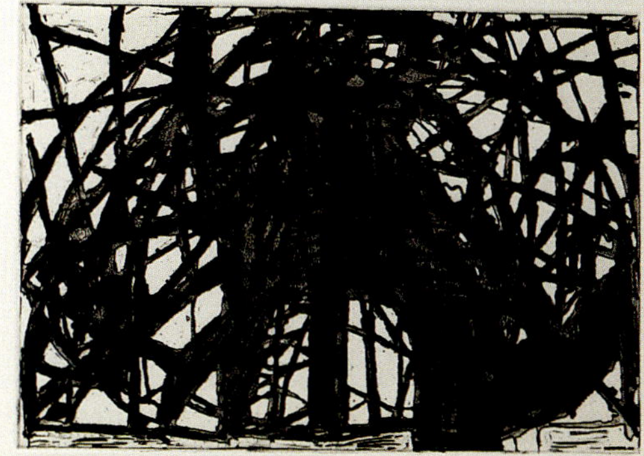

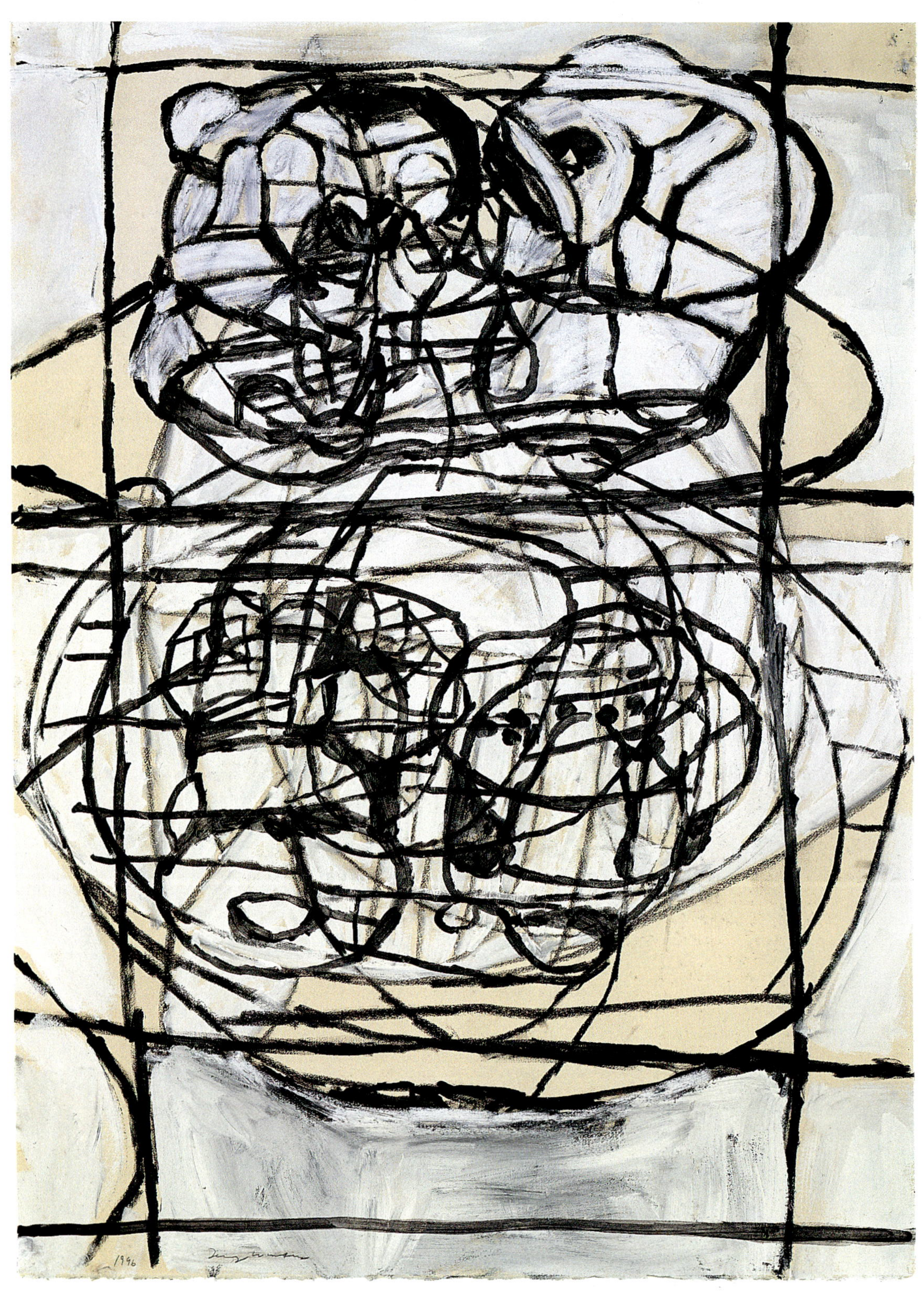

Multi-Form Visualization, 1996
Charcoal, ink, and acrylic on paper
41 5/8 x 29 3/4 in. (105.7 x 75.6 cm)
Collection of Maureen and Geof Kirsch

Connected Slice, 1996
Oil and acrylic on paper
41 5/8 x 29 3/4 in. (105.7 x 75.6 cm)
Brooklyn Museum of Art, New York,
Gift of the American Academy of Arts and Letters

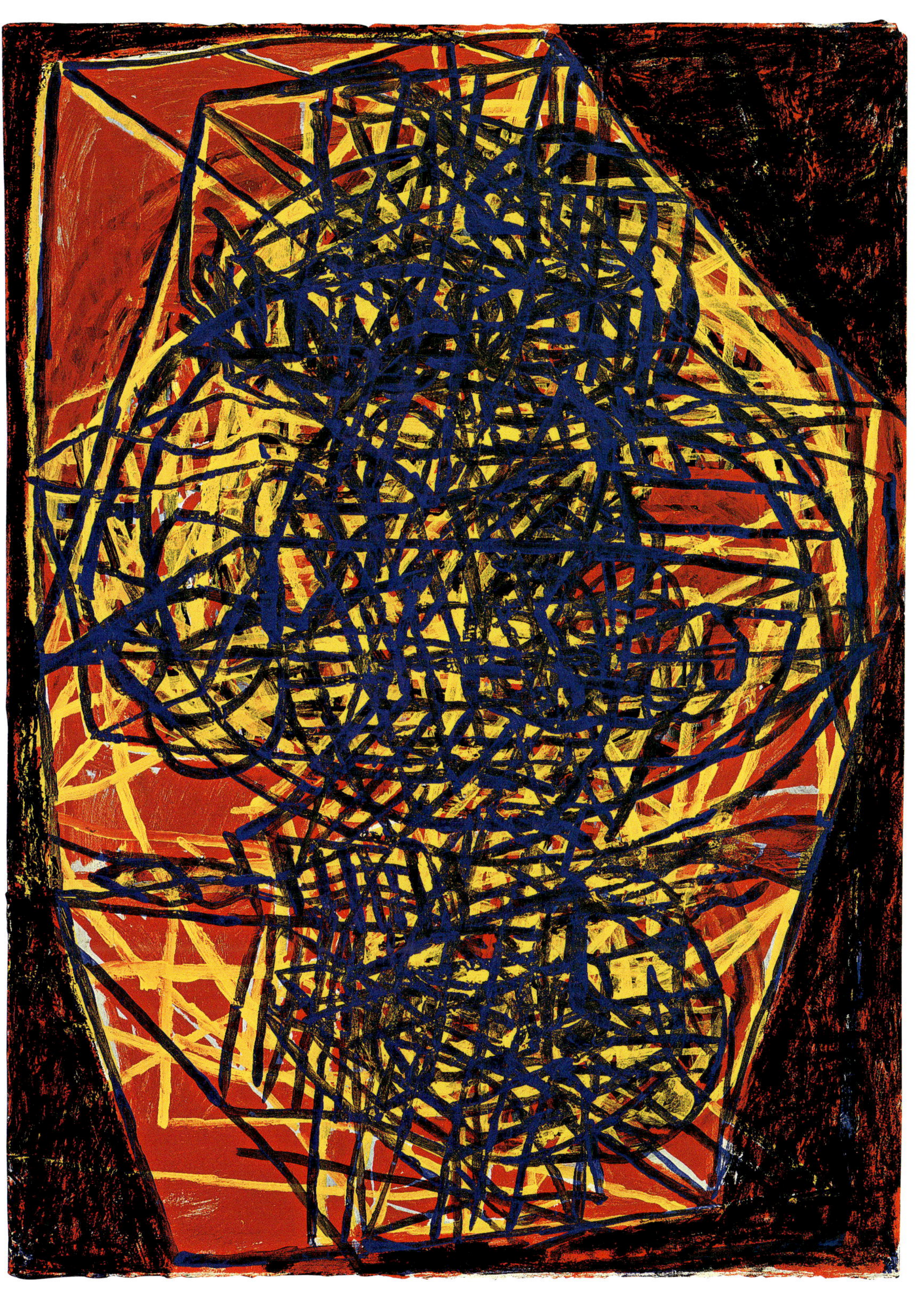

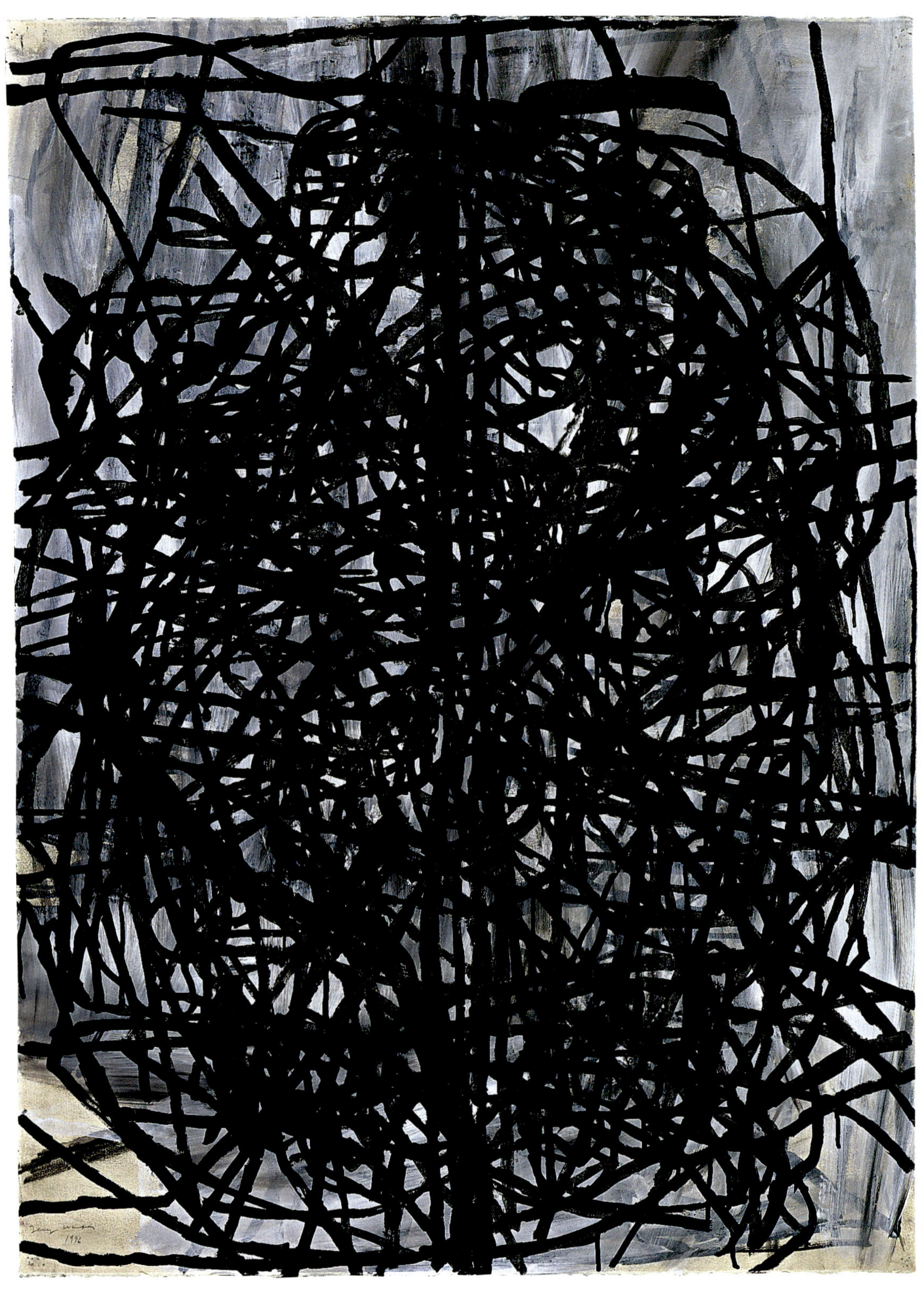

Vector Field, 1996
Graphite, ink, and acrylic on paper
41 5/8 x 29 3/4 in. (105.7 x 75.6 cm)
Collection of Nicki and Harold Tanner

Scene Generation, 1997
Acrylic on paper
41 5/8 x 29 3/4 in. (105.7 x 75.6 cm)
Collection of Emily Glasser and Bill Susman

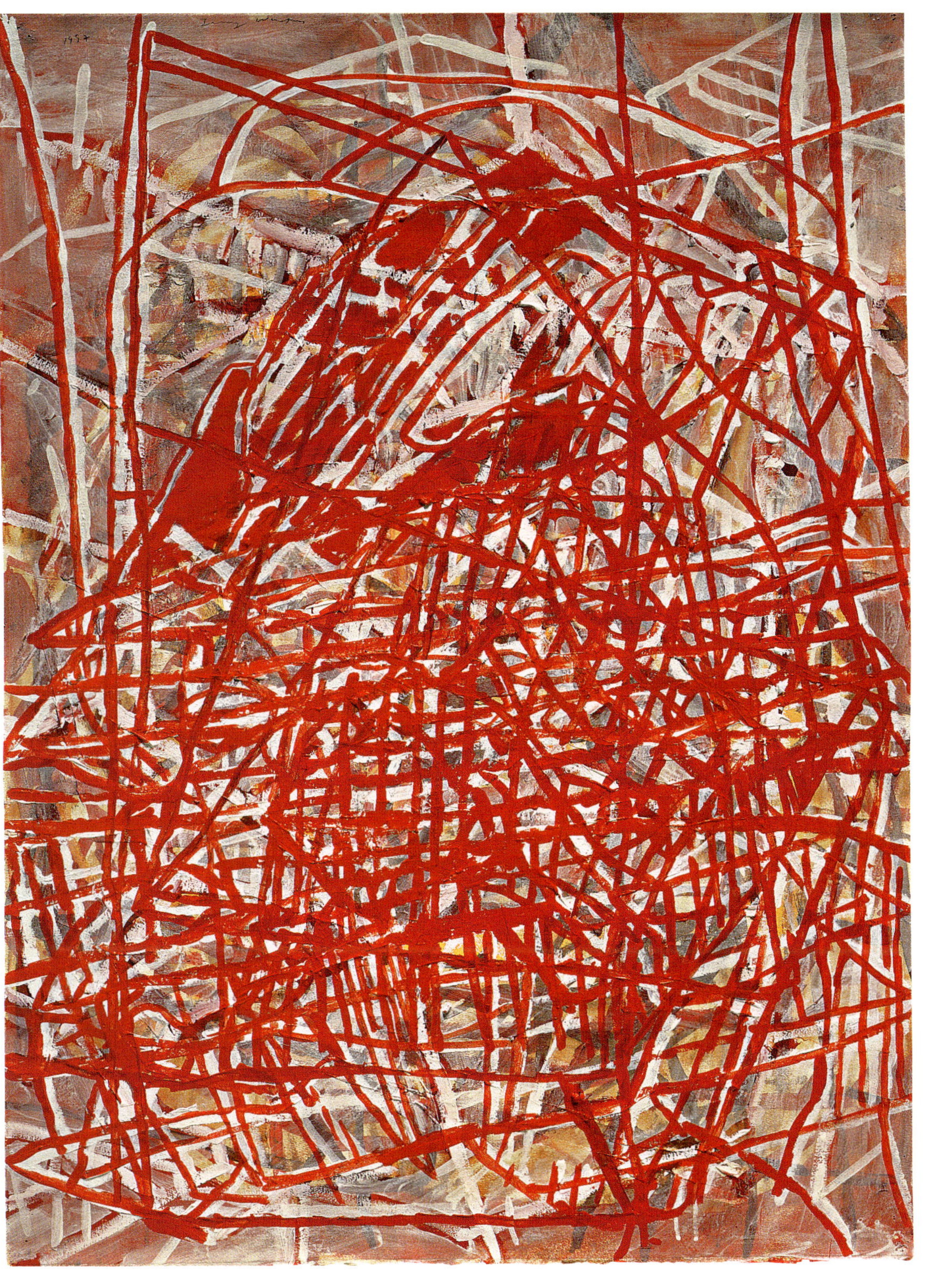

Animation, 1996
Charcoal, graphite, and oil on paper
41 5/8 x 29 3/4 in. (105.7 x 75.6 cm)
Private collection, New York

Pages 64–65:
"Process," from *Ocular Proofs*, 2001 edition
Bound book, offset lithography
Open, 7 1/2 x 10 in. (19.2 x 25.4 cm)
Courtesy of the artist

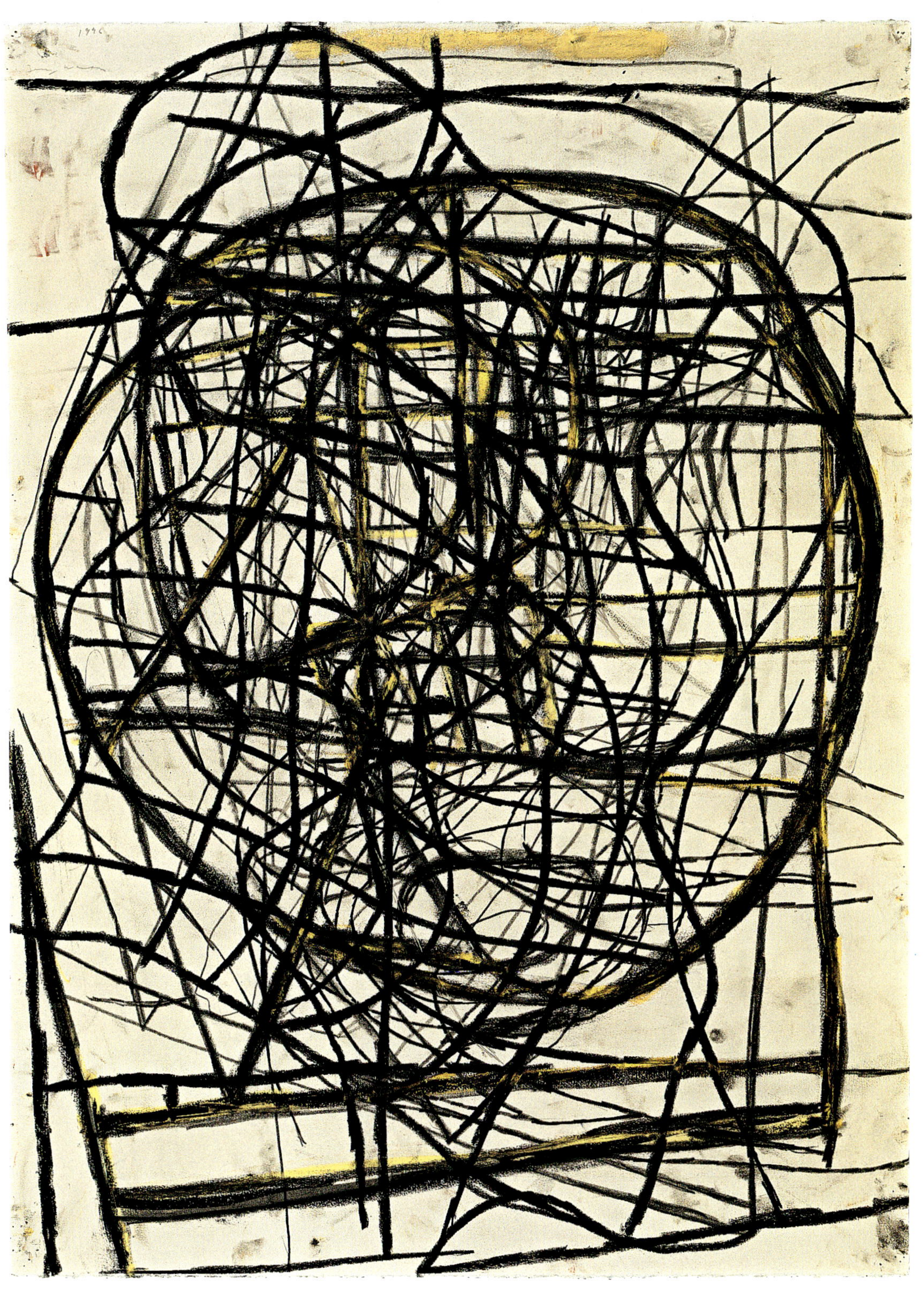

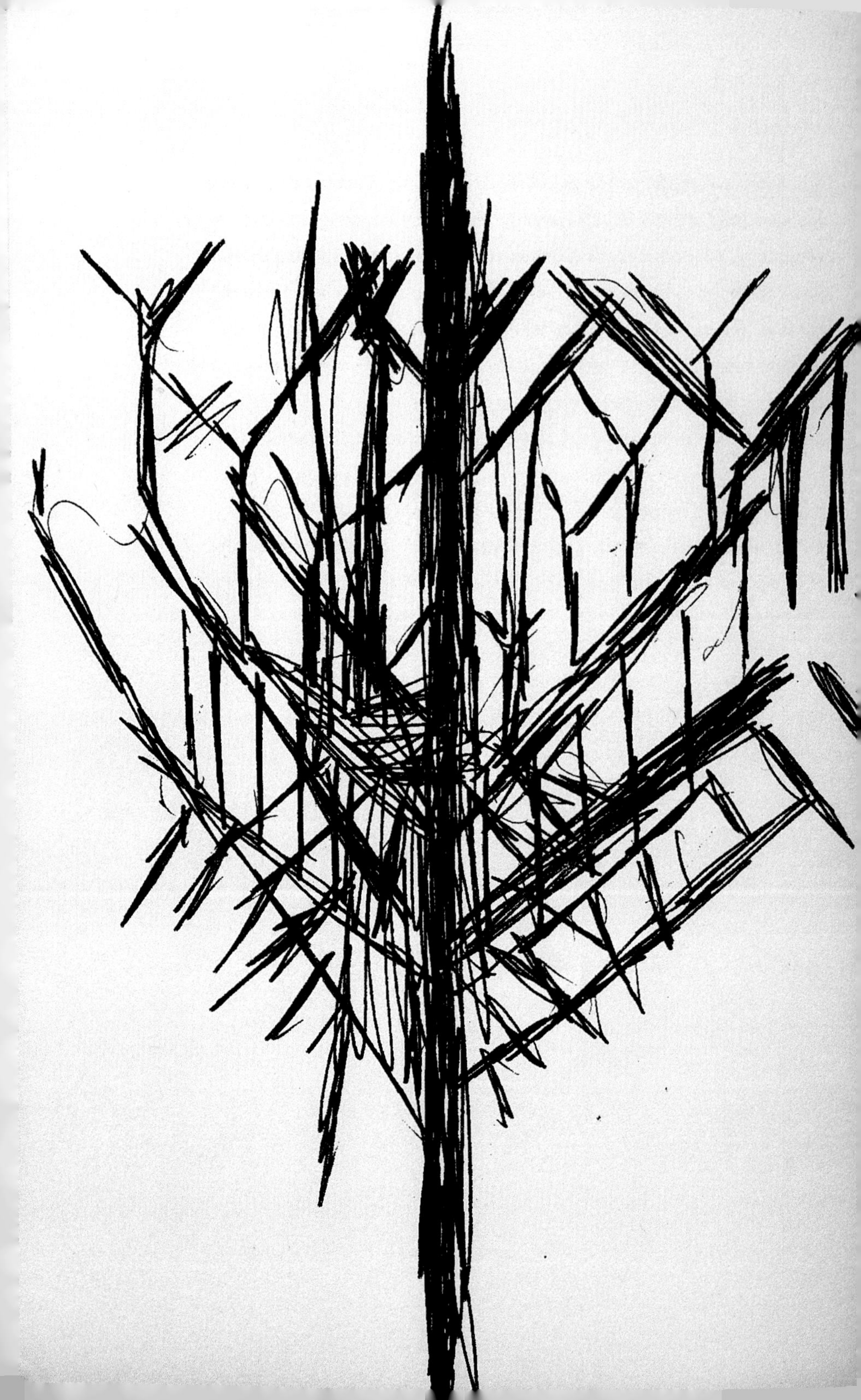

Process

the painting process demands display / a great deal of computing power is required by the circumstances / a medium-resolution gray must be as intense as each of the primary colors / a single bright image can display many levels of meaning / pictures can be read / paintings are strictly dedicated to building data / further graphic calculations require extreme visual orientations / unique material procedures produce irregular pictures / simple descriptions can be reduced or enlarged / more complex image operations free the main processor

GRAPHIC PRIMITIVES

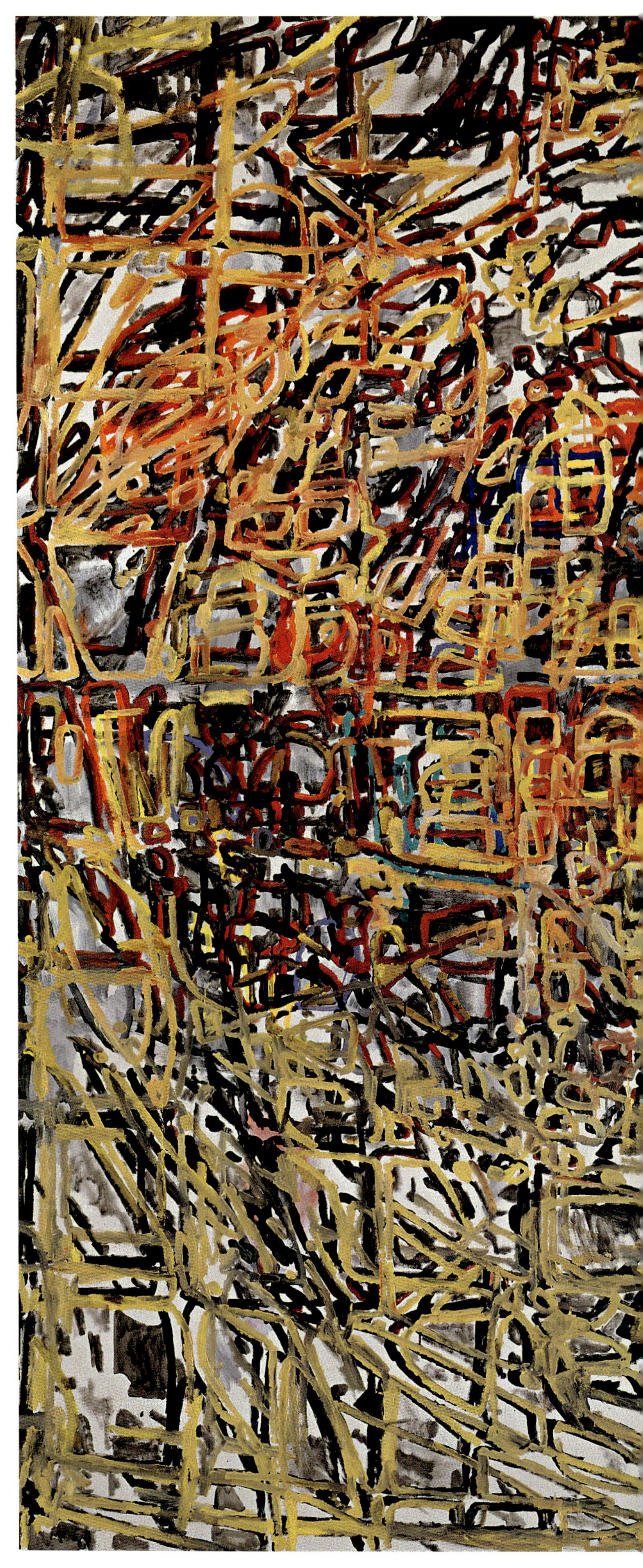

Color and Information, 1998
Oil and alkyd resin on linen
108 x 144 in. (274.3 x 365.8 cm)
Collection of Harry W. and Mary Margaret Anderson

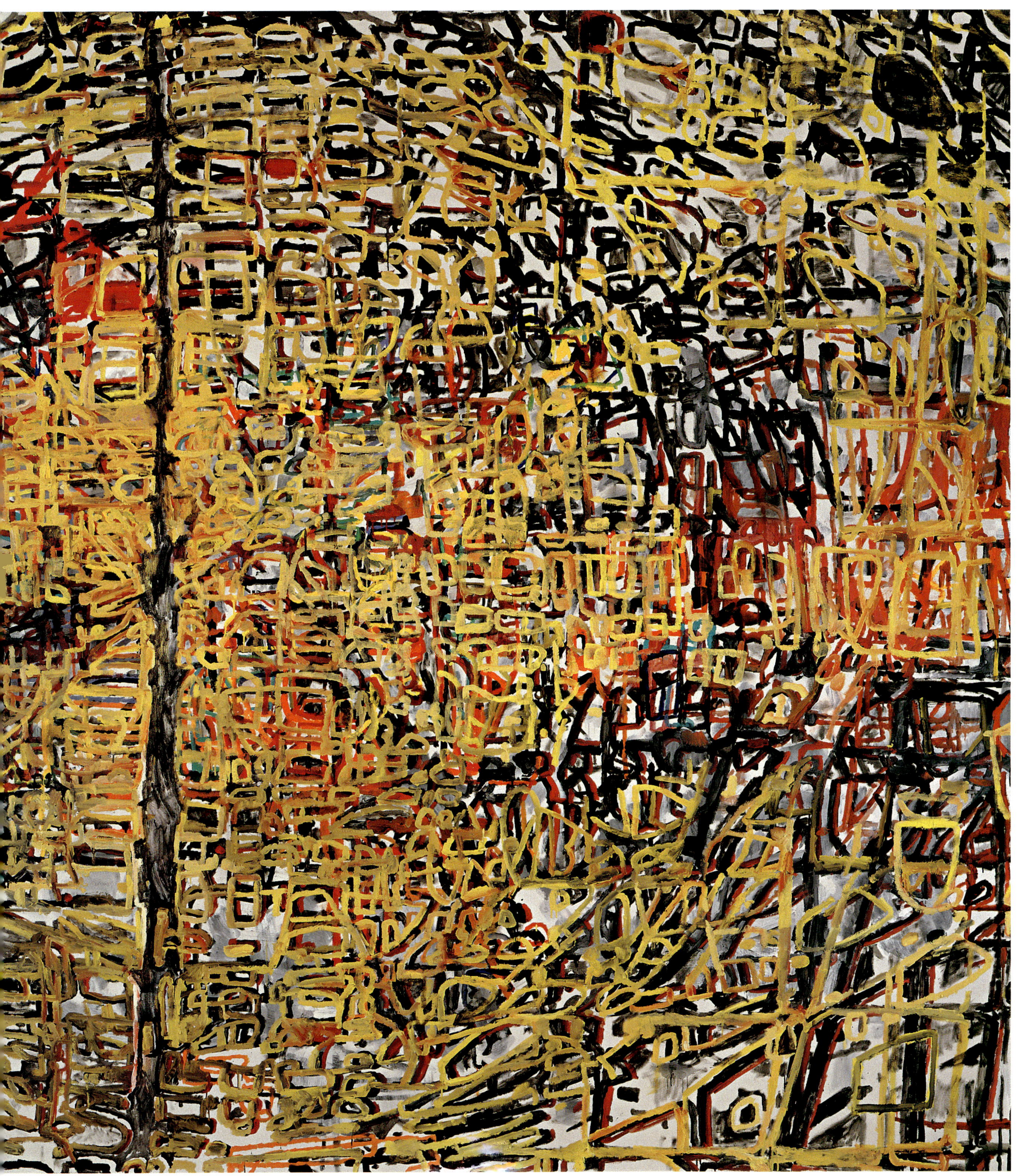

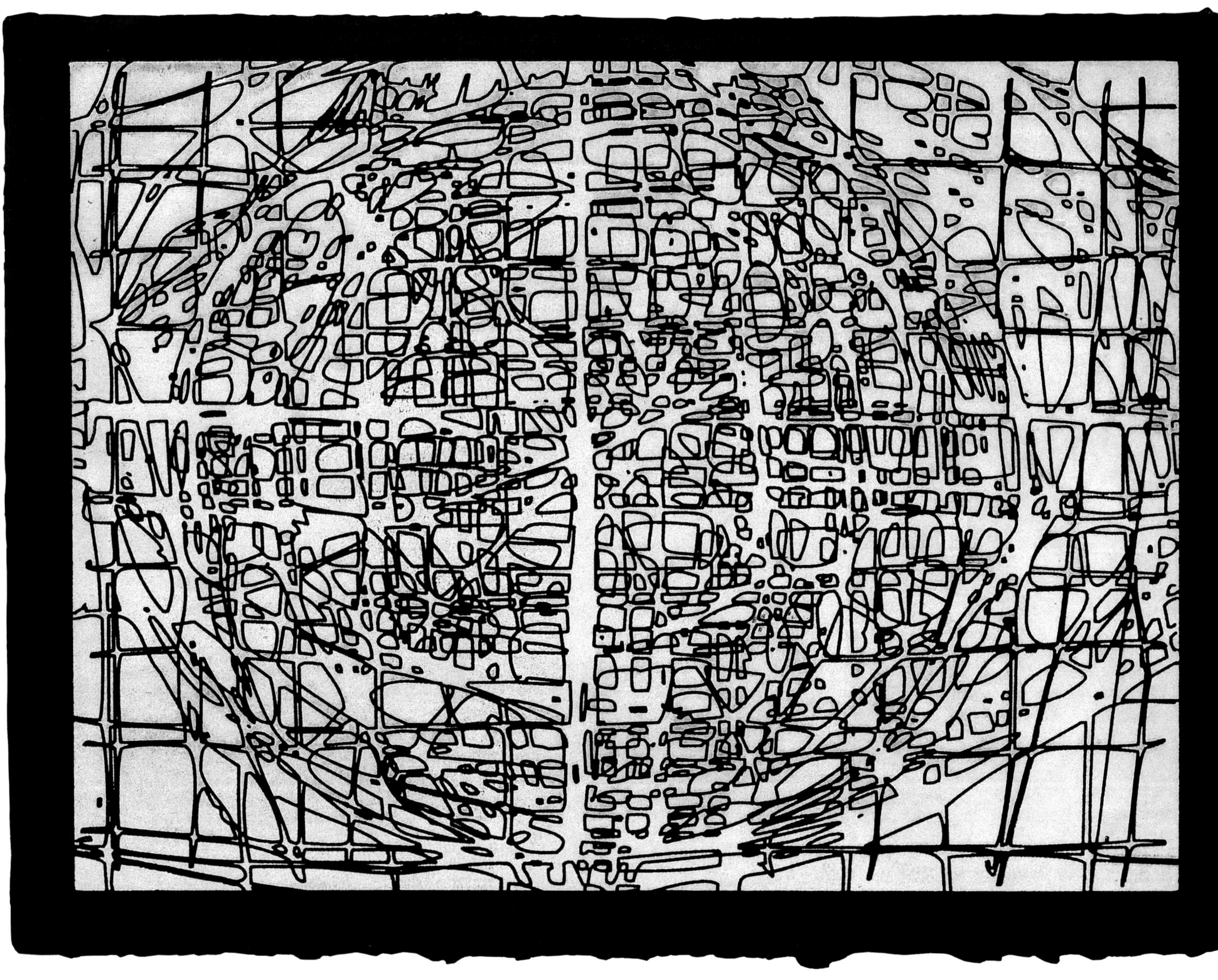

Graphic Primitives, 1, 1998
From a portfolio of 9 woodcuts
Rinsed-proof woodcut on paper
20 x 26 in. (50.8 x 66 cm)
Private collection, courtesy of Two Palms Press, New York

Graphic Primitives, 1–9, 1998
A portfolio of 9 woodcuts
Rinsed-proof woodcuts on paper
Each, 20 x 26 in. (50.8 x 66 cm)
Private collection, courtesy of Two Palms Press, New York

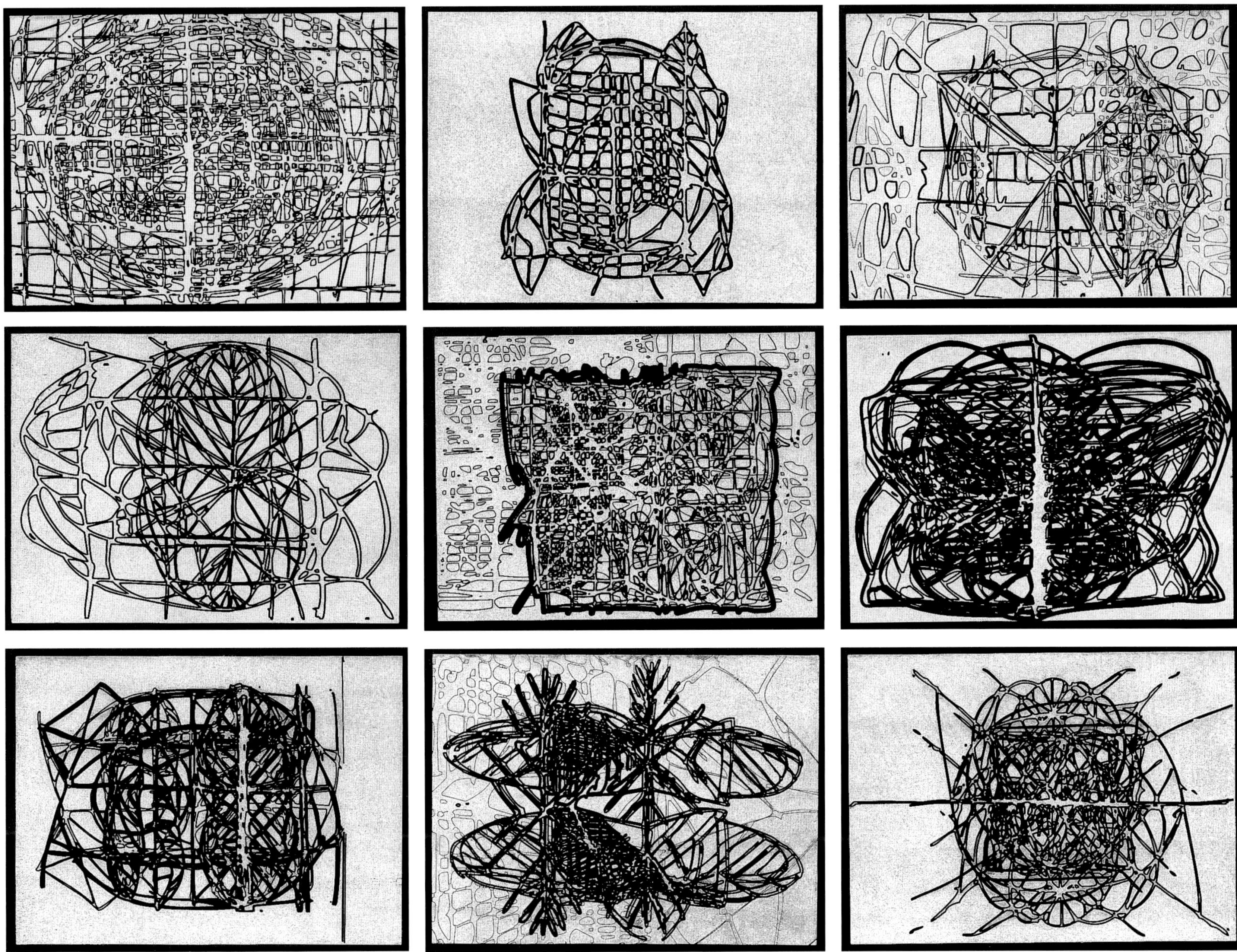

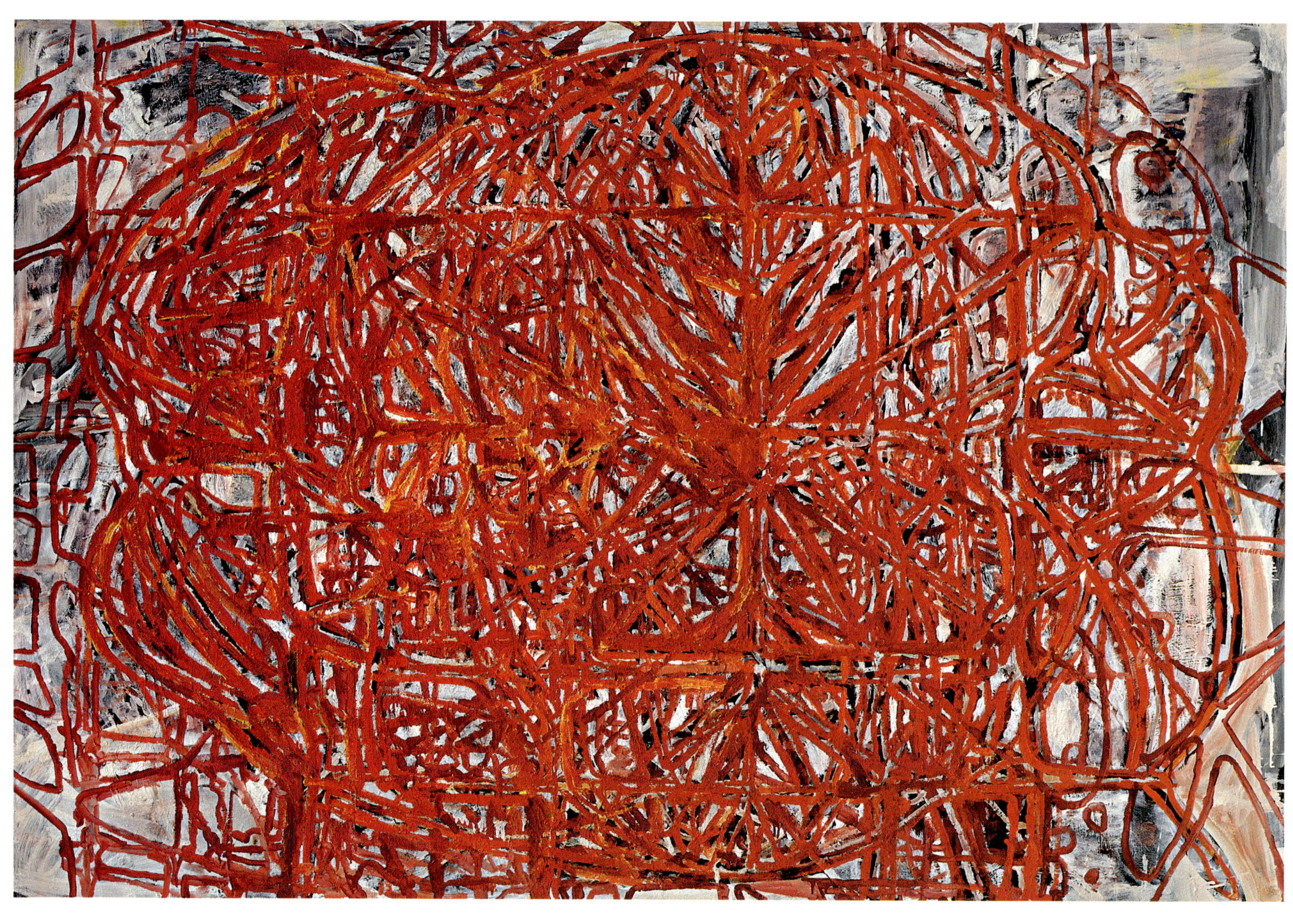

Graphic Primitives, 4, 1998
Oil and alkyd resin on linen
75 x 108 in. (190.5 x 274.3 cm)
Collection of the artist

Graphic Primitives, 6, 1998
Oil and alkyd resin on linen
75 x 108 in. (190.5 x 274.3 cm)
Private collection, London

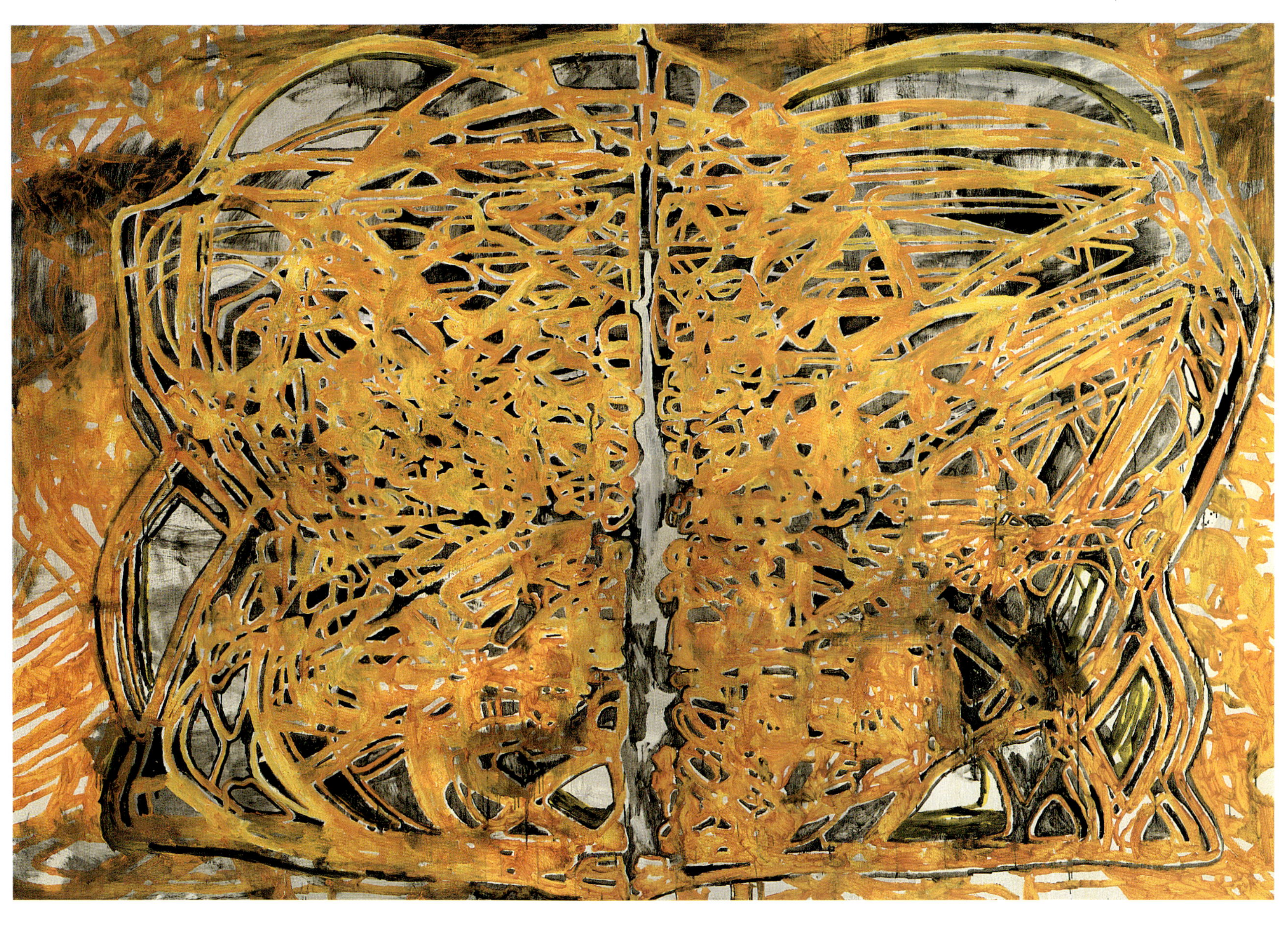

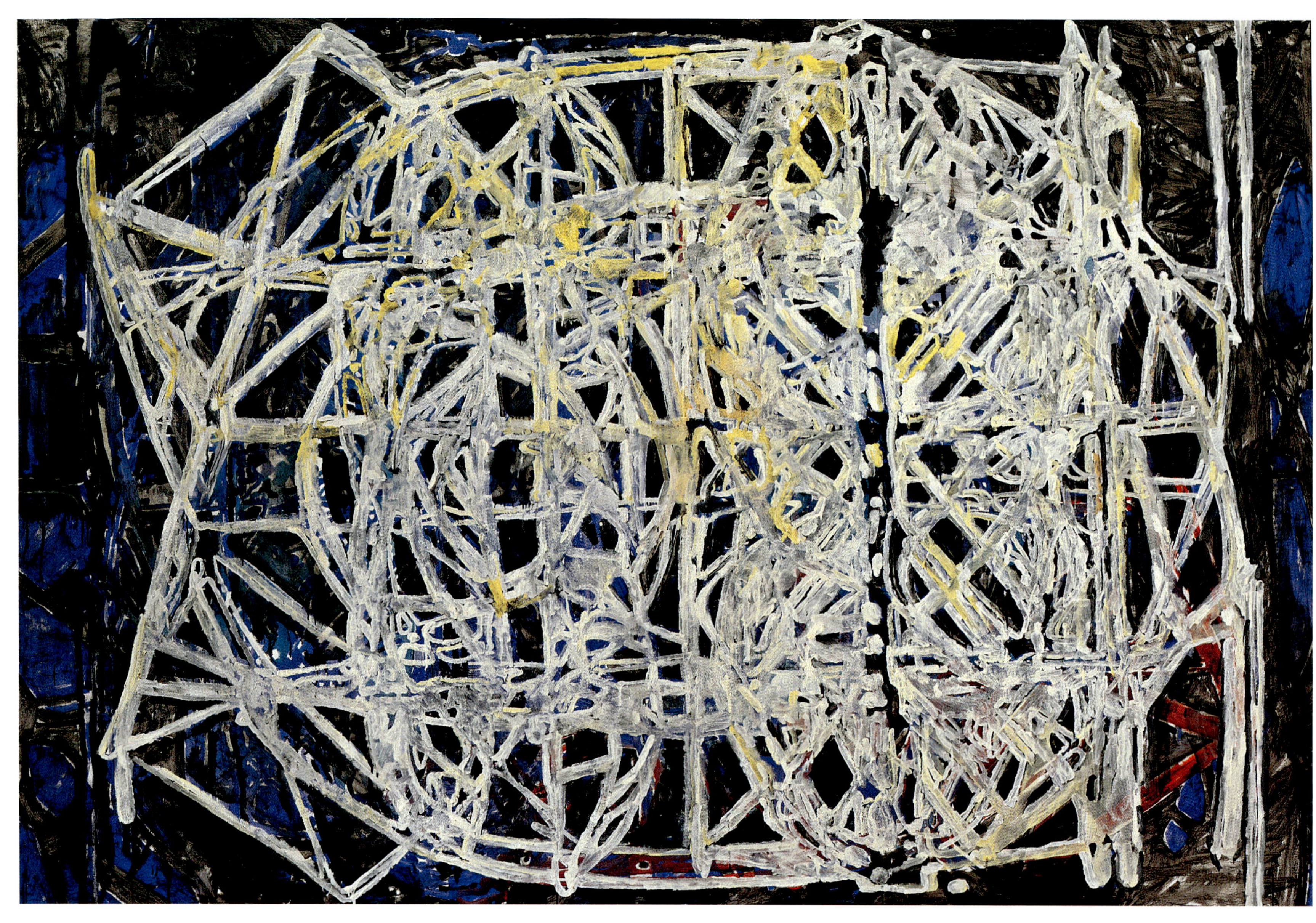

Graphic Primitives, 7, 1998
Oil and alkyd resin on linen
75 x 108 in. (190.5 x 274.3 cm)
Private collection

Graphic Primitives, 8, 1998
Oil and alkyd resin on linen
75 x 108 in. (190.5 x 274.3 cm)
Courtesy of Matthew Marks Gallery, New York

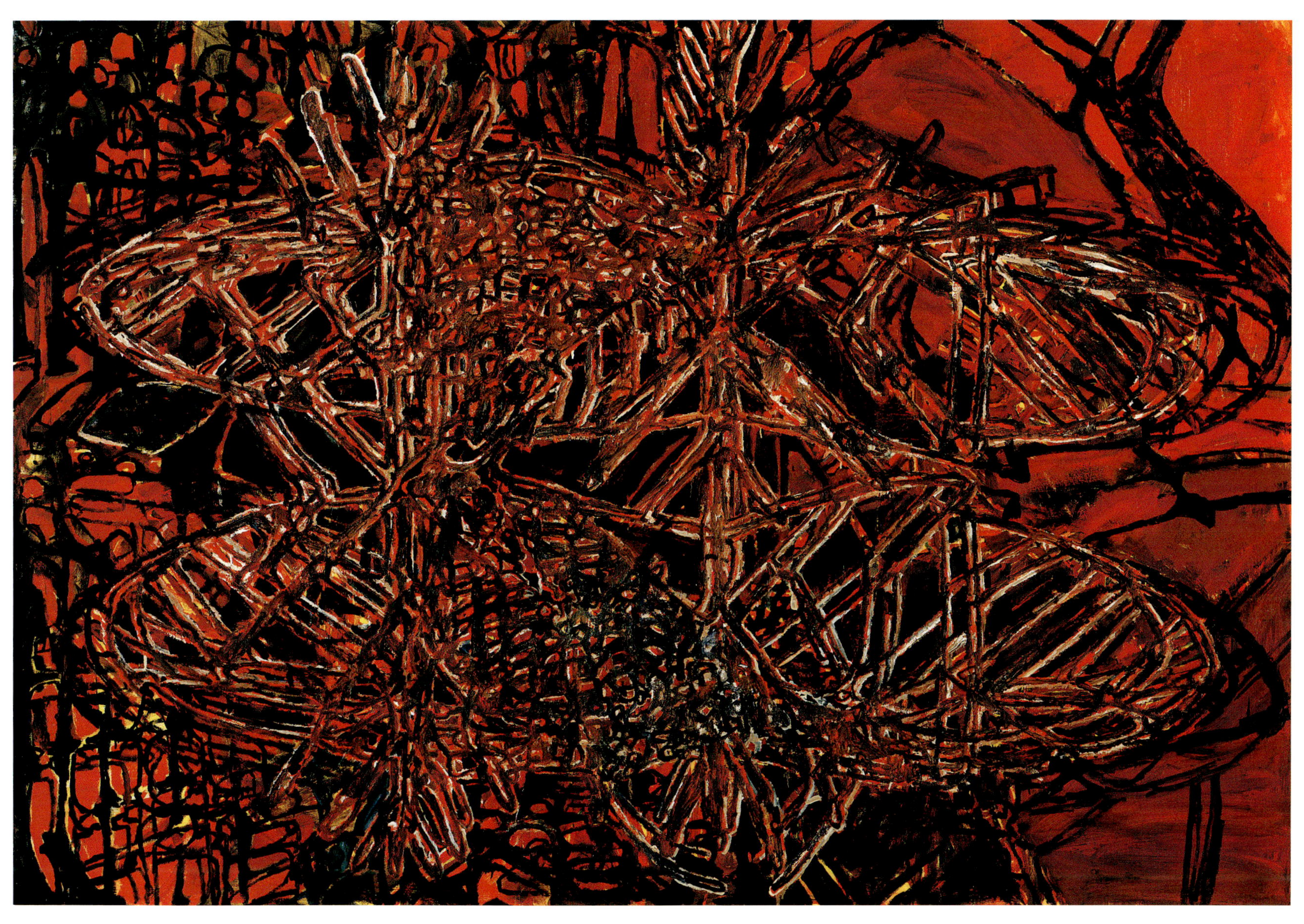

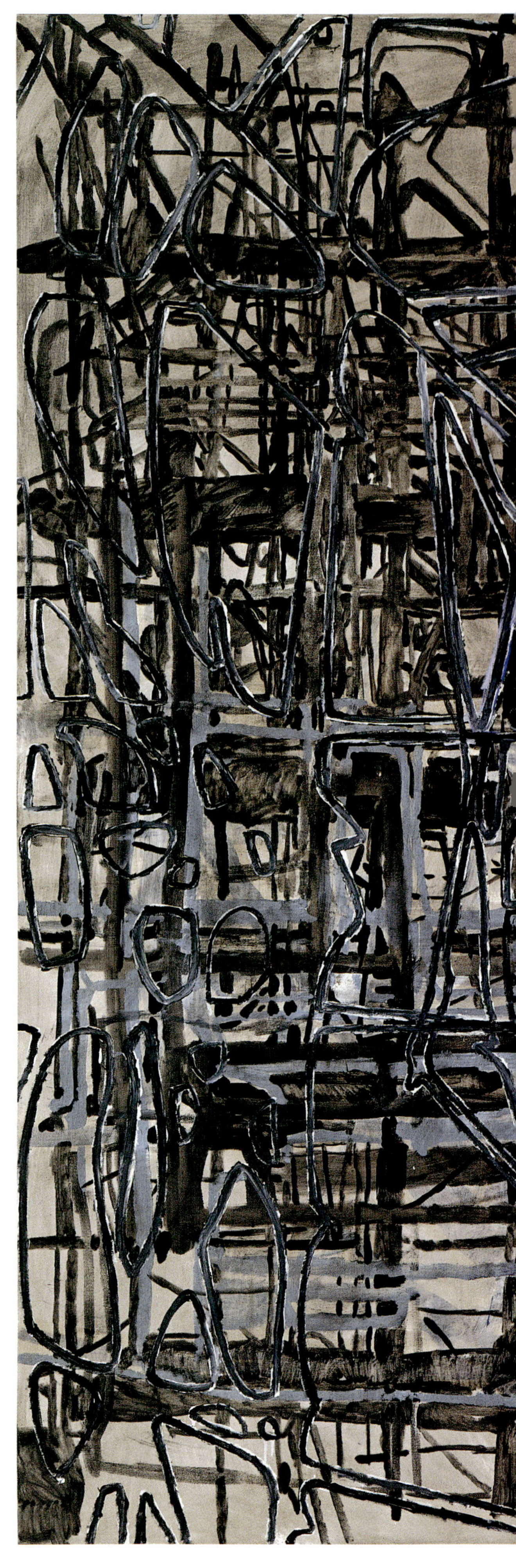

Gray-Scale Image, 1998
Oil on linen
96 x 120 in. (243.8 x 304.8 cm)
Collection of Rachel and Jean-Pierre Lehmann

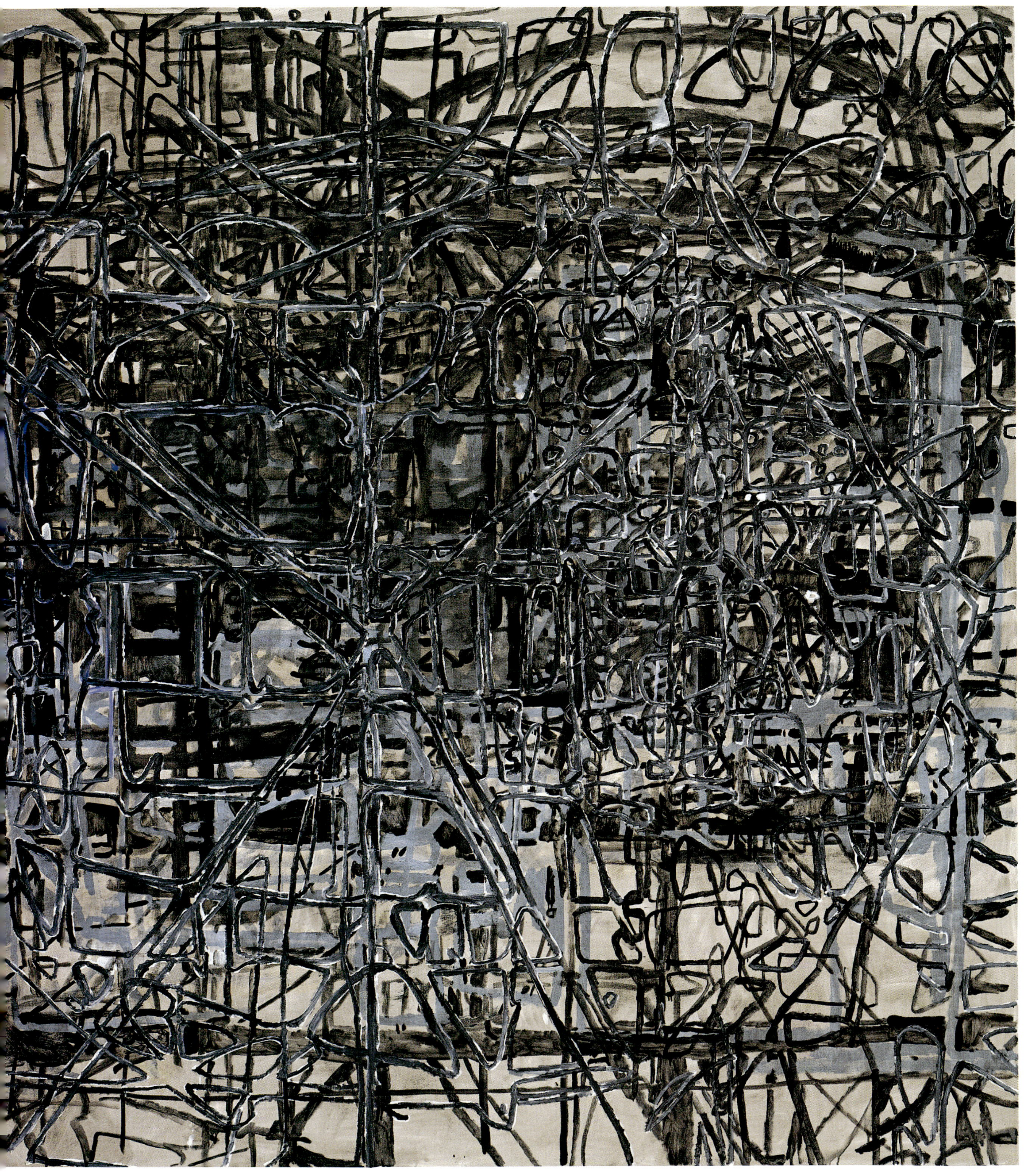

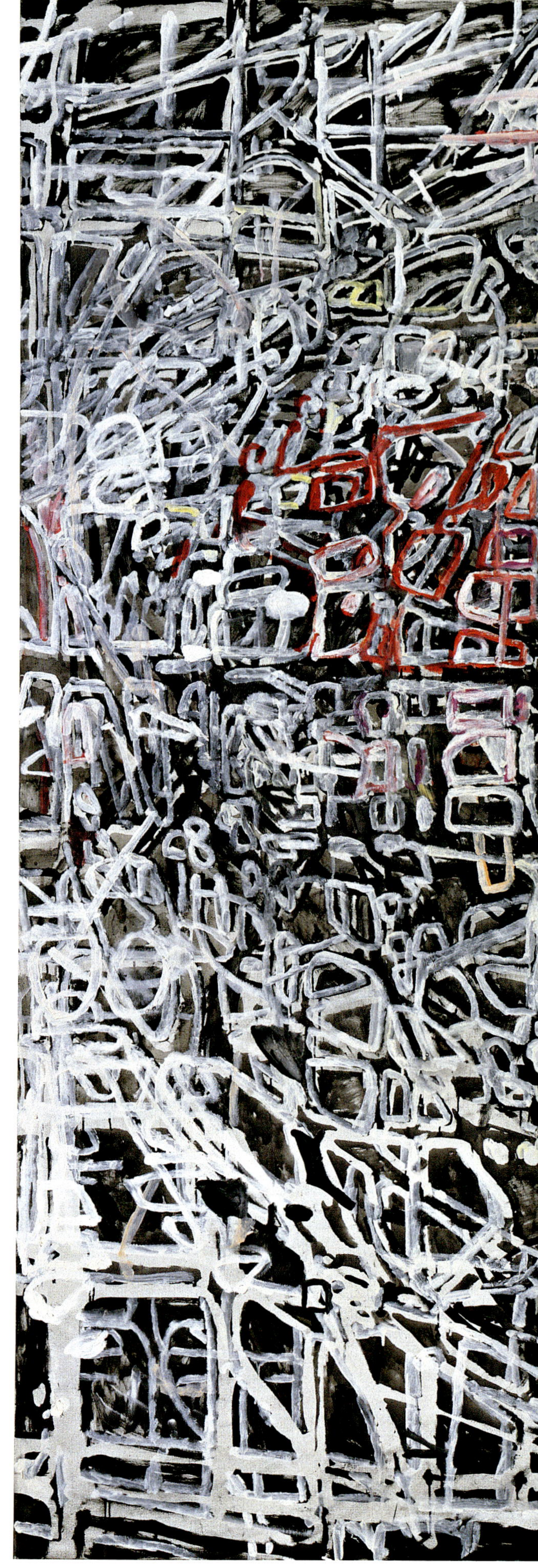

Graphics Tablet, 1998
Oil and alkyd resin on linen
96 x 120 in. (243.8 x 304.8 cm)
Collection of Robert and Jane Meyerhoff, Phoenix, Maryland

Page 81:
Intersections and Animations, Title Page, 1998
From a series of 50 drawings
Ink on vellum
12 x 9 in. (30.5 x 22.9 cm)
Courtesy of Matthew Marks Gallery, New York

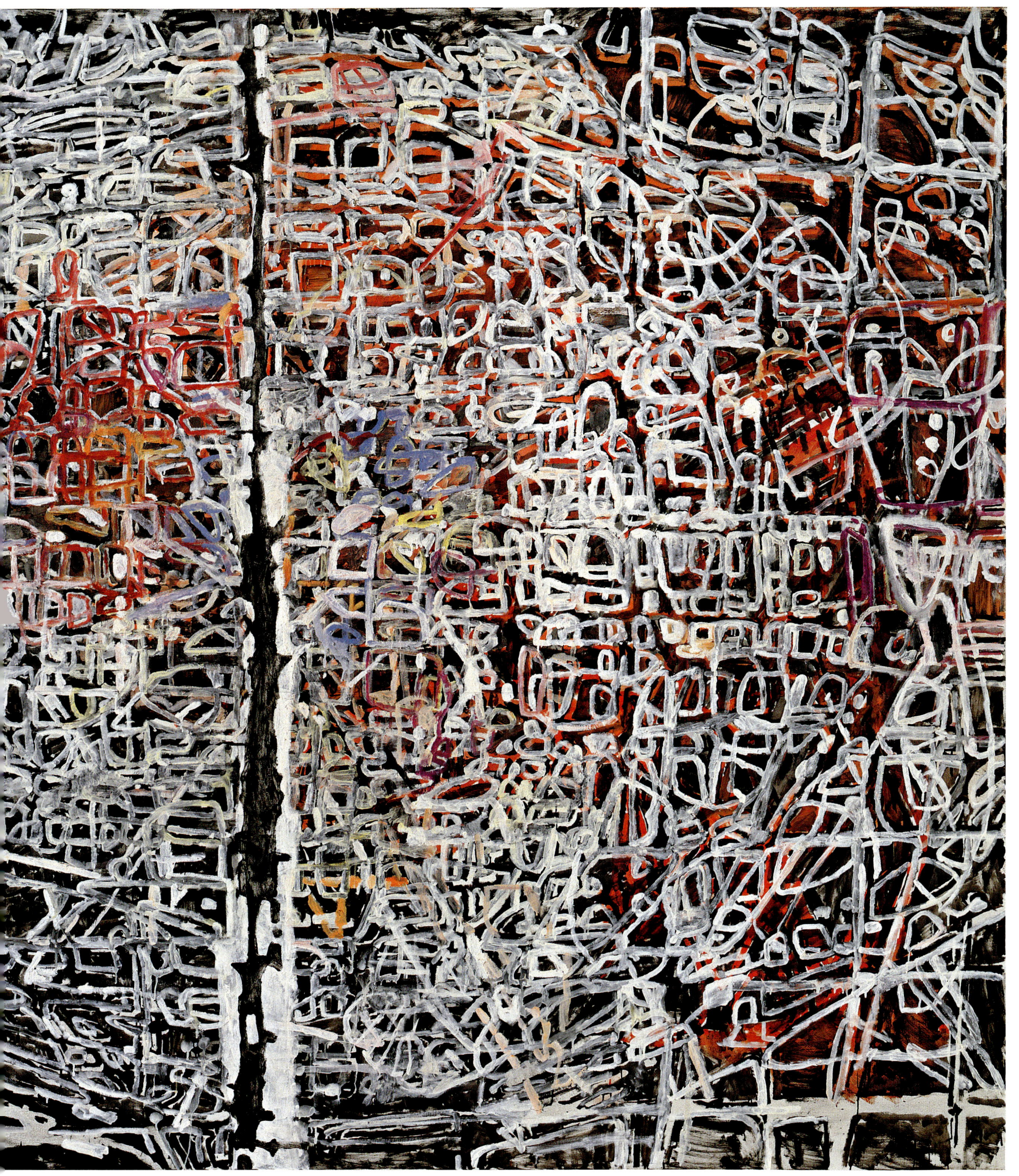

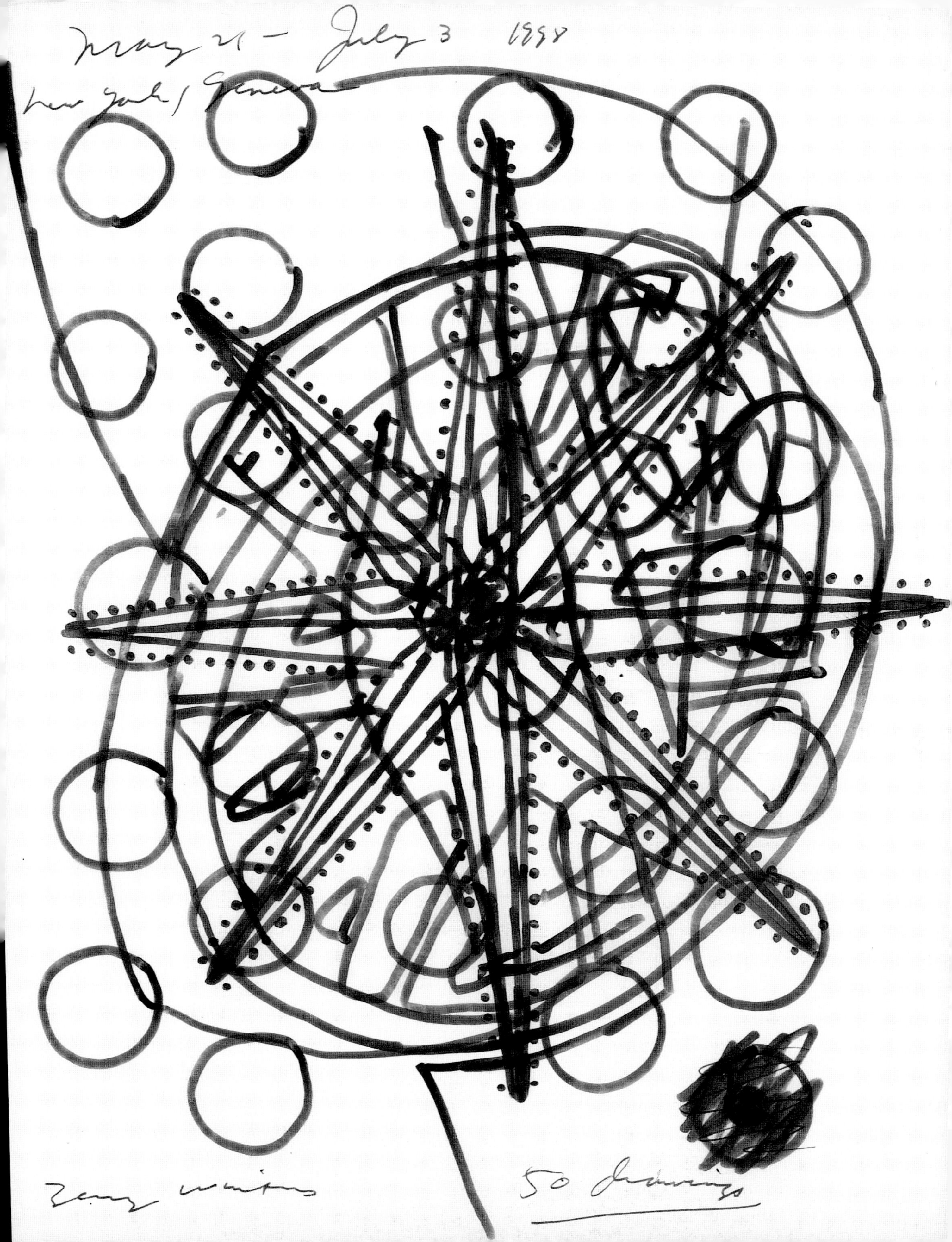
May 21 – July 3 1998
New York / Geneva
Terry Winters
50 Drawings

LOCATION PLAN

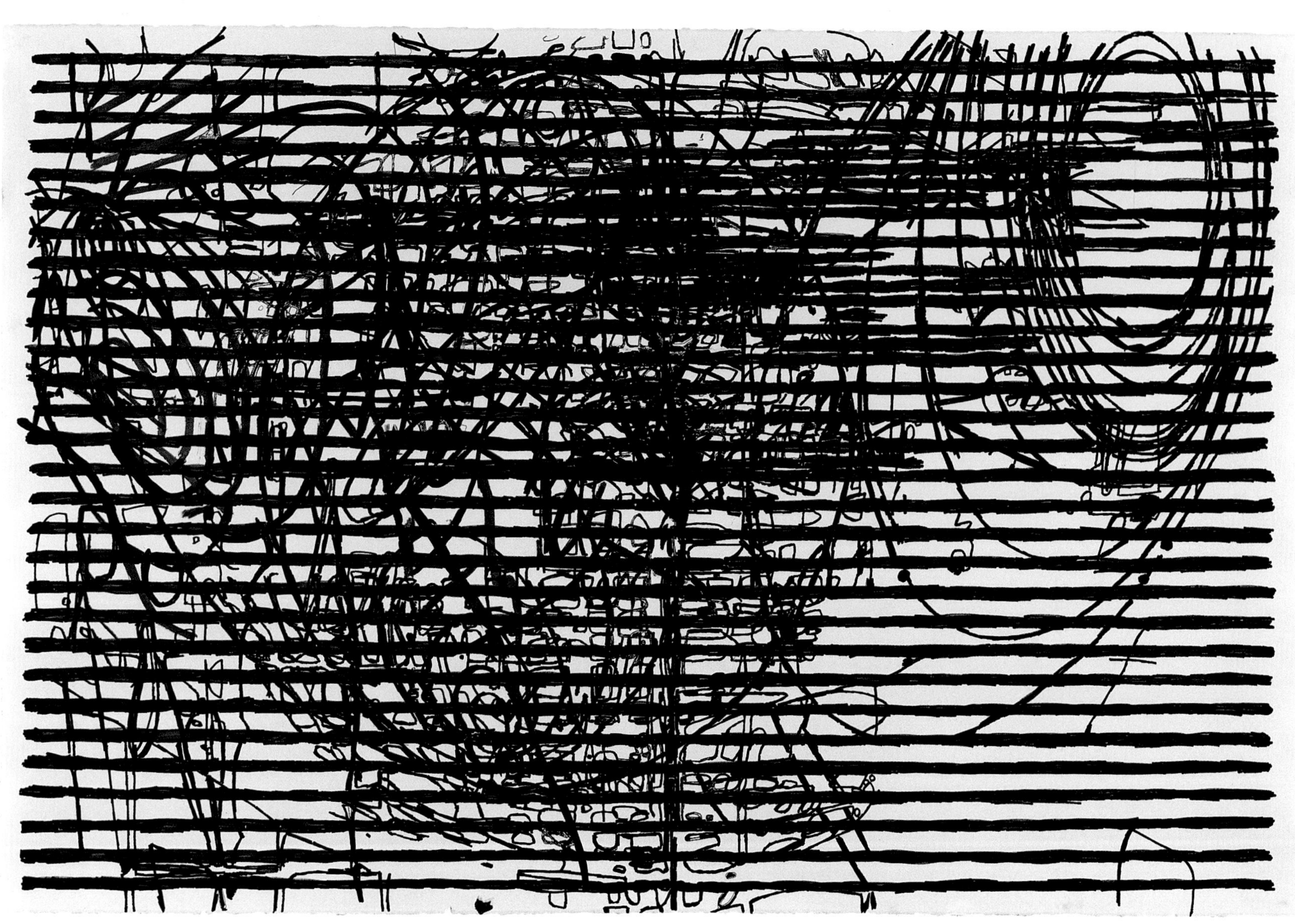

Linking Graphics, 1, 1999
Ink on paper
30 1/2 x 44 1/2 in. (77.5 x 113 cm)
Collection of the artist

Linking Graphics, 2, 1999
Ink, graphite, and colored pencil on paper
30 1/2 x 44 1/2 in. (77.5 x 113 cm)
The Museum of Modern Art, New York

Pages 86–87:
Trisha Brown Dance Company
Five Part Weather Invention, 1999, from *El Trilogy*
Music by Dave Douglas
Sets and costumes by Terry Winters
Lighting by Jennifer Tipton
Photograph by Joanne Savio

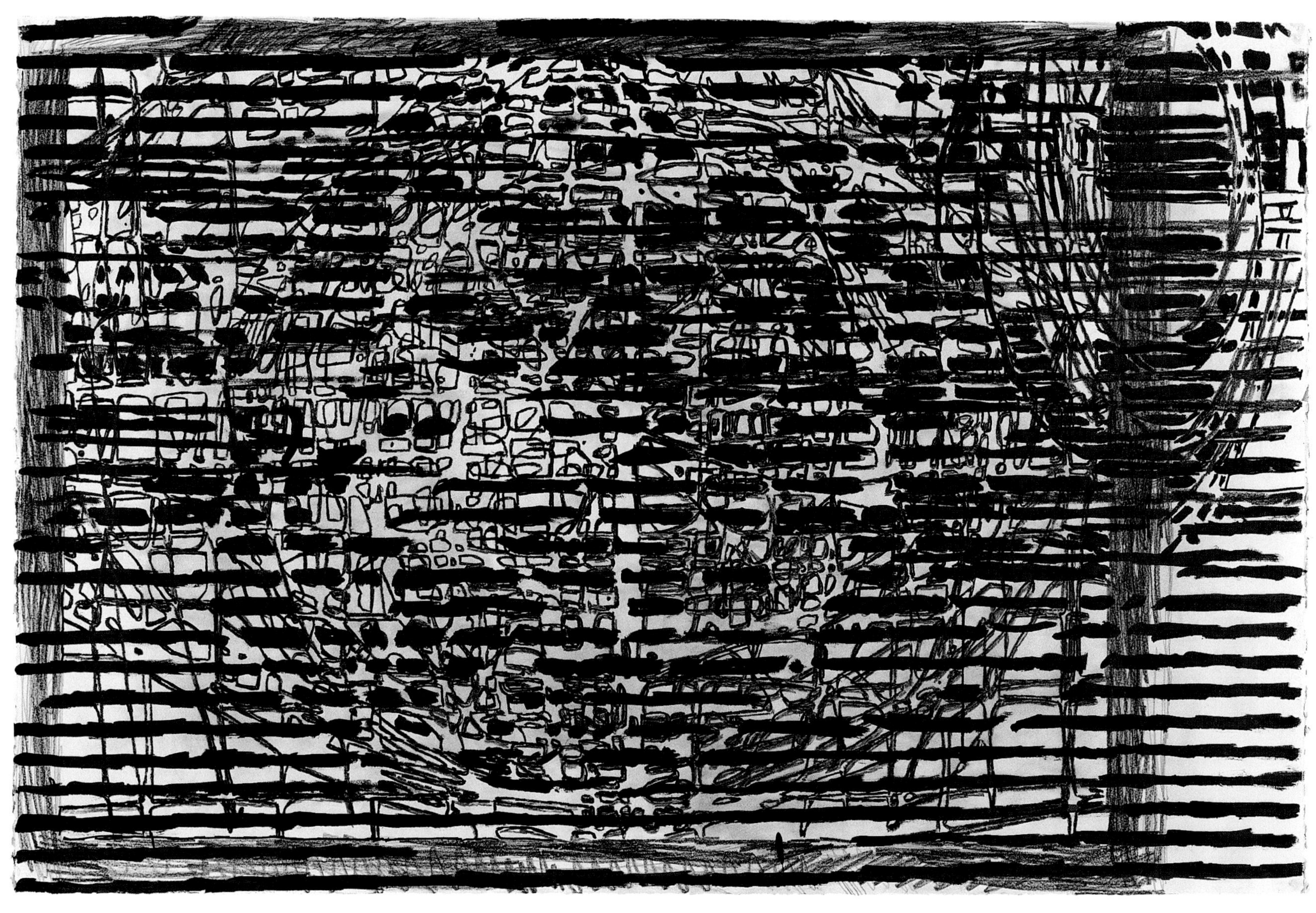

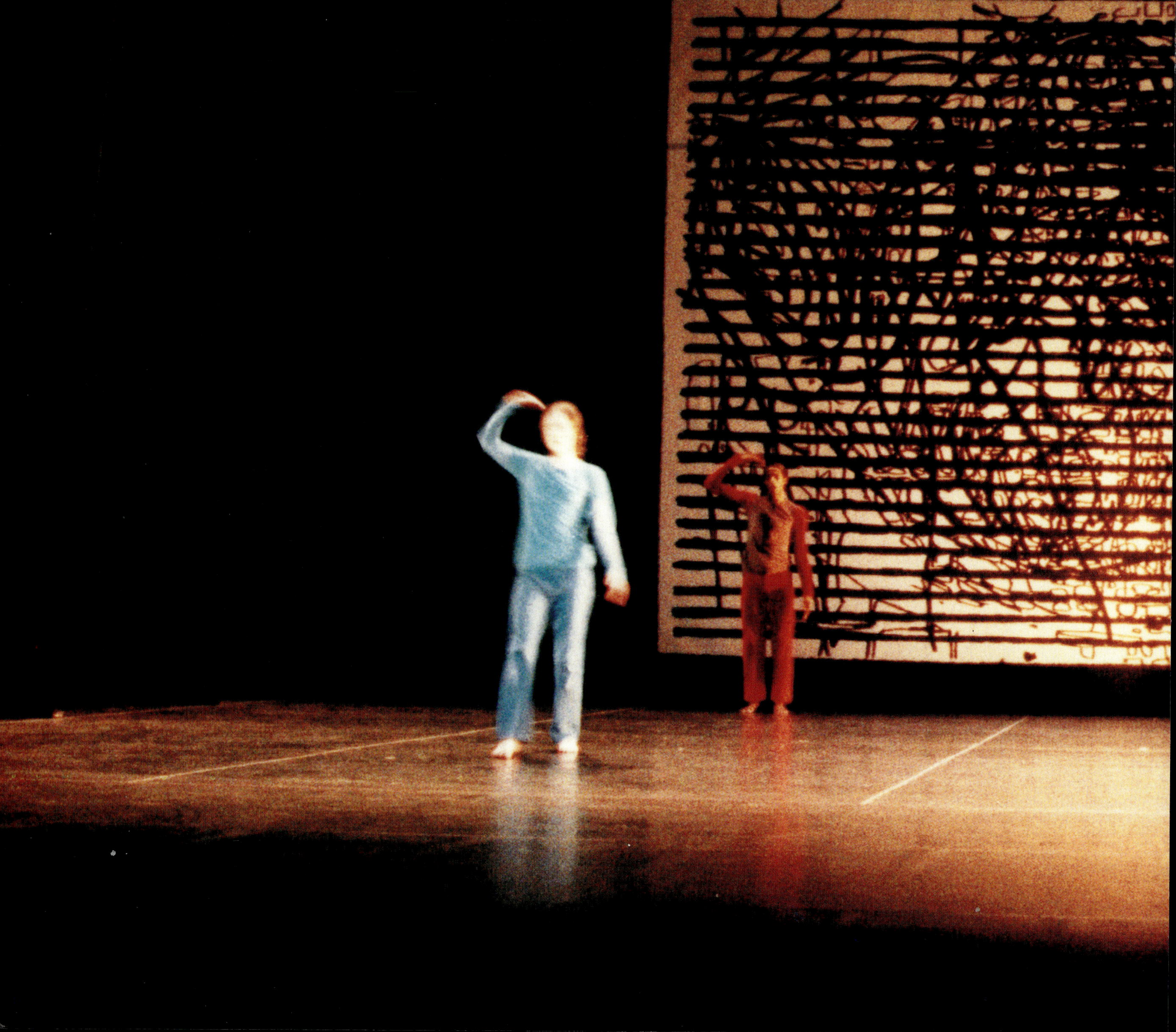

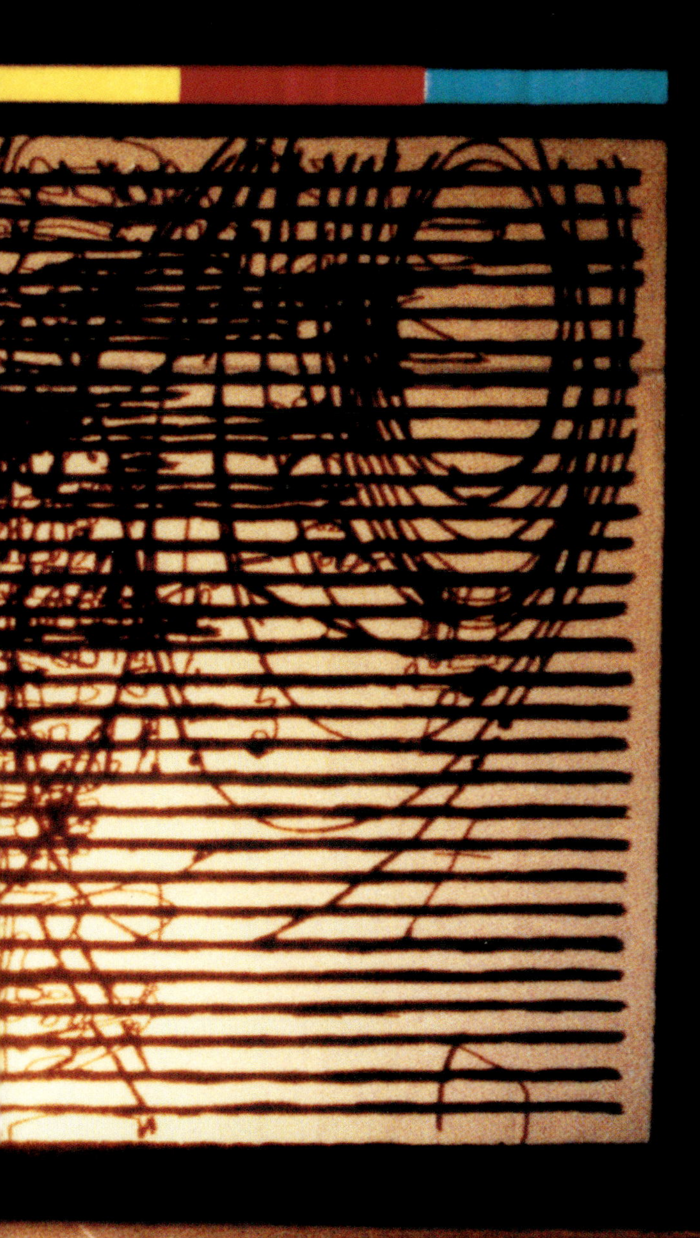
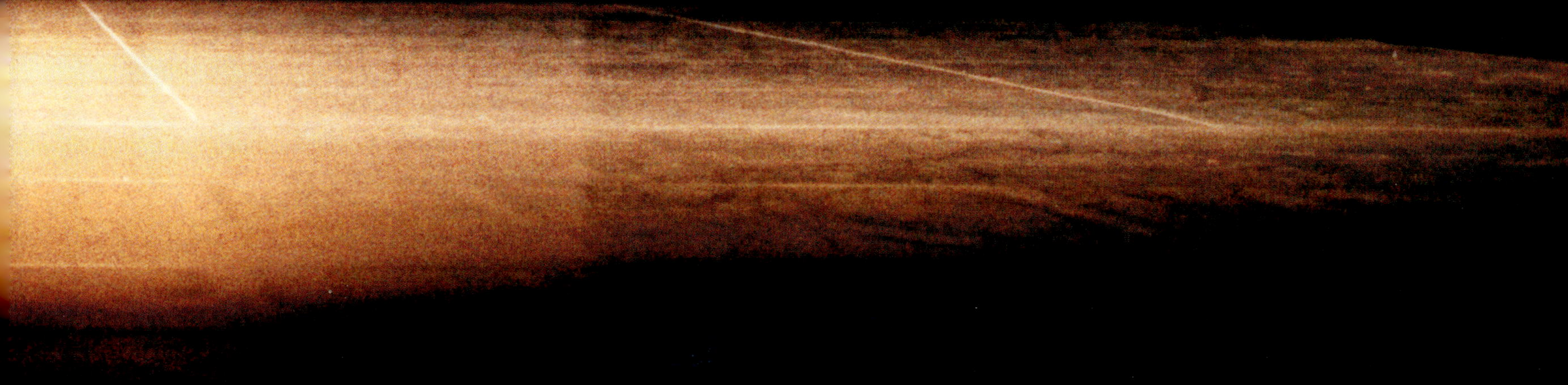

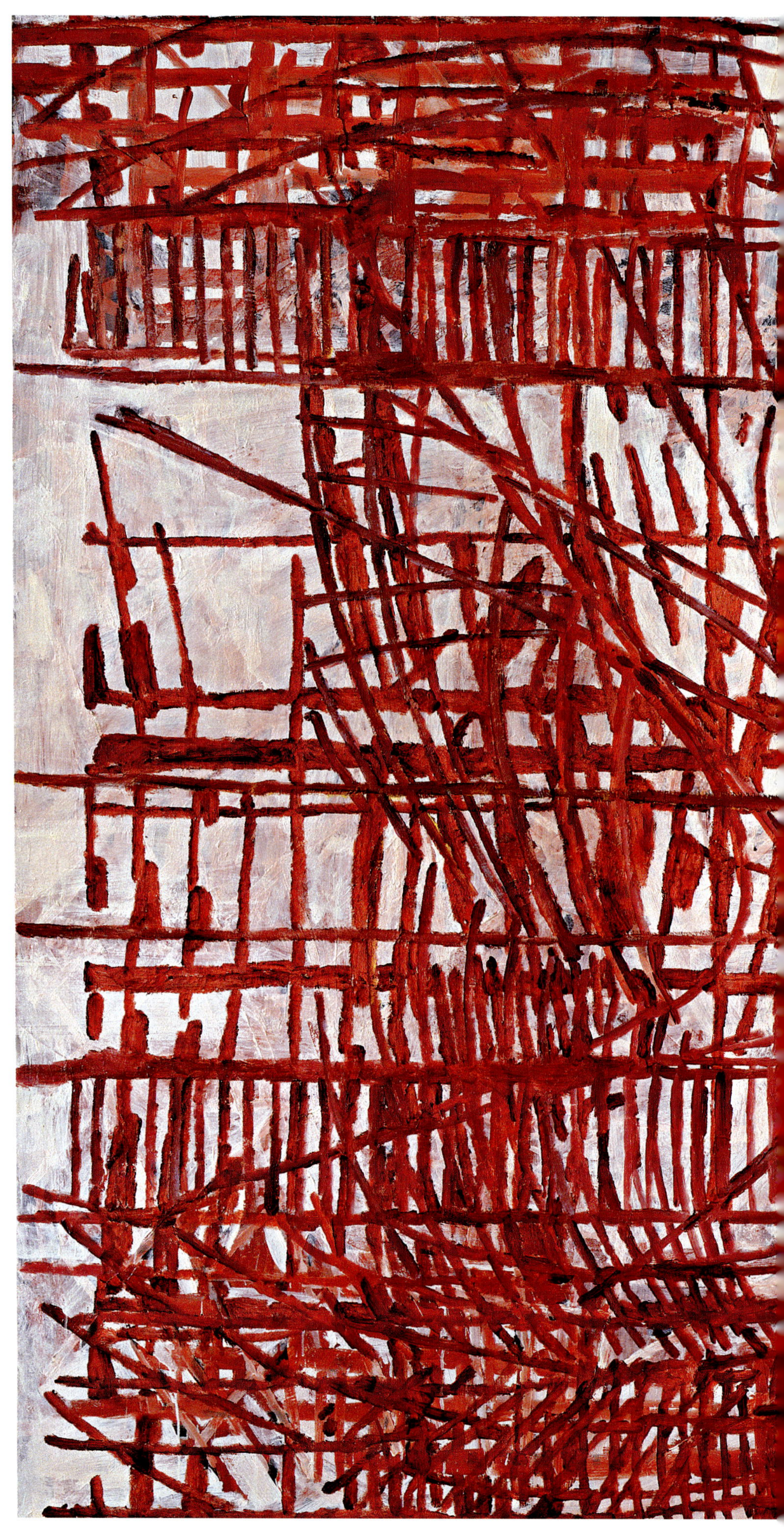

Graph of Curves, 1999
Oil on linen
94 5/8 x 133 3/4 in. (240.3 x 339.7 cm)
Private collection, courtesy of Matthew Marks Gallery, New York

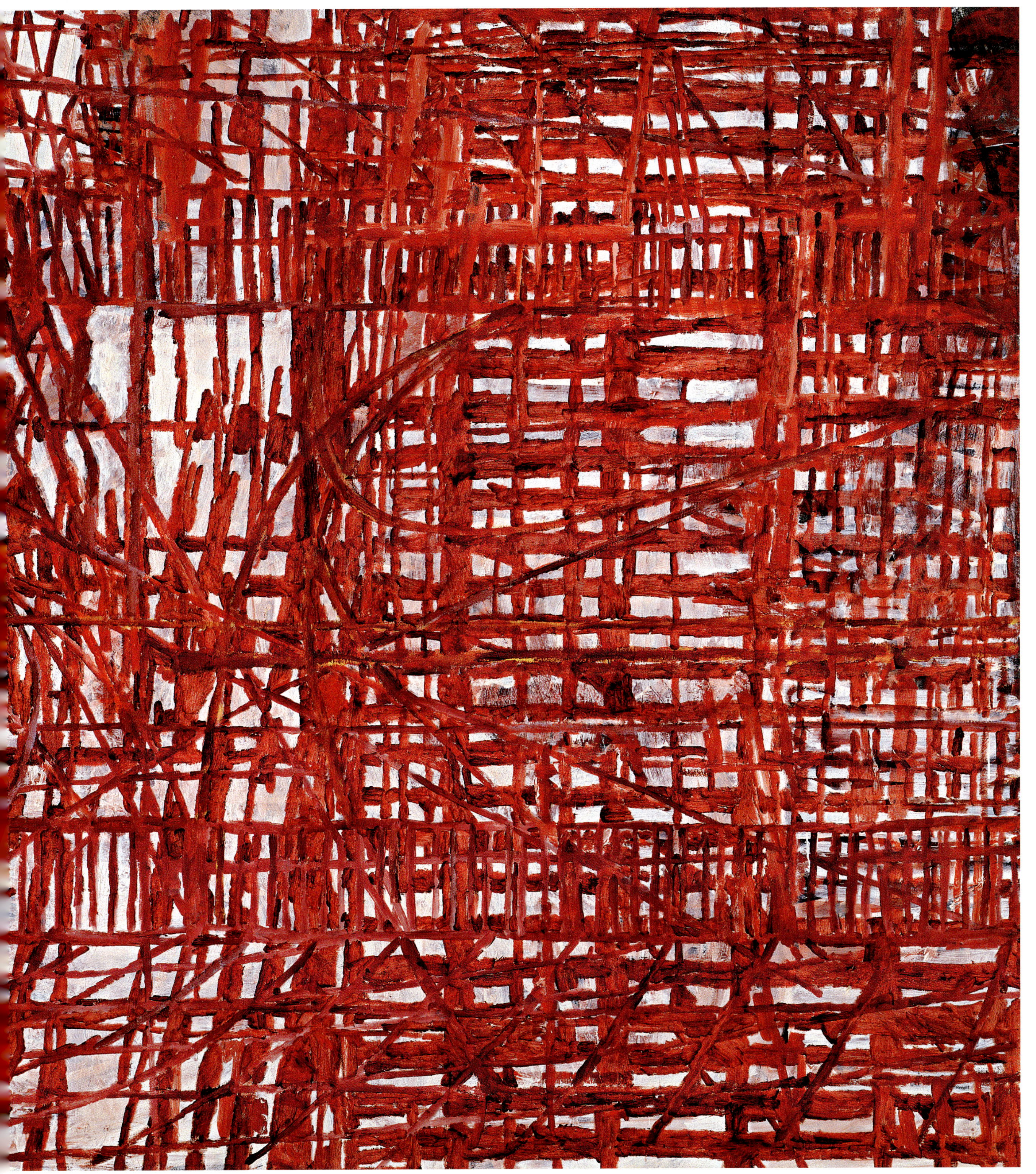

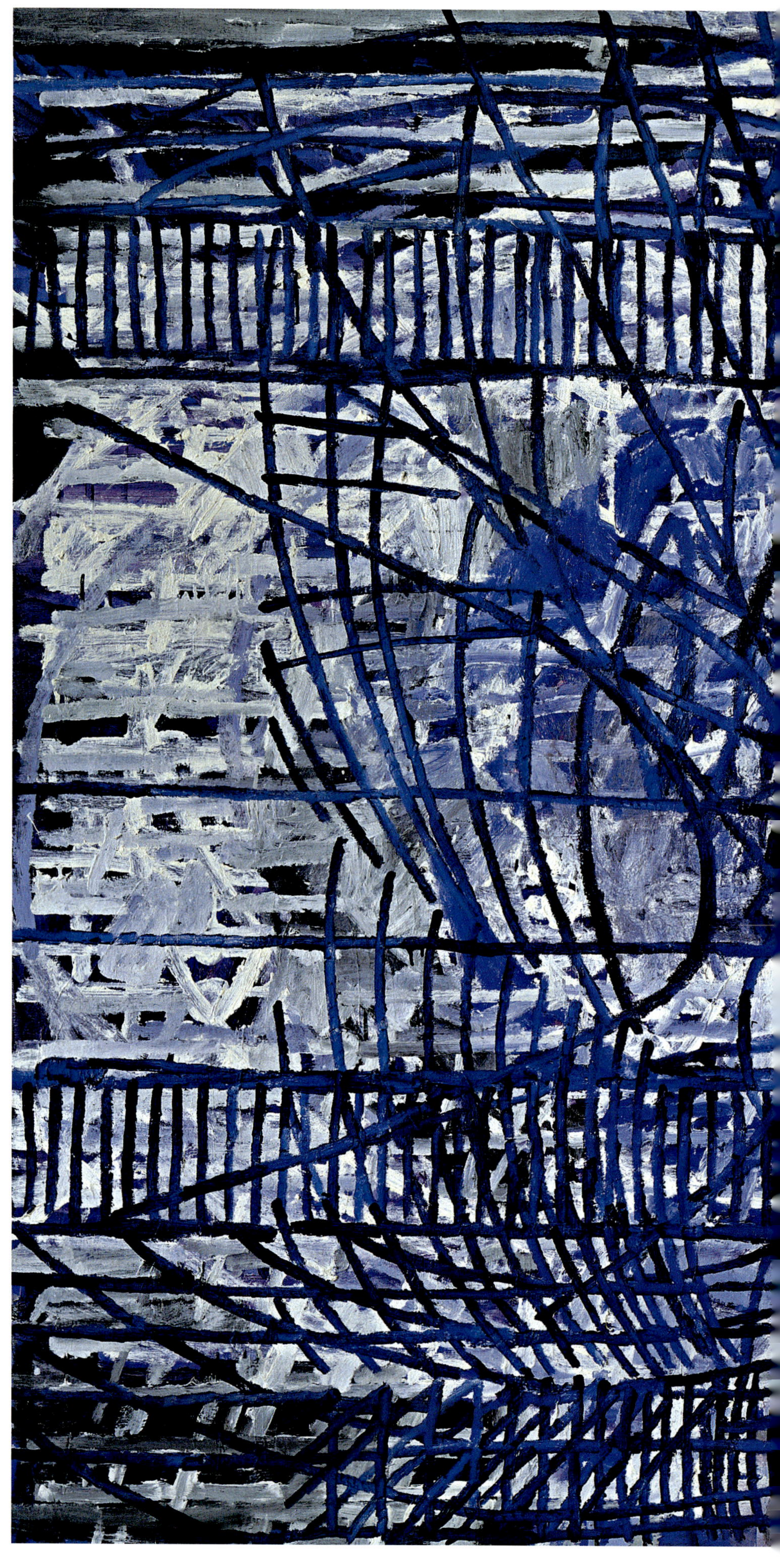

Blue Diagram, 1999
Oil on linen
70 7/8 x 100 3/8 in. (180 x 255 cm)
Private collection

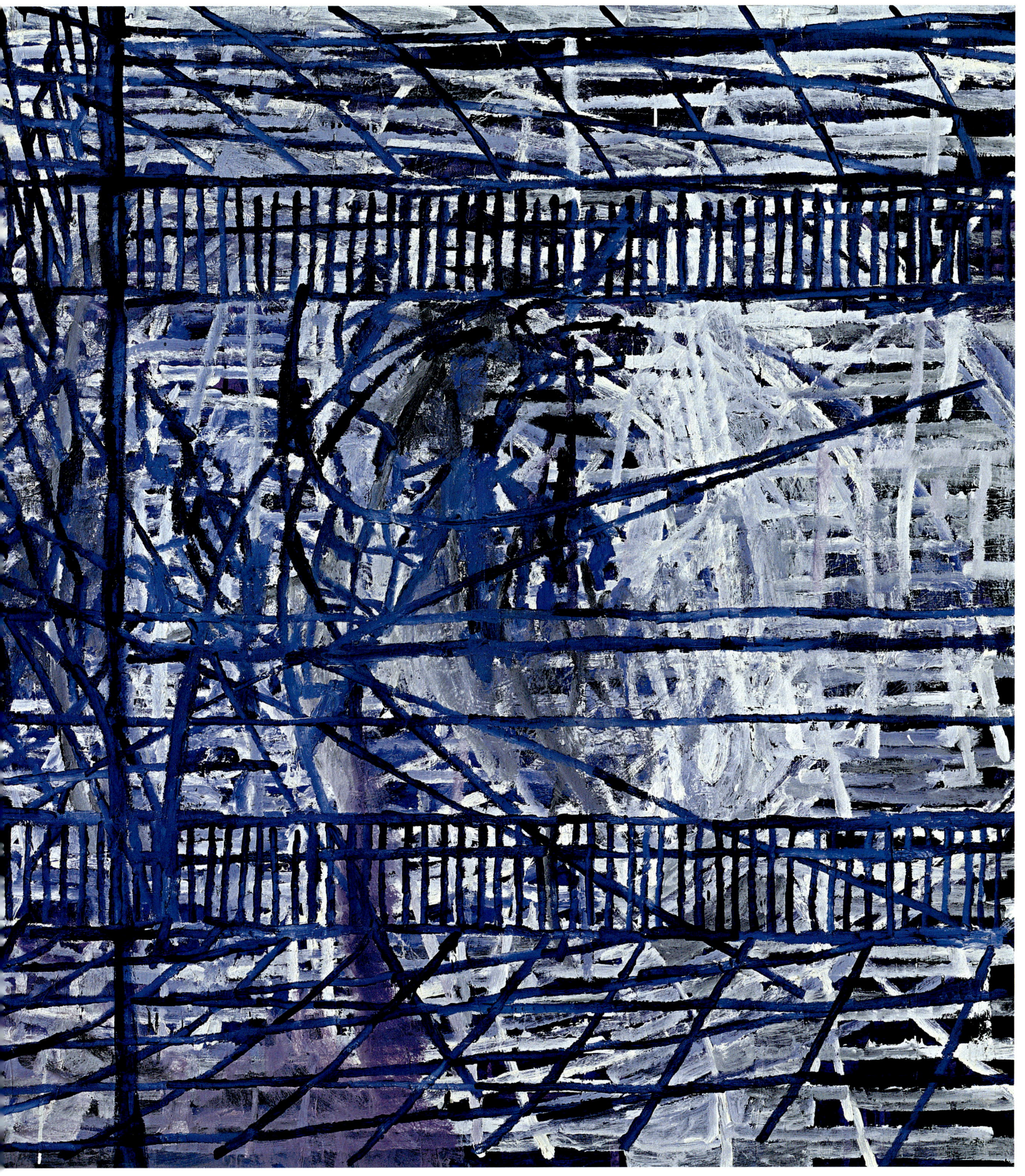

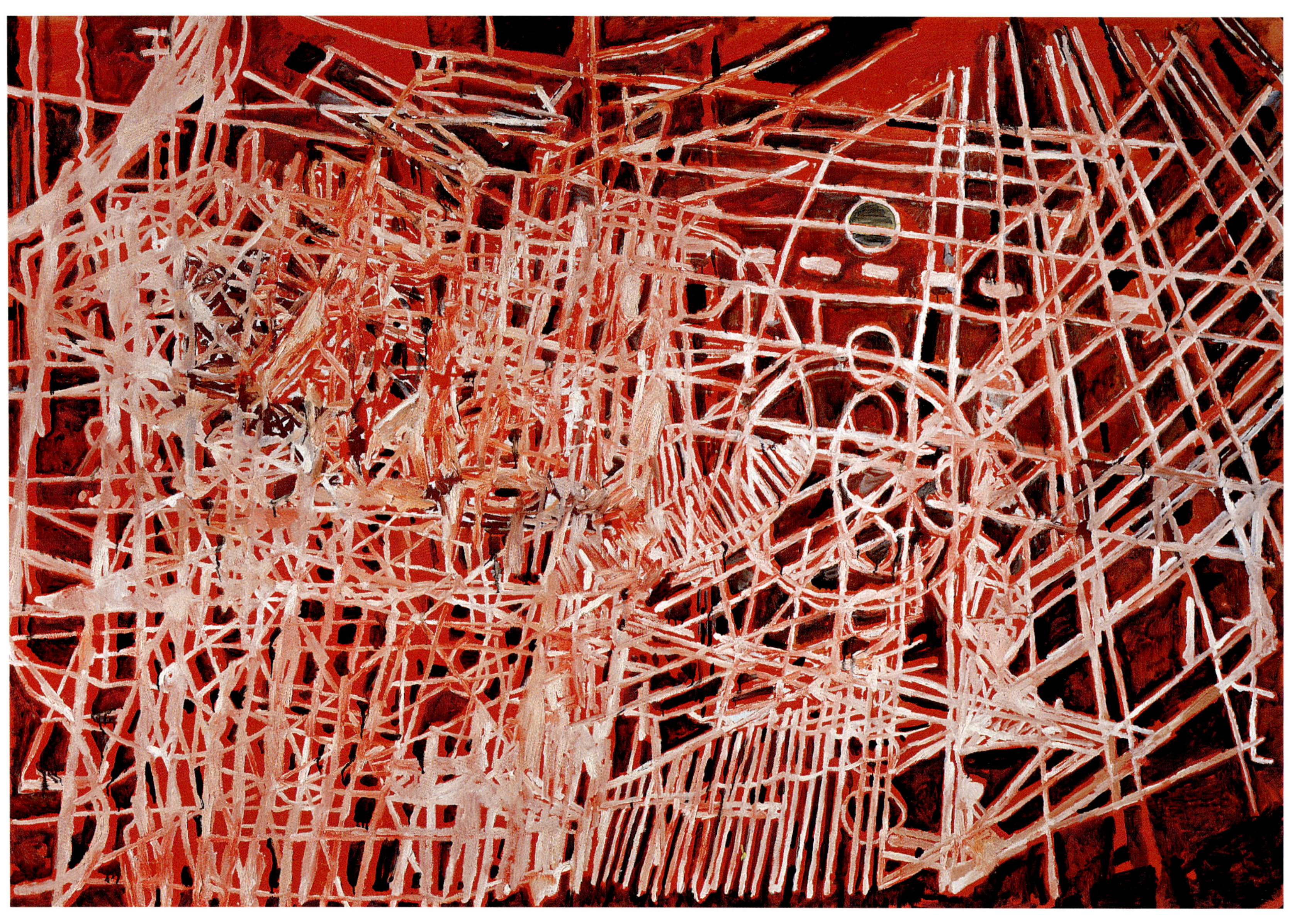

Forward Scattering, 1999
Oil on linen
82 5/8 x 116 3/16 in. (209.9 x 295.1 cm)
Courtesy of Matthew Marks Gallery, New York

Untitled, 1999
Oil on linen
57 1/16 x 82 3/4 in. (144.9 x 210.2 cm)
Private collection, Well, North Yorkshire

Pages 94–95:
Location Plan, 1999
A series of 30 drawings
Ink on vellum
Each, 11 1/2 x 16 3/8 in. (29.2 x 41.6 cm)
The Judith Rothschild Foundation, New York

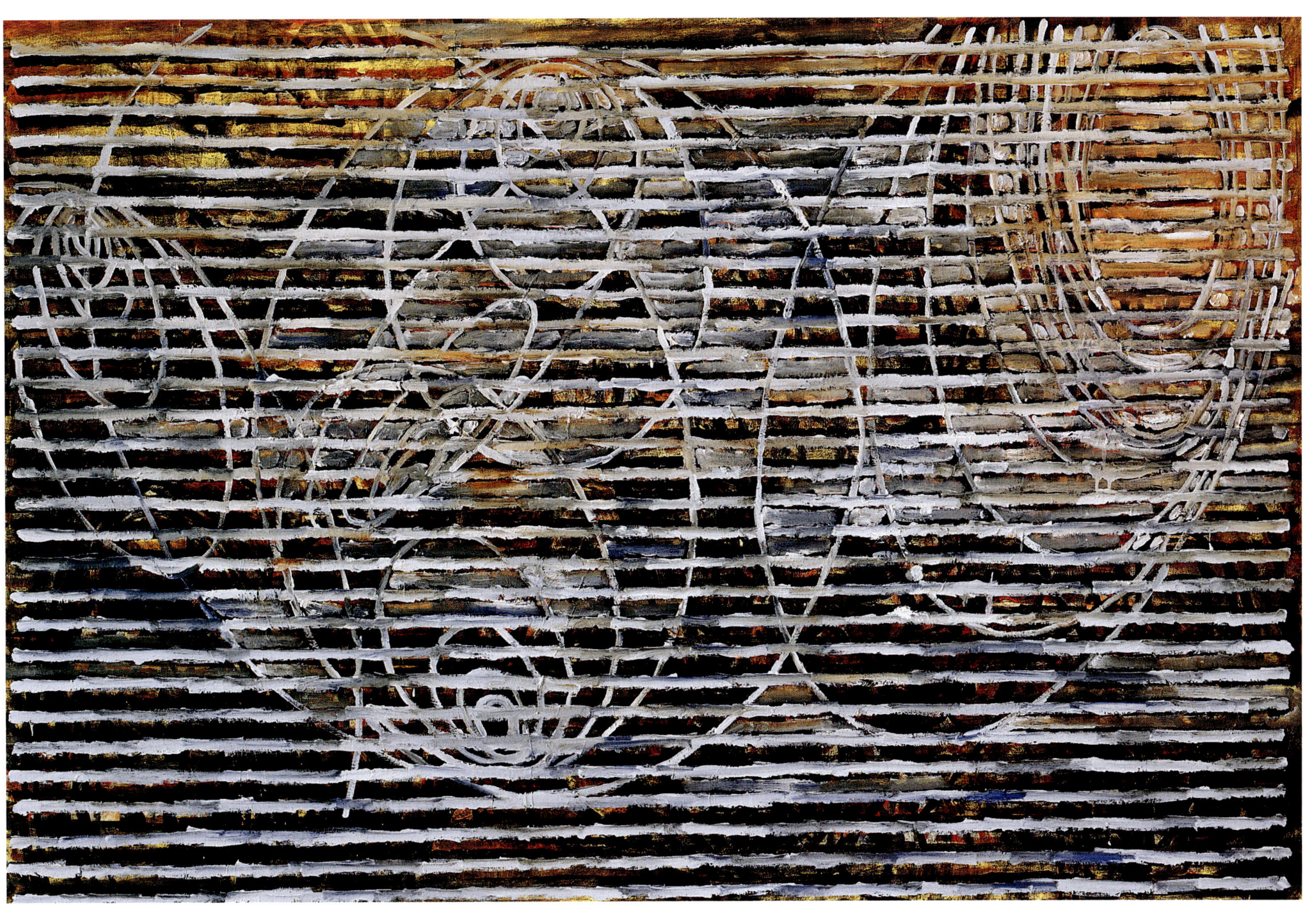

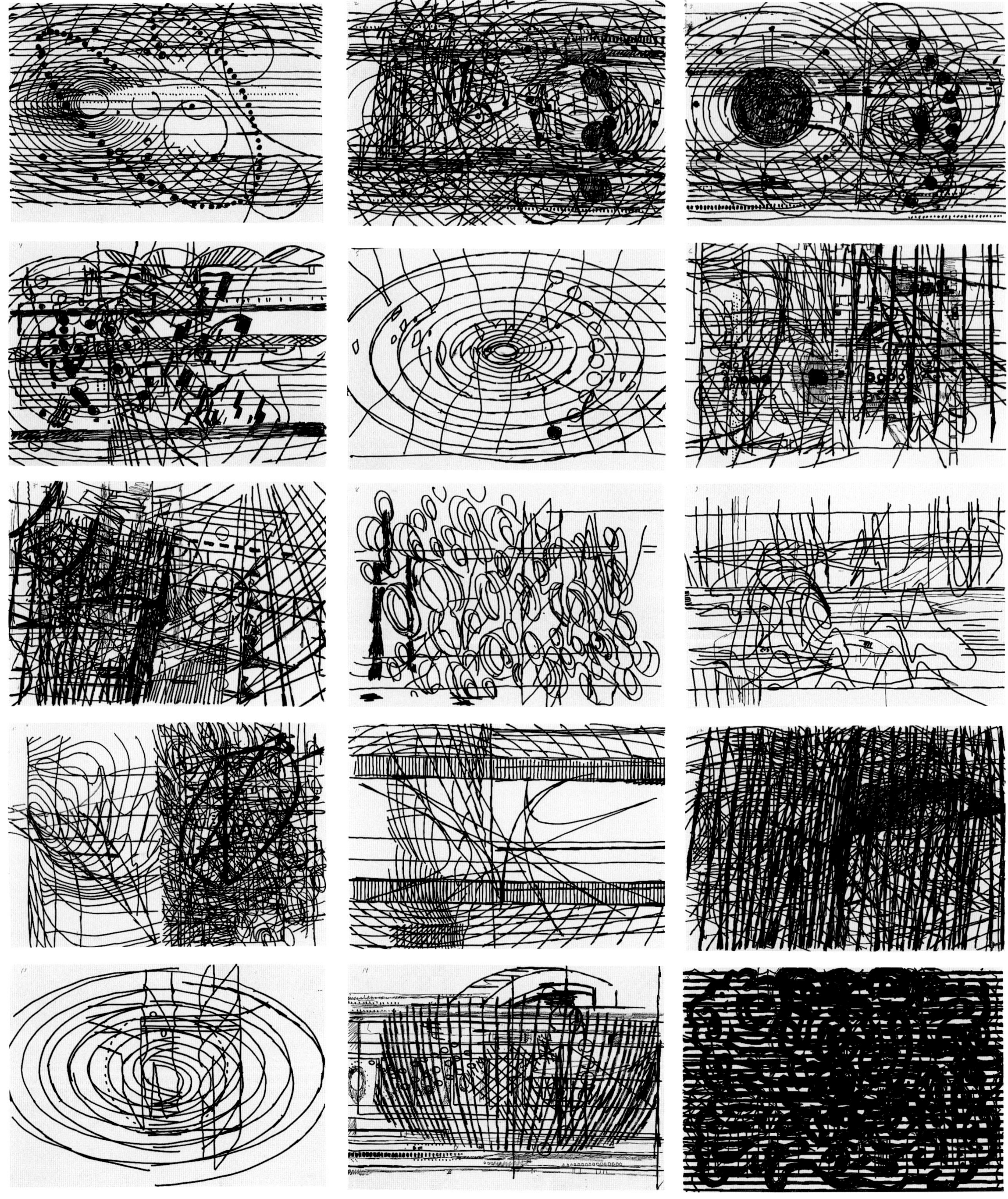

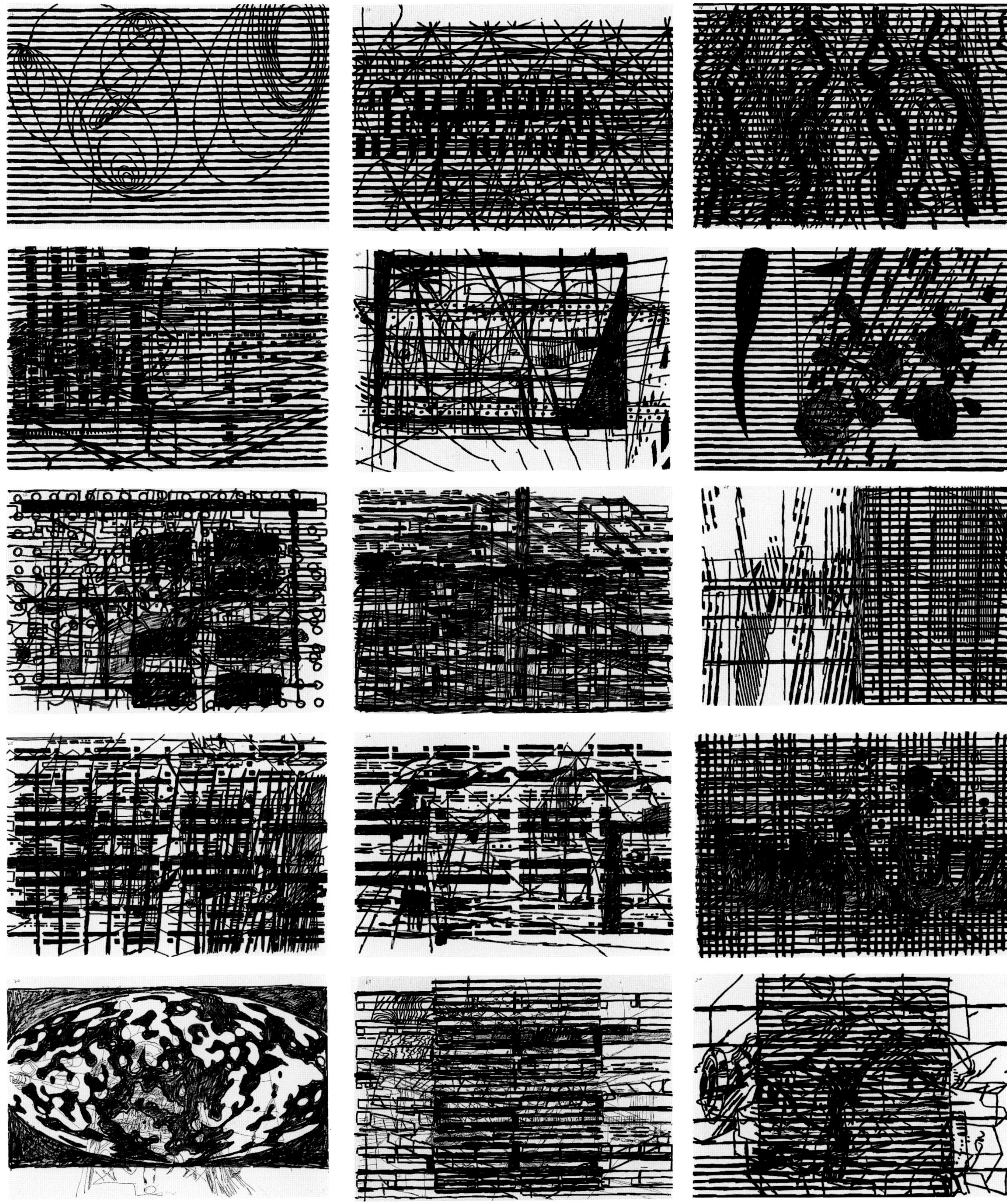

SET DIAGRAM

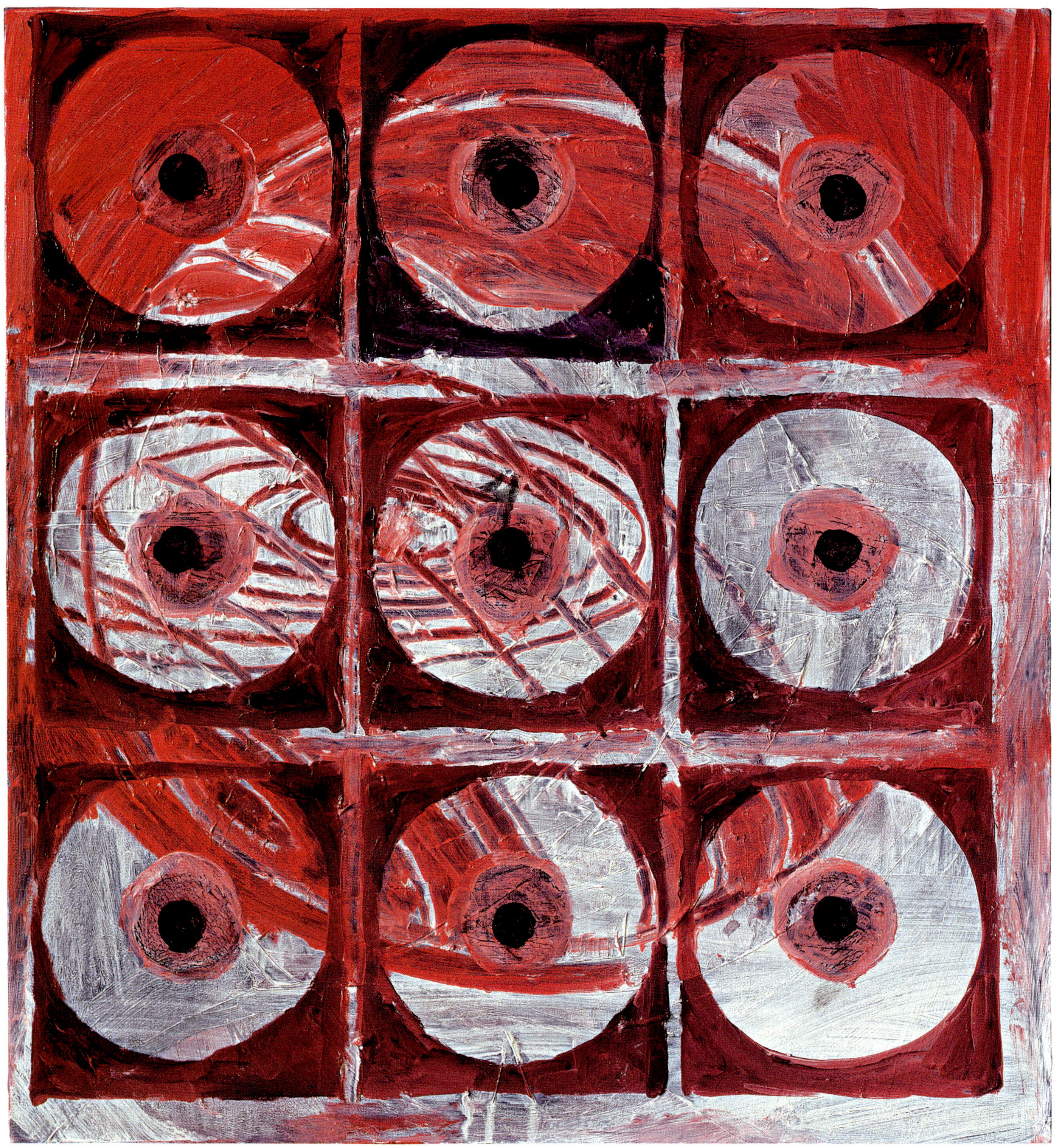

Set Diagram 41, 2000
Oil on linen
39 3/8 x 36 in. (100 x 91.4 cm)
Collection of the artist

Set Diagram 48, 2000
Oil on linen
39 3/8 x 36 in. (100 x 91.4 cm)
Collection of Neda Young, New York

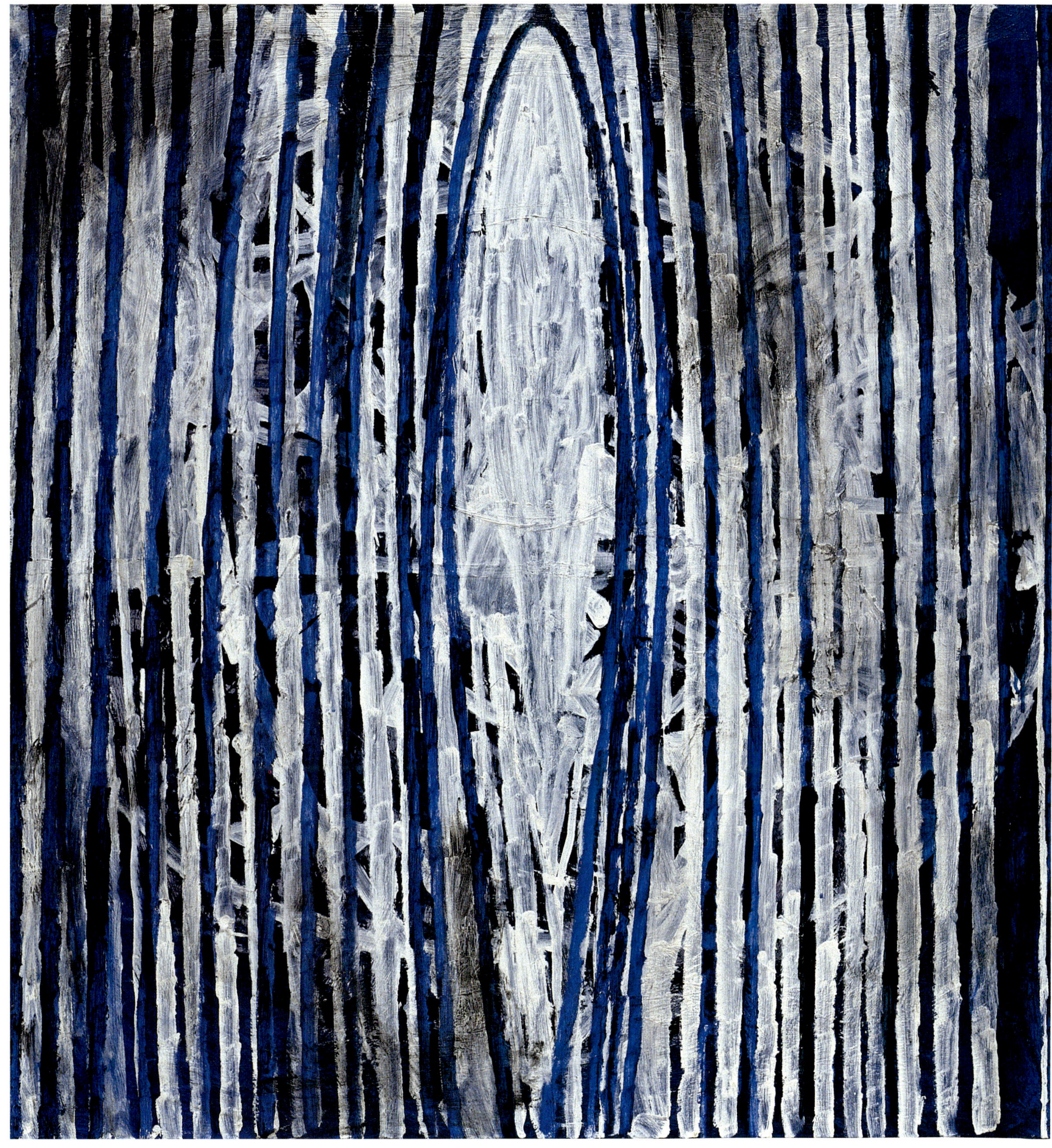

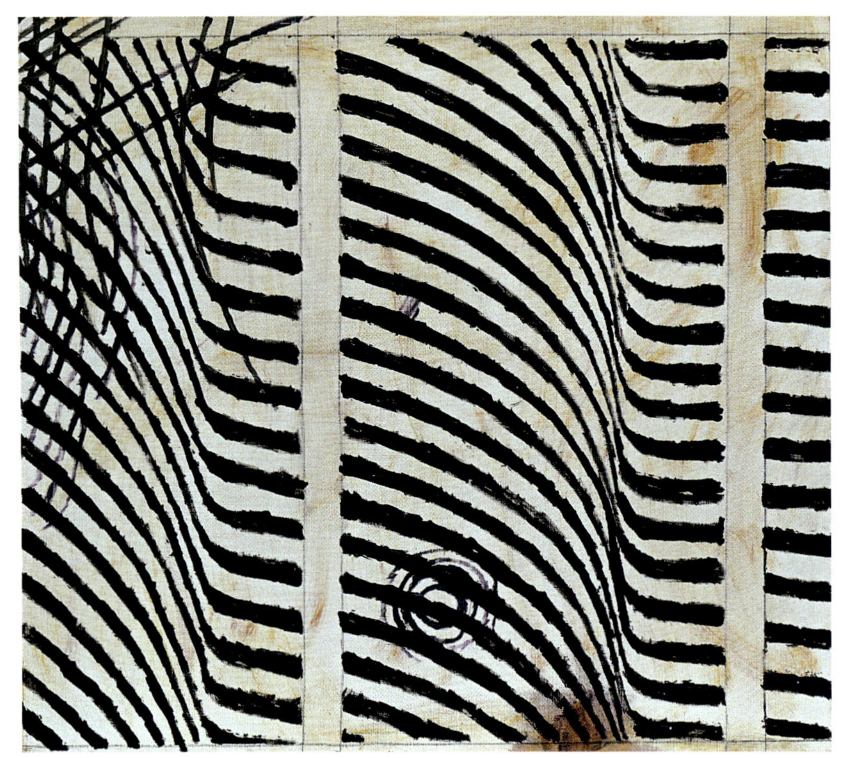

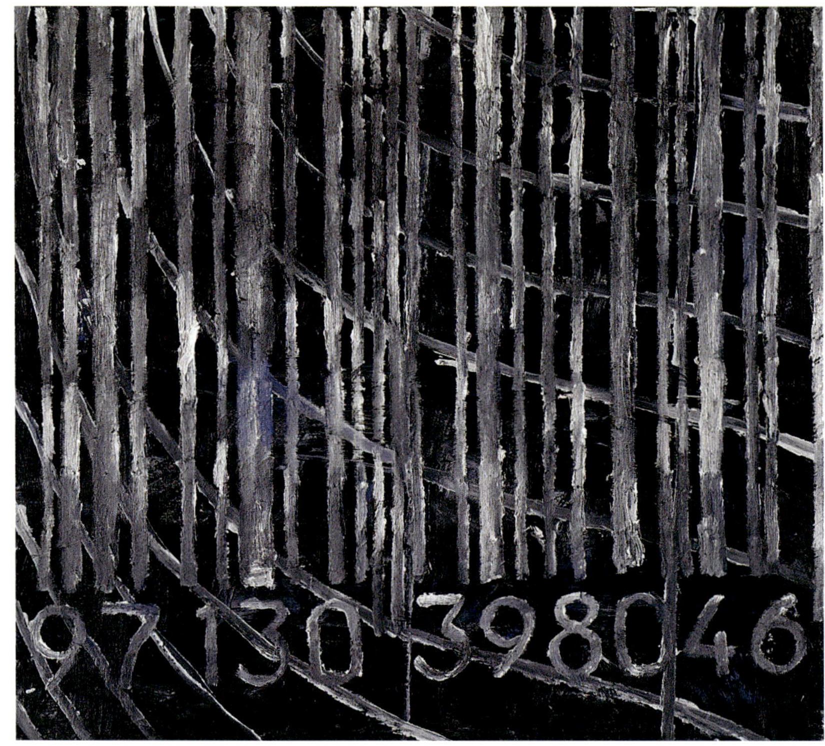

Set Diagram 27, 2000
Oil on linen
36 x 39 3/8 in. (91.4 x 100 cm)
Collection of the artist

Set Diagram 59, 2000
Oil on linen
36 x 39 3/8 in. (91.4 x 100 cm)
The Broad Art Foundation

Set Diagram 40, 2000
Oil on linen
39 3/8 x 36 in. (100 x 91.4 cm)
Collection of the artist

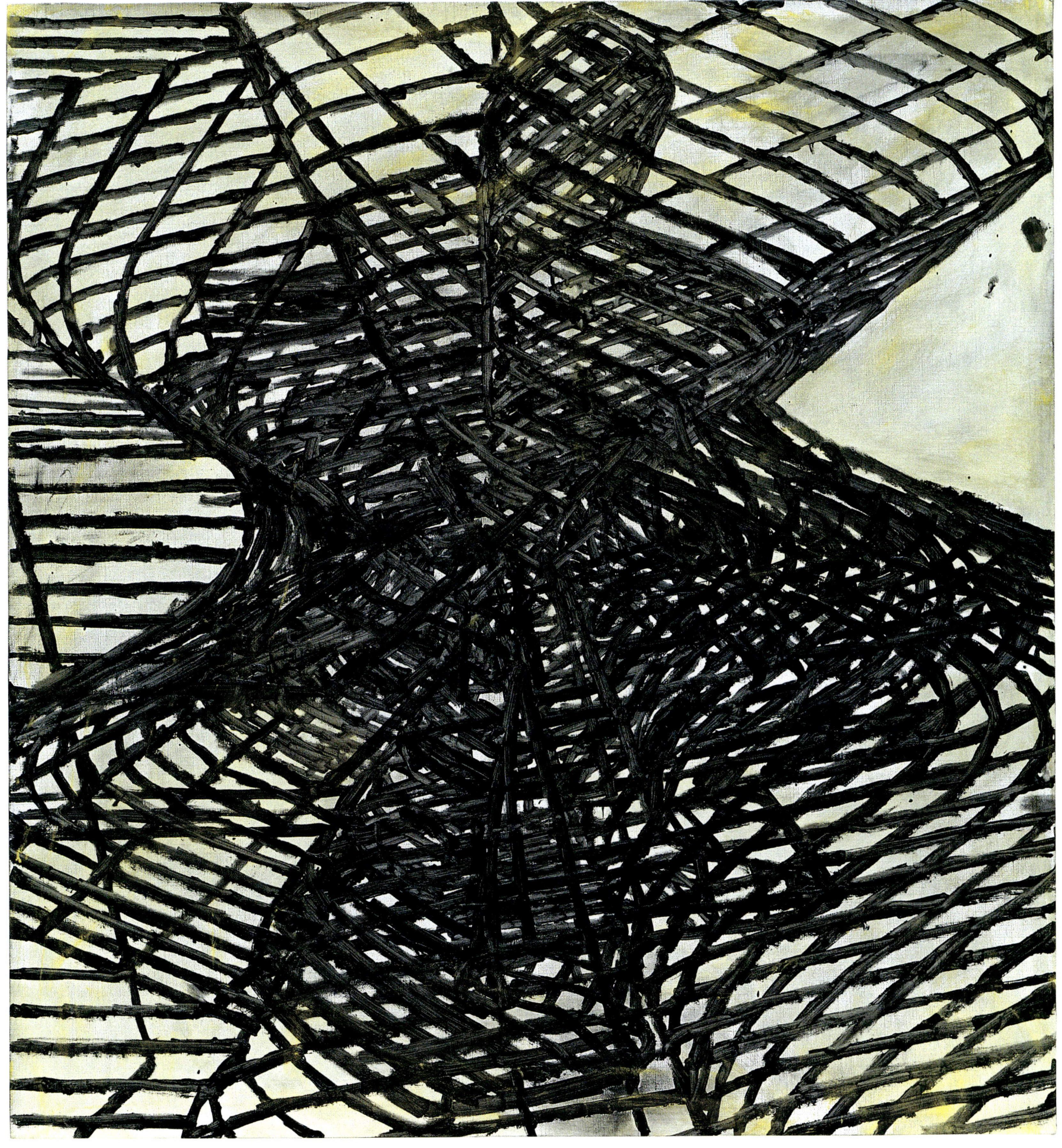

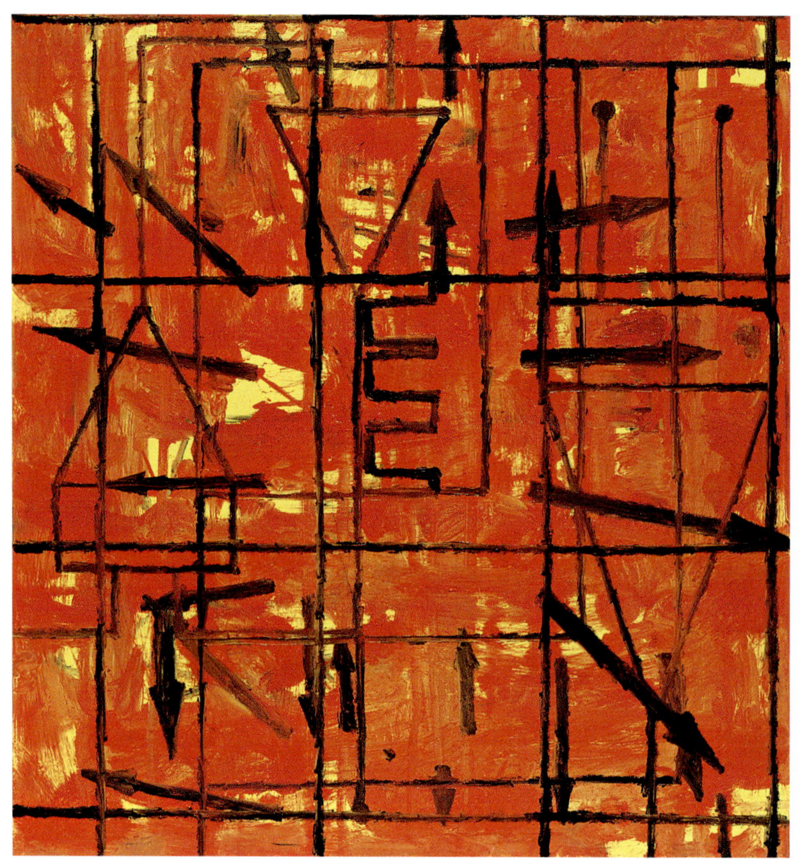

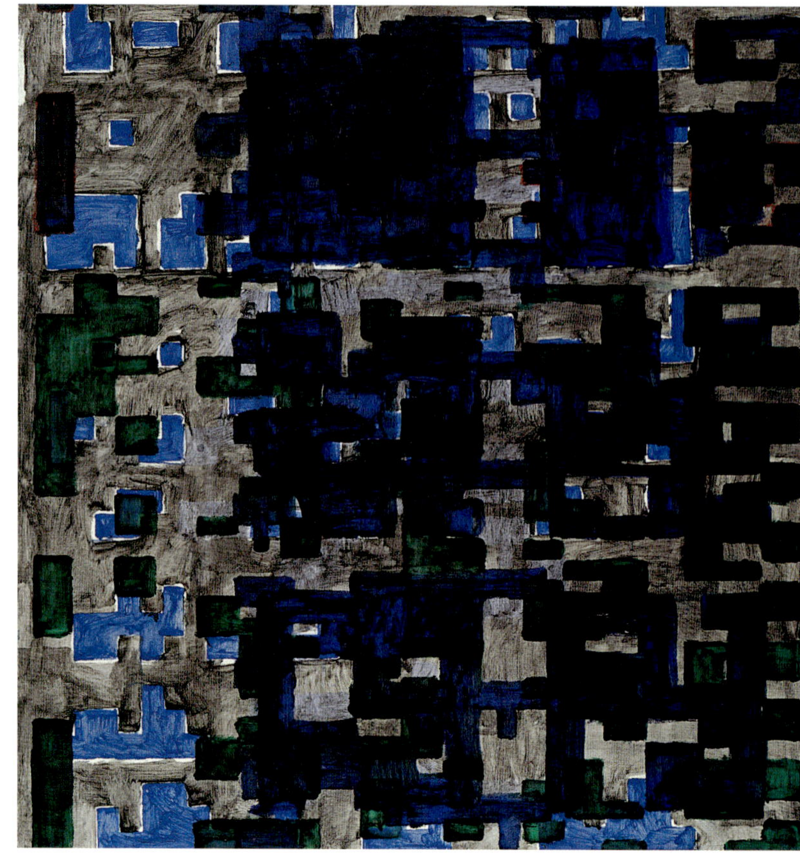

Set Diagram 52, 2000
Oil on linen
39 3/8 x 36 in. (100 x 91.4 cm)
The Broad Art Foundation

Set Diagram 62, 2001
Oil on linen
39 3/8 x 36 in. (100 x 91.4 cm)
Collection of Harry W. and Mary Margaret Anderson

Set Diagram 65, 2001
Oil on linen
39 3/8 x 36 in. (100 x 91.4 cm)
Private collection, courtesy of Matthew Marks Gallery, New York

Set Diagram 68, 2001
Oil on linen
39 3/8 x 36 in. (100 x 91.4 cm)
Courtesy of Matthew Marks Gallery, New York

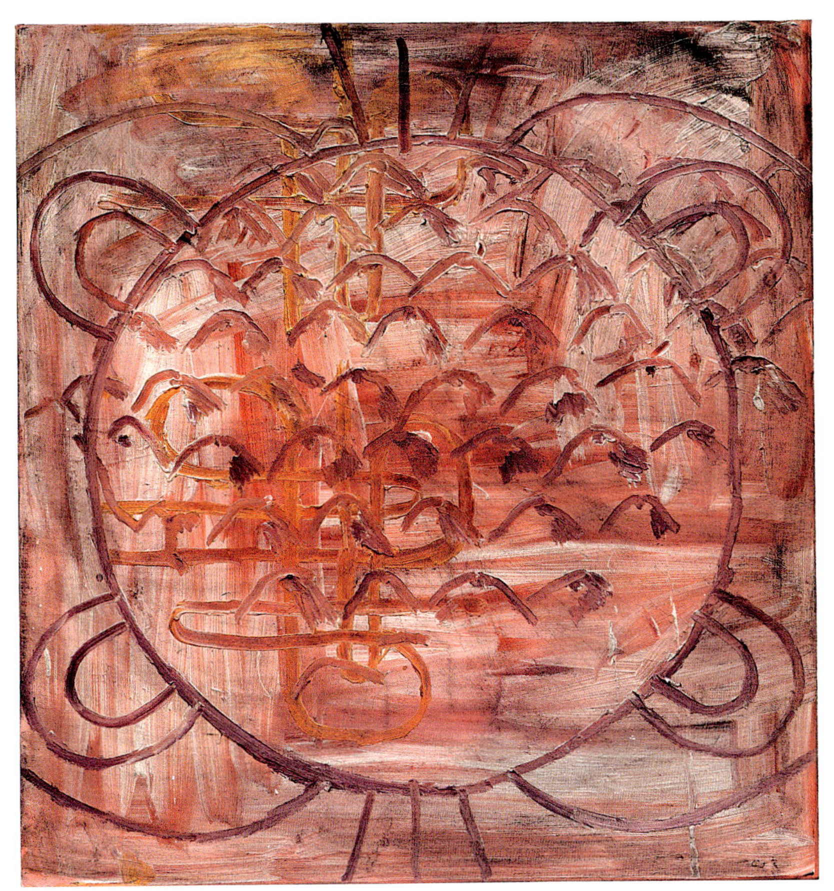

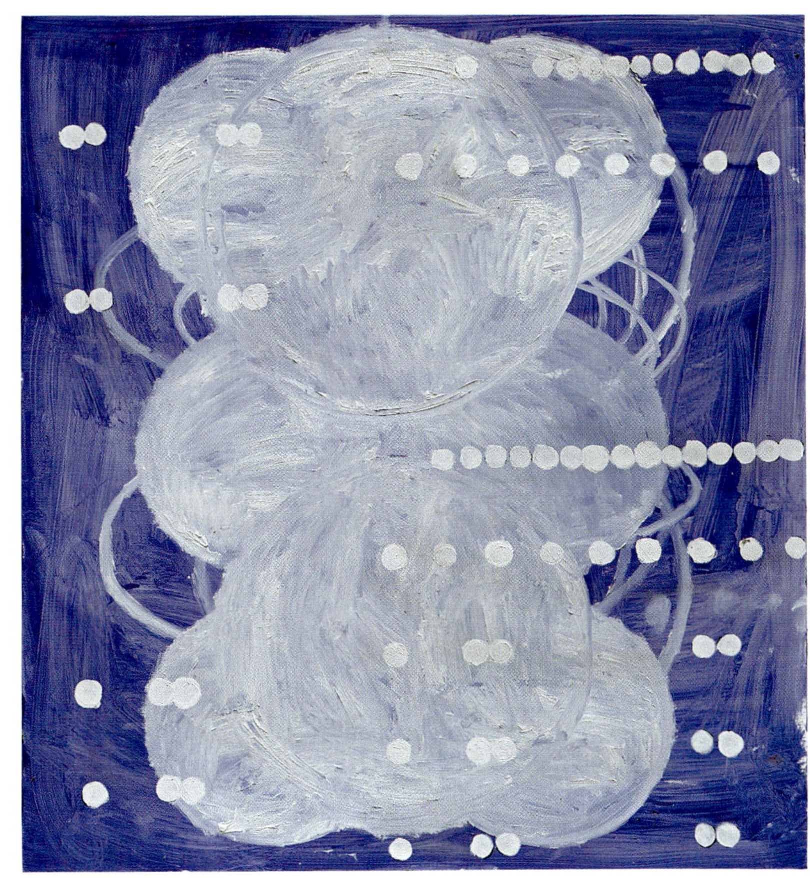

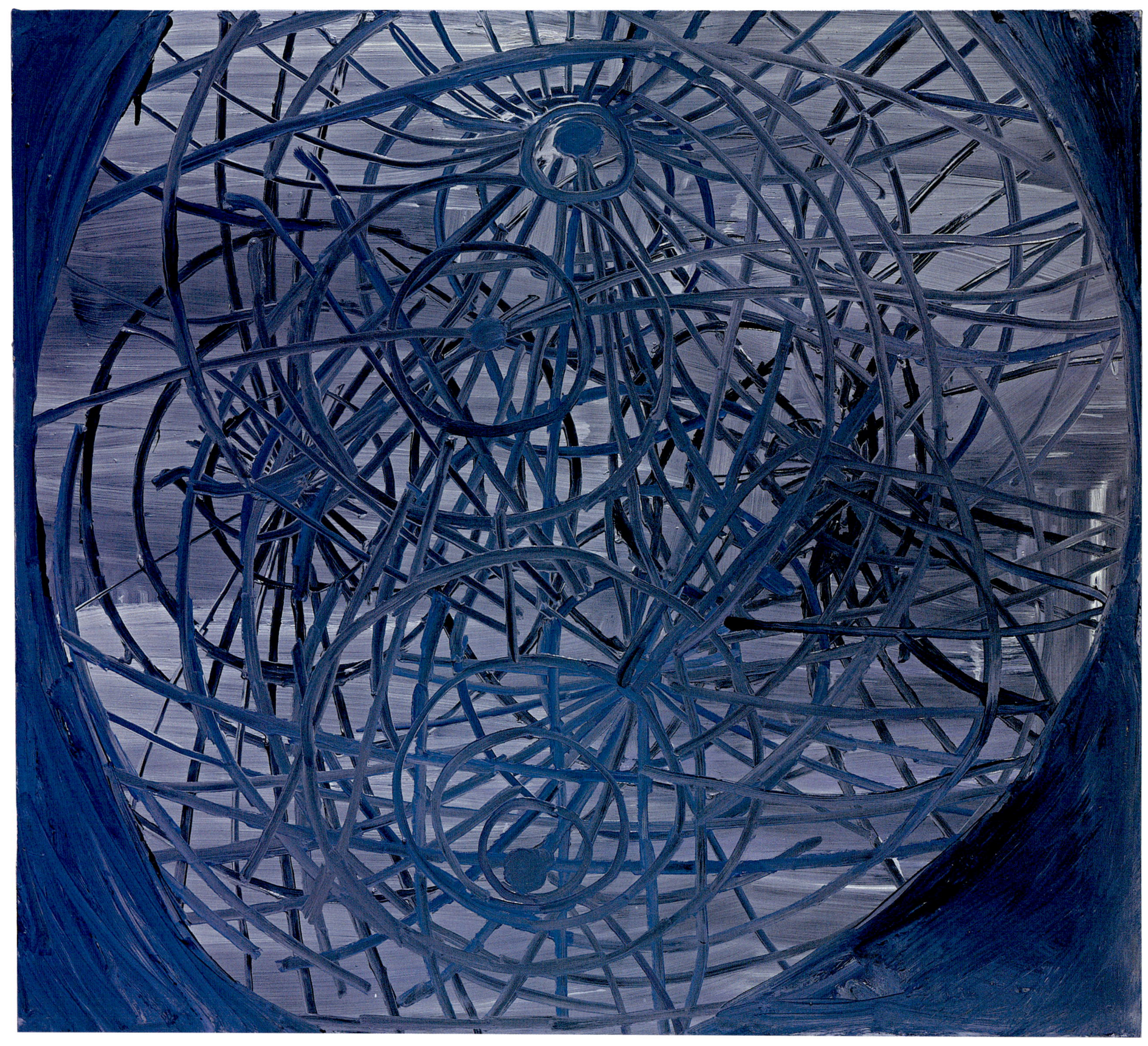

Set Diagram 67, 2001
Oil on linen
36 x 39 3/8 in. (91.4 x 100 cm)
Collection of Harry W. and Mary Margaret Anderson

Set Diagram 69, 2001
Oil on linen
39 3/8 x 36 in. (100 x 91.4 cm)
Courtesy of Matthew Marks Gallery, New York

Set Diagram 81, 2001
Oil on linen
39 3/8 x 36 in. (100 x 91.4 cm)
Collection of the artist

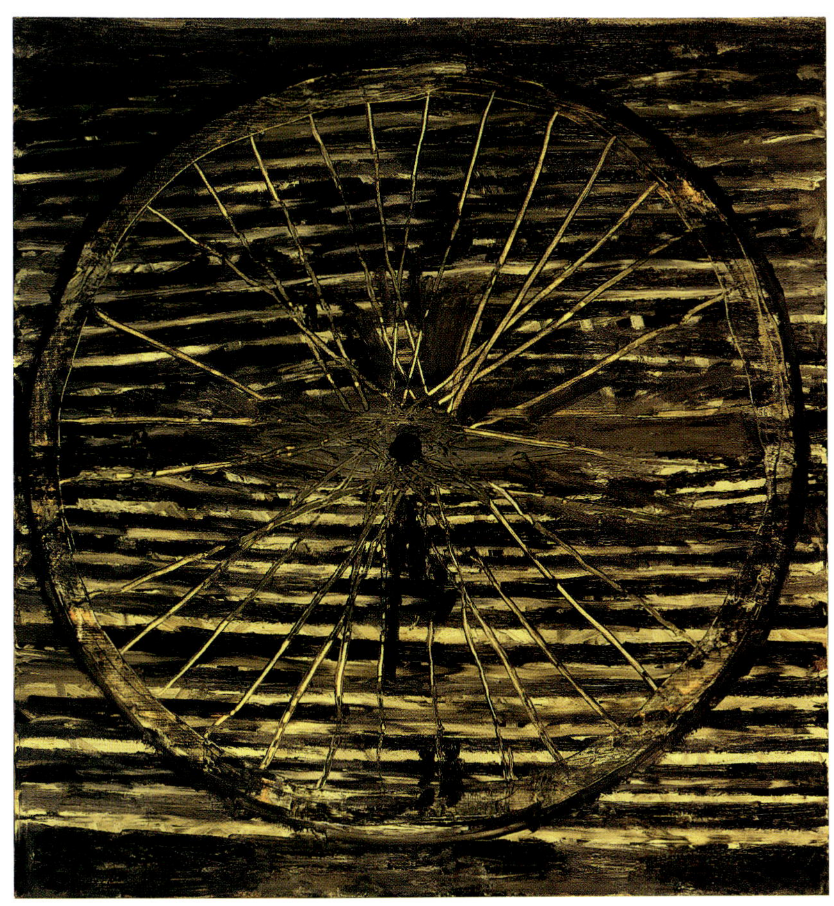

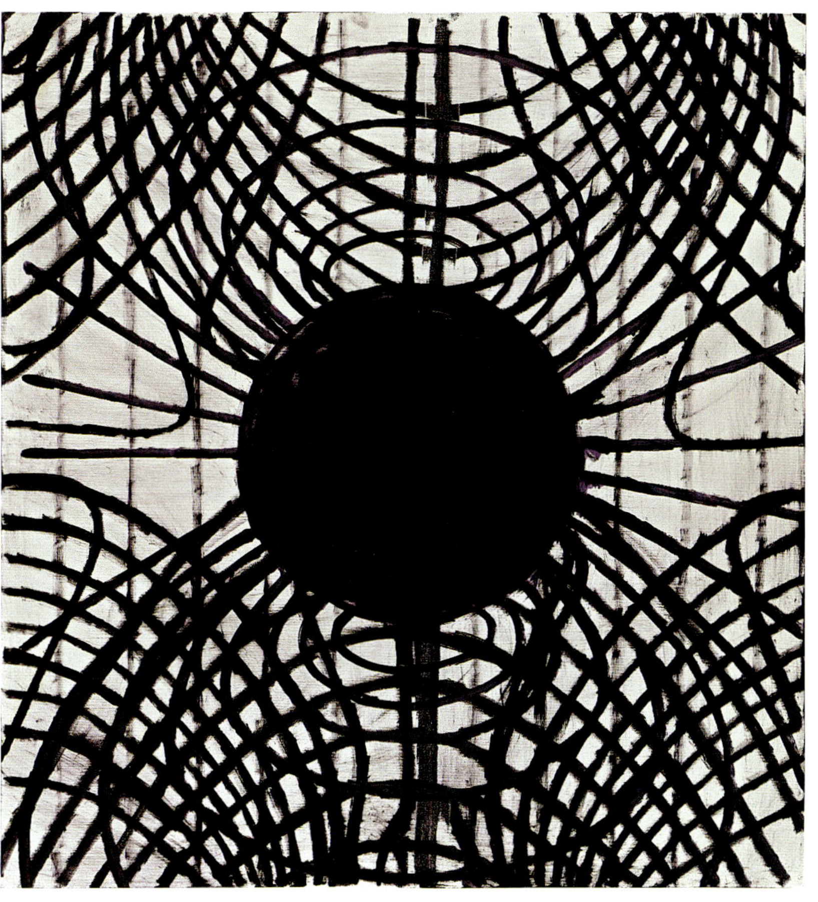

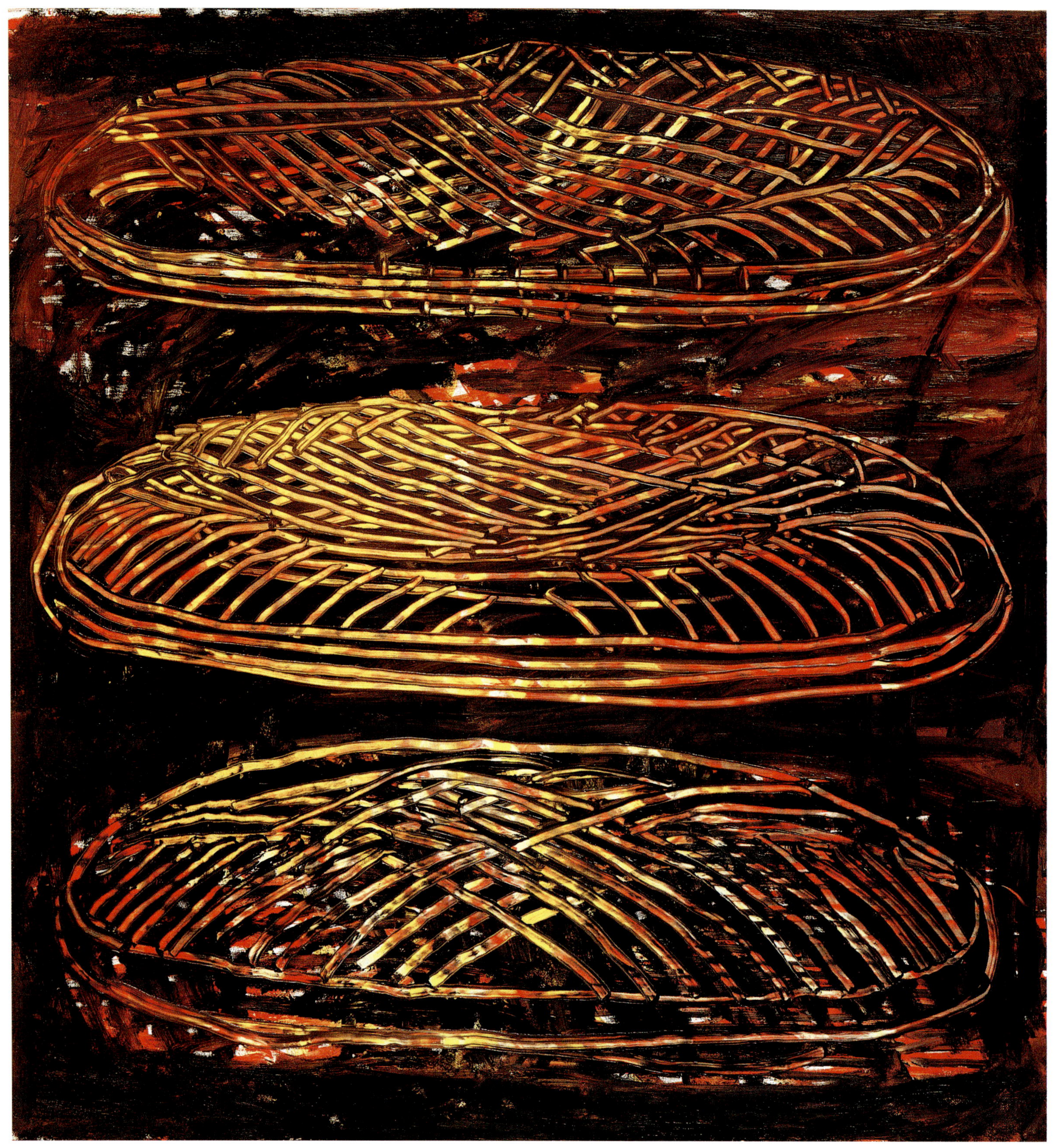

Set Diagram 88, 2002
Oil on linen
39 3/8 x 36 in. (100 x 91.4 cm)
Private collection, courtesy of Matthew Marks Gallery, New York

Set Diagram 100, 2002
Oil on linen
39 3/8 x 36 in. (100 x 91.4 cm)
Courtesy of Matthew Marks Gallery, New York

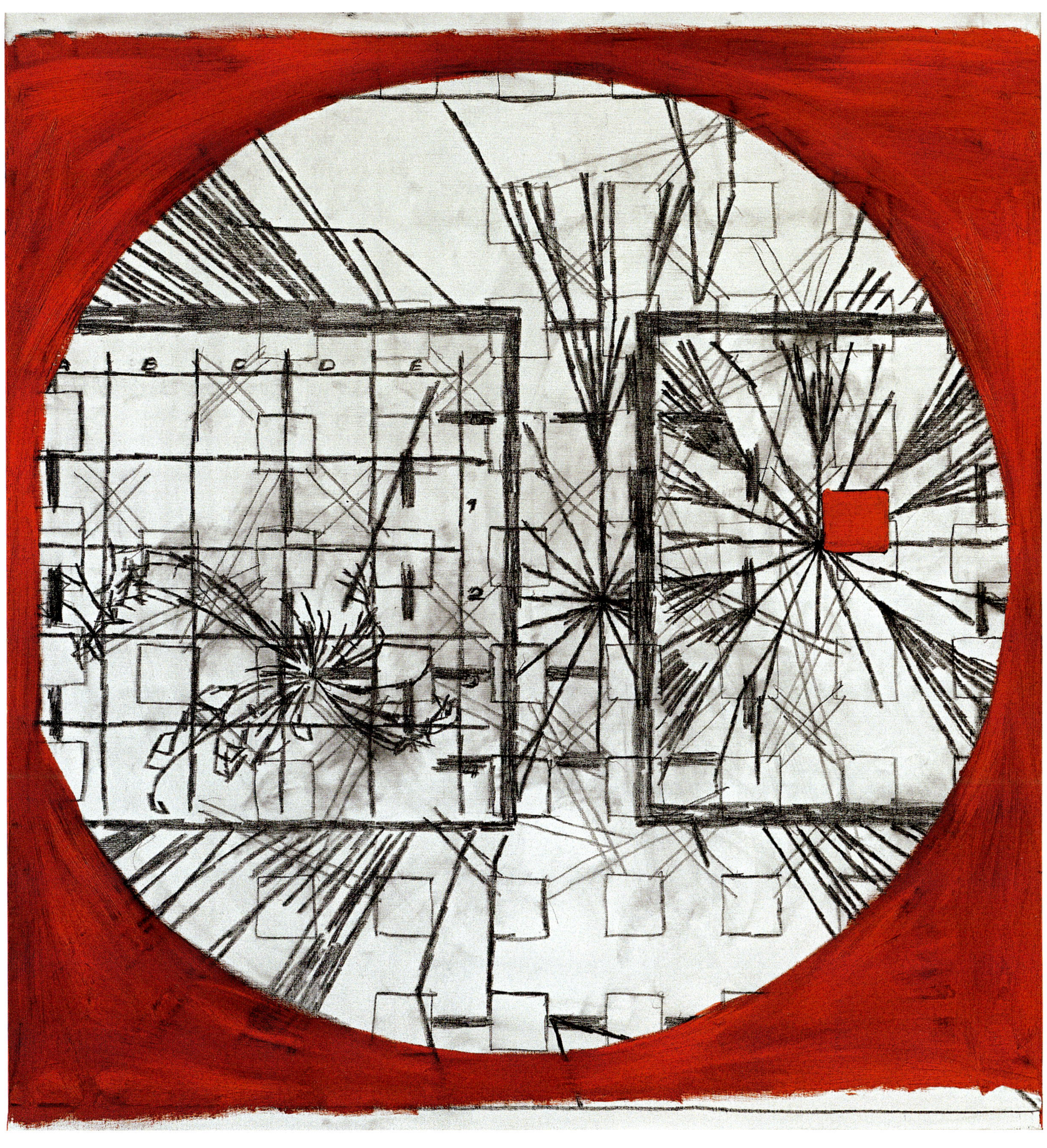

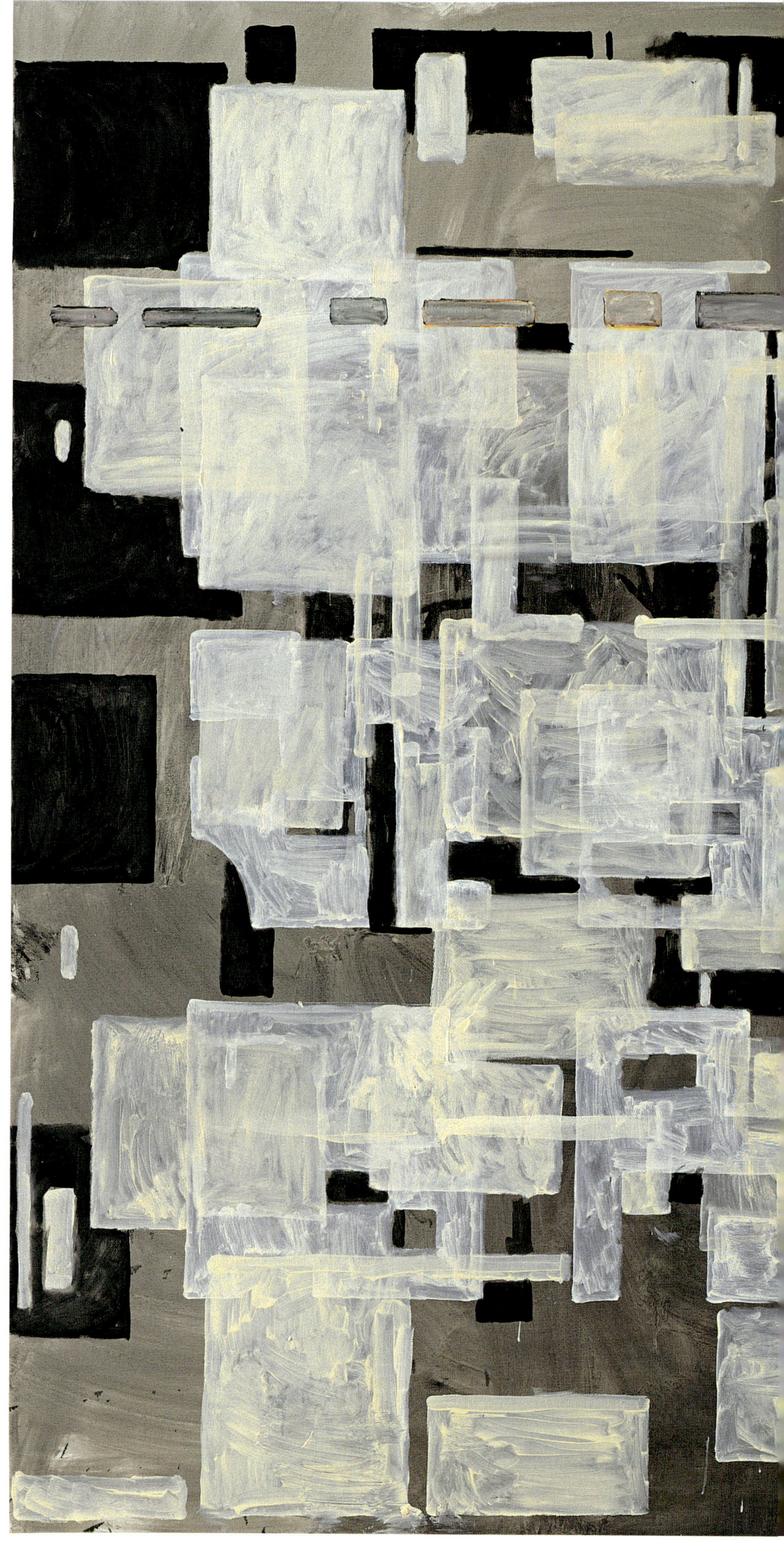

Case-Based Reasoning, 2000
Oil on linen
95 x 133 3/4 in. (241.3 x 339.7 cm)
Museo Nacional Centro de Arte Reina Sofía, Madrid

Pages 110–11:
Set Diagram, installation view, 2001
Lehmann Maupin Gallery, New York
Photograph by Todd Eberle

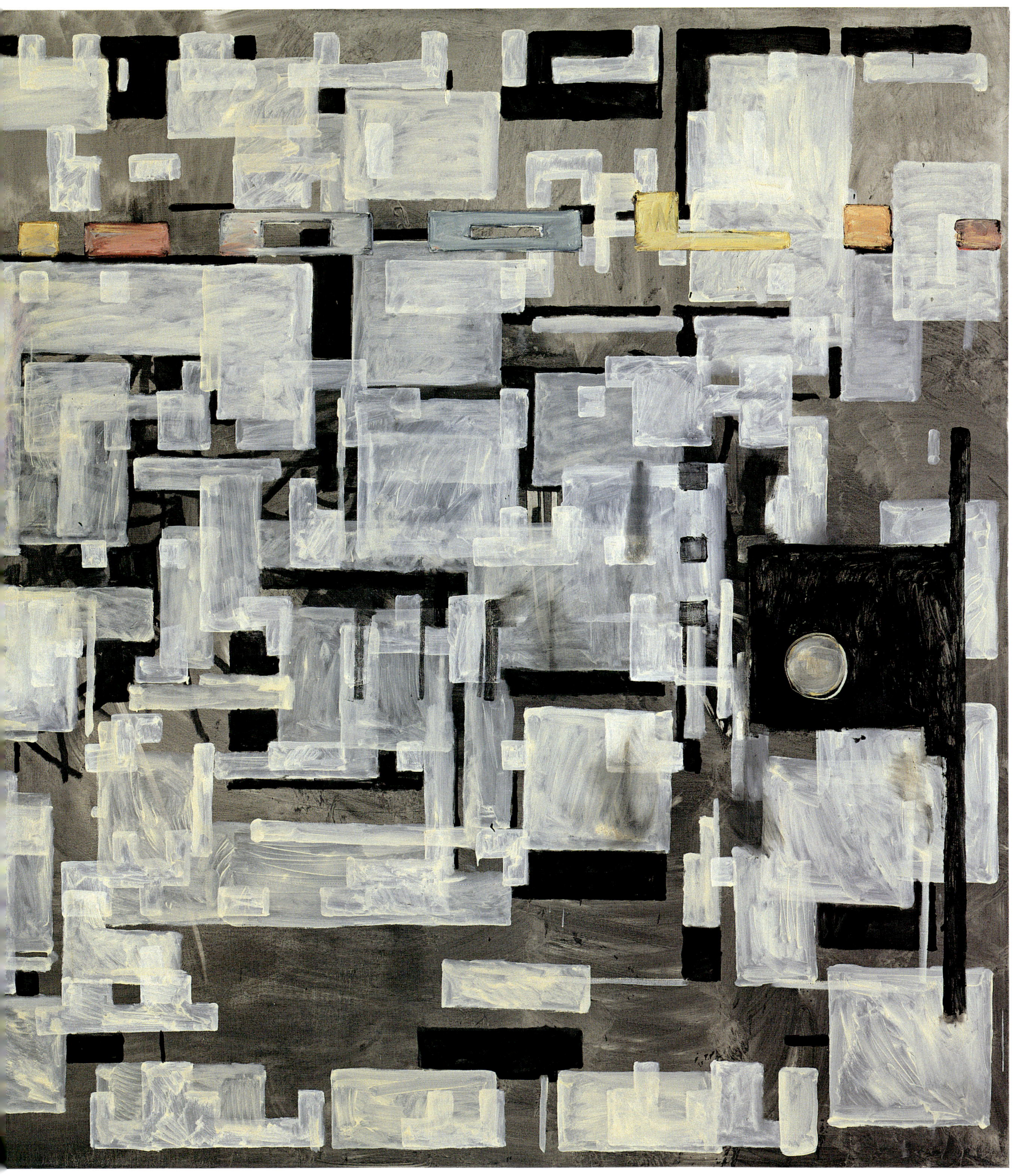

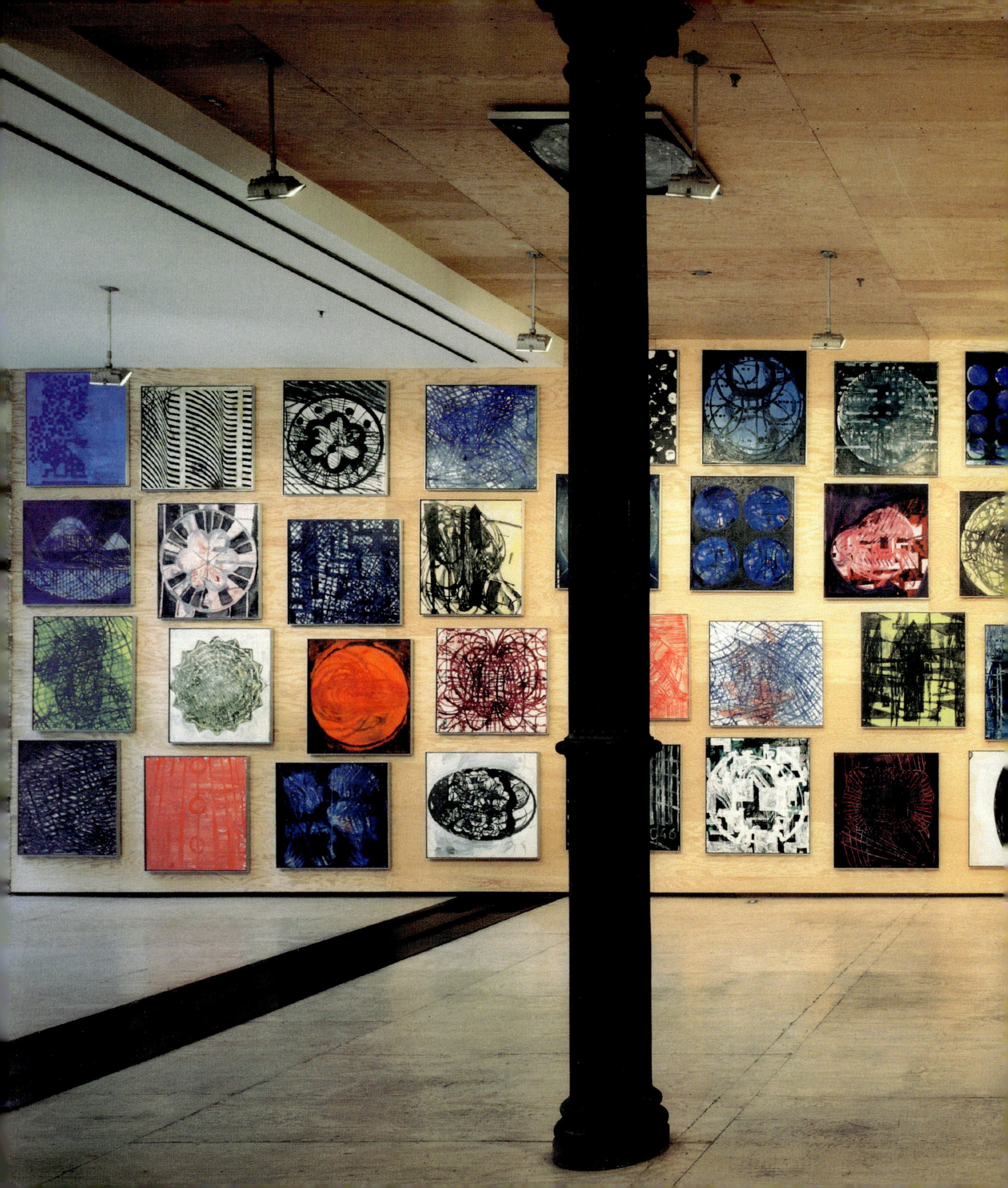

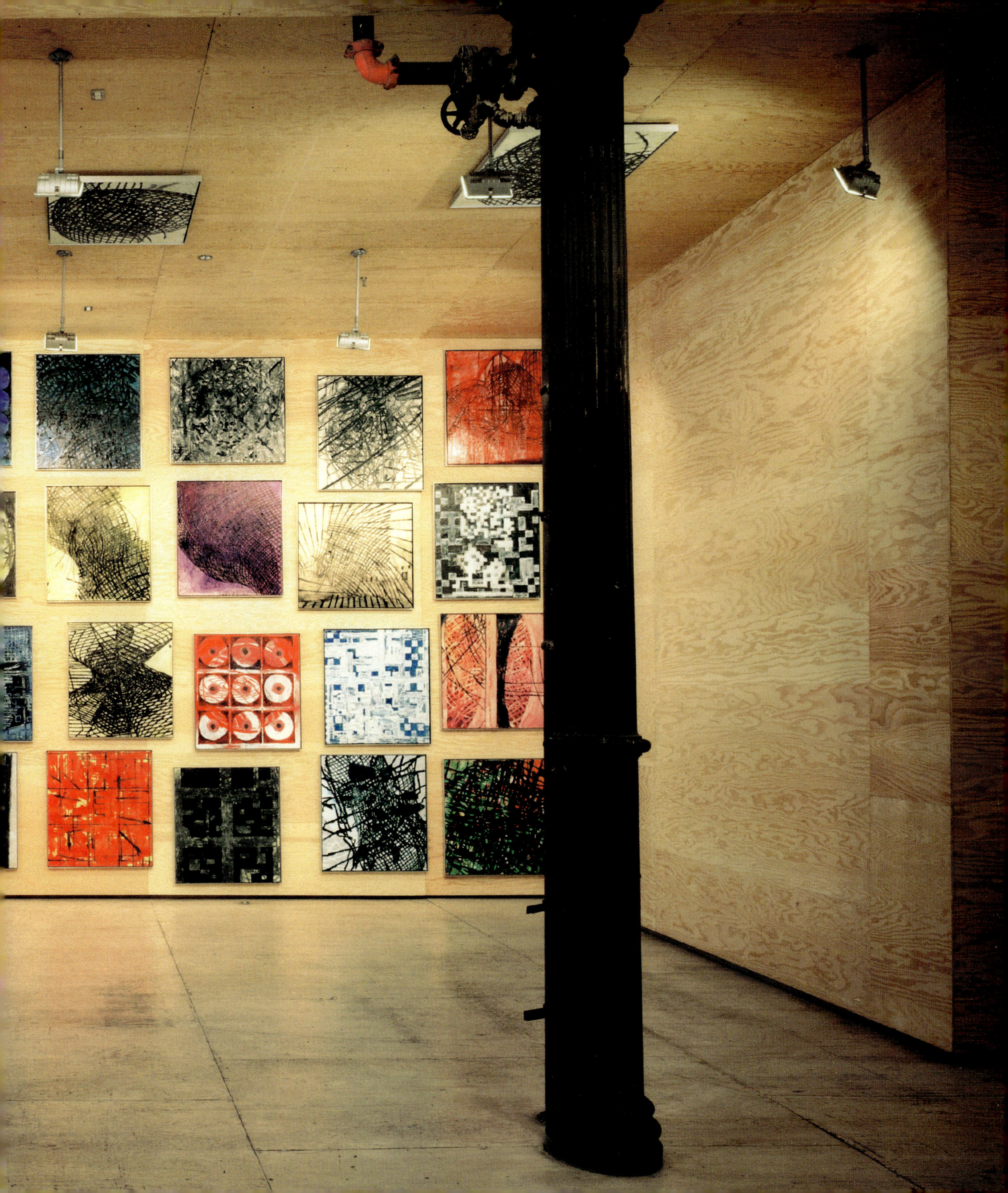

MESHWORKS

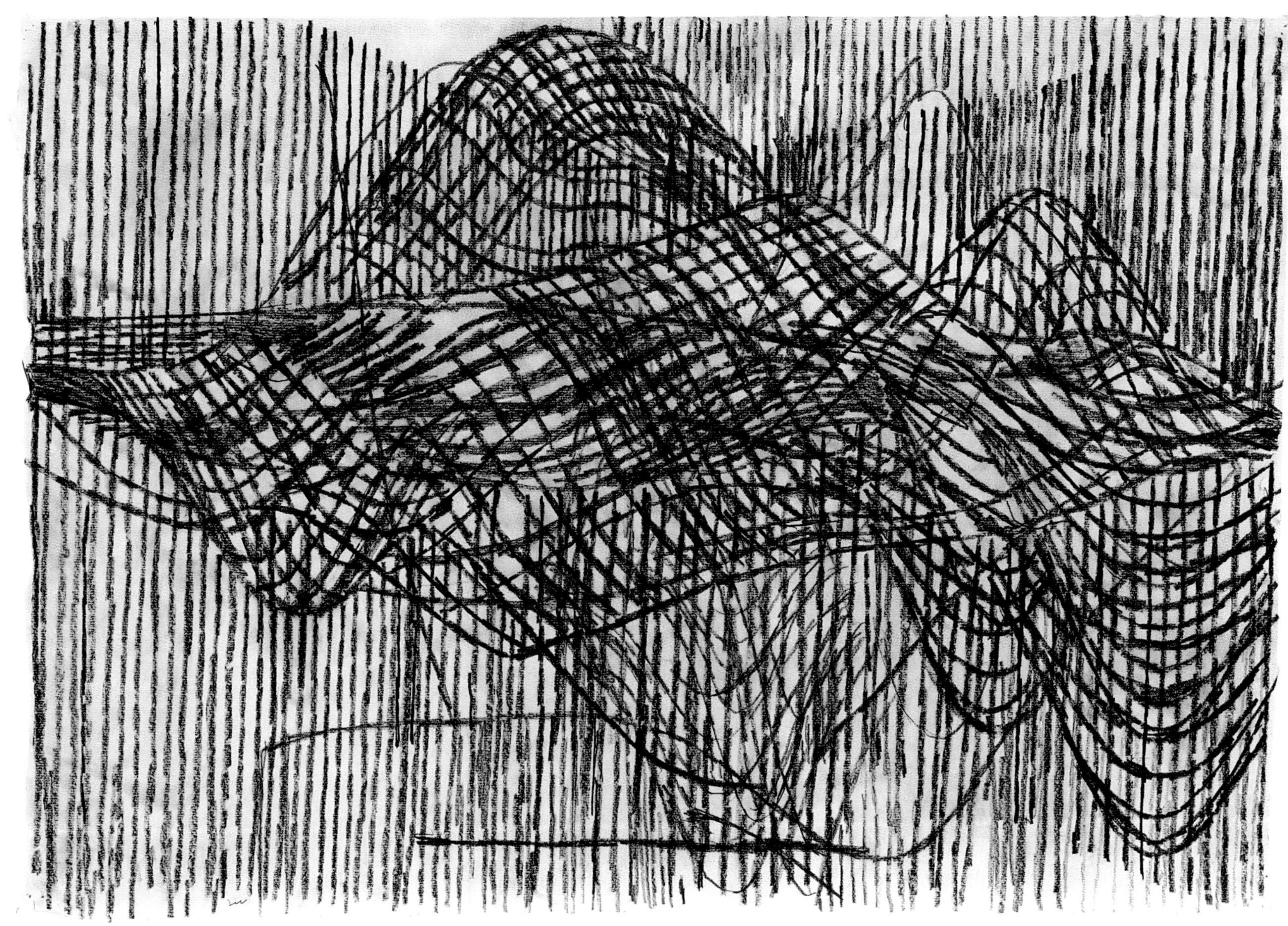

Meshworks, 1, 2000
Graphite on paper
20 x 28 in. (50.8 x 71.1 cm)
Private collection

Meshworks, 3, 2000
Graphite on paper
20 x 28 in. (50.8 x 71.1 cm)
Private collection

Meshworks, 6, 2000
Graphite on paper
20 x 28 in. (50.8 x 71.1 cm)
Collection of Joellin Comerford

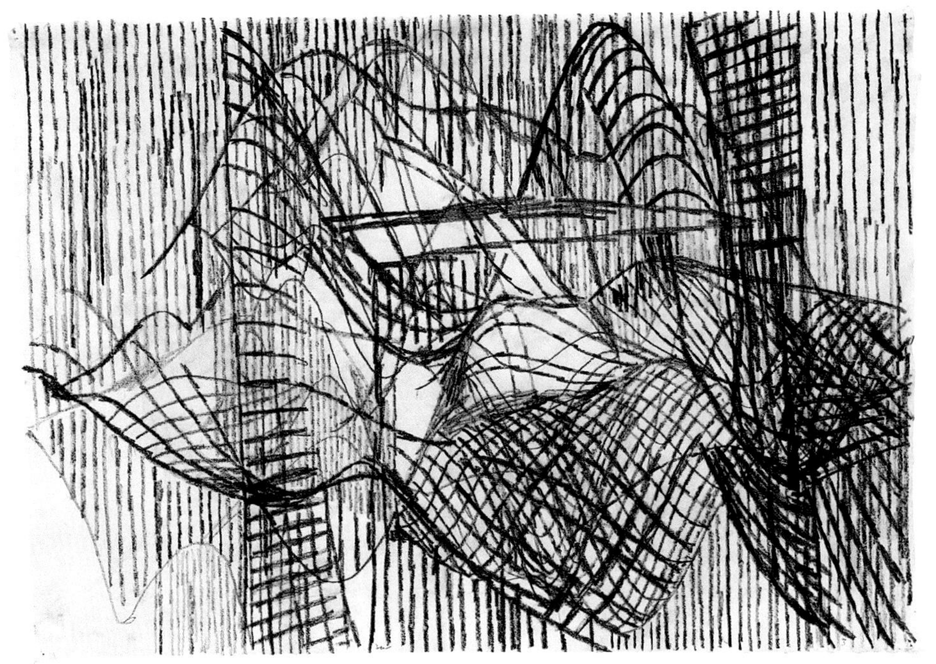

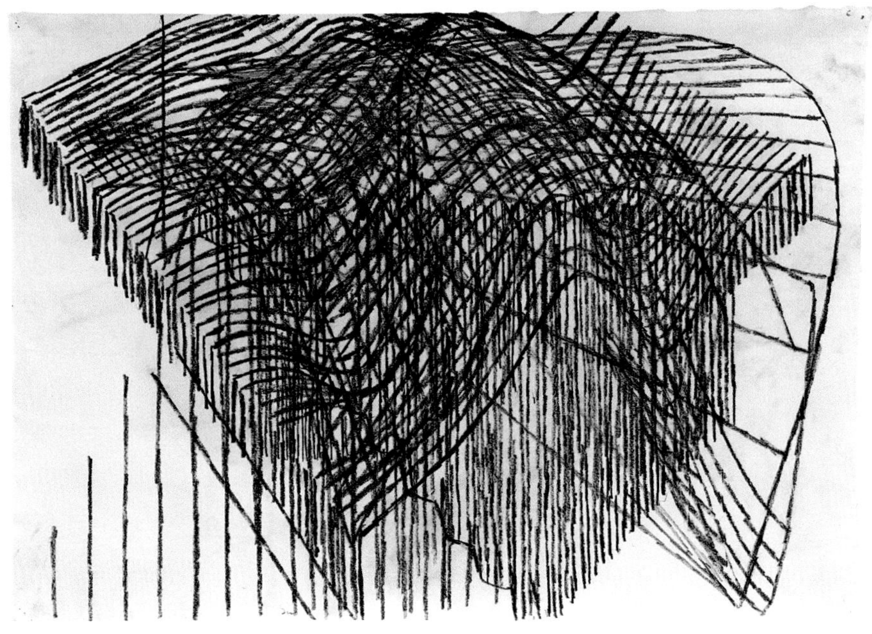

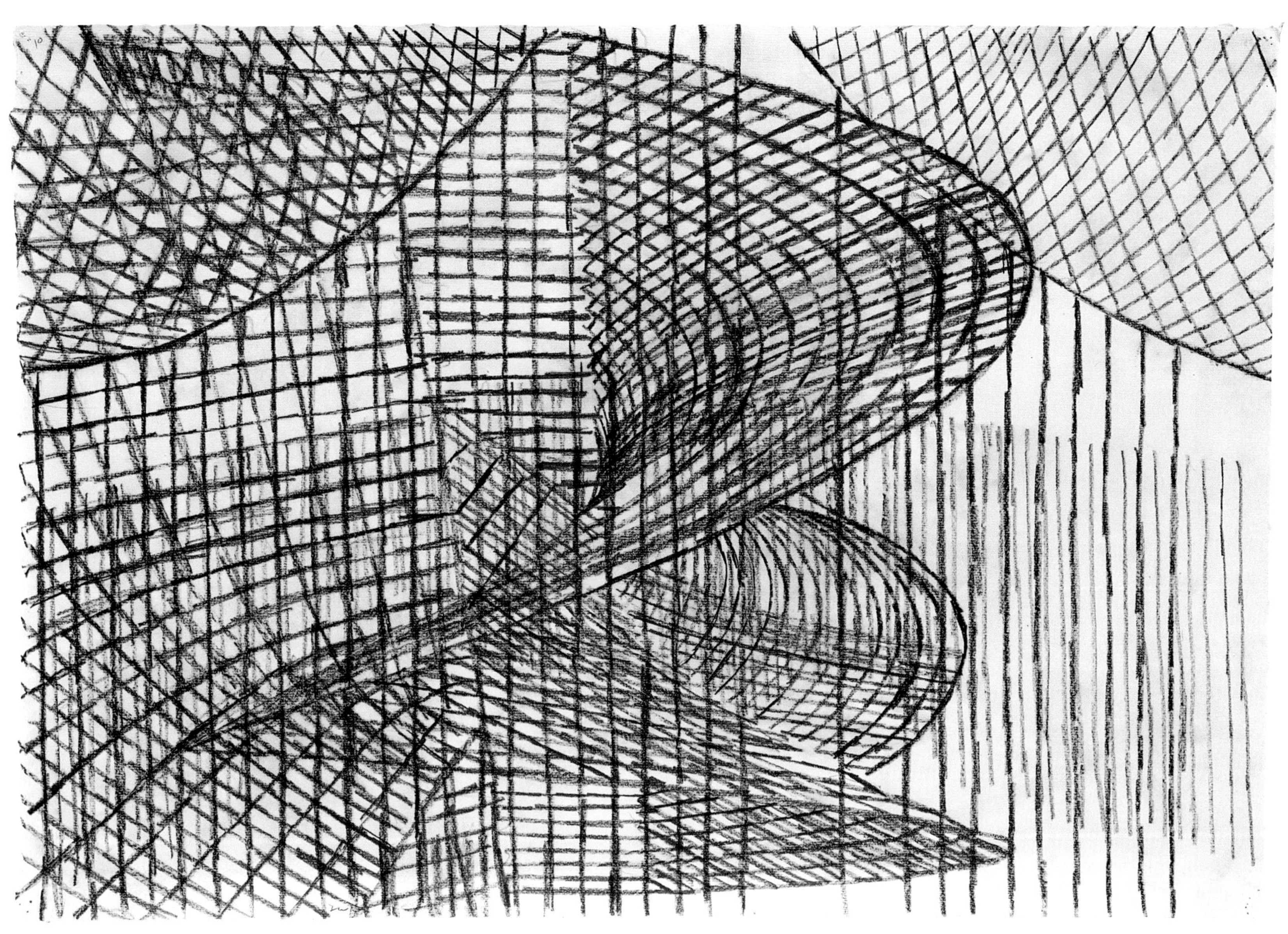

Meshworks, 10, 2000
Graphite on paper
20 x 28 in. (50.8 x 71.1 cm)
Private collection, courtesy of Matthew Marks Gallery

Meshworks, 7, 2000
Graphite on paper
20 x 28 in. (50.8 x 71.1 cm)
Private collection

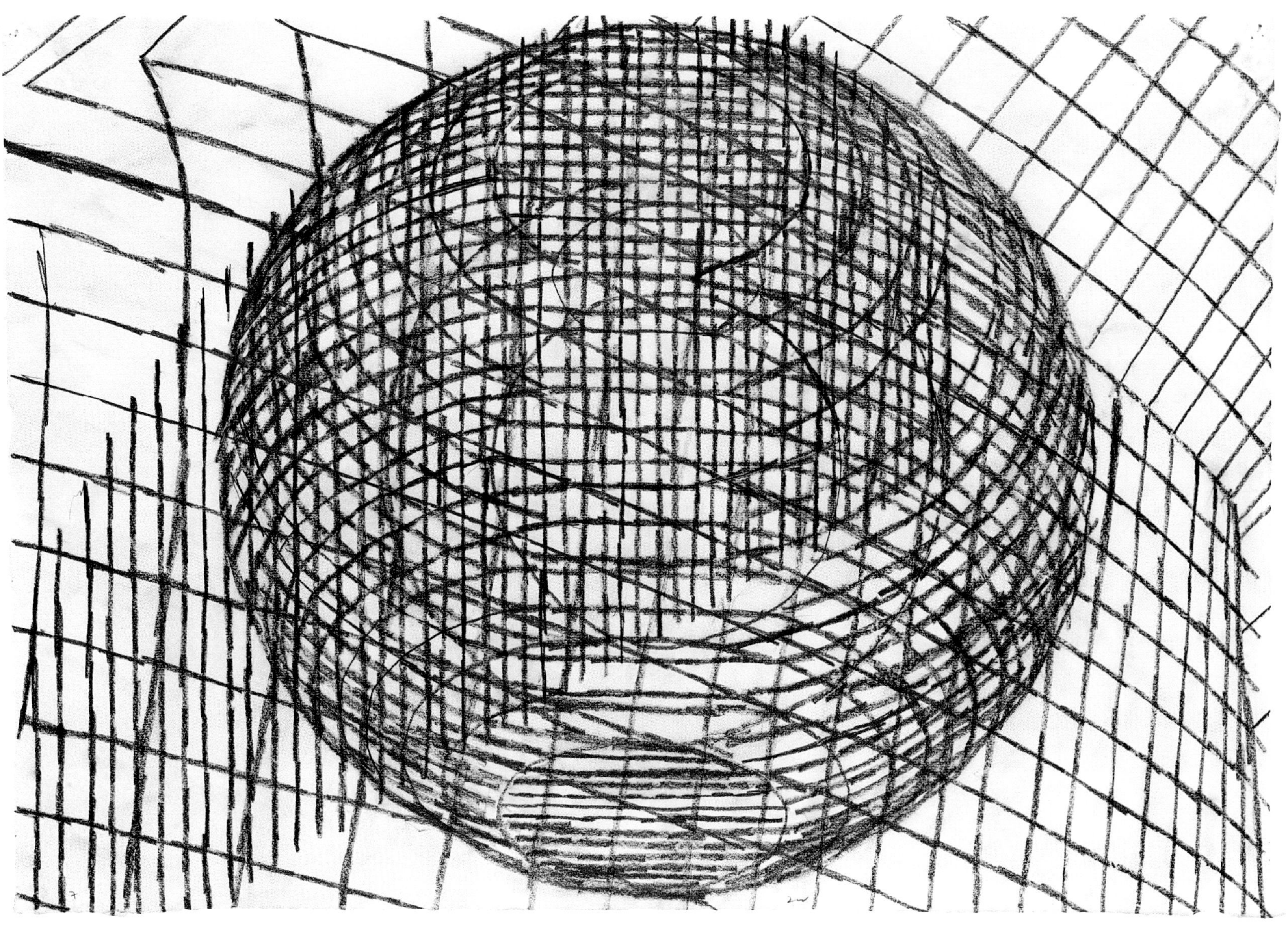

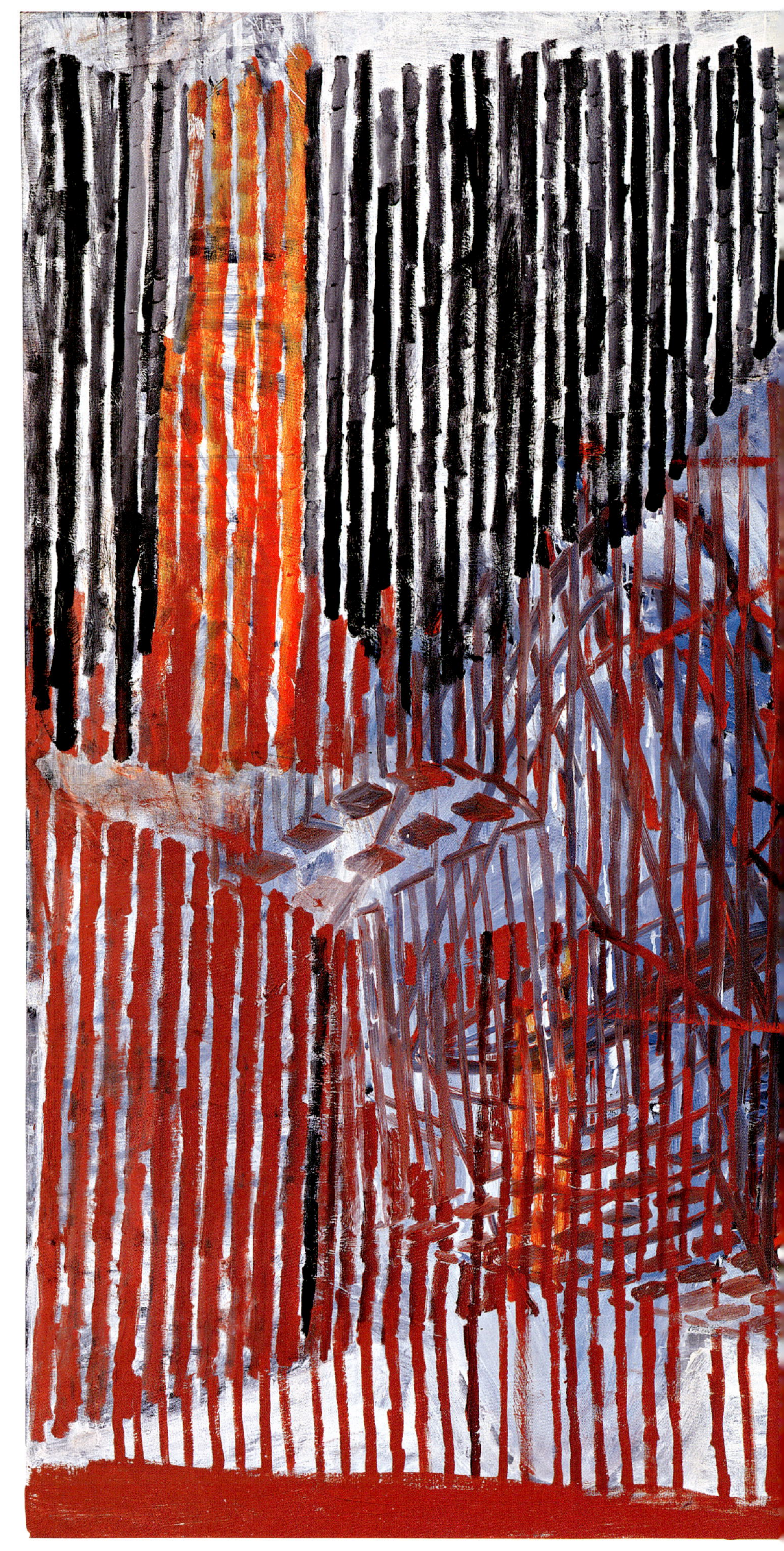

Functions, Vectors, and Speeds, 2001
Oil on linen
82 1/2 x 117 in. (209.6 x 297.2 cm)
Private collection

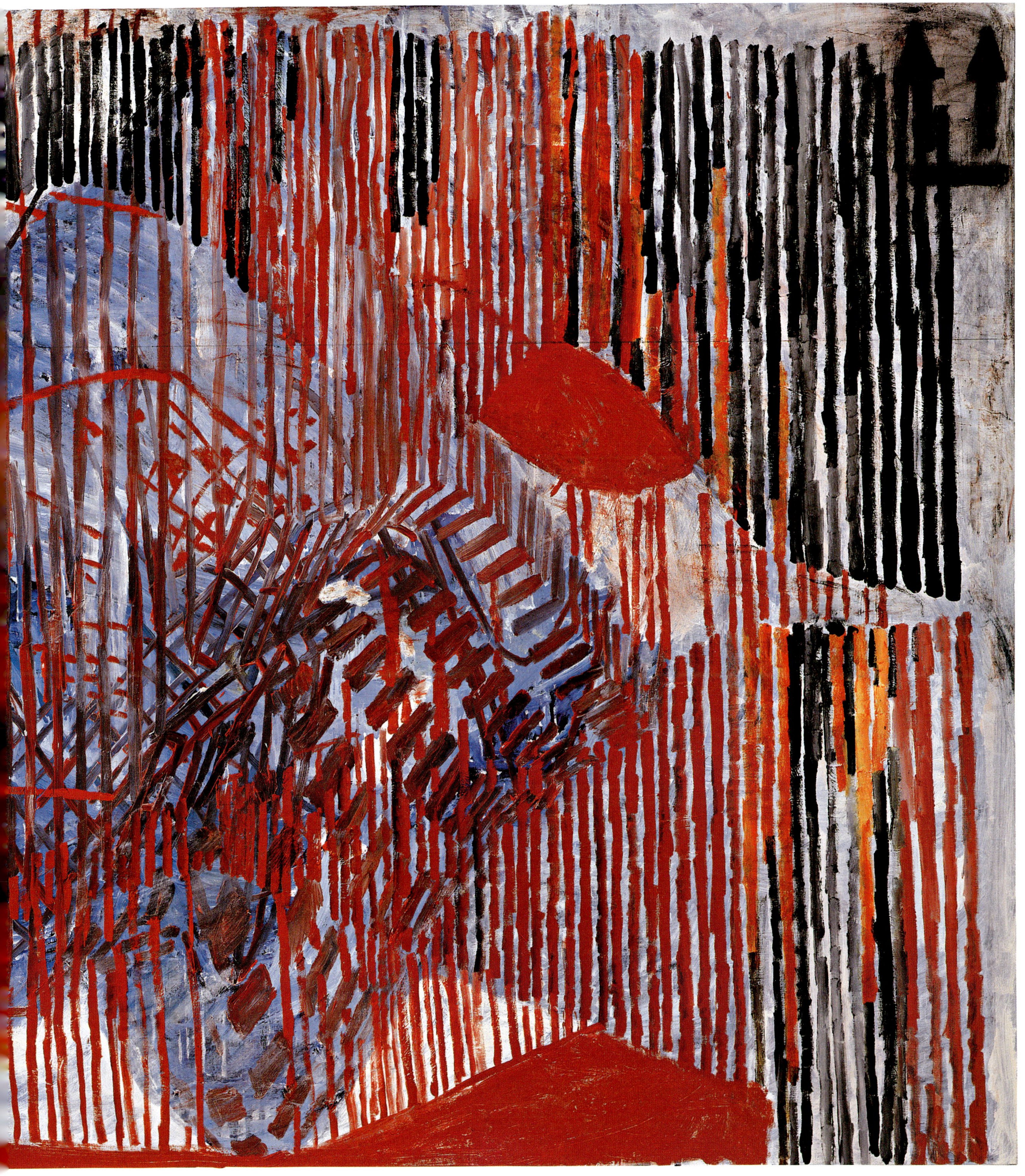

Untitled (1), 1999
Gouache on paper
44 1/4 x 30 1/2 in. (112.4 x 77.5 cm)
Private collection

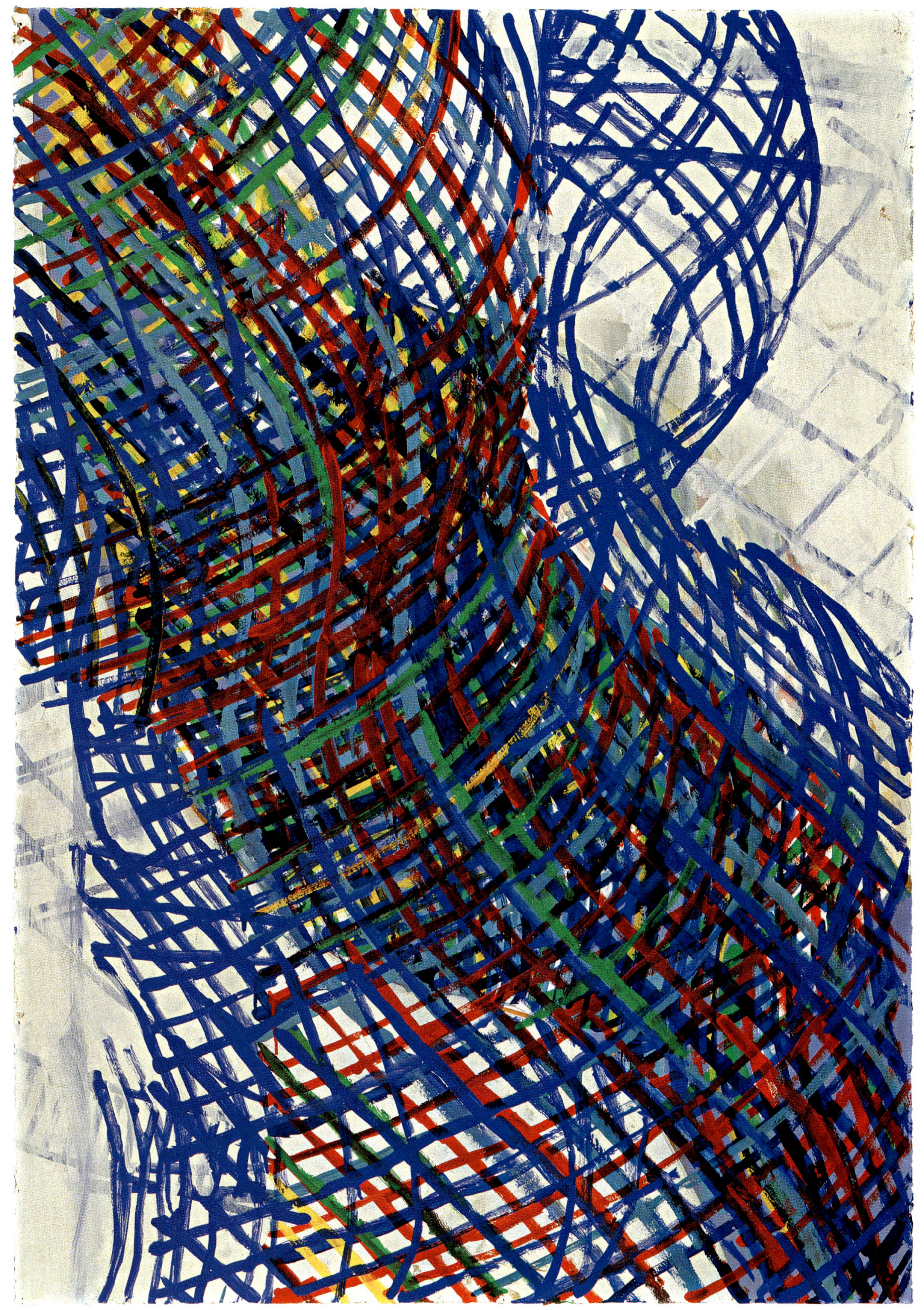

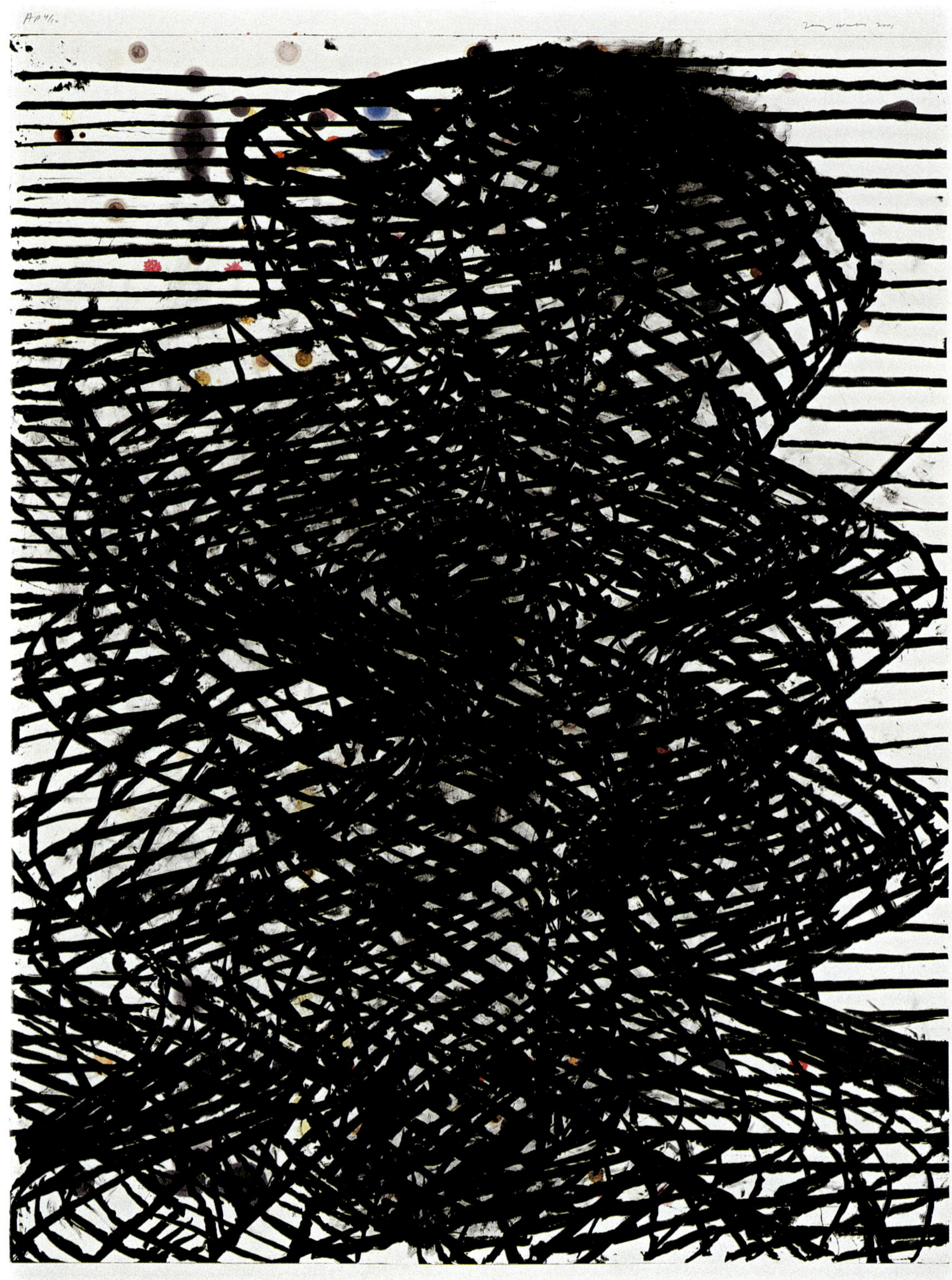

Pattern, 2001
Lithograph with pigmented inkjet on paper
52 x 39 3/4 in. (132.1 x 101 cm)
Private collection, New York

Amplitude, 2000
Sugar-lift aquatint and open-bite etching on paper
53 1/4 x 43 1/2 in. (135.3 x 110.5 cm)
Private collection, New York

Pages 124–25:
Merce Cunningham Dance Company
Loose Time, 2002
Music by Christian Wolff
Set and costumes by Terry Winters
Lighting by Aaron Copp
Photograph by Tony Dougherty

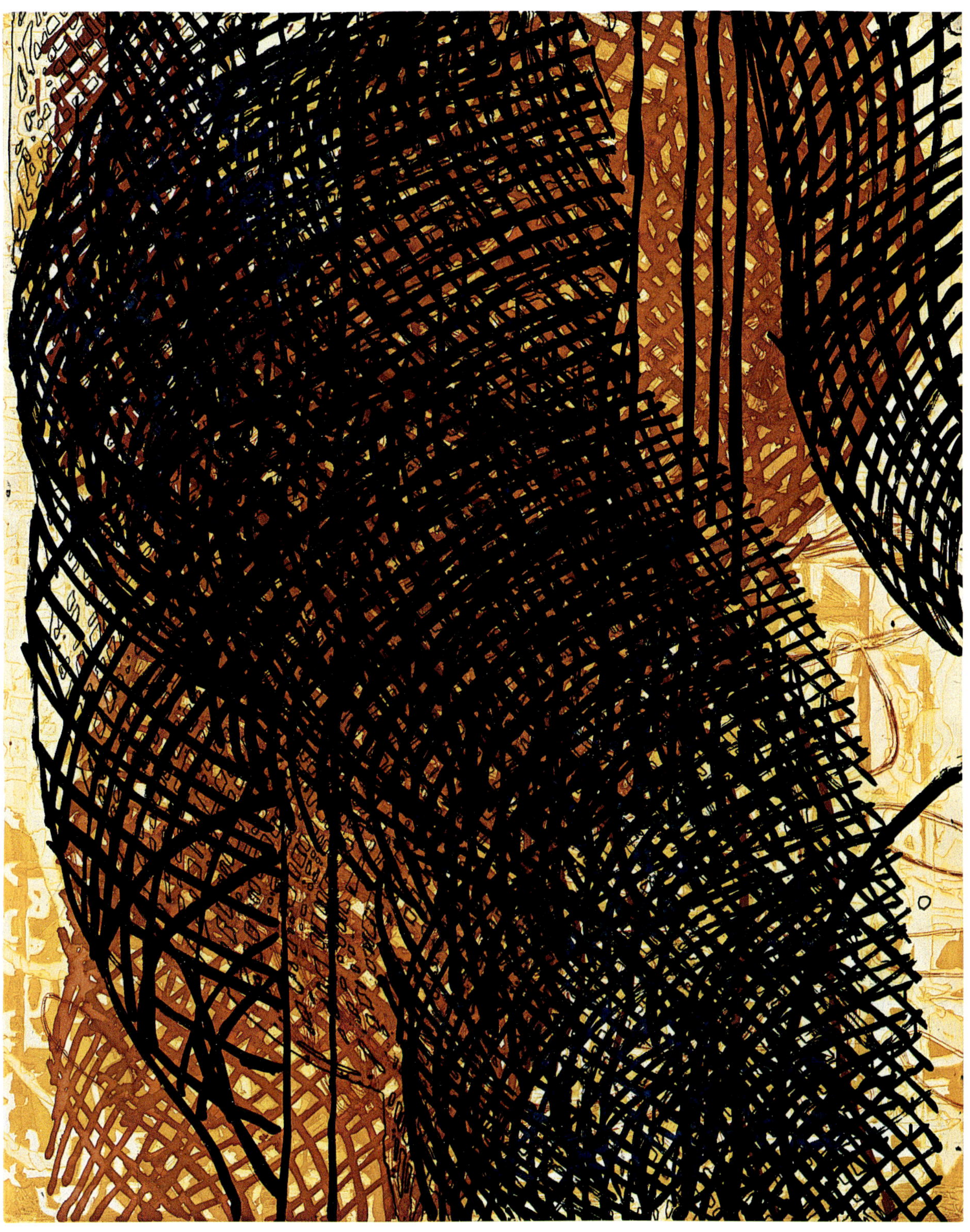

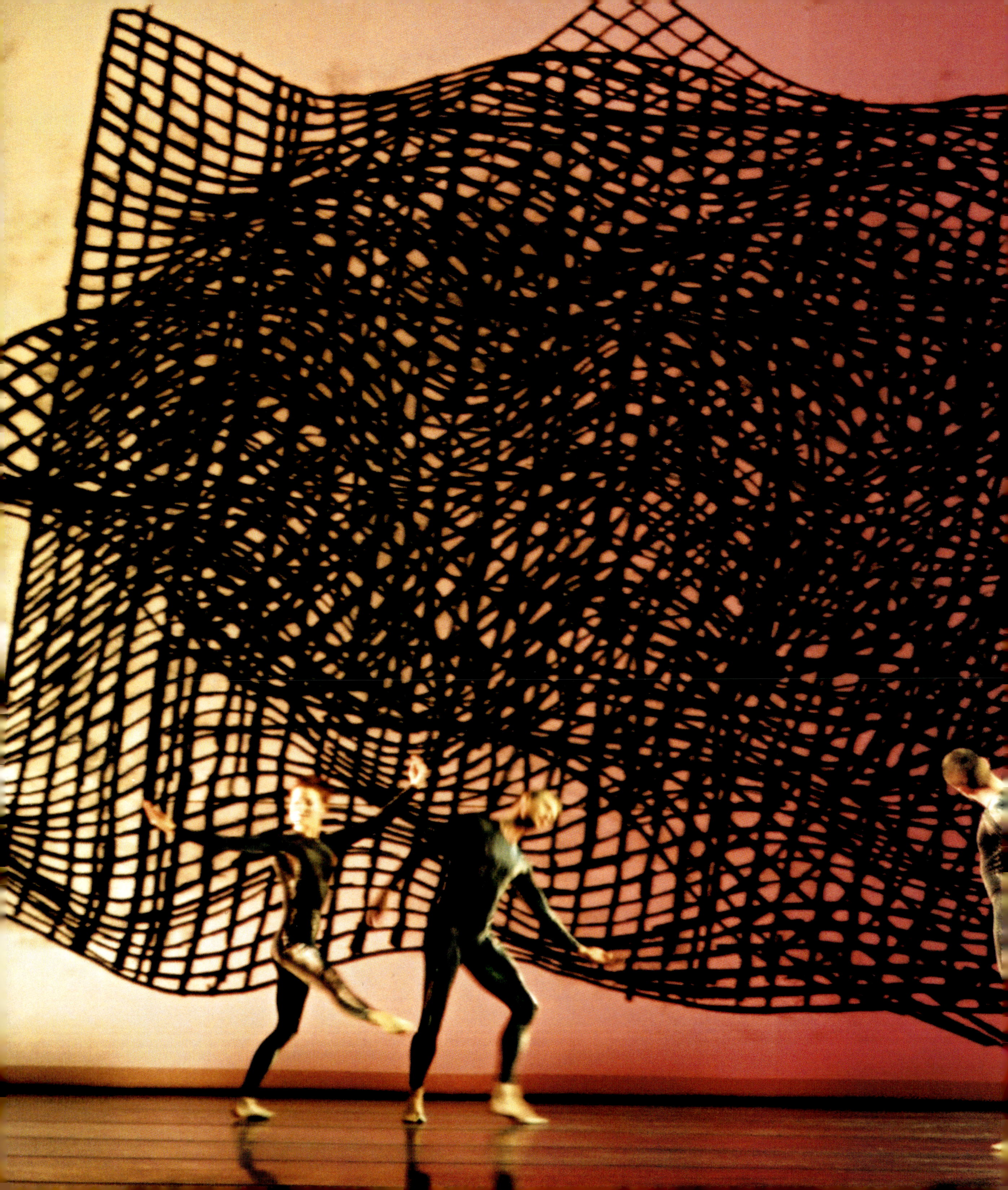

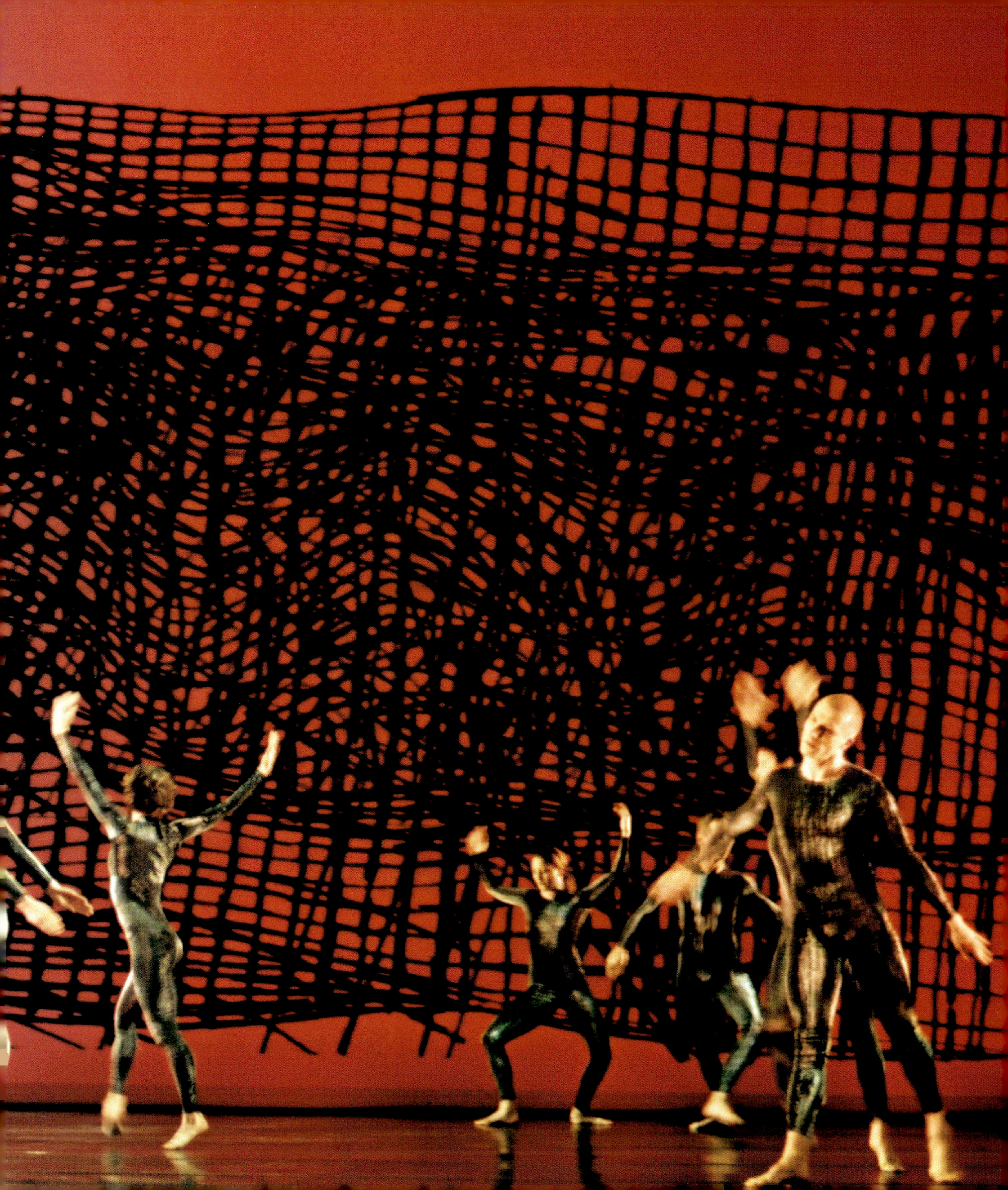

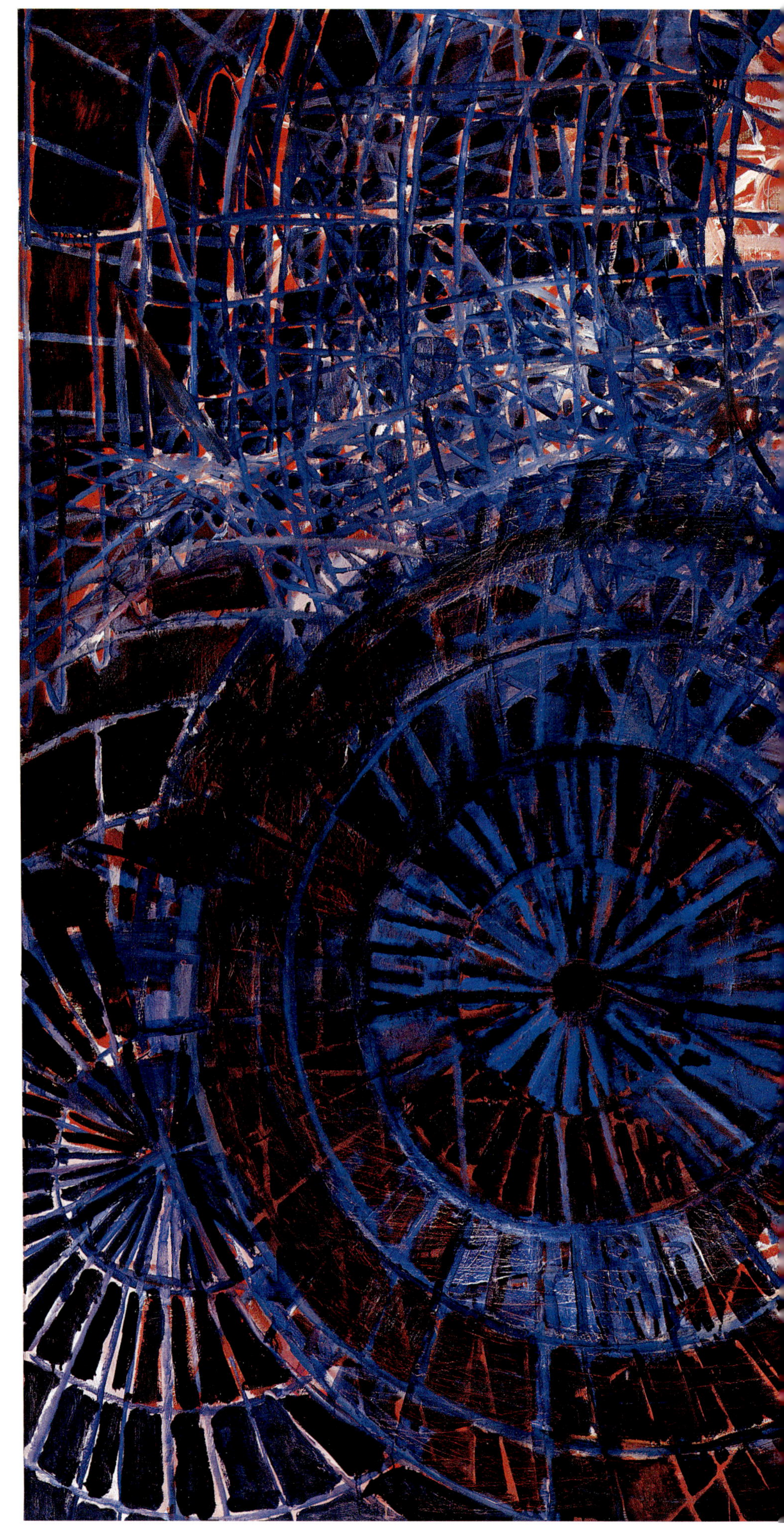

Composite, 2002
Oil on linen
82 3/4 x 117 in. (210.2 x 297.2 cm)
Dewey Art Collection

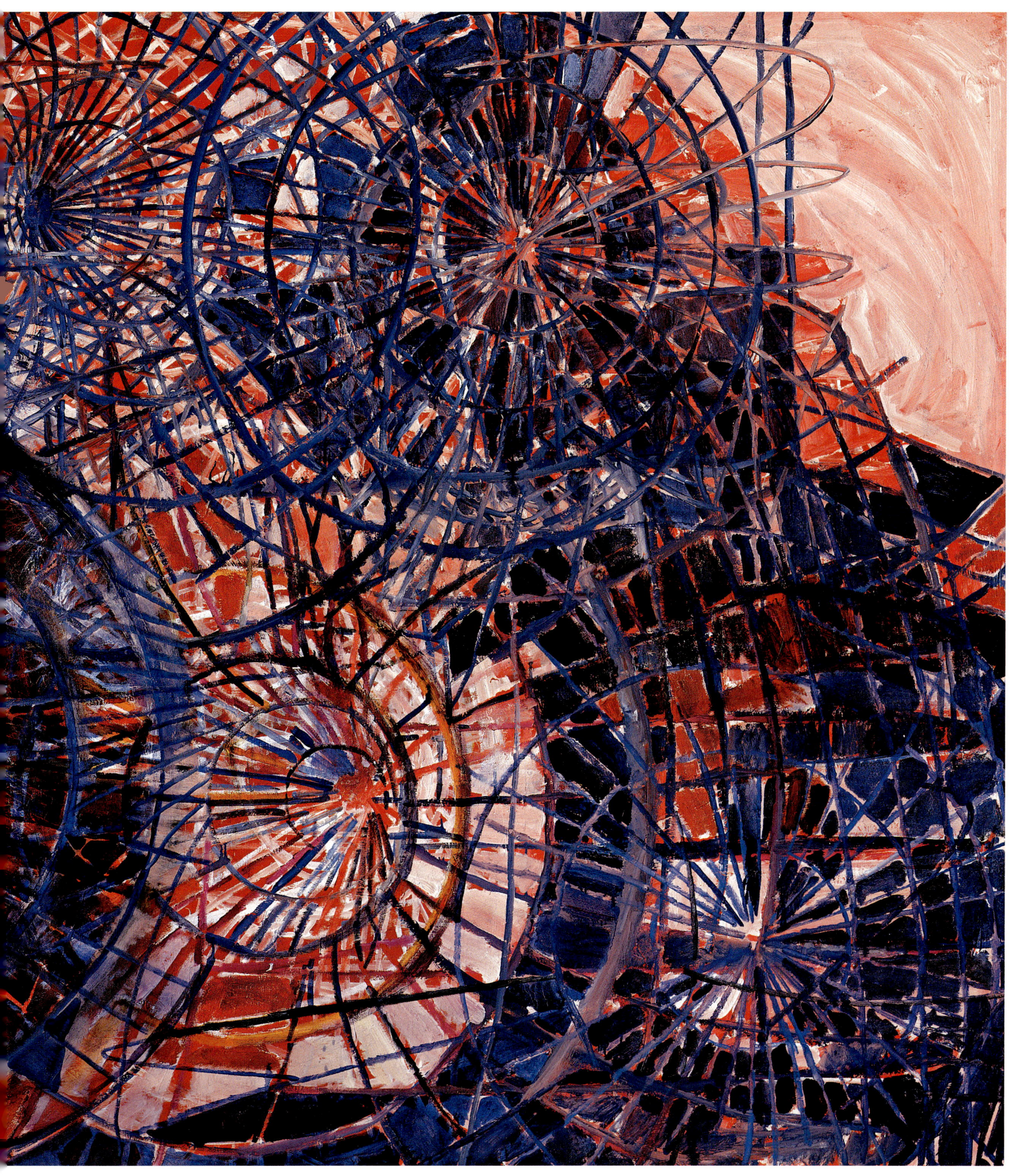

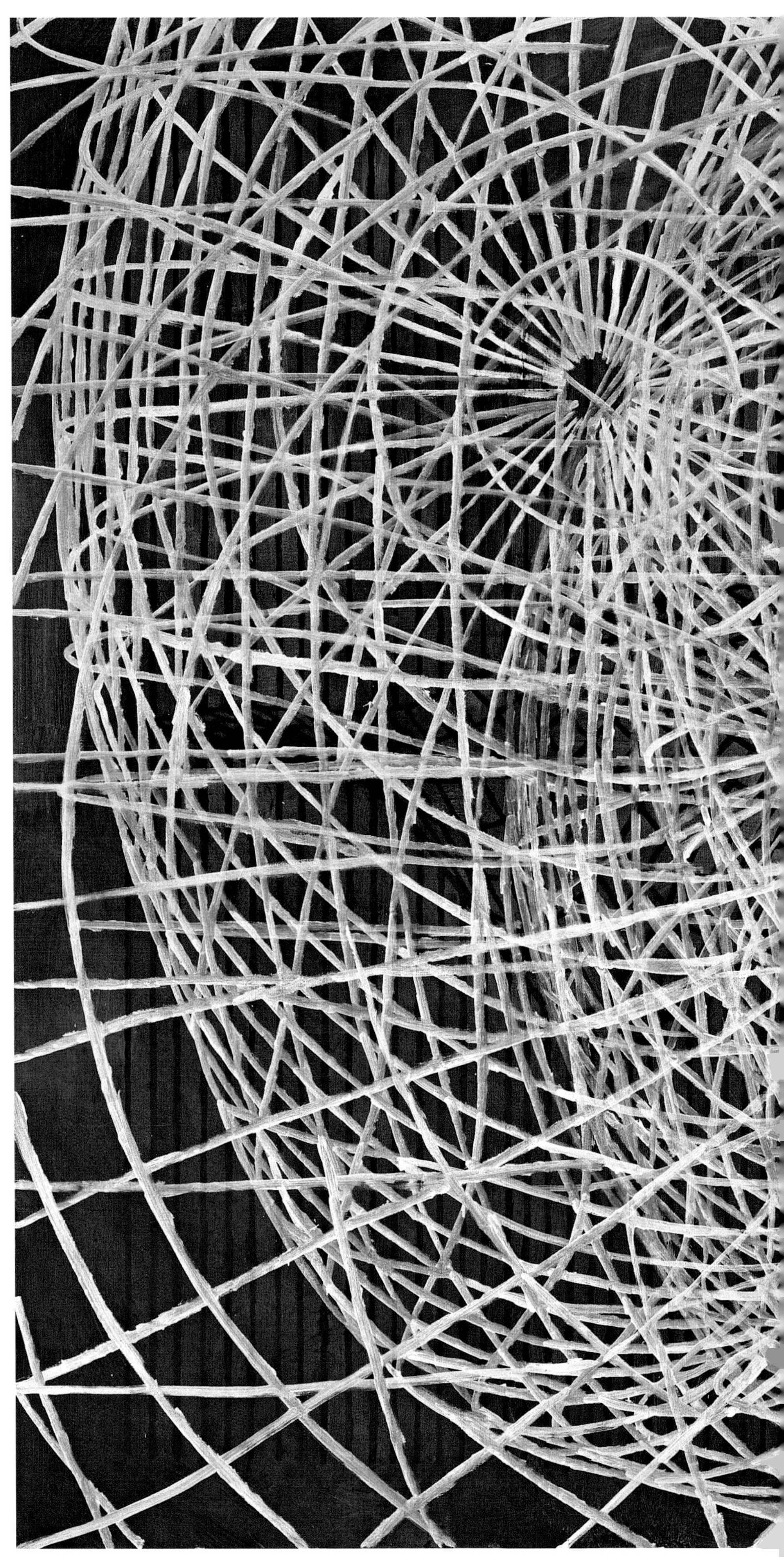

Luminance, 2002
Oil on linen
94 1/2 x 133 3/4 in. (240 x 339.7 cm)
Private collection

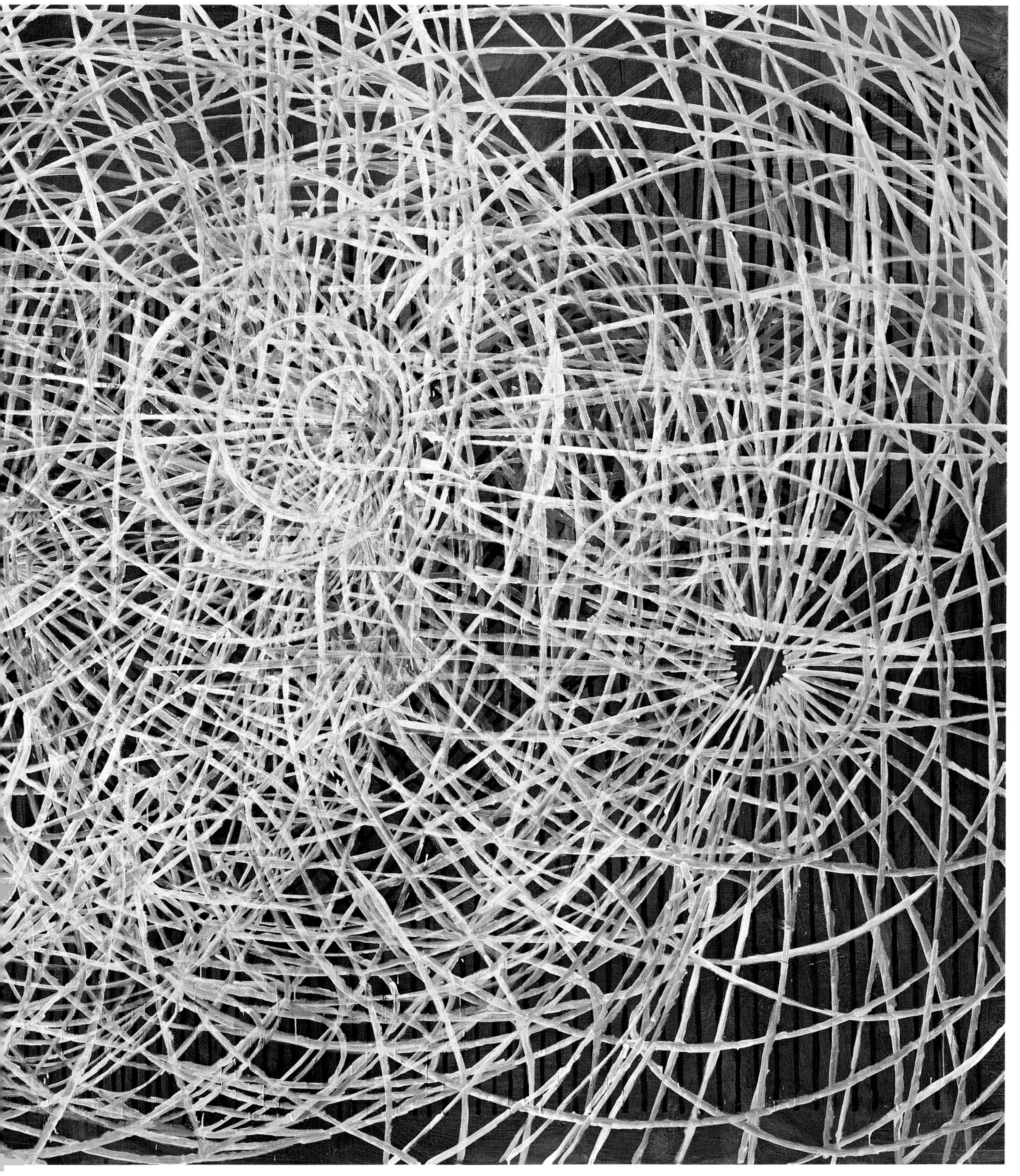

TURBULENCE SKINS

Boundary Layers/2, 2002
Graphite, gouache, acrylic, and charcoal on paper
59 7/8 x 40 1/8 in. (152.1 x 101.9 cm)
The Judith Rothschild Foundation, New York

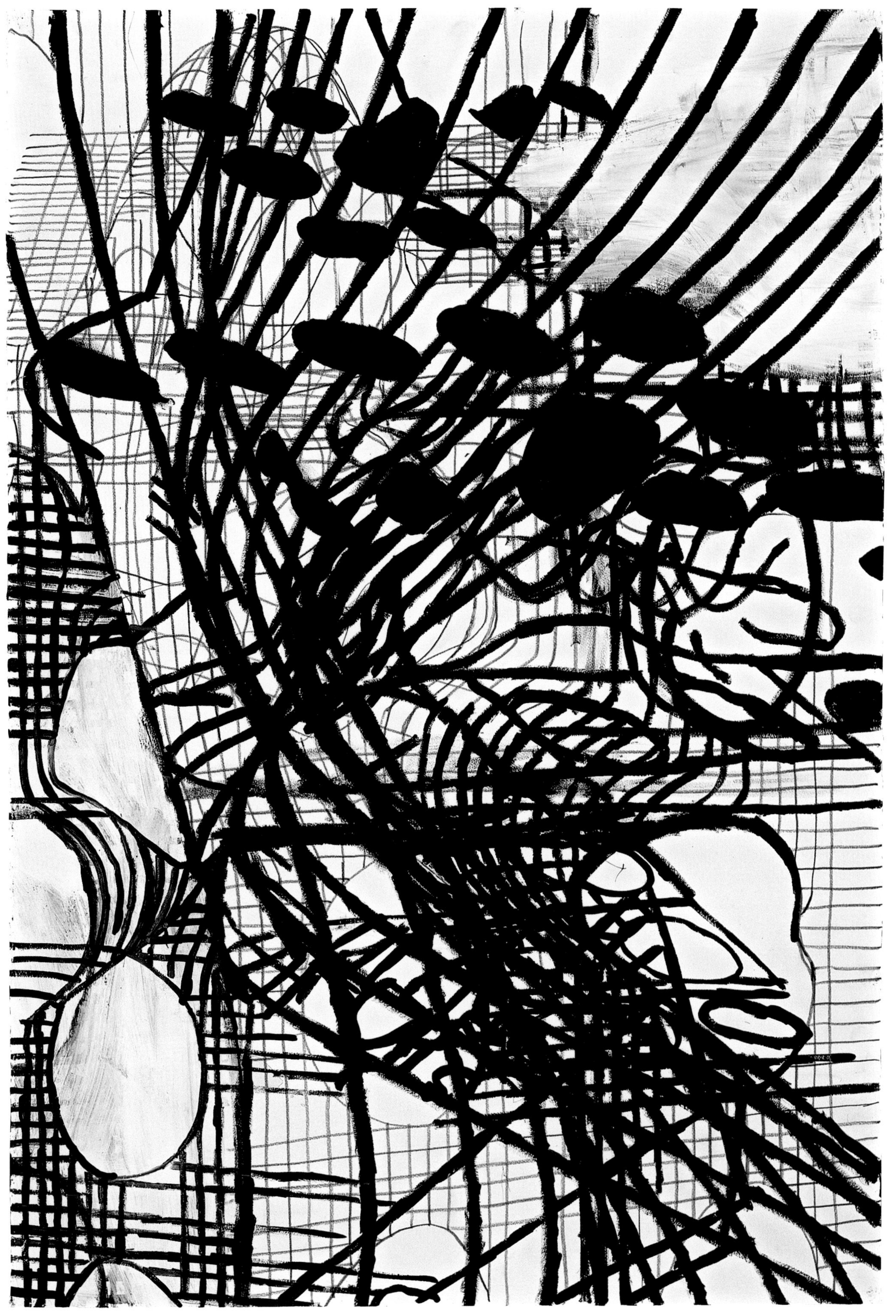

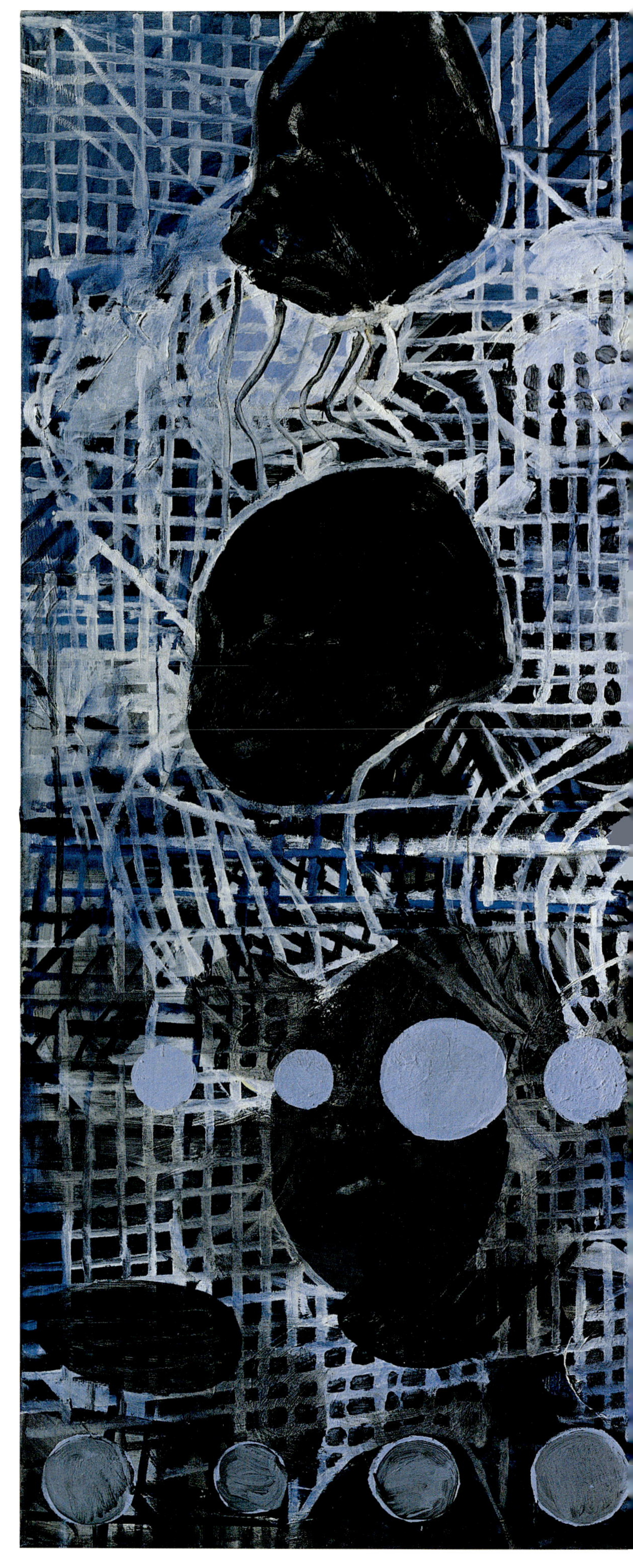

Standardgraph/1, 2003
Oil on linen
76 1/2 x 99 in. (194.3 x 251.5 cm)
Collection of Harry W. and Mary Margaret Anderson

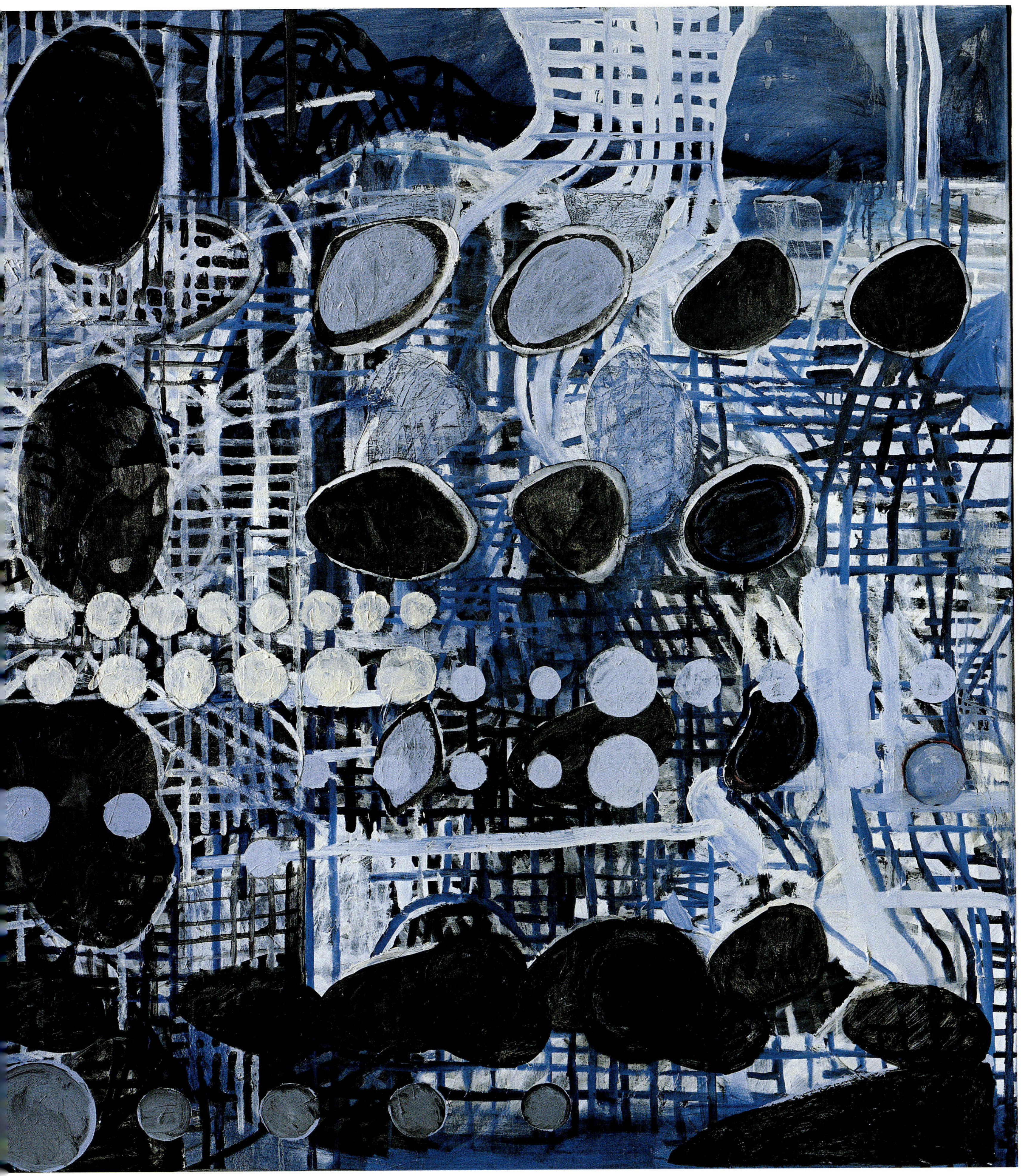

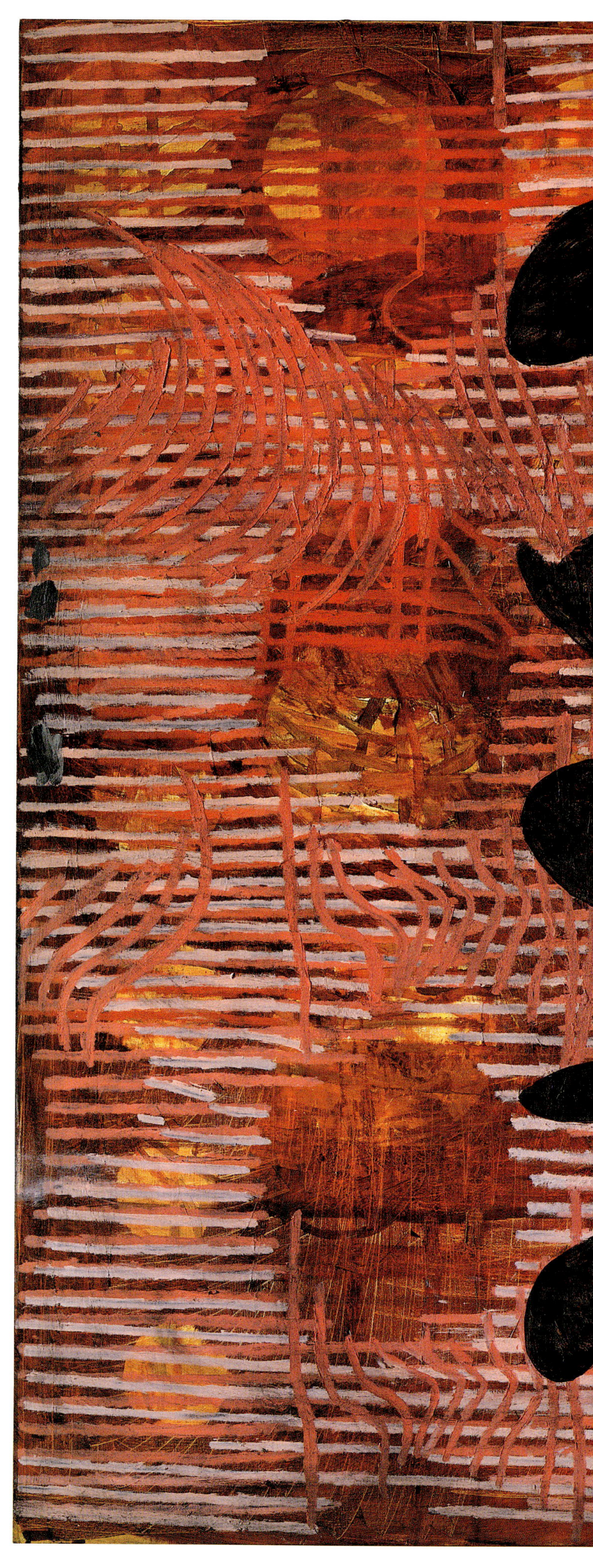

Standardgraph/2, 2003
Oil on linen
76 1/2 x 99 in. (194.3 x 251.5 cm)
Collection of Fran and Eric Rosenfeld

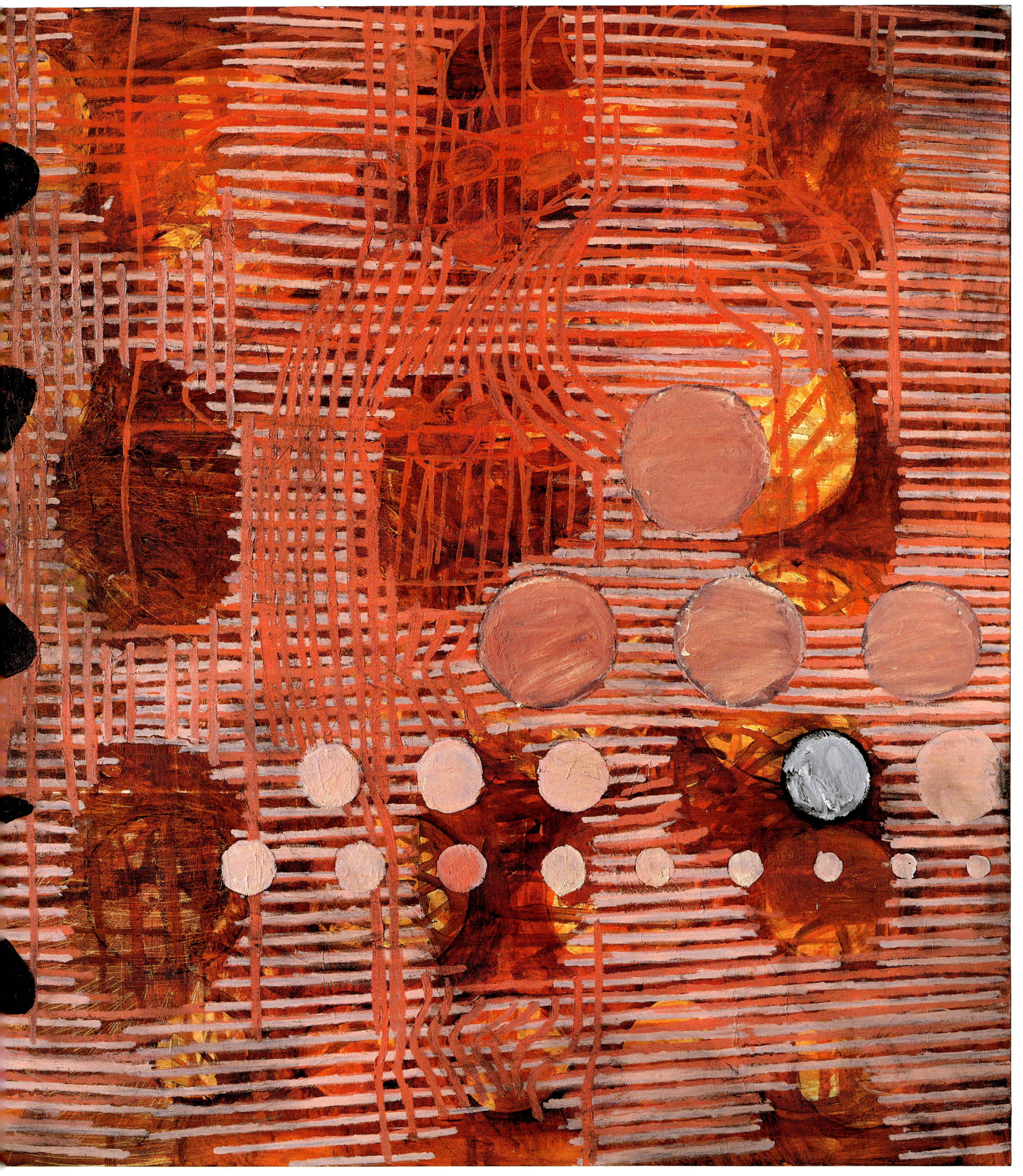

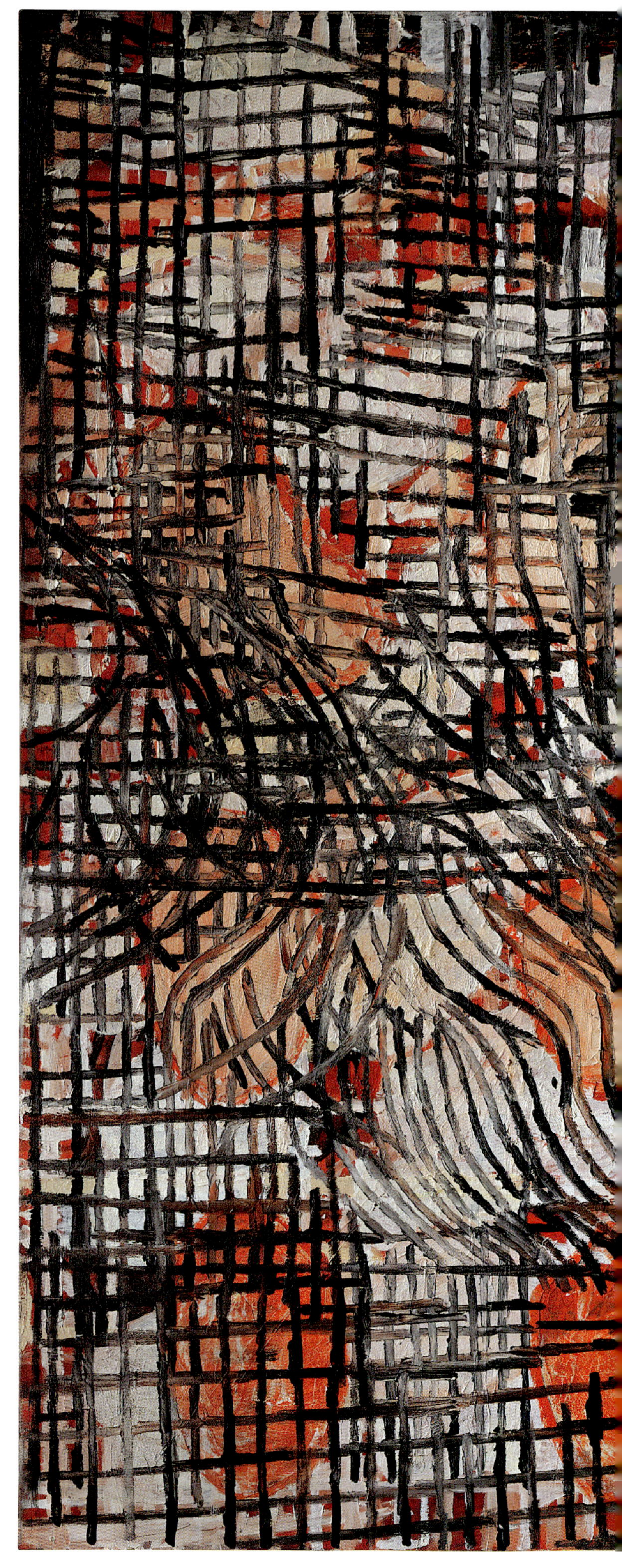

Standardgraph/3, 2003
Oil on linen
76 1/2 x 99 in. (194.3 x 251.5 cm)
Collection of Donald B. Marron

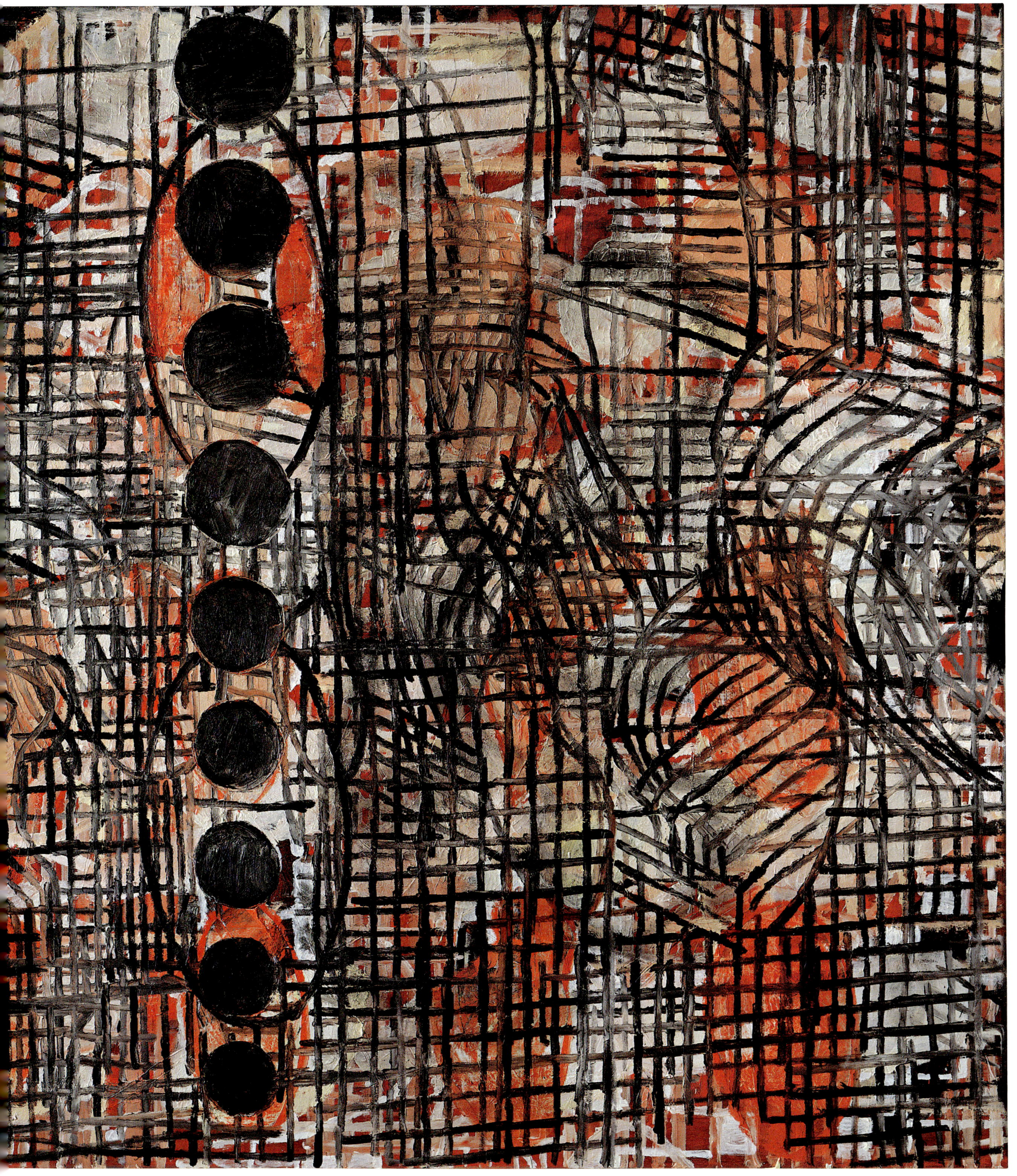

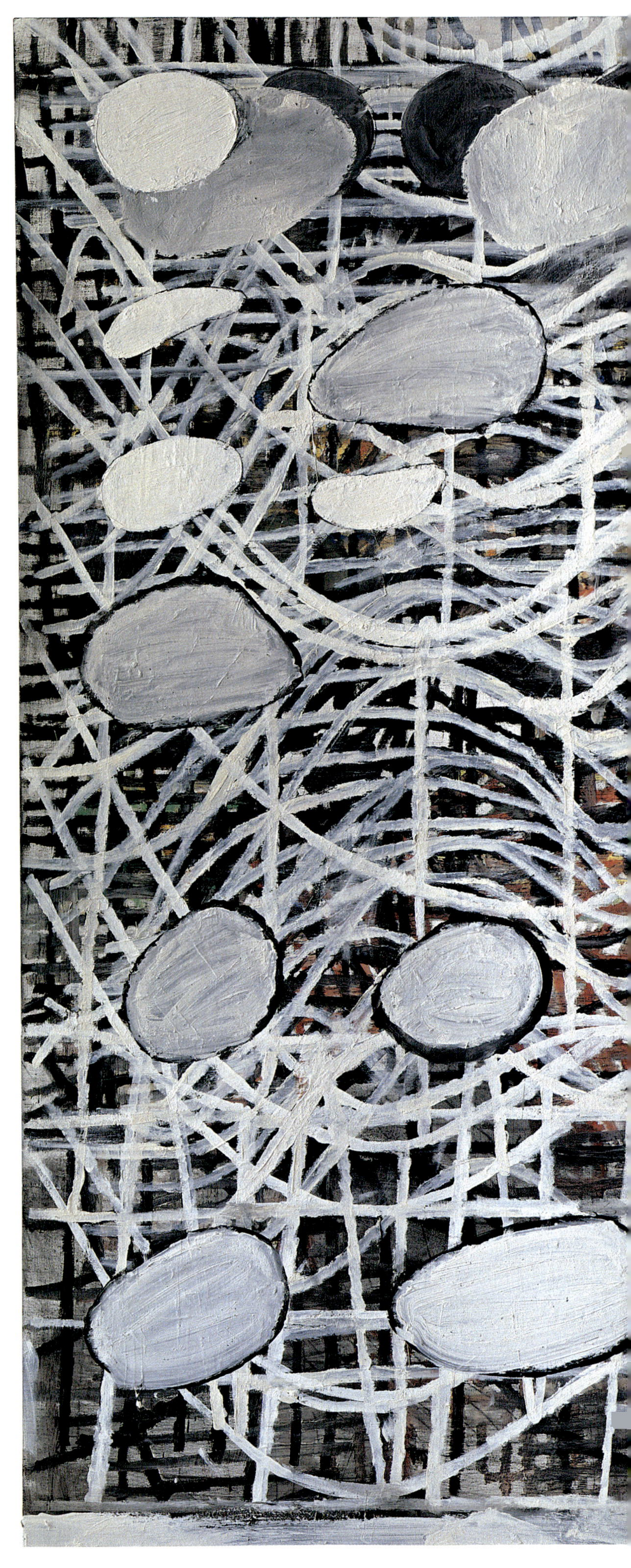

Standardgraph/4, 2003
Oil on linen
76 1/2 x 99 in. (194.3 x 251.5 cm)
Collection of Dr. and Mrs. Robert and Lisa Feldman

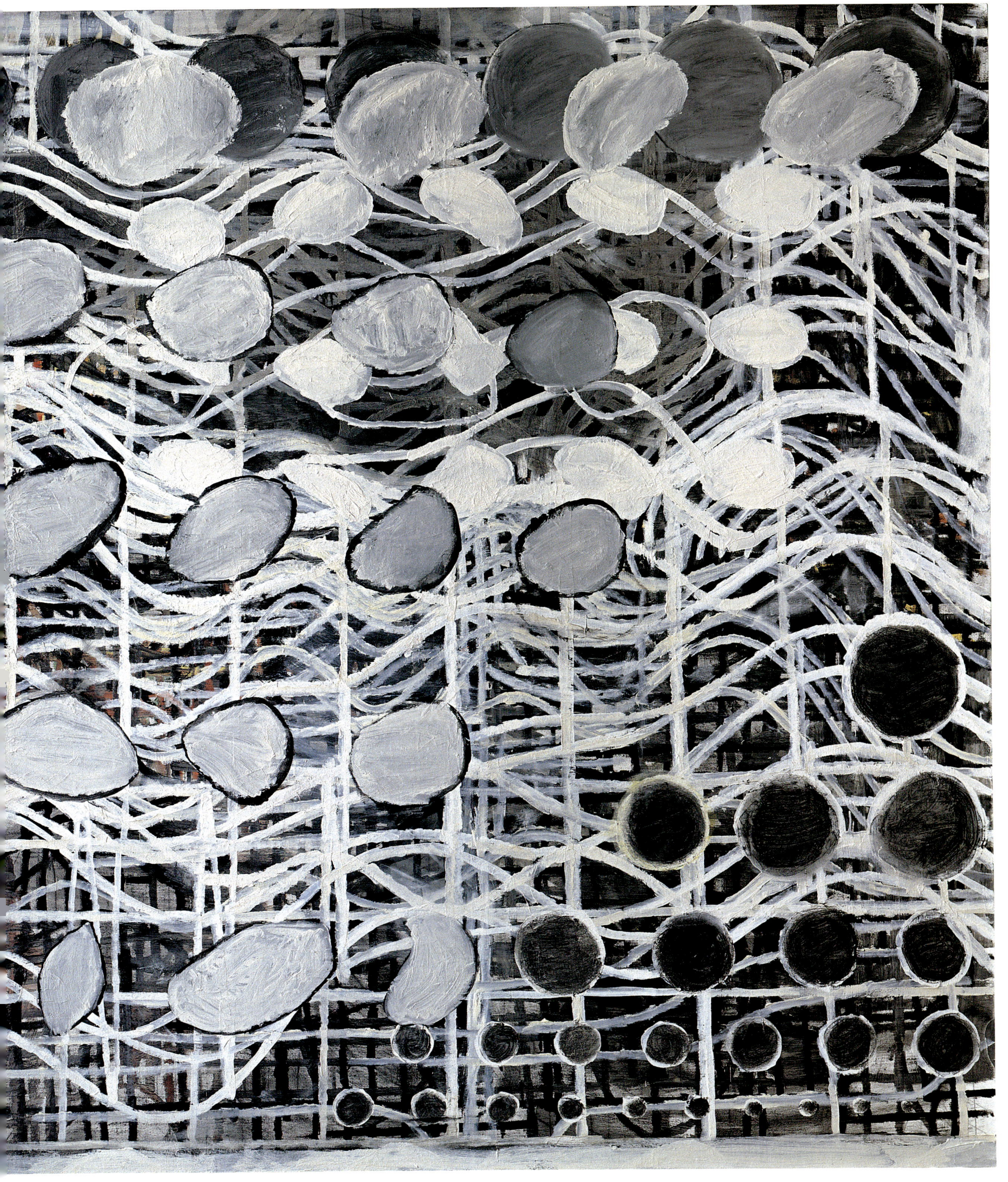

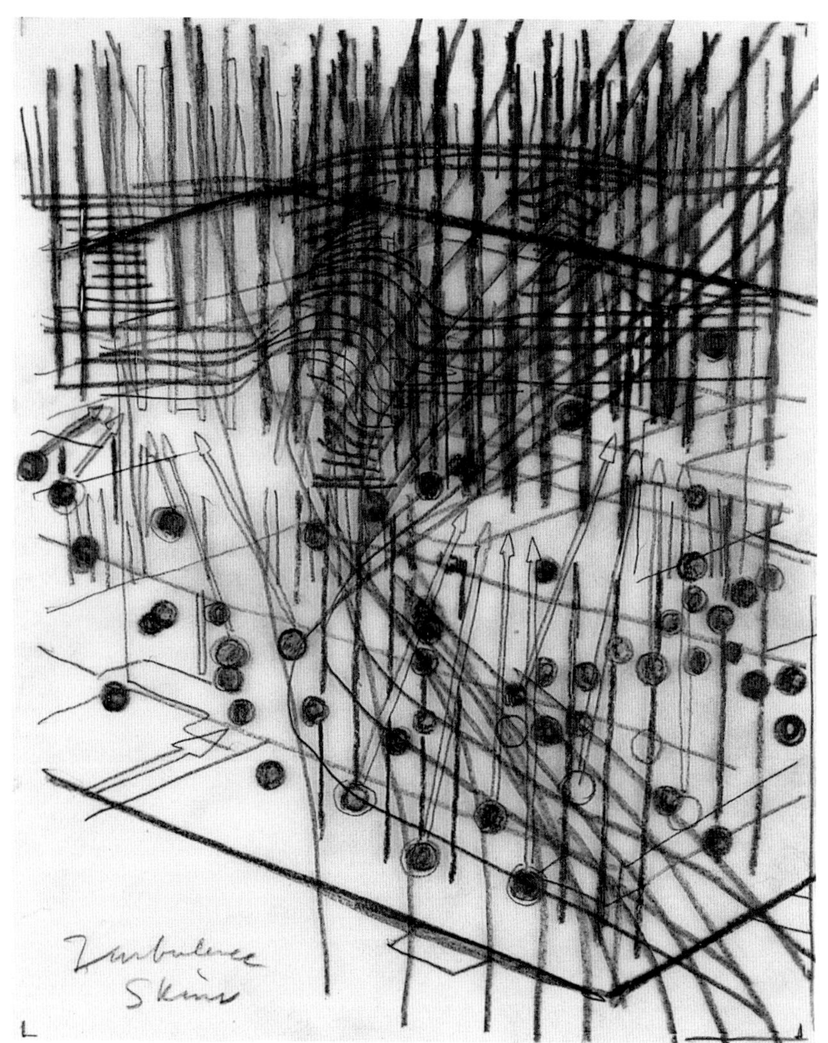

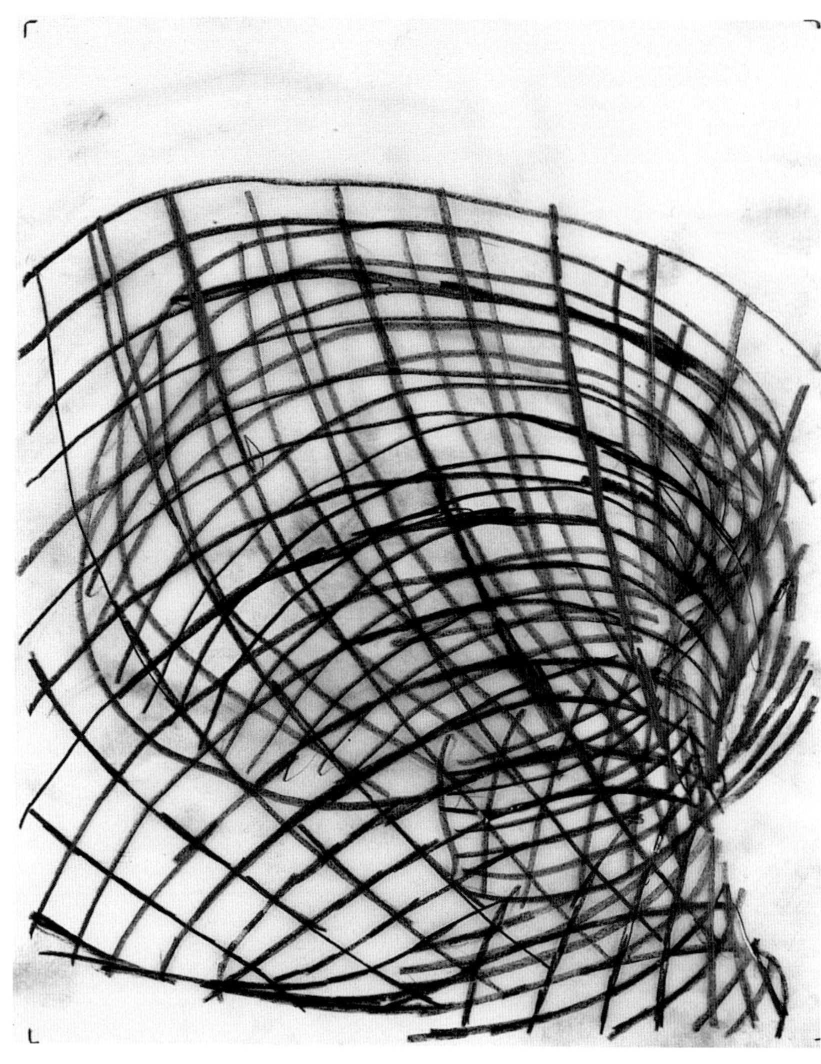

Pages 142–45:
Turbulence Skins, 2002
A series of 42 drawings
Graphite on vellum
Each, 14 x 11 in. (35.6 x 27.9 cm)
Collection of Harry W. and Mary Margaret Anderson

Pages 146–47:
Terry Winters with text by Ben Marcus
Turbulence Skins, 2004
From a portfolio of 42 prints
Lithographs on vellum
Each, 14 x 11 in. (35.6 x 27.9 cm)
Courtesy of the artist

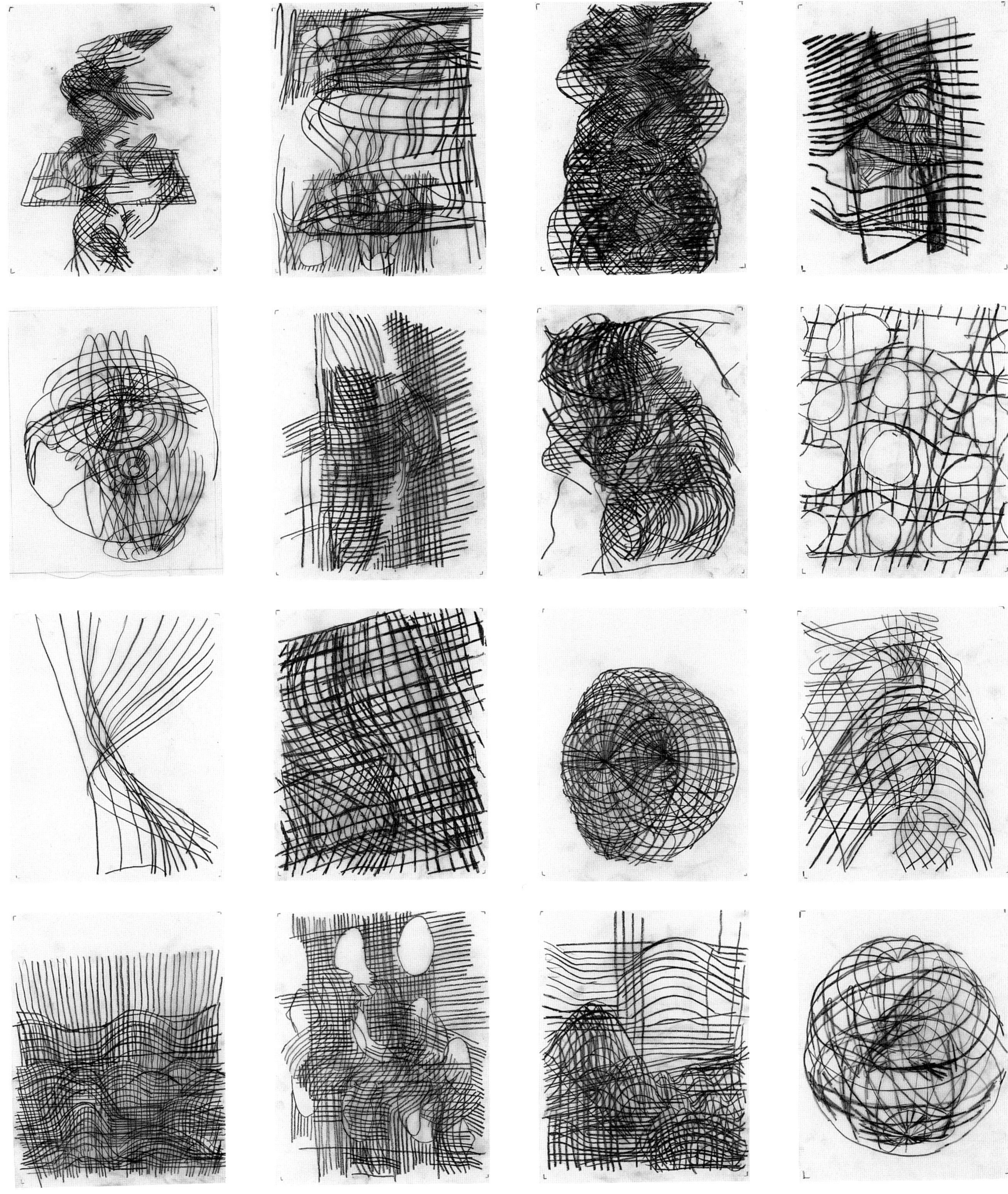

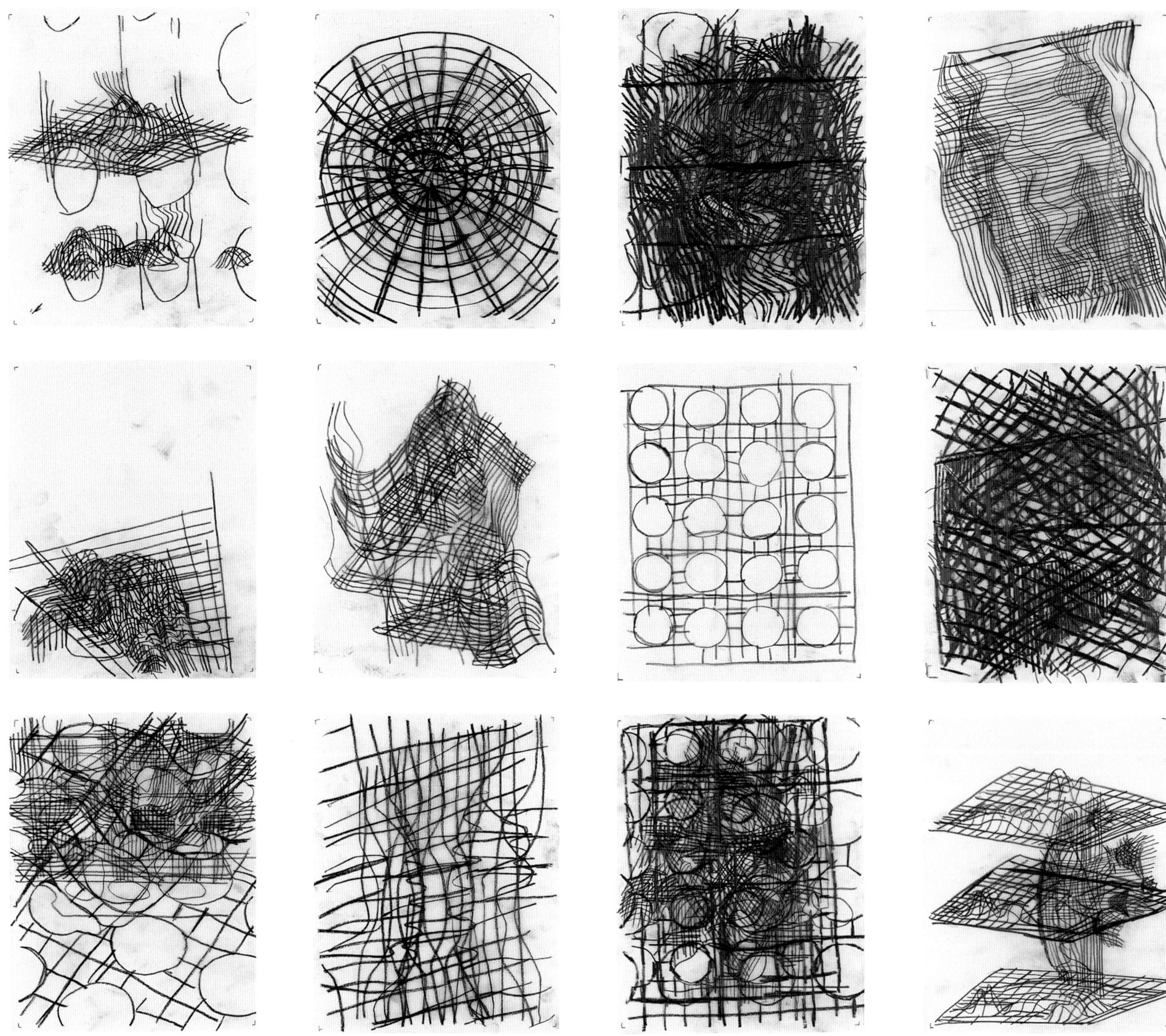

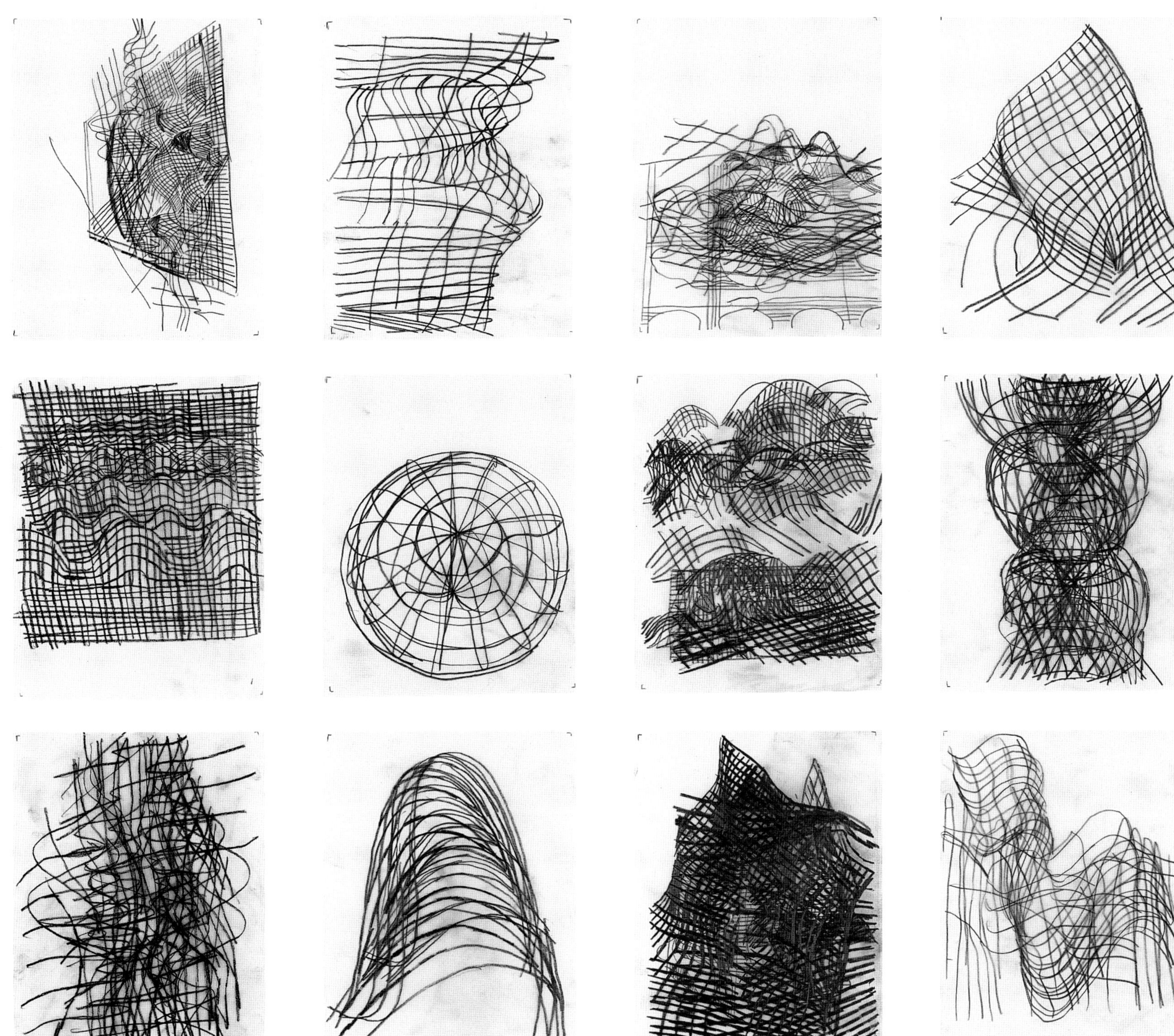

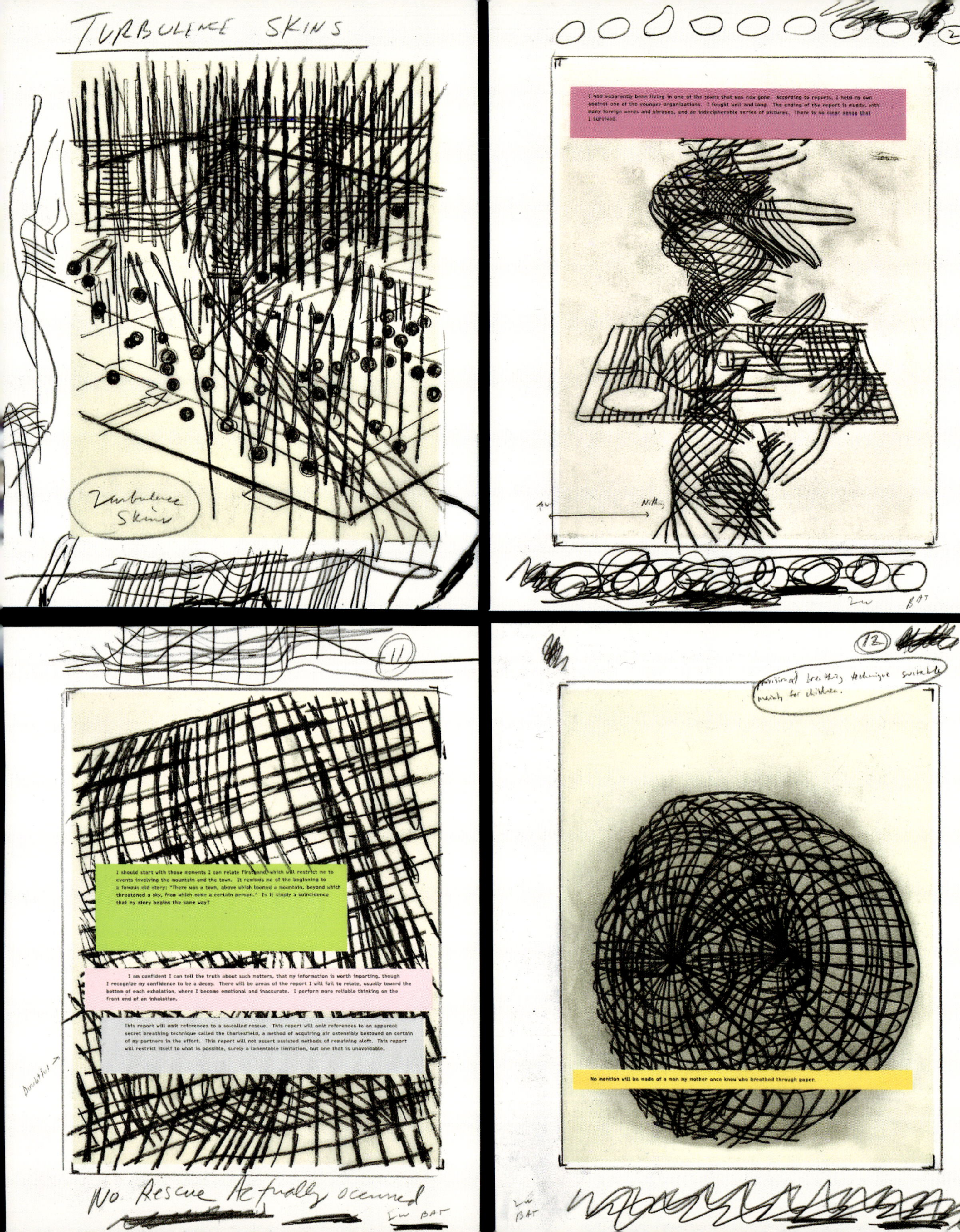
TURBULENCE SKINS
Turbulence Skins
I had apparently been living in one of the towns that was now gone. According to reports, I held my own against one of the younger organizations. I fought well and long. The ending of the report is muddy, with many foreign words and phrases, and an indecipherable series of pictures. There is no clear sense that I survived.
I should start with those moments I can relate firsthand, which will restrict me to events involving the mountain and the town. It reminds me of the beginning to a famous old story: "There was a town, above which loomed a mountain, beyond which threatened a sky, from which came a certain person." Is it simply a coincidence that my story begins the same way?
I am confident I can tell the truth about such matters, that my information is worth imparting, though I recognize my confidence to be a decoy. There will be areas of the report I will fail to relate, usually toward the bottom of each exhalation, where I become emotional and inaccurate. I perform more reliable thinking on the front end of an inhalation.
This report will omit references to a so-called rescue. This report will omit references to an apparent secret breathing technique called the Charlesfield, a method of acquiring air ostensibly bestowed on certain of my partners in the effort. This report will not assert assisted methods of remaining aloft. This report will restrict itself to what is possible, surely a lamentable limitation, but one that is unavoidable.
No Rescue Actually occurred
provisional breathing technique suitable mainly for children.
No mention will be made of a man my mother once knew who breathed through paper.

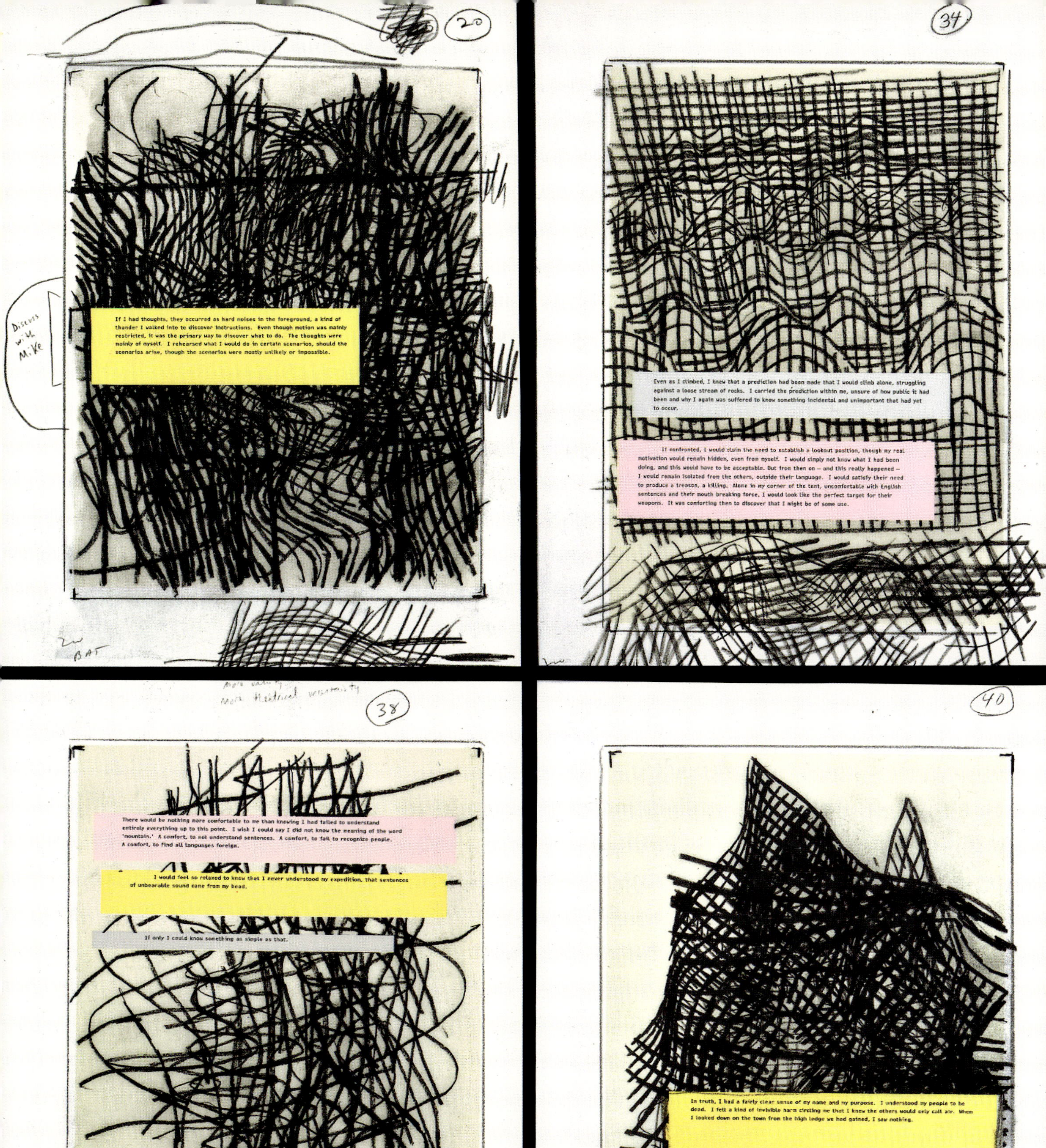
20
Discuss with Mike
If I had thoughts, they occurred as hard noises in the foreground, a kind of thunder I walked into to discover instructions. Even though motion was mainly restricted, it was the primary way to discover what to do. The thoughts were mainly of myself. I rehearsed what I would do in certain scenarios, should the scenarios arise, though the scenarios were mostly unlikely or impossible.
34
Even as I climbed, I knew that a prediction had been made that I would climb alone, struggling against a loose stream of rocks. I carried the prediction within me, unsure of how public it had been and why I again was suffered to know something incidental and unimportant that had yet to occur.
If confronted, I would claim the need to establish a lookout position, though my real motivation would remain hidden, even from myself. I would simply not know what I had been doing, and this would have to be acceptable. But from then on – and this really happened – I would remain isolated from the others, outside their language. I would satisfy their need to produce a treason, a killing. Alone in my corner of the tent, uncomfortable with English sentences and their mouth breaking force, I would look like the perfect target for their weapons. It was comforting then to discover that I might be of some use.
38
There would be nothing more comfortable to me than knowing I had failed to understand entirely everything up to this point. I wish I could say I did not know the meaning of the word 'mountain.' A comfort, to not understand sentences. A comfort, to fail to recognize people. A comfort, to find all languages foreign.
I would feel so relaxed to know that I never understood my expedition, that sentences of unbearable sound came from my head.
If only I could know something as simple as that.
40
In truth, I had a fairly clear sense of my name and my purpose. I understood my people to be dead. I felt a kind of invisible harm circling me that I knew the others would only call air. When I looked down on the town from the high ledge we had gained, I saw nothing.

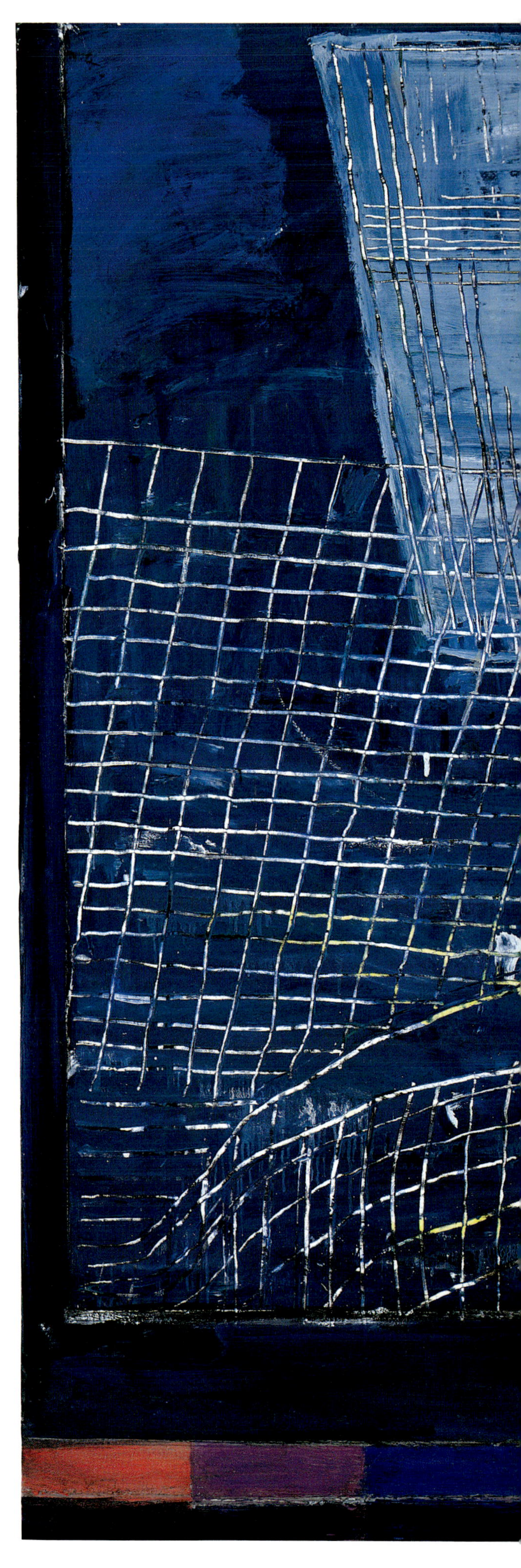

Scale, 2003
Oil on linen
70 x 87 in. (178 x 221 cm)
Collection of Donald B. Marron

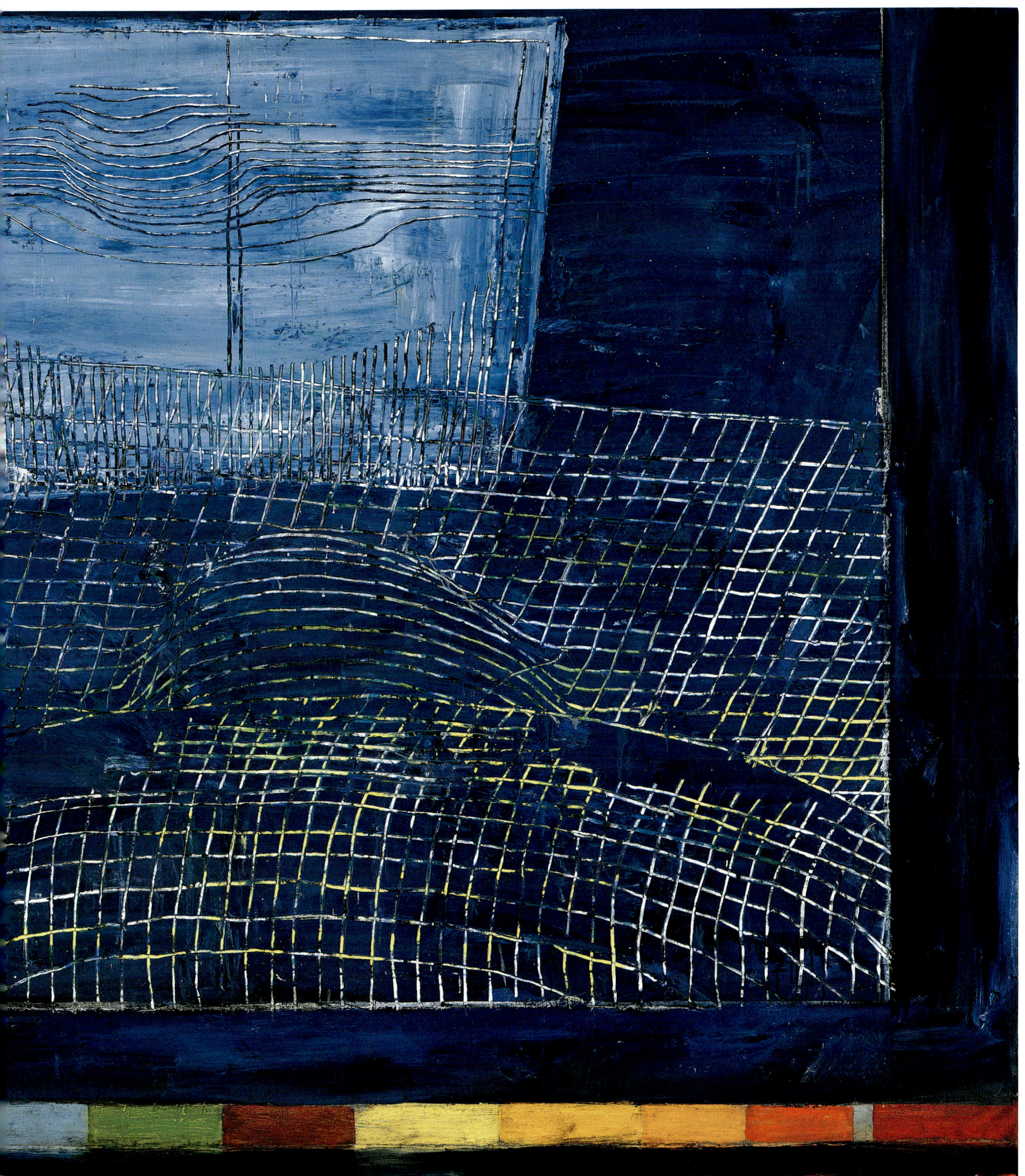

Untitled (Red), 2003
Oil on linen
77 x 59 1/2 in. (195.6 x 151.1 cm)
Private collection

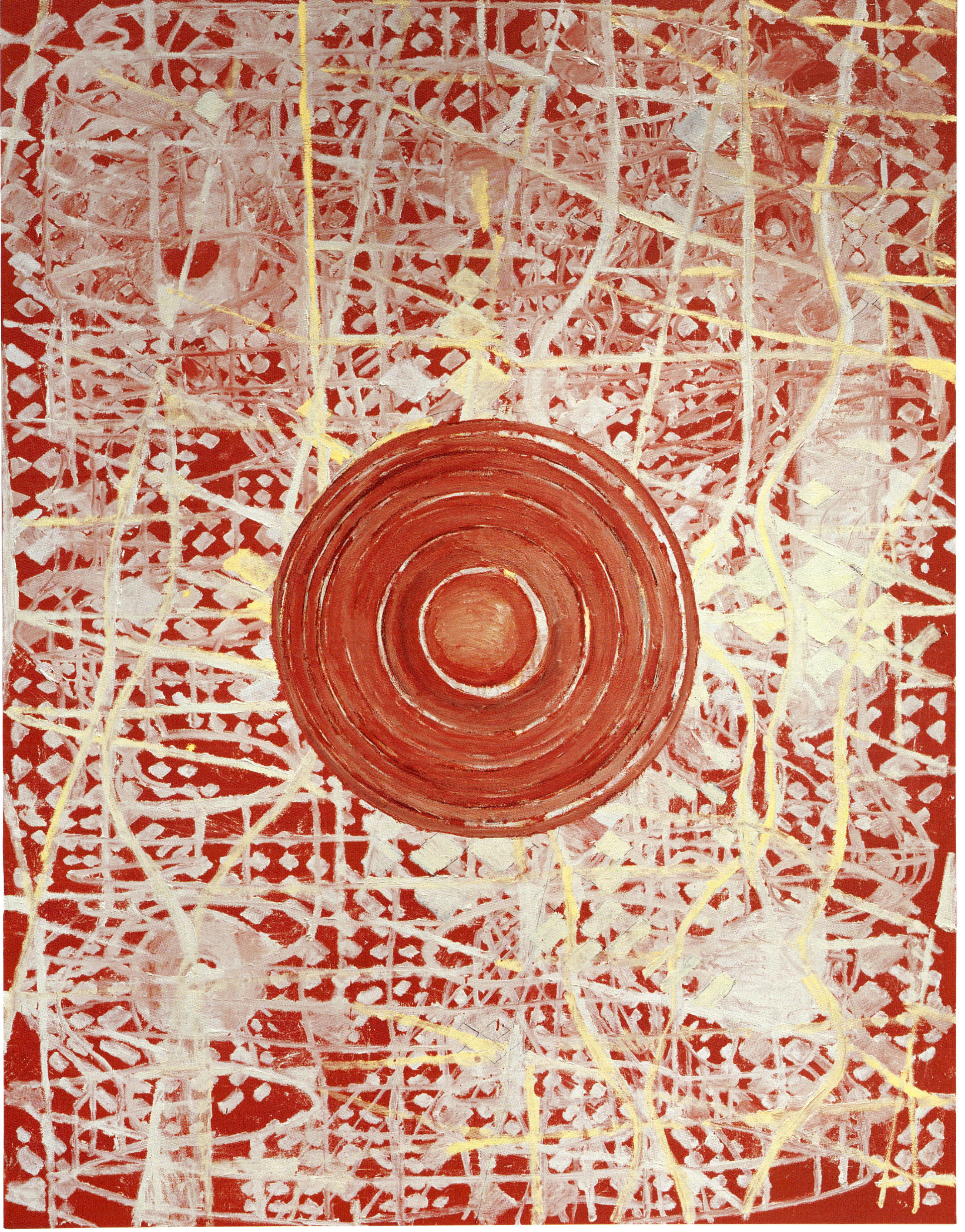

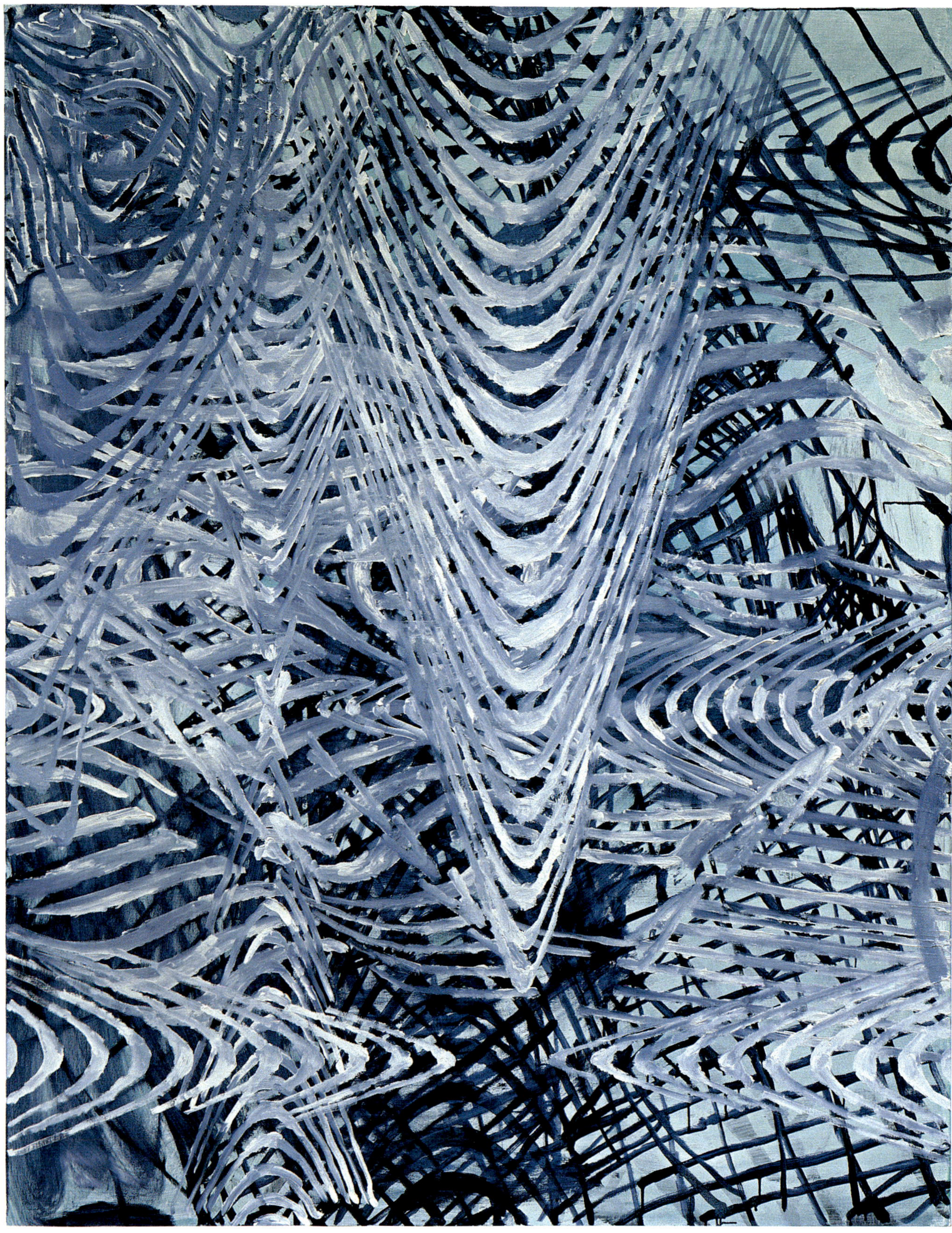

Untitled (Indigo), 2003
Oil on linen
77 x 59 1/2 in. (195.6 x 151.1 cm)
Private collection

Untitled (Violet), 2003
Oil on linen
77 x 59 1/2 in. (195.6 x 151.1 cm)
Collection of Hendel Teicher, New York

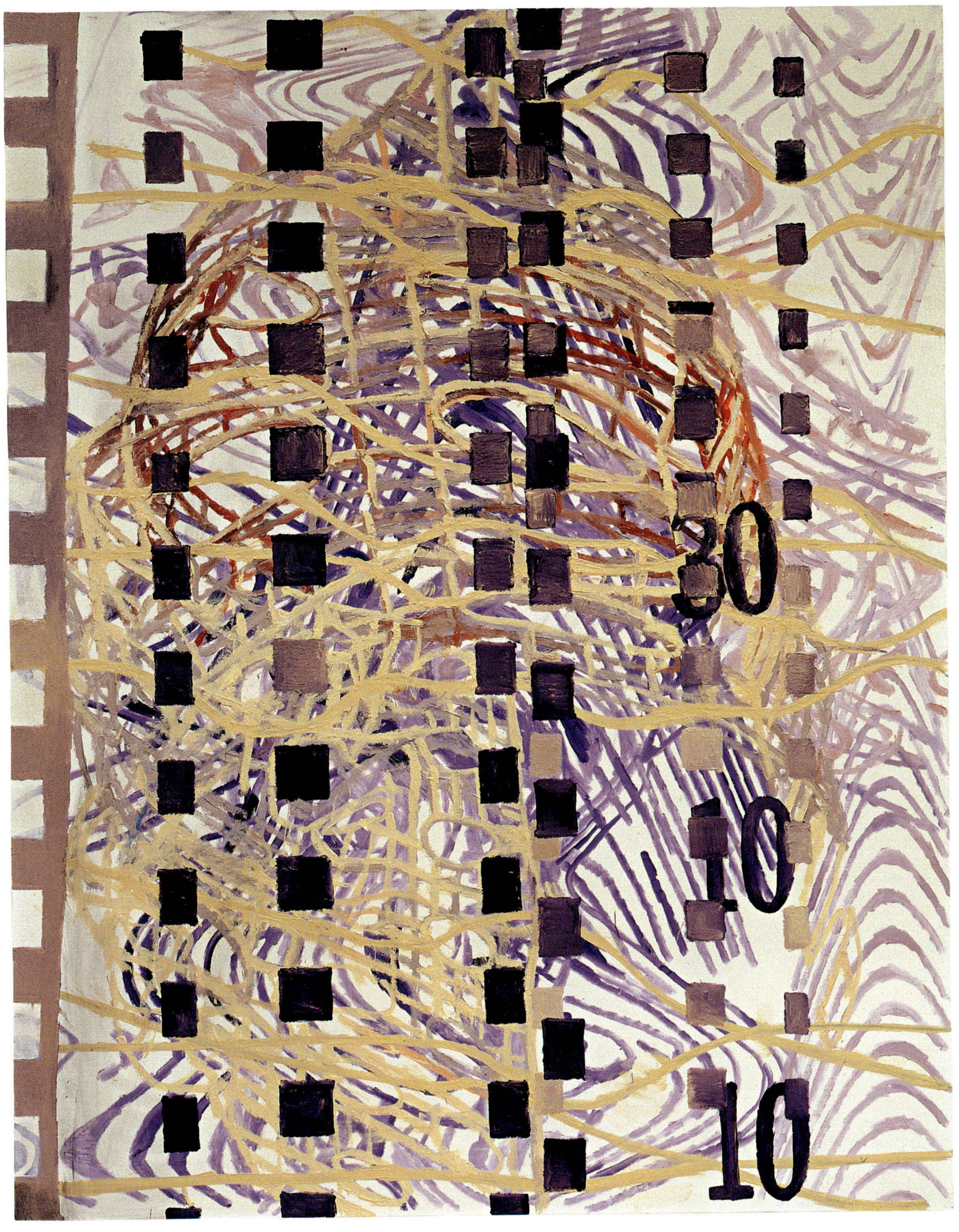
30
10
10

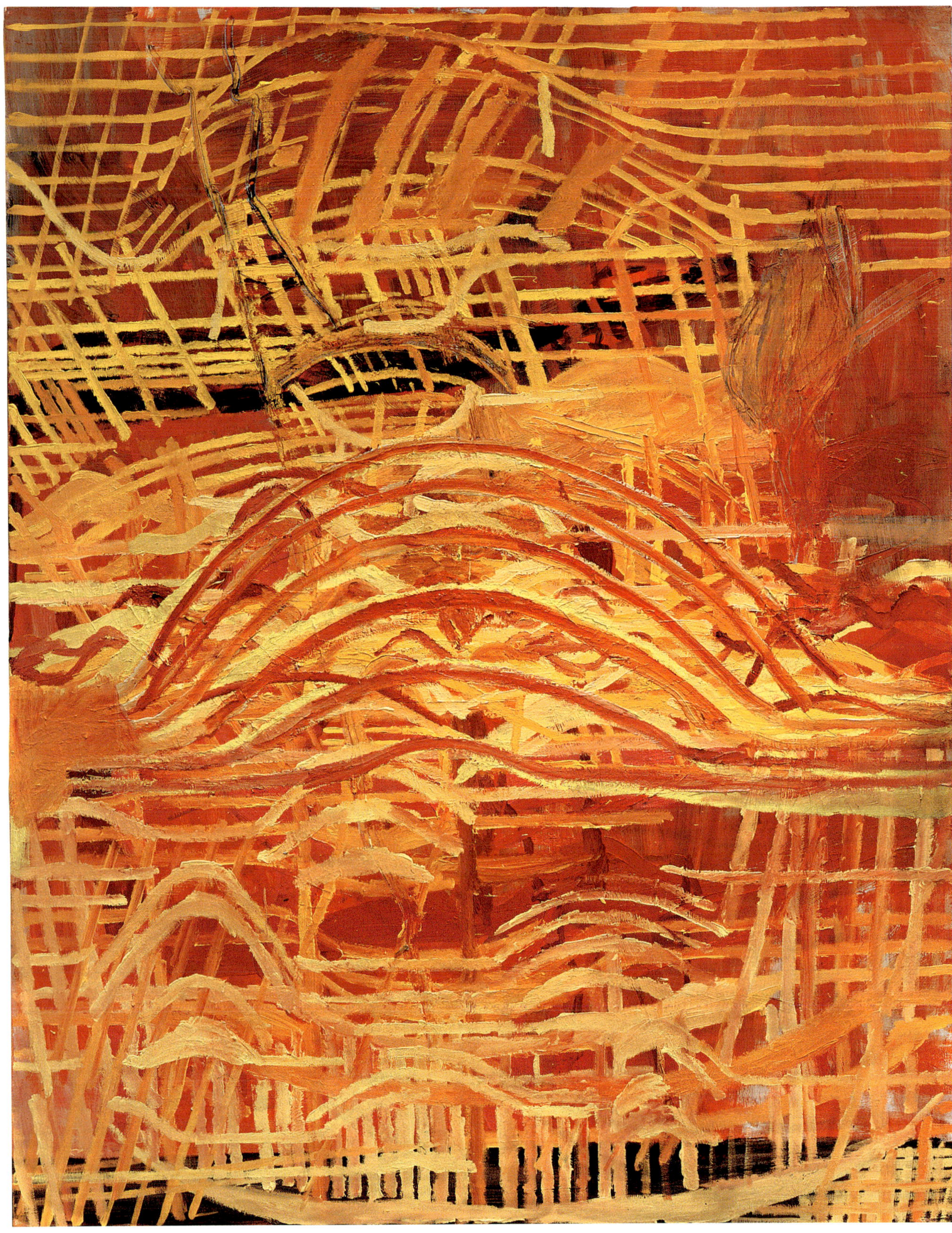

Untitled (Yellow), 2003
Oil on linen
77 x 59 1/2 in. (195.6 x 151.1 cm)
Private collection

Untitled (Blue), 2003
Oil on linen
77 x 59 1/2 in. (195.6 x 151.1 cm)
Collection of Buck A. Mickel

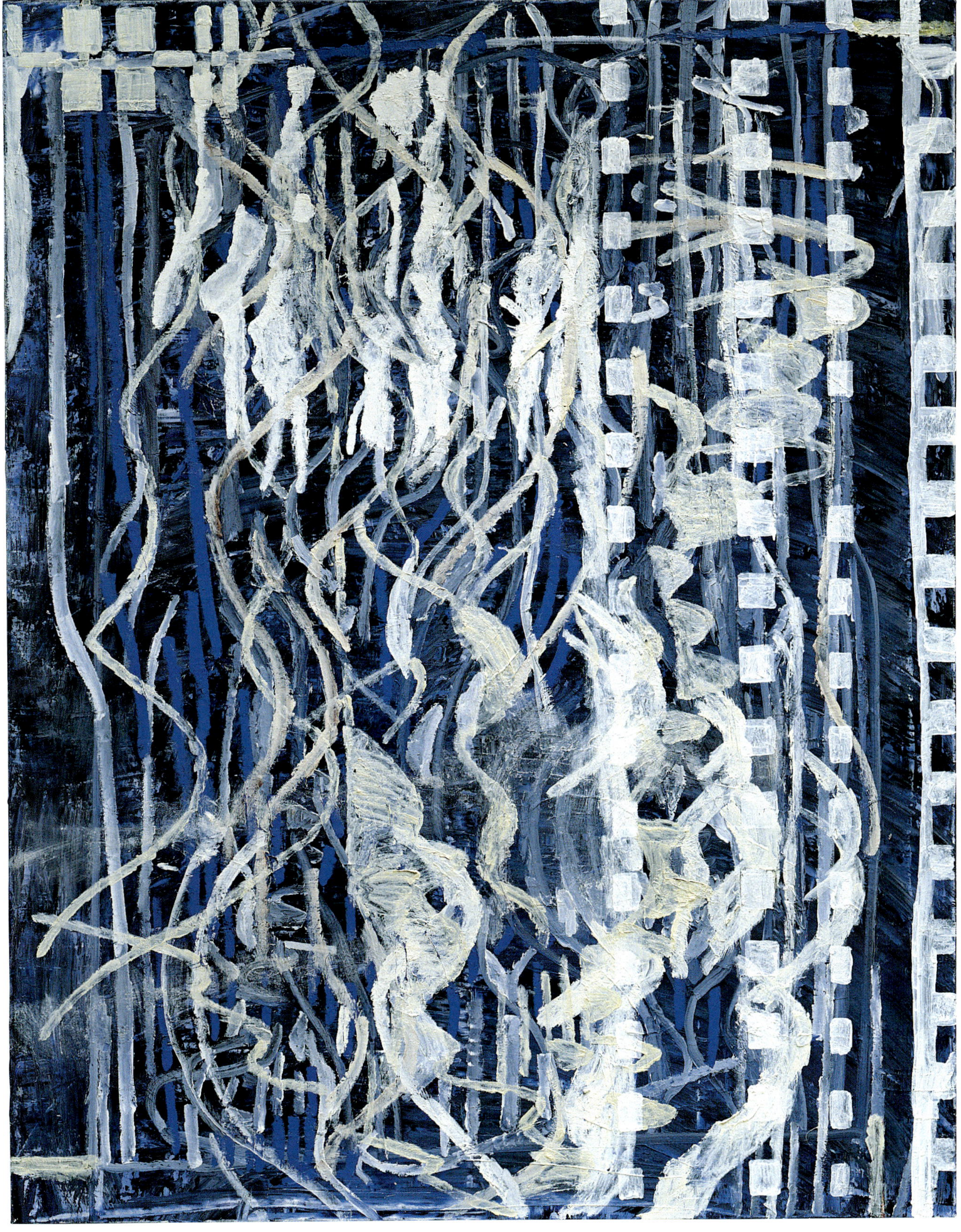

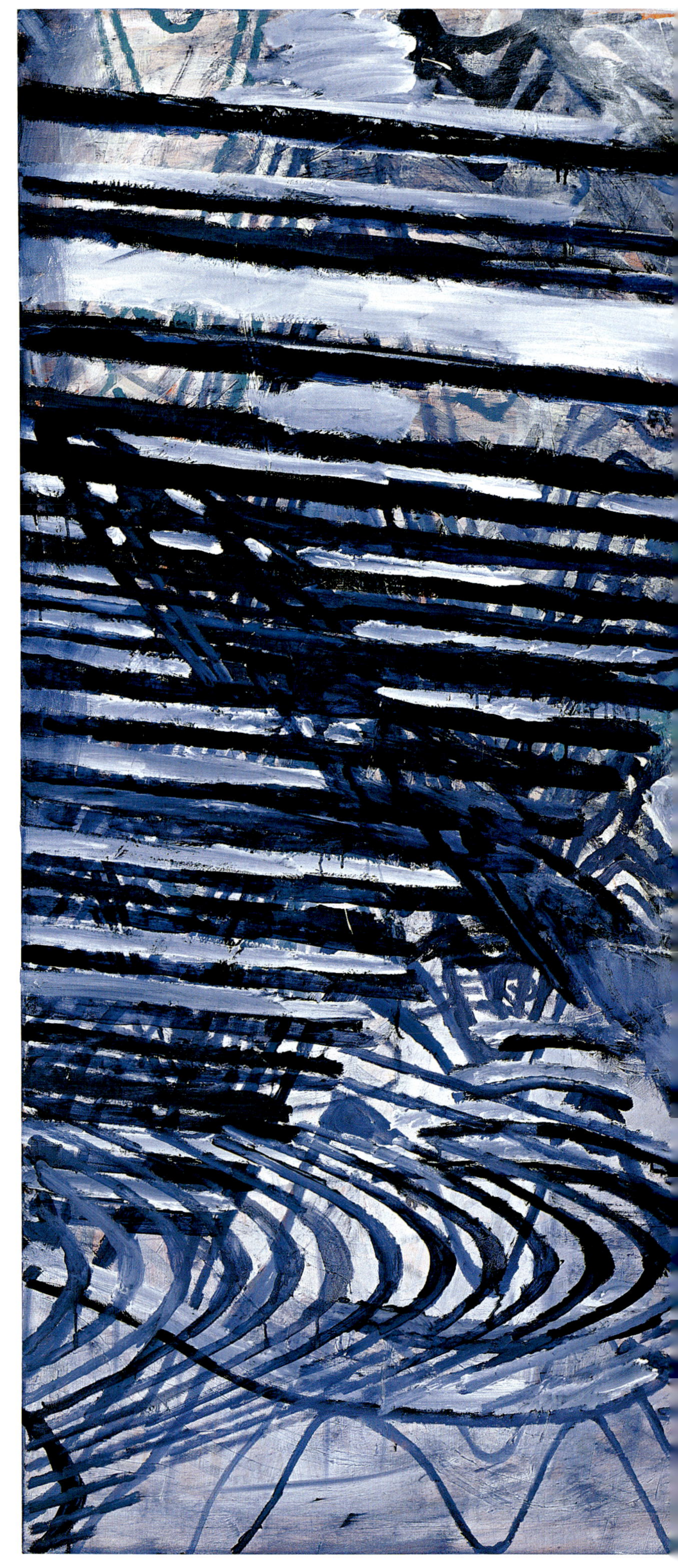

Untitled, 2003
Oil on linen
68 x 88 in. (172.7 x 223.5 cm)
Collection of Harry W. and Mary Margaret Anderson

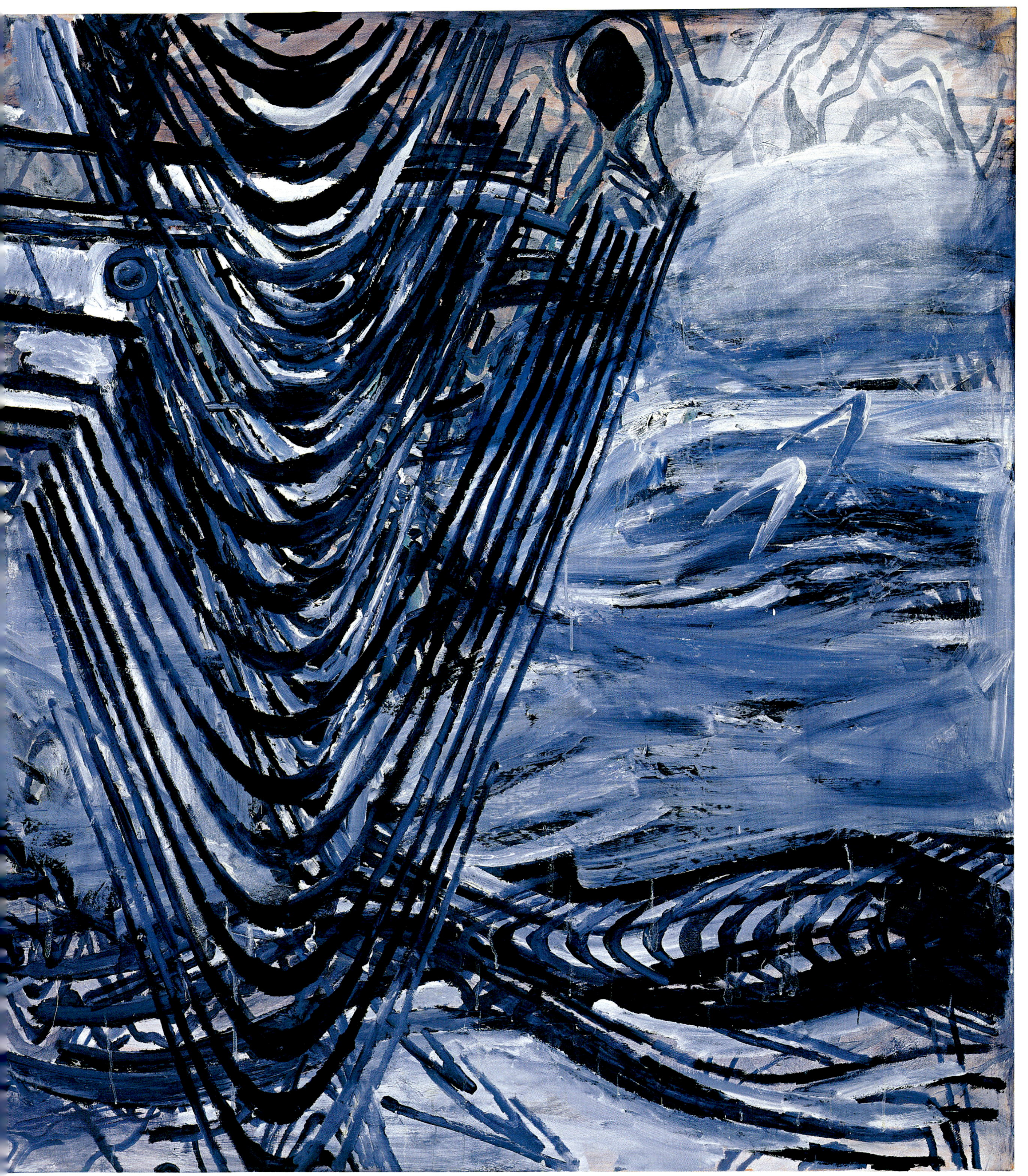

FOUNDATIONS AND SYSTEMS

Information is a consistent theme in the diverse drawings, paintings, and prints Terry Winters has created since 1994. His work repeatedly explores how information is communicated, that is, how effects of verisimilitude are achieved and denied in techno-scientific visualization strategies. "I like the way graphs, charts, maps, and blueprints look," he has explained. "I like the way they are set up as pictures that describe the way the world is, or how something works."[1] Sometimes, as with the barcode that appears in *Set Diagram 59* or the structural diagrams that are the impetus of the *Meshworks* drawings, he explicitly employs information science as the pretext for a painting or drawing. But, these references to informatics can be misleading. Winters's real interest is in information as a form of intelligence. He is not as concerned with the individual datum or even the scientific forms of visualization that he often uses in his work as he is in transmitting a more synthetic and subjective form of knowledge garnered from a broad range of sources.

Winters's fascination with information can be characterized by the term "flatbed picture plane" Leo Steinberg coined to describe "any receptor surface on which objects are scattered, on which data is entered, on which information may be received, printed, impressed—whether coherently or in confusion."[2] Winters's work—be it on paper or canvas—adheres to this model of a receptor surface that records the information encoded in everything from the imagery depicted to the manner in which he laid down the paint. Steinberg went on to explain that the orientation of the flatbed "is no longer the analogue of a visual experience of nature but of operational processes."[3] In his argument, Robert Rauschenberg's flatbed marked a paradigm shift from nature to a postmodern dimension of culture. Winters reverses Steinberg's trajectory back to nature, albeit his is the nature of a techno-scientific age, that is, nature as it is now visualized by scientists and engineers.

Tenon's Capsule, a series of six large-scale drawings from 1994 (pp. 36–39), exemplifies Winters's approach to information and describes his complicated relationship to the binary pairing of nature and culture. The drawings vacillate between coherence and confusion. Dense with a sense of experimentation, an effort to picture something is palpable even though the images remain resolutely abstract. Lines, fluctuating in density and direction, flow across the surface of the drawings in choreographed configurations. All the drawings repeat the same compositional elements—an oval form within a rectangular field—yet each drawing is a distinct permutation on the theme. As a counterbalance to the repeated composition, individual lines collide, creating a dizzying depth that is strangely subsumed to surface effects.

Tenon's Capsule marks a new direction for Winters's work, as it capitalizes on smaller-scale experimentation. In the fifty *Foundations and Systems* drawings made concurrently with the *Tenon's Capsule* series, Winters explored the same data set—line,

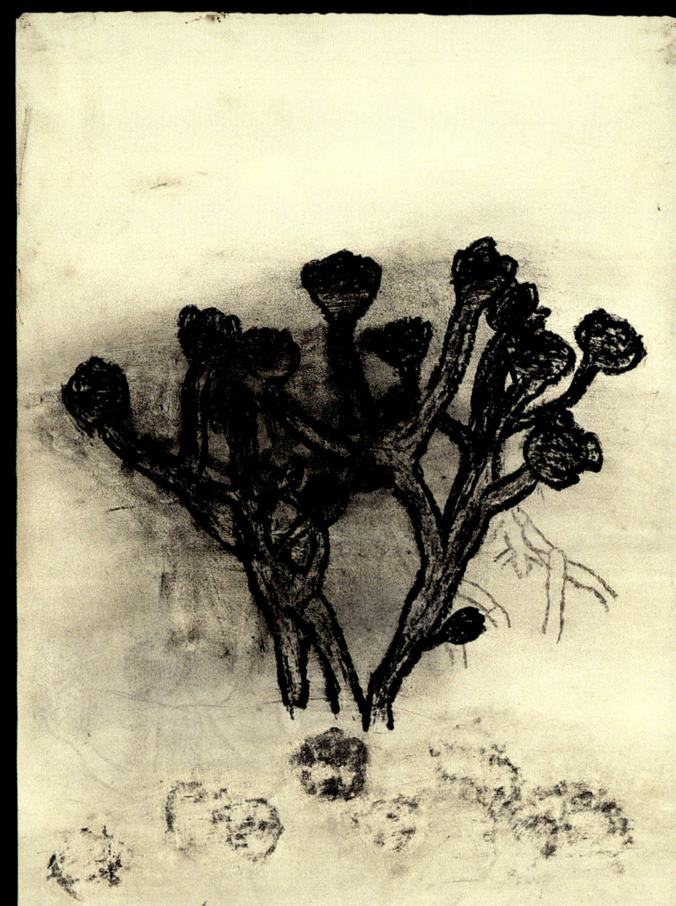

1

ground, surface—expressed with different degrees of pressure, angle, and intensity. Each *Foundations and Systems* drawing highlights different variables. The *Tenon's Capsule* drawings accumulate and extend the experiments into ambitious and independent works. *Tenon's Capsule* is more than the fusion or culmination of these related drawings, the series is also indebted to work made in the 1980s. Like Winters's earlier paintings of biological and botanical specimens, the *Tenon's Capsule* drawings emerge from existing imagery. "I am always working from something," Winters has said. And his titles sometimes betray those sources. Tenon's capsule, for example, is a medical term for the thin membrane that holds the eye in its socket.

The *Tenon's Capsule* drawings contain many ocular references. Their common oval composition, in a very schematic way, recalls the skull's orbital sac. Likewise, the drawings'

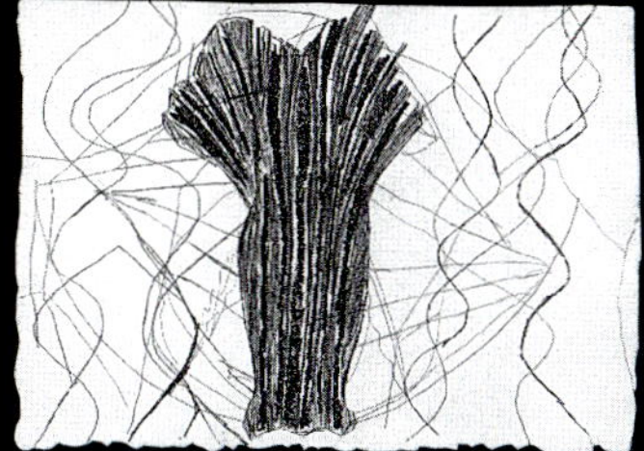

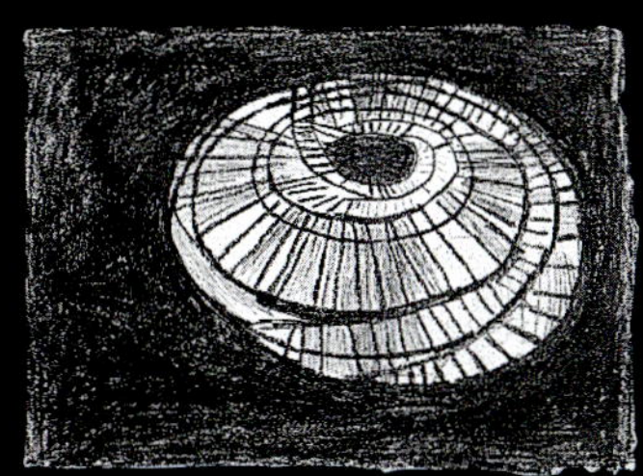

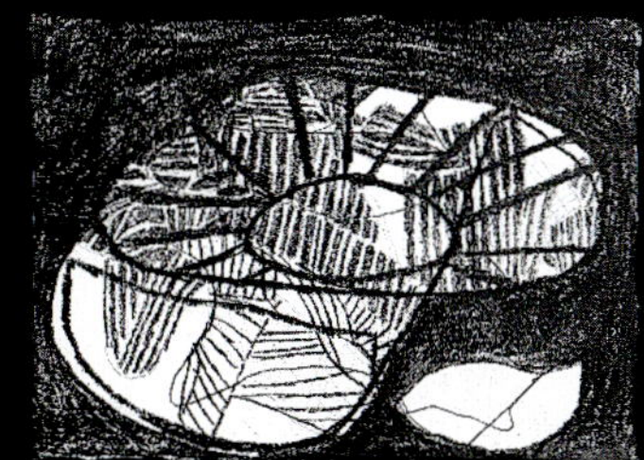

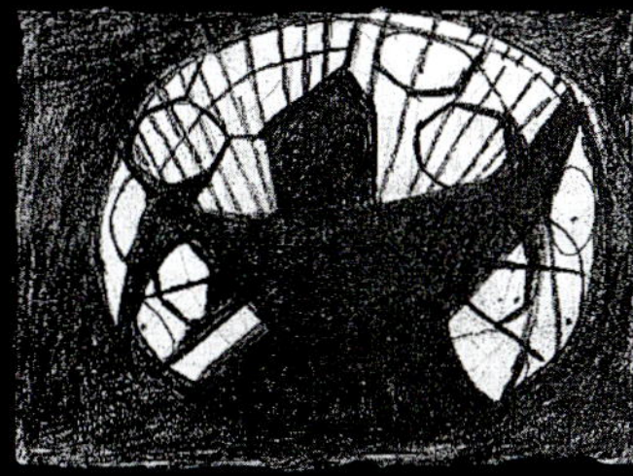

2 / 3 / 4 / 5

shared focus on interconnected linear networks that trace a circular orbit suggest the fibrous Tenon's capsule tissue.

The drawings, however, do not represent the membrane. Instead, the drawings play on the poetics of connectivity, specifically the tenuous link between eye and body, suggested by the title's allusion to the medical terminology.

Winters works directly from source material, but does not illustrate the images to which his titles refer. He describes his technique as an interactive transformation of existing forces, informed as much by his choice of pencil or pen as by his selection of appropriated photograph or diagram. His is a process of manipulation and mutation that produces evocative analogues.

Winters discovered the dynamic, abstract line present in *Tenon's Capsule* by turning his attention to the ground plane of his images. In *Lens* and *Compressed Model*, both from *Foundations and Systems*, for example, he laid down a heavily worked field of graphite on top of a linear network that was apparently previously applied. This superimposed ground frames the lines so that it forms a window to the tracery beneath. He repeats the effect in most of the *Tenon's Capsule* drawings. In number *1* a white ground encloses the central circular form. The palette is reversed in numbers *2, 4, 5* and *6*, which feature black frames. These shifts between foreground and back create disorienting effects and shifts in focus. Especially when the applied ground is woven into the linear networks, as in numbers *2, 5*, and *6*, it seems as if figure and ground are somehow intertwined. In *Tenon's Capsule*, as well as in *Foundations and Systems*, it is difficult to discern what is figure, what is ground, and how the two relate.

Shifting, mutating, rising grounds are a recurring motif throughout Winters's work from the 1990s. A similar concern appeared in the writing of philosopher John Rajchman, whose concept of ungrounding outlined new approaches towards the pragmatics of thinking and making shared by artists interested in the writing of philosopher Gilles Deleuze. Rajchman described the concept of ungrounding as a rejection of the series of oppositions that has historically defined how a built form relates to its context. In architecture, as in painting, figure-ground relationships had been described in binary terms—natural and artificial, organic and abstract, figural and geometric, contextual and autonomous. "Some would like to try to revalorize the first pole of these oppositions—the natural, the organic, the figural, the contextual, the 'site-specific,'" Rajchman wrote. "I would like to look instead at several attempts to get out from under these oppositions themselves, finding other spaces lying in between them—in other words, to *unground* them."[4]

Ungrounding is a philosophical inquiry into the interstitial spaces between systems in opposition, such as the ambiguous territory between nature and culture, and the connective Tenon's capsule tissue. It describes a potential for imaging that exists underneath, behind, and before the ground plane resolves into a clearly delimited figure and ground. "Attention to form-giving movement prior to the ground," Rajchman wrote, "releases a dynamic abstract line." This line "no longer moves within figure-ground relations as in the case of abstraction that is content to simply reduce or purify away figures from a basically immobile, rectilinear extensive space."[5] Instead, ungrounding produces a new kind of imaging, a form of abstraction that is free from any reference to figuration. This undulating, varying, dynamic line found beneath and before the ground propelled a decade of Winters's work.

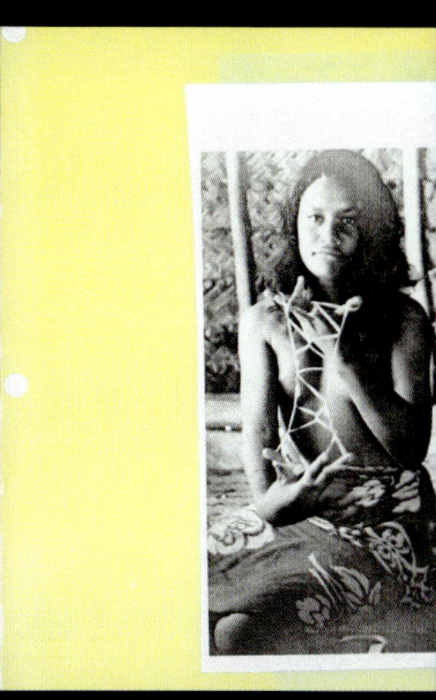

6

1
Terry Winters
Dark Plant 11, 1982
Crayon and charcoal on paper
41 1/2 x 29 1/2 in. (105.4 x 74.9 cm)
Collection of the artist

2 / 3 / 4 / 5
Terry Winters
Foundations and Systems, 1994/1995
From a series of 50 drawings
Graphite on paper
Each, 10 7/8 x 14 3/4 in. (27.6 x 37.5 cm)
2
Abstract Flash Frame, 1994
Private collection
3
Compressed Model, 1994
Private collection, courtesy of
Galerie Fred Jahn, Munich
4
Lens, 1994
Private collection, courtesy of
Galerie Fred Jahn, Munich
5
Geometric and Kinematic Methods, 1995
Collection of the artist

6
Terry Winters
Page from *Ocular Proofs*, 2001 edition
Offset lithography on paper
Each, 8 1/2 x 5 1/2 in. (21.6 x 14 cm)
Courtesy of the artist

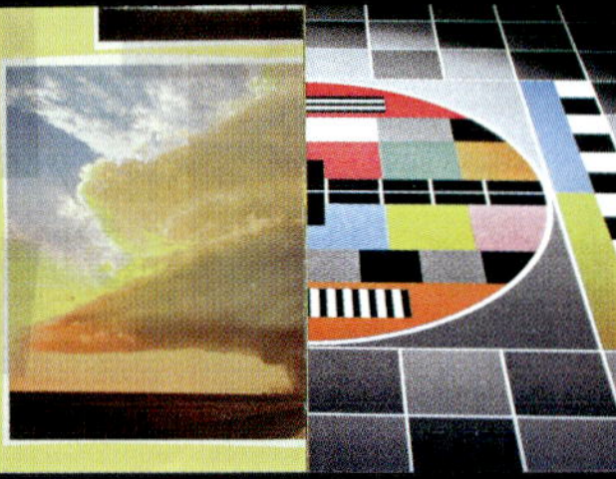

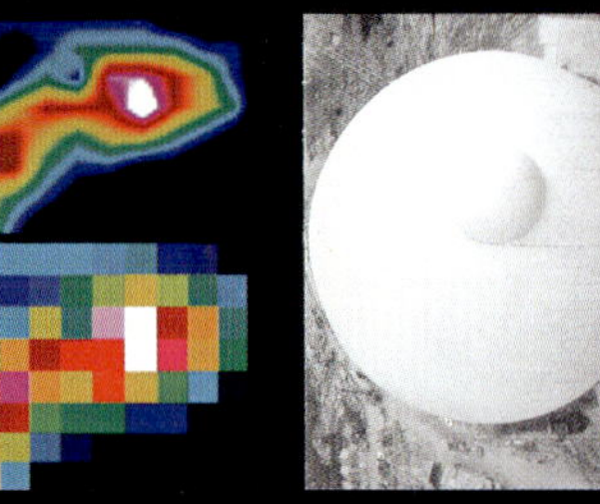

7 / 8

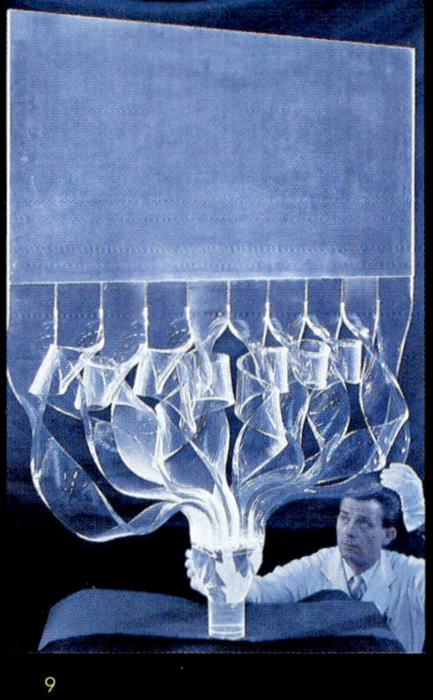

9

COMPUTATION OF CHAINS

Linear networks race across the surface of *Computational Architecture*, 1995 (pp. 42–43). Either deftly laid down in one forceful gesture or emphatically retraced, almost etched, onto the surface of the canvas, the lines intermittently diverge and integrate. Red bars across the top and bottom, joined by vertical members, superimpose a potent geometry onto the swirling yellow maelstrom at the heart of this turbulent painting.

The red grid on the surface of the painting defines the composition. A unique use of shading behind the vertical members highlights the fact that Winters literally imposed this grid, which he first worked out in the preceding *Computation of Chains*, #34, drawing (p. 53). The grid, a traditional modernist structure, establishes order as the subject of the painting. It imposes organization upon the chaos of his linear networks in the same way that computational architecture provides the sequencing system that makes the computer's stored data useful.

Ocular Proofs, a collection of images and texts Winters first published in 1995—the same year he painted *Computational Architecture*—expands on the analogy of computing and painting found in many of his works from this period. In a neither straight-forward nor rational manner, the book articulates Winters's oblique engagement with his source material. The book is composed of forty-seven stanzas, each paired to a line drawing. Winters made the ink drawings specifically for the project and the one-color process used to print the book. A grouping of heterogeneous photographs was appended as a coda to the book's second edition published in 2001. The artist pilfered the texts and photographs from a promiscuous variety of medical, mathematical, philosophical, aesthetic, and advertising materials and then assembled the text fragments into the individual stanzas. The photographs, appropriated texts, and sketches simultaneously assert that "a great deal of computing power is required" while explaining that "painting is the subject."

The book was not his first experimentation with text. In 1994 he had made *Models for Synthetic Pictures*, a portfolio of intaglio prints that includes extended notes on the preface page. A suite of drawings made in 1998, *Intersections and Animations*, was published the next year as offset lithographs in a book that includes short texts interspersed with the images. *Ocular Proofs* was, however, the first time since the 1970s that Winters integrated image and text.

"Process," one of *Ocular Proofs'* text-image pairings (pp. 64–65), at first appears to be rife with internal rupture. The text is carefully segregated from the drawing. Within the text midphrase breaks and backslashes accentuate the disjunction and make it difficult to determine the relationships between phrases.

The drawings, on the other hand, achieve symmetry and synthesis. Most of the drawings are made with lines that double back against themselves and are scratched into the surface of the paper. The inked lines suggest hesitation and instability, but they are joined together in branching structures that maintain a bilateral symmetry (which is reiterated in the design of the book's wraparound cover and interior flaps). Echoing the format of the book, all of the drawings are composed around a strong central vertical.

The *Ocular Proofs* drawings, despite all their shaky suggestiveness, rehearse many ways in which it is possible to build something new from the juxtaposition of disparate, even fractured, information. Like William Burroughs's cut-ups that search for new nonlinear narrative modes, Winters's accumulation of text and image proposes a process of finding new structures and new images by exploring the irrational spaces between unlikely pairings such as image and text or computing and painting.

7 / 8
Terry Winters
Double-page spreads from *Ocular Proofs*, 2001 edition
Offset lithography on paper
Each, 8 1/2 x 11 in. (21.6 x 27.9 cm)
Courtesy of the artist

9
Terry Winters
Page from *Ocular Proofs*, 2001 edition
Offset lithography on paper
8 1/2 x 5 1/2 in. (21.6 x 14 cm)
Courtesy of the artist

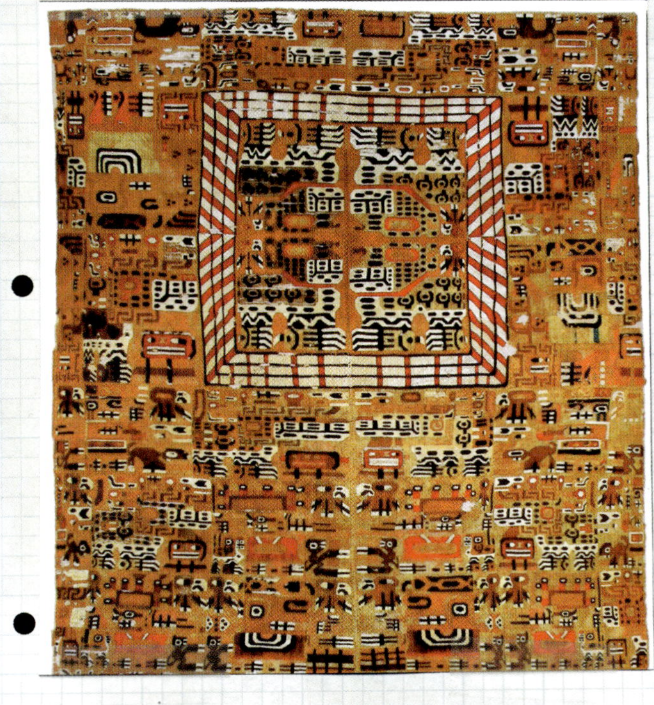

10

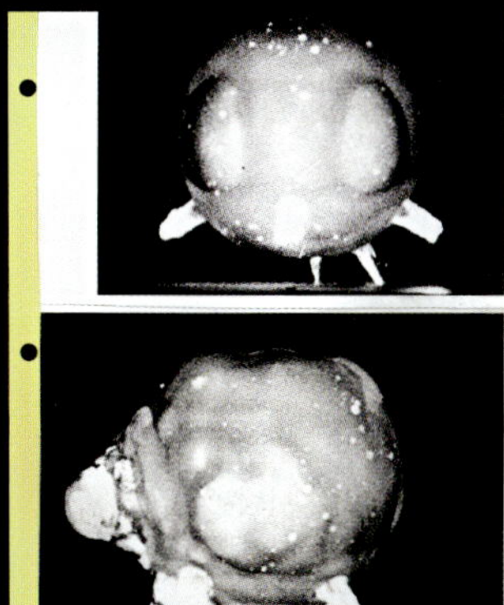

11

GRAPHIC PRIMITIVES

Color and Information (pp. 68–69) is an atomic blast to the senses.[6] Its chemical palette of acidic yellows and superheated reds burns into your retina. A shockwave of graphic intensity radiates from the unbreached cleft at its core. Information is the fallout of the beguiling explosion of color that emanates from the painting.

The color in *Color and Information* is markedly different from the earthy, natural, often handmade pigments that Winters used throughout the 1980s. The titanium white, chrome green, and iridescent turquoise share a sharpness and artificiality not seen before in his work. The painting pushes intensity and temperature to new extremes on his color scale.

Winters began to probe the unrestrained effects of color by first controlling the variable of information. *Color and Information* uses the same composition as in *Graphics Tablet*, the lunar pendant to its solar intensity (pp. 78–79). Both paintings share patterning and a design that was first worked out in *Graphic Primitives 1* and its eponymous woodcut (p. 70); all of these works are from 1998. To make the prints, Winters scanned drawings into an image-editing program. Manipulating the computer's tools to layer images, change the scale of shapes, and play with composition, he was able, as he describes it, to "pull information out of each line and see the potential in the virtual spaces between the lines."[7] He then output his design to a computer-guided laser that incised the wood-blocks used to make the prints. This technique served to distance Winters even further from what was by now the rote information encoded in the blocks.

Winters's approach intentionally discounts graphic information. By allowing the design to stabilize, color replaces line as the emotive element in this body of work. His painting process calls to mind the approach of ancient weavers who repeated the same patterns for generations, creating designs according to the parameters of patronage or heraldic code. In some of the ancient Andean textiles that inspire Winters the graphic substrates remain while color and proportion complicate, and intentionally confuse, the traditional patterns. In his work, Winters manipulates color as another layer of information that distorts, but nevertheless powerfully shapes, the graphic content.

Just as it is impossible to separate the force from the heat of a nuclear blast, color and information are inexorably intertwined. There may be a vertical chasm that divides the painting, but every other aspect of *Color and Information*—the circular motif, the allover grid, and the common depth—conspires to unify the work. The color threatens to blow; the graphic information keeps the painting stable.

10
Page from Terry Winters's notebook showing Andean (Wari) textile
Courtesy of the artist

11
Page from Terry Winters's notebook showing photographs of atomic bomb blasts (by Harold Edgerton)
Courtesy of the artist

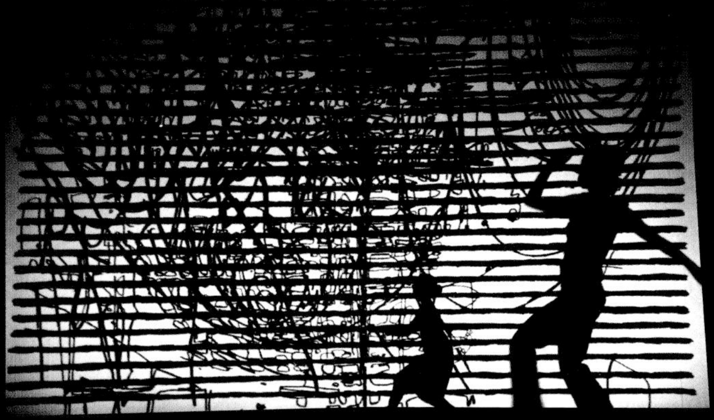

12

LOCATION PLAN

As its title suggests, *Linking Graphics, 1*, is an amalgam of many images (p. 84). Each layer of the drawing, a composition of horizontal bars superimposed onto looping forms over discrete rectangles, seems as if it could exist as an independent unit. In fact, the basic composition is reminiscent of the *Graphics Primitives, 1*, woodcut from 1998 (p. 70), and later Winters would repeat the concentric circles in *Location Plan, #16*, a drawing from 1999, as well as the large-scale painting *Luminance* from 2002 (pp. 128–29). Layering and repetition, or what could otherwise be described as structured improvisation, is the theme of the *Linking Graphics* and *Location Plan* series.

The overt presence of black horizontal, and sometimes vertical, lines is a defining feature of these drawings and paintings. The stripes, which sometimes read as bars obscuring access to the drawings below, emphasize Winters's improvisation with repeated compositional elements within the regularity of the series of thirty *Location Plan* drawings (pp. 94–95). The calibrated bars promise a set rhythm and yet the inflection of individual lines suggest a subtle syncopation that shifts the accent of the work by calling attention to other graphic elements.

This body of work is redolent with connotations of rhythm, pacing, improvisation, and other musical associations. While creating these paintings and drawings, from 1999 to 2000, Winters collaborated with choreographer Trisha Brown and composer Dave Douglas on *El Trilogy*, a complex five-part performance that explores weather, musical structure, improvisation, and the set-changing work of stagehands. Winters provided multiple sets, including bold graphic backdrops, spaces illuminated by colored light, costumes, and, in one striking scene, nine suspended cymbals. For *Five Part Weather Invention*, the first choreography in *El Trilogy*, Winters used *Linking Graphics, 1*, as the central element of the set. For the stage Winters enlarged the drawing to monumental scale, added at the top a gray-scale on the left and a color bar on the right, and had it printed onto a backdrop. As is often the case, the process of repetition and mutation lead to something new in Winters's work. The strong horizontal lines circumscribe the field and stage while also emphasizing the effect of calibration at play in the drawing, dance, and music.

Intrinsically and extrinsically, *Linking Graphics, 1*, resonated with Brown's dance and Douglas's score. In the same way that music is shaped by the architecture in which it is played, Winters's drawing affected *El Trilogy*. The dancers interacted with the drawing's patterning and movement in three dimensions. Carolyn Lucas, Brown's assistant, explained that the choreography "had to do with foot patterns and rhythm."[8] It is easy to imagine a dancer in counterpoint to the looping lines of the drawing as they move up and down, across the bars from bottom register to top, carrying the dance along the drawing's lyrical trajectory. Simultaneously, the bars lay down a beat in the same way that Greg Cohen's bass provides the pulse for *Five Part Weather Invention*, and the curving lines underneath wander and weave akin to Douglas's trumpet. The proximity of the dancers' bodies to Winters's abstract spaces soon began to affect his work. The *Location Plan* drawings that appear on the backdrop for the final section of the trilogy, *Groove and Countermove*, achieve a looseness and liberation of the hand that is, like Douglas's jazz and Brown's choreography, accomplished through rigorous constraint. Together the drawing, dance, and score examine the boundaries of genre and the common ground revealed through improvisational collaboration.

12
Trisha Brown Dance Company
Five Part Weather Invention, 1999,
from *El Trilogy* (see also pp. 86–87)
Music by Dave Douglas
Sets and costumes by Terry Winters
Lighting by Jennifer Tipton
Photograph by Joanne Savio

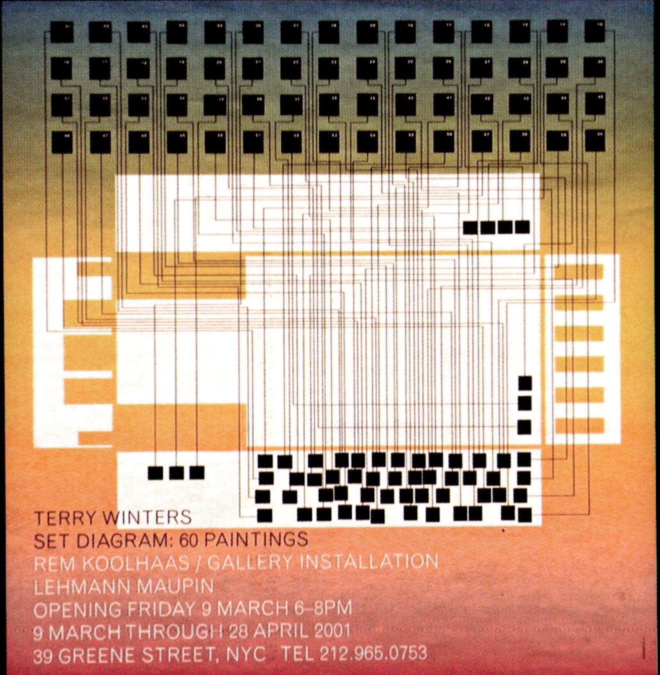

13

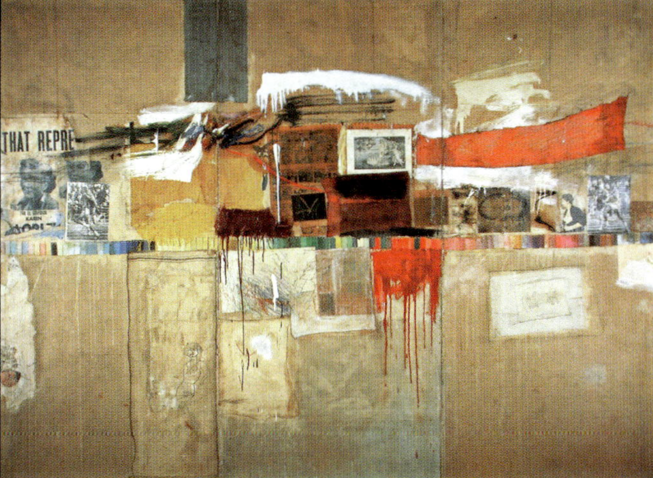

14

SET DIAGRAM

Set Diagram is the collective title of a series of one hundred paintings Winters made between 2000 and 2002, each of which measures one meter by one yard (pp. 98–107). To create the paintings Winters worked within the confines of number and scale—both of which were determined before he began to paint. The rigid parameters for the series facilitated a great diversity of image and technique in the individual works. In some cases, such as *Set Diagram 67* and *100*, the artist recapitulated the ocular structures and rising grounds that he first experimented with in 1994. Other paintings are more prospective. Numbers *10* and *13* clearly relate to *Amplitude*, an etching printed in 2000 (p. 123), the same year as those paintings, while the gouged mark-making in number *22* predicts the incised surface of *Scale* from 2003 (pp. 148–49). Some works, such as *Set Diagram 27* and *59*, are unlike anything Winters had made before.

The format of the paintings, as well as their integration into an architectural system designed the paintings shifted position and even slid onto the ceiling. Cultivating a liberation from the standard vertical wall-based orientation, the installation emphasized the idea of the paintings as interchangeable units.

In writing about the earlier *Graphic Primitives* paintings and prints, John Rajchman proposed that Winters had replaced Rauschenberg's flatbed picture plane with the Deleuzean concept of a "table of information in which things slide back and forth, images emerging from other images rather than from external things."[9] *Set Diagram*, with its modularity and image accretion across the series, would seem to embody this description of Winters's work. Set within the installation system and including overt references to computation, such as the bar code in number *59*, the paintings seem to be representative of Rajchman's information-based cognition, or in his words, a "city-brain consciousness."

As always with Winters's work, things are not simply binary. *Set Diagram* diverges from Rajchman's model natural world envisioned by the processes of tabulation. Winters's paint handling, the scraping and carving that appear in *Set Diagram*, suggest that his images are present in the paint itself and emerge through the painting process. In number *69* Winters carved the design of a simple Duchampian bicycle wheel directly into the gold and black bars that composed the painting's surface. Moving quickly, he delineated spokes and hub into the still wet paint. He used the same sgraffito technique to incise the surface of several *Set Diagram* paintings, as well as *Scale*. Approaching the idea of ungrounding with an impassive logic so direct as to be plainspoken, he literally dug through the ground to produce an image that his technique suggests was encountered in the material medium of the ground.[10]

Throughout his oeuvre, from his earliest incidental drawings in the 1970s and his cellular motifs in the 1980s, Winters's paintings insist upon the inherent iconicity of paint. In 1974 Rosalind Krauss opened the door for an understanding of the iconic dimension of paint in her that the images of flowers, fruit, or whatever, are contained by, literally embedded in, a material substance."[11] In a particularly evocative parallel with Winters's art she described Rauschenberg's panoply of images as "layered into the surface like so much material, embedded within the pictorial matrix like biological specimens floating in fluid under glass."[12]

The images in *Set Diagram* are too embedded within the pictorial matrix to slide and shift the way their installation suggested. Unlike the model proposed with Steinberg's "flatbed picture plane," however, the paintings do not abandon nature or propose the computer as a new form of cognition. Adamantly linked to the material medium of the paint itself, the series stakes a claim for the unpredictable potential inherent to painting's materiality.

13
Poster for Terry Winters, *Set Diagram: 60 Paintings* exhibition, 2001, graphic design by 2x4. Courtesy of the artist.

14
Robert Rauschenberg (United States, b. 1925)

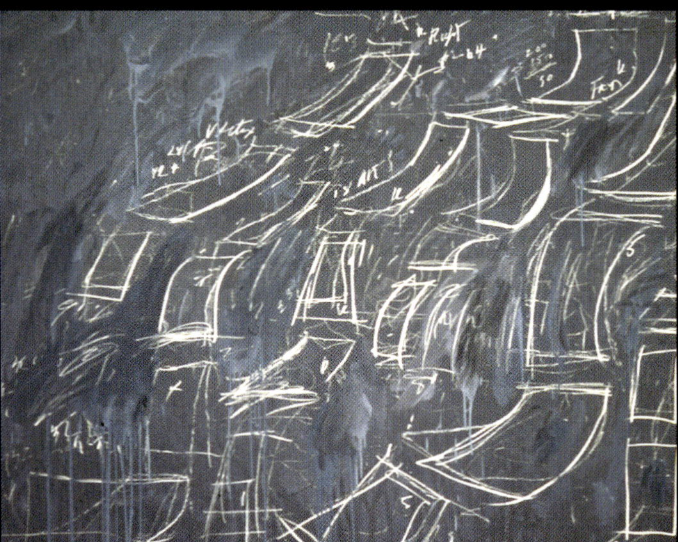

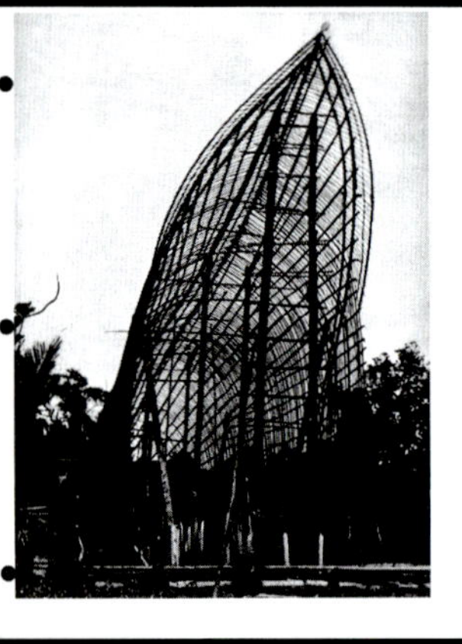

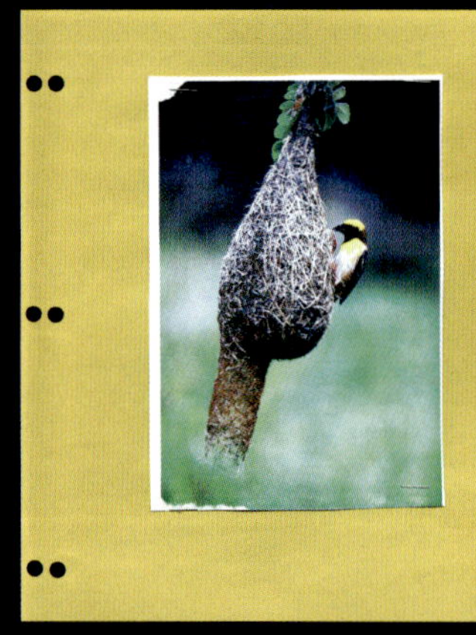

15 / 16 / 17

MESHWORKS

The *Meshworks* drawings delineate a disorienting range of spatial constructions, from folded space to vortexes (pp. 114–17). The overlapping planes, gridded shapes, and wave patterns almost seem recognizable as a computational form of structural analysis. In this series of large-scale drawings Winters simulates wire-frame imaging, the vernacular of advanced architectural rendering, as the impetus of the work. The drawings, however, juxtapose this techno-scientific form of visualization with the hand-wrought. The deckled edge of the paper, the smudged graphite, and the intentional stuttering within his line emphasize the nonmechanical nature of the drawings. What at first appear to be some of Winters's most direct appropriations of a scientific form of imaging expand and explode in the related paintings—*Composite* and *Functions, Vectors, and Speeds* (pp. 126–27, 118–19)—into works that advance a critique of the objective forms of representation that clearly fascinate him.

Winters uses *Meshworks* to propose an anexact, arational approach to information. His facture accentuates the extraneous—what a scientist would perceive as "noise"—as an integral aspect of his work. He intentionally calls attention to the smudges or smears that might have been incidental effects of his handling. The blurred yellow lines in *Computational Architecture*, for example, consciously emphasize the chaotic materiality in a painting that is otherwise focused on control. In his more recent work, such as the painting *Untitled* from 2003, momentary and incidental imperfections evolve into the subject of the piece (pp. 156–57).

This focus on materiality expressed with blemishes and stains reveals Winters's long-term engagement with Cy Twombly's work. Specifically, his approach to information is a dual homage to Rauschenberg's combines and Twombly's scumbled canvases. In his "blackboard" paintings from the mid-1960s, Twombly, in reaction to Minimal and Conceptual art, returned to the black and white palette that predominated in his painting of the early 1950s. In his reprise of the blackboard theme, Twombly replaced the scratched graffiti typical of his early work with what seemed to be geometric equations or mathematical formulations of crude spatial constructions. Just as his earlier work had violated the sanctity of the Abstract Expressionist gesture, the new paintings sullied the rigid objectivity of Minimal art. Twombly paintings suggest, as the philosopher Roland Barthes has explained, that "ideas (in the Platonic sense) are not shiny, metallic Figures in conceptual corsets, but somewhat shaky maculations, tenuous blemishes on a vague background."[13]

Winters approaches what at first appear to be engineered images with Twombly's aura of implausibility. His smeared and splotchy surfaces suggest an intuitive form of building, architecture, or painting that capitalizes on incident. Although the serial format and the routine of repetition define his process, the idiosyncrasies, the blips, and the blemishes that emerge from this process shape the work. Informed by his admiration of vernacular and animal architecture, as opposed to the computational form of architecture alluded to in *Meshworks*, Winters celebrates the instinctual as a rigorous method of examination.

15
Cy Twombly (United States, b. 1928)
Untitled, 1969
Oil and crayon on canvas
78 x 103 in. (198.1 x 261.6 cm)
Whitney Museum of American Art, purchase with funds from Mr. and Mrs. Rudolph B. Schulhof, 69.29

16
Page from Terry Winters's notebook with image of vernacular architecture
Courtesy of the artist

17
Page from Terry Winters's notebook with image of animal architecture
Courtesy of the artist

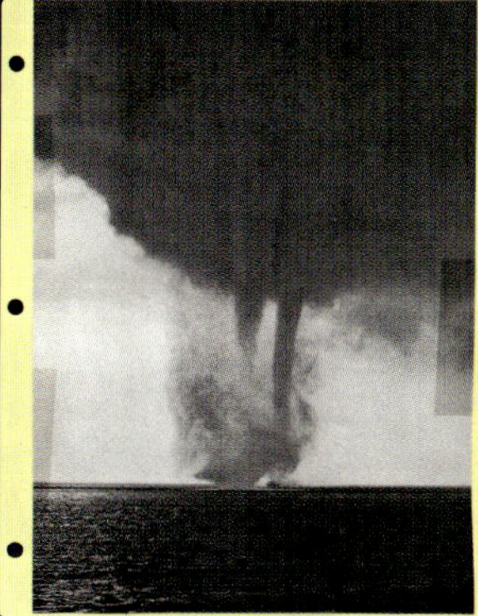

18

TURBULENCE SKINS

Turbulence is a concept that is at once the literal subject of the *Turbulence Skins* drawings and related paintings, while it is also an allusive, abstract concept beyond easy visualization. It is typical of Winters's many scientific and aesthetic motifs. Ethereal and yet describable with techno-scientific means, turbulence is the perfect emblem of a vision of nature that is mediated by culture. The term itself, like so many of the ideas at play in Winters's work, is open to a variety of connotations from the political to the scientific. It is a metaphor for both the content and his approach to his work that, in the end, always returns to the material specificity of paint.

Swirling air causing midflight commotion is probably what the word *turbulence* first calls to mind. It physically evokes invisible natural phenomena, which have been a subject of Winters's paintings since the 1980s. Where he once portrayed microscopic cellular worlds, he now graphs eddies of air and water across the planar skins of these drawings. Although seemingly clearly depicted on paper, the agitation recorded in the gridded space has only a glancing relationship to the natural world.

The turbulence in these drawings, and throughout Winters's oeuvre, is the quivering expressivity of his

The works from this period chart turbulent flows of paint. In *Untitled*, 2003 (pp. 156–57), linear skins break apart, melt, into a trembling pool of paint that recalls the rich loamy grounds from the 1980s that first gave rise to his biological imagery. *Scale*, 2003, with its calibrated planar shifts, calls attention to paint in a different manner (pp. 148–49). Extending across the bottom of the canvas, a color scale stabilizes the painting. The scale collapses competing definitions of space into the one indigo field that composes the work as a whole. It brings together, holds down, unifies, and synthesizes the competing elements of the painting. It produces the effect of a new space where all the planes can be perceived simultaneously. This space is neither actual nor virtual; it is instead a place of potentiality. The new space defined in *Scale* is that of painting's own potential as a medium and a practice.

Winters's oeuvre, with its fluctuating velocities of image and material, meditates on deeply rooted traditions within the history of the medium while it also acknowledges, as he calls it, "painting's low-tech, shape-shifting capabilities and extremely wide bandwidth." He has repeatedly experimented with forms of knowledge and means of manipulating materials—computer graphics, architecture, and dance to name a few—that expand the parameters of his practice. In a

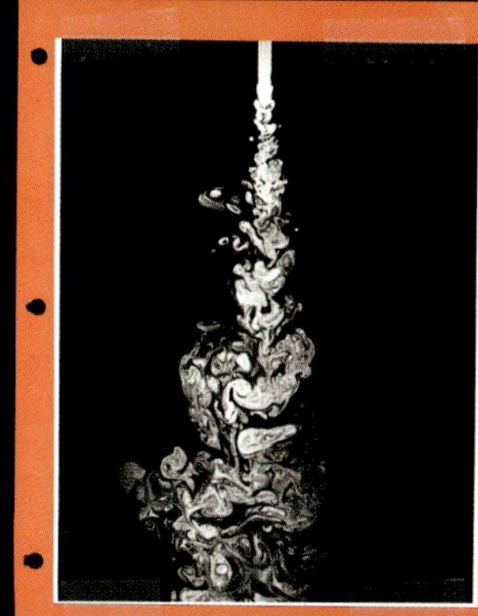

19

NOTES

1. Terry Winters, interview by author, March 2001. Subsequent quotes from the artist that are otherwise unattributed are drawn from interviews by the author in February 2003.
2. Leo Steinberg, "Other Criteria," *Other Criteria: Confrontations with Twentieth-Century Art* (New York: Oxford University Press, 1972), 84.
3. Ibid.
4. John Rajchman, *Constructions* (Cambridge, Mass.: The MIT Press, 1998), 80.
5. Ibid., 135.
6. Ronald Jones compared *Color and Information* to Harold Edgerton's photo of an atomic blast that Winters kept in his notebook (Ronald Jones, "Notebook," *Terry Winters: Graphic Primitives* [New York: Matthew Marks Gallery, 1999], 36–37).
7. Terry Winters, interview by author, June 2000.
8. In Hendel Teicher, ed., *Trisha Brown: Dance and Art in Dialogue, 1961–2001* (Andover, Mass.: Addison Gallery of American Art, Phillips Academy, 2002), 224.
9. John Rajchman, "Painting in the Brain-City," *Terry Winters: Graphic Primitives*, 10.
10. Christopher Knight first identified this "impassive logic" in Winters's earliest works (Christopher Knight, "Terry Winters," in *Terry Winters: Painting and Drawing*, ed. Phyllis Plous [Berkeley and Los Angeles: University of California Press, 1987], 21).
11. Rosalind Krauss, "Rauschenberg and the Materialized Image," *Artforum* 13, no. 4 (December 1974): 39.
12. Ibid., 40.
13. Roland Barthes, "The Wisdom of Art," *The Responsibility of Forms* (New York: Hill and Wang, 1985), 180. Originally published in *Cy Twombly, Paintings and Drawings, 1954–1977* (New York: Whitney Museum of American Art, 1979).

TERRY WINTERS

Born 1949 in Brooklyn, New York
B.F.A., Pratt Institute, Brooklyn, New York, 1971
Lives in New York City and Columbia County, New York

This documents the years 1991 through 2003. For the years 1977 to 1990, see Lisa Phillips, ed., *Terry Winters* (New York: Whitney Museum of American Art, 1991).

SELECTED INDIVIDUAL EXHIBITIONS

1991
Terry Winters/Zeichnungen, Galerie Max Hetzler, Berlin

1991–92
Terry Winters, Whitney Museum of American Art, New York (catalogue). Traveled to the Museum of Contemporary Art, Los Angeles (1991).

1993
Terry Winters, Galleria Massimo Valsecchi, Milan

1994
Terry Winters, Sonnabend Gallery, New York
Terry Winters, Gallery of Art, Johnson County Community College, Overland Park, Kansas (brochure)
Terry Winters, Galerie Lehmann, Lausanne
Terry Winters, Galerie Max Hetzler, Berlin

1995
Terry Winters: Drawings, Sonnabend Gallery, New York
Terry Winters: Foundations and Systems, Galerie Fred Jahn, Munich (catalogue)

1996
Terry Winters: Drawings, Galerie Lawrence Rubin, Zurich (catalogue)
Terry Winters: Arbeiten auf Papier, Galerie Max Hetzler, Berlin

1997
Terry Winters: Recent Works, School of the Museum of Fine Arts, Boston (catalogue)
Terry Winters: Oeuvres sur papier, Galerie Samia Saouma, Paris
Terry Winters: Early Works, Akira Ikeda Gallery, Tokyo
Terry Winters: Computation of Chains, Matthew Marks Gallery, New York (catalogue)

1998
Terry Winters: Graphic Primitives, White Cube, London
Terry Winters Prints: 1982–1998, Detroit Institute of Arts (catalogue)
Terry Winters: Folio, Victoria and Albert Museum, London

1998–99
Terry Winters, IVAM Centre del Carme, Valencia, Spain (catalogue). Traveled to Whitechapel Art Gallery, London.

1999
Terry Winters: Graphic Primitives, Matthew Marks Gallery, New York (catalogue)
Terry Winters: Arbeiten auf Papier, Galerie Fred Jahn, Munich
Terry Winters, Fogg Art Museum, Harvard University, Cambridge (brochure)

2000
Terry Winters, Kunsthalle, Basel (catalogue)
Terry Winters: Location Plan, Susan Inglett, New York
Terry Winters: Prints, Bowdoin College Museum of Art, Brunswick, Maine (brochure)

2001
Set Diagram: 60 Paintings, Lehmann Maupin Gallery, New York
Terry Winters: Drawings, Matthew Marks Gallery, New York (catalogue)
Terry Winters: Printed Works, The Metropolitan Museum of Art, New York (catalogue)

2002
Terry Winters: Paintings, White Cube2, London
Terry Winters: Drawings and Paintings, Galerie Fred Jahn, Munich

2003
Terry Winters: Zeichnungen/Drawings, Staatliche Graphische Sammlung/Pinakothek der Moderne, Munich (catalogue)
Terry Winters: Paintings and Drawings, Matthew Marks Gallery, New York (leaflet)

SELECTED GROUP EXHIBITIONS

1991
Sieben Amerikanische Maler, Staatsgalerie Moderner Kunst, Munich (catalogue)
Artists' Sketchbooks, Matthew Marks Gallery, New York (catalogue)
Bourgeois, Turrell, Winters: Portfolios, A Common Thread, G.H. Dalsheimer Gallery, Baltimore
Master Drawings 1520–1990, Janie C. Lee Master Drawings, New York, and Kate Ganz Ltd., London (catalogue)
Sherrie Levine, John Baldessari, Louise Bourgeois, Terry Winters, Helmut Federle, James Turrell, Reynolds/Minor Gallery, Richmond, Virginia
Visions/Revisions, Denver Art Museum
Gulliver's Travels, Galerie Sophia Ungers, Cologne (catalogue)
Paintings and Drawings, Daniel Weinberg Gallery, Santa Monica, California
Mito y Magia en America: Los Ochenta, Museo de Arte Contemporaneo de Monterrey, Mexico (catalogue)
Postmodern Prints, Victoria and Albert Museum, London
20th-Century Collage, Margo Leavin Gallery, Los Angeles
Large Scale Works on Paper, John Berggruen Gallery, San Francisco (catalogue)
Mel Bochner, Carroll Dunham, Barry Le Va, Terry Winters, Galerie Faust, Geneva
New Editions from ULAE, Greg Kucera Gallery, Seattle
43rd Annual Academy-Institute Purchase Exhibition, American Academy and Institute of Arts and Letters, New York
An Overview of Drawing, David Nolan Gallery, New York
Universal Limited Art Editions, Gallery of Art, Johnson County Community College, Overland Park, Kansas

1992
American Art of the 80s, Museo d'Arte Contemporanea di Trento e Rovereto, Trento, Italy
Allegories of Modernism: Contemporary Drawings, The Museum of Modern Art, New York (catalogue)
Drawing Redux, San Jose Museum of Art, San Jose, California (catalogue)
Jasper Johns, Brice Marden, Terry Winters: Drawing, Margo Leavin Gallery, Los Angeles (catalogue)
Slow Art: Painting in New York Now, P.S. 1 Contemporary Art Center, Long Island City, New York
Drawn in the '90s, Katonah Museum of Art, New York (catalogue). Traveled to Fine Art Gallery, Indiana University, Bloomington; Illingwork Kerr Gallery, Alberta College of Art, Calgary; Hunstville Museum of Art, Alabama; Worcester Art Museum, Massachusetts; Lamont Gallery, Phillips Exeter Academy, Exeter, New Hampshire; University Art Gallery, San Diego State University.
Emerging New York Artists, Fine Arts Building, College of Fine Arts, University of Nebraska at Omaha

Marking the Decade: Prints, 1960–1990, Baltimore Museum of Art
Not for Sale: Loans for the Private Collections of New York Art Dealers, Tel Aviv Museum of Art
28th Annual Exhibition of Art on Paper, Weatherspoon Art Gallery, University of North Carolina at Greensboro

1993
Terry Winters/John Cage, Bernard Toale Gallery, Boston
Master Drawings, 1907–1993: Spring 1993, Janie C. Lee Master Drawings, New York (catalogue)
Painting: Carroll Dunham, Bill Jensen, Harriet Korman, Suzanne McClelland, Stephen Mueller, Pat Steir, Michael Tetherow, Matthew Weinstein, Terry Winters, Texas Gallery, Houston
Drawings: 30th Anniversary Benefit for the Foundation for Contemporary Performing Arts, Castelli Gallery, New York
The Return of the Cadavre Exquis, The Drawing Center, New York
Merce Cunningham Dance Company Benefit Art Sale, 65 Thompson Street, New York (brochure)
Living with Art: The Collection of Ellyn and Saul Dennison, Morris Museum, Morristown, New Jersey (catalogue)
The Language of Flowers, Paul Kasmin Gallery, New York

1994
Drawing in Black and White, The Museum of Modern Art, New York
American Academy Invitational Exhibition of Painting and Sculpture, American Academy of Arts and Letters, New York
The Assertive Image: Artists of the Eighties, Armand Hammer Museum of Art and Cultural Center, UCLA, Los Angeles
Abstract Works on Paper, Robert Miller Gallery, New York
Metamorphosis: Surrealism to Organic Abstraction, 1925–1993, Marlborough Graphics, New York
Prints from Solo Impression, College of Wooster Art Museum, Wooster, Ohio (catalogue)
Portfolios and Suites, Greg Kucera Gallery, Seattle

1995
10 + 10, New York Studio School, New York
Reinventing the Emblem, Yale University Art Gallery, New Haven (catalogue)
Repicturing Abstraction: Basic Nature, 1708 Gallery, Richmond, Virginia (catalogue)
Mit dem Auge des Kindes: Kinderzeichnung und moderne Kunst, Lenbachhaus, Kunstbau, Munich, and Kunstmuseum Bern (catalogue)
Yamantaka Donation (Tibet House Benefit), Gagosian Gallery, New York
1995 Biennial Exhibition, Whitney Museum of American Art, New York (catalogue)
Printmaking in America: Collaborative Prints and Presses, 1960–1990, Mary Leigh Block Gallery, Northwestern University, Evanston (catalogue). Traveled to Jane Voorhees Zimmerli Art Museum, Rutgers, State University of New Jersey, New Brunswick; Museum of Fine Arts, Houston; National Museum of American Art, Smithsonian Institution, Washington, D.C.
New York Abstract, Contemporary Arts Center, New Orleans (catalogue)
Summer Fling, Basilico Fine Arts, New York
Art Works: The PaineWebber Collection of Contemporary Masters, Museum of Fine Arts, Houston (catalogue). Traveled to Detroit Institute of Arts; Museum of Fine Arts, Boston; Minneapolis Institute of Arts; San Diego Museum of Art; and Center for the Fine Arts, Miami.
Malerei, Galerie Max Hetzler, Berlin
25 Years: An Exhibition of Selected Works, Margo Leavin Gallery, Los Angeles (catalogue)
25 Americans: Painting in the 90s, Milwaukee Art Museum (catalogue)
Drawings from the Collection of Agnes Gund, The Century Club, New York

1996
Natural Process, Center Gallery, Bucknell University, Lewisburg, Pennsylvania
Sonnabend Collection, Deichtorhallen, Hamburg
Works in Progress: Recent Graphics by Carroll Dunham, Julian Lethbridge, Terry Winters, Susan Sheehan Gallery, New York
The Meaning (IN) Between: Koons Salle Winters, Galerie Lehmann, Lausanne
On Paper, Marlborough Gallery, New York (catalogue)
Nuevas Abstracciones, Palacio de Velázquez (Museo Nacional Centro de Arte Reina Sofía), Madrid (catalogue). Traveled to Kunsthalle, Bielefeld; Museu d'Art Contemporani, Barcelona.
The Robert and Jane Meyerhoff Collection, National Gallery of Art, Washington, D.C. (catalogue)
John Chamberlain, Carroll Dunham, Barry Le Va, John Newman, Al Taylor, Richard Tuttle, Terry Winters, Galerie Brigitte Ihsen, Cologne
Malerie I: S. Anzinger, G. Condo, R. Bleckner, A. Kassebröhmer, A. Oehlen, T. Winters, Monika Sprüth Galerie, Cologne
Thinking Print, The Museum of Modern Art, New York (catalogue)
An American Story, Whitney Museum of American Art, New York
Limited Edition Artists' Books Since 1990, Brooke Alexander, New York
Just Past: The Contemporary in MoCA's Permanent Collection, 1975–96, Museum of Contemporary Art, Los Angeles
Family Values: Amerikanische Kunst der achtziger und neunziger Jahre; Die Sammlung Scharpff in der Hamburger Kunsthalle (Family Values: American Art in the Eighties and Nineties; The Scharpff Collection at the Hamburg Kunsthalle), Hamburger Kunsthalle, Hamburg (catalogue)

1997
8 Paintings: Vija Celmins, Philip Guston, Jasper Johns, Giorgio Morandi, Jackson Pollock, Myron Stout, Philip Taaffe, Terry Winters (curated by Steve Wolfe), Luhring Augustine Gallery, New York
The View from Denver: Contemporary American Art from the Denver Art Museum, Museum Moderner Kunst, Vienna (catalogue)
Views from Abroad: European Perspectives on American Art 3/American Realities, Whitney Museum of American Art, New York (catalogue)
Spiders and Webs: Louise Bourgeois, Vija Celmins, Jim Hodges, Kiki Smith, Rosemarie Trockel, Terry Winters, Barbara Krakow Gallery, Boston
icon/iconoclast, Marlborough Chelsea, New York

1997–99
Proof Positive: 40 Years of Contemporary American Printmaking at ULAE, 1957–1997, Corcoran Gallery of Art, Washington, D.C. (catalogue). Traveled to UCLA at the Armand Hammer Museum of Art and Cultural Center, Los Angeles; Sezon Museum of Art, Tokyo; Kitakyushu Municipal Museum of Art, Kitakyushu City, Japan; and others.

1998
American Academy Invitational Exhibition of Painting and Sculpture, American Academy of Arts and Letters, New York
Prints in the 90s from ULAE, Marlborough Chelsea, New York
Bartlett, Johns, Marden, Rauschenberg, Murray, Shapiro, Winters: Early Works, Mukai Gallery, Tokyo
Master Drawings of the Twentieth Century, Mitchell-Innes and Nash, New York (catalogue)
Elements of the Natural: 1950–1992, The Museum of Modern Art, New York
Exhibition of Work by New Members and Recipients of Awards, American Academy of Arts and Letters, New York
Large Scale: Works on Paper, Danese Gallery, New York
Von Baselitz bis Winters: Vermächtnis Bernd Mittelsten Scheid, Staatliche Graphische Sammlung Munchen, Munich (catalogue)
Now and Forever: Part I, Matthew Marks Gallery and Pat Hearn Gallery, New York

David Lasry: Drawings, Prints, Collaborations, Wynn Kramarsky, New York
Young Americans 2: New American Art at the Saatchi Gallery, Saatchi Gallery, London (catalogue)

1999

The American Century: Art and Culture, 1900–2000, Part II, Whitney Museum of American Art, New York (catalogue)
To the Rescue: Eight Artists in an Archive, International Center of Photography, New York (catalogue). Traveled to Miami Art Museum and Contemporary Arts Museum, Houston.
Trisha Brown/Terry Winters: Works on Paper, MASS MoCA, North Adams, Massachusetts
Twenty Years of the Grenfell Press, Paul Morris Gallery, New York
20 Years/20 Artists, Aspen Art Museum, Colorado (catalogue)
American Painting after 1950: Pollock, Stella, Johns, Kelly, Winters, Fogg Art Museum, Harvard University, Cambridge

2000

Hard Pressed: 600 Years of Prints and Process, AXA Gallery, New York (catalogue). Traveled to Boise Art Museum; Museum of Fine Arts, Santa Fe; and Naples Art Museum, Florida.
Lasting Impressions: Contemporary Prints from the Bruce Brown Collection, Portland Museum of Art, Maine (catalogue)
Arbeiten auf Papier: Carroll Dunham, Luis Gordillo, Barry Le Va, Terry Winters, Michael Hasenclever Gallery, Munich
Art at Work: Forty Years of the Chase Manhattan Collection, Queens Museum of Art, New York (brochure)
Lux et Tenebrae, Peter Blum Edition, New York
00: Drawings 2000, Barbara Gladstone Gallery, New York (catalogue)
Druckgraphische Trouvaillen, Galerie Franke, Stuttgart
Celebrating Modern Art: The Anderson Collection, San Francisco Museum of Modern Art (catalogue)
An American Focus: The Anderson Graphic Arts Collection, Fine Arts Museums of San Francisco, California Palace of the Legion of Honor (catalogue). Traveled to Palm Springs Desert Museum; Albuquerque Museum.
Open Ends, The Museum of Modern Art, New York (catalogue)

2001

Mythic Proportions: Painting in the 1980s, Museum of Contemporary Art, North Miami
Works on Paper from Acconci to Zittel, Victoria Miro Gallery, London
Repetition in Discourse, Painting Center, New York (brochure)
American Identities: A New Look, Brooklyn Museum of Art, New York
New Installations and Acquisitions, The Broad Foundation, Santa Monica, California
Tenth Anniversary Exhibition: 100 Drawings and Photographs, Matthew Marks Gallery, New York (catalogue)
Thirty-Five Drawings, Richard Gray Gallery, Chicago (catalogue)

2001–03

Under Pressure: Prints from Two Palms Press, Lyman Allyn Museum of Art, Connecticut College, New London (catalogue). Traveled to Shick Art Gallery, Skidmore College, Saratoga Springs, New York; Meadows Museum, Southern Methodist University, Dallas; University Gallery, University of Massachusetts at Amherst; Kent State University Art Gallery, Kent, Ohio; Arthur A. Houghton Jr. Gallery, Cooper Union, New York.

2002

New York Renaissance: From the Whitney Museum of American Art, Palazzo Reale, Milan (catalogue)
Early and Late Work: Willem De Kooning, Tony Smith, Ellsworth Kelly, Brice Marden, Terry Winters, Matthew Marks Gallery/The Art Show, New York
177th Annual Exhibition, National Academy of Design, New York (catalogue)
From Twilight to Dawn: Postmodern Art from the UBS PaineWebber Art Collection, Frist Center for the Visual Arts, Nashville (catalogue)
Drawn from a Family: Contemporary Works on Paper, Colby College Museum of Art, Waterville, Maine (catalogue)
Trisha Brown: Dance and Art in Dialogue, 1961–2001, Addison Gallery of American Art, Phillips Academy, Andover (catalogue)
25th Anniversary Benefit Selections Exhibition, The Drawing Center, New York
Premio Biella per l'incisione 2002, Museo de Territorio Biellese, Biella, Italy
ArtWorks for Merce, Merce Cunningham Studio, New York

2003

Visions and Revisions: Art on Paper Since 1960, Museum of Fine Arts, Boston
Terry Winters and Barry Le Va: Zeichnungen, Galerie Zell am See, Austria
On Paper: Masterworks from the Addison Collection, Addison Gallery of American Art, Phillips Academy, Andover
Trisha Brown Dance Company Art Show and Benefit Sale, Pace Gallery, New York
Game Over, Grimm/Rosenfeld Gallery, Munich

SELECTED BIBLIOGRAPHY

Except for publications by the artist, this documents the years 1991 through 2003.

BOOKS & PROJECTS BY TERRY WINTERS

"Siren: Nine Drawings." *The Paris Review 26* (Fall 1984): 197–206.
Shapiro, David. *After a Lost Original: A Book of Poems.* Frontispiece etching by Terry Winters. New York: Solo Press, 1991; 2nd ed., Woodstock, N.Y.: Overlook Press, 1994.
Ocular Proofs. New York: Grenfell Press, 1995; 2nd ed., with additions, New York: Dome Editions, 2001.
"6-Field Sequence." *Sulfur 39* (Fall 1996): 74.
Intersections and Animations: 50 Drawings. New York: Dome Editions, 1999.
Trisha Brown Dance Company. *El Trilogy.* Sets and costumes by Terry Winters. First performance at the American Dance Festival, Durham, North Carolina, June 29, 2000.
Merce Cunningham Dance Company. *Joyce Event.* Set by Terry Winters. First performance at the Joyce Theater, New York, November 7, 2000.
Perfection, Way, Origin. With text by Jean Starobinski. West Islip, N.Y.: Universal Limited Art Editions, 2002.
Merce Cunningham Dance Company. *Loose Time.* Decor and costumes by Terry Winters. First performance at Zellerbach Hall, University of California, Berkeley, February 1, 2002.
Turbulence Skins. With text by Ben Marcus. New York: Columbia University Neiman Center, 2004.

MONOGRAPHS & EXHIBITION CATALOGUES

1991

Phillips, Lisa, ed. *Terry Winters.* Exh. cat. Essays by Lisa Phillips and Klaus Kertess. New York: Whitney Museum of American Art.

1994

Terry Winters. Exh. brochure. Essay by Jerry Saltz. Overland Park, Kans.: Johnson County Community College, Gallery of Art.

1995

Terry Winters: Foundations and Systems; Fifty New Drawings by Terry Winters (Fünfzig neue Zeichnungen von Terry Winters). Exh. cat. Essay by Michael Semff. Munich: Verlag Fred Jahn.

1996

Terry Winters Drawings 1996. Exh. cat. Foreword by Gabriele Lutz. Zurich: Galerie Lawrence Rubin.

1997

Terry Winters: Computation of Chains. Exh. cat. Conversation with Adam Fuss, studio photographs by Judy Linn. New York: Matthew Marks Gallery.
Terry Winters: Recent Works. Exh. cat. Essays by Lelia Amalfitano and Raphael Rubinstein. Boston: School of the Museum of Fine Arts.

1998

Terry Winters. Exh. cat. Essays by Enrique Juncosa and Ronald Jones. Valencia: IVAM/Institut Valencià d'Art Modern; London: Whitechapel Art Gallery.

1999

Sojka, Nancy. *Terry Winters Prints: 1982–1998, A Catalogue Raisonné.* Detroit: Detroit Institute of Arts.
Terry Winters: Graphic Primitives. Exh. cat. Texts by Ronald Jones and John Rajchman. New York: Matthew Marks Gallery.
Terry Winters: Fogg Art Museum, Harvard University. Exh. brochure. Essay by Linda Norton. Cambridge: Harvard University Art Museums.

2000

Terry Winters. Exh. cat. Essays by Peter Pakesch and W.G. Sebald. Basel: Kunsthalle Basel.

2001

Rosenthal, Nan. *Terry Winters: Printed Works.* Exh. cat. New York: The Metropolitan Museum of Art; New Haven and London: Yale University Press.
Terry Winters: Drawings. Exh. cat. Essay by Scott Rothkopf. New York: Matthew Marks Gallery.

2002

Terry Winters: Shadowgraphs. Essay by Susan Tallman. New York: Two Palms Press.

2003

Terry Winters: Zeichnungen/Drawings. Exh. cat. Essays by Michael Semff and Harry Cooper. Munich: Staatliche Graphische Sammlung/Pinakothek der Moderne.

SELECTED ESSAYS, ARTICLES, & REVIEWS

1991

Baker, Kenneth. "10 Years of Terry Winters: Retrospective at L.A.'s MoCA." *San Francisco Chronicle*, October 27.
Gutterman, Scott. "Facts of Life: Terry Winters Describes the Irreducible Nature of Existence—In Paint." *Journal of Art* 4, no. 7 (September): 38–40.
Knight, Christopher. "Winters Growth: Sensual Fusion of Culture, Nature." *Los Angeles Times*, September 18.
Saltz, Jerry. "Terry Winters." *Tema Celeste*, no. 31 (May/June): 82–83.
Smith, Roberta. "Artists' Sketchbooks." *New York Times*, April 5.

1992

Anfam, David. "New York: Winters, Wegman, de Kooning, and Tansey." *Burlington Magazine* 134, no. 1072 (July): 466–67.
"Fertile Regions: The Ever-Growing Art of Terry Winters." Interview by Robert Enright. *Border Crossings* 11, no. 2 (Spring): 14–23.
Kimmelman, Michael. "Cells, Crystals, Bugs, and Shells, Rendered in Paint." *New York Times*, March 8.
Pagel, David. "A Trio of Masterpiece Makers." *Los Angeles Times*, May 7.
Saltz, Jerry. "The Embryonic Vision: Terry Winters' *The Psychological Corporation*, 1990." *Arts Magazine* 66, no. 5 (January): 21–22.
Schjeldahl, Peter. "The Dearth of Painting." *Village Voice*, March 31, 97.
"Terry Winters." Interview by Bob Holman. *BOMB*, Spring, 42–47.
Wallach, Amei. "Works in Process at the Whitney." *New York Newsday*, March 6.
Winters, Terry. "L'Idealizzazione della forma." *Tema Celeste Arte Contemporaneo*, no. 35 (April/June): 69.

1993

Ackley, Clifford. "Terry Winters and Clifford Ackley: A Conversation." *Art New England* 14, no. 4 (June/July): 29–31.

1994

Adams, Brooks. "Terry Winters at Sonnabend." *Art in America* 82, no. 10 (October): 130–31.
Jones, K. Marriott. "Terry Winters." *Artforum* 32, no. 10 (Summer): 91.
Kimmelman, Michael. "Terry Winters." *New York Times*, February 25.
Rubinstein, Raphael. "Winters in Bloom." *ARTnews* 93, no. 5 (May): 153.

1995

Cotter, Holland. "A Critic's Dozen to Catch at the Biennial." *New York Times*, March 12.
Cotter, Holland. "Terry Winters/Drawings." *New York Times*, May 12.
Kuspit, Donald. "Terry Winters." *Artforum* 34, no. 3 (November): 88.

1996

Princenthal, Nancy. "Artist's Book Beat." *Print Collector's Newsletter* 27, no. 2 (May/June): 67–69.

1997

Kimmelman, Michael. "Terry Winters." *New York Times*, October 31.

Schjeldahl, Peter. "The Redeemer." *Village Voice*, October 28, 93.

Temin, Christine. "An Abstract Winters Tale." *Boston Globe*, March 5.

Yablonsky, Linda. "Terry Winters." *Time Out New York*, no. 117 (December 18–25): 57.

1998

Green, Roger. "Winters Wonderland: DIA Retrospective Traces Career of Nonpareil Printmaker." *Ann Arbor News*, October 24.

James, Merlin. "Terry Winters at Matthew Marks." *Burlington Magazine* 141, no. 1151 (January): 65–67.

Rubinstein, Raphael. "Nine Lives of Painting." *Art in America* 86, no. 9 (September): 90–99.

Schwabsky, Barry. "Terry Winters/Matthew Marks Gallery." *Artforum* 36, no. 6 (February): 92–93.

1999

Cumming, Laura. "He'd Start One Drawing...." *Observer* (London), March 7.

Dorment, Richard. "Striking a Balance When Things Fall Apart." *Daily Telegraph* (London), March 4.

Johnson, Ken. "Terry Winters/Graphic Primitives." *New York Times*, June 11.

Packer, William. "The Cosmos Captured in Intuitive Abstraction." *Financial Times*, March 9.

Searle, Adrian. "Who Needs Drugs, When You Can Paint Like This?" *Guardian* (London), February 23.

"Working Proof: Terry Winters/Graphic Primitives." *Art on Paper* 3, no. 5 (May/June): 58.

2000

Falkenstein, Michelle. "Performance Anxiety." *ARTnews* 99, no. 5 (May): 51.

Gladstone, Valerie. "Filling the Stage with Her Inventions." *New York Times*, April 30.

Kisselgoff, Anna. "It Takes Two to Jitterbug, Sometimes More." *New York Times*, May 11.

Russel, John. "Making Pen and Ink Seem Passé: The Proliferation of New Ways to Draw." *New York Times*, August 18.

2001

Baird, Daniel. "Printed Works: Terry Winters at the Metropolitan Museum of New York." *Brooklyn Rail*, October–November, 26.

Eleey, Peter. "In Conversation with Terry Winters." *Brooklyn Rail*, October–November.

Everett, Deborah. "Terry Winters: Printed Works." *NYArts*, September, 41.

Kastner, Jeffrey. "An Energetic Imagist Who Dances with Chance." *New York Times*, August 19.

McDonough, Tom. "Terry Winters at Lehmann Maupin and Matthew Marks." *Art in America* 89, no. 6 (June): 125–26.

Princenthal, Nancy. "Perfect like a Hedgehog: The Printed Works of Terry Winters." *Art on Paper* 6, no. 1 (September/October): 50–56.

"Working Proof: Terry Winters and Jean Starobinski; Perfection, Way, Origin (2001)." *Art on Paper* 5, no. 6 (July/August): 65.

2002

Anderson, Jack. "Exploring Austerity and Then Excitement." *New York Times*, December 10.

Johnson, Ken. "For Those in Search of Calm, an Armory Full of Modernists." *New York Times*, February 22.

Kisselgoff, Anna. "Cunningham Celebrates in a Fugue for 16 Dancers." *New York Times*, July 26.

"Working Proof: Terry Winters." *Art on Paper* 6, no. 3 (January/February): 80–81.

2003

Brennan, Michael. "Terry Winters/Matthew Marks Gallery." *Brooklyn Rail*, December 2003–January 2004, 12.

"Fiebrige Striche, die Technik und Natur verbinden." *Süddeutsche Zeitung*, May 22.

Glueck, Grace. "Terry Winters." *New York Times*, December 12.

Häntzschel, Jörg. "Kristalle, Schwämme, Nervenstränge." *Süddeutsche Zeitung*, August 8.

Oliv, Freia. "Systeme mit Tiefang." *Münchner Merkur*, June 3.

Palmer, Reinhard. "Winters' verborgene Welten in der Pinakothek der Moderne." *Und*, August 8.

Reitter, Barbara. "Transformationen." *Passauer Neue Presse*, July 3.

Sachs, Brits. "Man hört den Morast blubbern." *Frankfurter Allgemeine*, July 11.

"Thick and Thin: A Roundtable." *Artforum* 41, no. 8 (April): 174.

GROUP EXHIBITIONS: BOOKS & CATALOGUES

1991

Gulliver's Travels. Exh. cat. Cologne: Galerie Sophia Ungers and DuMont Buchverlag.

Large Scale Works on Paper. Exh. cat. San Francisco: John Berggruen Gallery.

Mito y Magia en America: Los Ochenta. Exh. cat. Introduction by Miguel Cervantes. Monterrey: Museo de Arte Contemporaneo de Monterrey.

Sieben Amerikanische Maler. Exh. cat. Edited by Carla Schulz-Hoffman. Munich: Staatsgalerie Moderner Kunst.

1992

Drawing Redux. Exh. cat. Curated by Phyllis Tuchman. San Jose: San Jose Museum of Art.

Drawn in the '90s. Exh. cat. Essays by Joshua P. Smith and Sean Rainbird. New York: Katonah Museum of Art and Independent Curators Incorporated.

Jasper Johns, Brice Marden, Terry Winters: Drawings. Exh. cat. Essay by Jeremy Gilbert-Rolfe. Los Angeles: Margo Leavin Gallery.

Rose, Bernice. *Allegories of Modernism: Contemporary Drawing*. Exh. cat. New York: The Museum of Modern Art.

1993

Living with Art: The Collection of Ellyn and Saul Dennison. Exh. cat. Essays by Lisa Dennison and Gary Sangster. Morristown, New Jersey: Morris Museum.

Master Drawings, 1907–1993: Spring 1993. Exh. cat. New York: Janie C. Lee Master Drawings.

1994

Flam, Jack D., and Daniel Shapiro. *Western Artists/African Art*. Exh. cat. Curated by Daniel Shapiro. New York: Museum for African Art.

Prints from Solo Impression. Exh. cat. Essays by Ruth E. Fine and Kathleen McManus Zurko. Wooster, Ohio: College of Wooster Art Museum.

1995

Fineberg, Jonathan David. *Art Since 1940: Strategies of Being*. Englewood Cliffs, New Jersey: Prentice Hall.

Fineberg, Jonathan David. *Mit dem Auge des Kindes: Kinderzeichnung und moderne Kunst*. Bern: Kunstmuseum Bern; Munich: Städtische Galerie im Lenbachhaus; Stuttgart: Verlag Gerg Hatje.

Kertess, Klaus. *1995 Biennial Exhibition*. Exh. cat. New York: Whitney Museum of American Art.

Margo Leavin Gallery: 25 Years. Exh. cat. Los Angeles: Margo Leavin Gallery.

New York Abstract. Essay by Lew Thomas. New Orleans: Contemporary Arts Center.

The PaineWebber Art Collection. Exh. cat. Introduction by Jack Flam, commentaries on the plates by Monique Beudert and Jennifer Wells. New York: Rizzoli International.

Printmaking in America: Collaborative Prints and Presses, 1960–1990. Exh. cat. Essays by Trudy V. Hansen, Barry Walker et al. New York: Harry N. Abrams.
Reinventing the Emblem: Contemporary Artists Recreate a Renaissance Idea. Exh. cat. Edited by Leslie K. Baier. Essays by Allison B. Leader and Richard S. Field. New Haven: Yale University Art Gallery.
Repicturing Abstraction. Exh. cat. Essays by Arthur C. Danto et al. Richmond: Anderson Gallery, Virginia Commonwealth University; Marsh Art Gallery, University of Richmond; Virginia Museum of Fine Arts; 1708 Gallery.
25 Americans: Painting in the 90s. Exh. cat. Text by Dean Sobel. Milwaukee: Milwaukee Art Museum.

1996
Family Values: Amerikanische Kunst der achtziger und neunziger Jahre; Die Sammlung Scharpff in der Hamburger Kunsthalle (Family Values: American Art in the Eighties and Nineties; The Scharpff Collection at the Hamburg Kunsthalle). Exh. cat. Essays by Stephen Schmidt-Wulffen and Christoph Heinrich. Ostfildern-Ruit, Germany: Cantz.
Nuevas Abstracciones. Exh. cat. Essays by Arthur C. Danto and Enrique Juncosa. Madrid: Museo Nacional Centro de Arte Reina Sofía; Barcelona: Museu d'Art Contemporani de Barcelona.
On Paper. Exh. cat. New York: Marlborough Gallery.
Rosenthal, Mark. *The Robert and Jane Meyerhoff Collection.* Exh. cat. Washington, D.C.: National Gallery of Art.
Tallman, Susan. *The Contemporary Print: From Pre-Pop to Postmodern.* New York: Thames and Hudson.
Wye, Deborah. *Thinking Print: Books to Billboards, 1980–95.* Exh. cat. New York: The Museum of Modern Art.

1997
Enright, Robert. *Peregrinations: Conversations with Contemporary Artists.* Winnipeg, Canada: Bain & Cox Publishers.
Kalman, Tibor. *Chairman: Rolf Fehlbaum.* Baden, Switzerland: Lars Müller Publishers.
Proof Positive: Forty Years of Contemporary American Printmaking at ULAE, 1957–1997. Exh. cat. Essays by Jack Cowart, Tony Towle, and Sue Scott. Washington, D.C.: Corcoran Gallery of Art.
The View from Denver: Contemporary American Art from the Denver Art Museum. Exh. cat. Forewords by Lorand Hegyi and Lewis I. Sharp. Vienna: Museum moderner Kunst and Denver Art Museum.
Views from Abroad: European Perspectives on American Art. Exh. cat. *Vol. 3, American Realities.* Essays by Nicholas Serota, Sandy Nairne, and Adam D. Weinberg. New York: Whitney Museum of Art.

1998
American Art of the Twentieth Century: Treasures of the Whitney Museum of American Art. Essays by David A. Ross, Adam D. Weinberg, and Beth Venn. New York: Whitney Museum of American Art.
Art of the 20th Century. 2 Vols. Edited by Karl Rurhrburg. Cologne: Taschen.
Master Drawings of the Twentieth Century. Exh. cat. New York: Mitchell-Innes and Nash.
Von Baselitz bis Winters: Vermächtnis Bernd Mittelsten Scheid. Exh. cat. Essays by Brita Sachs and Michael Semff. Munich: Staatliche Graphische Sammlung.
Young Americans 2: New American Art at the Saatchi Gallery. Exh. cat. Essays by Brooks Adams and Lisa Liebmann. London: Saatchi Gallery.

1999
Phillips, Lisa. *The American Century: Art and Culture, 1950–2000.* Exh. cat. New York: Whitney Museum of American Art in association with W.W. Norton.
Reimschneider, Burkhard, and Uta Grosenick. *Art at the Turn of the Millennium.* Cologne: Taschen.
To the Rescue: Eight Artists in an Archive. Exh. cat. Introduction by Carole Kismaric and Marvin Heiferman, curators. New York: Lookout for the American Jewish Joint Distribution Committee.
20 Years/20 Artists. Exh. cat. Curated by Suzanne Feldman. Essays by Suzanne Farver and Robert Hobbs. Seattle: University of Washington Press; Aspen, Colorado: Aspen Art Museum.

2000
00: Drawings 2000 at Barbara Gladstone Gallery. Exh. cat. Essay by Klaus Kertess. New York: Barbara Gladstone Gallery.
Breuer, Karin. *An American Focus: The Anderson Graphic Arts Collection.* Exh. cat. San Francisco: Fine Arts Museums of San Francisco; Berkeley and Los Angeles: University of California Press.
Celebrating Modern Art: The Anderson Collection. Exh. cat. San Francisco: San Francisco Museum of Modern Art; Berkeley and Los Angeles: University of California Press.
Lasting Impressions: Contemporary Prints from the Bruce Brown Collection. Exh. cat. Essays by Bruce Brown and Aprile Gallant. Portland, Maine: Portland Museum of Art.
Modern Contemporary: Art at MoMA Since 1980. Edited by Kirk Varnedoe, Paola Antonelli, and Joshua Seigel. New York: The Museum of Modern Art.
Platzker, David, and Elizabeth Wyckoff. *Hard Pressed: 600 Years of Prints and Process.* Exh. cat. New York: Hudson Hills Press.
Strange and Charmed: Science and the Contemporary Visual Arts. Edited by Siân Ede. Preface by A.S. Byatt. London: Calouste Gulbenkian Foundation.

2001
American Visionaries: Selections from the Whitney Museum of American Art. Introduction by Maxwell L. Anderson. New York: Whitney Museum of American Art.
At the Louvre and At Present: Contemporary Prints for the Chalcographie du Louvre. Essay by Rainer Michael Mason. Paris: Chalcographie du Louvre.
Lambert, Susan. *Prints: Art and Techniques.* London: V&A Publications.
Tenth Anniversary Exhibition: 100 Drawings and Photographs. Exh. cat. New York: Matthew Marks Gallery.
Thirty-Five Drawings. Exh. cat. Chicago: Richard Gray Gallery.
Under Pressure: Prints from Two Palms Press. Exh. cat. Essay by Barry Schwabsky. New London, Conn.: Lyman Allyn Museum of Art at Connecticut College.

2002
The 177th Annual: An Invitational Exhibition, May 1–June 9, 2002. Exh. cat. New York: National Academy of Design.
ArtWorks for Merce. New York: Cunningham Dance Foundation.
Drawn from a Family: Contemporary Works on Paper. Exh. cat. Foreword by Hugh J. Gourley III. Waterville, Maine: Colby College Museum of Art.
From Twilight to Dawn: Postmodern Art from the UBS PaineWebber Art Collection. Exh. cat. Essay by Mark Scala. Nashville: Frist Center for the Visual Arts and PaineWebber.
New York Renaissance: From the Whitney Museum of American Art. Exh. cat. Essay by Maxwell Anderson. New York: Whitney Museum of American Art; Milan: Electa.
Premio Biella per l'incisione 2002. Essay by Jeremy Lewison. Biella, Italy: Museo del Territorio Biellese.
Trisha Brown: Art and Dance in Dialogue, 1961–2001. Exh. cat. Edited by Hendel Teicher. Essays by Maurice Berger et al. Andover, Mass.: Addison Gallery of American Art, Phillips Academy.
A Visual Handbook: Staatliche Graphische Sammlung München. Edited by Michael Semff. Munich: Staatliche Graphische Sammlung.
Gillick, Liam, "Terry Winters: Graphic Primitives, 11 September–17 October 1998." *White Cube Exhibitions, May 1993–September 2002.* 2:72–73. London: White Cube.

IMAGE CREDITS

All artworks by Terry Winters © 2004 Terry Winters
Artwork © 2004 The Estate of Francis Bacon/ARS, New York/DACS, London, p. 26
Lawrence Beck, p. 20 bottom, 36–39
Cathy Carver, pp. 30, 50–53, 56–57, 64–65, 133, 146–47
Sheldon C. Collins, p. 164 top
D. James Dee, pp. 58–60, 63, 70–71, 84–85
Artwork © 2004 The Willem de Kooning Foundation/Artists Rights Society (ARS), New York; photograph by Hickey-Robertson, Houston, p. 27 bottom
Tony Dougherty, pp. 124–25
Todd Eberle, pp. 110–11
Artwork © 1991 Hans Namuth Estate, Center for Creative Photography, The University of Arizona, p. 27 top
Jen Nelson, pp. 158–61, 163 left, 164 bottom left and right, 165
© Robert Rauschenberg/Licensed by VAGA, New York, p. 163 right
Joanne Savio, pp. 86–87, 162
Steven Sloman, pp. 20 top, 42–48, 61, 68–69, 72–79, 88–95, 98–109, 114–17, 121, 126–29, 134–41, 151–55
Oren Slor, pp. 81, 118–19, 142–45, 148–49, 156–57
Courtesy United Press, Inc., New York, p. 163 left
Courtesy Universal Limited Art Editions (ULAE), Bay Shore, NY, pp. 55, 122–23

ADDISON GALLERY OF AMERICAN ART STAFF

Julie Bernson, Director of Education
Brian Coleman, Preparator
Anthony F. Conners, Museum Security
Roger E. Cowley, Museum Security
Susan C. Faxon, Interim Director and Curator of Art before 1950
Ralph R. Gallo, Museum Security
John Jeknavorian, Museum Security
Denise J.H. Johnson, Registrar and Financial Administrator
Allison N. Kemmerer, Curator of Photography and of Art after 1950
BJ Larson, Director of Museum Resources
Jennifer E. Lawlor, Administrative Assistant
Leslie Maloney, Chief Preparator
Dolores I. Mann, Museum Security
Juliann D. McDonough, Curatorial Associate
David J. Olivares, Head of Security
Hector Rivera, Custodian
Gilda Rossetti, Museum Security
Rachel Schiller, Education Fellow
Austin E. Sharpe, Assistant Preparator
Emily Shubert, Charles H. Sawyer Curatorial Fellow
James M. Sousa, Assistant Registrar for Collections and Archives
Janet I. Thoday, Museum Security
Theresa C. Zucchi, Museum Security

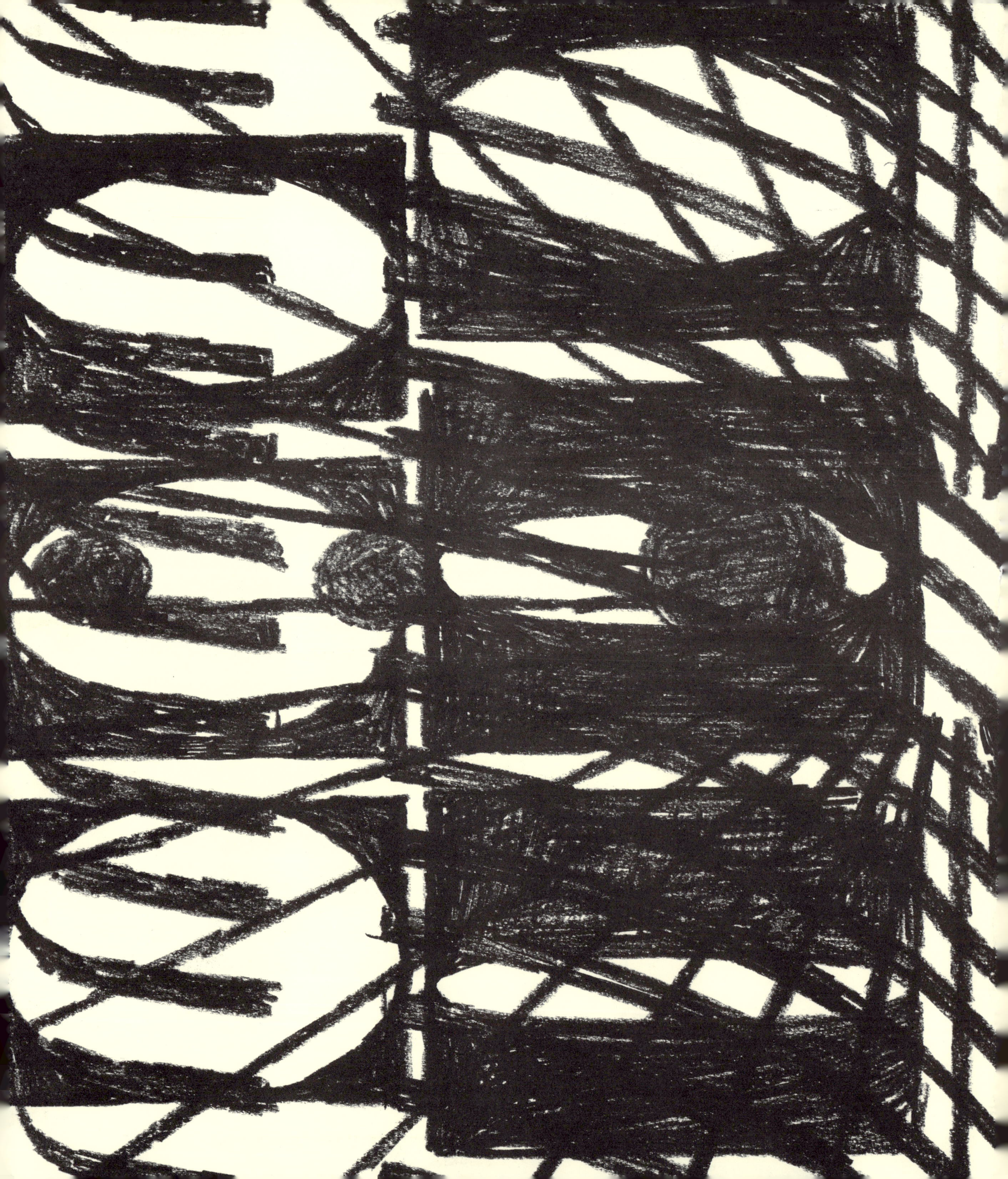

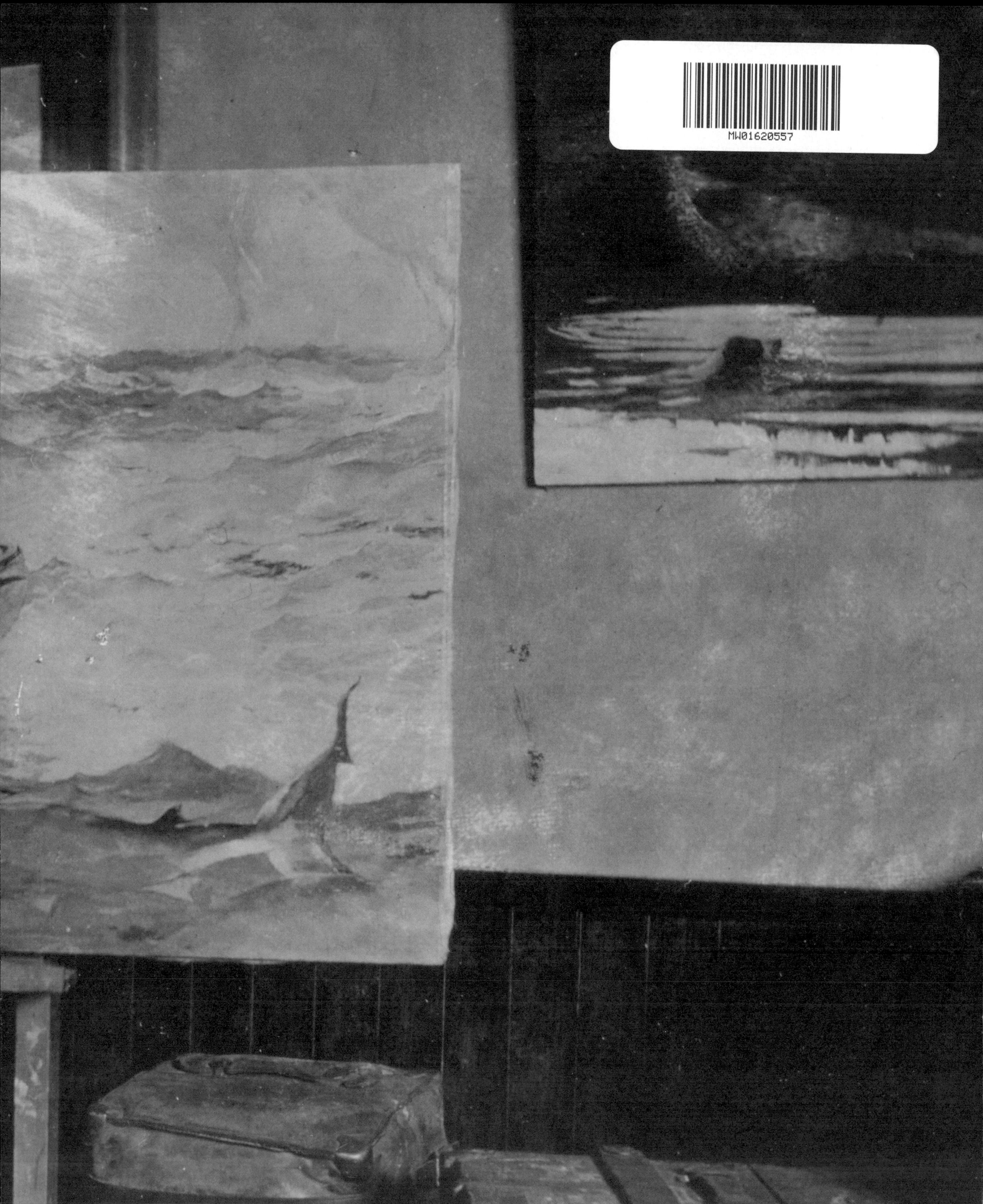

Winslow Homer and the Camera

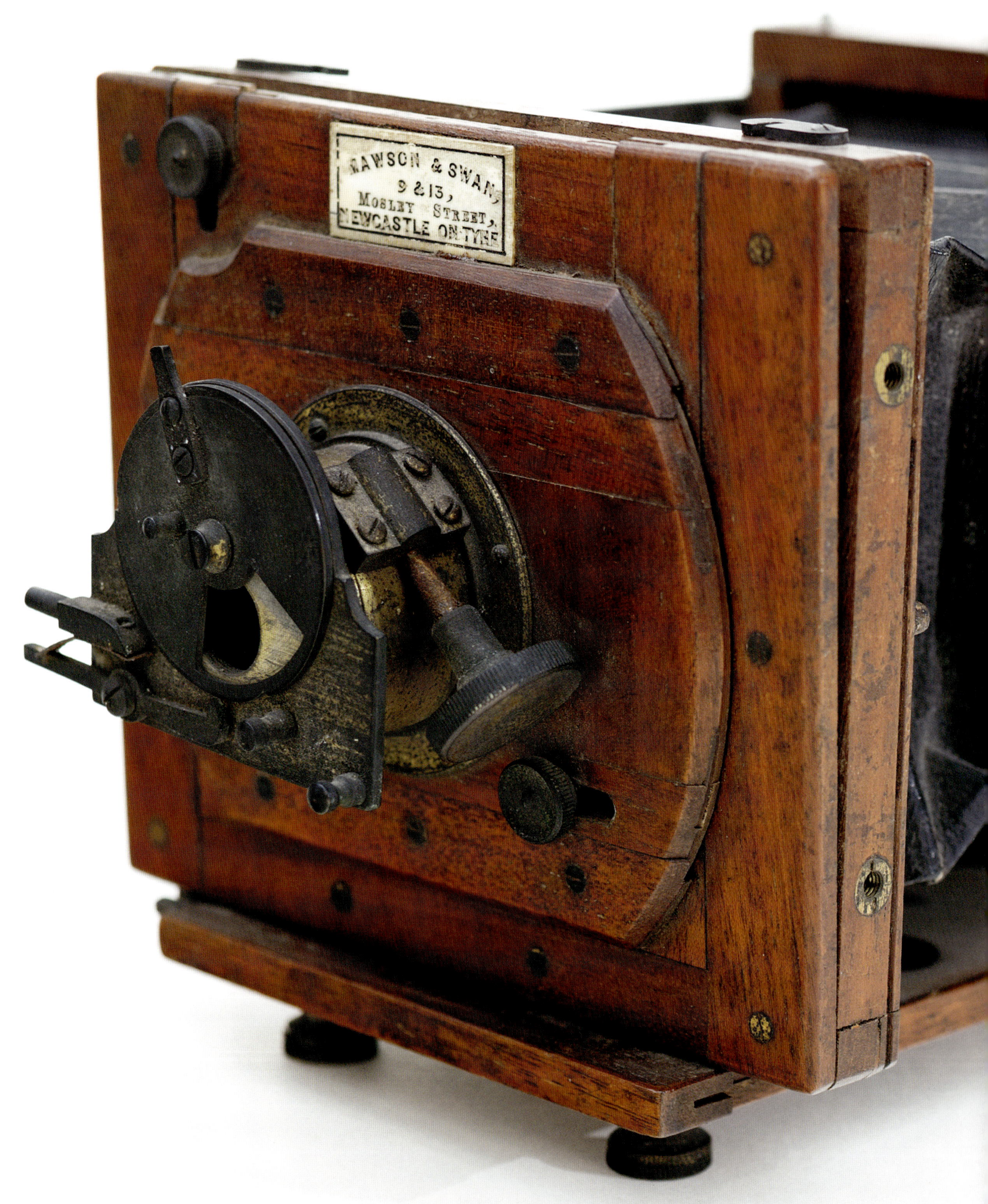
RAWSON & SWAN,
9 & 13,
MOSLEY STREET,
NEWCASTLE ON-TYNE

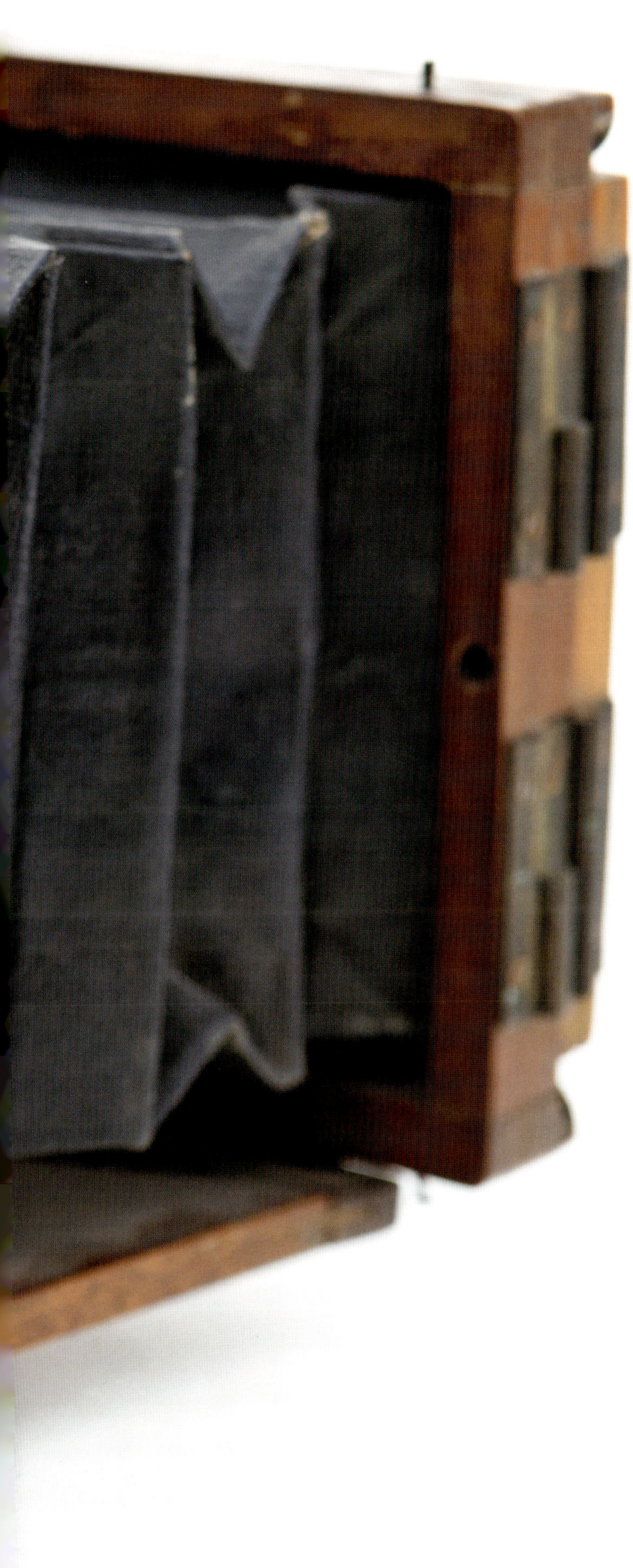

Winslow Homer and the Camera

PHOTOGRAPHY AND THE ART OF PAINTING

Dana E. Byrd

Frank H. Goodyear III

Bowdoin College Museum of Art
in association with
Yale University Press
New Haven and London

Published on the occasion of the exhibition *Winslow Homer and the Camera: Photography and the Art of Painting*, organized by Bowdoin College Museum of Art.

Bowdoin College Museum of Art, Brunswick, Maine
June 22 to October 28, 2018
Brandywine River Museum of Art, Chadds Ford, Pennsylvania
November 17, 2018, to February 17, 2019

yalebooks.com/art

Designed and set in Adagio Serif, Adagio Sans Serif, and Aperçu by Laura Lindgren
Printed in China by 1010 Printing International Limited

Library of Congress Control Number: 2017948833
ISBN 978-0-300-21455-0

A catalogue record for this book is available from the British Library.

The paper in this book meets the requirements of ANSI/NISO Z39.48-1992 (Permanence of Paper).

10 9 8 7 6 5 4 3 2 1

Cover illustrations: *(front)* Simon Towle, *Winslow Homer and a Group at the Water's Edge*, c. 1884 (detail of Goodyear essay, fig. 28D); *(back)* Winslow Homer, *Jumping Trout*, 1889 (detail of plate 50)
Endpapers: *(front)* Unidentified photographer, *Winslow Homer with "The Gulf Stream" in His Studio*, c. 1900 (detail of Goodyear essay, fig. 36); *(back)* Simon Towle, *The Ark and Winslow Homer's Studio*, c. 1884 (detail of Goodyear essay, fig. 28F)
Frontispiece: Mawson & Swan camera owned by Winslow Homer, c. 1882. Bowdoin College Museum of Art, Brunswick. Gift of Neal Paulsen, in memory of James Ott and in honor of David James Ott '74 [2013.29]

CONTENTS

PREFACE

In 2013, the Bowdoin College Museum of Art was given an English-made camera that once belonged to Winslow Homer. Acquired by the artist in 1882, during the two years he lived in Cullercoats, England, this object joined a large collection of Homer's art and archival materials at the Museum, including more than a hundred photographs either taken or collected by him. We appreciate greatly the generosity of Neal Paulsen, a resident of Scarborough, Maine, for presenting this camera to the Museum in memory of James Ott and in honor of David James Ott '74. This gift—together with the rich resources of the Winslow Homer Collection—inspired this project.

Dana E. Byrd, assistant professor of art history at Bowdoin, and I have collaborated on the research for this volume since the start. At first, we were not certain what to say about the camera, nor did we fully grasp the authorship or significance of the different photographs in the Winslow Homer Collection. In reviewing the scholarly literature, we found that several historians—especially Nicolai Cikovsky, Jr., Helen Cooper, Patricia Junker, Frank Kelly, David Tatham, and John Wilmerding—had noted the presence of photography in his practice, but that none had devoted prolonged consideration to its importance. We are grateful for their work in setting the stage for this study. Also, we must acknowledge Philip C. Beam, a Bowdoin art historian, the former director of the Museum, and the individual primarily responsible for working with Homer's family to secure the personal archive in which these photographs resided. He used many of these images in *Winslow Homer at Prout's Neck* (1966), but spoke only in passing about Homer's interest in photography. We are indebted to Beam for preserving this archive and for amassing during his tenure such a rich collection of graphic works by the artist.

Over the recent past, Dana and I have sought to understand better this group of photographs and the role that photography played in Homer's artistic practice. As he did not acquire his first camera until the early 1880s—when he was in his mid-forties—we were curious about the medium's influence on his art prior to that time. What was his relationship to the photographers who—like him—figured scenes and persons associated with the Civil War, or to those photographers who—also like him—traveled to picture resort communities or wilderness destinations during the era of Reconstruction? We wanted to know whether Homer acquired a camera solely to record personal memories and travels, or whether, as an artist devoted to a faithful portrayal of the larger world, he saw this new visual technology as a tool that might aid his painting, drawing, and printmaking. Similarly, how did his experience with the camera compare with that of other artists of his era, a period during which the medium became more affordable and easier to use after the introduction of dry plate negatives and the Kodak camera? Given the different photographic portraits of the artist in the Museum's collection, we were also interested in exploring to what degree he used photography to shape his public identity. These were some of our initial questions regarding this group of photographs.

In many ways, this project is comparable to *Eakins and the Photograph* (1994), Susan Danly and Cheryl Leibold's study of photography's importance to Thomas Eakins's artistic practice. Though the two artists did not work together, they both acquired their first cameras in the early 1880s. Their art was also concerned with many of the same questions, and they both experimented with various mediums throughout their careers. Because of the large number of extant photographs by Eakins, it appears that the Philadelphia artist had a more prolonged and active interest in photography. Yet, while Homer's photographic output was much smaller, we came to appreciate that his engagement with photography and its influence was no less significant.

During Homer's two-year sojourn in England, the artist acquired two cameras, both of which are included in this exhibition. As Nicolai Cikovsky, Jr., and Frank Kelly argued in the National Gallery of Art's exhibition *Winslow Homer* (1995), Homer went to England in the spring of 1881 looking to forge a new direction for his art. Returning to the United States in the fall of 1882, he had changed much about his artistic style and his choice of subjects. While photography was not primarily responsible for this transformation, his interest in making his own photographs and in looking at the work of other photographers was part of a broader creative exploration. Settling at Prout's Neck, Maine, he continued to experiment, often creating compositions of the same subject in different mediums, a characteristic of his practice since his early years as an artist. At times, a work in one medium might serve as a study for a work in another medium. On other occasions, he created a similar composition in two or more different mediums. In part, he was motivated by the commercial potential of a range of work, though this movement between art forms also interested him as one who was long engaged in probing the way things look and the challenge of portraying them realistically. During the last three decades of his life, photography became increasingly a part of this investigation, both at Prout's Neck and during travels beyond Maine.

The relationship between photography, painting, and other artistic mediums has long interested scholars of American art. With Van Deren Coke's *The Painter and the Photograph* (1964) as an important early study of this exchange, scholars have continued to probe photography's intersection with the wider world of the fine arts. *Shared Intelligence: American Painting and the Photograph* (2011), edited by Barbara Buhler Lynes and Jonathan Weinberg, is an important collection of recent essays that explores this history from its beginnings in the mid-nineteenth century to today. While essayists mention Homer in this volume, his engagement with photography goes largely unaddressed. Much scholarly work has also focused on the effort to advance photography as a fine art medium, and this literature—especially concerning photographers in the late nineteenth and early twentieth centuries—has also shaped our inquiry.

Like most painters of the late nineteenth century, Homer never spoke directly about photography, nor did he ever exhibit such images in any formal manner. Yet, during his lifetime he owned at least three cameras. He also collected photographs by others and posed occasionally for his portrait both outdoors and in photographers' studios. As one attuned to appearances and constantly experimenting with how to represent them, Homer understood that photography as a new technology of sight had much to reveal. While he privileged his own vision, and saw painting as the most compelling means to figure the world, he grew to learn that photography—despite its limitations and problematic reputation in the world of the fine arts—was a medium that did not undermine, but instead complemented, his larger artistic interests.

In my essay, I look broadly at Homer's career as a whole, from the artist's beginnings as an illustrator in Boston through his time in New York City to his final years in Maine. My goal is to think anew about his artistic practice by examining his engagement with photography and the larger image economy during the latter half of the nineteenth century. Dana's essay takes a different approach, focusing specifically on his travels to the Bahamas, Cuba, and Florida during the 1880s. Yet, she is likewise concerned with the influence of a new visual culture that shaped Homer's response to these tropical locales. Together, the two essays aim to add a new chapter to an appreciation of Homer and his art, and to complicate his reputation as a painter. In addition to resetting our understanding of Homer's oeuvre, this publication also aspires to contribute to a broader study of American art by considering his work as an important precursor to the emergence of modernism in the United States. Homer was one of the most celebrated painters of the late nineteenth century, but, as this study hopes to demonstrate, his achievement owes a debt to new modes of vision that the medium of photography helped to create.

Frank H. Goodyear III
Co-Director, Bowdoin College
Museum of Art
Brunswick, Maine

ACKNOWLEDGMENTS

This project has benefited greatly from exchanges with scholars and students at Bowdoin College and beyond. In particular, we want to acknowledge Elizabeth Athens, Susan Danly, Linda Docherty, Kathleen Foster, Abigail Booth Gerdts, Eleanor Harvey, Mike Kolster, Rodney Laughton, Philip Von Stade, and John Wilmerding. Also, Catherine Cyr '17, a summer intern at the Museum in 2015, provided invaluable research assistance at a critical moment. Students enrolled in the spring 2016 art history course "Winslow Homer and American Art" pushed this project along through their probing questions and insightful analyses regarding Homer's art and legacy. A two-day symposium at Bowdoin in 2016, co-sponsored by the Department of Art History and the office of the Dean for Academic Affairs and entitled "Across the Divide: Intermediality and American Art," was especially enriching, and we are thankful for the presentations and conversations on that occasion with others who are exploring the historical exchange between different artistic mediums.

We are pleased to be able to travel this exhibition after its presentation in Brunswick to the Brandywine River Museum of Art in Chadds Ford, Pennsylvania. Our thanks to Thomas Padon, the James H. Duff Director, for his enthusiastic support of this project.

For assistance in the development of this catalogue, we are grateful to the editorial staff of Yale University Press. To Amy Canonico, Mary Mayer, Raychel Rapazza, and Kate Zanzucchi, as well as to freelance copyeditor Jane Friedman, proofreader Maddy Kloss, and indexer Cathy Dorsey, thank you for the care you have shown in guiding this volume to publication. Also, our appreciation to Laura Lindgren, who created the catalogue's design.

Closer to home, we thank numerous colleagues at the Bowdoin College Museum of Art, including John Eric Anderson, Caroline Baljon, Rebekah Beaulieu, Suzanne Bergeron, Anne Collins Goodyear, Michelle Henning, Jo Hluska, Joachim Homann, Laura Latman, Liza Nelson, Steve Perkins, José Ribas, Ellen Tani, and Honor Wilkinson. At Bowdoin College, our thanks to Michael Archibald, Allison Crosscup, Scott Meiklejohn, Ann Ostwald, Heidi Peterson, and Jennifer Scanlon. As always, we thank Dean for Academic Affairs Elizabeth McCormack and President Clayton Rose.

While nearly two-thirds of the works in the exhibition derive from the Museum's collection, twenty-five institutions and private collectors have generously lent works that have added complexity and nuance to this presentation. In particular, we want to acknowledge our colleagues at other institutions, including Judith Dolkart, Susan Faxon, and Alison Kemmerer, Addison Gallery of American Art; Anne Pasternak and Kimberly Orcutt, Brooklyn Museum; Sharon Corwin and Elizabeth Finch, Colby College Museum of Art; Jonathan Walz, The Columbus Museum; Caroline Baumann and Caitlin Condell, Cooper-Hewitt National Design Museum, Smithsonian Institution; Chris Brownawell and Michael Komanecky, Farnsworth Art Museum; Joanne Bloom, Fine Art Library, Harvard College Library; Tim Burgard, Fine Arts Museums of San Francisco; Martha Tedeschi and Ethan Lasser, Harvard Art Museums; David Little, Mead Art Museum, Amherst College; Jonathan Binstock, Memorial Art Gallery, University of Rochester; Stacy Cerullo, New Britain Museum of American Art; Lawrence Wheeler and John Coffey, North Carolina Museum of Art; Chris Kintzel, Peabody Art Collection, Maryland; Mark Bessire and Jessica May, Portland Museum of Art; Janie Cohen and Andrea Rosen, Robert Hull Fleming Museum, University of Vermont; Jessica Nicoll and Linda Muehlig, Smith College Museum of Art; Stephanie Stebich and Eleanor Harvey, Smithsonian American Art Museum; Olivier Meslay, Sterling and Francine Clark Art Institute; Franz Jantzen and Maya Foo, Supreme Court of the United States; Elizabeth Glassman and Peter Brownlee, Terra Foundation for the Arts; Thomas Loughman and Linda Roth, Wadsworth Atheneum; Brad and Ann Willauer; Matthias Waschek and Elizabeth Athens, Worcester Art Museum; and Jock Reynolds and Pamela Franks, Yale University Art Gallery.

Financial support from many individuals, foundations, and Museum of Art endowments have made possible this exhibition and its catalogue. Major support is provided by the Mr. and Mrs. Raymond J. Horowitz Foundation for the Arts, the Elizabeth B. G. Hamlin Fund, the Stevens L. Frost Endowment Fund, the Becker Fund for the Bowdoin College Museum of Art, Peter J. Grua '76 and Mary G. O'Connell '76, the Devonwood Foundation, Robert Freson, and the Wyeth Foundation for American Art. Additional support has been provided by the Morton-Kelly Charitable Trust, Selina Little, Charles and Elizabeth Cabot Lyman, Judy Glickman Lauder, Steven P. Marrow '83 and Dianne A. Pappas P'21, Lee Sprague, Lile R. and John A. Gibbons, Jr. '64, the Karl R. Philbrick Art Museum Fund, Betsy Evans Hunt, the Roy A. Hunt Foundation, and Patricia Brown. At the Brandywine River Museum of Art, the presenting sponsor is the Robert J. Kleberg, Jr. and Helen C. Kleberg Foundation.

LENDERS TO THE EXHIBITION

Addison Gallery of American Art
Brooklyn Museum
Colby College Museum of Art
The Columbus Museum
Cooper-Hewitt National Design Museum, Smithsonian Institution
Farnsworth Art Museum
Fine Art Library, Harvard College Library
Fine Arts Museums of San Francisco
Harvard Art Museums
Mead Art Museum, Amherst College
Memorial Art Gallery, University of Rochester
New Britain Museum of American Art
North Carolina Museum of Art
Peabody Art Collection, Maryland
Portland Museum of Art
Robert Hull Fleming Museum, University of Vermont
Smith College Museum of Art
Smithsonian American Art Museum
Sterling and Francine Clark Art Institute
Supreme Court of the United States
Terra Foundation for the Arts
Wadsworth Atheneum
Brad and Ann Willauer
Worcester Art Museum
Yale University Art Gallery

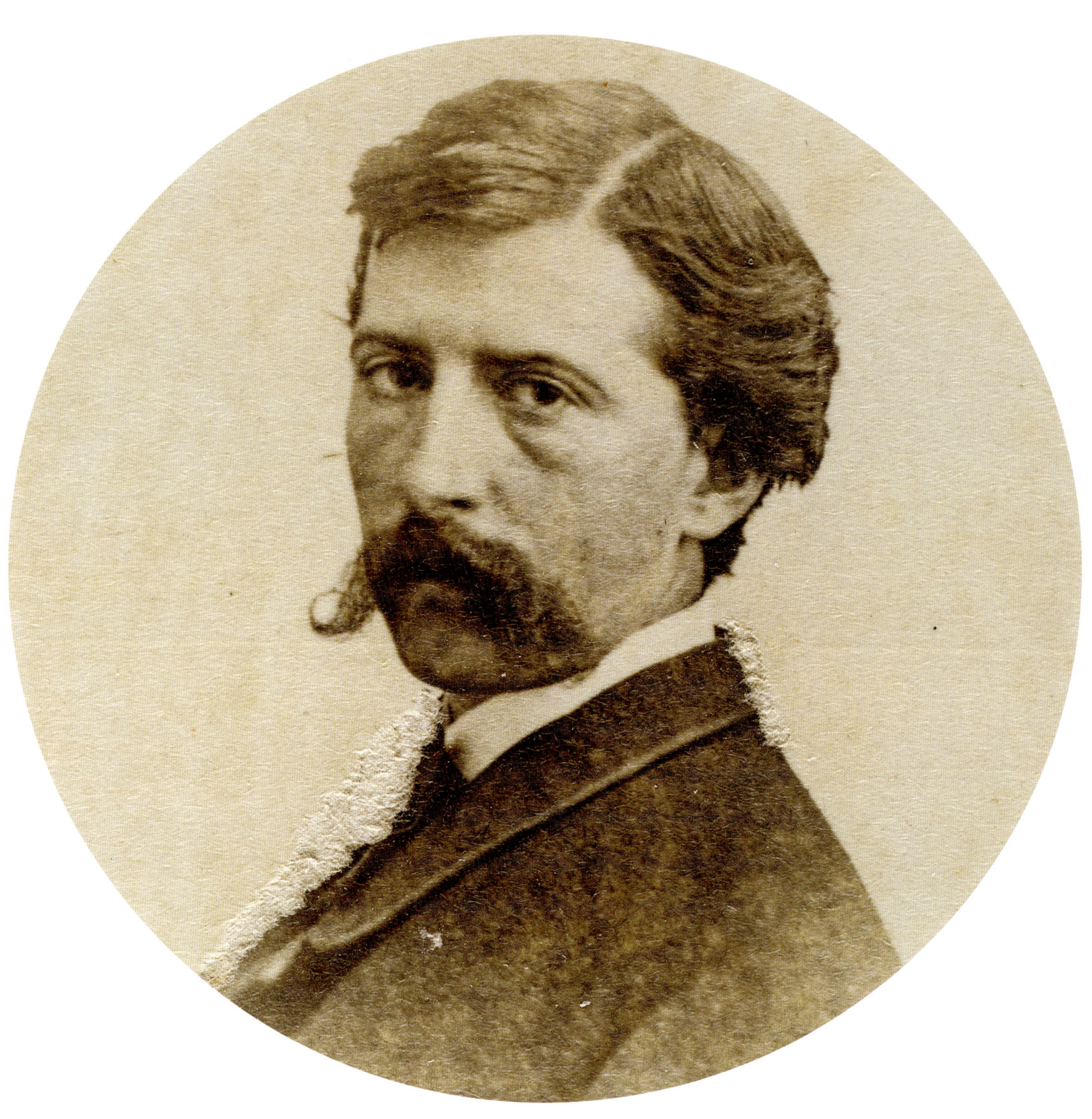

A Good Thing When He Sees It

Winslow Homer, Photography, and the Art of Painting

FRANK H. GOODYEAR III

There it is! You simply have to get it right.

—Winslow Homer to John Beatty, September 1903

Winslow Homer was a painter. He thought of himself as a painter and directed his greatest efforts toward this art form. Whether with oils or watercolors, he sought to push his painting to address large themes, and did so in a vocabulary that broke from many American traditions. As an artist devoted to the world as it is, he saw painting as an effort not only to record a particular place and time, but also to visualize and dramatize broader social and philosophical questions that were at once timeless and timely. His practice was characterized by experimentation and a keen awareness of contemporary society, and be it working in the studio or outdoors, he approached painting with a respect for the past, but, equally important, an openness to new creative possibilities. Fiercely independent, though hardly an artistic or social recluse, he tended to eschew direct association with other artists of the day as well as artistic schools, preferring instead to explore the art of painting on his own terms.

Homer's reputation as a painter was born during his lifetime and has continued mostly intact since his death in 1910.[1] While written profiles extolling his talents preceded his death, Kenyon Cox's assessment in *Scribner's Magazine* in 1914 did much to solidify the different ways in which Homer's art has been understood over the past century. An artist himself, though one who was indebted to traditional academic precedents and who veered toward idealized renderings of classical subjects, Cox identified Homer as a painter committed to portraying faithfully the subject before him: "He is not thinking of an audience at all, but only of the thing he has seen and of his effort to render it truthfully. He places himself in direct competition with nature, and if his work seems harsh or violent it has become so in the effort to match nature's strength with his own." Cox's description of Homer's dedication to the pursuit of the truth and to "the power and the grandeur of the elemental forces of nature" included an anecdote about his "portable painting house," a three-sided structure that permitted Homer to paint or draw outdoors at the water's edge in any season and during periods of extreme weather. This, among other details, exemplified

FIG. 1. Thomas Gray and Thomas Faris, *Winslow Homer in Boston*, 1863. Albumen silver print, 4 × 2 7/16 in. (10.2 × 6.2 cm), sheet. Bowdoin College Museum of Art, Brunswick. Gift of the Homer Family. [Homer Memorabilia 1]

the purity of his practice. "A flaming realist—a burning devotee of the actual," Homer was a unique talent, according to Cox, for "painting aspects of nature which another, if he had seen them, would consider unpaintable."[2]

Cox's tribute laid the foundation for subsequent critical appraisals of Homer and his art. While Cox evinced little interest in photography during his career, his profile casts Homer's artistic gift in the same language that one might use to characterize photographic vision. Inside his "portable painting house," looking out at the world, Homer is described as intently focused on the subject before him, blinkered from any distraction outside the frame. His eye is a polished lens that records accurately the scene before him. Cox's description of Homer's devotion to the actual posits him as a type of camera. Though effusive in his praise of Homer's achievements as an artist, Cox was also not hesitant to list some of Homer's shortcomings, among them being "a poor technician, an unequal colorist, [and] a powerful but untrained draughtsman." Furthermore, regarding some of the artist's late marine paintings, Cox claimed dismissively that they are "almost as effective in a good photograph as in the original."[3]

While celebrating Homer as an artist on the whole, Cox was troubled by the painter's commitment to realism, wary of an aesthetic that portrays the world in such an unmediated fashion. Author Henry James had expressed a similar concern about Homer forty years earlier, characterizing the artist's dedication to "perfect realism" as both a strength and a weakness. In James's view, Homer "cares not a jot for such fantastic hairsplitting as the distinction between beauty and ugliness. He is a genuine painter; that is, to see, and to reproduce what he sees, is his only care; to think, to imagine, to select, to refine, to compose, to drop into any of the intellectual tricks with which other people sometimes try to eke out the dull pictorial vision—all of this Mr. Homer triumphantly avoids. He not only has no imagination, but he contrives to elevate this rather blighting negative into a blooming and honorable positive . . . but there is nevertheless something one likes about him."[4] Artists—and writers—grappled intensely with the implications of this turn toward realism in nineteenth-century America. Photography's introduction in 1839 complicated and invigorated this debate and made the question of a painting's faithfulness to its subject a central concern. Some artists avoided photography, regarding it as offering few insights and considering it a far inferior medium for representing a subject. Others, however, were at least curious about it, recognizing that new visual technologies such as photography might complement and widen one's practice.[5] Homer wished to "get it right," as he explained to his friend John Beatty in 1903, and throughout an artistic career that spanned five decades, his work intersected frequently with this new medium.[6]

Whereas Cox and James might have one believe that his paintings were composed and completed predominantly *en plein air*, they were not the result of a brief, intimate outdoor encounter, but rather the product of often intense study, labor, and revision over the course of many weeks and sometimes years. Their complaints also fail to fully recognize the degree to which Homer's paintings were constructed and, more generally, how "perfect realism" was in fact a fiction in his art. A study of his oeuvre reveals the composite nature of many of his paintings. As devoted as he was to observation, Homer often created compositions that brought together disparate elements from other sources into a new, unified whole. This idea of cutting and pasting goes back at least as far as the Renaissance, yet in Homer's art the combination suggests both something more modern and something in part indebted to new modes of seeing. Photography and the larger image economy of the second half of the nineteenth century helped to make possible this new vision, and encouraged Homer to move away from an exclusively direct transcription of a subject in favor of a more hybrid practice and a lifetime fascination with optical experience. More forward-looking than backward, his work anticipated certain new directions explored by a subsequent generation of modernist artists, such as abstraction, montage, and seriality.

Homer came of age at a moment that witnessed a visual culture revolution. The advent of photography, lithography, and other forms of printmaking and advertising inundated the public with images—images largely considered cheap by fine artists.[7] This development resulted in giving jobs to many aspiring artists, including Homer, and compelling painters to reconcile their role and status with a rapidly changing art world. Homer's art from its beginning was shaped by photography and the new ways of seeing that it engendered. Of course, as a painter of this period interested in photography, Homer was not alone. From the medium's earliest days, others shared a similar fascination. In the nineteenth century, Albert Bierstadt, Frederic Church, Thomas Eakins, Thomas Moran, and William James Stillman, among others, understood that photography could aid their artistic practice. Yet, whereas many saw it as a means to render the details of a subject faithfully, few explored as did Homer the visual effects that the medium introduced or used its lessons to think anew about the art of painting. Photography was hardly the sole source of his accomplishments as an artist. Its presence, however, was always nearby and deeply felt. Having received only a limited academic art education, Homer found instruction in the image-rich world that surrounded him and used those experiences to craft a wholly independent artistic career.[8]

"Not a soldier, but a camp follower & artist," 1854 to 1866

Homer's earliest lessons as an artist were from his mother, Henrietta Benson Homer, a self-taught watercolorist whose observations of intimate details in nature foreground the importance of looking closely and seeing clearly. Painted directly from nature, these watercolors depict botanical specimens, birds, moths, and butterflies (fig. 2). Rarely do they include a wider scene or any type of imaginative flight of fancy. This commitment to portraying a subject as it appears was fundamental to her work as an artist. It also became a hallmark of her son's art. For a time after her death in 1884, he hung in his studio a display of her watercolors, a testament to a son's affection and the importance of her work.[9] Yet, when the aspiring artist began his professional career in the mid-1850s, as an apprentice designer of sheet-music covers and other paper products for the Boston lithographer John H. Bufford, he learned that the expanding image economy forced many commercial artists to create designs rapidly and in conjunction with other demands. Such work often left little space for the artist's imagination, but instead functioned

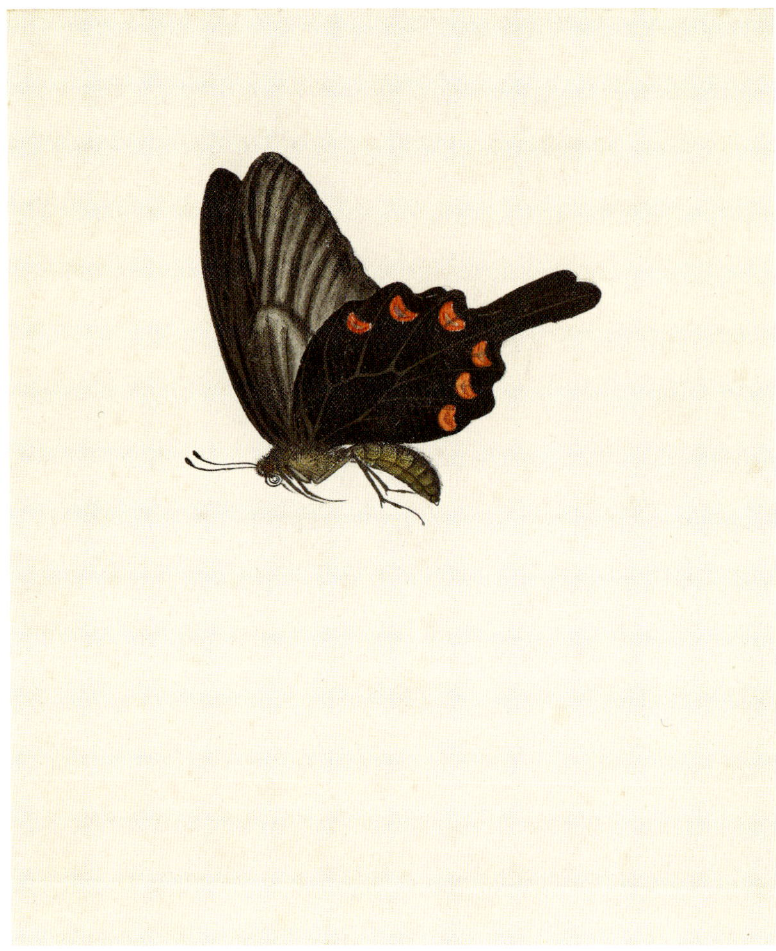

FIG. 2. Henrietta Benson Homer, *Untitled (Moth Study)*, n.d. Watercolor, gouache, and graphite, 7 3/16 × 6 in. (18.3 × 15.2 cm). Bowdoin College Museum of Art, Brunswick. Gift of the Homer Family. [1964.69.186.4]

merely as a secondary decorative ornament. The source materials for these prints varied widely, and copying was common. Unlike those artists who were academically trained by drawing from life or from plaster casts, Homer refined his drawing skills by fulfilling specific assignments, often by copying photographs by others. This first job seems to have been less than satisfying. As one critic concluded in 1878, "his sojourn there was a treadmill existence. Two years at the grindstone unfitted him for further bondage; and, since the day he left it, he has called no man master."[10] Though Homer was glad to throw off these shackles and hoped to begin a painting career, he was never far from this same marketplace for images.

Leaving Bufford's shop in 1857, Homer found work as a freelance illustrator in Boston and later in New York. While the range of his work during the four years before the Civil War's outbreak expanded significantly, the demand for images from illustrated newspapers such as *Ballou's Pictorial* and *Harper's Weekly* was similar. Deadlines were tight, editors often chose the subjects, and a news article or work of fiction frequently accompanied the image. In addition, much attention was paid to an engraving's legibility and credibility. Images helped sell papers, and the best images were easy to comprehend and conveyed a certain verisimilitude. Given these criteria, editors were increasingly interested in the journalistic possibilities of photography, a medium that captured detail well and that seemed to promise an objective rendering of its subject. Though the technology that enabled photomechanical reproduction had not yet been introduced, periodicals began using photographs as the source material for engravers. By crediting the photographer in the image's caption, the newspaper could assert its integrity.

Working freelance, Homer was selling upwards of two dozen images a year during this period. With the threat of war on the horizon and a continued rivalry with other New York–based newspapers and magazines, the editors at *Harper's* turned to Homer often for up-to-date images to accompany news stories. John Beatty recollected that "the Harpers were always very kind, taking all the drawings he made, and paying him at the rate of one hundred dollars for a full-page drawing."[11] As a draftsman, he developed an aptitude for working in black and white as well as an understanding of the relationship between dark and light values, skills that would prove valuable throughout his career. Desirous of embarking on a painting career, Homer took classes in the fall of 1859 at the National Academy of Design, though these sessions lasted only a few months. During this same period, his brother Charles also presented him with *Chevreul on Colours*, an 1859 English translation of Michel-Eugène Chevreul's *De la loi du contraste simultané des couleurs et de l'assortiment des objets colorés*, a volume that would greatly influence his thinking about painting, and that he later referred to as his "Bible."[12] In addition, he began to consider more intensive study in Europe, though he lacked the resources at this time to underwrite such travel. Homer wished to become a painter; however, as commissions from *Harper's* were often the sole source of his income, he rarely hesitated to take on new editorial assignments.

While many of his engravings for *Harper's* derived from original preparatory sketches, he did utilize photographs as a source material for some of this work. Most often, these images were portraits of prominent politicians and other public figures to whom he did not have access, but whose likeness the newspaper was eager to publish. Beginning in 1860, the celebrated photographic studio run by Mathew Brady became a frequent source for Homer. Located only five blocks south of his new studio on Washington Square, Brady's gallery on Broadway was a cornucopia of available images. Although there were dozens of photographers in New York at the time, many of whom sold portraits of notable individuals, Brady was especially successful at recruiting them to his door. A recognized leader in his field, he worked hard to market his images in different sizes and formats and to place them in the pages of the illustrated newspapers.[13] Whether Brady approached the editors at *Harper's* or Homer sought out Brady on his own, the aspiring painter completed more than a dozen engravings based on Brady's photographic portraits.

Homer's portrait of Abraham Lincoln exemplifies this work (plate 2). Published on the cover of the November 10, 1860, issue of *Harper's*, with a credit to Brady, the image was intended to celebrate the election of the new president only four days earlier. While the editors at *Harper's* had championed Lincoln's candidacy and likely asked Homer to prepare his engraving in advance of the vote, the portrait was done with a tight deadline in mind. Homer was not the first graphic artist to identify and use Brady's standing portrait of Lincoln (fig. 3). Originally taken eight months prior on the occasion of a major campaign speech at New York's Cooper Union, the photograph had been copied previously by other printmakers to promote his election. Homer's rendition brings forward much of what others had come to like about this image. In particular, it shows Lincoln as a serious gentleman, someone who seemed presidential in his bearing and not a

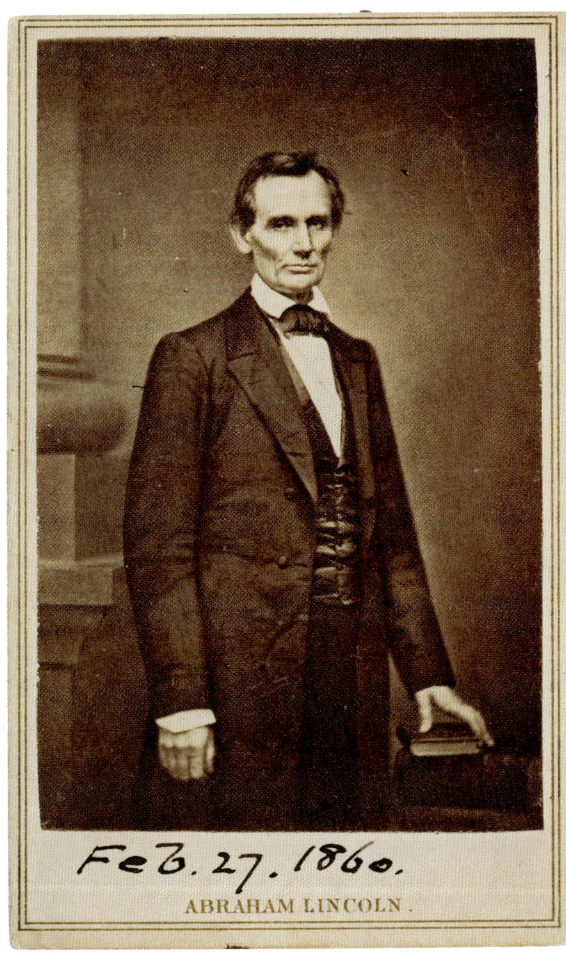

FIG. 3. Mathew Brady Studio, *Abraham Lincoln*, February 27, 1860. Albumen silver print, $3\frac{15}{16} \times 2\frac{3}{8}$ in. (10 × 6 cm). Courtesy of Special Collections, Fine Arts Library, Harvard University. [120.1976.10873]

backwoods lawyer from the Midwest frontier. Much of Homer's copy follows closely the details of Brady's portrait, and the resulting flatness of the print reflects his study of the photograph. Homer did, however, change the image not insignificantly. In addition to reducing the size of his subject's ears and lessening the shrunken quality of his cheeks, the artist introduced an imaginary backdrop not present in Brady's portrait. As a result, Lincoln is made to appear as though he is standing not far from an outdoor balcony. A branch of ivy crawls up and over the balcony, while a tasseled curtain frames the subject. Homer also introduced an inkwell to the table, on which previously only two books had resided. These changes to the photograph reflect a desire to improve the image by downplaying some of Lincoln's unique physical characteristics, accentuating certain qualities such as his writing, and situating him in a more believable setting rather than before a nondescript photographic backdrop.

Looking closely at a subject, adding and deleting details, revising elements, and gathering the parts into a larger whole were characteristics of Homer's graphic practice. This philosophy would also later inform his approach to painting. Artists have long adopted such strategies, yet during a period when new printing and photographic technologies were transforming the image economy, Homer forged a practice that borrowed as much from them as from more traditional artistic sources. This interest reveals itself early and often. In a series of prints for *Harper's* about four of the Southern states that had chosen to secede from the Union, Homer assembled a composite image that brought together within a single frame bust-length portraits of various seceding congressional delegations. For this commission, since these individuals were not available to the artist, he relied upon whatever images—photographs or prints—he could locate handily. In realizing the engraving of the two senators and five con-

FIG. 4. Attributed to Alexander Gardner, *The Inauguration of Abraham Lincoln*, March 4, 1861. Salt print, $10\frac{1}{8} \times 12\frac{3}{8}$ in. (26 × 31 cm). Bowdoin College Museum of Art, Brunswick. Museum Purchase, Lloyd O. and Marjorie Strong Coulter Fund. [2016.30]

gressmen in *The Seceding Mississippi Delegation in Congress*, for example, he was able to secure all of their likenesses from Brady (plate 3). As with Lincoln's portrait published three months earlier, he reconfigured Brady's work, trimming each portrait to a standard format and then arranging the likenesses together on a single sheet. There is nothing naturalistic about the grouping. With the two senators Jefferson Davis and Albert Brown positioned at the top and center, respectively, the composite image is meant simply to picture these individuals within the limited vertical space available in *Harper's*. Though perhaps easily dismissed as an unimaginative copy, this print and others demanded creative effort and imparted important lessons about how to approach graphic challenges. Relying at times upon borrowed images, Homer developed an artistic practice that was less conventional and more interconnected with the larger visual culture than that of many of his contemporaries.

Another example for which he likely relied upon photography to fulfill an editorial commission was the double-page engraving of Lincoln's inauguration (plate 4).[14] On assignment for *Harper's*, Homer traveled to Washington with the nation on the brink of war to create a series of views. Three photographers also showed up on this occasion, including

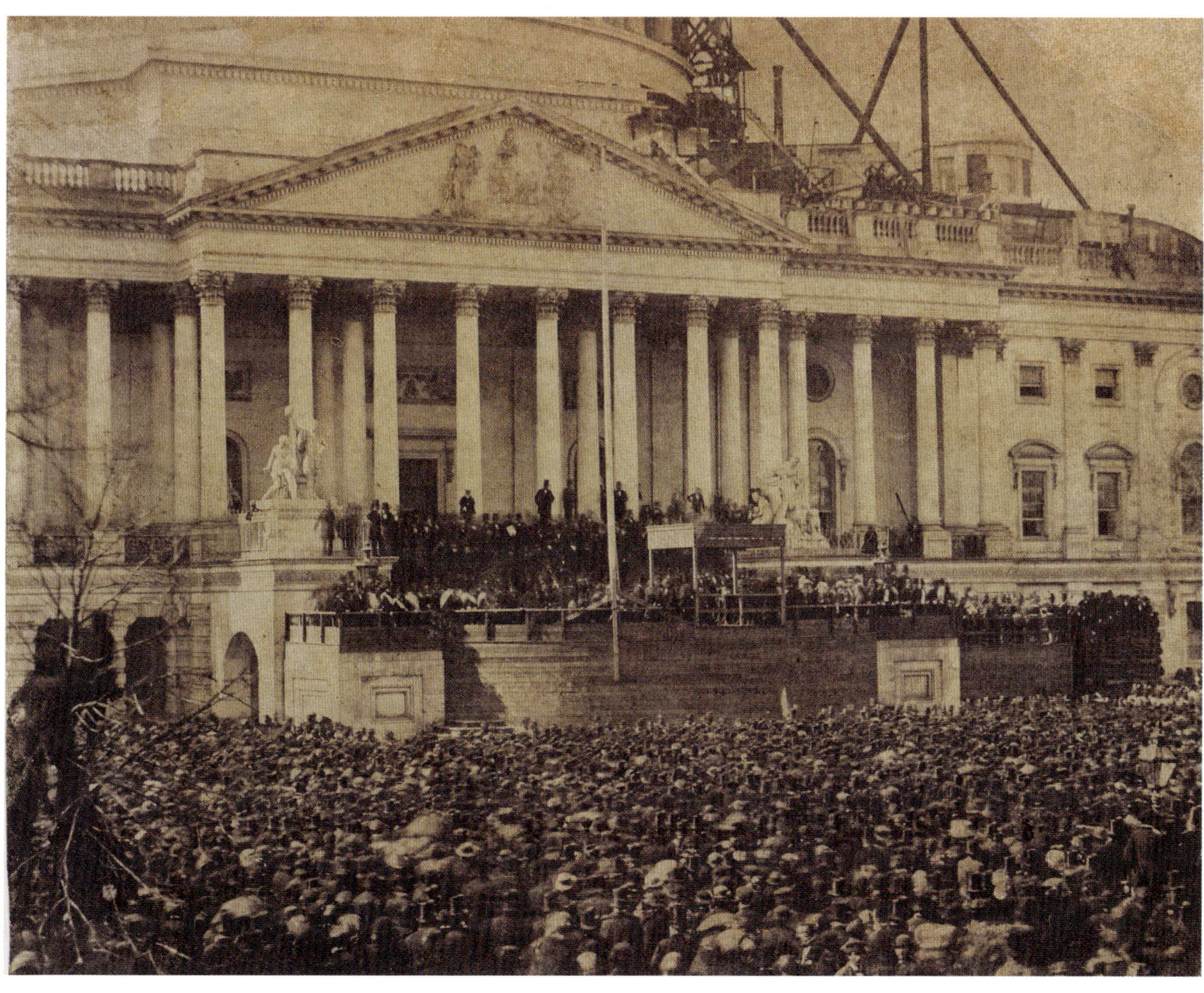

Alexander Gardner, Brady's Washington studio chief. Homer had never before been to the nation's capital, and likely had only an inkling of how he might approach this project. In the lead-up to the ceremony, a wooden platform was constructed about fifty yards from the front of the speaker's podium. Believed to have been built in order to realize a panoramic, elevated photograph of the proceedings, this structure became the perch for one of the photographers—likely Gardner. Working for *Frank Leslie's Illustrated Newspaper*—a rival of *Harper's*—this photographer could not overlook preparations such as where to position himself, especially given the cumbersome equipment and sensitive chemistry he carried and the large crowds that were expected. The resulting photograph became the source for an engraving that *Leslie's* published twelve days later (fig. 4).[15]

Homer's view depicts the same event—except that it positions the viewer looking at the scene from the right side of the crowd rather than the left, as represented in the photograph. Published on the same day as the *Leslie's* engraving, Homer's print of Lincoln's swearing-in was an ambitious undertaking; undoubtedly the drawing required at least several hours to complete, though likely many more. Given the relative brevity of the ceremony, he could not have finished it "on the spot," as the caption in *Harper's* declares. Instead, it was completed later and probably with the assistance of the same photograph now attributed to Gardner. Note the compositional resemblance between the two images. Both are depicted from a comparable elevated view, both situate the viewer at a similar distance from the new president, and both picture the Capitol approximately forty-five degrees off-center. Details in the Capitol's architecture and the temporary platform erected on its steps are likewise similar, and the gathered crowd is figured with an equal density. Homer added his own personal embellishments, among them a clearly visible American flag at left and an assortment of individualized portraits of onlookers in the print's foreground. With its unique ability to figure the scene in a near instant, the photograph provided him with the larger compositional structure for his print and with noteworthy details that one visit to the Capitol would not have permitted him to capture.

No records indicate whether Homer intersected with the three photographers at the Capitol that day. As an artist for *Harper's*, he was well versed in the use of photographic images as source materials for published engravings, and likely subscribed to the notion that this type of borrowing improved the quality of his final drawing. In this case, he would not have been able to realize an accurate study of Lincoln's inauguration without photography. After the medium's introduction, images across the artistic spectrum changed, as photography saw and represented sights that had not previously been rendered in still images. Artists in nineteenth-century America responded in different ways to photography. Whether or not they employed it in their work, they were compelled at least to consider its implications. Unlike others, Homer did not take up photography—at least not at this point in his career. Wishing to become a painter, he understood it instead as a means to assist his larger artistic practice.

Five weeks after this moment in Washington, the Civil War erupted with the Confederate assault on Fort Sumter in South Carolina. Over the next three years, Homer

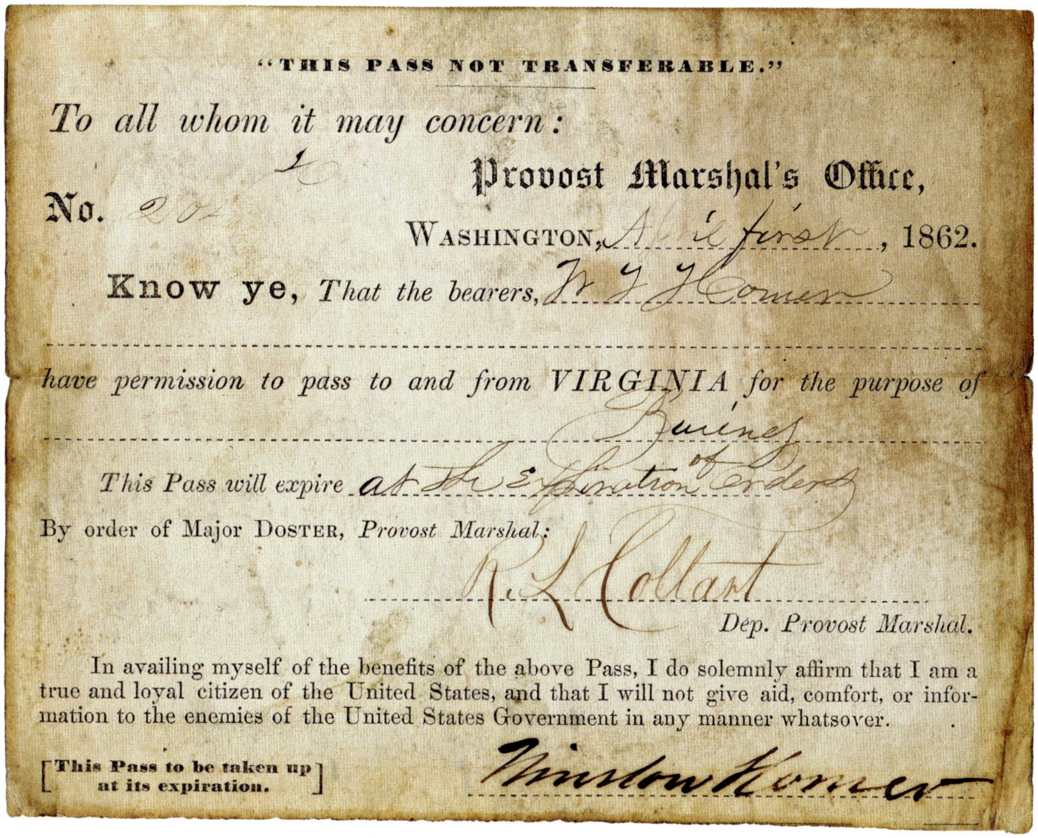

"THIS PASS NOT TRANSFERABLE."

To all whom it may concern:

Provost Marshal's Office,

No.

WASHINGTON, , 1862.

Know ye, *That the bearers,*

have permission to pass to and from VIRGINIA for the purpose of

This Pass will expire

By order of Major DOSTER, *Provost Marshal:*

Dep. Provost Marshal.

In availing myself of the benefits of the above Pass, I do solemnly affirm that I am a true and loyal citizen of the United States, and that I will not give aid, comfort, or information to the enemies of the United States Government in any manner whatsover.

[This Pass to be taken up at its expiration.]

FIG. 5. Army pass issued to Winslow Homer, April 1, 1862. Paper document, $4\frac{1}{2} \times 5\frac{5}{8}$ in. (11.4 × 14.3 cm). Bowdoin College Museum of Art, Brunswick. Gift of the Homer Family. [1964.69.152]

traveled from New York to Virginia at least three times to cover the conflict.[16] *Harper's* circulation increased during this period, and its editors were eager for up-to-date coverage from the front. Homer was an able draftsman by this time, and his training had taught him how to work quickly and create a drawing that was accessible to readers. He was joined in this effort by other artist-correspondents and also an equal number of photographers. Each was asked to register their request to work among the military and, if granted, was issued a pass from the Provost Marshal's Office (fig. 5). While some traveled unaccompanied by other image makers, many ventured forth with fellow artists or connected with them after arriving at the front. A respectful camaraderie—rather than a pitched rivalry—seems to have developed between artists and photographers.

In the spring of 1862, the Union launched a major military offensive—the Peninsula Campaign—into the Virginia tidewater region. Wanting to move on and potentially capture the Confederate capital at Richmond, Lincoln's forces looked to end the war with a large and concentrated assault. Homer had been in Virginia the previous fall to make sketches, and desired to return that spring. Embarking in early April from Alexandria, alongside a large Union force that included his cousin

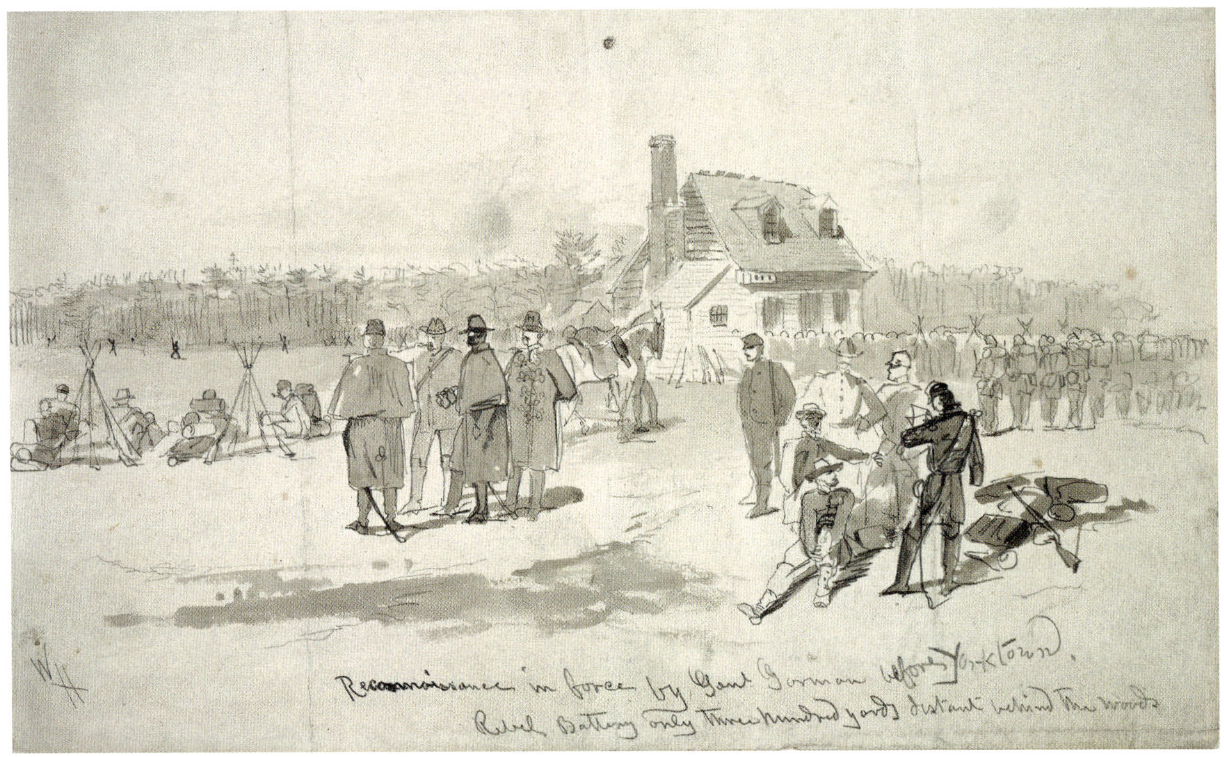

FIG. 6. Winslow Homer, *Reconnaissance in Force by General Gorman before Yorktown*, 1862. Graphite with brush and gray wash on cream wove paper, 8¼ × 13¼ in. (21 × 33.7 cm). Museum of Fine Arts, Boston. Gift of Maxim Karolik for the M. and M. Karolik Collection of American Watercolors and Drawings, 1800–1875. [50.3915]

Lieutenant Colonel Francis Channing Barlow, he traveled down the Potomac River into the Chesapeake before disembarking at Fort Monroe in Hampton. Shortly thereafter, fighting at Lee's Mill broke out, the result of which settled little and initiated a monthlong siege of the nearby town of Yorktown. Present much of this time, Homer endured periods with little food and witnessed considerable death and disease. He also created a number of drawings—works that focused more on individual soldiers, camp life, and troop movements than on actual battles.

Homer was hardly the only Northern artist or photographer around Yorktown then. Though the actual number is hard to confirm, it is known that at least several ventured into Virginia and other points to the south that spring. They include the prolific *Harper's* illustrator Alfred Waud, who witnessed the siege and likely crossed paths with Homer.[17] Both men contributed drawings to the engraving *Our Army before Yorktown, Virginia*, published in *Harper's* on May 3, 1862, the same day that Confederate forces escaped from the area largely unbowed (plate 5). Homer's *Reconnaissance in Force by General Gorman before Yorktown* is the source for the scene in the upper right section, and is one of seven small vignettes in this double-page engraving (fig. 6). In the graphite and watercolor drawing, he shows officers and enlisted men stopped temporarily outside a farmhouse to discuss strategy, noting in his written caption that a "rebel battery [was] only three hundred yards distant behind the woods." Brought together in a single composite print, this and six other scenes provide an overview of the Union Army's engagement at Yorktown, with an emphasis on the experience of the soldiers themselves. However, in both Homer's and Waud's work, no individual is singled out, nor do the scenes convey any larger psychological drama. Danger and heroism are referenced, though the effect is rather muted. *Our Army before Yorktown, Virginia* shares much with the descriptive reportage that accompanied it, which was rather matter-of-fact and touched little on the tension and anguish felt by many during the campaign. Though exceptions abound, Homer's graphic work during the war was more anecdotal—and less circumspect—in nature.[18]

Mathew Brady was similarly interested in realizing photographic views from the front lines, which he hoped to market to newspapers and the public alike. From Brady's Washington studio, Gardner that same spring sent into the field several colleagues, including John Wood and James Gibson, with express instructions

FIG. 7. John Wood and James Gibson, *Battery No. 1, near Yorktown, Virginia*, 1862. Albumen silver print, 7 × 9 1/8 in. (17.8 × 23.2 cm). Bowdoin College Museum of Art, Brunswick. Gift of the Lee Gallery, Inc. [2015.46]

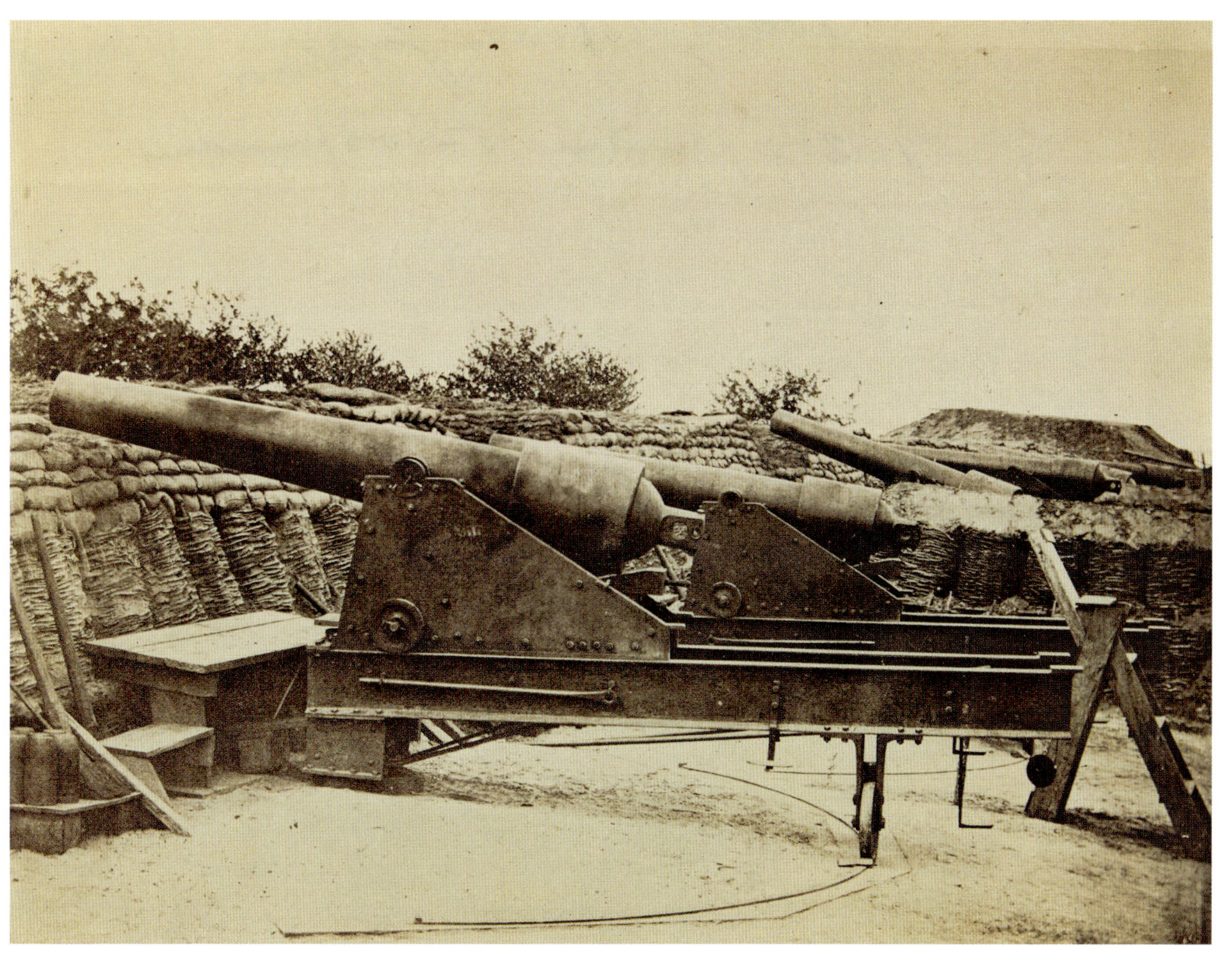

to document the Peninsula Campaign. They returned with several dozen photographs, most notably a series of views that picture the heavy artillery batteries that General George McClellan, the commander of the Union Army, had ordered constructed not far from Yorktown. Gardner thought highly enough of these pictures that he later included three of them in *Gardner's Photographic Sketch Book of the War* (1866). Like other images in this photographically illustrated history of the conflict, Wood and Gibson's *Battery No. 1, near Yorktown, Virginia*—another co-authored image—conveys photography's ability to transport the viewer behind the lines and peer directly into the scene of the conflict, and in this case, the weapons of modern warfare (fig. 7). Though soldiers appear in other views, this photograph presents a head-on visual encounter with the massive armaments recently introduced by the Union Army. It provides little context and no obvious human drama, though given the size and number of the guns, it evokes a devastating and awe-inspiring feeling. In Gardner's written description of the photograph, he emphasizes the unrivaled power of these guns, claiming that "experienced officers expressed the opinion that with this battery alone, the enemy could have been driven from their position in Yorktown."[19] No records exist that confirm whether Homer encountered Wood and Gibson there; however, as photographs by Gardner and his colleagues served as the source for engravings that began to appear shortly thereafter in *Harper's* and other periodicals, it is safe to say that Homer learned about this work at least by the time of its publication.

It was during the period immediately following Homer's return from the front that he started to paint in earnest. Though he would continue his steady supply of drawings to *Harper's* and others for the foreseeable future, he made a commitment to begin slowly moving beyond this trade. By contrast, magazine illustrators such as Theodore Davis, Edwin Forbes, and Waud continued to focus their efforts on producing sketches from the front lines. Homer's first painting, *Sharpshooter*, grew out of his recent experience at Yorktown (plate 6). Representing a Union sharpshooter perched in a tree with his eyes focused down the barrel of a rifle, it is a marked departure from most of his Yorktown prints. Rather than depicting a group in camp or on a traditional battlefield, Homer highlights a single soldier, and instead of contextualizing the scene in a wide landscape, he eliminates the ground altogether, directs the viewer's gaze upward at the figure seated above, and provides little background beyond the branches of the tree. In a letter to a friend more than forty years later, Homer recalled his handling of a rifle owned by a sharpshooter from Michigan, the experience he claimed inspired this painting: "I looked

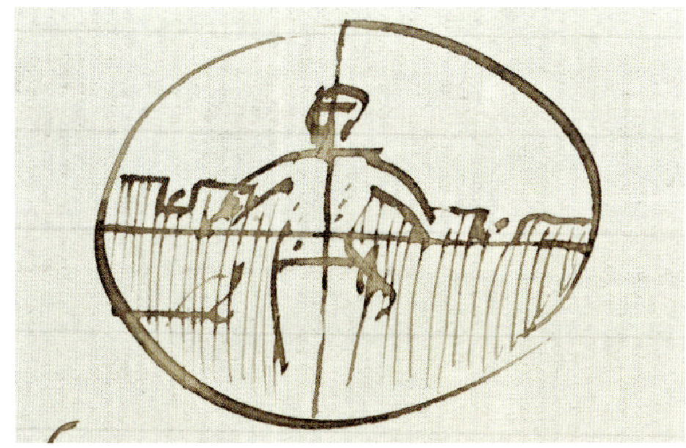

FIG. 8. Winslow Homer, Sketch in a letter to George G. Briggs, February 19, 1896. Paper document, $8^{5}/_{16} \times 5^{15}/_{16}$ in. (21 × 15 cm). Winslow Homer Collection, 1863–1945, Archives of American Art, Smithsonian Institution, Washington, D.C.

through one of their rifles once when they were in a peach orchard in front of Yorktown in April 1862. This is what I saw. I was not a soldier, but a camp follower & artist, the above impression struck me as being as near murder as anything I ever could think of in connection with the army & I always had a horror of that branch of the service."[20] Above the line "This is what I saw," he drew within the text of the letter a sketch of a targeted soldier within the crosshairs of a sharpshooter's telescopic sight (fig. 8).

Homer's emphasis on the gun as a killing machine bears similarities to Wood and Gibson's focus on the large cannons. Both Homer's painting and Wood and Gibson's photograph are close-up accounts of modern warfare. Unlike his and Waud's composite print from Yorktown, *Sharpshooter* is a study of a psychologically rich human drama. It achieves its power by employing techniques for which photography was particularly known: namely, a directed gaze, tight cropping, and nuanced details. For Homer, painting had the potential to convey sentiments that went beyond graphic reportage. With *Sharpshooter*, he rejected the sweeping battlefield panoramas that typified conventional representations of war, choosing instead to focus on a single soldier employing the most lethal hand-held weapon then available. Whereas most of his subject is rendered in rich, colorful detail, Homer chose to downplay the soldier's individuality by rendering his face largely featureless. As its title suggests, the painting is less a narrative about a specific soldier and more a meditation on the act of aiming a long rifle in order to kill one's enemy. It is about the cold precision and unflinching focus required to succeed—and survive—in a new age of warfare. Of note, in the wood engraving for *Harper's* created after this painting, the soldier's face is depicted in greater detail, a change that shifts the composition's focus toward the type of eyewitness reportage that *Harper's* sought.

Sharpshooter is a painting about vision and, in this case, sight that has been focused by staring intently down the barrel of a gun. Dramas that center on the act of looking and the exchange of gazes among figures emerged at this time as important subjects for Homer. In particular, he frequently portrayed structures and instruments that were used to magnify or clarify sight. Long-barreled rifles, lookout stations, and telescopes serve as noteworthy elements in several paintings and prints inspired by the war. In his engraving of the same year *The Approach of the British Pirate "Alabama"* (plate 7), for example, a ship's captain looks out through a spyglass at a distant enemy ship in a manner not unlike the soldier's pose in *Sharpshooter*. A group of women, including one with an infant child in her arms, crowd around him, awaiting information about what the captain sees. In this and other works, the act of looking is as fraught with tension as any physical encounter.

Homer also found individuals who were the object of someone else's gaze a rewarding subject. Though painted a year after *Sharpshooter* and depicting an episode believed to be unrelated to the Peninsula Campaign, *Defiance* can be understood as a companion to his painting of the Union sharpshooter perched in a tree (plate 8).[21] In this work he has flipped the perspective, choosing instead to center his composition on a reckless Confederate soldier who stands atop an earthen bulwark inviting a shot from across the line. It is a portrait of misplaced courage, and the exploding fire of two Union guns—represented as two small white dots amid a dark background at left—indicate that the man is indeed the target of distant sharpshooters. Like the subject in *Sharpshooter*, the man's face in *Defiance* is largely nondescript; similarly, the painting's antagonist is not entirely visible. The drama of these two works derives from the act of looking. Less interested in recording a specific individual or battle scene than in exploring the psychological tensions that front-line soldiers confronted, Homer structured these compositions around what it meant to be the shooter and the target in a period that witnessed the emergence of more advanced weaponry and new warfare tactics.

Like telescopic sights and spyglasses, the medium of photography was an instrument that altered the manner in which one saw and apprehended the wider world. By capturing a moment in time, it served as an aide-mémoire that provided a believable, though only approximate, representation of a chosen subject. While it could clarify sight by structuring a scene and fixing certain details, it also transformed those elements. A photograph's lack of color, its spatial flatness, and its inability to capture motion or provide a unified focus were understood as distinct limitations of the medium during this period. The remarks of British painter John Ruskin are typical of the simultaneous admiration and disdain that many artists felt for it. About a series of recent drawings, he told a friend in 1846: "My drawings are truth to the very letter—too literal perhaps; so says my father, so says not the Daguerreotype, for it beats me grievously." Declaring that "I have allied myself with [photography]," he continued, "[i]t is certainly the most marvelous invention of the century. . . . As regards art, I wish it had never been discovered, it will make the eye too fastidious to accept mere handling."[22] Ruskin's recognition of photography's power and his worry over its influence suggest that he—like other artists at the time—saw photographic images as problematic. Deceptively faithful, they transformed vision and distorted their subjects. Years later, after much experimentation, he rejected photography altogether.

Homer's work with photography introduced him to the medium's unique visual qualities. While he learned to use them effectively in his graphic illustrations for *Harper's*, his first attempt to create a painted portrait of a specific individual based on a photograph served to illustrate the shortcomings of this approach. In the portrait of his friend Albert Kintzing Post, an officer in the 45th Regiment of the Massachusetts Infantry, Homer is believed to have worked directly from a tintype (plate 9).[23] As the original photograph is now lost and the exact circumstances are unknown, it is difficult to ascertain the extent to which he based his image on this source. Given that tintype portraitists frequently employed a blank backdrop and that the medium had limited capacity to record both a subject in the foreground and deep space, Homer likely fabricated the camp scene in the painting's background. The smoking fire in front of Post—another subject that a tintype was largely incapable of representing—was also probably a figment of Homer's imagination. Yet, the direct frontal view and standing pose are characteristic of this type of photography. The flatness of the figure also shares similarities with the artist's earlier print of Lincoln based on Brady's photograph. Relative to other paintings of the period, the portrait is not entirely successful, as the figure seems lifeless and does not fit convincingly within the larger scene. A small work intended as a memento of Post's military service, it was likely a private painting not meant for wider exhibition. That said, the exercise of painting a portrait based on a photograph was presumably useful to Homer, as it demonstrated the challenges of trying to convey a likeness based exclusively on a photograph.

During this formative period in his painting career, Homer came to learn that photography was a medium not to be used explicitly to replicate a particular subject, but rather to be a source from which he might draw ideas and learn certain lessons. It was to be studied and interacted with, but was not to serve as a substitute for other preparatory studies, especially drawing, a medium he relied upon to outline a painting's composition and to work out many of its details. His drawing *Marching Infantry Column* exemplifies this dual function (plate 10). Though a painting was never realized from this study, the graphite and charcoal sketch manifests Homer's thoughts concerning the portrayal of a large group of Union soldiers marching through an open field. Unfolding diagonally across the sheet, the column fills the pictorial space much more realistically than in his portrait of Albert Post. In addition, he experiments here with how to capture figures in motion. From detailed renderings of soldiers at left front to more generalized outlines of soldiers in the middle ground, Homer used drawing as a means to solidify ideas before turning to the painting easel.

Whereas drawing was instrumental in solving these graphic quandaries, photography became a place to think more broadly about new strategies for depicting a particular subject. It enabled other perspectives on pictorial challenges. As the war came to an end, photographs by George Barnard, Alexander Gardner, Timothy O'Sullivan, and others did more than simply heroicize the Union victors.

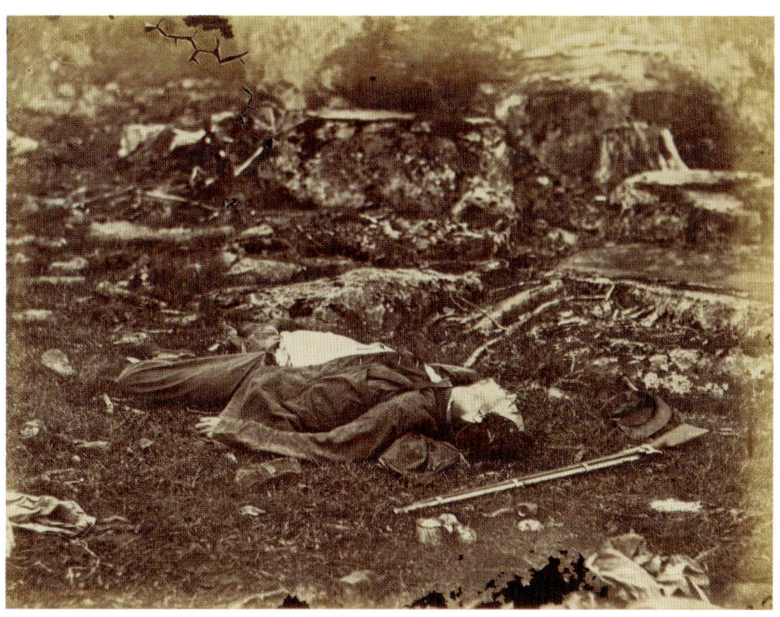

FIG. 9. Alexander Gardner, *A Sharpshooter's Last Sleep, Gettysburg, Pennsylvania*, 1863. Albumen silver print, 6⅞ × 8⅞ in. (17.5 × 22.5 cm). Library of Congress, Prints and Photographs Division, Washington, D.C. [E468.7.G2, v. 1, no. 40]

As Gardner's *A Sharpshooter's Last Sleep* attests, photographs were especially conducive to making visible the tragic sacrifice and widespread destruction caused by the conflict (fig. 9). The stark immediacy of Gardner's portrait of a dead sharpshooter brought home the human costs of the war. In *Trooper Meditating beside a Grave*, Homer captures an equally poignant moment, as a Union soldier looks down at a wooden cross marking a grave amid a dark forest (plate 14). In both compositions, the viewer's gaze is led down to the ground.

What differentiated Homer's painting of the war from that of his contemporaries was his commitment to exploring the larger psychologically charged experiences and issues of the conflict. Specific places, events, and individuals were less important than engaging with larger questions regarding the nature of warfare and the life of a soldier: for example, what does it mean to kill, what does it mean to be a target, and what is the impact of so much death and suffering? Whereas other American painters grappled with the war either through symbolism or by constructing traditional battle scenes, Homer—a loyal Union supporter—was most interested in the physical hardships and emotional traumas central to the human experience of war. He did not rely on age-old artistic conventions and academic training to guide his work, but instead came to value observation and direct encounter. In this period photography aided that effort, introducing the artist to new subjects and new modes of seeing. By freezing time, photography helped Homer to think more deeply about what he had seen. The result was the development of a hybrid practice that combined personal sight and an engagement with a wider range of sources and strategies for developing a composition. In the years after the war, he would continue to draw lessons from the rich visual culture that surrounded him.

"Painting a better picture," 1867 to 1880

Upon meeting Homer for the first time in 1897, as a fellow jurist for the Carnegie Institute International in Pittsburgh, the painter Cecilia Beaux was surprised by the older artist's appearance and demeanor: "This personage I took to be a high official in the world of the Institute, or of coal and steel. He was a spare, oldish man, with a short, dark, almost unnaturally dark, moustache. Everything he wore, and even his cane, was new; gloves, necktie, hat, suit, never had been worn before, and seemed to oppress the wearer a little. He remained absolutely silent during the drive. . . . He looked, I whispered to myself, as a diamond expert might, if I had ever seen one. There was something intense, observant, in his quiet. His new clothes seemed like a disguise. I inquired of Mr. Beatty, who was the operating angel of our destiny. Mr. Beatty looked at me in wonder—'Why, Winslow Homer, of course.' He was amazed that I did not know him, had not met him."[24]

Beaux's anecdote, though not published until 1930, has added to the myth that emerged about the artist well before his death. Her characterization of his anonymity, quietness, and discomfort with the trappings of formal society bears similarities to other descriptions.[25] Homer's relocation in 1883 from the center of the American art world in New York to the remote coastal outpost at Prout's Neck, Maine, also supports this narrative, as does his interest in painting outdoors among the elements—and not within genteel domestic interiors like Beaux and others. Yet, as scholar Sarah Burns has written, that image of a disengaged, nature-bound artist was "largely a fiction," and accounts neither for his active involvement with the art marketplace nor for his deep engagement with contemporary society.[26]

While Homer did value his independence and enjoyed the wilderness, this reputation also fails to account for how self-conscious he was of his public image. As a primarily self-taught artist in New York, he worked to cultivate a reputation—from the outset of his career—that suggested both his sophistication and his desire to be known for working beyond the traditional studio. His involvement with artistic colleagues in Greenwich Village and—beginning in 1864—his membership in the National Academy of Design were important in establishing a professional network. During this same period, photography also served as a vehicle to shape his public persona. In 1863, coincident with the first exhibition of his paintings and the publication of his first lithographic print series, *Campaign Sketches*, he visited the Boston photographers Thomas Gray and Thomas Faris to have his photographic portrait made (see fig. 1). This occasion may have been the first ever that Homer posed before a photographer's camera. He was then visiting his family in Belmont outside Boston and was also working with the Boston-based lithographer Louis Prang on *Campaign Sketches*. The silhouetted carte-de-visite portrait shows the twenty-seven-year-old artist formally dressed with his body in profile, his hair neatly combed, and his head turned three quarters to the left. This pose against a blank backdrop is traditional in format and conveys a confidence and seriousness of purpose befitting an upwardly mobile professional. As multiple copies of the photographic print could be ordered, the portrait likely served as a personal keepsake, a gift to Homer's family, and a calling card of sorts.

It is useful to compare this photograph with the self-portrait caricature he produced the following year. In *Our Special*, he represents himself less as an urbane gentleman and more as a dashing cavalier working heroically amid the war's front lines (fig. 10). His decision to include this likeness in the series *Life in Camp*, a collection of twenty-four small-format chromolithographs of different characters connected to the war, suggests his interest in being associated with the recent military campaigns. Seated on a cannon with long hair, a Van Dyck beard, and a wide-brimmed hat—none of which he ever had—he casts his work as a *Harper's* illustrator in

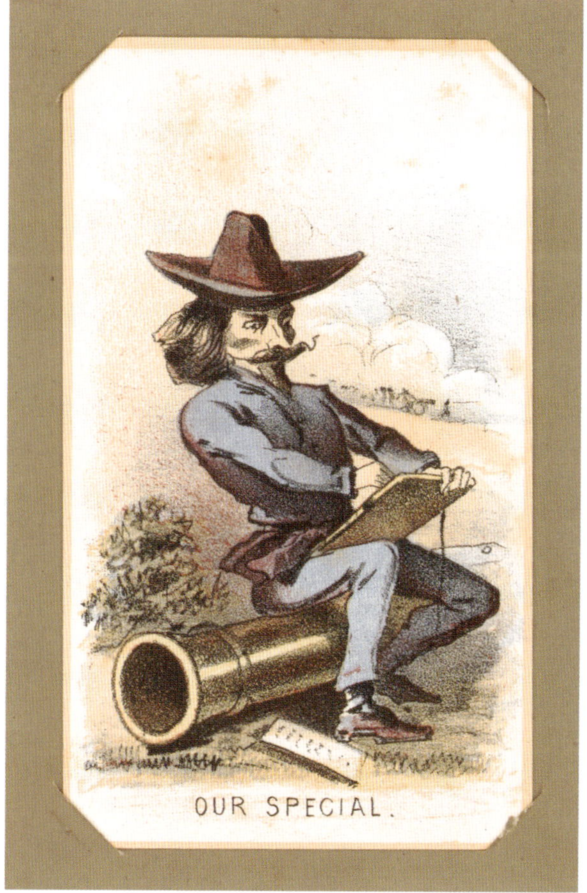

FIG. 10. Louis Prang, after Winslow Homer, *Our Special*, from the series *Life in Camp, Part 2*, published by L. Prang & Co., c. 1864. 12 prints (1 page): chromolithograph; 4 × 2 3/8 in. (10.3 × 6.2 cm) each. Library of Congress, Prints and Photographs Division, Washington, D.C. [LC-DIG-pga-07125]

romantic terms. *Our Special* is the first in a series of portraits—mostly photographic—from throughout his life that figure him outdoors within a space coded masculine. Though an obvious humor pervades this and other works in *Life in Camp*, these images contributed to the burgeoning idea of Homer as an artist working both within and apart from the artistic mainstream.

In the aftermath of the Civil War, with public acclaim for recently exhibited paintings such as *Prisoners from the Front* (1866, Metropolitan Museum of Art), Homer gained a reputation as a rising talent in American art circles. Though he was still creating illustrations for *Harper's* and others, he wanted to focus more attention on his painting. Accepting his promotion to a full academician at the National Academy of Design in 1866, he was required to contribute a work to that institution's prestigious collection. His submission of the small painting *Croquet Player* (1865, National Academy of Design) and his statement at the time that he "would like to have the privilege of painting a better picture" suggest both his ambition and a lingering discontent with his current work.[27] Homer had wanted to visit Europe since the start of the war. Like many American artists at the time, he saw France as an auspicious place to continue his education. With the war's end and support from his family and from promised commissions for *Harper's*, the opportunity to travel finally presented itself.

In December 1866, he sailed from Boston en route to Paris, where he would spend a year painting and studying the collections at the Louvre and other French galleries. Yet, unlike many of his artistic peers, he chose not to enroll in the traditional academic classes then readily available. Several historians have written about Homer's sojourn in France. Regrettably, few documents from his time abroad exist, apart from nineteen small paintings and three illustrations he created there, and disagreement persists as to whether this trip profoundly reshaped his practice.[28] Much of what he did produce was created in the countryside outside Paris and manifests an interest in rural life, especially the roles that women played in farming communities. A familiarity with Jean-François Millet and other artists of the French Barbizon School is evident, an influence that continued to resonate following Homer's return to America. He was also exposed to Japanese art at this time, the first major international exhibition of which was then being held at the Paris Exposition Universelle, where he exhibited two of his recent Civil War paintings. Japanese art made an impact then, as well as later in his career.[29] Yet, Homer was never strictly indebted to a particular artistic movement but, as evident from his early work as an illustrator, borrowed freely from a variety of sources.

While in Paris, Homer sought out a new photographic portrait. Then living with Albert Kelsey, a fellow painter and friend from Belmont, he visited the photographic studio of Bautain, where a series of likenesses of the two men was made. In his individual portrait, Homer sports a new hairstyle, has waxed his mustache to full dramatic effect, and wears a fashionable, wide-lapelled jacket and vest from which a watch chain hangs (fig. 11). He is the epitome of the well-appointed artist, confident in his public stature, notwithstanding the fact that his financial resources were limited at this time. In fact, Homer was so strained fiscally that he wrote his friend Charles

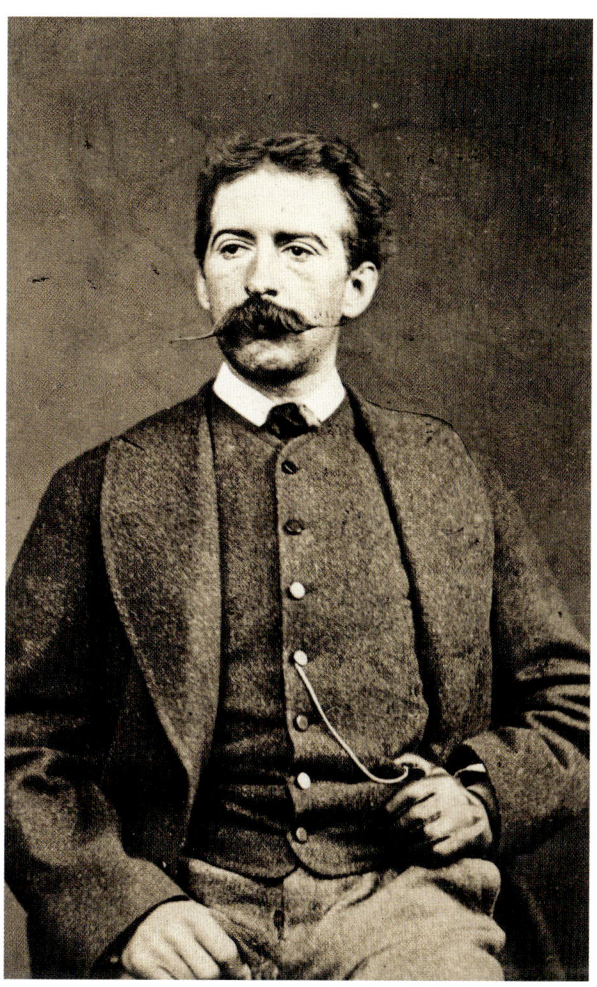

FIG. 11. Bautain, *Winslow Homer in Paris*, 1867. Albumen silver print, 3 11/16 × 2 1/4 in. (9.4 × 5.7 cm). Bowdoin College Museum of Art, Brunswick. Gift of the Homer Family. [1964.69.179.1]

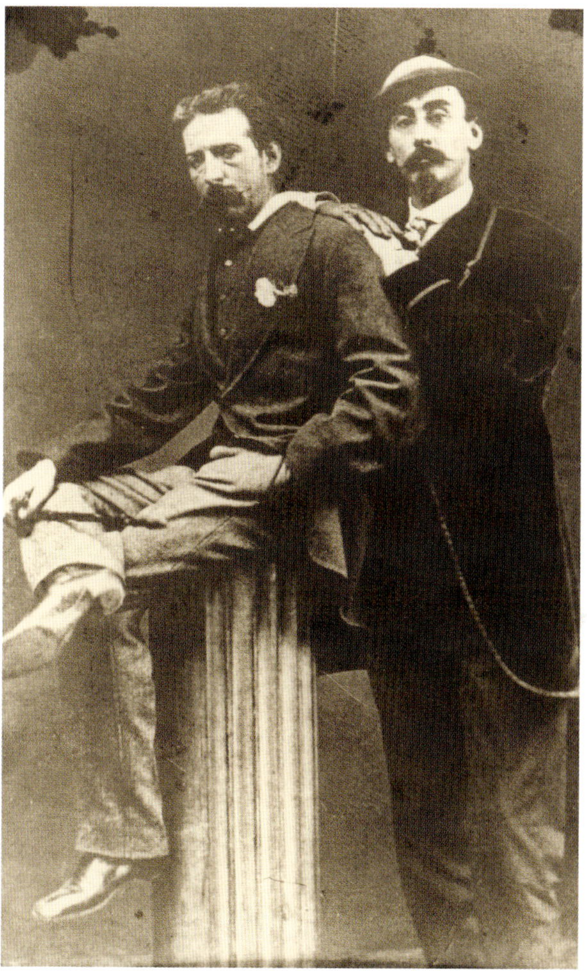

FIG. 12. Bautain, *Winslow Homer and Albert Kelsey*, 1867. Albumen silver print, 3 3/4 × 2 5/16 in. (9.5 × 5.6 cm). Bowdoin College Museum of Art, Brunswick. Gift of the Homer Family. [1964.69.185]

Voorhees in New York that summer asking whether he would buy one of his paintings so that he could extend his stay.[30] A photograph of the two artists together was also created on this occasion (fig. 12). It is a playful and irreverent portrait, as Homer sits with his legs crossed atop a truncated column then serving as a prop in Bautain's studio. Kelsey stands behind him with his hands resting on Homer's back. Homer inscribed the title "Damon and Pythias" on the verso of the small print, referencing the famous Greek story about male friendship. This photograph was a private memento of their time together in Paris. Though such photographs likely had no direct use in his art, they indicate Homer's interest and understanding of the medium along with his ease in interacting with photographers.

Like other Americans in Paris, Homer was also a tourist during his year abroad. The painting *The Gargoyles of Notre Dame* (1867, private collection) suggests his interest in Parisian architecture and in climbing Notre Dame's towers to gain an elevated, 360-degree view of the city. The figure standing at right—believed to be Kelsey—peers out at the city in a pose similar to the stone gargoyles seated upon the cathedral's stone railings. Several photographers in Homer's day and earlier had taken images from this famous perch. Regardless of whether Homer was inspired by these photographs to create this painting, he would at least have known about the long tradition of creating views from atop Notre Dame, a history that predates photography's invention.[31] Compositionally, his painting bears similarities to photographs by Charles Nègre and others. In common with these other images, *The Gargoyles of Notre Dame* is about the activity of looking and the sense of wonder and beauty—even terror—one experiences from this rare height. With his hand placed across his mouth, the figure stands transfixed before the view. Like *Sharpshooter*, it delivers a particular sensation through a study of a single figure and, in this case, the awe-inspiring vista that surrounds him. While Homer's paintings were rarely based directly on photographic sources, many were indebted to ways of seeing that photography helped to popularize.

Returning to New York in the fall of 1867—supposedly with a return fare paid for by Kelsey—Homer reestablished himself in his old, cramped studio in the University Building, a space that one critic described as "altogether too small for a man to have a large idea in."[32] The following spring he relocated to a new studio in the Mercantile Library Building at Astor Place, and in 1872 resettled again—this time to the Tenth Street Studio Building, a building popular with both young and established artists in the heart of Greenwich Village. For much of his career, Homer led a peripatetic existence, traveling often to sites well beyond his immediate home. Though New York served as a base during this period, his studio was rarely a permanent, fixed space, but instead was reassembled at different destinations in temporary, often makeshift quarters. Taking advantage of improved railway and other transportation networks, he was able to travel with relative ease, especially compared with American artists of an earlier generation.

These dislocations seemed to suit him temperamentally and afforded him access to the subjects he wished to paint as well as sports such as fishing that he enjoyed.[33] As in Paris, Homer acted much like a tourist in these pursuits, though now he allied himself with a class of recreational travelers who sought out places apart from the city and known for their outdoor activities. During the late 1860s and 1870s, he traveled to a variety of popular camps and resorts. His destinations included mountainous sites such as the White Mountains in New Hampshire and the Catskills and Adirondacks in upstate New York, and coastal communities like Manchester and Gloucester in Massachusetts, East Hampton on New York's Long Island, and Long Branch in New Jersey. All had been discovered previously by earlier artists, and were at the time the favored subjects of other contemporary painters as well. These trips may have been inspired by commercial assignments from the illustrated magazines or by the prospect of creating new works that might appeal to collectors, many of whom visited these same places. For Homer, they represented an opportunity to continue his work out in the field and away from the traditional centers of artistic production. It is interesting to note that, unlike many other painters of the period, he never visited Niagara Falls or felt inclined to travel to the West.

While during these trips he created paintings, drawings, and—beginning in 1873—watercolors that privileged an untouched, unpeopled wilderness, Homer was not blind to the larger enterprise of tourism, nor to the other artists who frequented these places. In fact, he made these individuals and their recreational pursuits the subject of several compositions. His series of works in the White Mountains completed during the summers of 1868 and 1869, for example, suggest his fascination more with the people who ascended these hills as a type of adventure than with the landscape itself or the scenic views from these elevated perspectives. Paintings such as *White Mountain Wagon* (plate 15) and *Artists Sketching in the White Mountains* (plate 16) epitomize this interest in the people who gathered at such sites. In *Artists Sketching*, three painters sit before their easels on an open mountaintop, and all look off in the same direction at a subject—presumably a mountain peak or valley—that is beyond the painting's edge. By representing their backs instead of their faces and positioning them one in front of the other, Homer invites the viewer to participate in the same act of looking. As with other paintings and prints of tourist landscapes, he infuses the scene with a subtle, cutting humor. Indeed, unlike the outdoorsman who desires to get beyond the beaten path, these artists sit together at a popular gathering spot and gaze out in unison toward a landscape we cannot see. While he sought to nurture an independent vision, Homer was surely aware that he participated in a similar enterprise as these other artists. In the print based on this painting that he created for *Appletons' Journal*—titled *The Artist in the Country*—he transformed its focus by eliminating two of the artists and inserting a female figure who stares over the painter's shoulder (plate 17). Now in a vertical format and with wildflowers included in the foreground, the print is less about gazing at a faraway view and instead about an intimate, perhaps romantic encounter between a young man and woman. Both the painting and the print share the same central figure and the same mountain setting, yet their emphasis is markedly different. Given his experience as an illustrator, he was attuned to graphic experimentation and adept at building compositions that added and subtracted elements from various sources.

His travel to such places also introduced him to a new type of photographer, namely, those professionals who established businesses that catered to the recreational traveler, as well as the hotels and railways that served them. At most of these sites, photographers had established studios or traveled there to create views that promoted tourism and that could be sold as souvenirs. As in the past, Homer worked often in close proximity with these photographers. They were both rivals and partners in an artistic exchange. He learned from their work, and they learned from him. In the White Mountains, several artists and photographers, including Albert and Edward Bierstadt, Nathan Pease, and John Soule, produced photographic views of noteworthy landmarks. Most successfully, Benjamin and Edward Kilburn of Littleton, New Hampshire—the Kilburn Brothers—marketed several hundred different photographic images of the White Mountains, mainly stereographic

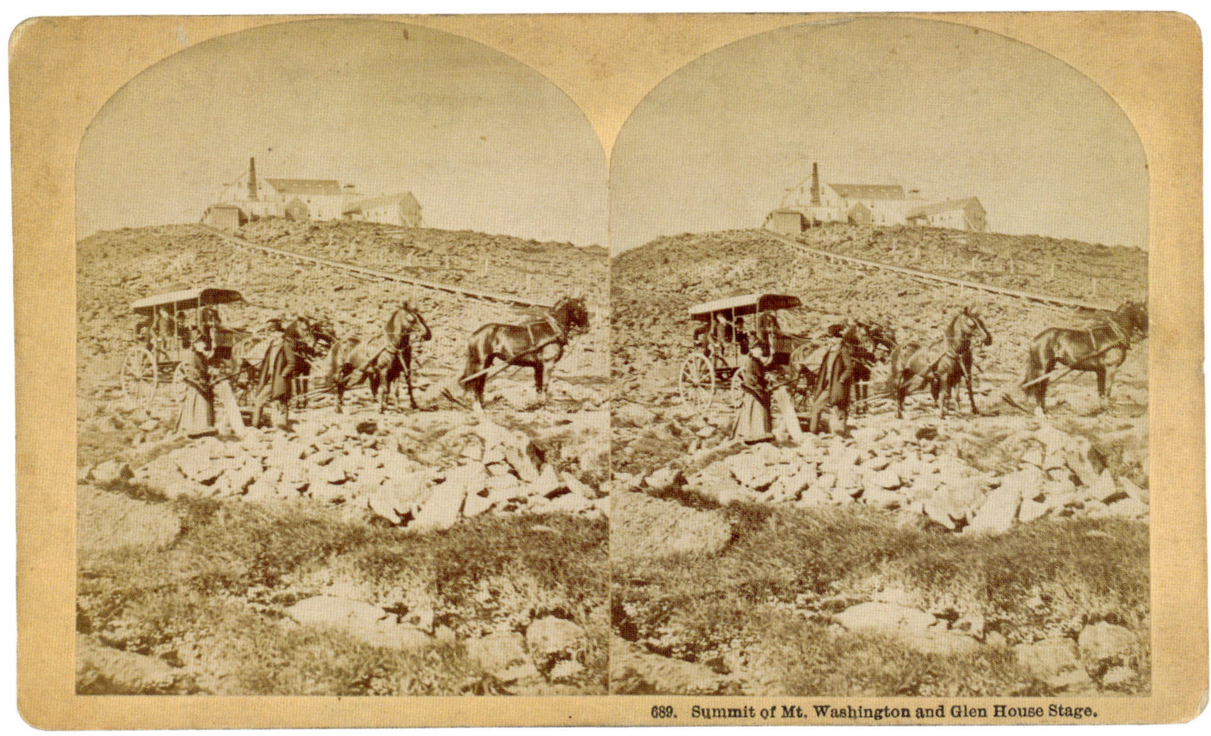

FIG. 13. Kilburn Brothers, *Summit of Mt. Washington and Glen House Stage*, c. 1870. Albumen silver print, 4 × 7 in. (10.2 × 17.8 cm). Robert Dennis Collection of Stereoscopic Views, Photography Collection, Miriam and Ira D. Wallach Division of Art, New York Public Library. [91-F30.2692]

views, beginning in the late 1860s. Perhaps not surprisingly, the arrival of these photographers coincided with the completion in 1868 of the Mount Washington Cog Railway, a daring engineering enterprise that transported visitors to the summit and made New England's highest mountain not only an iconic landmark but also a popular tourist destination.[34]

Though Homer did not portray the railway, his visit to Mount Washington depended upon this new transportation system. There, he likely encountered images such as the Kilburn Brothers' *Summit of Mt. Washington and Glen House Stage* (fig. 13), for photography's influence reveals itself in several works, including *White Mountain Wagon*. Depicting a horse-drawn carriage operated by the Glen House, a resort hotel near Mount Washington, this oil study portrays it as having momentarily stopped. Homer's primary interest is not necessarily the passengers, but rather the carriage itself, especially the wheels, each of whose polished wooden spokes is slightly different due to the sunlight. Photography is a medium that relies on light, and the resulting prints often reveal subtle light effects. Homer made light and its infinite manifestations a core element of his practice. While he was not working from a specific photographic likeness to create *White Mountain Wagon*, the completion of this composition owes a debt to the medium. Photographers such as the Kilburn Brothers gave him images from which he could learn.

Given the limitations of the photographic medium at this time—in particular, the small size, the glossy surface, the lack of color, the pictorial flatness, and the inability to capture motion—these images were no substitute for the tried-and-true practice of close personal observation. Direct studies executed in oil or graphite permitted the artist to work through important decisions concerning such elements as composition, lighting, and pose, and Homer subscribed wholeheartedly to this practice from the start of his painting career. With their unique ability to freeze time, however, cameras captured additional details about these aspects while introducing other optical experiences—for example, glare, blur, and shadow—that the eye alone might not immediately perceive. Because subjects move and changes occur in a scene's lighting or atmospheric conditions, photographs—no matter their quality or the taint associated with their commercial production—could capture a moment in time and provide useful information to an artist. Stereographic images also gave the illusion of three-dimensional sight, and though perspectives were distorted in these images, they informed, as well as challenged, artists. In short, photography provided a type of fresh, immediate visual encounter that interested artists who were dedicated to portraying subjects as they appeared.

At other times, photography could serve a very practical purpose. Homer possessed a strong entrepreneurial spirit and, as noted earlier, explored a variety of commercial opportunities, especially in the graphic arts. During this period, he regularly supplied illustrations not only for magazines but also for books, in particular volumes of poetry. In 1871, Louis Prang commissioned him to create illustrations to accompany *The Courtin'*, an extended poem by American author James Russell Lowell that the Boston bookseller James R. Osgood was publishing in a deluxe edition. Though he was pursuing painting as his primary focus, he accepted this assignment and others in part because of the reliable paycheck. The decision to create a series of silhouettes was made, and Homer delivered the seven images to Prang that spring (plate 19). However, as he noted in a letter to Prang, "the drawings vary in size, but they can be fixed when they are reduced by photog'y."[35] At the time of their creation, Homer was unsure about the exact size that would be required for publication. Knowing that they would be reproduced as heliotypes, an early photomechanical reproduction technique for which Osgood held an exclusive right, he recognized that the size of his silhouettes did not matter, for photography would correct the issue. During a career that coincided with sweeping changes in reproduction technology, Homer published his work using numerous printing methods. As photography was increasingly a part of these processes, he learned more about the medium's characteristics and capabilities through these assignments.

While New York and Boston remained important centers that nurtured Homer as an artist, he made them neither the subject nor the backdrop of his paintings. His turning away from the urban context where he lived during these formative years suggests that the subjects he prized were outdoors, predominantly in rural settings. For him, a studio-centered practice produced work that lacked vital connections with the wider world. In a profile of the artist published in 1882, the critic George Sheldon paraphrased Homer's complaint: "No matter how carefully drawn the figure, nor how admirably composed the composition, nor how exquisite the sentiment, nor how brilliant and harmonious the color scheme, the picture cannot be true unless it has been executed in part at least under the all-embracing sky. One of the chief causes of the failure of some of our finest executants with the brush is their ignorance or neglect of this essential condition." According to Homer, a good exemplar of this tendency was William-Adolphe Bouguereau. Sheldon quotes Homer's assessment of the celebrated French artist: "His pictures look false; he does not get the truth of that which he wishes to represent; his light is not out-door light; his works are waxy and artificial. They are extremely near being frauds."[36]

The desire to avoid the "false" and the "artificial" led Homer away from the city for weeks and months at a time. Though Sheldon asserts that "he paints what he has seen; he tells what he has felt; [and] he records what he knows," Homer did not rely on his eye alone, but continued to engage in a practice that involved different methods and sources, including photography.[37] Two photographs of Homer on a beach—believed to have been taken in Marshfield, Massachusetts, in 1869—indicate that he posed for an unidentified photographer during a sketching trip to the coast (figs. 14 and 15). He looks away from the camera in both photographs, while his dog Jack rests at his feet. In one view, he holds a parasol, ostensibly to avoid the direct sunlight, as it appears to be a bright day. Given its position, however, it was not then serving that function. In the other photograph, he looks downward in a contemplative pose, not unlike the female figure in *The Artist in the Country*. As the camera required a tripod and the process for its operation involved several steps, there was nothing accidental or spontaneous about these views. Instead, they were composed images taken by someone with knowledge of photography. While neither the creator of the images nor their larger purpose can be ascertained, they were likely figure studies to aid his work. Homer also brought sketch paper to the beach, and returned with his oil paints and canvas as well. In his practice, he saw photography, drawing, and oil studies as companions that complemented each other.

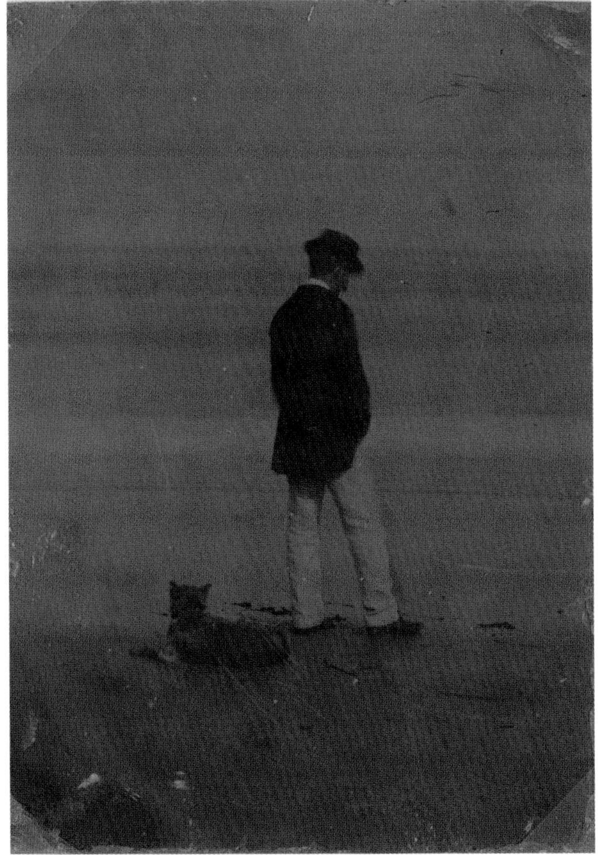

FIG. 14. Unidentified photographer, *Winslow Homer at Marshfield*, c. 1869. Tintype, 3⅞ × 2¾ in. (9.8 × 7 cm). Bowdoin College Museum of Art, Brunswick. Gift of the Homer Family. [1964.69.153.7]

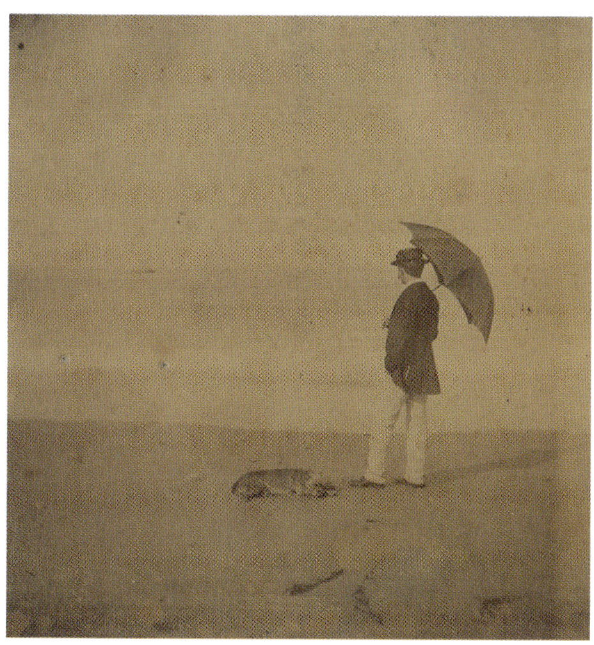

FIG. 15. Unidentified photographer, *Winslow Homer at Marshfield*, c. 1869. Albumen silver print, $3^{1}/_{2} \times 3^{1}/_{4}$ in. (8.9 × 8.3 cm). Bowdoin College Museum of Art, Brunswick. Gift of the Homer Family. [1964.69.179.2]

From these different studies, Homer created a series of paintings and prints of beach scenes. The larger setting of these works—sandy flats and gentle surf—bears similarities to the place where these two photographs were created. The locations and dates of some of these paintings can be confirmed, though in several instances, the details are elusive. *On the Beach at Marshfield* is one such picture that was painted *en plein air*, and that may have been worked on indoors at a later time (plate 20). Relative to these two photographs, he has broadened horizontally the painting's composition, added a foreground landscape, and developed a narrative that includes five individuals. Of note, two of the figures hold parasols similar to the one that Homer holds in the photograph. In the print that relates to this painting, he altered the view once again, reducing its horizontality, eliminating two figures, and enlarging the central female figure with a parasol (plate 21). A detailed drawing of this young woman exists, which shows how he repositioned the angle of the parasol. In this new configuration, which Homer used in the print, the woman now hides behind it and steals a fleeting glimpse of the couple seated together back on the beach. She is no longer a nondescript individual leaving the beach, but a defeated rival for the affection of a man who appears in the distance sitting closely with another woman. Reproduced in *Harper's* with the title *On the Beach—Two Are Company, Three Are None*, the print conveys more effectively than the painting the drama of this romantic incident. Again, the act of looking gives the scene its emotional resonance. Attuned to appearances, yet desirous of delving beneath the surface of things, Homer throughout his career consistently sought to explore moments of psychological significance.

Whereas he concentrated on presenting human dramas in works set in the White Mountains and in coastal communities like Marshfield, he found the Adirondacks a place that promised more of an unspoiled wilderness experience. Likely influenced by William Murray's *Adventures in the Wilderness; or, Camp-Life in the Adirondacks*, a popular romance published in 1869 and credited with precipitating a new era of tourism in the region, Homer first ventured into the so-called North Woods during the summer of 1870 with the artists Eliphalet Terry and John Lee Fitch. He found the area and its outdoor activities so appealing that he returned no fewer than nineteen times, and in 1888 joined the North Woods Club, an elite sportsman's group. In his work there, Homer emphasized the rugged terrain and the solitude of the place, especially relative to the crowds he encountered at other resort destinations. A vast forested and mountainous landscape full of lakes and rivers, the Adirondacks were sparsely populated and in 1870 welcomed only three thousand visitors, a small fraction of the number that other tourist sites attracted.[38]

Because of the dramatic growth in wilderness tourism, however, approximately a quarter of a million people were annually visiting the Adirondacks by the century's end. Large hotels and small inns, privately owned camps and clubs, and railway and stagecoach service made travel easy and increasingly comfortable. In addition, industrial logging in the region became a big business during this period. Homer was witness to this extraordinary transformation, yet, as scholar Patricia Junker has argued, he was less interested in portraying the place as it was, and more in perpetuating certain mythic ideas that had become associated with the area and its inhabitants.[39] During the last quarter of the nineteenth century, the Adirondacks were not a pristine wilderness populated only by rustic guides, though these individuals and the activities they supported were where he decided to focus his attention. Homer was not the first artist to discover this region, and in his paintings, prints, and watercolors, he took his cue from many of his predecessors. A photograph from 1874 of a group of nattily attired artists on the Ausable River, which flowed through the Adirondacks' popular Keene Valley, includes Homer in the back row at center (fig. 16). This image suggests his involvement in the larger artistic community there, and his commitment to portraying many of the same sites.

In addition to the writers and artists who helped to develop and popularize the region's reputation, various photographers also played a significant role, especially Seneca Ray Stoddard. Having opened a photographic studio in Glens Falls, New York, in 1867, Stoddard made his first trip to the Adirondacks during the summer of Homer's initial visit. He returned nearly every year for the next four decades, creating—like the Kilburn Brothers in the White Mountains—an extensive body of photographs that introduced to would-be travelers and recalled for visitors the area's natural beauty. By 1874, the year in which Homer posed on the Ausable River, Stoddard had assembled a catalogue of nearly seven hundred views, the great majority of which were stereographs. Adding to Stoddard's reputation as the leading purveyor of information about the area, the photographer authored the first map for tourists and in 1874 published *The Adirondacks: Illustrated*, a guidebook he updated and republished annually until 1914.[40]

Homer's Adirondack work has much in common with Stoddard's photography. Both picture the region as a portal to escape the crowds and demands of the wider world. Though the extent to which the two men knew one another is unclear, their pictures suggest that each learned from the other. For an outside visitor like Homer, Stoddard's views directed him to certain destinations and educated him as to how to see these sites. Compare, for example, *The Angler* (plate 25) with Stoddard's stereograph *Lake View House from Birmingham Falls* (fig. 17), one of dozens of

FIG. 16. John Francis Murphy, *Artists on the Ausable River*, 1874 (printed later). Gelatin silver print, 7 × 5 in. (17.8 × 12.7 cm). Adirondack Experience on Blue Mountain Lake. [1982.006.0001]

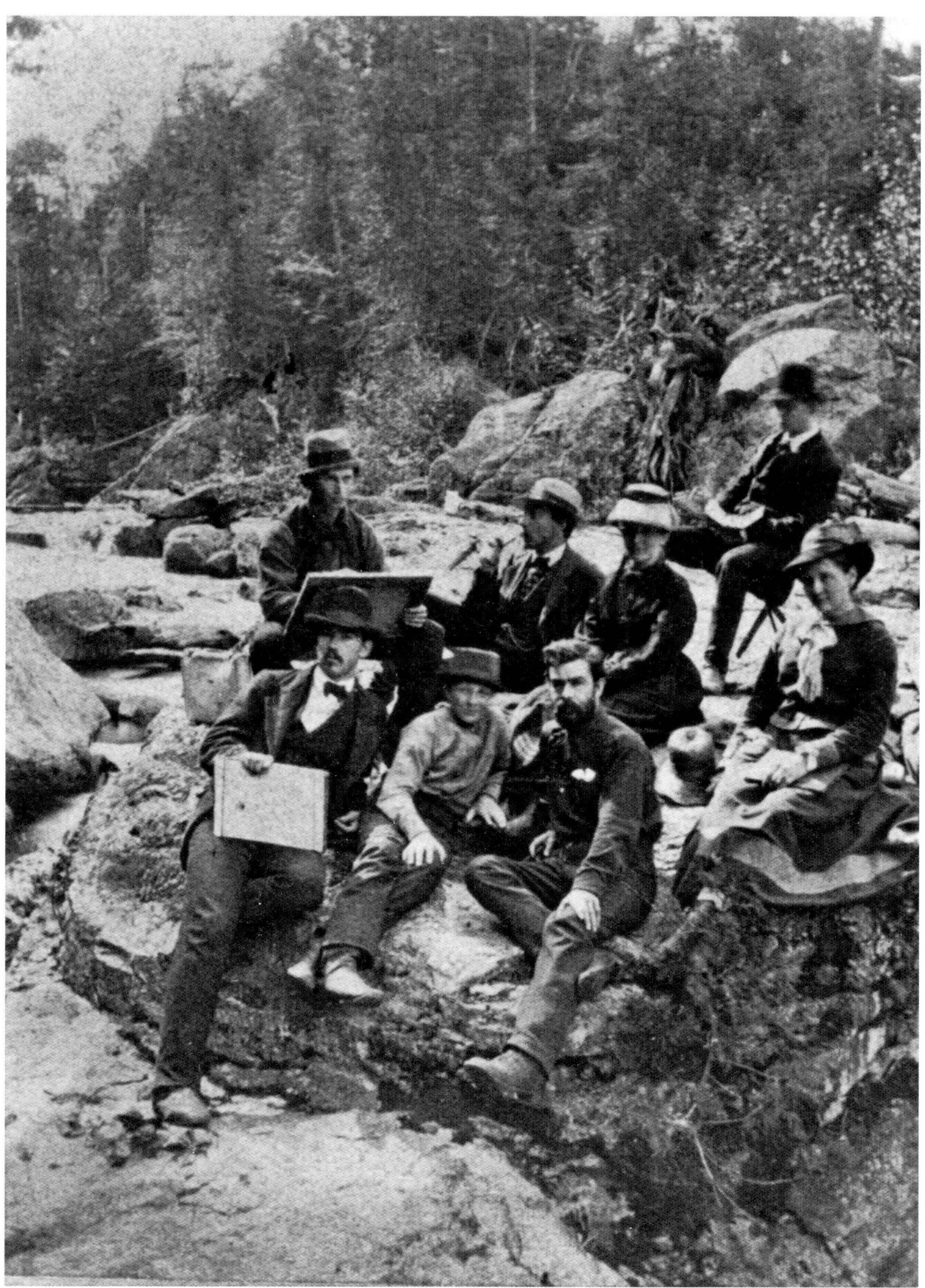

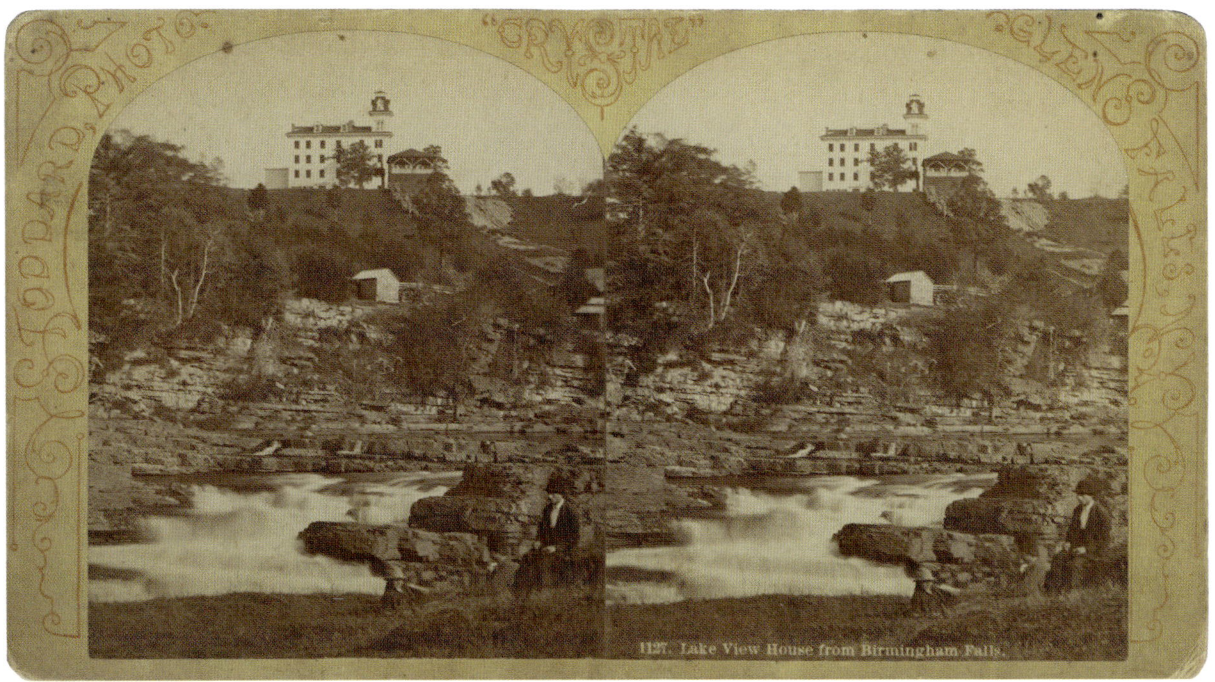

FIG. 17. Seneca Ray Stoddard, *Lake View House from Birmingham Falls*, c. 1875. Albumen silver print, 4 × 7 in. (10.2 × 17.8 cm). Seneca Ray Stoddard Adirondack Stereoviews, Adirondack Experience on Blue Mountain Lake. [1975.020.0537]

views of this popular stretch of the Ausable River. Homer's painting—believed to have been created during his 1874 trip—presents a fisherman casting by the water's edge, his intense gaze locked upon a spot on the river's surface beyond the frame. While photography was limited in its ability to capture a figure in motion, it could provide useful information about other details, including in this case a river's topography and foliage. Views such as Stoddard's also helped him to think about the structure of his compositions, especially spatial relationships. It is important to note that Stoddard's stereograph includes a large hotel prominently featured in the background. Given his relationship with various hotels and other tourism enterprises, Stoddard was often eager to promote notable accommodations in the wilds of the Adirondacks. In contrast, Homer figured the Adirondacks as a wilderness untouched by modern civilization. Yet, as his travels suggest, he enjoyed modern comforts and tended not to venture well beyond the places where he was staying.

In his interactions with photographers, Homer was not the sole beneficiary. They also learned much from him and other artists during this period. Desirous of elevating the artistic status of their work, many photographers, including Stoddard, looked to paintings and prints for compelling subjects and for lessons about composition and lighting. Again, although no direct evidence of their engagement exists, Stoddard was likely familiar with Homer's work in the Adirondacks. In photographs such as *Game in the Adirondacks*,

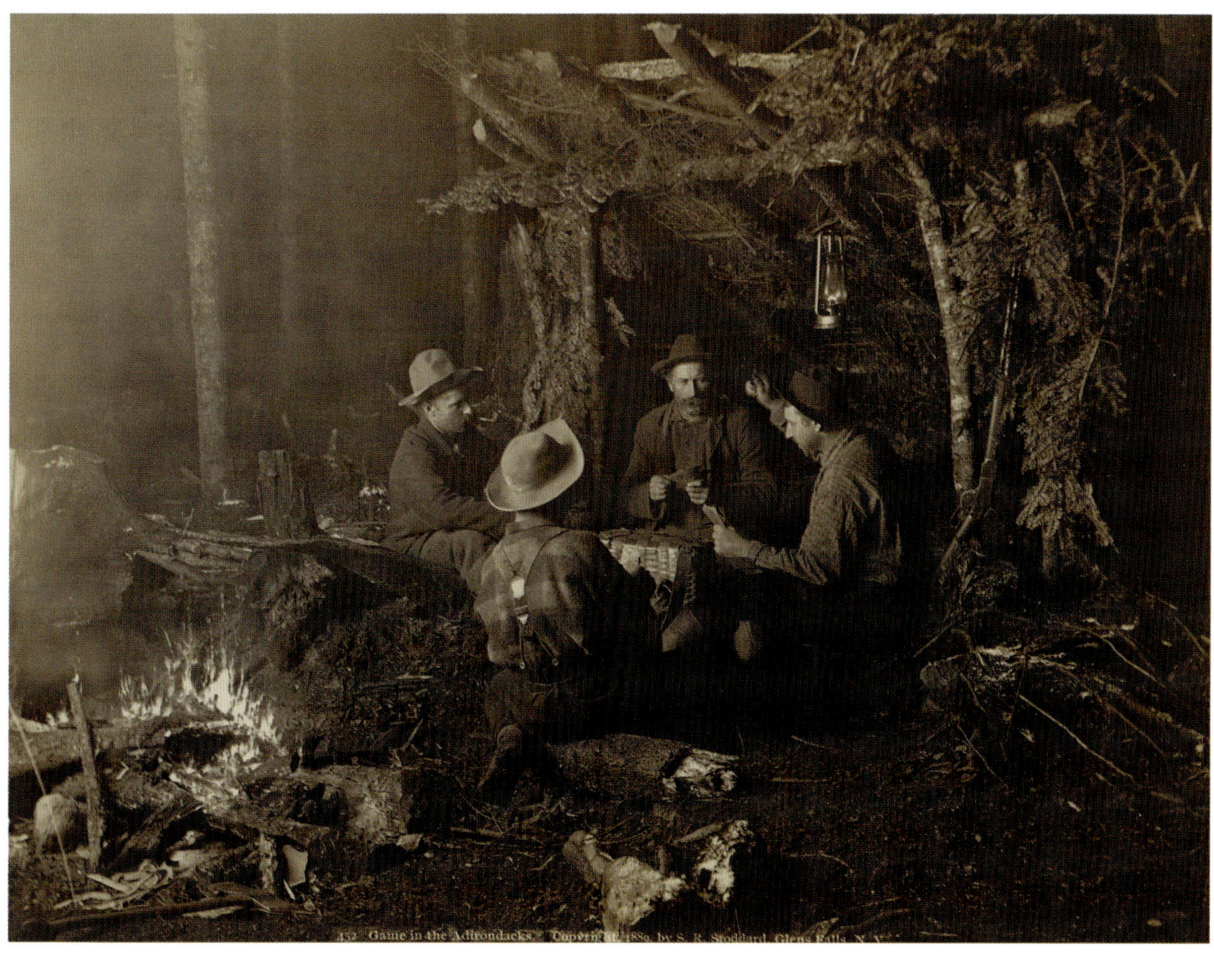

FIG. 18. Seneca Ray Stoddard, *Game in the Adirondacks*, 1889. Albumen silver print, 7 × 9 in. (17.8 × 22.8 cm). Adirondack Experience on Blue Mountain Lake. [1966.060.2499]

he draws inspiration from the artistic tradition of nocturnal camp scenes (fig. 18). Showing four men playing a game of cards next to a thatched-roof lean-to and a campfire, this image represents a marked departure in Stoddard's photography. It is not the type of scenic view on which he had built his commercial reputation, but rather a work that reveals a new interest in presenting notable individuals within a specific narrative. *Game in the Adirondacks* was also the product of Stoddard's recent experiments with magnesium flash photography—a new innovation in photography—though, as his use of gouache to add definition to the fire at left suggests, photography was still unable to capture accurately such details as smoke and fire. Stoddard often sought to expand the range of photographic products he offered to Adirondack visitors, and in this example he crafted a new image that borrowed liberally from non-photographic precedents.

One such work might have been Homer's *Camp Fire* (plate 30). Created during and immediately after his 1877 trip to the North Woods, it was exhibited in New York to enthusiastic reviews that fall and again in 1880. Picturing two fishermen resting in the darkness of night alongside their tent and before a roaring fire, it is reminiscent of night scenes by other artists of the period and before. Critics were especially keen on Homer's handling of the fire. As a writer for the *New York Times* opined, "with a boldness which emulates Japanese draughtsmen . . . Mr. Homer follows the airy trail of the sparks from his camp-fire, and gives at length and in full, against the dark background, what the eye only sees for a moment and in motion."[41] His ability to capture an instantaneous moment in a darkened space, along with the quietude of the scene, impressed viewers, making *Camp Fire* one of the standout paintings of the year. Rendering a nighttime scene more convincingly than Stoddard did with his photograph, Homer continued to explore techniques and strategies for representing subjects as they appeared. Lessons from different sources, among them Japanese drawing, informed this pursuit, as suggested by the *New York Times* critic. Similarly, photographers such as Stoddard looked to the example of visual images in other mediums.

By the end of the 1870s, critics and collectors celebrated the individuality of Homer's paintings. The praise of a reviewer in 1878 exemplifies this idea: "No two of Mr. Homer's pictures look alike. Every canvas with his name attached bears the reflex of a distinct artistic impression. His style is large and free, realistic and straightforward, broad and bold; and many of his finished works have somewhat of the charm of open-air sketches—were, indeed, painted outdoors in the sunlight, in the immediate presence of Nature; while in the best of them may always be recognized a certain noble simplicity, quietude, and sobriety, that one feels grateful for in an age of gilded spread-eagleism."[42] Though known then for working at a remove from the artistic mainstream, he had nevertheless become a part of an established network of artists in New York, as a member of the National Academy of Design, the American Watercolor Society, the Century Association, and the Tile Club, and a regular contributor to their exhibitions and others. Two portraits created in 1880 by Napoleon Sarony—like Brady, a New York photographer famous for celebrity portraits and a fellow Tile Club member—picture Homer as a self-assured and fashionable gentleman who seemed to move comfortably in fine art circles (figs. 19 and 20). Indeed, he looks little different from his artistic peers.

Yet, his frequent extended stays outside of New York and his decision to abandon—at least temporarily—commissioned work for the illustrated magazines may indicate a longing for greater independence. In the summer of 1880, he returned to Gloucester, where he lived alone on an island in the harbor, a spot that "was precisely to his liking," according to a later recollection by his friend the Boston dealer J. Eastman Chase.[43] Leaving behind his oil paints, he completed a large number of ambitious watercolors that summer, and reports suggest that he enjoyed the company of the local fishermen.[44] Homer was not necessarily growing antagonistic toward New York, for he would continue in the coming years to have relationships with dealers and collectors there—not to mention his older brother, Charles, and sister-in-law Martha, who lived in Brooklyn. Instead, it was more a case of ambivalence toward an artistic establishment that he wished increasingly to keep at arm's

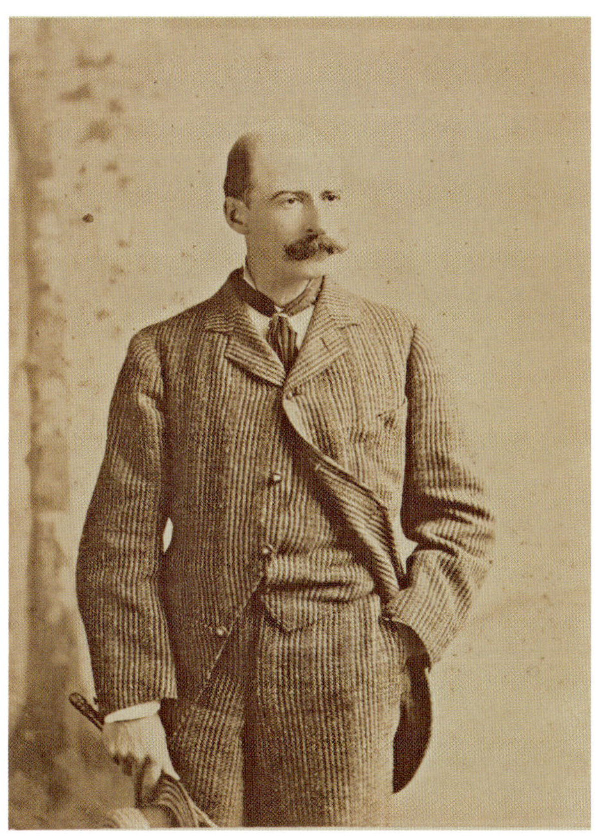

FIG. 19. Napoleon Sarony, *Winslow Homer in New York*, 1880. Albumen silver print, 5 15/16 × 4 1/8 in. (15.1 × 10.5 cm). Bowdoin College Museum of Art, Brunswick. Gift of the Homer Family. [1964.69.179.3]

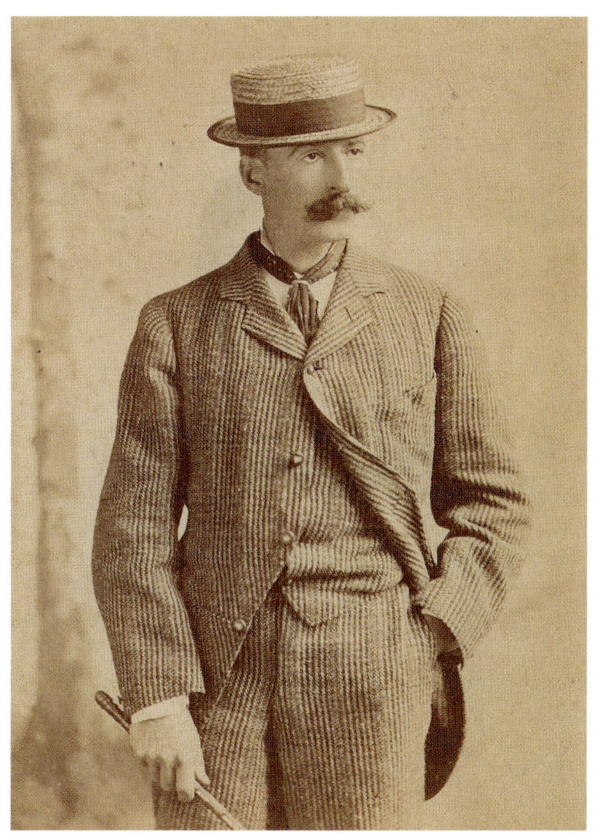

FIG. 20. Napoleon Sarony, *Winslow Homer in New York*, 1880. Albumen silver print, 5 7/8 × 4 1/4 in. (14.9 × 10.8 cm). Bowdoin College Museum of Art, Brunswick. Gift of the Homer Family. [1964.69.179.5]

length. In addition, he was looking at this time for fresh inspiration in his work. Believing that a new outlook required space apart from the familiar, Homer sailed from New York in March 1881 en route to England.

"Many studies in black and white," 1881 to 1882

Describing Homer's twenty-month sojourn in England, his first biographer, William Downes, argued that it constituted a "turning point in the artist's career." He continued by observing that while critics "found his earlier work crude, harsh, and awkward," they "hastened to acclaim the English series as masterpieces." In his study Downes tended to agree, and further suggested that Homer's subsequent paintings after England represented the pinnacle of his artistic achievement.[45] Though this assessment is far too dismissive of the painter's earlier career, it is evident in the work completed over the last thirty years of his life that Homer's time abroad in 1881–82 led to changes in his practice. Apart from the brilliantly colored paintings and watercolors he created on winter trips to Florida and the Caribbean, his palette became darker and the color combinations more complex. His painting technique became more studied, while at the same time his finished surfaces became looser and more expressive. During the first part of his career, his subjects and the tone of his compositions varied widely—from the innocent frivolity of children at play and the wholesome excitement of sportsmen and tourists on holiday, to the grim uneasiness of soldiers at war and the sense of alienation endured by African Americans. The natural world served primarily as a backdrop for these dramatic narratives. Beginning in England, however, the power of larger natural forces became more pronounced, and individuals were increasingly portrayed as either isolated from the rest of humanity or captive to their surroundings. This stylistic evolution happened over more than two years, but it became especially evident following Homer's relocation from New York. Desirous of a new chapter in his life and his art, he saw England—and later Maine—as a deliberate break from this past.

Homer never explained his motivations directly, leaving recent scholars to speculate about broken relationships and frustration with the direction of his work.[46] Whereas his European trip fifteen years earlier to France occurred at the outset of his painting career—likely inspired by an urge to see Paris and to encounter firsthand the center of the Western art world—he traveled to England in 1881 with his reputation established and a career no longer dependent on commercial magazine assignments. During the initial few weeks, he was in London—the artist's first trip to that cosmopolitan city—where, among other outings, he spent time studying drawings at the British Museum. Given that museum's outstanding collection of Old Masters, one might presume that he studied drawings from that era, though the opportunity existed to see works that ranged to the present day. This visit suggests that the chance to study and to think anew about his work was at least part of Homer's reasoning. As the annual exhibitions of the Society of Painters in Watercolours and of the Royal Academy opened in April, it is likely that he ventured out as well to see the latest examples of British contemporary art.[47]

Yet, he did not stay in London more than a month, deciding instead to establish a temporary residence in Cullercoats, a small fishing village and summer artists' colony on the North Sea nearly three hundred miles north of the British capital. Similar in remoteness and natural beauty to many of the rural destinations he enjoyed in America, Cullercoats allowed him to work largely separate from the wider art world. Based in a cottage overlooking the ocean, he embarked on a new series of compositions related to the people of this coastal community. As during the previous summer in Gloucester, his focus was not primarily painting. Instead, as Downes relates, he "made many studies in black and white, using a variety of mediums, such as charcoal, crayon, lead pencil, chalk, India ink, and watercolor wash, on paper of various tints."[48] Homer had worked with these different graphic instruments and materials before, but at no previous time had he used them with such intensity, nor in combination.

His compositions also reflected a new level of experimentation with perspective and structure. *Beach Scene with People and Fishing Boats* is a study in charcoal that suggests this exploration (plate 34). Though small in size and not intended for exhibition, it shows him combining at least four different elements together in a single drawing: a group assembled in the foreground, two larger-sized men in fishing hats at right, a fleet of boats in the middle and background, and a piece of the shoreline jutting into the composition in the right background. This type of drawing exercise informed his finished work of this period, including *Perils of the Sea*, an ambitious watercolor completed during his first year in Cullercoats (plate 36). With its complex configuration of individuals at distinct locations within the scene, it reflects his determination to create a narrative concerning the danger and occasional anguish that this fishing community endured. By conceiving an elevated foreground space on which the two principal female figures stand and by flattening the composition, he has brought into close proximity the two women peering out to sea with a larger group of men who have gathered below to do the same. The watercolor emphasizes both the homosocial culture that characterized Cullercoats and the shared sense of foreboding that gripped the local men and women alike. Homer experimented with, refined, and reused this new split-scene compositional strategy on various occasions in the years ahead.

Given his desire to experiment, it is significant that he bought his first two cameras while abroad. One was an English-made Marion & Company "Academy" camera, which produced square plates measuring 1¼ inches (fig. 21). A "miniature"-type camera, the Academy was advertised as "the most useful article ever invented for artists and tourists," which could be "carried in the pocket with ease, and will produce acceptable little photographs."[49] Though the camera survives,

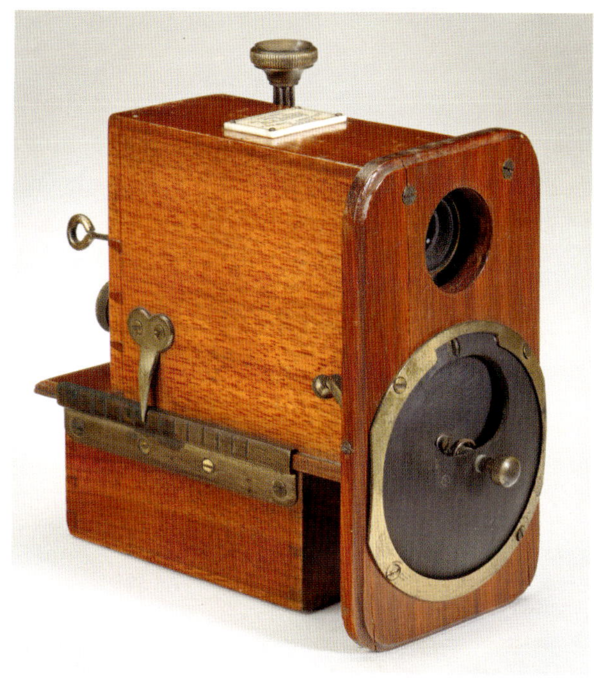

FIG. 21. Marion & Company "Academy" camera owned by Winslow Homer, c. 1881. Wood with metal and glass components, 5 × 2⅝ × 5½ in. (12.7 × 6.6 × 14 cm). Worcester Art Museum. Mrs. Kingsmill Marrs Collection. [1925.613]

no photographs by Homer of this size are extant, and one scholar has surmised that "he couldn't make it work."[50] He acquired the other camera from Mawson & Swan, a leading regional photographic business in the city of Newcastle-on-Tyne, less than ten miles from Cullercoats (see frontispiece). This camera produced images that were approximately 3 by 4 inches. After buying it, Homer inscribed his initials and the date "August 15, 1882" on the camera's wooden plate holder. Regarding the initials, he was always diligent about labeling his possessions. The significance of the date is not known, though it may indicate the time of its purchase. Both cameras were designed for the serious amateur rather than the studio professional, and they were notable for their portability and ease of use.

Only one photograph is known to exist from his time in England (plate 37). Mounted inside his copy of *Chevreul on Colours*, the book that his brother Charles had presented to him twenty years earlier, it pictures a man hoisting a sail on a coble fishing boat and includes a caption, "Sept. 1882 Cullercoats."[51] The photograph's size and date suggest that it was likely made with the Mawson & Swan camera. Though the image is technically poor, it depicts a subject that Homer represented often during his time in Cullercoats. While several drawings and watercolors present this type of boat from a similar perspective, *The Breakwater, Cullercoats* includes a near-exact rendering of this photograph as a distinct element on the watercolor's right side (plate 38). In this instance, photography did not guide the larger structure of the composition, though it did serve to provide useful information regarding how to represent a darkened sail in the middle distance. Other watercolors created in Cullercoats indicate that he followed a similar approach in his rendering of coble fishing boats. These examples reaffirm that the artist continued to view painting as a hybrid practice.[52]

The decision to save the photograph and to add a caption suggests that he valued the image, despite its shortcomings. Given the purchase of two cameras, Homer likely took other photographs during this period as well, though their current whereabouts are unknown. Maggie Jefferson Storey, one of his Cullercoats models, later told a friend that she posed for a series of photographs, some of which he presented to her in an album, now lost.[53] Storey appears in several drawings and watercolors, including as the subject of *Head of a Woman* (plate 35). As this drawing and others from Cullercoats demonstrate, however, Homer generalized the features of his subjects and did not strive to accentuate their individuality. In a manner reminiscent of his earlier figure compositions, Homer saw Storey and other models as representatives of a particular type of person who lived by the sea. Although fascinated by how things appear and committed to an accurate rendering of the larger world, he was also routinely reshaping what he saw, especially in his depiction of the human face.

While living in Cullercoats, Homer was not alone in pursing an interest in taking his own photographs. With the recent introduction of dry plates and new cameras designed for amateur practitioners, the popularity of photography grew significantly at this moment. Despite its distance from London and other major cities, the northeast coast of England supported a thriving photographic community. In Newcastle-on-Tyne, Mawson & Swan sponsored annual exhibitions at a local art gallery and awarded prizes in various categories. A competitive exhibition mounted in the fall of 1881 featured nearly two hundred images from about fifty different individuals.[54] To support this interest, a local camera club was established there in 1882, with its first secretary being from Cullercoats. No evidence indicates whether Homer participated in any of these programs, though plenty of assistance was certainly available for an aspiring photographer.

The men and women involved in the fishing economy on the coast constituted a frequent theme for British artists and photographers. As many during this period were drawn to the laboring classes as a subject matter, these individuals became viewed as an ideal representation of that nation's pre-industrial

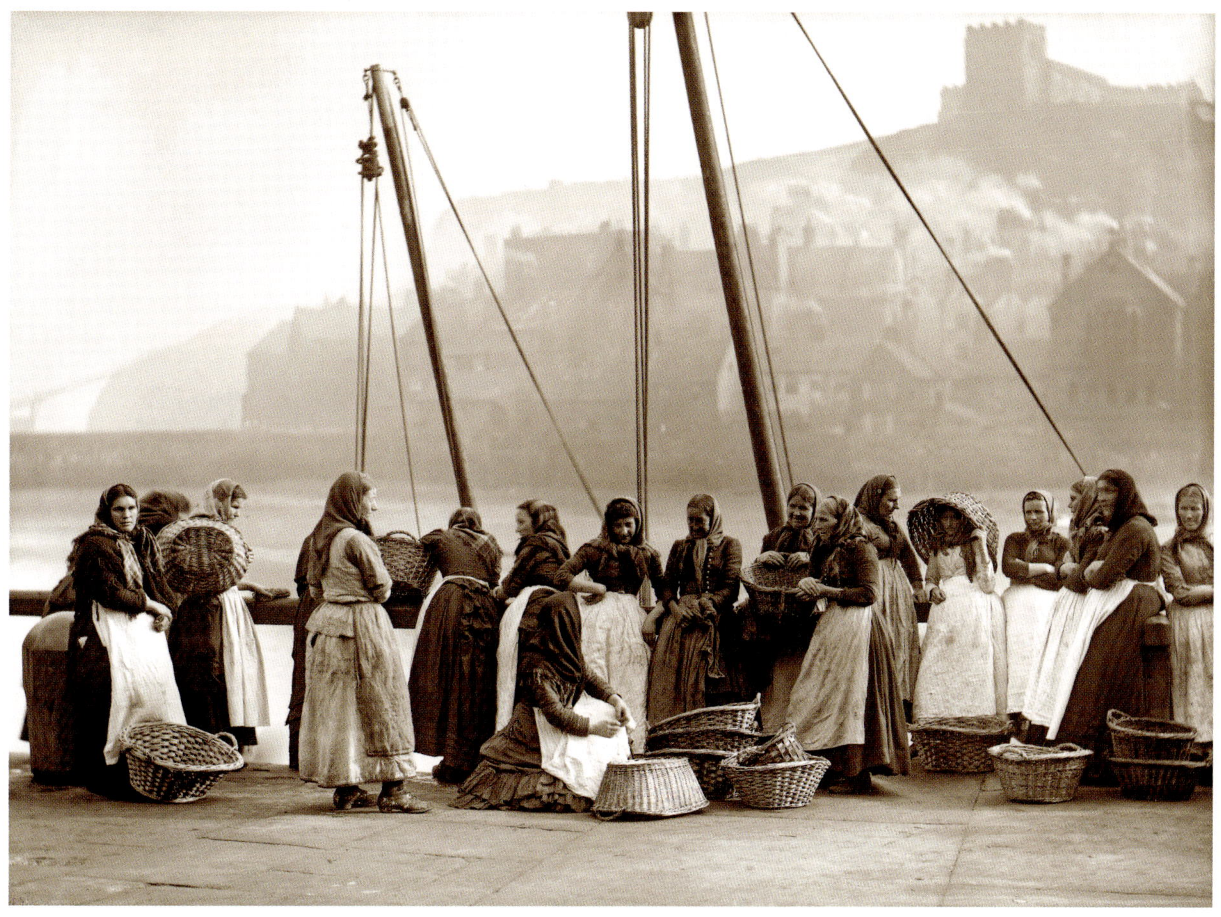

FIG. 22. Frank Meadow Sutcliffe, *Fisherwomen Leaning on Harbour Rail, Whitby Harbour*, c. 1880 (printed later). Gelatin silver print, 12 × 16 in. (30.5 × 40.6 cm). Courtesy of The Sutcliffe Gallery.

past and the living continuation of its age-old economies and cultures.[55] Women carrying handmade baskets and wearing light-colored smocks over their dark dresses and men in water-resistant suits and hats attracted much attention from those with cameras, especially when posed on the beach or a wharf. With the growth of tourism, painters and photographers found a ready market for such images. One of the leading commercial photographers in the region and a frequent exhibitor was Frank Sutcliffe, who lived down the coast from Cullercoats in Whitby. Beginning in 1876, he operated a successful portrait studio there, though he also gained a reputation for his photographs of the village and its inhabitants. Views such as *Fisherwomen Leaning on Harbour Rail, Whitby Harbour* exemplify the approach that made him popular (fig. 22). In this photograph, Sutcliffe posed a group of women by the water's edge, with the town of Whitby and its famous abbey visible across the bay. The masts and rigging of a vessel appear behind the group, a marker of these women's proximity to the maritime trade. No hint of recent developments—social, economic, or technological—is

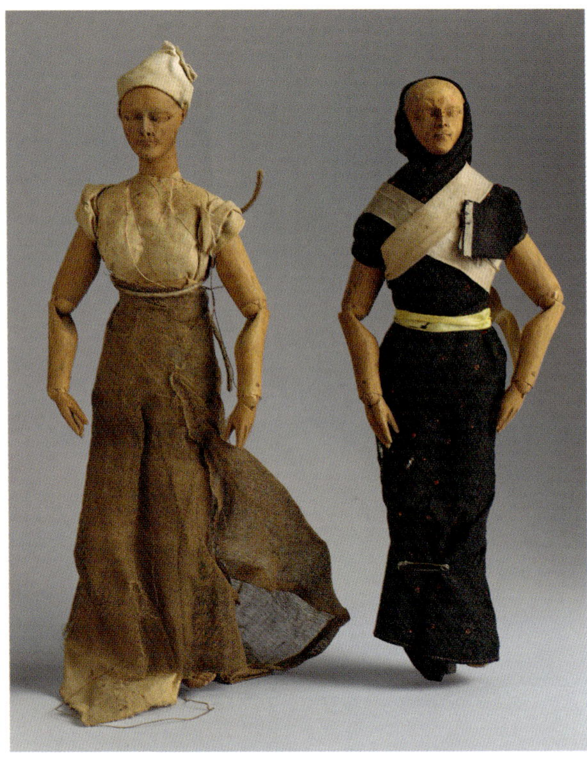

FIG. 23. Two dolls bought by Winslow Homer in England, c. 1881–82. Wood and cloth. Bowdoin College Museum of Art, Brunswick. Gift of the Homer Family. [1964.69.189.1 and 1964.69.189.3]

visible. Like many of the artist's views, the photograph presents a timeless image of a traditional working-class population. Seeking to elevate photography's status, Sutcliffe was later a founding member of the Brotherhood of the Linked Ring, an influential fine art photography society in England.[56]

Both the figures that Homer chose to depict during this period and their poses share many similarities with the individuals pictured by Sutcliffe and other regional photographers and suggest a like disregard for the rapid transformations that were reshaping fishing communities on the North Sea.[57] Though created a year after his return to America, *Fisher Girls on Shore, Tynemouth* is a good example of Homer's interest in and prolonged study of the young women who worked gathering bait, repairing nets, and serving the local economy (plate 40). Similar to Sutcliffe, he was not especially interested in highlighting the individuality of these fisherwomen. Instead, they act like characters in a romantic drama set in this rustic seaside community. Notably, Homer acquired three wooden dolls during his time in England. Small enough to hold in one's hand, two of them wore outfits that approximated the traditional customs of these working-class women (fig. 23). They could also be manipulated to assume different poses. The stiff posture of the female figures in *Fisher Girls* and other drawings, watercolors, and paintings of this period suggests that he might have used them in the service of his work. Homer was dedicated to working out of doors in an effort to accurately capture colors, light effects, and myriad other details. During this period, he also learned and drew inspiration from photographs, drawings at the British Museum, and perhaps even wooden dolls.

It is not entirely surprising that England was the place where the artist first experimented with making his own photographs. Not only was it an ocean apart from his home and a place where he hoped to redirect the trajectory of his work, but it was also a fertile ground for conversations regarding the relationship between painting and photography. In the latter half of the nineteenth century, British photographers played a leading role in championing the fine art status of photography by creating work that moved the medium into new artistic realms. The combination printing practice and allegorical subjects of Oscar Gustave Rejlander and Henry Peach Robinson, the inventive portraits and mythological studies of Julia Margaret Cameron and Charles Lutwidge Dodgson, and the atmospheric landscape photography of Peter Henry Emerson—to name only a few well-known figures—made a strong case for photography as a fine art. With innovations in camera technology and photographic supplies, the number of practitioners—many with artistic ambitions—grew exponentially, especially in the 1880s. Exhibitions, publications, and camera clubs increased alongside this boom. Painters and printmakers took notice, including those associated with the influential Pre-Raphaelite movement in Britain. Many drew lessons from photography, and some even experimented with the camera.[58]

Yet, the medium's association with commerce and technology prevented broad acceptance within the artistic establishment for decades. Walter Woodbury, a pioneering photographic inventor, described with frustration the reluctance of many artists toward the medium in an 1882 article in the British journal *The Photographic News*: "That painters do make great use of photography, although they are loth to own it, is an acknowledged fact. There is a new class of shop lately sprung up in Paris, whose specialty consists in studies of all kinds—trees, rocks, stones, bits of foreground, cattle, sheep, figures, in costume and out of it, whose customers, I am told by the proprietors, are mainly artists. How is it that they seem to be ashamed to acknowledge the great assistance they derive from our art?"[59] Homer was interested in photography's potential to reveal visual insights that might aid his painting, though, like many at the time, he did not publicize this interest or make known any photographs that he might have made. He was recognized for and committed to painting, an investment that did not permit public forays into the photographic arts.

In America during the latter half of the nineteenth century, a similar story unfolded. Well-regarded landscape painters such as Albert Bierstadt, Frederic Church, and Thomas Moran collected or created photographs that influenced their choice of subjects and the evolution of their painting style. Though few spoke about photography, the medium interested them, as their canvases reveal. Indeed, examples abound of instances where—like Homer—they modeled compositions or elements in a painting or print on photographs. Most famous, however, is the example of Philadelphia painter Thomas Eakins, who acquired his first camera in 1880.[60] As scholar Mary Panzer has observed, Eakins embraced "new standards of scientific observation" as part of his artistic practice, a stance promulgated by British philosopher Herbert Spencer and other leading artistic commentators of the day. Rather than portraying a classicized ideal, Spencer came to believe that painters should take a positivist approach to studying their subjects.[61] Eakins conveyed this sentiment in a letter to his father while studying in Paris in 1868: "I think that Herbert Spencer will set them right on painting. The big artist does not sit down monkey like & copy a coal scuttle or an ugly old woman like some Dutch painters have done nor a dungpile, but he keeps a sharp eye on Nature & steals her tools. He learns what she does with light the big tool & then color then form and appropriates them to his own use."[62] In Eakins's practice, photography became an invaluable tool, and during the last two decades of the century, he, his wife, Susan Macdowell Eakins, and his students at the Pennsylvania Academy of the Fine Arts created more than a thousand photographs that served as preliminary studies. These images included portraits, figure and animal studies, landscapes, and chronophotographs. While Homer did not correspond about photography with American artists such as Eakins, his interest coincided with their investigations and with larger debates about photography's status as a fine art and its role as an aid to painting.

For Eakins, photography provided a type of precision and specificity that he sought in his artistic practice. As a painter, Homer was less wedded to such exactitude, especially in his representation of figures. Nevertheless, he shared with Eakins a desire to understand better the manner in which structures worked and how they appeared. He did not utilize photography as ambitiously and creatively as Eakins, but as an artist he—like Eakins—wished to move beyond the conventional idealization that characterized much academic painting of this period. Both were interested in optical experiences, and photography proved an important tool for engaging with the larger world. Homer's decision to purchase two cameras in England cannot fully account for the turn in his career. Other factors also influenced these changes. Yet, his acquisition did complement his search for a new artistic identity. Though his work with these cameras never equaled Eakins's, photography would continue to be a noteworthy part of his practice. After twenty productive months in England, Homer returned to America. Arriving in New York at the beginning of the winter of 1882–83, he brought with him both cameras—not to mention many new watercolors and drawings, but only three oil paintings created during his time abroad. In the years ahead, he would pursue oil painting again with fervor, though in a fashion that constituted a marked departure from his work of previous decades.

"A painter who knows a good thing when he sees it," 1883 to 1910

During John Beatty's visit with Homer at Prout's Neck in 1903, the inquisitive fine arts director of the Carnegie Institute asked him whether "beauty exists in nature" and how it might "be discovered and revealed." "Quick as a flash," Homer responded, "'Yes, but the rare thing is to find a painter who knows a good thing when he sees it . . . it is a gift to be able to see the beauties of nature. . . . You must not paint everything you see. You must wait, and wait patiently until the exceptional, the wonderful effect or aspect comes. Then, if you have sense enough to see it—well . . . that is all there is to that.'"[63] By this time, Homer had been living in Maine for twenty years and knew well what he was looking for. He was also then both critically successful and economically comfortable. Yet, in returning to America in 1882, he faced an uncertain future. Despite productive study in England, he had sold few paintings and seemed torn about his next step. Few documents exist from this period that might reveal insights into why he returned from Cullercoats when he did and why only six months after returning to New York he decided to leave again, and this time for good. A notice in the *Boston Globe* on July 1, 1883, suggested that he "has had so little financial encouragement in New York that he proposes to leave the city. He will have a studio-dwelling not far from Portland, where he will paint to please himself, expecting to give exhibitions of his work occasionally in Boston, his native city."[64] Such notices helped to perpetuate the popular idea that Homer had withdrawn from the wider art world.

Whatever the state of his affairs might have been upon his return, he left New York then in part out of habit. Like many other urban-based artists, he had long favored getting outside the city during the warm summer months. Recent developments with his larger family shaped his decision to visit Maine. During the previous year his younger brother, Arthur, had purchased land on Prout's Neck and had begun to build a cottage that became known as "El Rancho." Arthur had honeymooned on Prout's Neck seven years earlier, and though he, his wife, Alice, and two young sons lived half a continent away in Galveston, Texas, he saw Maine as an attractive place to spend summers. Desirous of creating a family gathering place, Homer's older brother, Charles—a successful New York–based chemist—financed the purchase of a more extensive property there in the spring of 1883 and began work on a seaside home, the "Ark," that was finished later that summer. Over the next twenty years, the family would acquire other large sections of land, eventually securing much of the southern half of this 1,500-acre coastal peninsula.[65]

It was there that the forty-seven-year-old artist would spend the summer of 1883, painting almost exclusively watercolors based on studies created in England and of the rocks and breakers at Prout's Neck. *Surf at Prout's Neck* is characteristic of his work that summer (plate 41). Picturing a rolling wave approaching the rocky shore, it departs compositionally from watercolors of the previous decade. Homer's emphasis is entirely on the wave itself, as the foreground and background are largely, though not completely, eliminated from the view. While he enjoyed watching and studying the incoming surf, often devoting hours at a time to this activity, lessons drawn from photography also informed his artistic decisions. Note, for example, how the flat pictorial plane and the radical cropping of the composition direct the viewer's gaze and highlight the wave's movement and power. *Surf and Rock near Cannon Rock, Prout's Neck*, a charcoal and chalk drawing created the following season, achieves a similar effect, though of a slightly different subject (plate 42). In this instance, his focus is more on the ragged rocks that constitute the shoreline. The splash of a crashing wave drawn in white chalk animates the scene, though the greater emphasis is on the rocks themselves. Again, he isolates a specific subject for study and creates a tightly cropped work, dispensing with figures and other details that might provide another type of narrative.

At Prout's Neck, Homer took up photography again, though probably only sporadically. Regrettably, only a single photograph exists from the period immediately following his return from England, making it difficult to assess fully his commitment to the medium at this time. Created with the Mawson & Swan camera only feet from the ocean, *Cliff at Prout's Neck* bears similarities to the watercolors and drawings he was creating of the nearby coast (plate 43). It pictures a wave rolling up on the rocks and the rock formations that comprise the shore, including a jagged vertical cliff that rises dramatically at left. The view lacks the drama of the previously discussed watercolor and drawing, in part

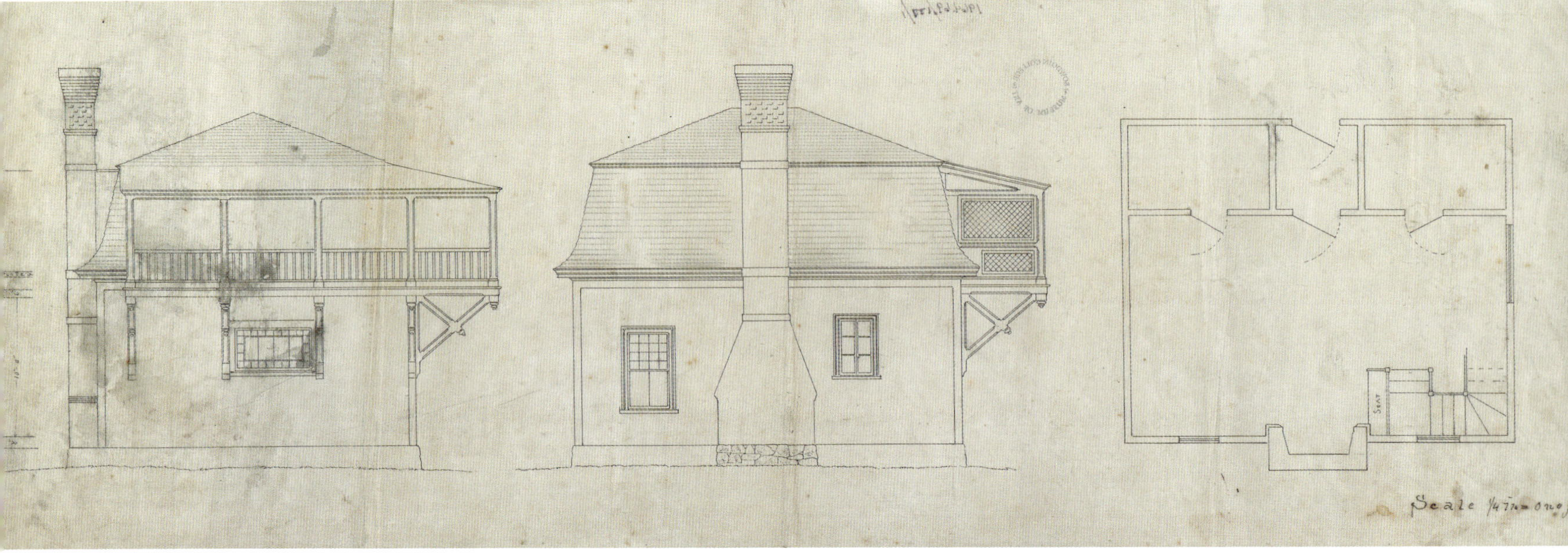

FIG. 24. John Calvin Stevens, *Design for Conversion of Stable into Winslow Homer's Studio*, 1883. Ink, 10 5/16 × 30 1/16 in. (26.2 × 76.4 cm). Bowdoin College Museum of Art, Brunswick. Gift of the Homer Family. [1964.69.177.1]

because it seems to have been photographed on a relatively calm day.

Those who knew Homer remarked that he liked to depict the sea during and after storms, when the surf was larger, the winds stronger, and the skies anything but blue. Beatty recalled a day when a gale arrived there: "Homer was in a fever of excitement, and searched for an extra palette and colors that I might join him in painting, arranging everything so that we might not lose a moment when the rain should abate. While waiting, we paced the coast, clad in heavy raincoats. Sometimes we clung to the wiry shrubs that grew from the crevices between the rocks; at other times we braced ourselves against the driving wind as best we could. Homer was in his element. He watched the shifting clouds with intense interest and was alive to every changing mood. It was for this he had waited."[66] Given the relative fragility of his camera and the importance of keeping this equipment safe and dry, photography was less well-suited for the days that Homer most cherished. Nevertheless, this photograph provided him with useful details, especially about the rocks, which might have informed how he pictured them in other works. As the camera cropped its subject by what the lens could capture, photographs introduced all sorts of unusual compositional structures as well.

Homer had been to Prout's Neck in 1875 on the occasion of his brother's honeymoon trip. From his letters, it is apparent that he came to enjoy his time there. "I am delighted with this place," he told his sister-in-law Martha during his first summer back.[67] Comfort with his new surroundings and recognition that he wanted to devote his artistic energies to working by the sea led him to leave New York and resettle permanently in Maine, a decision almost certainly made during the winter of 1883–84. Purchasing four lots to the east of the Ark from his brother Charles, he hired local Portland architect John Calvin Stevens to convert a stable or carriage house into a studio. Stevens's design for this conversion included an outdoor porch on the second floor that extended beyond the building's southern exterior wall, a structure that was supported by diagonal braces (fig. 24). Facing the ocean, this porch, or "piazza" as he called it, became a place where Homer went to look out from an elevated height at the wider scene.[68] He is not known to have painted from this porch, but instead used it simply to view the scene and to think. At the time, the studio was closer to the water's edge than all of the other local cottages, and the addition of this unique architectural element provided an unparalleled panoramic perspective.

As Rupert Holland, the early historian of Prout's Neck, wrote in 1924, "the sea was his constant companion."[69] At times, Homer was loath for any other. Ensconced in this new abode by the beginning of July 1884—ten weeks following his mother's death in Brooklyn—Homer turned again to his artistic work, though like the preceding summer creating predominantly works on paper. He worked on more ambitious oil paintings largely after the summer crowds had departed. Both that summer and in future summers, the studio served as a type of sanctuary that enabled him to remain somewhat apart from the rest of the community. He needed such a place, as Prout's Neck and the environs surrounding the nearby town of Scarborough supported a growing tourism industry with more than half a dozen hotels and inns, including the Checkley House, which local resident Ira Foss founded in 1873 and expanded to nearly a hundred guest rooms by the century's end. While located only a short distance away on the other side of the Ark, the Checkley and its guests rarely interested Homer and never appeared in his work. The individuals who modeled for him were local men and women, not summer visitors. In a letter to his brother Charles in September about the crowds, he remarked that "I like my home more than ever as people thin out."[70] Given the small size of the community, Homer did grow over the years somewhat self-conscious about the perception that he was deliberately aloof. In a letter to his friend Louis Prang in 1893, he wrote: "I deny that I am a recluse as is generally understood by that term. Neither am I an unsociable hog. . . . This is the only life in which I am permitted to mind my own business. I suppose I am today the only man in New England who can do it. I am perfectly happy and contented."[71]

Homer saw the studio as a place to retire. Paraphrasing Job, he joked in a caption that accompanied a small drawing of the studio that the space was a retreat "where the women cease from troubling, and the wicked are at rest" (fig. 25). Yet, with its second-floor balcony looking out to the ocean—not unlike a camera lens directed at its subject—it also functioned in the manner of a viewing device that focused his sight. Indeed, the studio was Homer's laboratory for thinking about vision and the challenge of portraying what one sees. In this regard, it served a similar purpose to the cameras he purchased in England. Many artists at the century's end established studios in the country or on the coast as a summertime retreat. Their cottages, however, tended

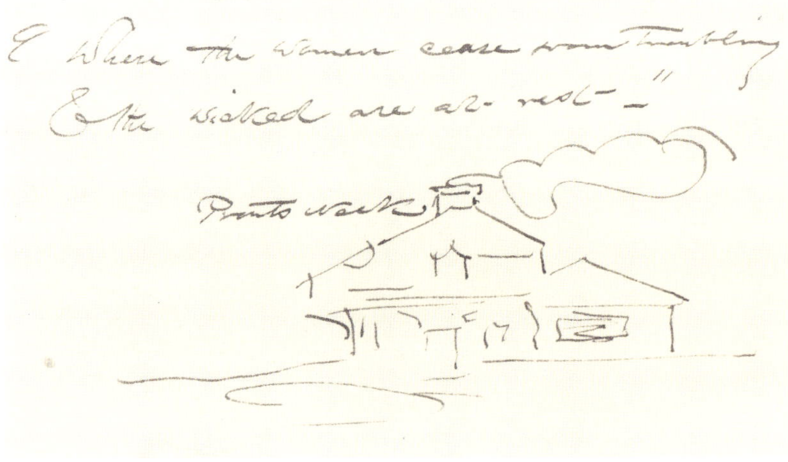

FIG. 25. Winslow Homer, Sketchbook drawing, c. 1898. Graphite, 3 1/8 × 5 1/8 in. (7.9 × 13 cm). Bowdoin College Museum of Art, Brunswick. Gift of the Homer Family. [1964.69.1]

to resemble other summer homes and were not set up as anything other than comfortable domiciles. Homer's, by contrast, was a place to pursue his interest in the close observation of the larger world. While drawings and watercolors of momentary impressions were often completed in relatively short order, many of his paintings upon his return from England took months, sometimes years to finish. The studio gave him a space to work through his thoughts about a subject and to consider solutions to specific pictorial challenges. Though Homer's penchant for long looking might seem worlds apart from the instantaneity of photography, both served to inform his painting practice.

A photograph of the studio—likely taken in 1884—shows a female figure (his sister-in-law Martha?) standing on the balcony looking out (fig. 26). The photograph was acquired by Homer, although it is not known who created the image—perhaps Homer himself—or for what purpose. Given the absence of the Ark and other nearby structures, however, one might surmise that it served to mark the recent completion of the studio. The image also manifests the type of looking that the studio made possible. Paintings from this same period spotlight a similar activity. In *Taking an Observation*, for example, a grisaille oil sketch completed in 1884 for installation in the cabin of his brother Arthur's sailboat, he depicts a mariner peering through a sextant with no land in sight (plate 45). The model may be Arthur himself, who served in the Navy during the Civil War. The painting is a study of concentration and a celebration of a sailor's expertise in understanding his place within the wide ocean. Sextants were used to calculate a ship's location based on the angle of the sun and stars, and served as a critical navigational tool. The abilities to use this instrument and to read the sky and waters were analogous to Homer's own artistic practice. Both depended on comprehending what was seen in front of them, an activity aided by certain tools of the trade.

Two years later Homer created a larger, more finished painting, *Eight Bells* (plate 47), a work whose composition borrowed significantly from *Taking an Observation* as well as an earlier, 1881 watercolor (also entitled *Taking an Observation*, private collection). Each of these works functions as a type of self-portrait. *Eight Bells* is particularly revealing, for though the painting includes two figures, they act as two halves of a single individual. Nearly identical in appearance and outfit, both hold

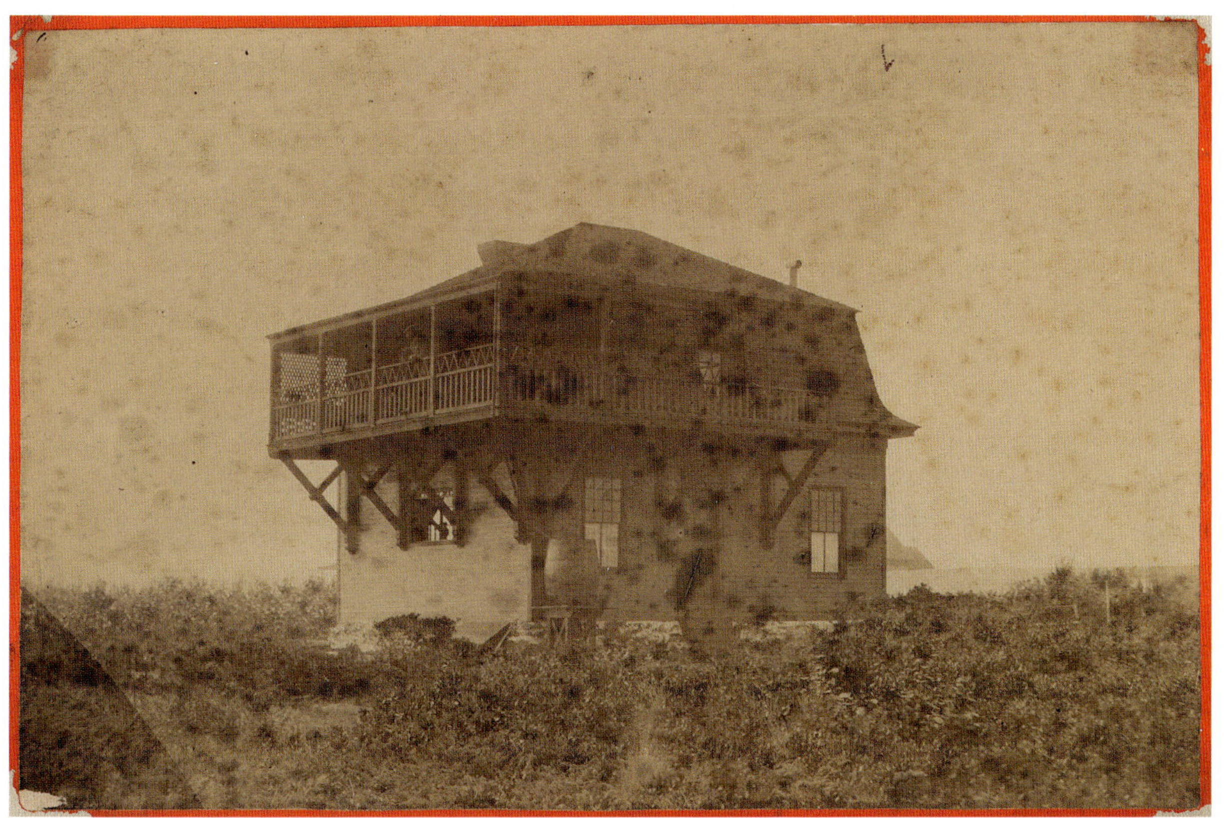

FIG. 26. Unidentified photographer, *Winslow Homer's Studio*, c. 1884. Albumen silver print, 4 7/16 × 6 11/16 in. (11.3 × 17 cm). Bowdoin College Museum of Art, Brunswick. Gift of the Homer Family. [1964.69.153.11]

similar nautical instruments. While one looks through it out to the sea—not unlike an observer on Homer's second-floor balcony—the other looks down at his instrument—not unlike a painter studying his palette. The pair presents two types of looking, one peering out in the distance, the other focused on something close at hand. In their spatial relationship, the two individuals in *Eight Bells* also call to mind the subjects represented in the motion study photographs of Homer's contemporaries Thomas Eakins, Eadweard Muybridge, and the French scientist Étienne-Jules Marey. Beginning in the 1870s, but even more so in the 1880s, these three men took a leading role in pioneering the field of chronophotography.[72] They were fascinated by the desire to capture motion in people and animals in order to both understand physiology better as well as comprehend how to portray a moving body. Muybridge's *Animal Locomotion (Plate 287)* records a naked man running and reaching to the ground to pick up a ball (fig. 27). In the larger series of which this photograph was a part, a project undertaken in Philadelphia between 1883 and 1887, Muybridge published 781 collotypes of men, women, and animals engaged in different actions. His effort to capture movement with his multiple-camera apparatus was hugely influential on various

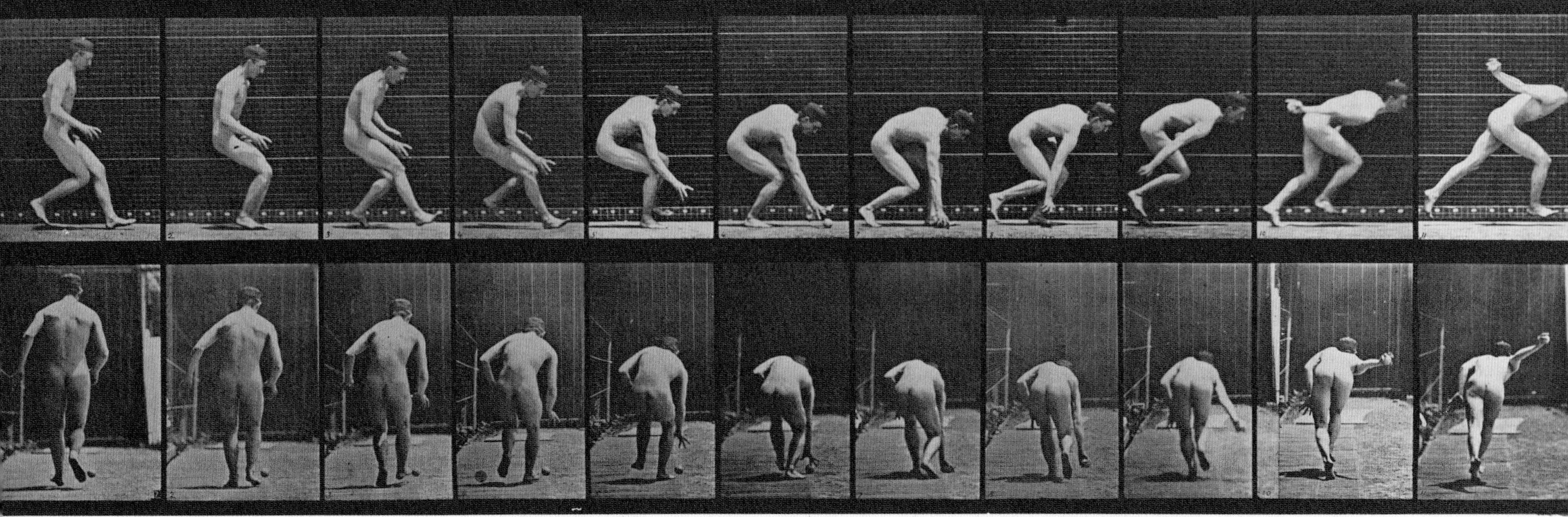

FIG. 27. Eadweard Muybridge, *Animal Locomotion (Plate 287)*, 1887. Collotype, 5¾ × 18 in. (14.5 × 45.7 cm). Bowdoin College Museum of Art, Brunswick. Gift of Paula and Mack Lee. [2006.16]

disciplines, including the fine arts. While there is no record that Homer saw or was aware of Muybridge's work, the pair in *Eight Bells* suggests a kindred interest in understanding the body in motion.

Prout's Neck was Homer's base of operations for the remainder of his life. Though he enjoyed his independence, living there put him in the proximity of many other artists and photographers. With New York artist Thomas Cole's 1844 trip to Mount Desert Island as an early inspiration, Maine became a destination for many out-of-state painters, the great majority of whom created romantic landscapes that foreground the region's rugged natural beauty. The number of visiting artists was fast growing in the years after the Civil War, especially with expanded passenger service on the Boston and Maine Railroad. A new railway station in Scarborough, a short distance from Prout's Neck, opened in 1873, enabling Homer to travel with ease and opening up the area to visitors. The number of local artists was also expanding, with nearby Portland and Cape Elizabeth comprising an important locus of activity. The Brush'uns, a plein-air painting group that frequented different places along the coast, was founded in 1860, and the Portland Art Society was established in 1884 in a building designed by John Calvin Stevens (architect of Homer's studio). Homer befriended several local artists during this time, though he never participated in their exhibitions, preferring instead to show in Boston, New York, and other, larger cities.[73]

Portland was also home to an active contingent of commercial and amateur photographers. If he needed photographic equipment, supplies, or advice, several sources were near at hand. Indeed, by 1887 nine separate photographic businesses operated there, a large figure given that Portland's population did not exceed fifty thousand until after 1900.[74] Many ran portrait studios, though a few also ventured into the business of creating landscape views and stereographs. The scenic coast was a common destination for these individuals. As in England, the introduction of dry plate negatives and easier-to-operate cameras led to the rapid growth in the number of amateur practitioners in the area, including some who actively sought to use the camera for artistic purposes. To support these ambitions, the Portland Camera Club was founded in 1899.[75] The extent to which Homer interacted with photographers in the region is unknown, though an article in a Portland newspaper after his death describes him as the "best friend" of Robert Knight, a local art dealer and photographer. In Knight's obituary, it was stated that "Knight was one of the first to realize the value of the now omnipresent view photograph as a valuable factor in the art world."[76]

During this period Homer was familiar—perhaps even friends—with at least one artist whose practice combined painting and photography. Samuel Peter Rolt Triscott was an English-born artist who settled outside Worcester, Massachusetts, in 1871 and became a founding member of the Boston Society of Watercolor Painters in 1885. He was one of the first artists to discover Monhegan Island off the coast of Maine, where he bought land and visited during the summer. Triscott learned photography in the 1880s and used it to produce landscape views that frequently served as source material for his watercolors.[77] Triscott and Homer shared the same Boston dealer, J. Eastman Chase, and seemed to have met through this association. In using photographs as the basis for watercolor paintings, Triscott tended to replicate the compositional structure of the photograph. While he copied specific details, like Eakins and others, he often "improved upon" the photograph by eliminating certain elements and reconfiguring others. The color and expressionistic brushwork of the resulting watercolors also distinguished them from the photographs.

For Homer, Triscott, and other painters, photography had the ability to stop time and to fix the ever-shifting light before them. Unlike Triscott, however, Homer did not borrow so literally from photographs during this period. His interest in the medium was less about replicating details, as it had been earlier in his career, and more about thinking broadly about this visual technology's contributions to understanding vision and the larger natural world. In 1865, during a moment when photography's potential was first being debated, photographer John Moran—the older brother of painter Thomas Moran—wrote about the "relation of photography to the fine arts," and argued that "it is the power of seeing and deciding what shall be done, on which will depend the value and importance of any work, whether canvas or negative."[78] Homer did not make photographs as distinct works of art, as Moran did, though he subscribed to a similar notion: that at the foundation of the visual arts lay a commitment to looking outward and deciding on a composition to pursue.

In a more prosaic albeit no less significant connection to the medium, Homer also participated in the popular activity of collecting family photographs and compiling photographic scrapbooks. At Prout's Neck, he and his family collected dozens of photographic images, some of which were framed and hung on the wall and others gathered into albums. In some instances, they interacted directly with photographers who visited the area. One example is Simon Towle, a commercial photographer from Lowell, Massachusetts, who created a series of photographs of the Homer family during their first years at Prout's Neck (figs. 28A–H). Towle had visited and photographed at Prout's Neck prior to the Homers' purchase of land there. During the summer of 1883 and again in 1884, he returned with two cameras—one to create medium-format views and a second to create stereographs. How Towle came to know the Homers is unknown. They may have met during one of Towle's trips to Maine, as the photographer visited often in order to create views that he could sell either directly to summer visitors or through his commercial gallery in Lowell. It is also possible that Homer's brother Charles and sister-in-law Martha intersected with Towle in Lowell. Martha was raised in nearby West Townsend, Massachusetts, and she and Charles often returned there. En route to or from Maine, they would have passed through Lowell, and might have connected with him then.

That said, this series, of which ten views are extant, remains a bit of a mystery. Who encouraged its creation, and what was the larger purpose? All of the photographs were taken outdoors and variously feature groups of people enjoying themselves or the recently constructed dwellings that the Homers had built. Winslow appears in three of the photographs. In one, he stands alongside his father and his dog Sam; in a second, he is with a group of family members and others by the water's edge; and in the third, he joins a large party at a corn roast on the rocks. In this last photograph, a woman in the back of the group holds an American flag in her hand, perhaps an indication that Towle has captured a Fourth of July celebration. Other photographs in the series depict the Ark, El Rancho, and scenic views of the rocks and ocean at Prout's Neck. Given the size of Towle's camera, he relied upon a tripod to operate it. His photographs were not spontaneous snapshots but carefully composed views that required coordination with his subjects. He did a good business creating photographs for individuals and groups, and it is likely that one of the Homers commissioned him to create these views. Yet, the photographs were not all made in the same year, an indication that Towle's relationship with the Homers was not a one-off or random occurrence.

What Towle's photographs show is a tight-knit family that enjoyed their time outdoors at Prout's Neck. They also manifest a sense of pride for the new family venture they had launched there, alongside a sense of belonging with the wider community. As the Homers began to market and sell lots from their different properties to others, these photographs might also have complemented their real estate investment. No evidence exists, however, to suggest that these images circulated. Importantly, what the photographs do not show are the nearby hotels and the sporting activities that were at the center of visitors' vacations, subjects that Towle did photograph on other occasions. Despite the proximity of the Checkley House, the Homers tried to remain at a distance from it. These views are also a far cry from the close studies of the rocks and oceans that Homer had previously drawn and photographed. While several feature the coastline, the place that Homer looked out upon from his studio and that he would repeatedly revisit as a subject, it is not believed that he used these photographs as part of his artistic practice.

Towle's photographs do, however, indicate Homer's continuing engagement with the medium. He lived in a world increasingly dominated by such images. The introduction of new reproduction processes associated with photography, including halftone, photolithography, and photogravure, had by the century's end made the medium the leading source for images in books, newspapers, magazines, and advertisements. Photography mediated people's understanding of the larger world, a fact that resonated with a painter such as Homer. Though he privileged painting's ability to convey truth and beauty, he also did not shy away from photography. Indeed, every painter during this period was compelled to reconcile their practice in light of photography's popularization. In an era of mass visual culture, what was the status of those artists who worked with paint on canvas? Each responded in their own way, though their work was also inflected by other developments—artistic, social, economic, and technological. As Homer came to understand as an apprentice illustrator, painting reigned supreme in the hierarchy of the arts and gave its practitioners a privileged seat from which to speak.

Despite the authority of painting, he became increasingly accustomed to supplying photographic copies of his oil canvases to publishers. At an earlier moment, engravers had been required to accomplish this work, and the resulting images were predictably different—significantly so—from the original. Desirous of broadening the visibility of his paintings and the quality of these reproductions, he worked with several photographers to prepare images for publication. William Kurtz, whose New York studio specialized in halftone printing, was highly favored by Homer. In a letter to Martha Homer in 1895, he discussed the process for copying paintings: "The best place to have a picture copied is Kurtz in the American Art Building, Madison Square. . . . Do not cut that sketch off the block until it is photographed—unless it is uneven on the surface. I fixed it so that it would not rub & in doing it may have wobbled up—(if so it must be cut off and mounted flat)."[79] Notwithstanding the lack of color and other shortcomings, photographic reproductions of artworks transformed the public's understanding and appreciation of painting and other fine arts.

These copies impressed Homer enough that for a time he seems to have considered marketing photographic reproductions of his paintings. In 1884, he discovered the etching process and completed *The Life Line*, the first in a series of etchings based on important paintings and watercolors of the period (plate 44). Though he had largely ceased working on commission for illustrated magazines, he remained on the lookout for opportunities to make money from his work. Sales of watercolors and etchings were important to him. Perhaps inspired by their success, he had at least two paintings photographed, and affixed the resulting images on cardboard mounts to which he added his signature, a presentation format that was then common for works on paper and fine art photographs (fig. 29). One such painting was *The Coming Away of the Gale*, a work that he had painted and first exhibited in 1883. As one of the first major oils to be completed after his return from England, Homer had great expectations that it would receive critical praise. Anticipating that acclaim, he had the painting photographed and prepared the copy for sale. Like his watercolors and etchings, it was another product

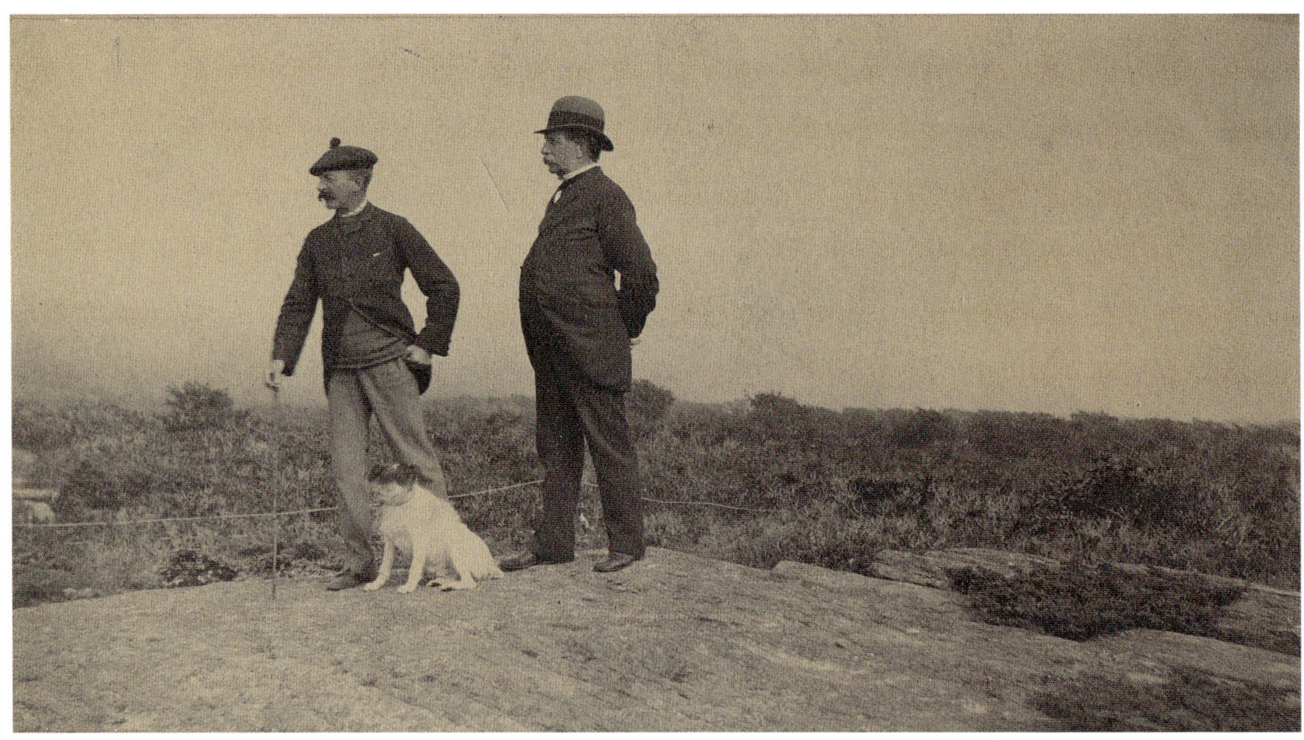

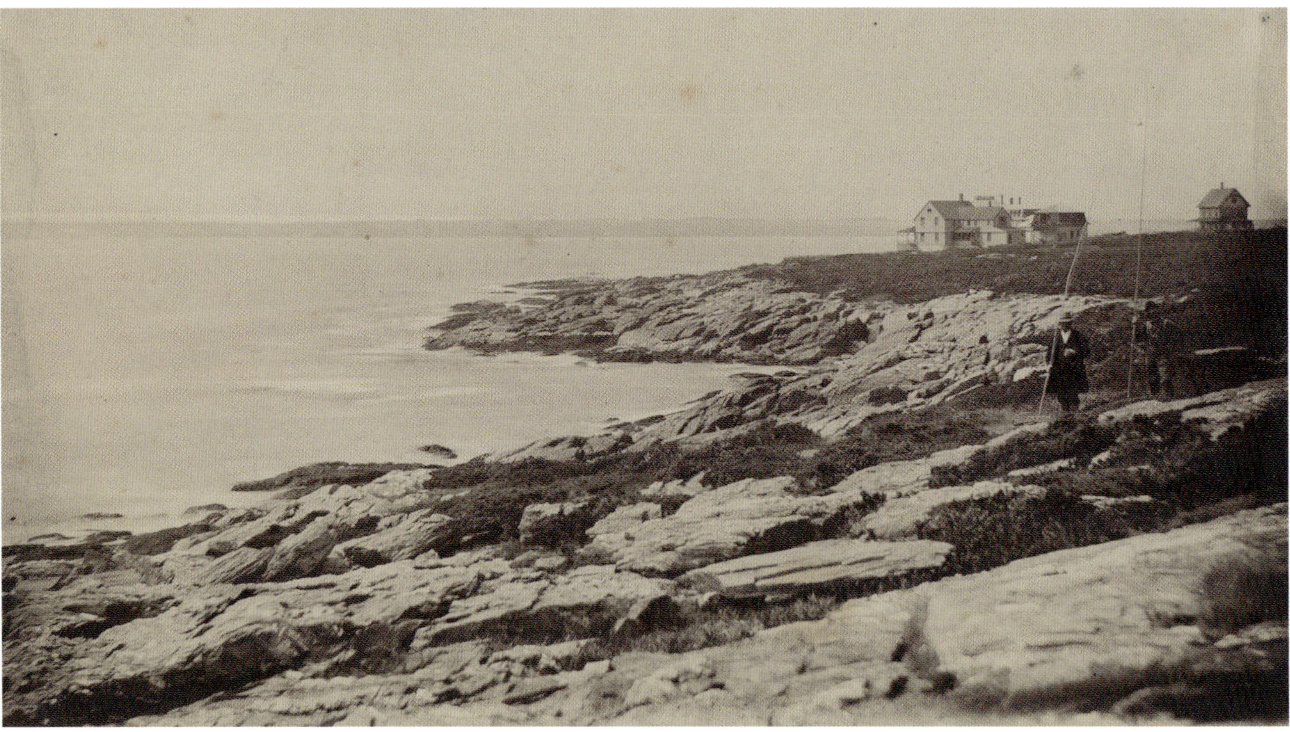

FIG. 28A. Simon Towle, *Winslow Homer, His Dog Sam, and His Father Charles Savage Homer, Sr., at Prout's Neck, Maine*, c. 1884. Albumen silver print, 3⁷/₈ × 7 in. (9.8 × 17.7 cm). Bowdoin College Museum of Art, Brunswick. Gift of the Homer Family. [1964.69.153.3]

FIG. 28B. Simon Towle, *View of the Ark from a Distance*, c. 1883. Albumen silver print, 3⁷/₈ × 6³/₄ in. (9.8 × 19 cm). Bowdoin College Museum of Art, Brunswick. Gift of the Homer Family. [1964.69.177.22]

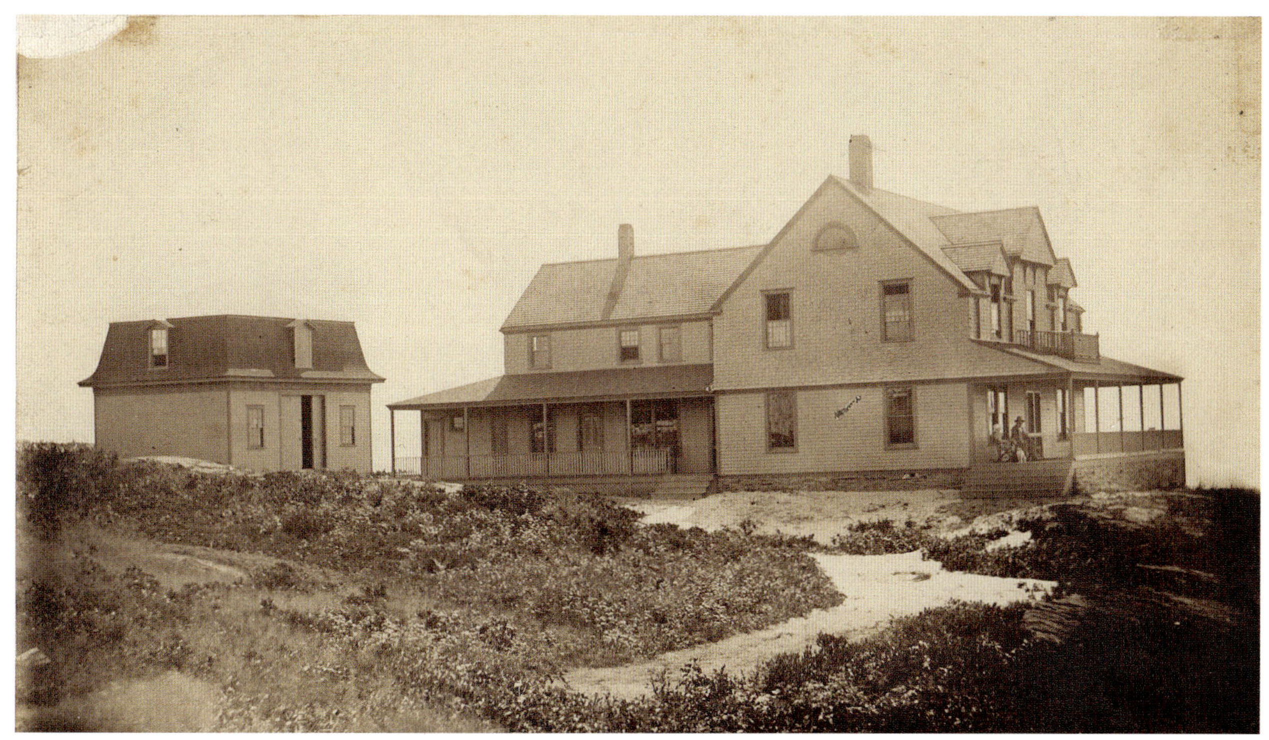

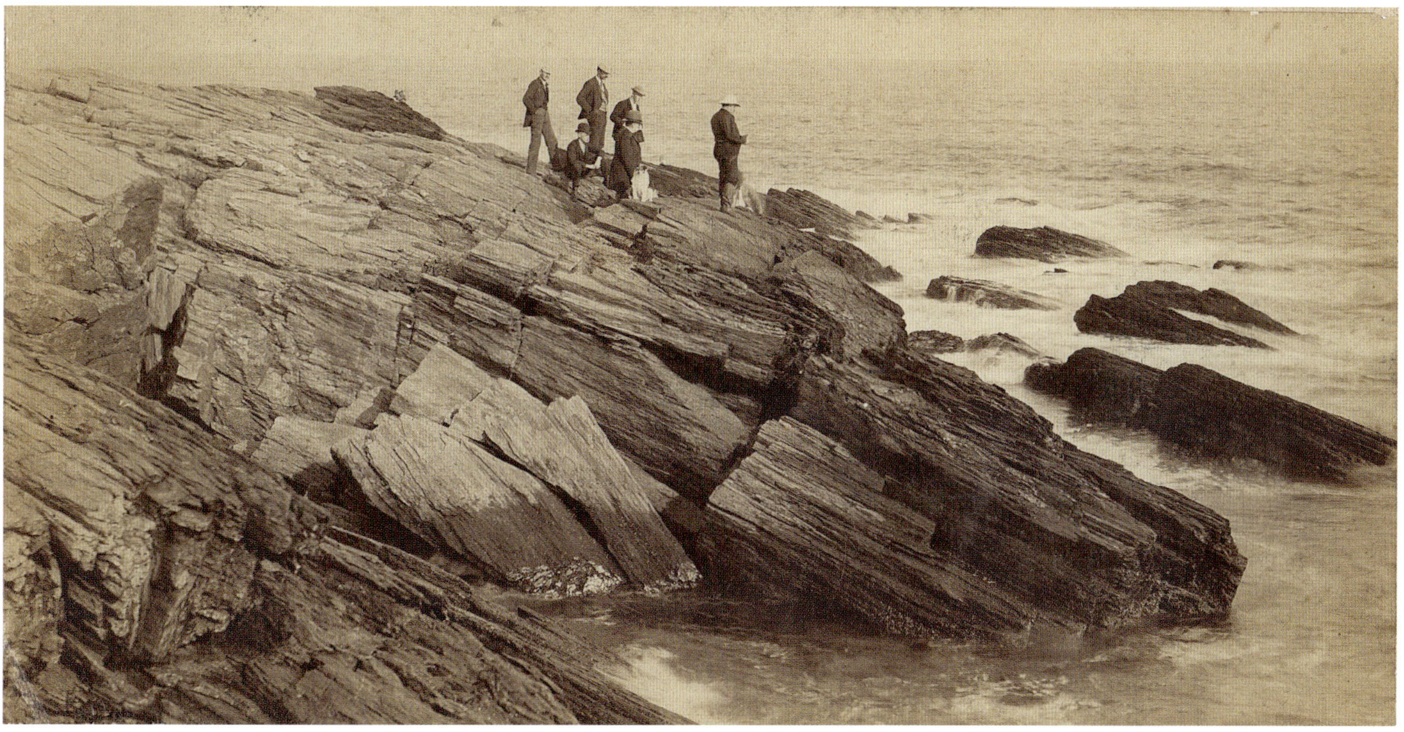

FIG. 28C. Simon Towle, *The Ark and Stable*, c. 1883. Albumen silver print, $4^{3}/_{16} \times 7^{1}/_{8}$ in. (10.6 × 18.1 cm). Bowdoin College Museum of Art, Brunswick. Gift of the Homer Family. [1964.69.153.10]

FIG. 28D. Simon Towle, *Winslow Homer and a Group at the Water's Edge*, c. 1884. Albumen silver print, $3^{15}/_{16} \times 7^{1}/_{2}$ in. (10 × 19.1 cm). Bowdoin College Museum of Art, Brunswick. Gift of the Homer Family. [1964.69.177.16]

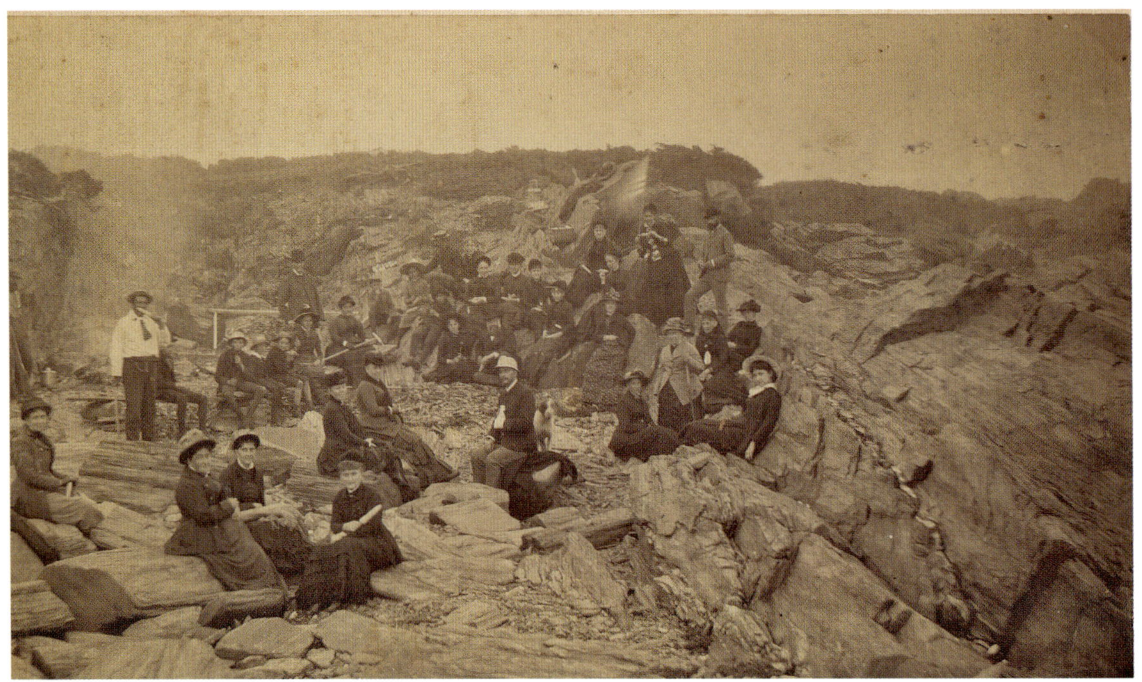

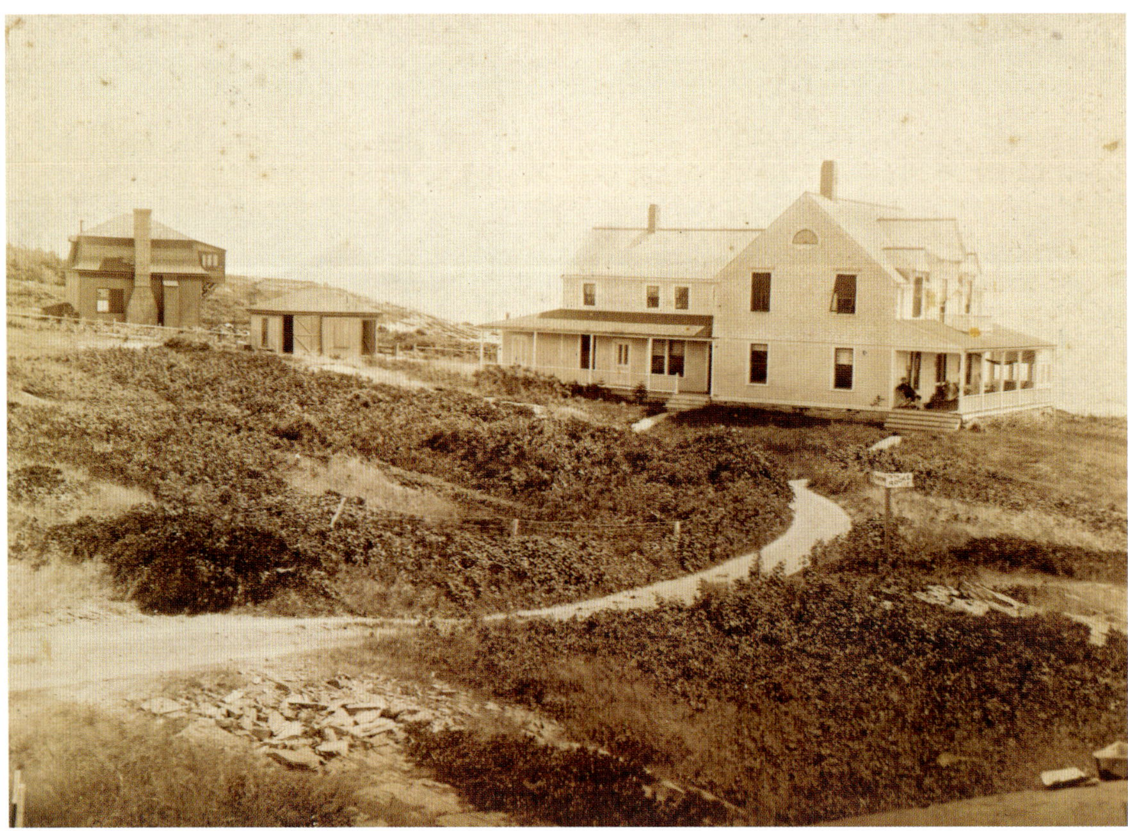

FIG. 28E. Simon Towle, *Corn Roast*, c. 1884. Albumen silver print, 4 5/16 × 7 3/16 in. (10.9 × 18.3 cm). Bowdoin College Museum of Art, Brunswick. Gift of the Homer Family. [1964.69.177.17]

FIG. 28F. Simon Towle, *The Ark and Winslow Homer's Studio*, c. 1884. Albumen silver print, 6 5/8 × 9 1/16 in. (16.8 × 23 cm). Bowdoin College Museum of Art, Brunswick. Gift of the Homer Family. [1964.69.177.25]

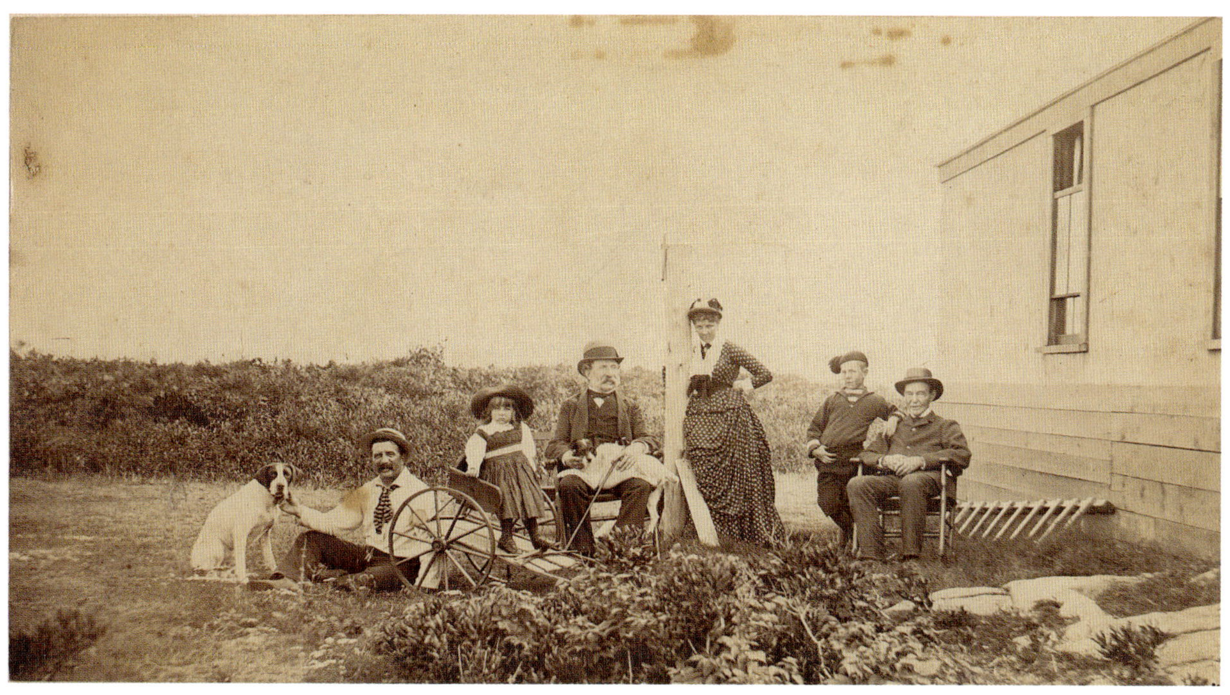

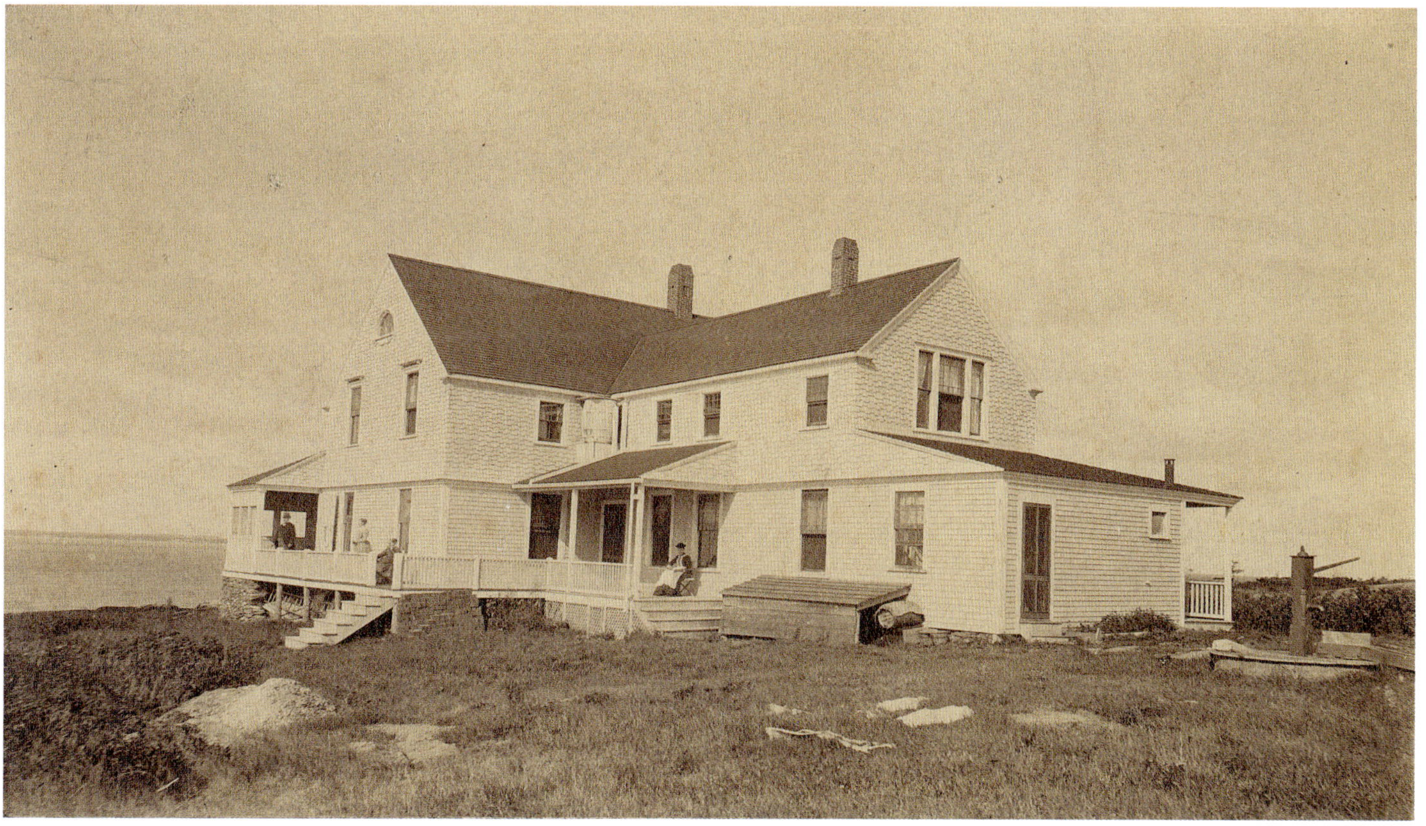

FIG. 28G. Simon Towle, *Homer Family Seated beside El Rancho*, c. 1884. Albumen silver print, 4 1/16 × 7 3/16 in. (10.3 × 18.3 cm). Bowdoin College Museum of Art, Brunswick. Gift of the Homer Family. [1964.69.177.20]

FIG. 28H. Simon Towle, *The Ark*, c. 1884. Albumen silver print, 4 1/2 × 7 3/4 in. (11.4 × 19.7 cm). Bowdoin College Museum of Art, Brunswick. Gift of the Homer Family. [1964.69.177.24]

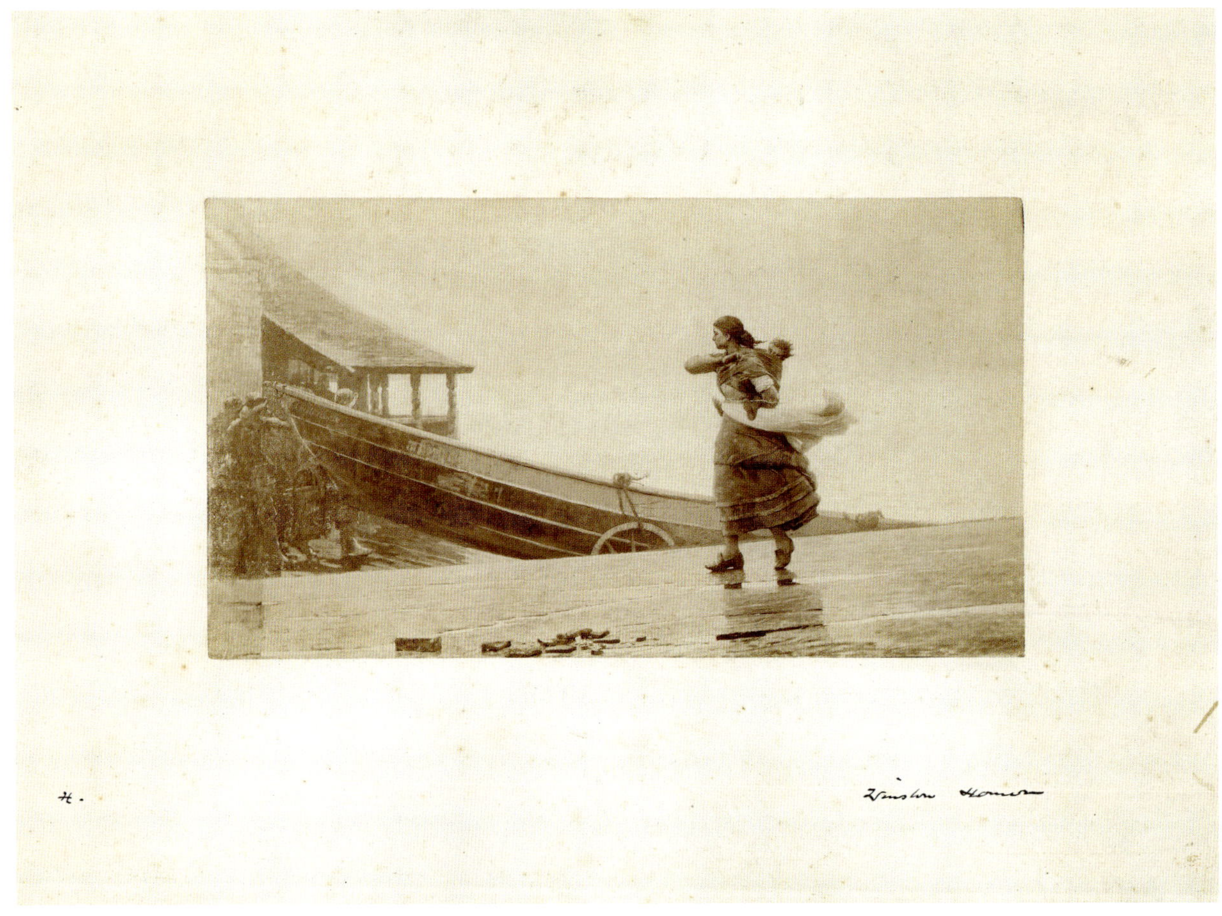

FIG. 29. Unidentified photographer, *Winslow Homer's "The Coming Away of the Gale,"* c. 1883. Albumen silver print, 4 7/8 × 8 11/16 in. (12.4 × 22.1 cm). Bowdoin College Museum of Art, Brunswick. Gift of the Homer Family. [1964.69.176.2]

that he could market to audiences who might not want or could not afford a much-costlier painting. When the painting received only lukewarm reviews, he brought it back to his studio, where he reworked it over the next ten years and later retitled it *The Gale* (plate 55). Though the idea of marketing photographic copies of this painting did not succeed, he later returned to other reproduction techniques for producing salable copies of his paintings.

In preparation for embarking on a new painting, Homer never abandoned drawing. As a means to focus his thinking on a given subject, it was one of the core elements of his practice. His commitment to drawing, however, was more sporadic during the last two decades of his painting career. At times, he employed it, though increasingly his work began with time spent looking and thinking, followed by plein-air study, and subsequent refinements to a composition in the studio based in part on memory. His early biographer William Downes recalled during this period: "He was accustomed to do a great deal of looking before he decided upon a subject to paint; and sometimes he would spend whole days just looking at the sea, without touching a brush. Although he was one of the first painters in America to take the trouble to carry a canvas several miles for the purpose of making a study from nature in some place which had interested him, yet he did not always work directly from nature. His extraordinary memory for visual impressions served him so well, that at times he could record a scene he wished to paint without any preparation except the slightest of notes and the hastiest memoranda."[80] He used drawing in the preparation for his watercolor painting, especially as an understudy that could guide his application of color washes. Relative to earlier in his career, however, drawing was a less pronounced part of his process. Photography did not replace drawing, but it did play a role, especially in revealing details that might be difficult to capture with the eye alone or when time was limited and there was much to record.

Finding the long, cold winters at Prout's Neck difficult to endure without some type of respite, Homer traveled often to warmer destinations such as Florida, Bermuda, and islands in the Caribbean, sometimes by himself, but often with his brother Charles. He also went away during other seasons, especially to pursue his passion for fishing. In 1889, he traveled to the Adirondacks for the first time in fifteen years. He returned there often during the next several years, and in 1893 added the Tourilli Fish and Game Club in Quebec as an alternate fishing destination. These many trips afforded him plenty of opportunities to create new work, and he returned to Maine each time with a dozen or more watercolors. The portability and ease of watercolor made it his preferred medium for painting while away from the studio at Prout's Neck.

On several of these journeys, he brought with him a Kodak #1, a lightweight, hand-held camera that the George Eastman Company first introduced in 1888. Charles gave it to him in the lead-up to one of these trips, though the exact date is unknown.[81] Marketed with the slogan "You Press the Button, We Do the Rest," the Kodak #1 came preloaded with enough film to take a hundred exposures. The resulting images were round in format due to the type of lens it utilized, a feature that Eastman "corrected" in later models. At Prout's Neck, Homer and members of his family made the camera part of their social activities (figs. 30 and 31). Taken on the porch of the Ark, these views exemplify the personal, informal snapshots for which the camera became known and suggest how integrated photography was in the social rituals of the family. Simpler to operate than his Mawson & Swan camera, the Kodak #1 presented a new recreational activity for the family.

A survey of the Kodak #1 images that Homer created beyond Maine shows that he was less interested in using the camera to create family portraits and more so in bringing the camera into the field in order to capture certain wilderness sites and distinct visual effects (plates 60A–K). In Florida, for example, his eye gravitated to stands of tall palms on the banks of swamps and rivers. The mirrored reflections of these trees on the water fascinated him enough to capture them with his camera. Homer made many of these views from his seat in a fishing boat, an indication that he traveled with the camera by his side and that he envisioned such trips as a

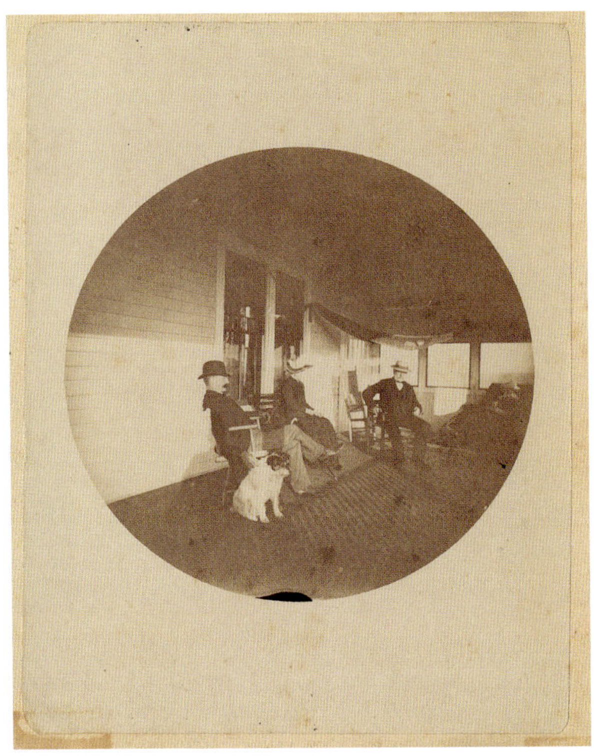

FIG. 30. Unidentified photographer, *Winslow Homer, Martha Homer, and Charles Homer, Sr., Sitting on the Porch at the Ark*, c. 1895. Gelatin silver print, 2⅝ × 2⅝ in. (6.7 × 6.7 cm), image. Bowdoin College Museum of Art, Brunswick. Gift of the Homer Family. [1964.69.153.4]

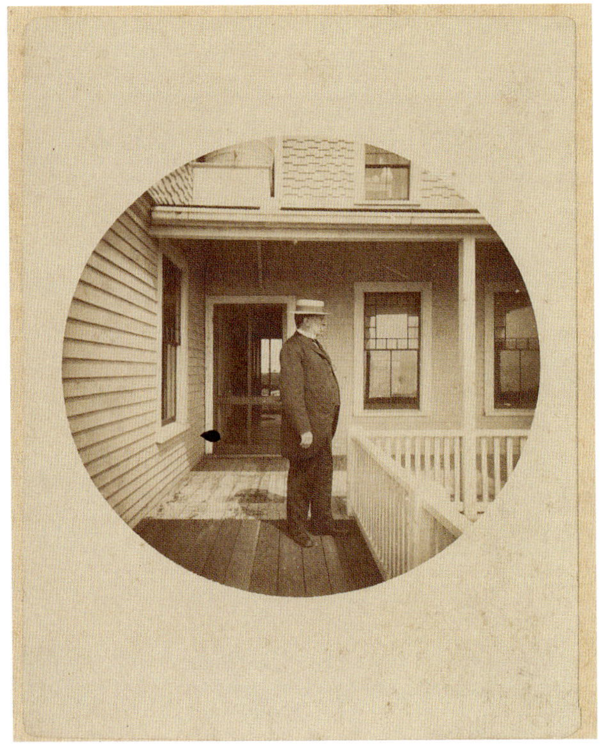

FIG. 31. Unidentified photographer, *Charles Homer, Sr., Standing on the Porch at the Ark*, c. 1895. Gelatin silver print, 2⅝ × 2⅝ in. (6.7 × 6.7 cm), image. Bowdoin College Museum of Art, Brunswick. Gift of the Homer Family. [1964.69.181.6]

combination of sport and artistic exploration. Several Florida watercolors bespeak a similar interest in stands of palms by the water's edge. *The Turkey Buzzard*, for example, may not replicate these photographs, but it was the result of much looking at this subject and thinking about how to convey its distinct forms and light effects (plate 64).

The extant photographs from his travels to Quebec share similar qualities with the Florida photographs. In both instances, Homer studied unique subject matter that a camera was well suited to represent. In Quebec, several photographs depict a figure in a canoe in the middle distance. These were not meant as portraits of his traveling companions. Instead, they are about noting visual details on the water's surface and understanding the relationship of a moving canoe within a larger scene. This type of momentary impression could not be rendered effectively in a drawing, especially as he might not have wanted or been able to stop. Such photographs also introduced the idea of the blur, an optical result that shed insight into the complex nature of vision. In watercolors from Quebec, such as *Under the Falls, the Grand Discharge* (plate 62) and *Canoe in Rapids* (plate 63), water is as important a protagonist as the individuals in their canoes. Understanding how to portray the substance convincingly

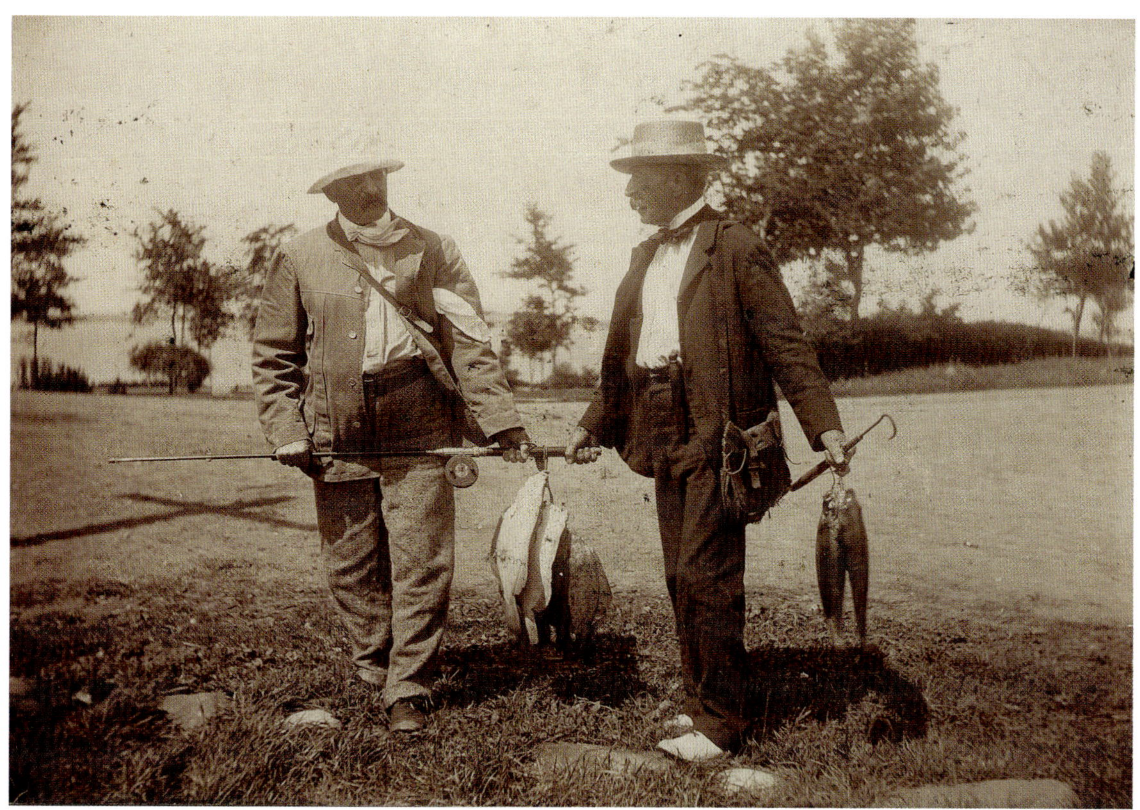

FIG. 32. Unidentified photographer, *Charles Homer, Jr., and Winslow Homer Carrying Fish*, c. 1900. Gelatin silver print, 4¾ × 6¾ in. (12.1 × 17.2 cm). Bowdoin College Museum of Art, Brunswick. Gift of the Homer Family. [1964.69.153.2]

in its various guises and to factor in an element like a canoe was a difficult task. Homer enjoyed watercolor for its ability to convey a fleeting moment. With its ability to stop time, photography shed light on this challenge.

Embraced by many as a device to record faces, places, and personal memories, the Kodak #1 camera served Homer in other ways. Though he did not avoid participating in family photographs, such as posing with his catch alongside his brother, he saw photography as a tool for better understanding the wider world (fig. 32). Travel and fishing are both pursuits centered primarily on active looking and movement. While photography's capacity to capture motion was still in its infancy, recent achievements in chronophotography and the birth of filmmaking ushered in a new era for the portrayal of moving subjects. Homer's watercolors of leaping fish—a subject that he depicted frequently during his travels—intersect with this larger interest. With its complex array of colors and its focus on the dramatic action of the sport, watercolors such as *Jumping Trout* broke new ground in the artistic rendering of fish (plate 50). His ability to portray a fish as a live creature leaping for a fly distinguished him from other artists of the period, most of whom recorded their subjects dead on the water's edge. As historian

Paul Schullery has shown, however, Homer's fish rarely replicated the actions of an actual fish striking its target. Not only were the poses he created inaccurate, but the handling of the water out of which the fish arose was often unrealistic.[82] He worked primarily from memory in composing these watercolors. Photography's promise to render the world in unrivaled detail led artists to respond in various ways. With Homer, it encouraged him to figure these fish in a new fashion—one that was more believable to the eye.

Motion photography also reinvigorated the tradition of sequential imagery. The idea of creating multiple representations of a particular subject over time predated photography's introduction. Yet, its ability to create several exposures in short order—a hallmark of the Kodak #1 and other roll-film cameras—made such imagery more ubiquitous in the 1890s. Motion picture films also furthered this phenomenon. At times, Homer demonstrated an interest in pairing works together or establishing a related series of images. Two watercolors from an 1892 trip to the Adirondacks, *Deer Drinking* and *The Fallen Deer*, suggest the artistic potential of this approach (plates 53 and 54). In the first watercolor, a deer straddles a fallen log to drink from a body of water; in the second, it has fallen into the water, its head partially submerged and its body suddenly lifeless. With this pairing, the viewer is made to infer what has transpired in the interval: namely, the shooting of the deer by a hunter beyond the frame of the composition. The absence of the gunshot and a bloody wound does not lessen the violence of the image. By involving the viewer in this imaginative narrative, Homer created a scene just as powerful, if not more, as one that depicted the subject directly. Innovation characterized his work in watercolor during this period, and though he claimed that watercolor was "something that I can sell for what people will give," he saw it as a place to experiment with his practice.[83]

Evidence suggests that Homer was not the sole photographer on these trips. Indeed, several photographs may feature the artist himself. J. Ernest Yalden, a family friend whom he met in the Adirondacks, recalls that he created a number of photographs of Homer there.[84] Whether or not he used Homer's camera is unknown, though the idea that Homer might have posed suggests that being the author was less important than the resulting image. For an artist who rarely pictured himself in his own paintings and prints, yet who created work that was often deeply felt, his inclusion in these photographic views also points to his own invisible presence in works from throughout his career. Yalden is the subject of *Paddling at Dusk*, a watercolor created in 1892 that portrays the New York University student in a canoe on Mink Pond (plate 52). Yalden recalled years later that "it has always been a puzzle to me how he was able to get the effect he did when it was almost too dark to distinguish one color from another."[85] Yalden's position in this composition—paddling away from the viewer in the middle ground—creates the suggestion that the artist was with him on the water. Except for the light shimmering off the ripples, the water is dark; the background is nearly monochromatic and more abstract than representational. Long fascinated by the nocturne, Homer drew lessons from the blur of photography to render the darkness of the scene. Thirty-four years older than Yalden, he also saw in his friend a shadow of his younger self.

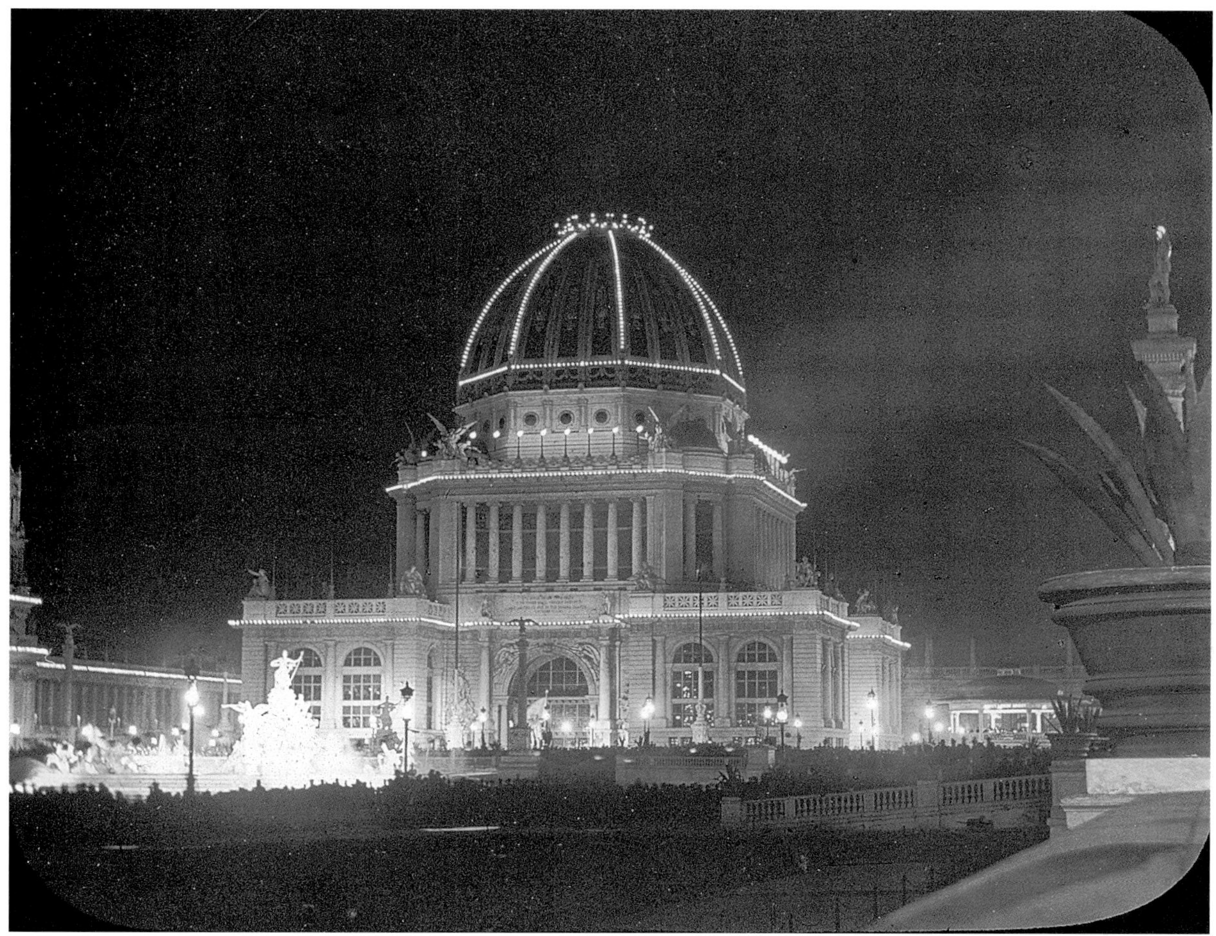

FIG. 33. Starks Lewis, *World's Columbian Exposition, Administrative Building at Night*, 1893. Lantern slide, 3¼ × 4 in. (8.3 × 10.2 cm). Brooklyn Museum. Goodyear Archival Collection. [6.1.016]

The different light effects that break the night's darkness is also the primary subject of *The Fountains at Night, World's Columbian Exposition*, the only painting he completed during a trip to the 1893 world's fair in Chicago (plate 56). There to see an installation of fifteen of his paintings and to receive a gold medal from the fair's art committee, Homer was captivated—like many visitors—by the electric lights that lit up the fairgrounds at night. Chicago was the first world's fair to introduce electric light, and the nighttime scene was as popular as any of the exhibits. Numerous photographers created images of the exhibition buildings and the large lagoon at the center of the fairgrounds illuminated by electric light. A nighttime view of the Exposition's Administration Building, with Frederick MacMonnies's grand fountain in front, by Starks Lewis, an amateur photographer from Brooklyn, suggests the visual drama that awaited fairgoers (fig. 33). Homer was enthralled by the fair, and while there bought a souvenir booklet composed of photographs of its main attractions.[86]

Like many photographers—both professional and amateur—he lined up to represent a view similar to Lewis's. Artificial light had caught his interest three years earlier in *Summer Night* (1890, Musée d'Orsay), a painting that portrays two women dancing on an outdoor porch awash in electric or gas light, as the light of the moon shines down from above. In *The Fountains at Night*, the scene is again alive with motion and complex light effects: water shoots upward and out from the fountain, and a gondola in the foreground with two oarsmen and two passengers glides across the shimming waters of the lagoon. Painted exclusively in black, white, and various shades of gray, it has much in common with period photographs of the scene, except for the fact that Homer was able to capture motion more convincingly than any photographer. Though well aware of and influenced by a visual culture increasingly dominated by photography, Homer created paintings during this period that surpassed photography's ability to capture the complex interaction between form, light, and movement. He did so in part by adapting photography's lessons to his larger practice.

Depicting water in different weather conditions, seasons, and times of day was the challenge that preoccupied the artist most during his last two decades. Living almost literally atop the ocean at Prout's Neck, he understood how it could play tricks on the eye and that it could be at one moment light, calm, and almost transparent, and at another opaque, heavy, and more powerful than anything humans might produce to oppose it. Understanding the ocean's ever-shifting character consumed his attention. Two photographic albums from the turn of the century that belonged to his brother Arthur feature images of the rocky shoreline and crashing waves, including the photograph *High Rocks*, alongside images of family members in various recreational pursuits (fig. 34). Whether these photographs of the ocean were taken by Homer or simply inspired by him, they record this engagement with the water and its relationship with the rocks at the shoreline. Though sandy beaches were close by, Homer was not interested in painting them, choosing instead to focus on the sometimes violent confrontation between surf and rocks.

While photographs might capture interesting details and optical effects, they were not especially effective in getting below the surface of the water and in comprehending the source of the ocean's power. Homer meant his late marine painting to be felt by viewers. They were less about specific narratives and more about subjective experiences. Created in 1894, *High Cliff, Coast of Maine*, for example, lacks a human figure in the scene, though it places the viewer in an elevated position overlooking the action at the water's edge (plate 59). With its bold forms, subtle coloring, and grand scale, it conveys an energy far exceeding that of the photograph of the same scene. Photographs of this period, by comparison, present a very matter-of-fact rendering of the world. They describe their subjects well, and while they had the potential to excite a connection, their small size and technical limitations restricted their capacity to express larger themes. Homer's late paintings, by deflecting obvious conclusions, required extended contemplation and achieved a level of realism unsurpassed in contemporary American art circles.

Homer garnered numerous accolades during this period. Awards, exhibitions, invitations to serve on prestigious exhibition juries, and art purchases by museums and

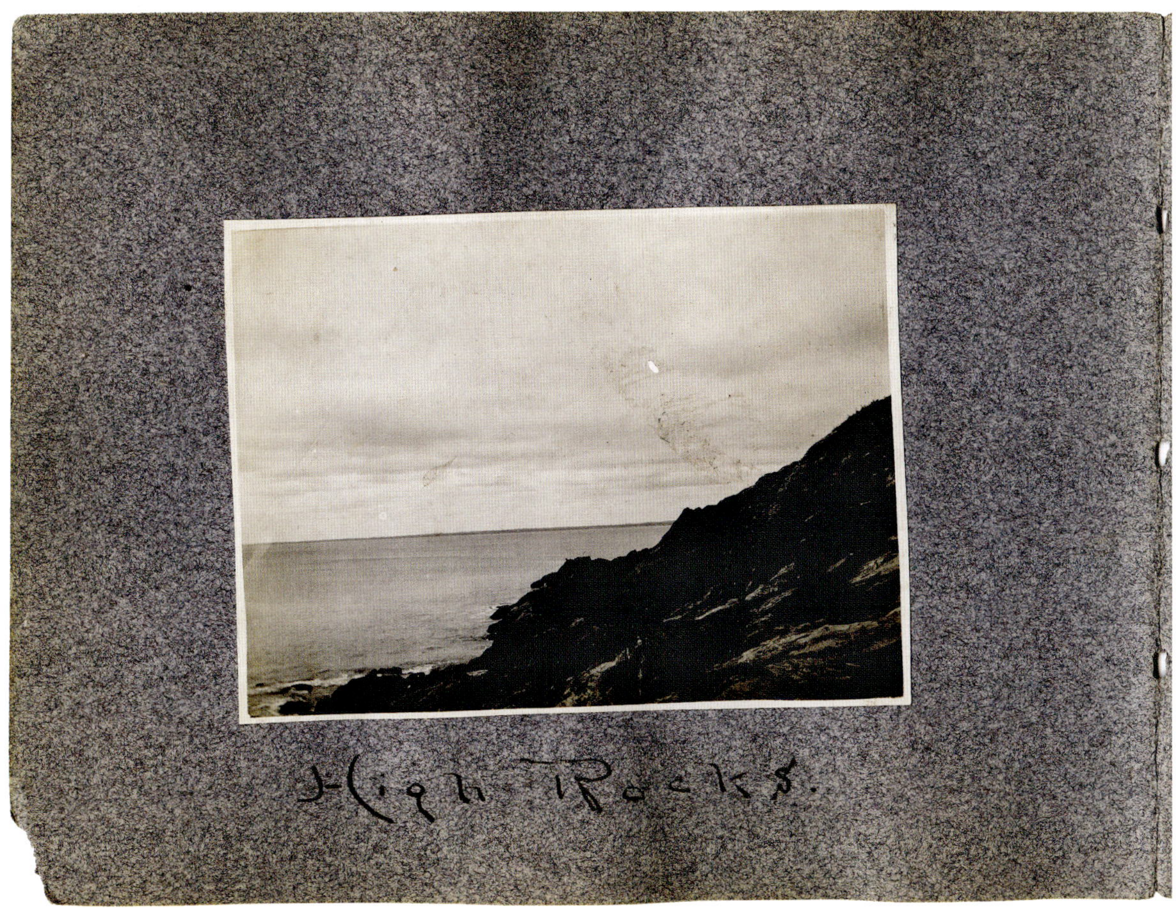

FIG. 34. Unidentified photographer, *High Rocks*, c. 1900. Gelatin silver print from an album owned by Arthur Homer, 4⅝ × 6½ in. (11.7 × 16.5 cm). Bowdoin College Museum of Art, Brunswick. Gift of the Homer Family. [Homer Memorabilia 27.k]

private collectors came regularly to him. This recognition pleased him, though at Prout's Neck, his newfound standing prompted greater attention than he sometimes wished. Anecdotes about efforts to keep visitors away from his studio are numerous. A desire for photographs of him was another by-product of this celebrity status. Requests came from different quarters, and Homer accommodated many of them by posing in commercial portrait studios and more informally in and around his home. At times, he posed alongside family members or close friends. These images were meant as personal keepsakes that reflected important relationships, and many were unconnected with his artistic practice. Two photographs taken at and within his studio by an unidentified individual at the century's end suggest that some wished for a portrait that captured the activity for which he was famous. In the first image, he poses outside the studio with Lewis Wright, an African American waiter whom Homer met in Boston and in 1895 invited to work for the family (fig. 35). Homer and Wright built a close relationship, and Wright continued to assist

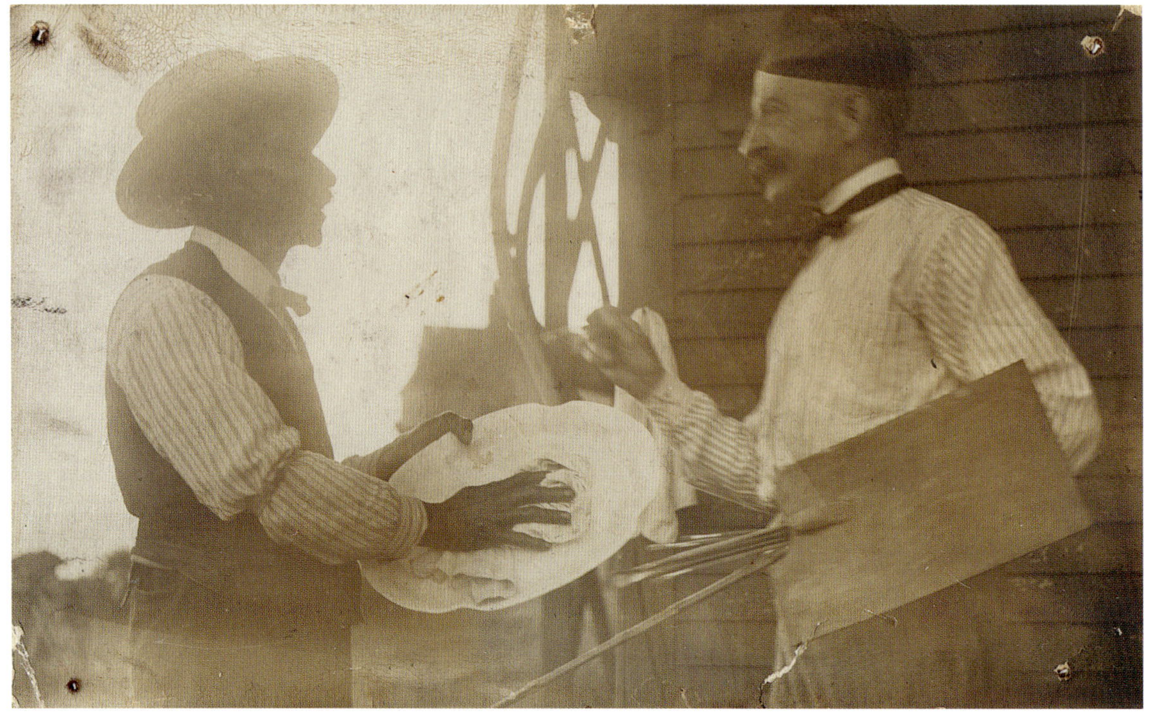

FIG. 35. Unidentified photographer, *Winslow Homer and Lewis Wright at the Studio*, c. 1900. Gelatin silver print, 3³/₈ × 5⁷/₁₆ in. (8.6 × 13.8 cm). Bowdoin College Museum of Art, Brunswick. Gift of the Homer Family. [1964.69.153.5]

the family at Prout's Neck until Homer's death. Homer holds a palette and brushes in his hands, while Wright wipes clean a plate. The specific circumstances are unknown, though Homer thought enough of the image to keep a copy and tack it on the wall of his studio.

In the other photograph, he stands alone—again with palette and brushes in hand—in front of his easel on which the painting *The Gulf Stream* (1899, Metropolitan Museum of Art) resides (fig. 36). This is the only photograph that shows him presumably at work in his studio. Though it was not reproduced during his lifetime, it has been published frequently since then, often serving as a window into his practice and a glimpse inside the studio. In this portrait, he does not look directly at the photographer, as he does in other formal portraits, but instead glances to the side. He might have been momentarily distracted, or perhaps he was annoyed by this interruption. Dressed in a dark jacket in front of his easel with other paintings visible on the wall behind him, Homer is depicted as a serious artist caught in the midst of his work on a large painting about an Afro-Caribbean man stranded on a boat that has lost its mast. In the painting sharks circle in the foreground, and a storm appears on the horizon. Human powerlessness in the face of unknowable forces of nature had emerged as a recurring theme in his late paintings, and was especially present in *The Gulf Stream*. This photographic portrait, which links the artist and the doomed subject of his painting, supported his posthumous reputation as someone who subscribed late in life

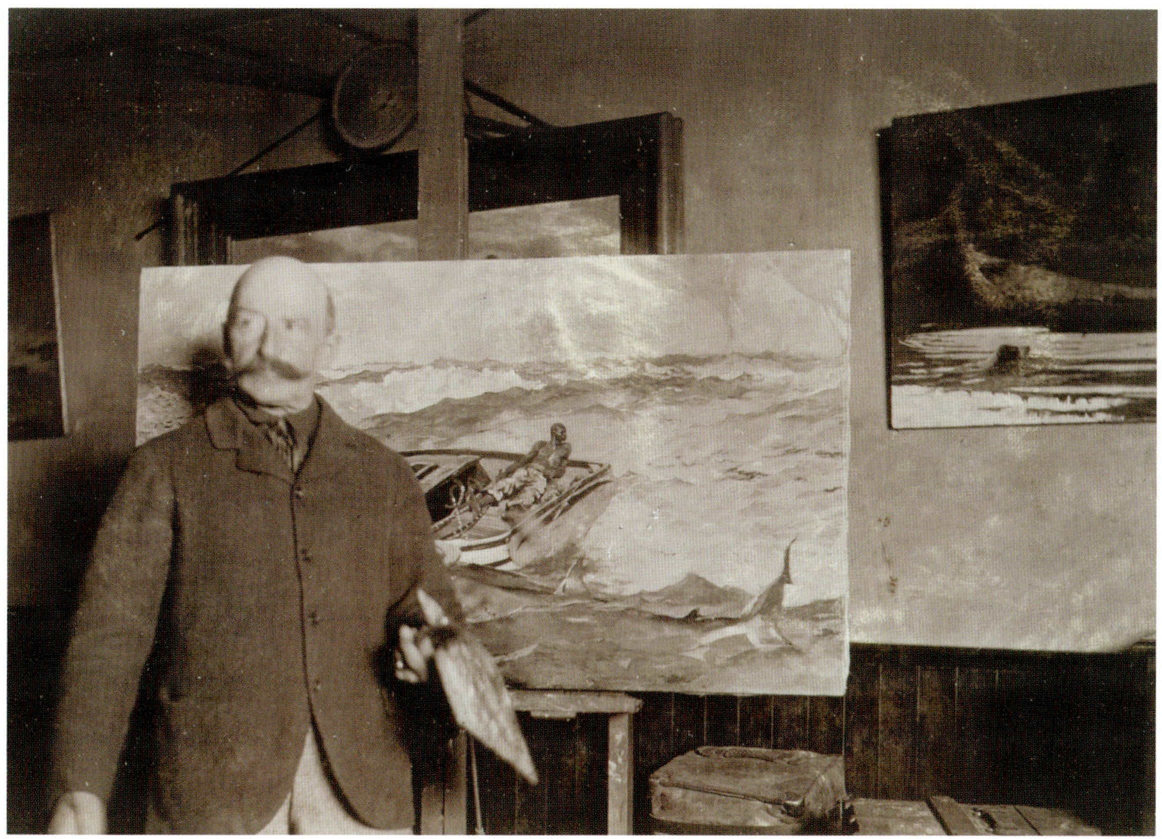

FIG. 36. Unidentified photographer, *Winslow Homer with "The Gulf Stream" in His Studio*, c. 1900. Gelatin silver print, $4^{11}/_{16} \times 6^{3}/_{4}$ in. (11.9 × 17.2 cm). Bowdoin College Museum of Art, Brunswick. Gift of the Homer Family. [1964.69.179.9]

to a more fatalistic attitude about the larger world. Seen together with the portrait that included Lewis Wright, it also suggests that *The Gulf Stream* might have held more personal significance than previously imagined.

As indicated in the other photographic portraits from this period, including the last photographic likeness, created in 1908, Homer remained a figure who chose not to reveal much about himself (fig. 37). Like earlier portraits going back to the Civil War, this photograph conveys a similar respectability and gravity, but says little about his relatively unconventional path to success or his fragile health. In May of that year, he suffered a stroke that affected his speech and, as he related in a letter to his brother Charles in July, left him unable to "tie his neck tie in the way that I have done for the past twenty years."[87] Though the exact month of this portrait is unknown, Homer appears, as always, well-dressed with his jacket and tie in the proper fashion. Having received a request for an interview from the Boston art critic William Downes in June, Homer replied after his recovery in August that he was unwilling to assist him: "It may seem ungrateful to you that after your twenty-five years of hard work in booming my pictures that I should not agree with you in regard to that proposed sketch of my life. But

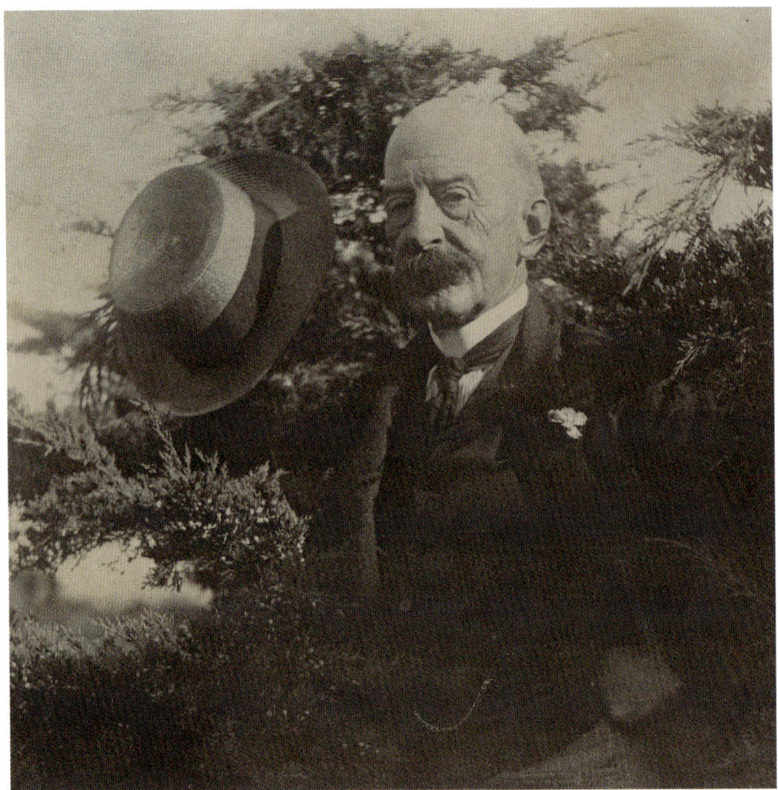

FIG. 37. Unidentified photographer, *Winslow Homer at Prout's Neck*, 1908. Gelatin silver print, 10 1/16 × 10 in. (25.6 × 25.4 cm). Bowdoin College Museum of Art, Brunswick. Gift of the Homer Family. [1964.69.179.16]

I think it would probably kill me to have such a thing appear, and as the most interesting part of my life is of no concern to the public I must decline to give you any particulars in regard to it."[88] Continuing to paint and travel throughout this period, Homer died two years later at his studio, with both his brothers in attendance.

. . . . . .

On February 21, 1895, the day before his fifty-ninth birthday, Homer wrote his brother Charles. Around this time, he corresponded regularly with him and his wife, Martha, often about small matters, though sometimes his letters became more reflective about his past. Hesitant to share such feelings with the larger public, he did confide private thoughts to those closest to him. He was in such a mood that winter day, and wrote about the previous twelve years in Maine: "I am very well with a birth day tomorrow. I suppose I may have 14 more, (That was mother's age 73 years) and what is 14 years when you look back. The life that I have chosen gives me full hours of enjoyment for the balance of my life. The sun will not rise, or set, without my notice, and thanks. Only think of my absolute freedom, I have gained in, one item, a year's time in the last 12 years."[89] In this short statement, he acknowledges both his own mortality and his contentment with the decision to live at Prout's Neck. He also hints at the centrality of the natural world, the significance of direct observation, and the importance of independence for him as an artist.

Homer sought to see clearly and to depict accurately what he saw. He could become annoyed when viewers misconstrued what he had attempted to capture. When a critic described the sun as a "silvery moon" in *The Artist's Studio in an Afternoon Fog* (1894), he remarked to a friend, "that oil is not a moonlight. No one but a first-class fool would take it for one."[90] Like other artists, Homer longed for audiences to look closely. Painted just several months before this letter, *The Artist's Studio* was Homer's only painting that figured the studio and the Ark (plate 57). In his art, as in his interactions with others outside of his family, Homer disclosed little about his private self. Though largely invisible, he is present in his work, and a review of his oeuvre suggests much about him and his understanding of the role that artists play in society. In *The Artist's Studio*, Homer came, as scholars Frank Kelly and Nicolai Cikovsky, Jr., have remarked, "as close to self-portraiture" as he ever got.[91] Whereas he had spent the previous twelve years looking out at the ocean, contemplating it in all its infinite variety, and seeking to convey something of its unknowable power, for this painting he looked back from the water's edge at his own home, and in a larger sense at his own self. Shrouded in fog with the sun looming over the scene and casting the buildings in a silhouetted darkness, the scene is people-less and reveals little about the man who lived there. He renders the buildings as ghostlike shadows that sit atop the water below, a place of solitude separate from the rest of humanity.

Though a unique optical experience serves as the basis of its drama, the painting is also an artistic creation composed of myriad decisions. Its vantage point, framing edge, color palette, and many other details reflect specific choices. This tension between naturalistic truth and composition was at the heart of Homer's practice, an idea that those who knew him often recalled. His acquaintance Augustus Moulton once remarked about his achievement, "the mere painting of a picture is nothing. It must be studied and thought out."[92] To Homer, paintings had the potential to make a subject not only legible, but understood more clearly than by sight alone. They permitted one to penetrate below the surface in order to appreciate a deeper, contemplative side of experience. To achieve these ends, he employed many strategies and devices. As John Beatty recalled, "he was interested in every aid offered by science."[93]

Working in an age increasingly dominated by photography, Homer understood its potential to serve as a source material for his art. Copying photographs was a part of his early art education. Over time, however, as he grew more familiar with the work of other photographers and he began making his own photographic views, his interest in the medium became more concerned with its unique visual effects. While photographs promised an objective rendering of a subject, he came to understand that they delivered something quite different. *The Artist's Studio* was not based directly on a photograph, though elements of the painting—the manner in which it is cropped, the blur of the background scene, and the flatness of the composition—owe a debt to photographic vision. For Homer, like many American and European painters of the late nineteenth century, photography invigorated his work and initiated a wider dialogue about the nature of representation. The medium's introduction gave rise to new rivalries in the world of the fine arts and within the larger and fast-growing marketplace of images. More often, though, photography acted as a site for experimentation and a tool that complemented and expanded his practice and that of others.

A tension between nature and technology also takes center stage in a consideration of Homer's career. Like many landscape painters of his age, Homer devoted much energy to investigating and depicting the mysteries and beauty of the natural world. At Prout's Neck, an ever-present, always visible and audible conflict between sea and land surrounded him and inspired the final chapter of his artistic life. Both before and after moving to Maine, he also ventured to often-remote wilderness destinations, places such as the Adirondacks, Florida, and the Caribbean, where rustic guides and local inhabitants were seemingly as unspoiled as the natural surroundings. Yet, these communities, where he found a sense of home in a frequently rootless life, were accessible to him thanks to new transportation systems, the birth of the tourism industry, and America's expanding industrial economy. Indeed, they were the products of broad changes—social, economic, and cultural—that were transforming all parts of the nation. Photography was only one of many technologies responsible for the wholesale reorganization of modern life. Though he cherished the natural world, he was well aware of these changes, and often made them themes of his work.

In the early twentieth century, Homer became a hero to many modern artists who were deliberately rejecting the academic models and conservative tendencies of an earlier generation. New York–based painters such as George Bellows, Robert Henri, Edward Hopper, Rockwell Kent, and others found his devotion to living apart from the city in close proximity to the natural world worthy of emulation. These artists ventured north to Maine, looking to replicate what Homer had achieved at Prout's Neck. In addition to admiring his rugged individuality, they also found much to appreciate in his painting style, or, rather, what they perceived as his lack of style. And they shared his commitment to seeking an essential relationship with his subjects, his yearning to penetrate reality's surface, and his connection with the laboring classes. In addition to living apart from the city, Homer seemed to work independent of others, rather than aligning himself with any one school or tradition. In a profile of Homer published in 1889 by Mariana G. Van Rensselaer, the American art critic foregrounded his career-long independence: "He was born with a different nature from most painters of his day, and with so strong a nature that he took no impress from their practice or ideas. . . . From beginning to end, and as regards alike essence and form, he has worked out his art for himself."[94] His experience with the larger image economy and his desire to follow his own path as a painter resonated deeply with those young artists pursuing new subjects and new painting styles.

For Homer, artists served as the eyes of the world. They prioritized what to look at and provided insight into how to think about important social and philosophical questions. From a young age, Homer privileged painting as the medium best suited to seeing. Yet, photography's introduction complicated the manner in which society looked at itself and compelled painters to consider anew their methods and subjects. As a source of visual information, as a reproduction technology, as a recreational pastime, and as a means to establish a public face, photography intrigued and influenced him. Like others, Homer experienced moments of doubt, periods when he struggled to realize his artistic goals. Photography did not resolve these uncertainties, just as he realized it could not reproduce reality as faithfully as some claimed. Yet, photography promoted a conversation about realism and how to portray the world before him. Adopting it alongside other strategies, he forged an artistic career grounded in an exploration of these mysteries.

NOTES

Epigraph: Winslow Homer to John Beatty, the director of the Department of Fine Arts at Pittsburgh's Carnegie Institute, about the art of painting during a conversation "in the presence of nature," at Prout's Neck, Maine, in September 1903. John Beatty, "Recollections of an Intimate Friendship," in Lloyd Goodrich, *Winslow Homer* (New York: Macmillan, 1944), 222.

1. Major works that consider the entirety of Homer's life and art include William H. Downes, *The Life and Works of Winslow Homer* (Boston: Houghton Mifflin, 1911); Goodrich, *Winslow Homer*; Philip Beam, *Winslow Homer at Prout's Neck* (New York: Little, Brown, 1966); John Wilmerding, *Winslow Homer* (New York: Praeger, 1972); Gordon Hendricks, *The Life and Work of Winslow Homer* (New York: Harry N. Abrams, 1979); Nicolai Cikovsky, Jr., and Franklin Kelly, *Winslow Homer* (New Haven, Conn.: Yale University Press, 1995); and Elizabeth Johns, *Winslow Homer: The Nature of Observation* (Berkeley: University of California Press, 2002).
2. Kenyon Cox, "The Art of Winslow Homer," *Scribner's Magazine* 56, no. 3 (September 1914): 377, 378. Beatty also mentions a "small booth, open to the sea," though "protected from the storm on three sides at least," from which he "painted a number of his most notable works." Beatty, "Recollections," 209.
3. Cox, "Art of Winslow Homer," 383, 388.
4. Henry James, "On Some Pictures Lately Exhibited," *Galaxy* 20 (July 1875): 93.
5. On the relationship between painting and photography, see Van Deren Coke, *The Painter and the Photograph: From Delacroix to Warhol* (Albuquerque: University of New Mexico Press, 1964); and Barbara Buhler Lynes and Jonathan Weinberg, eds., *Shared Intelligence: American Painting and the Photograph* (Berkeley: University of California Press, 2011).
6. The scholarly literature on the topic of American realism during the late nineteenth and early twentieth centuries is extensive. Authors in art history and literary studies have debated the concept. In particular, see Amy Kaplan, *The Social Construction of American Realism* (Chicago: University of Chicago Press, 1988); Michael Bell, *The Problem of American Realism: Studies in the Cultural History of a Literary Idea* (Chicago: University of Chicago Press, 1993); Edward Lucie-Smith, *American Realism* (New York: Harry N. Abrams, 1994); and Barbara Novak, *American Painting of the Nineteenth Century: Realism, Idealism, and the American Experience* (Oxford: Oxford University Press, 2007).
7. On this visual culture revolution, see Vanessa Schwartz and Jeannene Przyblyski, eds., *The Nineteenth-Century Visual Culture Reader* (New York: Routledge, 2004).
8. David Tatham and John Wilmerding were among the first historians to discuss photography's presence in Homer's art. In particular, see David Tatham, "Some Apprentice Lithographs of Winslow Homer," *Old-Time New England* 59, no. 4 (Spring 1969): 87–104; and Wilmerding, *Winslow Homer*.
9. Beam, *Winslow Homer at Prout's Neck*, 36.
10. "American Painters—Winslow Homer and F. A. Bridgman," *Art Journal* 4 (1878): 226.
11. Beatty, "Recollections," 215.
12. Ibid., 223.
13. About Mathew Brady, see Mary Panzer, *Mathew Brady and the Image of History* (Washington, D.C.: Smithsonian Institution Press, 1997); and Robert Wilson, *Mathew Brady: Portraits of a Nation* (New York: Bloomsbury, 2013).
14. Questions concerning the attribution of this print have been raised in the past. The print is not signed in the plate, nor was Homer or any other artist credited in the accompanying text. While Gordon Hendricks is skeptical of Homer's presence in Washington that day, primarily because of the poor execution of other works in *Harper's* from Lincoln's inauguration, a profile of the artist written during his lifetime as well as the account provided by Homer's first biographer, William Downes, mention his work there. Hendricks, *Life and Work of Winslow Homer*, 43; "American Painters—Winslow Homer and F. A. Bridgman," 227; and Downes, *Life and Works of Winslow Homer*, 39. See also David Tatham, *Winslow Homer and the Pictorial Press* (Syracuse, N.Y.: Syracuse University Press, 2003), 102.
15. In the *Leslie's* caption, George Stacy is identified as the photographer of this large-format salt print. Yet, more recently, it has been attributed to Gardner because of the print's process and size. Gardner commonly employed the salt print process during this period, and is known for his expertise

in creating oversized prints. Given the complexity of the composition and the success of the finished print, it seems more probable that Gardner was the author rather than Stacy, a New York–based maker of popular stereographs. "The Inauguration of Abraham Lincoln, the Sixteenth President of the United States of America," *Frank Leslie's Illustrated Newspaper* 11, no. 277 (March 16, 1861): 264–65.

16. On Homer and the Civil War, see Peter Wood and Karen Dalton, *Winslow Homer's Images of Blacks: The Civil War and Reconstruction Years* (Austin: University of Texas Press, 1988); and Eleanor Harvey, *The Civil War and American Art* (New Haven, Conn.: Yale University Press, 2012).
17. Frederic Ray, *Alfred R. Waud: Civil War Artist* (New York: Viking, 1974), 33–34.
18. David Tatham has written that Homer had thought his Yorktown drawings would not be engraved in combination with those by others. Later, the artist expressed disappointment to *Harper's* editors when he was paid less than he had expected and that his contribution was not credited in print. Tatham, *Winslow Homer and the Pictorial Press*, 114–16.
19. Alexander Gardner, *Gardner's Photographic Sketch Book of the Civil War* (New York: Dover, 1959), unpaginated.
20. Winslow Homer to George G. Briggs, February 19, 1896, letter in the Winslow Homer Collection, Archives of American Art, Smithsonian Institution.
21. A lack of consensus exists concerning the location depicted in this painting. The work's original title cannot be confirmed, and its association with the siege at Petersburg, Virginia, in 1864 seems to originate from a 1919 estate sale catalogue. Eight years earlier, William Downes suggested that the painting was based on an episode from the earlier Peninsula Campaign, while comparisons with drawings made during the Battle of the Wilderness support the idea that the painting derives from that campaign. Downes, *Life and Works of Winslow Homer*, 48; and Abigail Booth Gerdts and Lloyd Goodrich, *Record of Works by Winslow Homer*, vol. 1, *1846 to 1866* (New York: Spanierman Gallery, 2005), 316–18.
22. Quoted in Ken Jacobson and Jenny Jacobson, *Carrying off the Palaces: John Ruskin's Lost Daguerreotypes* (London: Quaritch, 2015), 47.
23. Gerdts and Goodrich, *Record of Works by Winslow Homer*, 359; and Sally Mills, "Portrait of Albert Post," in *Winslow Homer: Paintings of the Civil War*, by Marc Simpson et al. (San Francisco: Bedford Arts, 1988), 189–91. My thanks to Tim Burgard for assisting with the research on this painting.
24. Cecilia Beaux, *Background with Figures* (Boston: Houghton Mifflin, 1930), 211–12. My thanks to Linda Docherty for sharing this source.
25. In a separate account, artist Frank Duveneck, another jurist at the 1897 Carnegie Institute International, recalled meeting a "little chap" on the train to Pittsburgh. "We talked about everything but art." Only upon arrival at their hotel did Duveneck learn the identity of his traveling companion. Beatty, "Recollections," 218–19.
26. Sarah Burns, *Inventing the Modern Artist: Art and Culture in Gilded Age America* (New Haven, Conn.: Yale University Press, 1996), 189.
27. Winslow Homer, inscription on his diploma from the National Academy of Design, 1866, Winslow Homer Collection, Bowdoin College Museum of Art.
28. Each of the artist's biographers has written about his travels in France. In addition, see Albert Ten Eyck Gardner, *Winslow Homer: American Artist* (New York: C. N. Potter, 1961); and Henry Adams, "Winslow Homer's 'Impressionism' and Its Relation to His Trip to France," in *Winslow Homer: A Symposium*, vol. 26, ed. Nicolai Cikovsky, Jr. (Washington, D.C.: National Gallery of Art, 1990), 61–83.
29. On Homer and Japanese art, see Erica Hirschler, "North Atlantic Drift: A Meditation on Winslow Homer and French Painting," in *Weatherbeaten: Winslow Homer and Maine*, ed. Thomas A. Denenberg (New Haven, Conn.: Yale University Press, 2012), 71–83.
30. Goodrich, *Winslow Homer*, 40.
31. Wilmerding, *Winslow Homer*, 50, 78–79.
32. Thomas Aldrich, "Among the Studios," *Our Young Folks* 2, no. 7 (July 1866): 395.
33. About Homer and fishing, see Patricia Junker, ed., *Winslow Homer: Artist and Angler* (New York: Thames & Hudson, 2003).
34. On artists and landscape tourism, see Gail Davidson et al., *Frederic Church, Winslow Homer, and Thomas Moran: Tourism and the American Landscape* (New York: Bulfinch, 2006). About landscape photography in the East, see Diane Waggoner et al., *East of the Mississippi: Nineteenth-Century American Landscape Photography* (New Haven, Conn.: Yale University Press, 2017).

35. Winslow Homer to Louis Prang, May 16, 1871, copy of a letter in the collection of Abigail Gerdts.
36. George W. Sheldon, *Hours with Art and Artists* (New York: D. Appleton, 1882), 136–37.
37. Ibid., 136.
38. David Strauss, "Towards a Consumer Culture: 'Adirondack Murray' and the Wilderness Vacation," *American Quarterly* 39, no. 2 (Summer 1987): 281.
39. Junker, *Winslow Homer: Artist and Angler*, 106.
40. For Seneca Ray Stoddard, see Jeanne Adler, *Early Days in the Adirondacks: The Photographs of Seneca Ray Stoddard* (New York: Harry N. Abrams, 1997).
41. "Artists and Their Work," *New York Times*, April 9, 1880, 5.
42. "American Painters—Winslow Homer and F. A. Bridgman," 227.
43. J. Eastman Chase, "Some Recollections of Winslow Homer," *Harper's Weekly* 54 (October 22, 1910): 13.
44. Helen Cooper, *Winslow Homer Watercolors* (New Haven, Conn.: Yale University Art Gallery, 1986), 66.
45. Downes, *Life and Works of Winslow Homer*, 106.
46. Homer's decision to relocate to England has received much scholarly attention. In particular, see Cikovsky and Kelly, *Winslow Homer*; Johns, *Winslow Homer*; and David Tatham, *Winslow Homer in London: A New York Artist Abroad* (Syracuse, N.Y.: Syracuse University Press, 2010).
47. About Homer's time in London, see Tatham, *Winslow Homer in London*; and Judith Walsh, "More Skillful, More Refined, More Delicate: London," in *Watercolors by Winslow Homer: The Color of Light*, ed. Martha Tedeschi and Kristi Dahm (New Haven, Conn.: Yale University Press, 2008), 75–106.
48. Downes, *Life and Works of Winslow Homer*, 104.
49. Advertisement for Marion & Company, *Academy Notes* (1885): xxviii. My thanks to Elizabeth Athens for sharing this advertisement.
50. Hendricks, *Life and Work of Winslow Homer*, 157.
51. Winslow Homer, inscription in Homer's copy of *Chevreul on Colours*, private collection. See also David Tatham, "Winslow Homer's Library," *American Art Journal* 9, no. 1 (May 1977): 93.
52. Patricia Junker first identified the correspondence between this photograph and Homer's watercolor. Junker, *Winslow Homer in the 1890s: Prout's Neck Observed* (New York: Hudson Hills, 1990), 65.
53. Tony Harrison, *Winslow Homer in England* (Ocean Park, Maine: Hornby Editions, 2004), 26–28.
54. "Exhibition of Photographs at Newcastle," *British Journal of Photography* (November 25, 1881): 607.
55. About British photographers' interest in rural subjects during this period, see Sara Stevenson, *The Personal Art of David Octavius Hill* (New Haven, Conn.: Yale University Press, 2002); and John Taylor, *The Old Order and the New: P. H. Emerson and Photography, 1885–1895* (New York: Prestel, 2006).
56. About Frank Sutcliffe, see Michael Hiley, *Frank Sutcliffe: Photographer of Whitby* (Boston: D. R. Godine, 1974).
57. John Wilmerding, "Winslow Homer's English Period," *American Art Journal* 7, no. 2 (November 1975): 67; and Cikovsky and Kelly, *Winslow Homer*, 174–75.
58. On the Pre-Raphaelites' interest in photography, see Diane Waggoner et al., *The Pre-Raphaelite Lens: British Photography and Painting, 1848–1875* (London: Ashgate, 2010). See also Ellen Handy et al., *Pictorial Effect, Naturalistic Vision: The Photographs and Theories of Henry Peach Robinson and Peter Henry Emerson* (Norfolk, Va.: Chrysler Museum, 1994). A similar response to photography's rise also occurred in nineteenth-century France. See Kimberly Jones et al., *In the Forest of Fontainebleau: Painters and Photographers from Corot to Monet* (New Haven, Conn.: Yale University Press, 2008).
59. Walter Woodbury, "The Syren: Photography versus Art," *Photographic News* 26, no. 1222 (February 3, 1882): 55.
60. On Eakins's relationship with photography, see Susan Danly and Cheryl Leibold, eds., *Eakins and the Photograph: Works by Thomas Eakins and His Circle in the Collection of the Pennsylvania Academy of the Fine Arts* (Washington, D.C.: Smithsonian Institution Press, 1994); and Kathleen Foster et al., *Thomas Eakins Rediscovered: Charles Bregler's Thomas Eakins Collection at the Pennsylvania Academy of the Fine Arts* (New Haven, Conn.: Yale University Press, 1998).
61. Mary Panzer, "Photography, Science, and the Traditional Art of Thomas Eakins," in Danly and Leibold, *Eakins and the Photograph*, 105.
62. Thomas Eakins to Benjamin Eakins, March 6, 1868, letter in the Thomas Eakins Collection, Pennsylvania Academy of the Fine Arts. Also quoted in Kathleen Foster and Cheryl Leibold, *Writing about Eakins: The Manuscripts in Charles Bregler's Thomas Eakins Collection* (Philadelphia: University of Pennsylvania Press, 1989), 206; and Panzer, "Photography, Science," 105.

63. Beatty, "Recollections," 224.
64. "Art and Artists," *Boston Globe*, July 1, 1883, 13.
65. For the real estate transactions of the Homer family, see Kenyon Bolton, "'The Right Place': Winslow Homer and the Development of Prouts Neck," in Denenberg, *Weatherbeaten*, 29–47.
66. Beatty, "Recollections," 211–12.
67. Winslow Homer to Martha Homer, August 27, 1883, letter in the Winslow Homer Collection, Bowdoin College Museum of Art.
68. Winslow Homer to Martha Homer, June 24, 1884, letter in the Winslow Homer Collection, Bowdoin College Museum of Art.
69. Rupert Holland, *The Story of Prout's Neck* (Cambridge, Mass.: Cosmos, 1924), 50.
70. Winslow Homer to Charles Homer, September 1, 1884, letter in the Winslow Homer Collection, Bowdoin College Museum of Art.
71. Winslow Homer to Louis Prang, December 30, 1893, copy of a letter in the collection of Abigail Gerdts. Augustus Moulton, another acquaintance of Homer's, remarked that he was regarded by strangers as "reticent and austere, but to his intimates he was most genial and delightful." Augustus Moulton, *Old Prout's Neck* (Portland, Maine: Marks Printing House, 1924), 122.
72. For Eadweard Muybridge and the origins of chronophotography, see Philip Prodger, *Time Stands Still: Muybridge and the Instantaneous Photography Movement* (New York: Oxford University Press, 2003).
73. For painting in nineteenth-century Maine, see Gertrud Mellon and Elizabeth Wilder, eds., *Maine and Its Role in American Art, 1740–1963* (New York: Viking, 1963).
74. Grenville Donham, ed., *Maine Register; or, State Yearbook and Legislative Manual* (Portland, Maine: J. B. Gregory, 1887), 332.
75. On the history of Maine photography, see Libby Bischof, Susan Danly, and Earle Shettleworth, *Maine Photography: A History, 1840–2015* (Portland, Maine: Down East Books, 2016).
76. Clipping from the *Portland Evening Express and Advertiser*, November 12, 1910, in a scrapbook owned by the Portland Museum of Art; *Daily Eastern Argus* (Portland), February 15, 1910, 8; and Junker, *Winslow Homer in the 1890s*, 57.
77. For Samuel Peter Rolt Triscott, see Richard Malone and Earle Shettleworth, *Rediscovering S. P. Rolt Triscott: Monhegan Artist and Photographer* (Thomaston, Maine: Tilbury House, 2002).
78. John Moran, "The Relation of Photography to the Fine Arts," *Philadelphia Photographer* 2, no. 15 (March 1, 1865): 33.
79. Winslow Homer to Martha Homer, April 24, 1895, letter in the Winslow Homer Collection, Bowdoin College Museum of Art.
80. Downes, *Life and Works of Winslow Homer*, 113.
81. Junker, *Winslow Homer in the 1890s*, 57.
82. Paul Schullery, "Winslow Homer: Time in the Adirondacks," in Junker, *Winslow Homer: Artist and Angler*, 86–90.
83. Winslow Homer to Charles Homer, September 25, 1887, copy of a letter in the collection of Abigail Gerdts.
84. David Tatham, "Winslow Homer at the North Woods Club," in Cikovsky, *Winslow Homer: A Symposium*, 124.
85. J. Ernest Yalden to Robert McDonald, September 30, 1936, letter in the collection of the Memorial Art Gallery, University of Rochester; and David Tatham, *Seeing America: Painting and Sculpture from the Collection of the Memorial Art Gallery of the University of Rochester* (Rochester, N.Y.: University of Rochester Press, 2006), 109.
86. *Glimpses of the World's Fair: A Selection of Gems of the White City and the Midway Plaisance*, souvenir booklet, 1893, Winslow Homer Collection, Bowdoin College Museum of Art.
87. Winslow Homer to Charles Homer, July 3, 1908, letter in the Winslow Homer Collection, Bowdoin College Museum of Art.
88. Quoted in Goodrich, *Winslow Homer*, 197.
89. Winslow Homer to Charles Homer, February 21, 1895, letter in the Winslow Homer Collection, Bowdoin College Museum of Art.
90. Undated newspaper clipping in the Winslow Homer Collection, Bowdoin College Museum of Art.
91. Cikovsky and Kelly, *Winslow Homer*, 329.
92. Moulton, *Old Prout's Neck*, 120.
93. Beatty, "Recollections," 223.
94. Mariana G. Van Rensselaer, *Six Portraits: Della Robbia, Correggio, Blake, Corot, George Fuller, Winslow Homer* (Boston: Houghton Mifflin, 1889), 265–66.

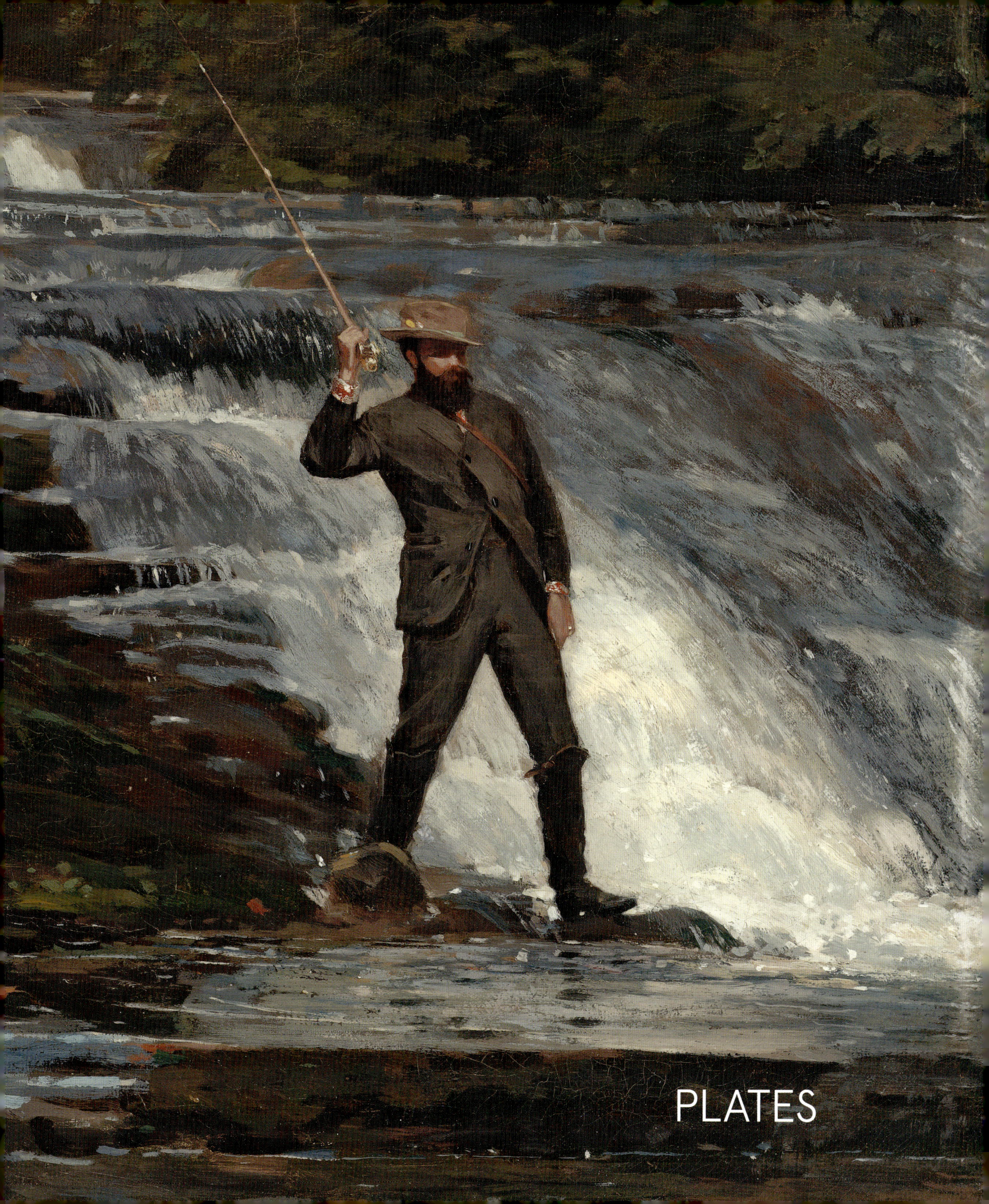

PLATES

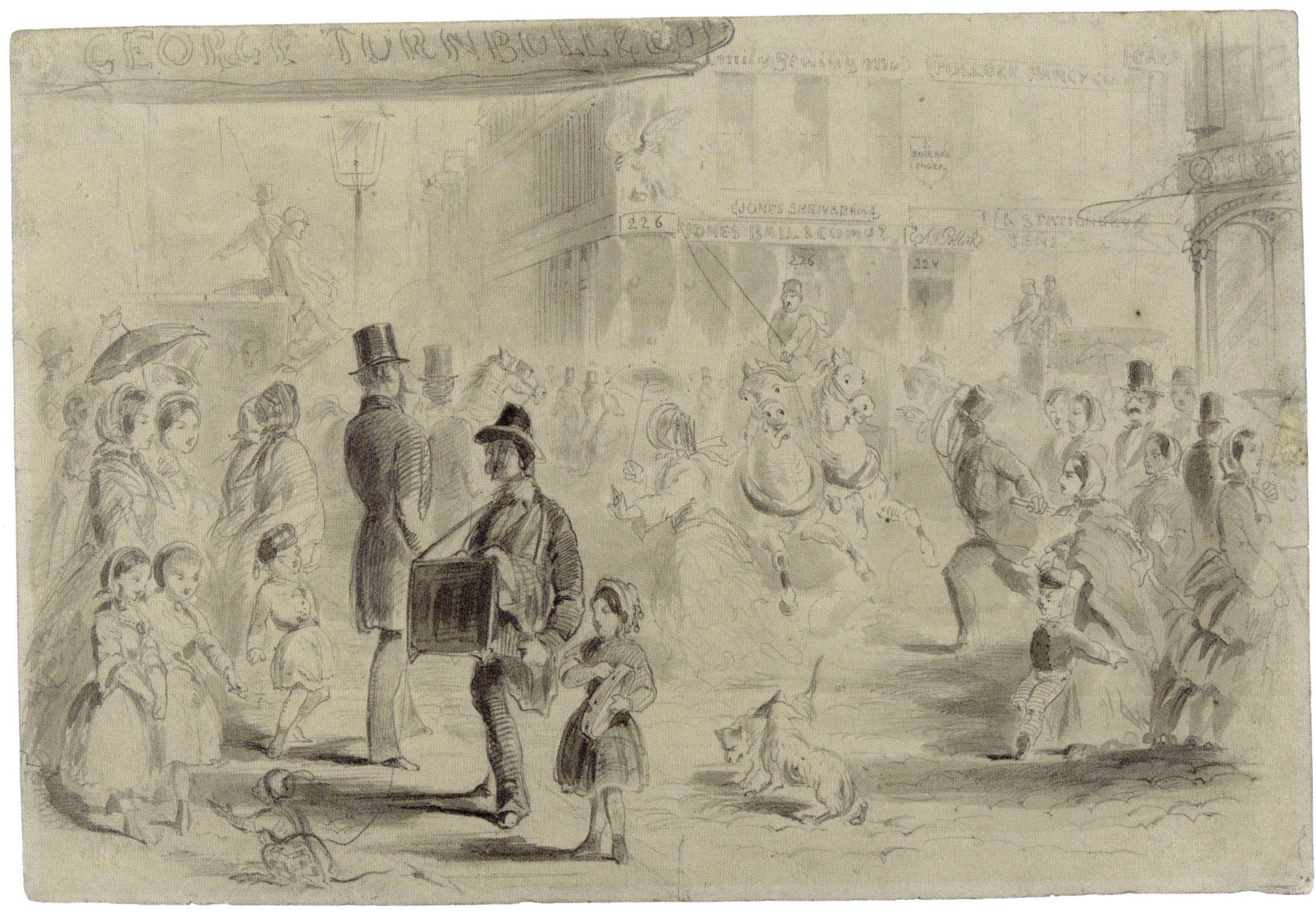

PLATE 1. Winslow Homer, *Corner of Winter, Washington, and Summer Streets, Boston*, 1857. Graphite, 7¼ × 9½ in. (18.4 × 24.1 cm). Bowdoin College Museum of Art, Brunswick. Gift of Lois Homer Graham, grandniece of the artist, in honor of Philip C. Beam, Henry Johnson Professor of Art and Archaeology Emeritus at Bowdoin College. [1991.110]

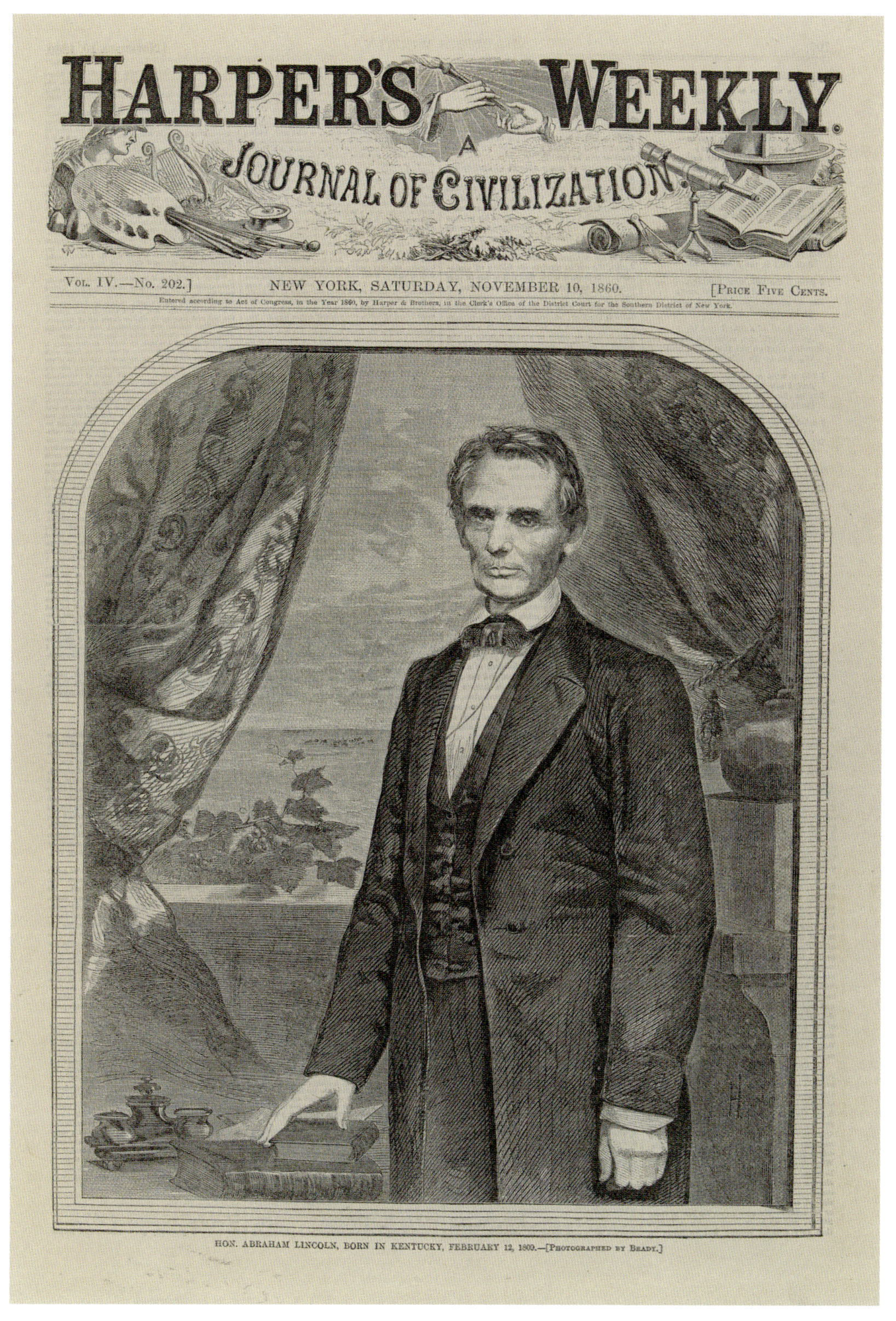

HARPER'S WEEKLY.
A JOURNAL OF CIVILIZATION.

VOL. IV.—No. 202.] NEW YORK, SATURDAY, NOVEMBER 10, 1860. [PRICE FIVE CENTS.

Entered according to Act of Congress, in the Year 1860, by Harper & Brothers, in the Clerk's Office of the District Court for the Southern District of New York.

HON. ABRAHAM LINCOLN, BORN IN KENTUCKY, FEBRUARY 12, 1809.—[PHOTOGRAPHED BY BRADY.]

PLATE 2. After Winslow Homer, *Hon. Abraham Lincoln, Born in Kentucky, February 12, 1809*, published in *Harper's Weekly*, November 10, 1860. Wood engraving. Bowdoin College Museum of Art, Brunswick. Museum and College Purchase, Hamlin, Quinby, and Special Funds. [1974.1.51]

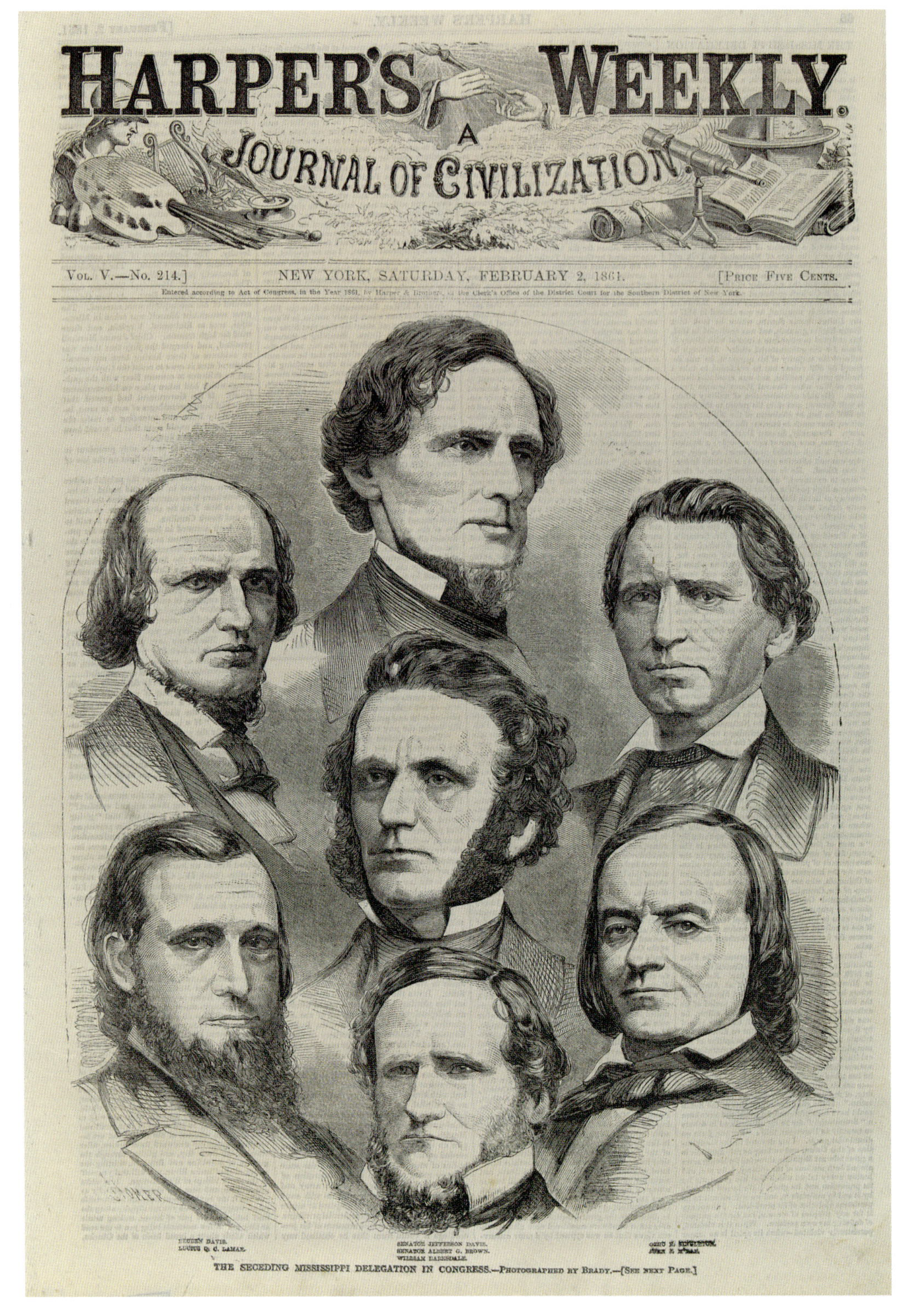

HARPER'S WEEKLY.

A JOURNAL OF CIVILIZATION.

Vol. V.—No. 214.] NEW YORK, SATURDAY, FEBRUARY 2, 1861. [Price Five Cents.

Entered according to Act of Congress, in the Year 1861, by Harper & Brothers, in the Clerk's Office of the District Court for the Southern District of New York.

REUBEN DAVIS.
LUCIUS Q. C. LAMAR.

SENATOR JEFFERSON DAVIS.
SENATOR ALBERT G. BROWN.
WILLIAM BARKSDALE.

THE SECEDING MISSISSIPPI DELEGATION IN CONGRESS.—Photographed by Brady.—[See next Page.]

PLATE 3. After Winslow Homer, *The Seceding Mississippi Delegation in Congress*, published in *Harper's Weekly*, February 2, 1861. Wood engraving. Bowdoin College Museum of Art, Brunswick. Museum and College Purchase, Hamlin, Quinby, and Special Funds. [1974.1.58]

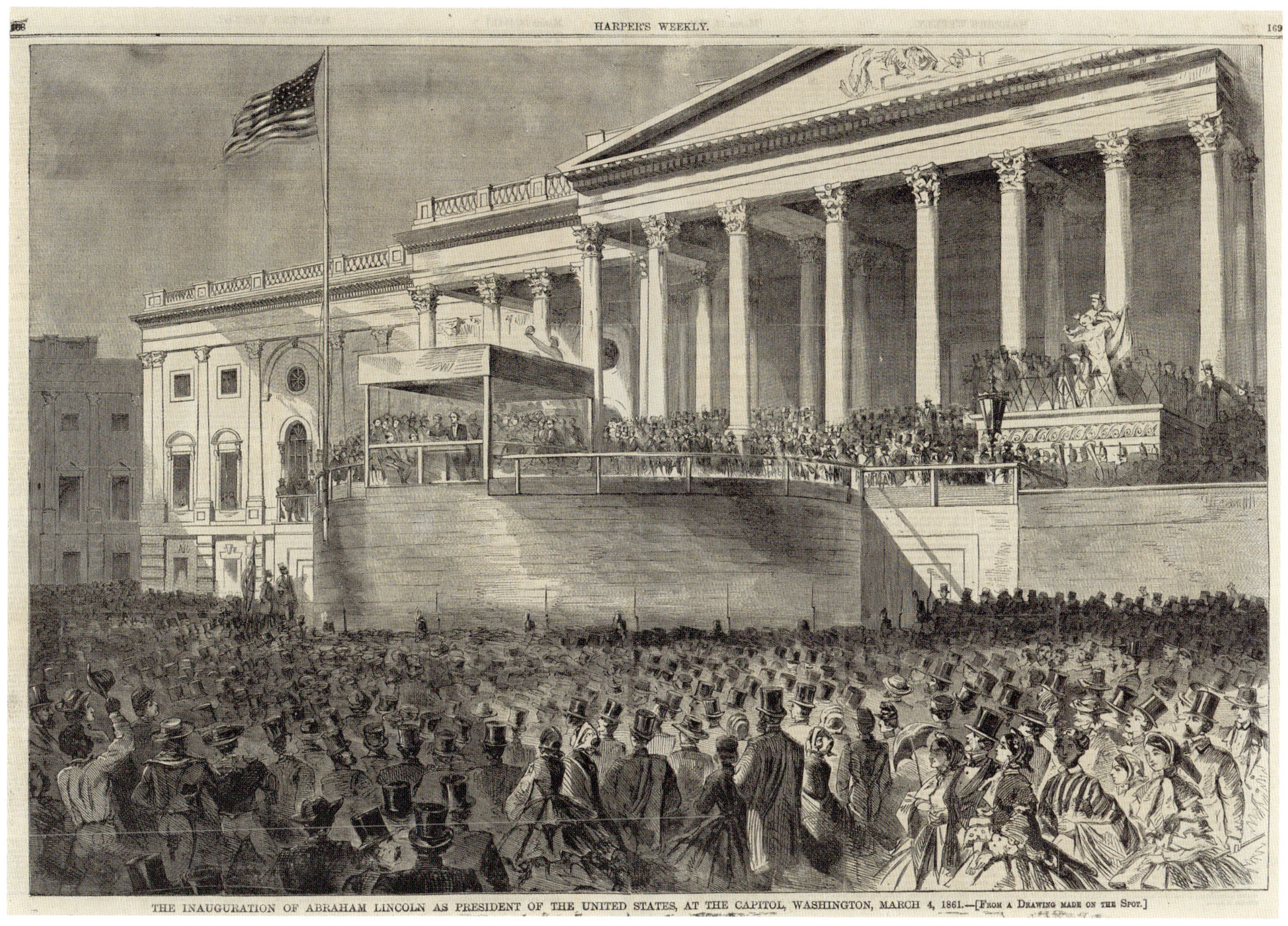

PLATE 4. After Winslow Homer, *The Inauguration of Abraham Lincoln as President of the United States, at the Capitol, Washington, March 4, 1861*, published in *Harper's Weekly*, March 16, 1861. Wood engraving. Bowdoin College Museum of Art, Brunswick. Museum and College Purchase, Hamlin, Quinby, and Special Funds. [1974.1.67]

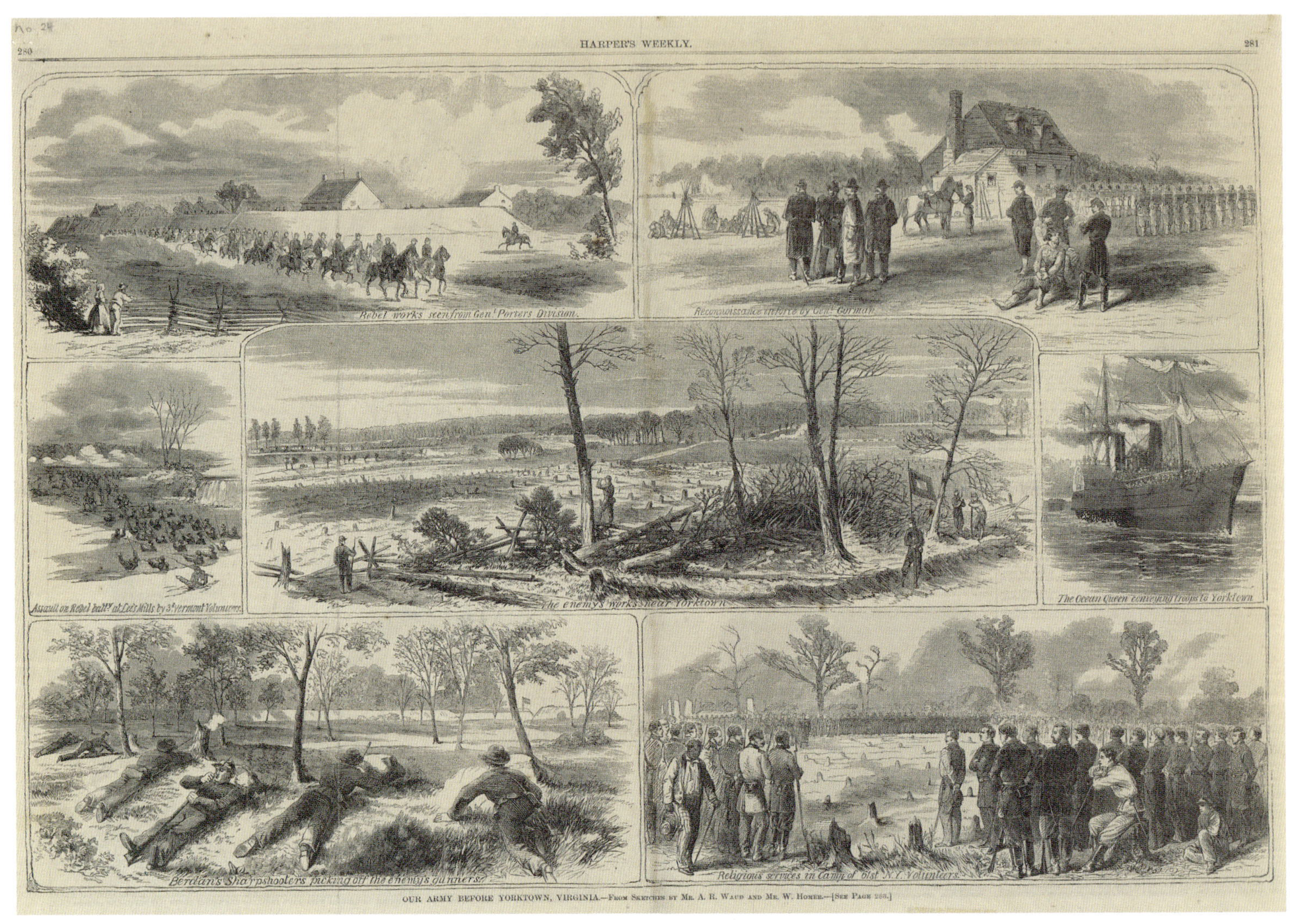

PLATE 5. After Winslow Homer and Alfred Waud, *Our Army before Yorktown, Virginia*, published in *Harper's Weekly*, May 3, 1862. Wood engraving. Bowdoin College Museum of Art, Brunswick. Museum and College Purchase, Hamlin, Quinby, and Special Funds. [1974.1.87]

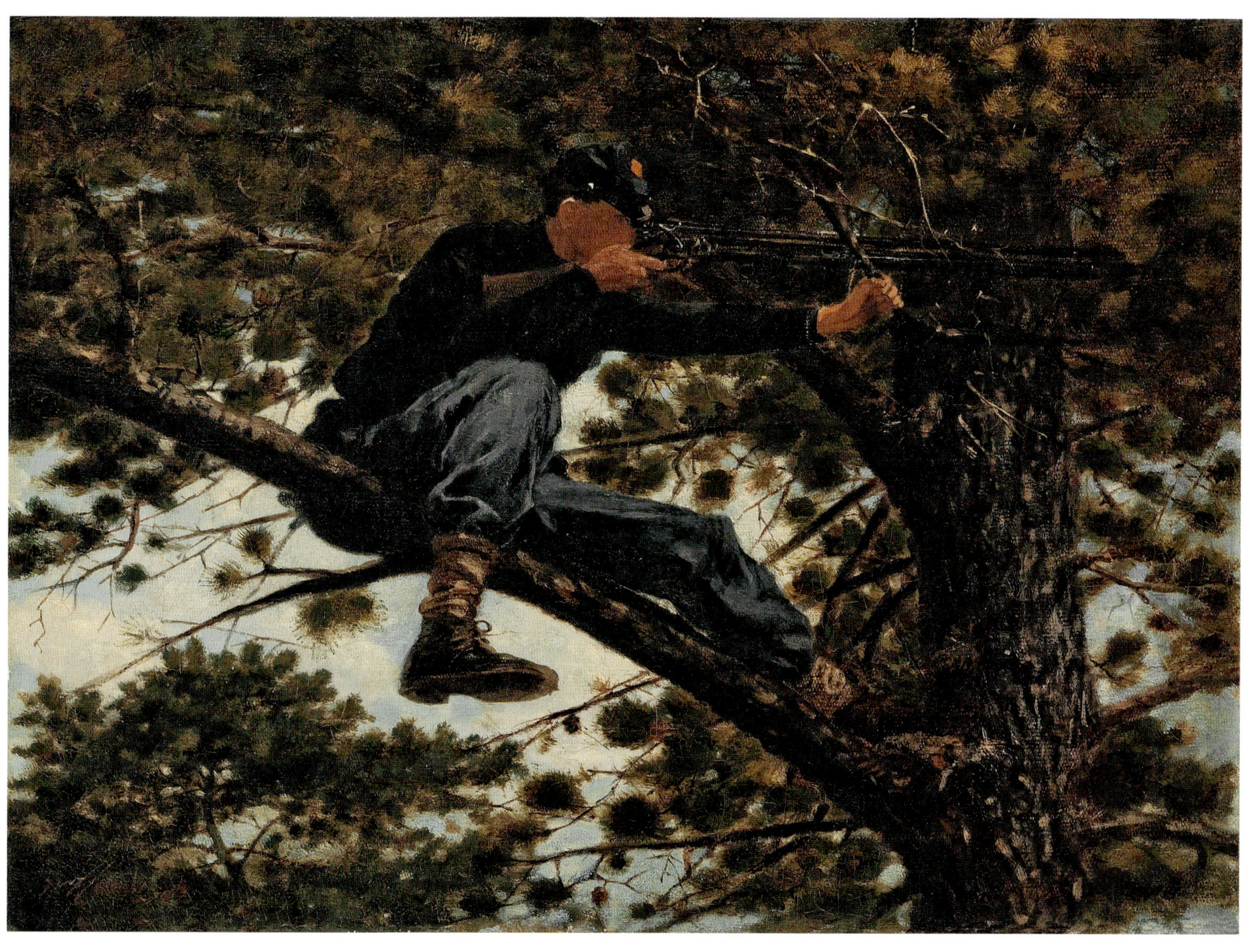

PLATE 6. Winslow Homer, *Sharpshooter*, 1863. Oil on canvas, 12¼ × 16½ in. (31.1 × 41.9 cm). Portland Museum of Art, Maine. Gift of Barbro and Bernard Osher. [1992.41]

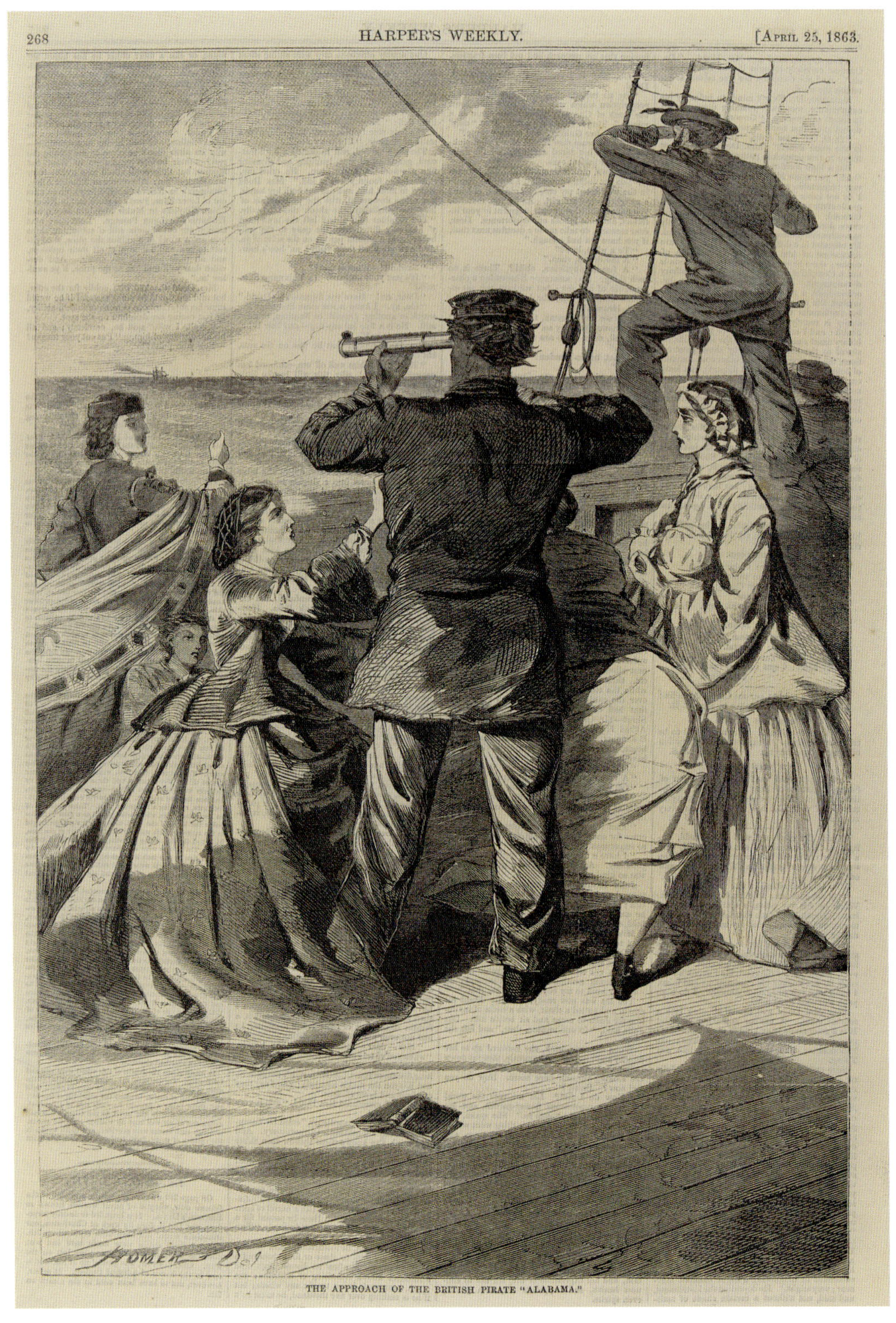
268 HARPER'S WEEKLY. [APRIL 25, 1863.

THE APPROACH OF THE BRITISH PIRATE "ALABAMA."

PLATE 7. After Winslow Homer, *The Approach of the British Pirate "Alabama,"* published in *Harper's Weekly*, April 25, 1863. Wood engraving. Bowdoin College Museum of Art, Brunswick. Museum and College Purchase, Hamlin, Quinby, and Special Funds. [1974.1.103]

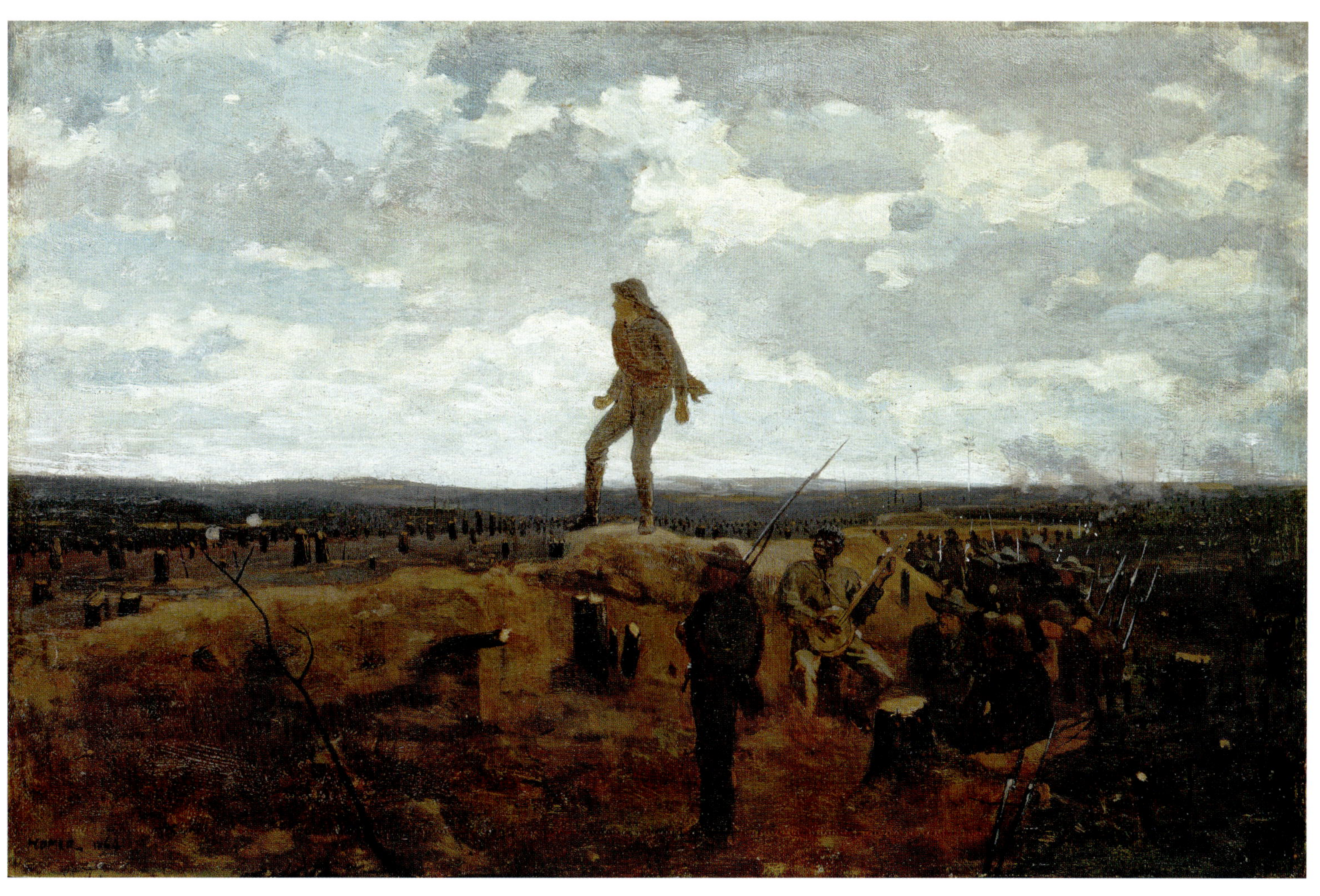

PLATE 8. Winslow Homer, *Defiance, Inviting a Shot before Petersburg*, 1864. Oil on panel, 12 × 18 in. (30.5 × 45.7 cm). Detroit Institute of Arts. Founders Society Purchase with funds from Dexter M. Ferry, Jr. [51.66]

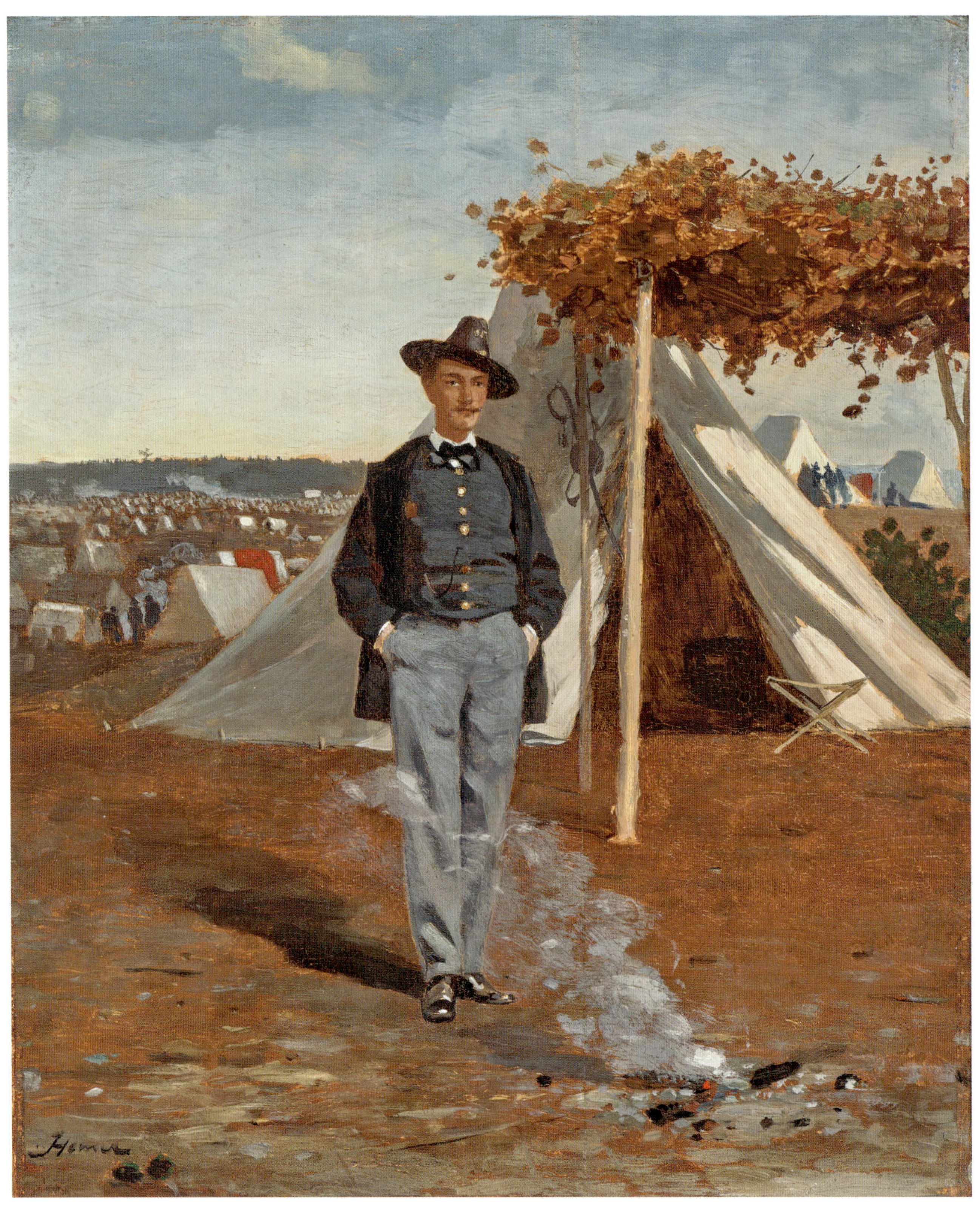

PLATE 9. Winslow Homer, *Albert Post*, c. 1864. Oil on panel, 12½ × 10½ in. (31.8 × 26.7 cm). Fine Arts Museums of San Francisco. Gift of Rollin K. and Diane Post. [1995.56]

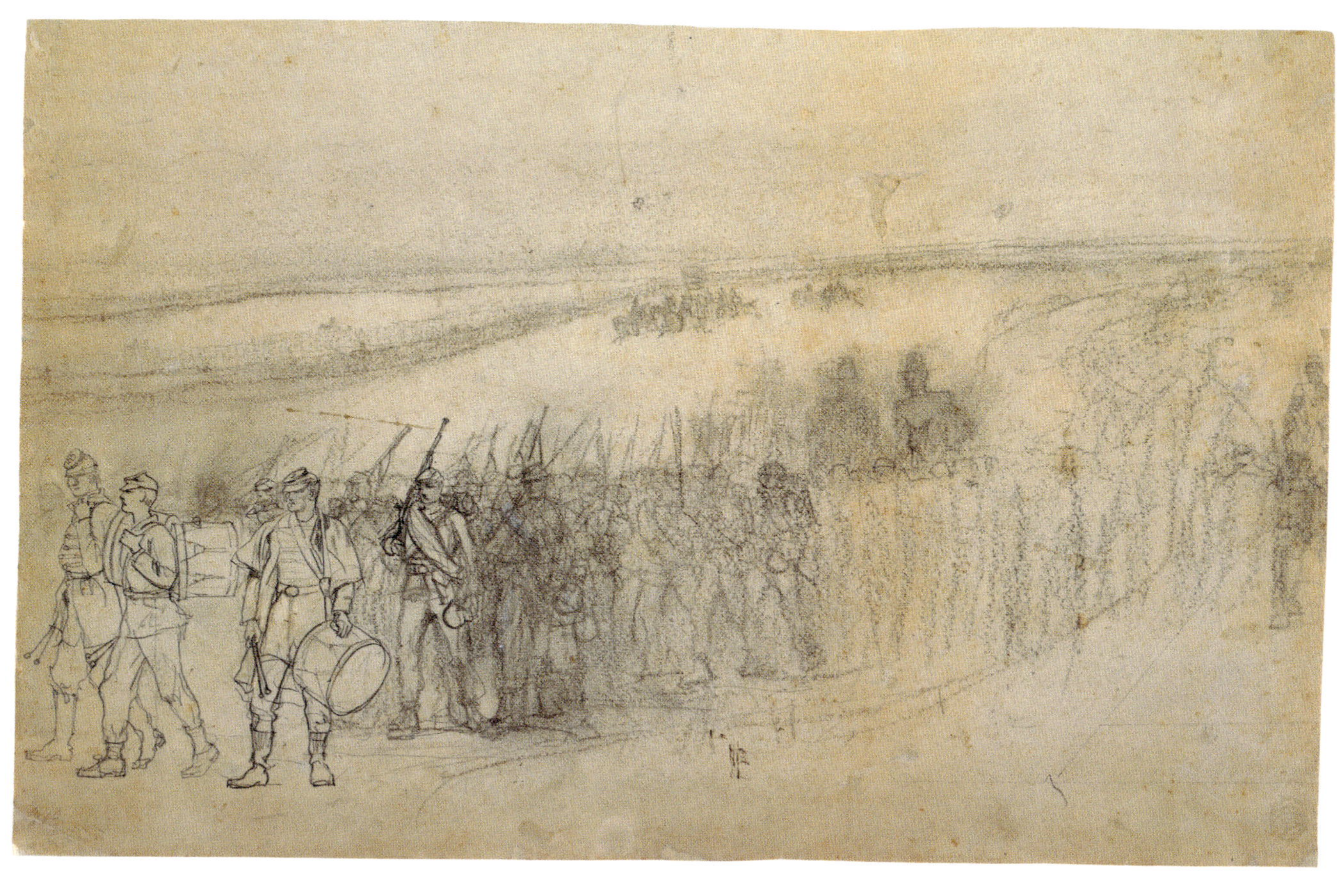

PLATE 10. Winslow Homer, *Marching Infantry Column*, c. 1862. Graphite, charcoal, brush, and white gouache, 13¼ × 20³⁄₁₆ in. (33.8 × 51.3 cm). Cooper-Hewitt, National Design Museum, Smithsonian Institution, New York. Gift of Charles Savage Homer, Jr. [1912-12-204-A]

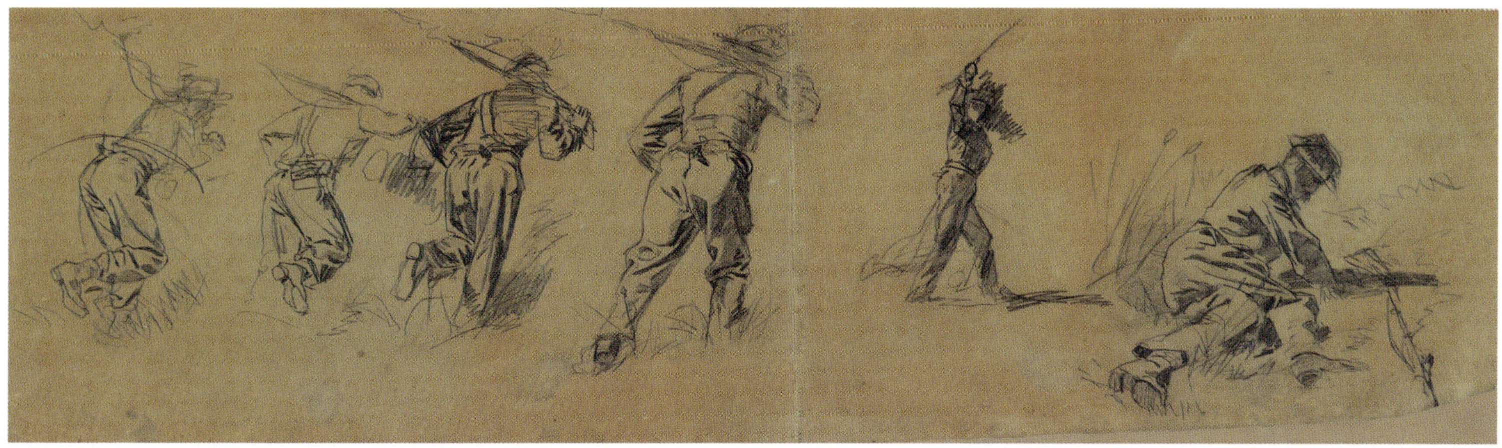

PLATE 11. Winslow Homer, *Study of Soldiers*, c. 1863–65. Graphite, 9⁹⁄₁₆ × 35⅝ in. (24.3 × 88.4 cm). Cooper-Hewitt, National Design Museum, Smithsonian Institution, New York. Gift of Charles Savage Homer, Jr. [1912-12-105]

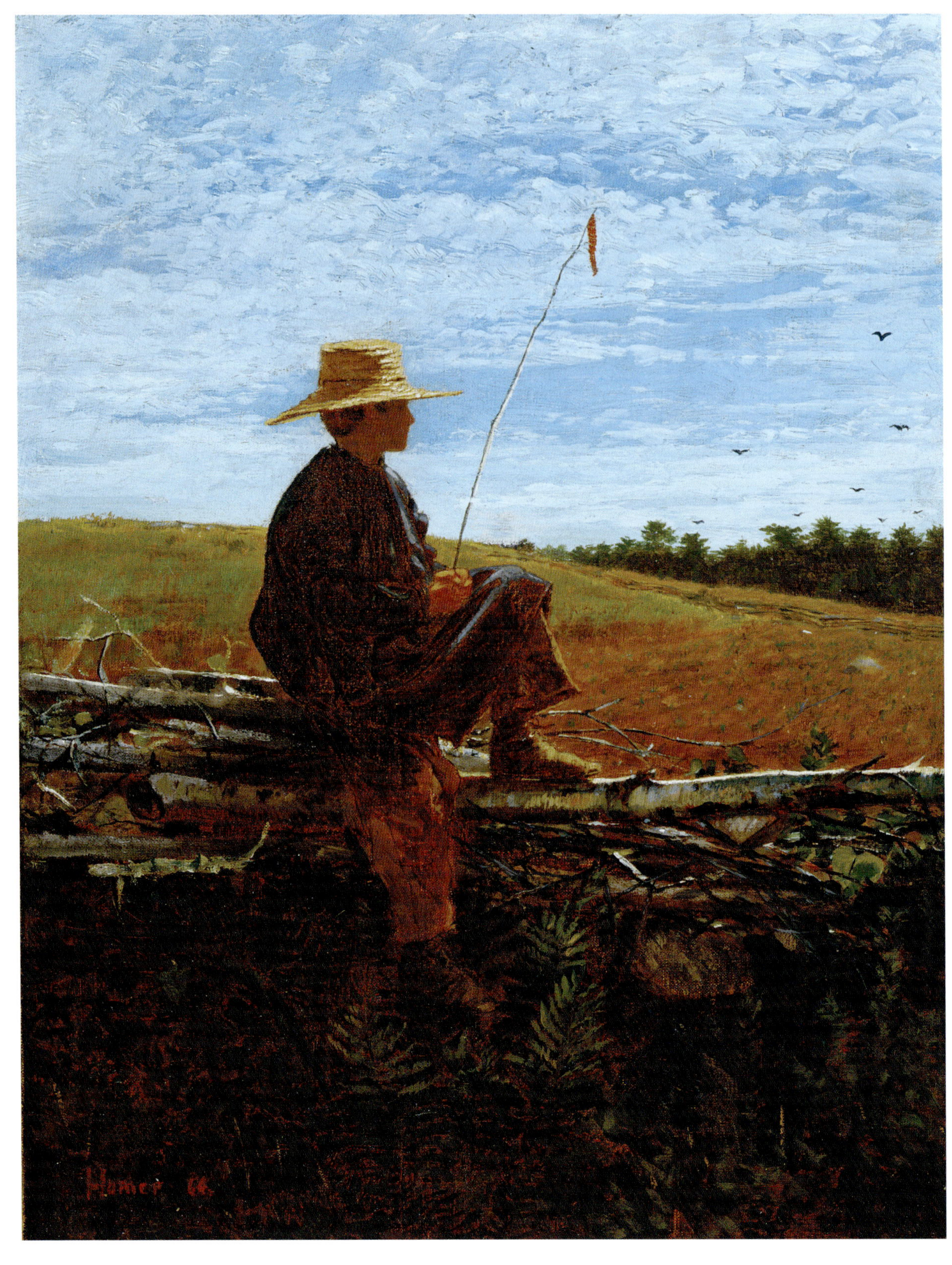

PLATE 12. Winslow Homer, *On Guard*, 1864. Oil on canvas, 12¼ × 9¼ in. (31.1 × 23.5 cm). Terra Foundation for the Arts, Chicago. Daniel J. Terra Collection. [1994.11]

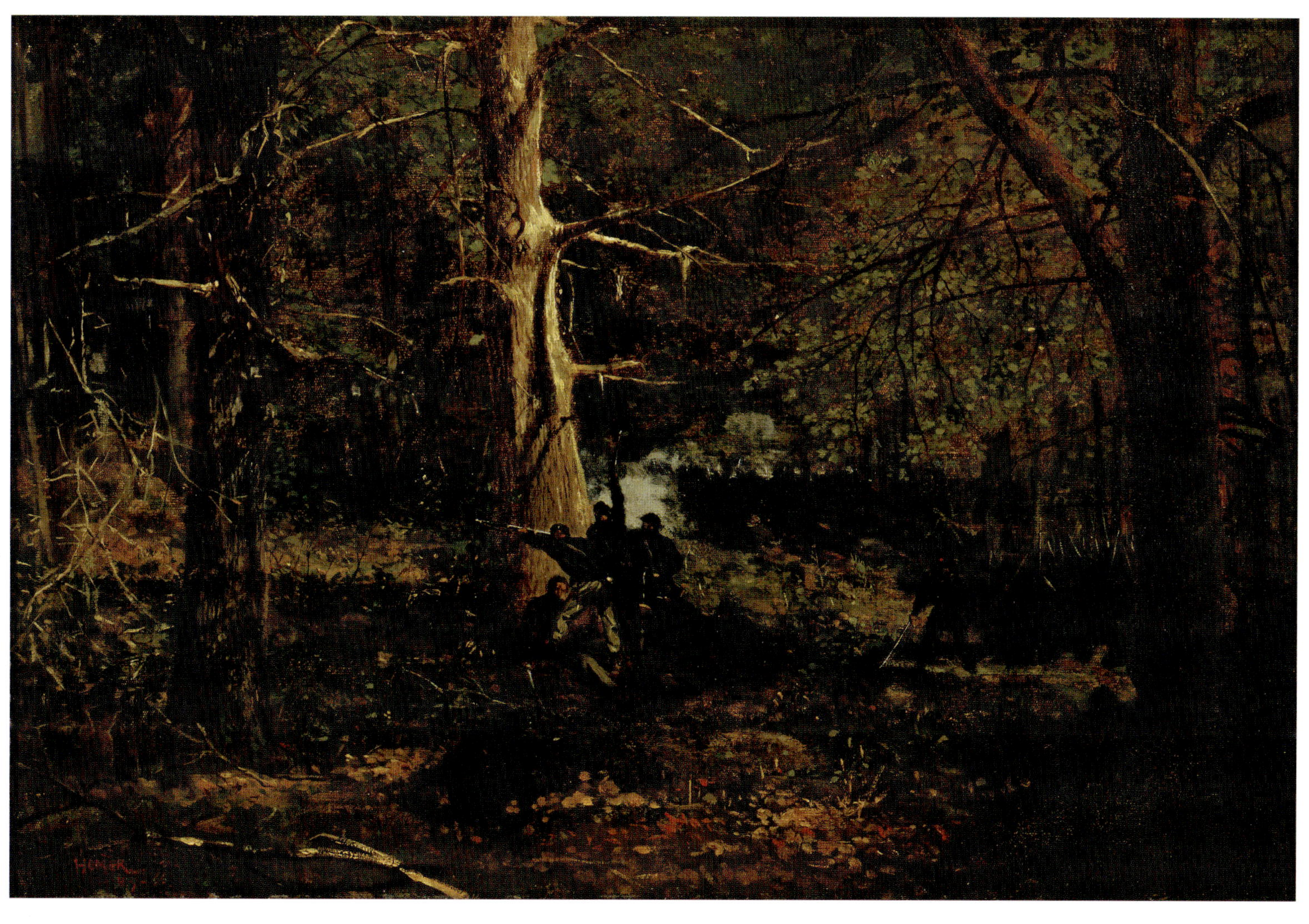

PLATE 13. Winslow Homer, *Skirmish in the Wilderness*, 1864. Oil on canvas, 18 × 26¼ in. (45.7 × 66 cm). New Britain Museum of American Art. Harriet Russell Stanley Fund. [1944.05]

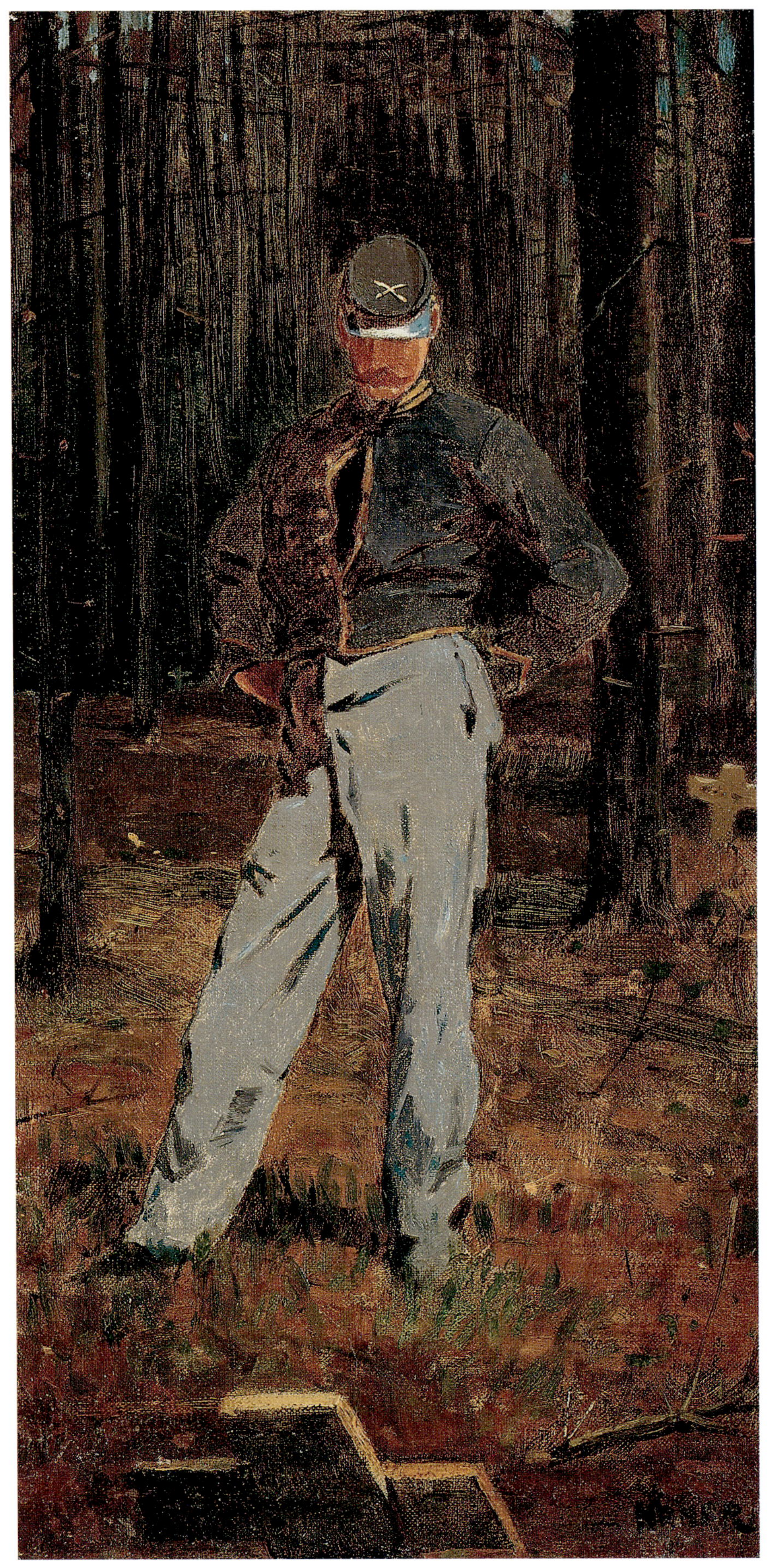

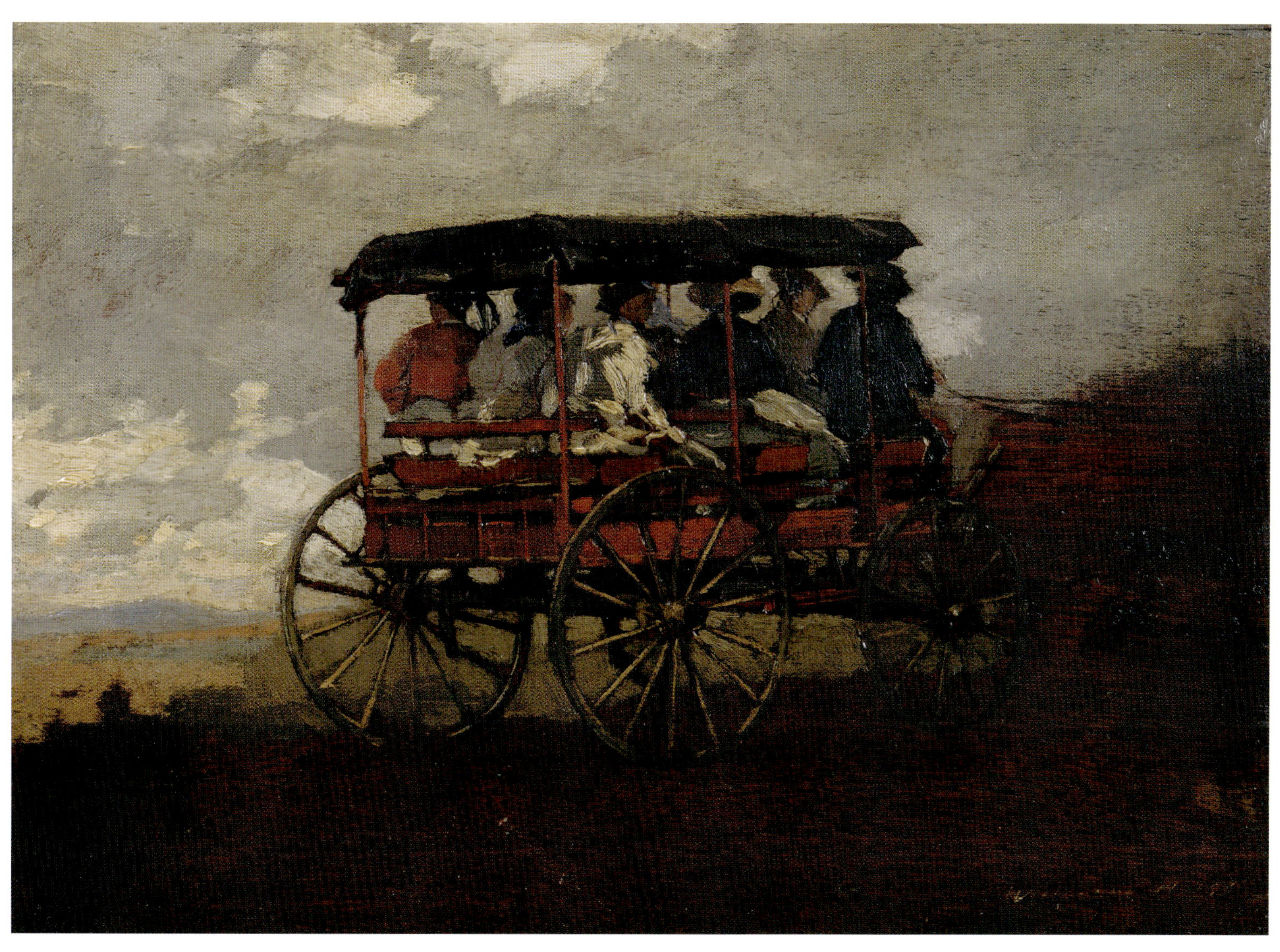

PLATE 15. Winslow Homer, *White Mountain Wagon*, c. 1869. Brush and oil paint on mahogany panel, 11¾ × 15¹³⁄16 in. (29.8 × 40.2 cm). Cooper-Hewitt, National Design Museum, Smithsonian Institution, New York. Gift of Mrs. Charles Savage Homer, Jr. [1918-20-9]

PLATE 14. Winslow Homer, *Trooper Meditating beside a Grave*, c. 1865. Oil on canvas, 16 × 8 in. (40.6 × 20.3 cm). Joslyn Art Museum, Omaha. Gift of Dr. Harold Gifford and Ann Gifford Forbes. [1960.298]

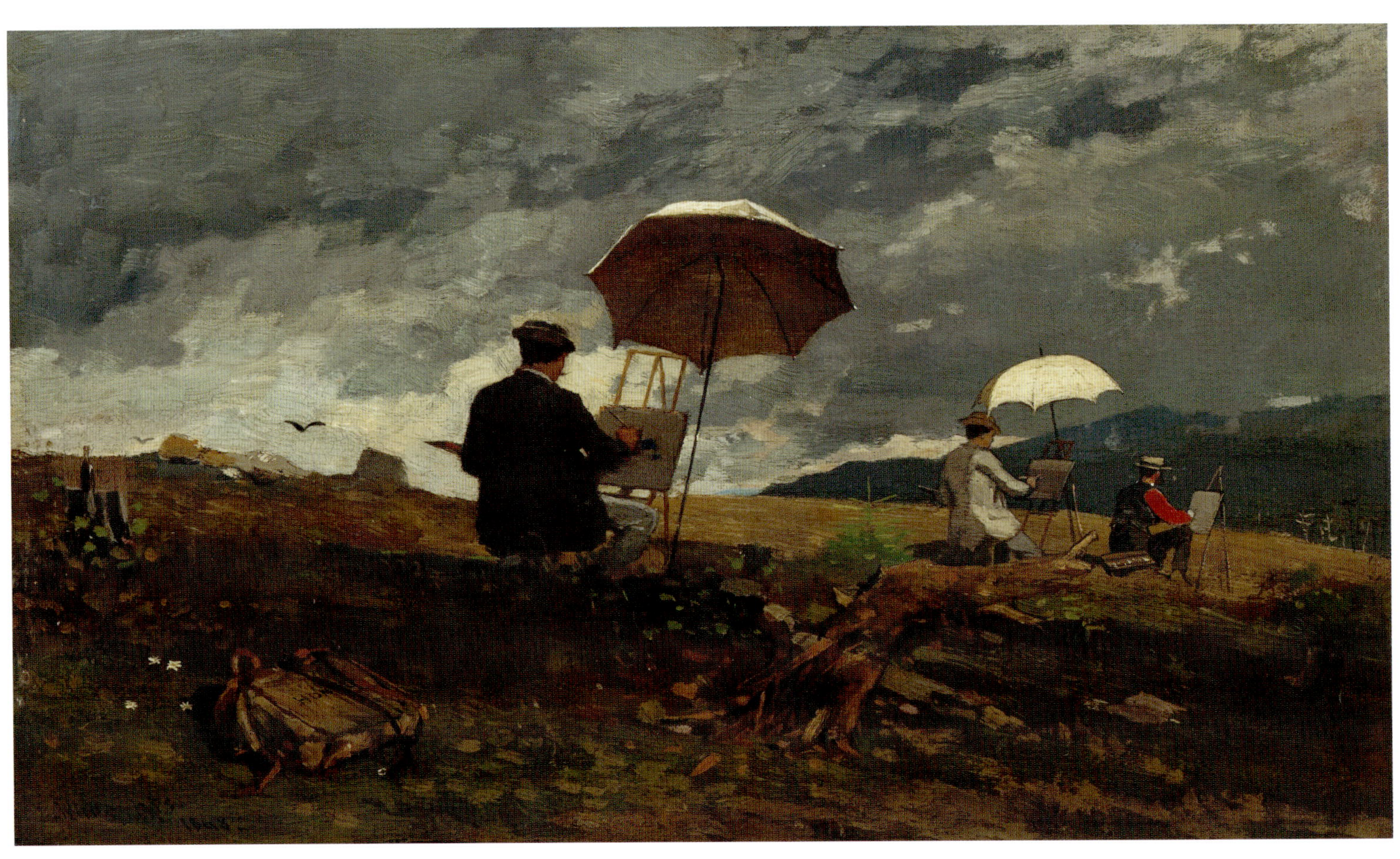

PLATE 16. Winslow Homer, *Artists Sketching in the White Mountains*, 1868. Oil on panel, 9 7/16 × 15 13/16 in. (24.1 × 40.3 cm). Portland Museum of Art, Maine. Bequest of Charles Shipman Payson. [1988.55.4]

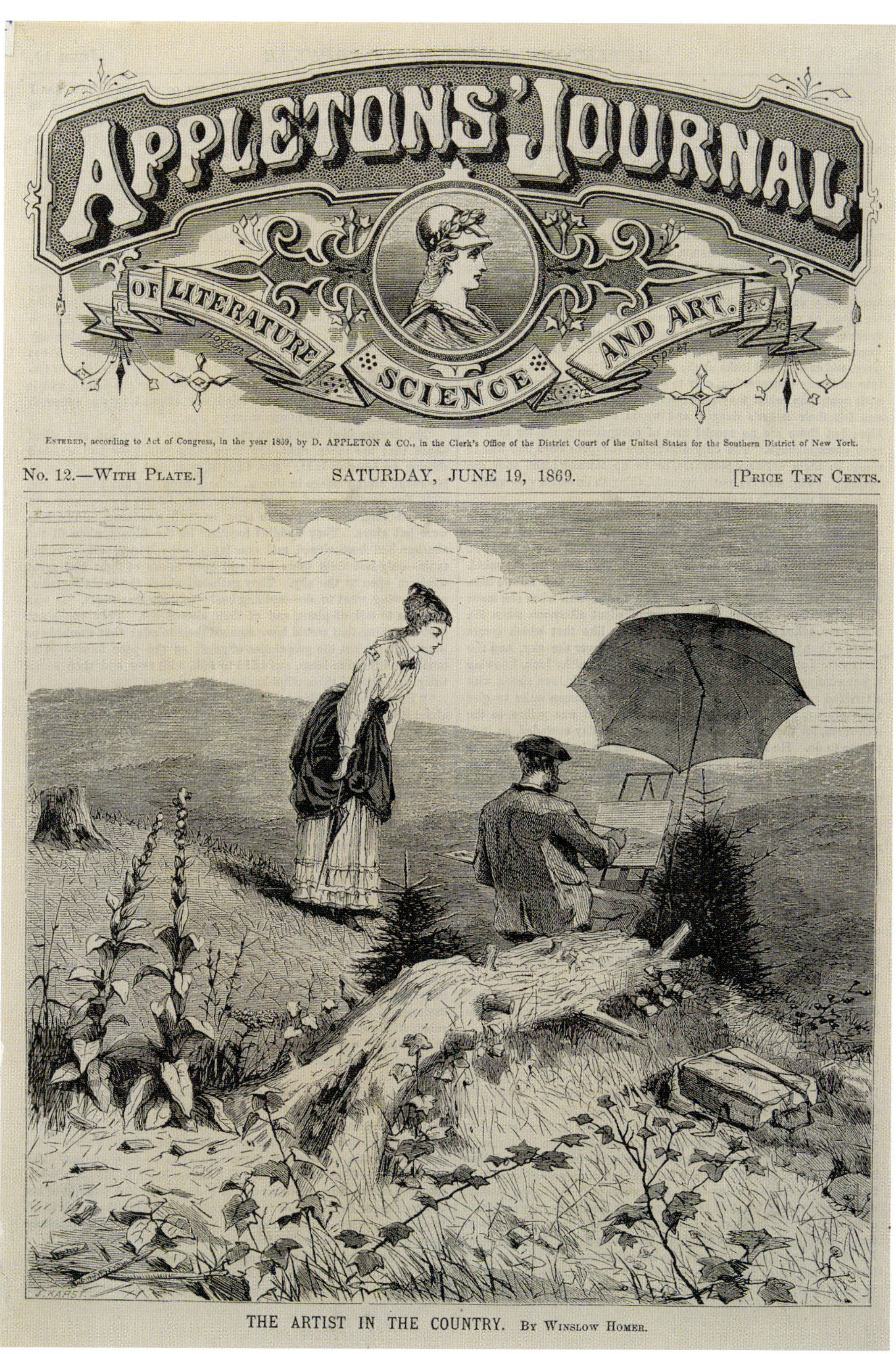

PLATE 17. After Winslow Homer, *The Artist in the Country*, published in *Appletons' Journal*, June 19, 1869. Wood engraving. Bowdoin College Museum of Art, Brunswick. Museum and College Purchase, Hamlin, Quinby, and Special Funds. [1974.1.141]

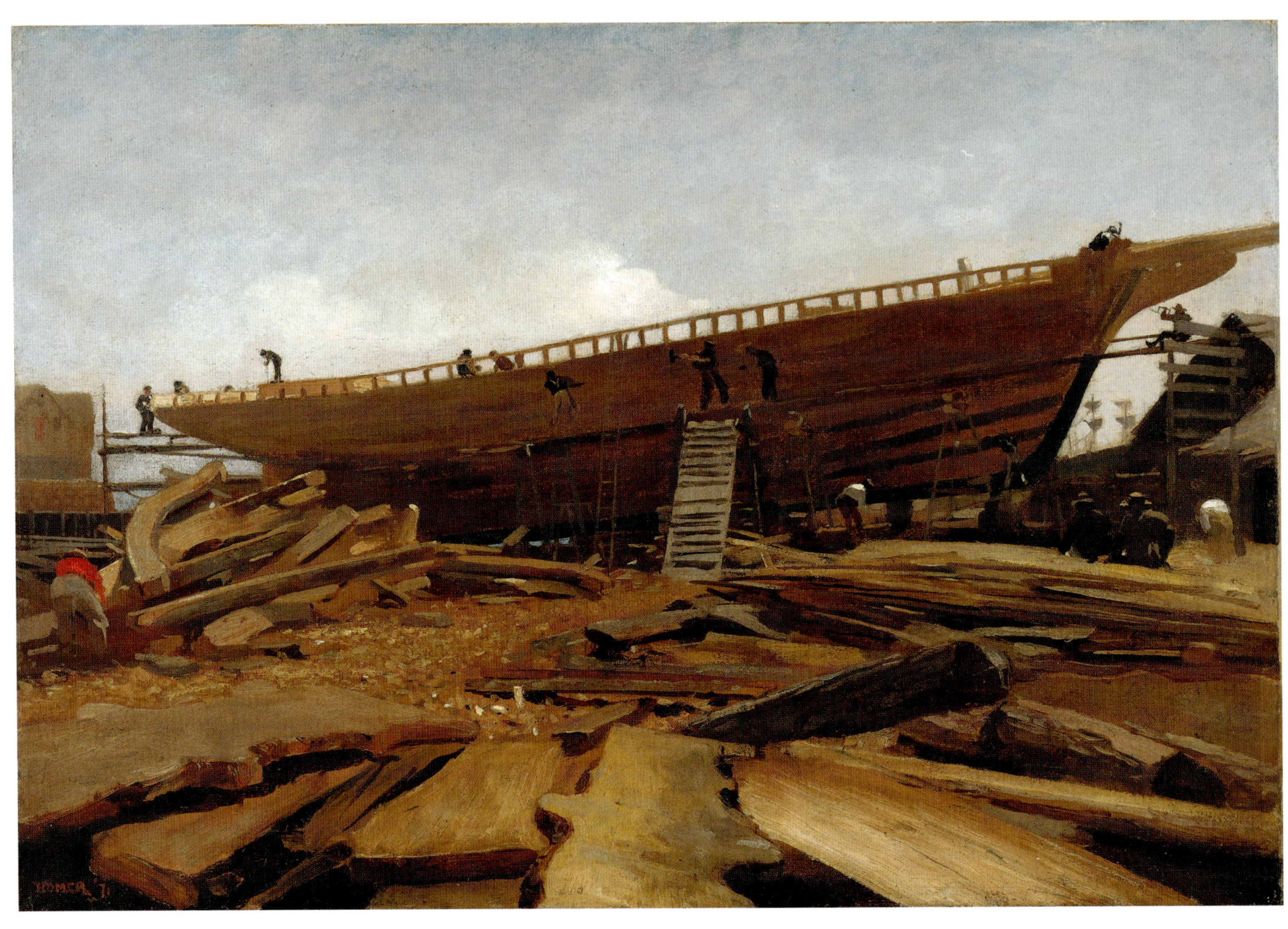

PLATE 18. Winslow Homer, *Shipyard at Gloucester*, 1871. Oil on canvas, 13½ × 19¾ in. (34.3 × 50.2 cm). Smith College Museum of Art, Northampton. Museum Purchase. [1950.99]

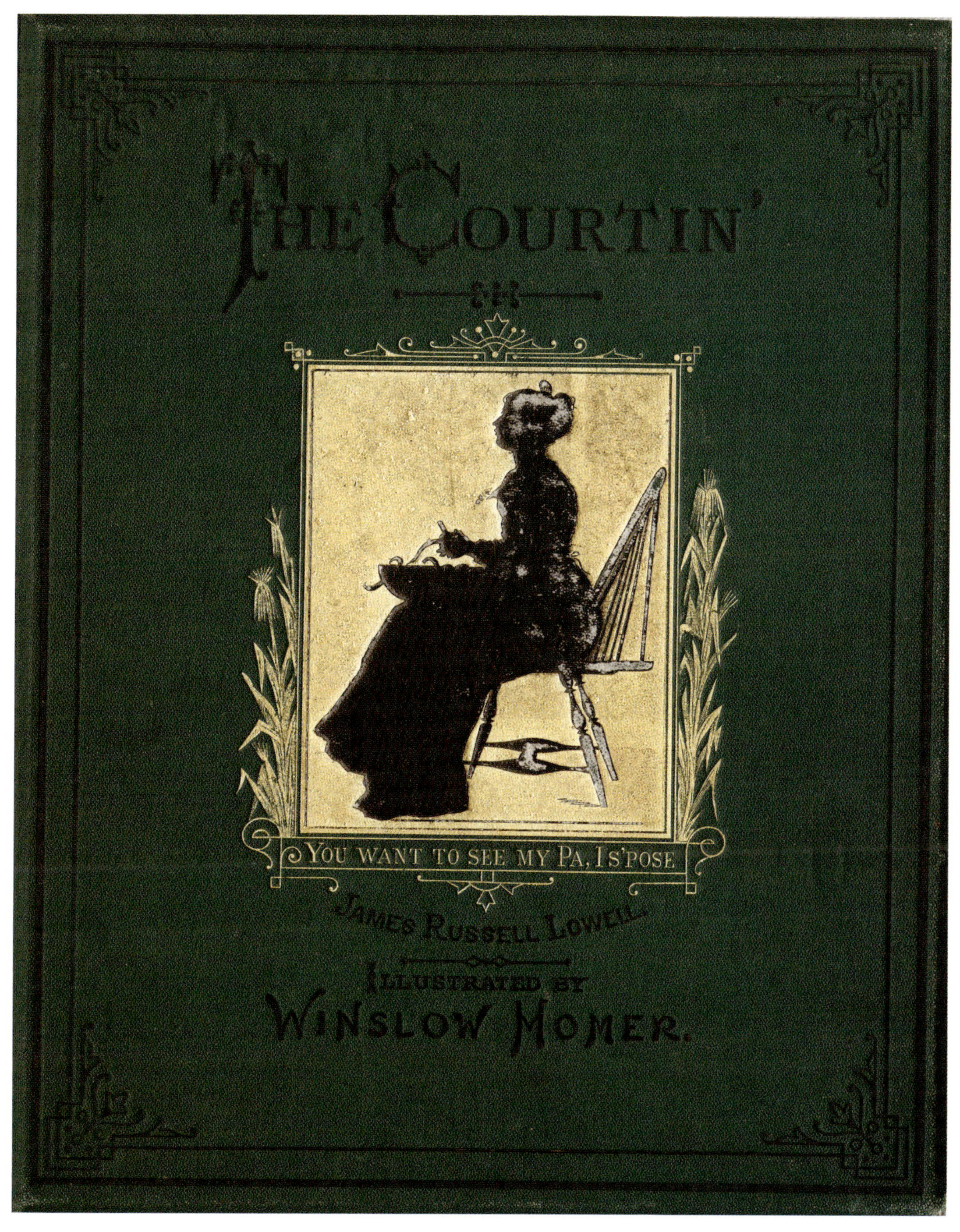

PLATE 19. Winslow Homer, *The Courtin'* by James Russell Lowell, 1874. Heliotype silhouette on bound volume. Bowdoin College Museum of Art, Brunswick. Gift of the Homer Family. [1964.69.167]

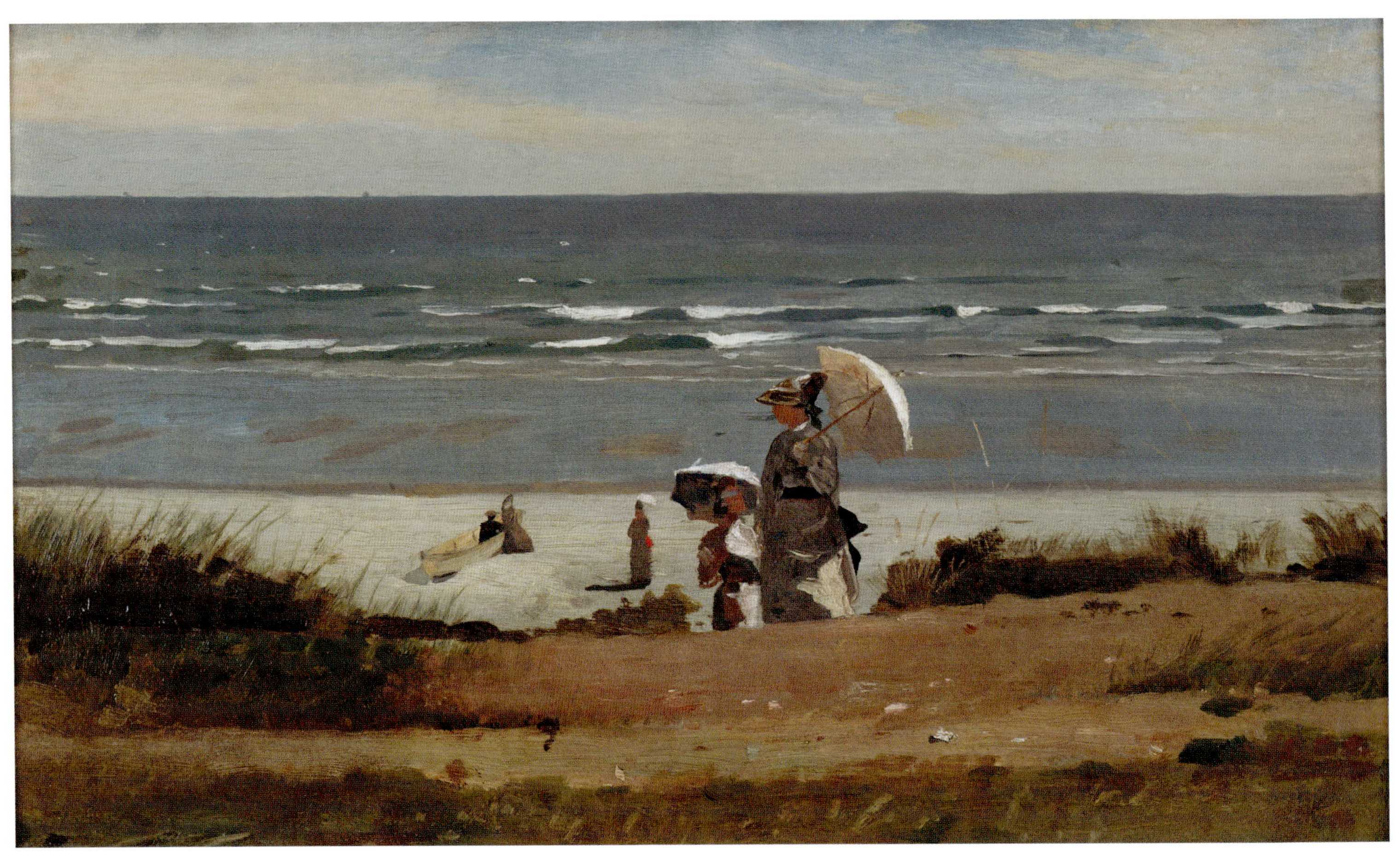

PLATE 20. Winslow Homer, *On the Beach at Marshfield*, c. 1872. Oil on canvas, 13¼ × 21½ in. (33.7 × 54.6 cm). Joyce and Erving Wolf, Houston.

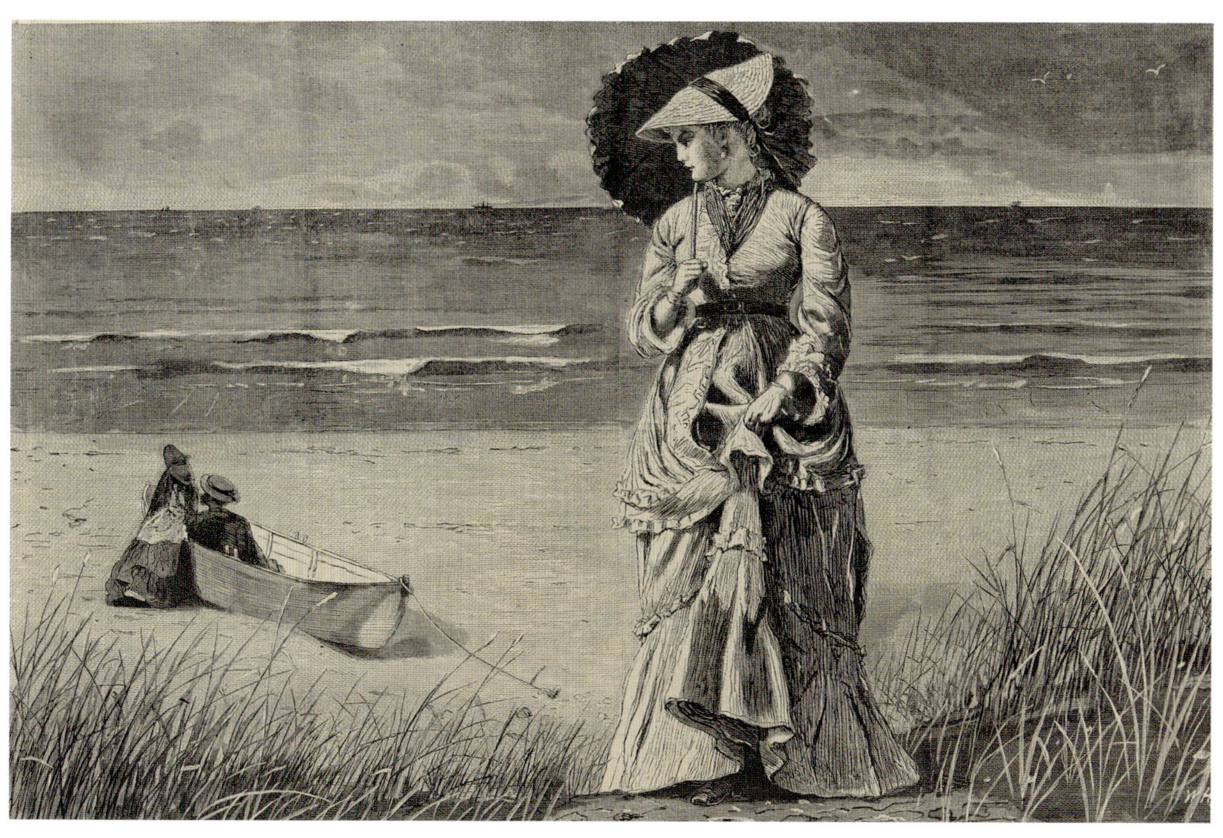

PLATE 21. After Winslow Homer, *On the Beach—Two Are Company, Three Are None*, published in *Harper's Weekly*, August 17, 1872. Wood engraving. Bowdoin College Museum of Art, Brunswick. Museum Purchase, Hamlin Fund. [1966.5]

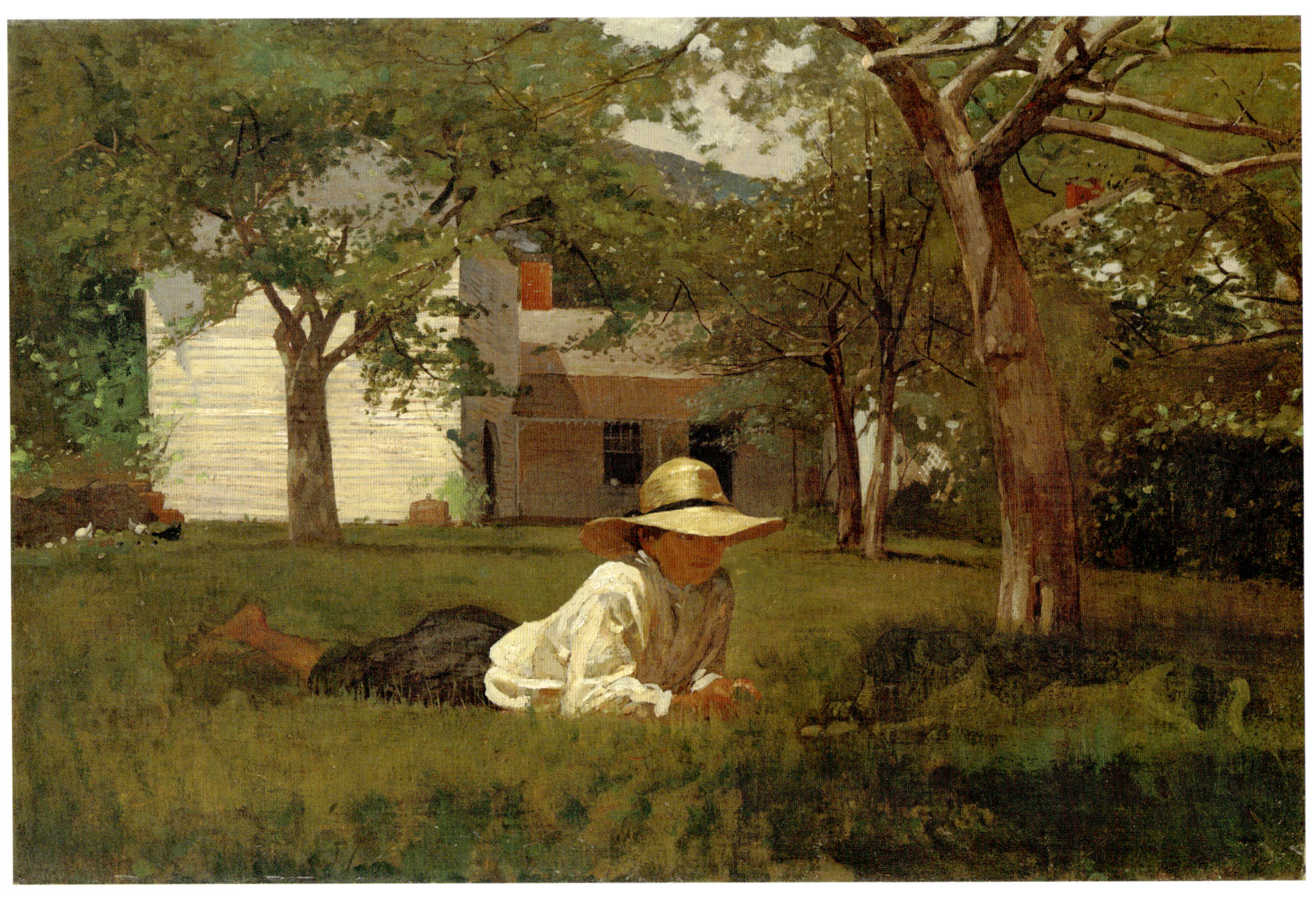

PLATE 22. Winslow Homer, *The Nooning*, c. 1872. Oil on canvas, 13 5/16 × 19 5/8 in. (33.9 × 49.9 cm). Wadsworth Atheneum Museum of Art, Hartford. The Ella Gallup Sumner and Mary Catlin Sumner Collection Fund. [1947.1]

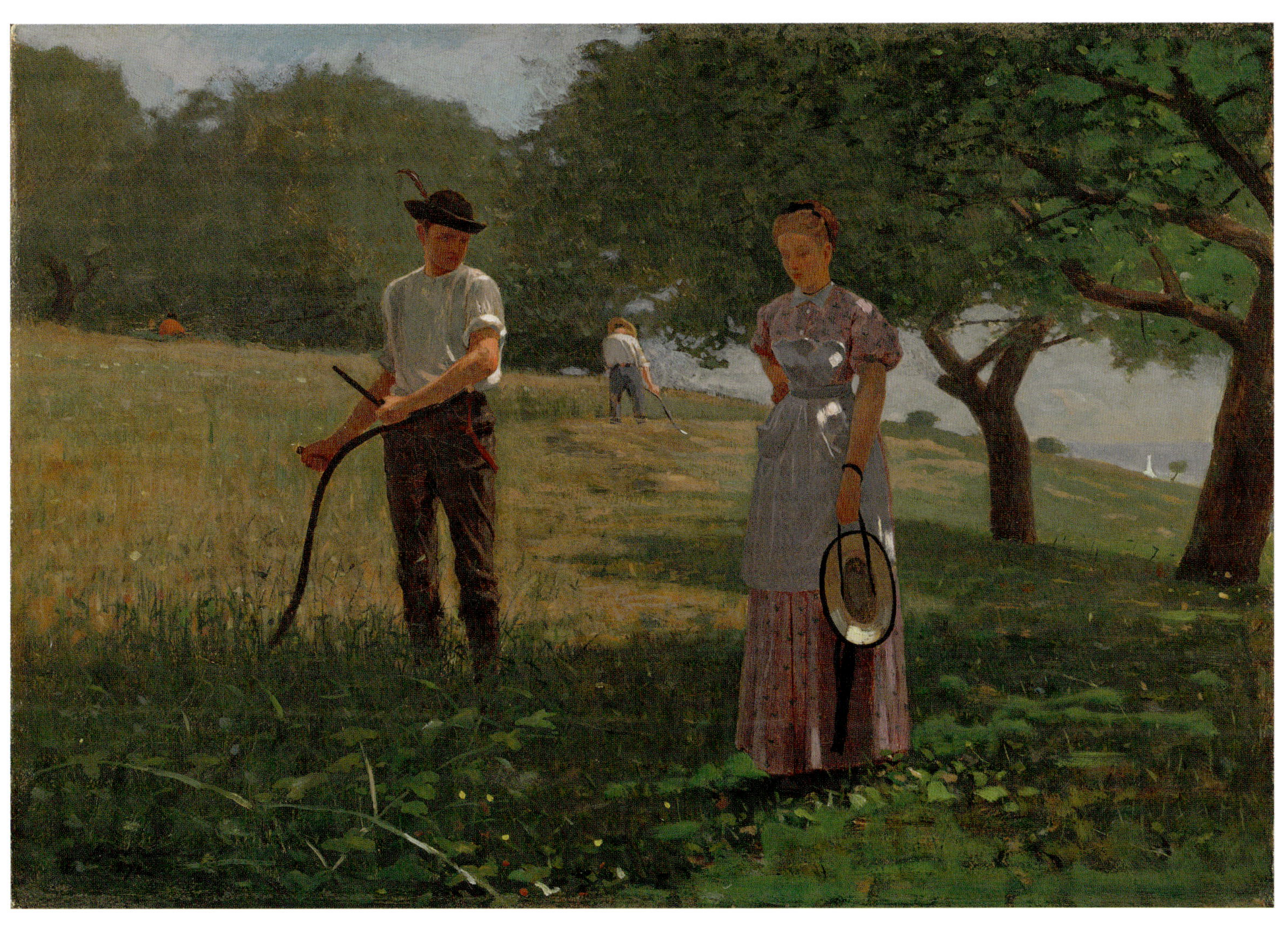

PLATE 23. Winslow Homer, *Waiting an Answer*, 1872. Oil on canvas, 12 × 17 in. (30.5 × 17.8 cm). Peabody Art Collection, Maryland. [MSA SC 4680-10-0034]

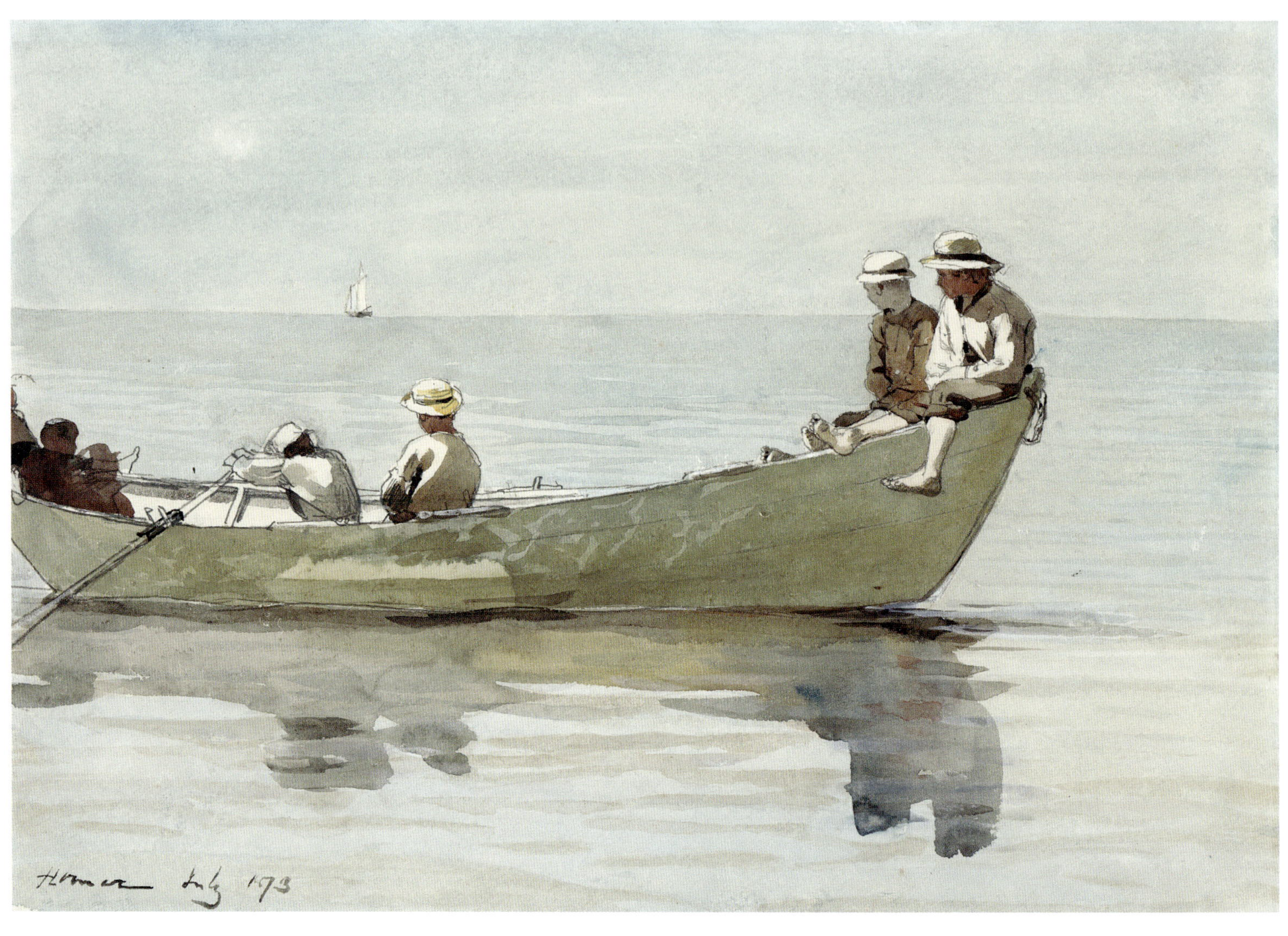

PLATE 24. Winslow Homer, *Seven Boys in a Dory*, 1873. Watercolor on paper, 9½ × 12½ in. (24.1 × 31.7 cm). Farnsworth Art Museum, Rockland, Maine. Anonymous Gift. [1999.22]

PLATE 25. Winslow Homer, *The Angler*, c. 1874. Oil on canvas, 23½ × 16 in. (59.7 × 40.6 cm). Private collection.

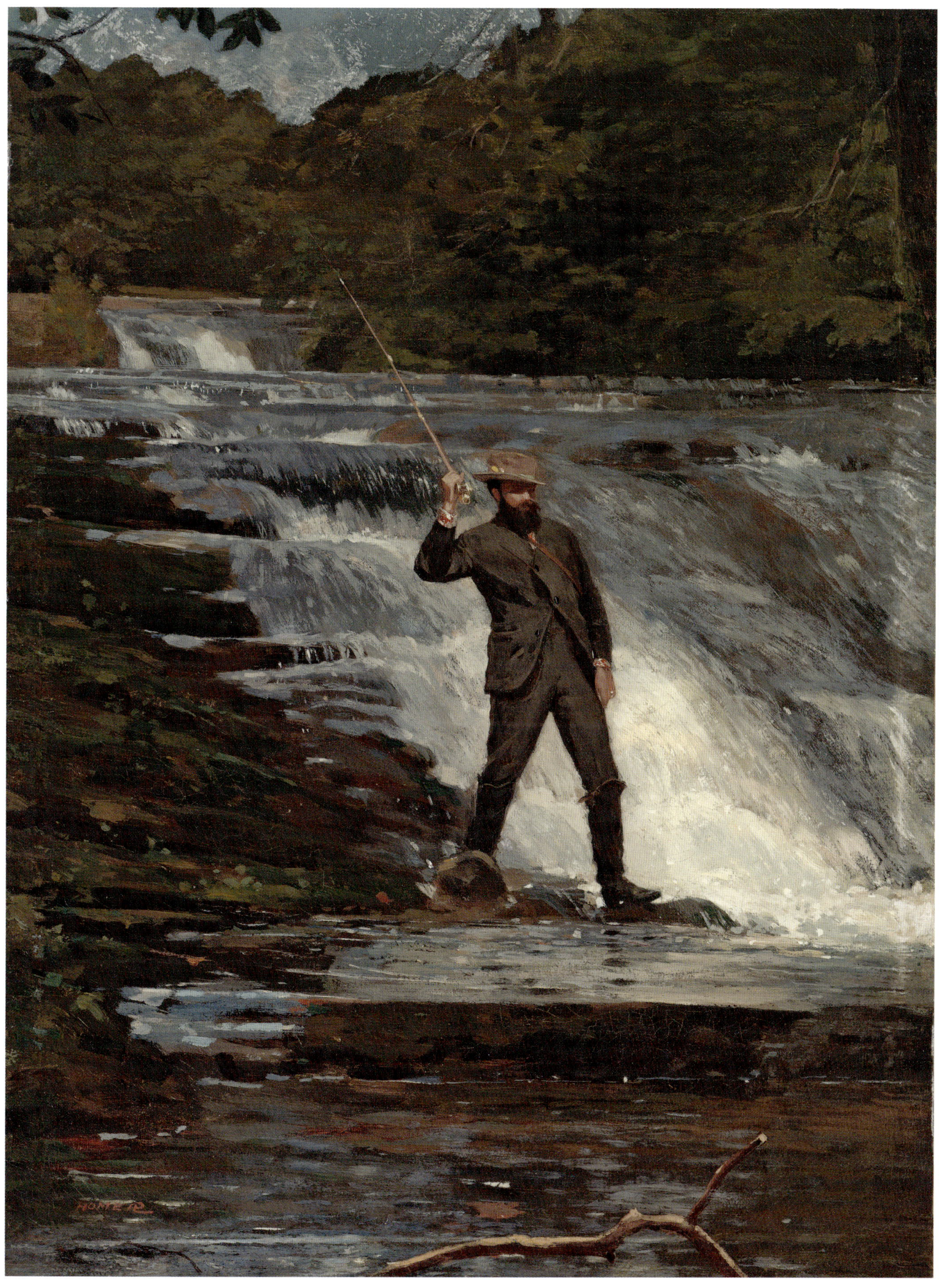

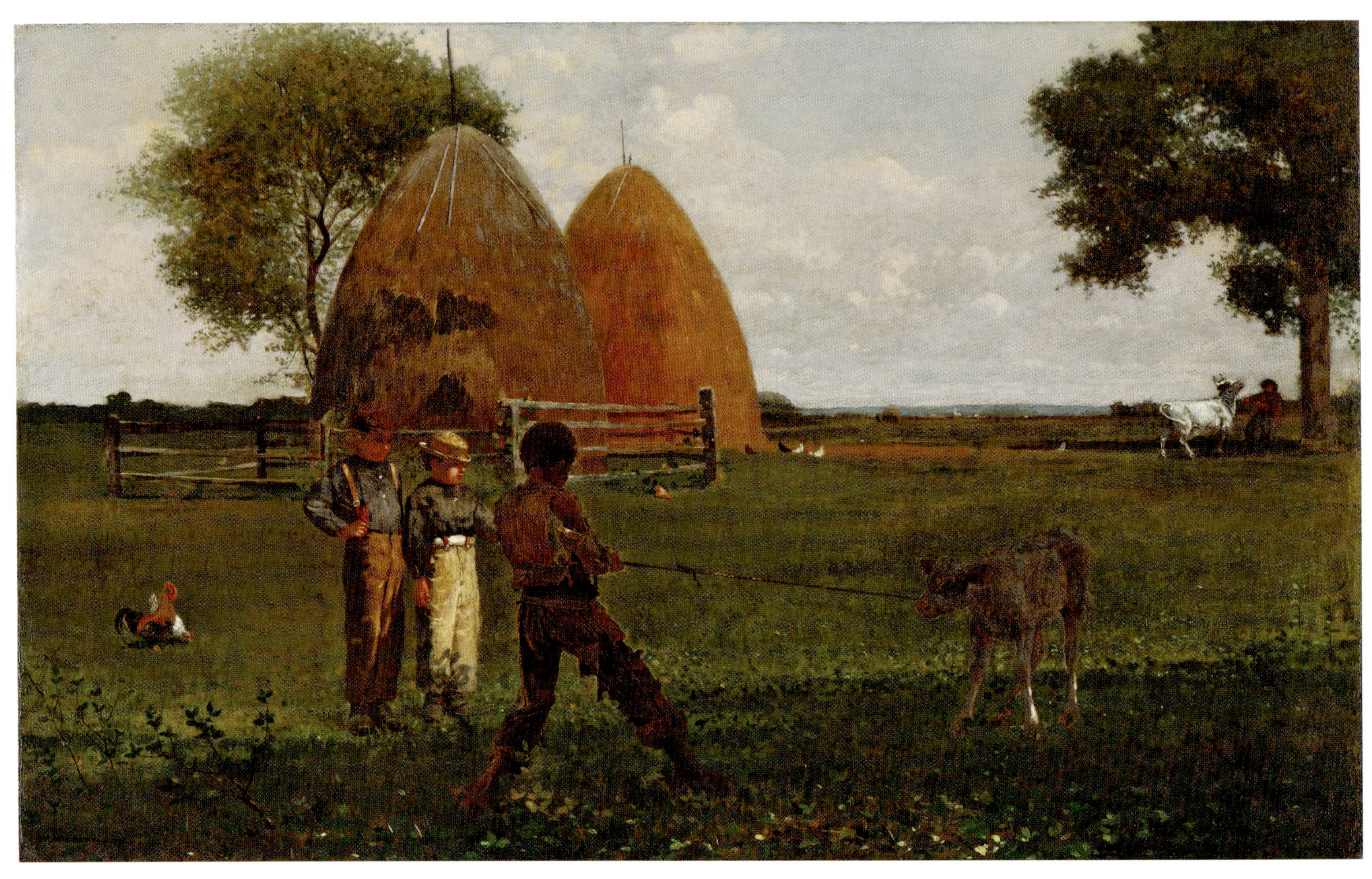

PLATE 26. Winslow Homer, *Weaning the Calf*, 1875. Oil on canvas, 24⅛ × 38¼ in. (61.3 × 97.2 cm). North Carolina Museum of Art, Raleigh. Purchased with Funds from the State of North Carolina. [1952.9.16]

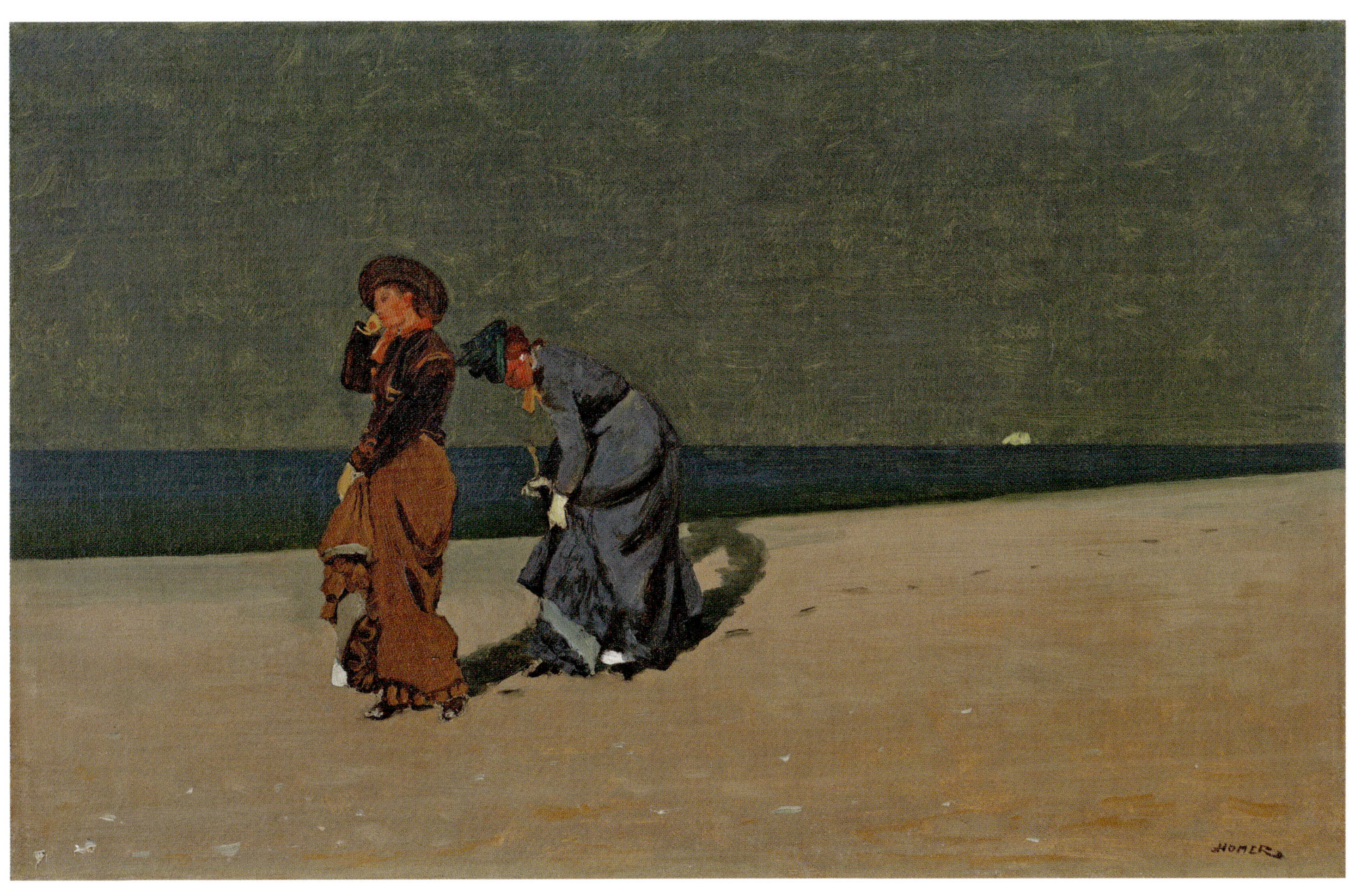

PLATE 27. Winslow Homer, *Evening on the Beach*, c. 1871–78. Oil on canvas, 12 × 19 in. (30.5 × 48.3 cm). Colby College Museum of Art, Waterville. The Lunder Collection. [27.2011]

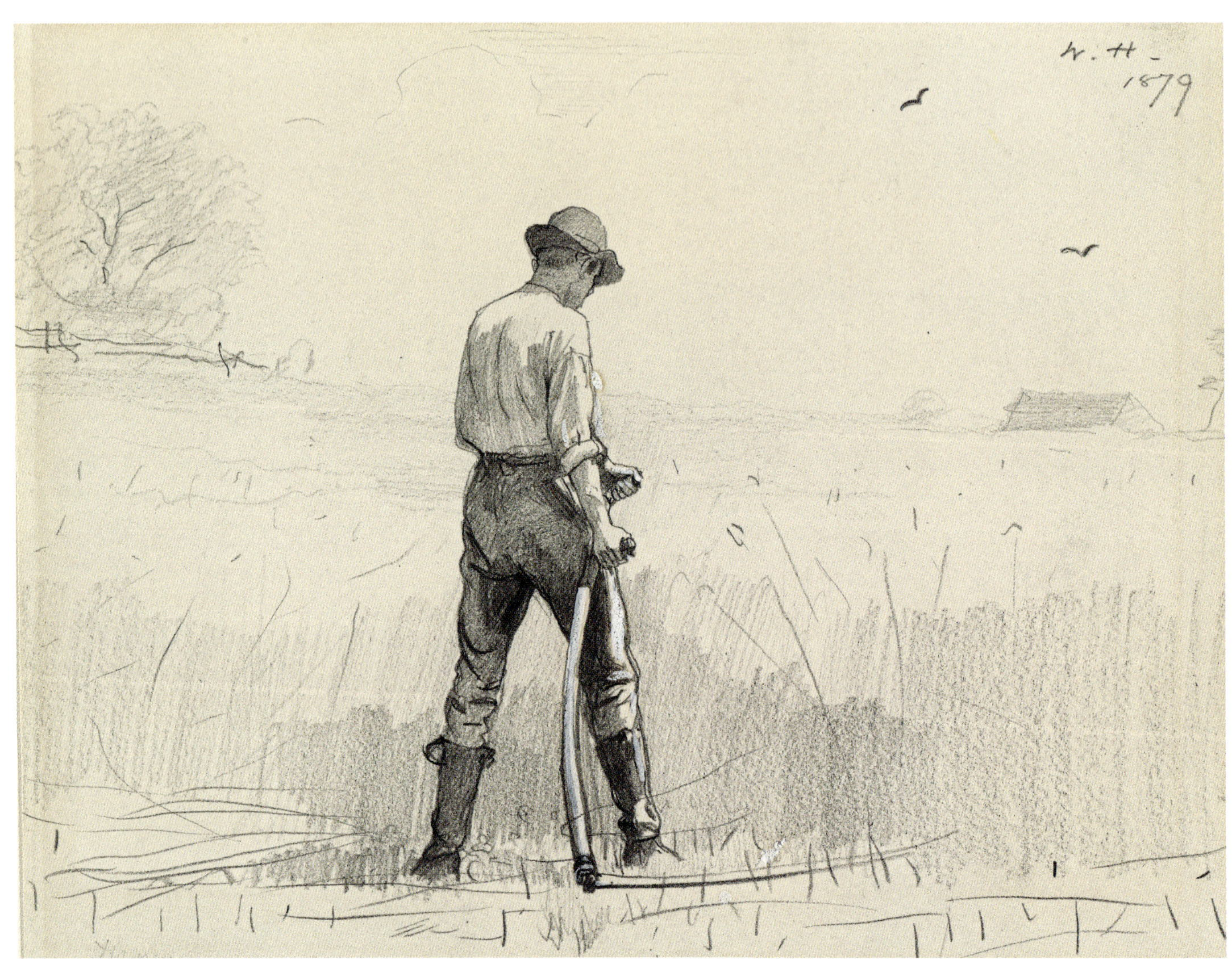

PLATE 28. Winslow Homer, *Man with Scythe*, 1879. Graphite and charcoal, 10 × 12½ in. (25.4 × 31.7 cm). Bowdoin College Museum of Art, Brunswick. Gift of Shorey M. Armstrong. [1991.44]

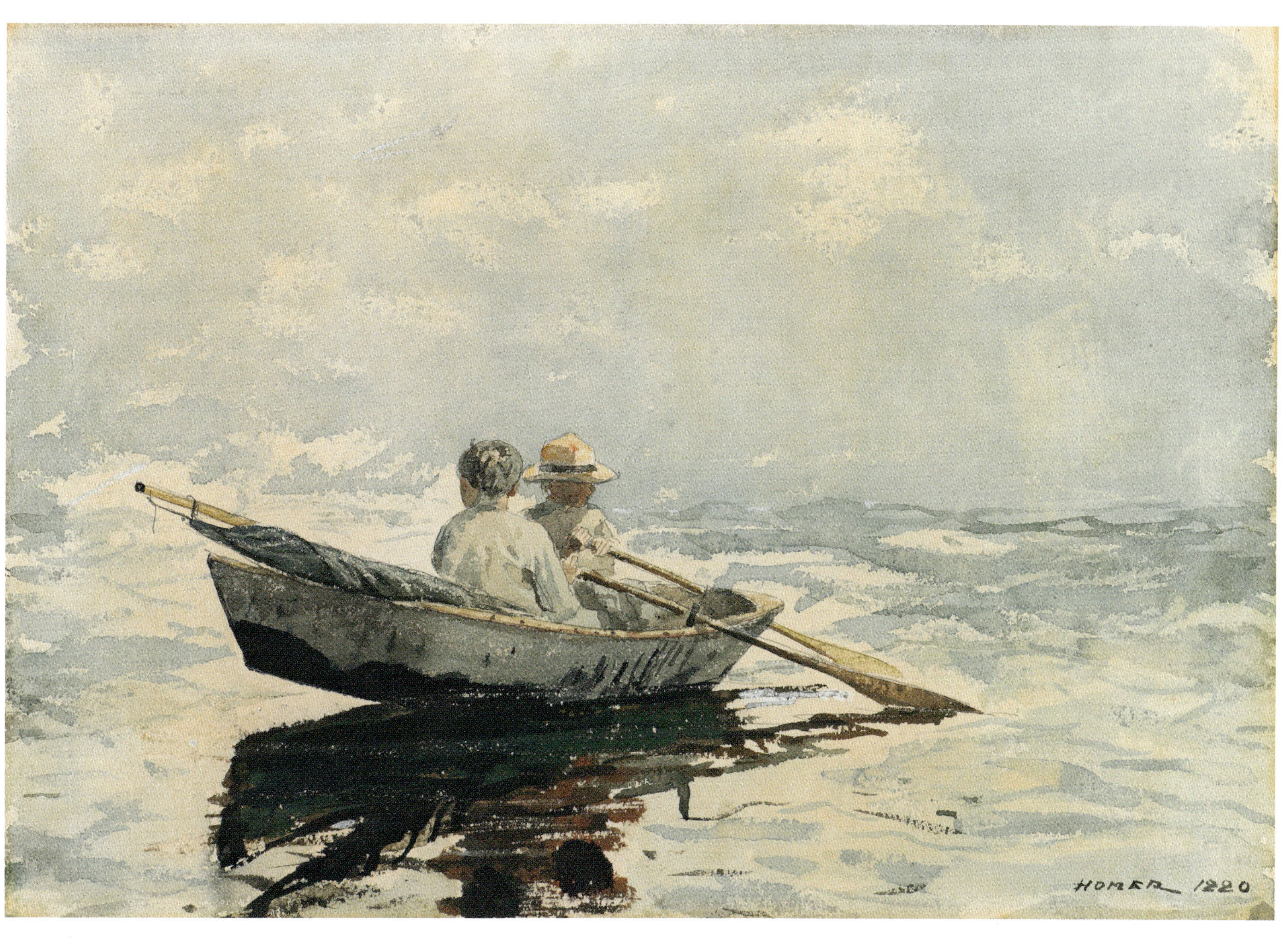

PLATE 29. Winslow Homer, *Rowboat*, 1880. Watercolor over graphite, 9⅞ × 13$\frac{15}{16}$ in. (25.1 × 35.4 cm). Bowdoin College Museum of Art, Brunswick. Gift of Henry Hill Pierce, Jr., in memory of William John Curtis, Class of 1875. [1991.45]

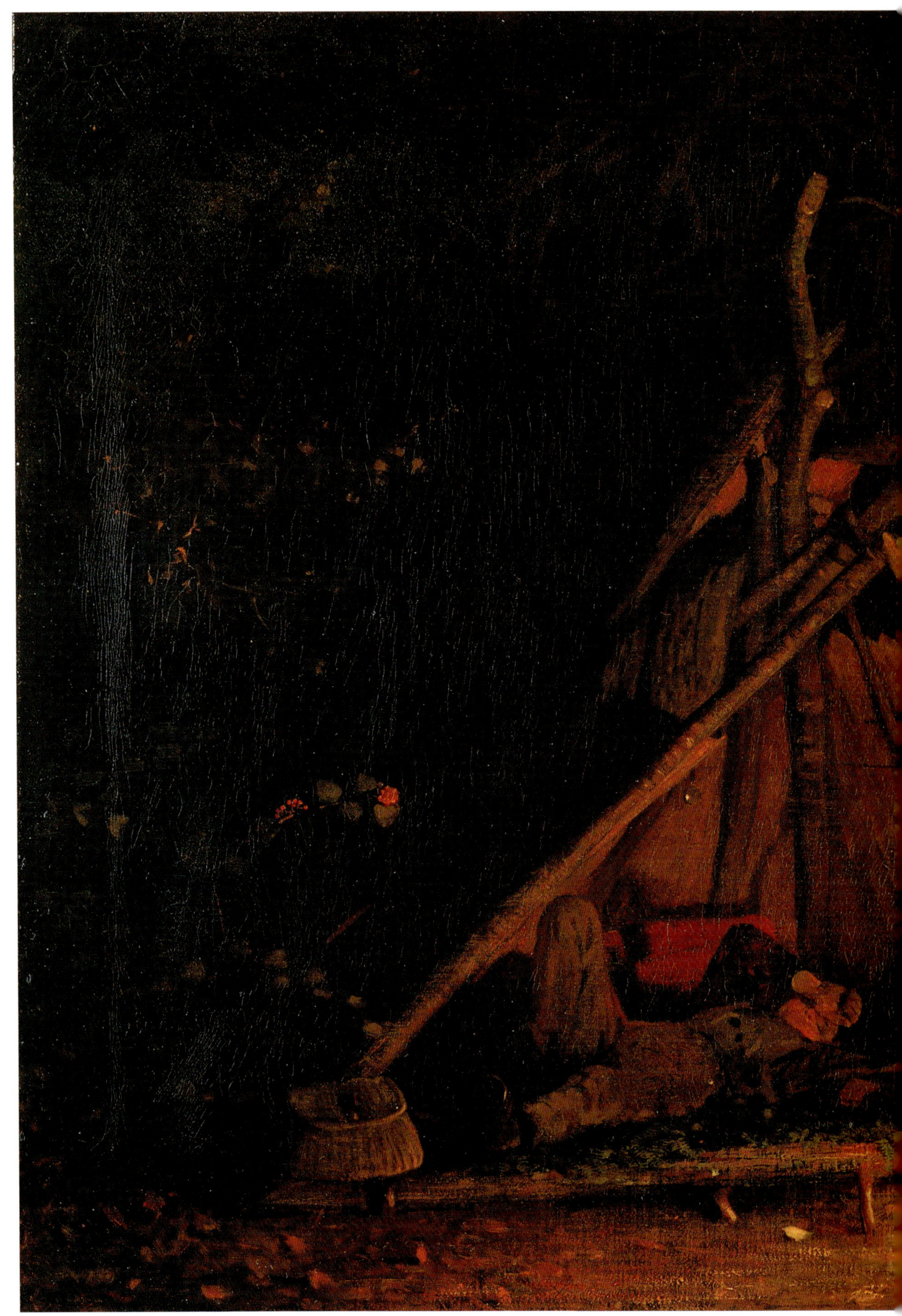

PLATE 30. Winslow Homer, *Camp Fire,* 1877–80. Oil on canvas, 23¾ × 38⅛ in. (60.3 × 96.8 cm). Metropolitan Museum of Art, New York. Gift of Josephine Pomeroy Hendrick, in the name of Henry Keney Pomeroy, 1927. [27.181]

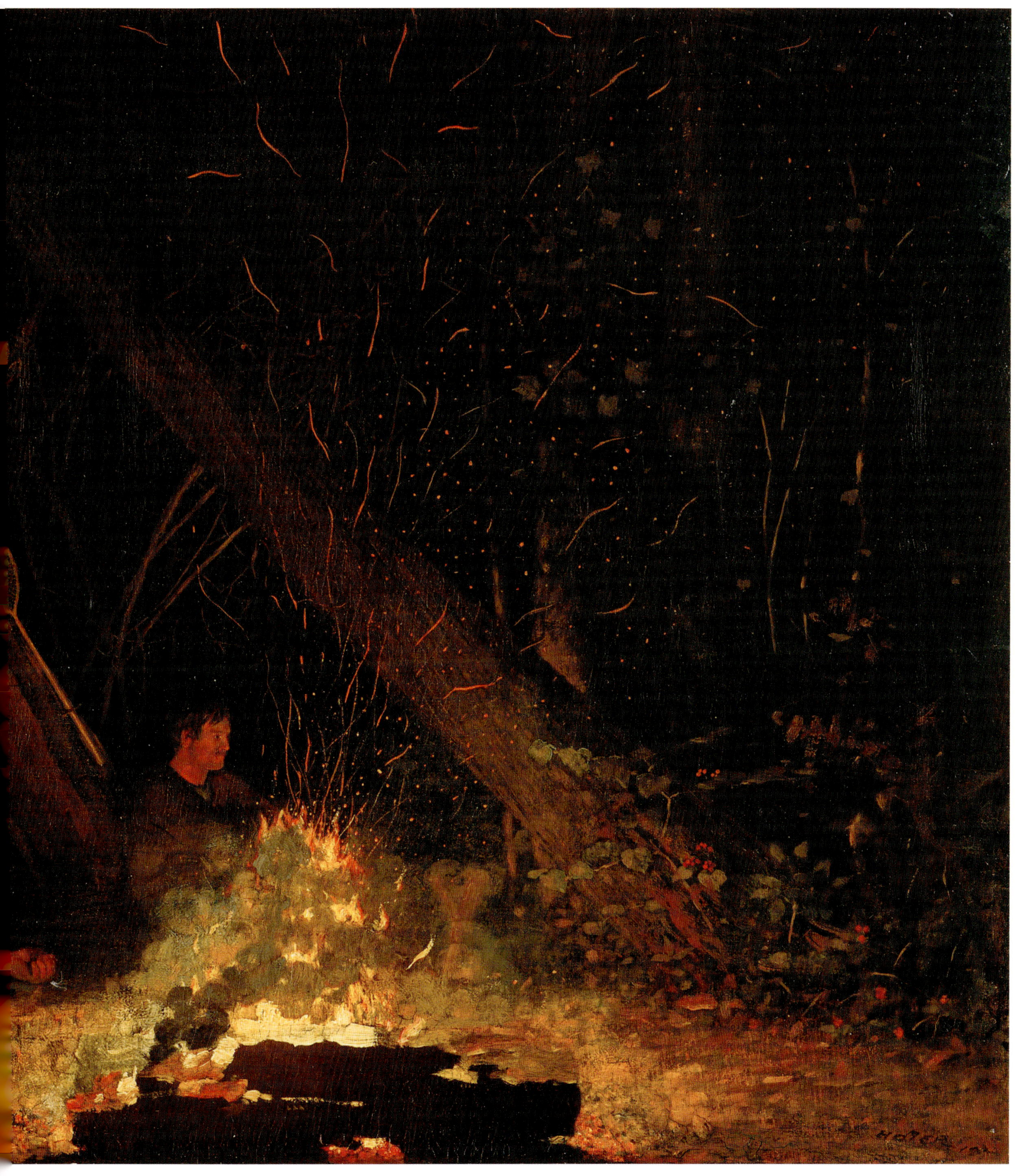

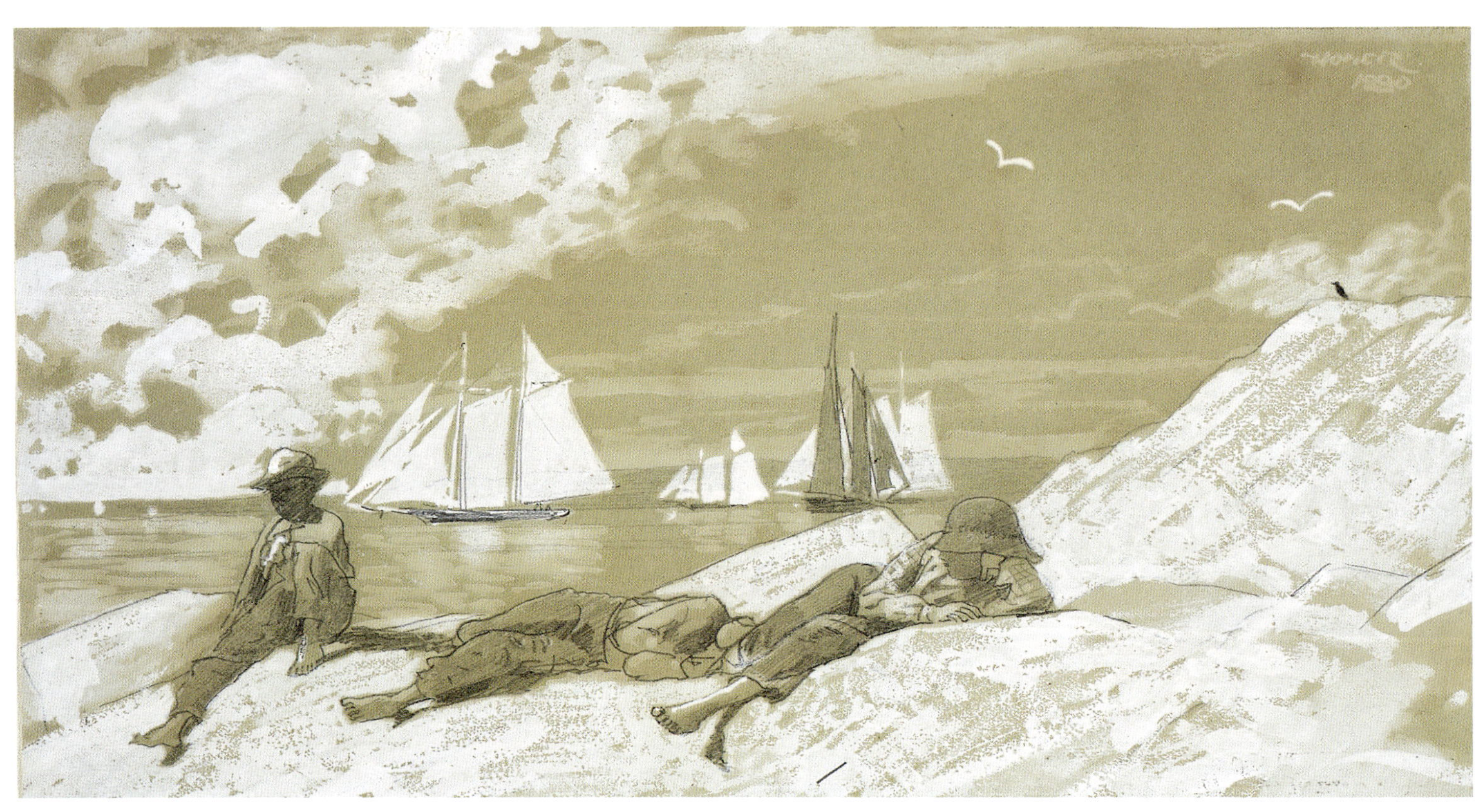

PLATE 31. Winslow Homer, *New England Coast—Sailing Ships in Harbor*, 1880. Graphite and white gouache on paper, 7¼ × 13⅜ in. (18.4 × 34 cm). Farnsworth Art Museum, Rockland, Maine. Museum Purchase. [1946.649]

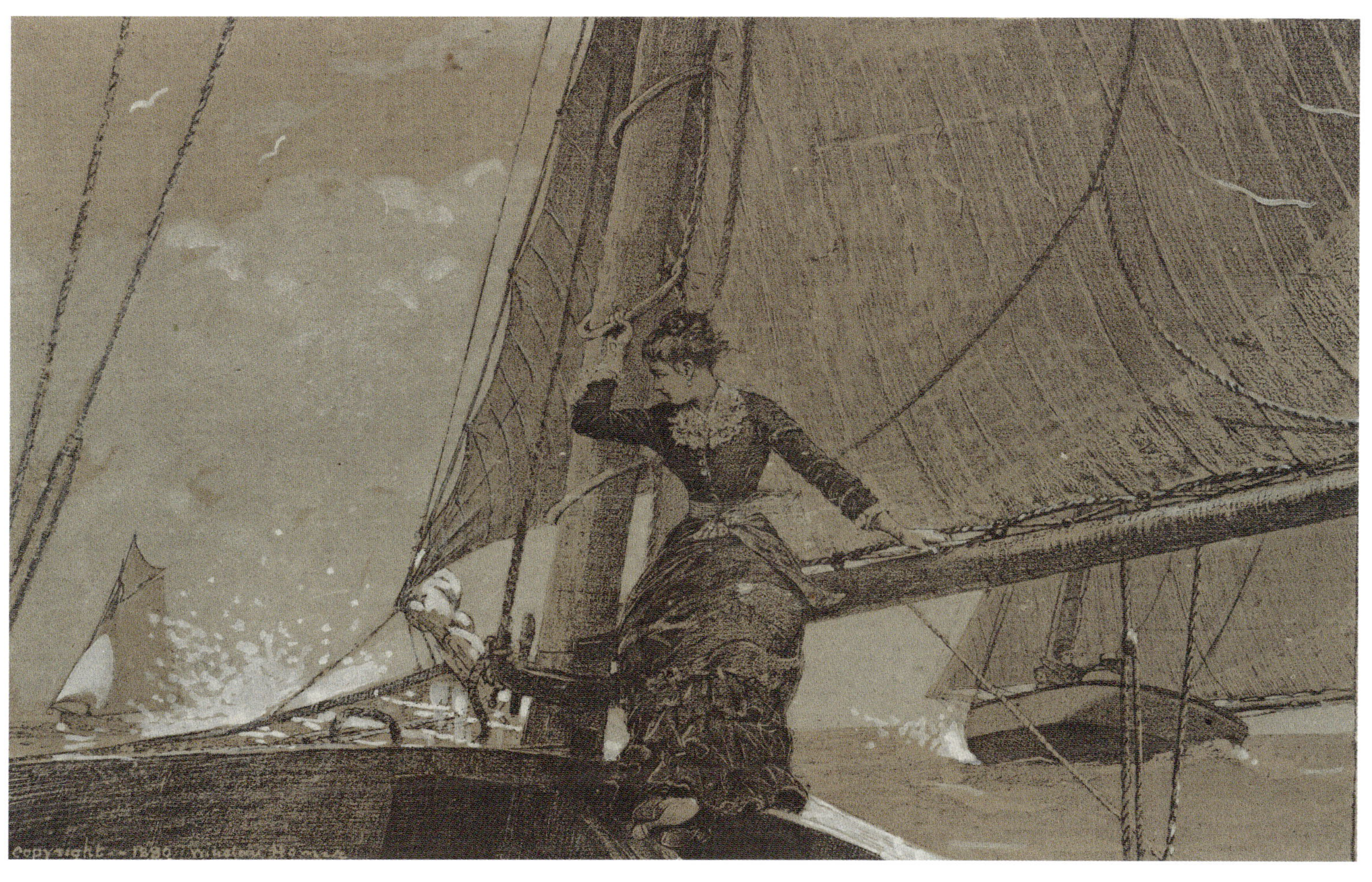

PLATE 32. Winslow Homer, *Yachting Girl*, 1880. Heliograph with gouache, $7\frac{7}{8} \times 12\frac{9}{16}$ in. (20 × 31.9 cm). Bowdoin College Museum of Art, Brunswick. Gift of Mrs. Lewis A. DeBlois. [1971.14]

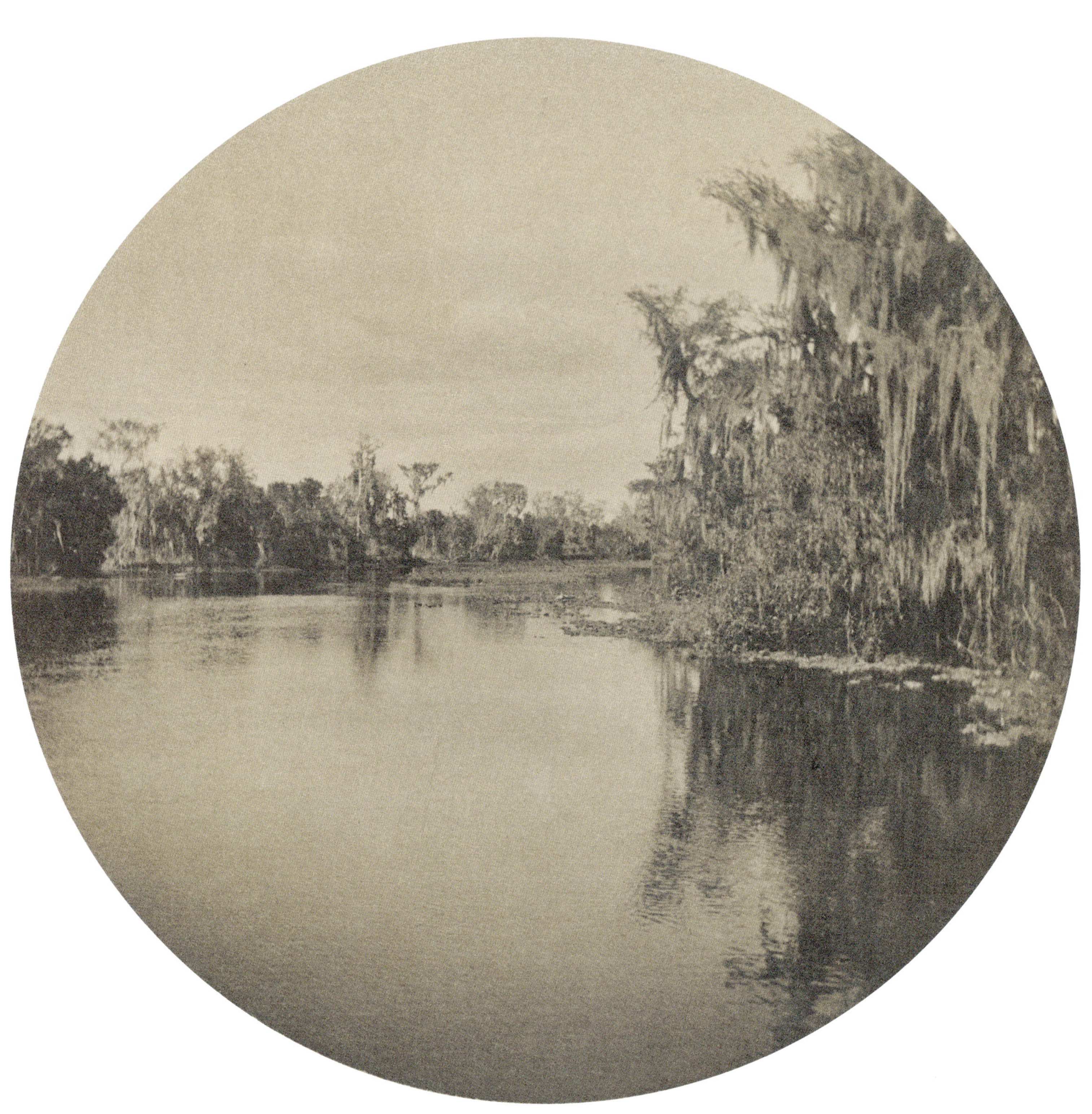

Trouble in Paradise?

Winslow Homer in the Bahamas, Cuba, and Florida, 1884–1886

DANA E. BYRD

The famed American artist Winslow Homer came of age amid the expansive visual world of the late nineteenth century, working across media to produce drawings, paintings, prints, and watercolors for consumption in the art market. To great success, the relationship between these works—from the translation of photographs into wood engravings to the incorporation of elements developed in his watercolors into finished oil paintings—has been well plumbed by scholars in order to offer a comprehensive and nuanced account of his body of work. Indeed, scholars have devoted a tremendous amount of attention to exploring virtually every aspect of Homer's career, as well as connections between his artistic output and the creations of other artists.[1] Although both the medium of photography and the artist himself emerged in the late 1830s and came of age at mid-century, the relationship of Homer's art to the medium of photography has been the subject of far less scrutiny than other aspects of his career.

In 1882, while on sojourn in England, Homer purchased his first and second cameras, an English-made Marion & Company "Academy" camera and a Mawson & Swan camera.[2] Homer had traveled there to visit major collections of art, including London's British Museum, and to make new work. He eventually settled in Cullercoats, a fishing village and a growing tourist destination near Tynemouth on the North Sea. It is reasonable to assume that Homer's purchase of the cameras launched a new phase in his interaction with photography. He was no longer merely viewing, commissioning, and incorporating photographs into his hybrid artistic practice, as had formerly been the case; he was now taking them as well. Although just one photograph from the two cameras is known to have survived, it is instructive to consider the benefits of each of these devices. Marion & Company's Academy hand-held camera was designed to be light and portable, and included a magazine, which held a number of plates that could be exposed successively, freeing the operator from having to hand load the camera after each shot.[3] The Mawson & Swan camera, which survives in the collection of the Bowdoin College Museum of Art, required a bit more attention from the operator, including the changing of plates between each shot (see frontispiece). The two cameras, however, were designed to be operated by amateurs, making them appropriate for travelers and belying Homer's interest in them.

Detail of plate 60B

Photographs, taken by and for travelers, were central to the late nineteenth century's visual culture of tourism. Photography was not the sole province of tourists; nonetheless, to be a tourist in the nineteenth century meant one likely had some involvement with the camera and its image-making possibilities. The concurrent development of photography and tourism gave rise to an impressive body of images by some of the nineteenth century's leading artists, including Frederic Church and Thomas Moran. Travel photographers documented historic and scenic places, from manmade marvels such as the Egyptian pyramids to natural phenomena like Niagara Falls, and tourists eagerly consumed the representations. By the 1880s, the newfound accessibility of cameras and other photographic equipment meant that tourists could take their own pictures, although professionals also disseminated images as souvenirs and documentation. Guidebooks played an indispensable role in the nineteenth-century travel experience. Publishers often relied on professional photographs of tourist destinations as fodder for their publications. A photograph of a popular tourist site could serve multiple uses: it might be included as a plate in a book, be translated into a wood engraving, or even serve as the basis for the lively word pictures that often accompanied illustrations. Guidebooks often combined photographs, illustrations, maps, and prose to promote a particular venue. While still at home, a potential traveler would use a guidebook first to plan a trip, then, when onsite, to navigate the unfamiliar territory, and finally, safely back at home, as a cherished souvenir through which to remember the trip and share the experience with others. Photographic technology here worked in the service not of self-reflection but of industry—a seemingly very modern use of the image.[4]

Homer, like many well-off travelers of his day, likely consulted tourist materials enriched by photography when planning his trip to England. The most successful examples were those, such as *Stanford's Guides*, a series of travel guides to England and parts of Europe published by Edward Stanton of London, and *Harper's Hand-Books*, launched in the United States in 1862 by Harpers Publishers, that crafted compelling narratives about given destinations that effectively removed any uncertainty about those destinations on the part of the reader.[5] For the traveler crafting an itinerary, these guides differentiate among particular aspects of the destination. A survey of Northumberland-region travel publications reveals several aspects of the community that were highlighted again and again, including the bracing sea air to be enjoyed on Cullercoats's beach, the picturesque local boats, and the compelling architecture, such as the Royal National Lifeboat Institution Station, which housed various lifeboats. Indeed, Homer's poignant portrayals of Cullercoats fisherfolk incorporate aspects of these suggested sights, while also engaging more broadly with the challenges faced by those villagers who made their living from the sea. His renderings highlight the visual appeal of the North Sea's fisherfolk, while capturing the sense of danger inherent in their work. As a tourist, Homer may have been directed to popular sites by guides, but as an artist, he transformed aspects of these destinations into powerful compositions.

Material evidence drawn from Homer's surviving personal library suggests that while in Cullercoats, he had begun to explore the connections across media. Art historian David Tatham notes that among the books Homer had in England were his dog-eared copy of a translation of Michel-Eugène Chevreul's *De la loi du contraste simultané des couleurs et de l'assortiment des objets colorés* as well as Friedrich Ernst Feller's *New English and French Pocket Dictionary*. The two texts represent a continued negotiation between Homer's roles as artist and tourist: Homer's brother Charles had gifted the Chevreul book to him in 1860; and the Feller dictionary had been purchased in anticipation of a Channel crossing to France after his stay in Cullercoats had ended. As Homer traveled, he used the Chevreul volume as a "memory book" and recorded notes and sketches in the margins of the text. Notably, the book is embellished with an undated sketch of his brother Charles, sketches of two female figures, lists of triads, autographs, and pencil markings. Intriguingly, Homer pasted into the front endpapers "a photograph showing in silhouette one of the small fishing boats and fisherman of Cullercoats."[6] Likely taken with the Mawson & Swan camera, this image signals the growing importance of photography to the artist's practice. In a volume that was instrumental in the development of the artist's painting, the addition of this memory-making marginalia is a material manifestation of the intersections between painting, photography, and travel in Homer's art-making practice.

On Homer's next international trip, he was accompanied by his father, Charles Savage Homer, travel guides, and art supplies, but no camera.[7] The 1884–85 Bahamas trip was prompted by a commission from *Century Magazine* to produce pictures for a feature article promoting Bahamas tourism. A growing American interest in tropical travel may have prompted the *Century* project and Homer's decision to accept it (in the previous decade the artist had sworn off commercial illustration). The resulting Bahamas watercolors are just a part of Homer's highly celebrated 1880s tropical oeuvre. Since their execution, these works made in the Bahamas, Cuba, and Florida—rendered in a medium traditionally prized for its spontaneity—have been much admired, with authors in recent years addressing both their subject matter as well as the what and the when of their creation.[8] One important aspect of these images that remains underexplored concerns their relationship to Homer's involvement with the image world of late nineteenth-century tourism, including the photographs, illustrations, and guidebooks that supported the burgeoning travel industry. The present essay seeks to fill this lacuna, situating the artist's depictions of these lush and scenic destinations in the context of the rich visual culture. It does so by drawing on a number of archival sources, which, in addition to the pictures produced by and for Homer, include his own writing, histories of these tropical locales, and tourist materials, including images, guidebooks, and period accounts of the tropics.

The artist had likely had his curiosity about the tropics, an interest shared by many Americans at this time, stoked by the region's growing tourist industry. During the 1860s, tourism promoters, backed by colonial administrators, relied on guidebooks, postcards, and illustrated lectures to market the islands in the Caribbean, including the Bahamas, Cuba, and Jamaica, as picturesque "tropical" paradises. They hired photographers and artists to create carefully fashioned representations designed to convey the experience that hoteliers sought to provide to guests. Journalists were courted to visit the region and to report their experiences in local papers across the states. Indeed, Homer was one of numerous visual artists and writers who would go on to shape the image of the Bahamas and Florida in travelogues, literary representations, and pictures, while relying on guides to plan their own excursions. Circulating internationally, these marketing campaigns were oriented toward an influx of tourists from Canada and the United States who were privileged to engage in leisure travel.

Homer's first tropical pictures celebrate the visual pleasures of the region while hinting at a darker side of each of the popular locales. Tourism materials are produced to inform and persuade, and as such, they are meant to be inherently positive and celebratory. Watercolors of sparkling azure seas and lush orange trees in Homer's oeuvre certainly participate in these promotional practices. Moodier pictures in muddier palettes, however, indicate that Homer was not reproducing a set of stock tropical motifs and instead was also engaging with the work of gloomier forces. Indeed, Homer went to great lengths to distinguish *between* the Bahamas, Cuba, and Florida, and in each place produced mini-oeuvres revealing his complex understanding of each destination. The artist absorbed, rather than abandoned, his hard-earned conception of individual places, continuing to ruminate on them throughout the remainder of his career and redeploying them to great effect in his later oil paintings.

The Bahamas, Grand Sanitarium of the Western Hemisphere

> We find a place where the invalid . . . may enjoy the finest and most equable climate in the world, during the winter months, absolutely free from all danger of epidemic disease . . . and other dangers and disadvantages usually incident to tropical countries, good society, fine educational and religious privileges . . . recreations of varied and healthful character.
>
> —*Guide to Nassau, Island of New Providence, Bahamas, West Indies*, 1876

Winslow Homer's arrival in the Bahamas—a group of twenty-nine islands off the coast of North America, north of Cuba and Santo Domingo, at the easternmost edge of the Gulf of Mexico—coincided with the territory's proud assumption of the mantle of a fall and winter tourist destination for the sick and healthy alike. Representations of the Bahamas in picture and print alternated between describing them as a safe haven with the modern conveniences of home, and highlighting such elements of island life as temperate climates and stunning vistas, to entice potential visitors. Drawing on a long relationship between the United States and the Bahamas, such promotional materials targeted prospective American travelers. Like other territories of the British crown, the Bahamas were overseen by a colonial governor who was both an executive and a holder of legislative authority. Under British rule, the islands were a comfortable destination for Americans; English was spoken, and, as in the United States, "Conch" or white Bahamian society was stratified and organized around various social pursuits, including dinner parties and costume balls.[9]

The Bahamas had long been in the American public's consciousness. The islands benefited greatly from the U.S. Civil War. As the federal blockade prevented British ships from reaching Southern ports, blockade runners from the Confederacy met British ships in the Bahamas, illicitly trading cotton for British goods. Many Americans regarded this tacit British Bahamian support of the renegade Confederacy as a betrayal of the United States, and the ensuing prosperity of Bahamians ill-gotten and tainted. The end of the Civil War, and the highly charged project of suturing the United States back together, marked the end of prosperity for the blockade runners and, thus, the Bahamas. In the 1870s, seeking a new source of revenue and in hopes of rehabilitating the region in the eyes of many Americans, the Bahamian colonial government and hoteliers began aggressively promoting the islands as a tourist destination particularly amenable to the ill and infirm during the winter months.[10] The colonial regime and other boosters hoped that tourism would continue to grow on the strength of Nassau's beautiful setting, its temperate climate, and the "spontaneous, hearty kindness offered by the people universally."[11] Travel guides to the Bahamas were published in London and New York throughout the 1870s and 1880s, and popular national periodicals such as *Frank Leslie's Illustrated Newspaper* and *Harper's Monthly* regularly carried articles extolling the virtues of the so-called Isles of Eden. Local newspapers from Albany to Cincinnati to Montreal featured the island paradise in articles and advertisements. Once coupled with text, Homer's *Century* commission was intended to boost the Bahamas as a place of leisure and healing, thus overwriting its recent history as a haven for Confederates. It was one element in the editorial leadership's project of using pictures and prose to knit together the United States's fractured factions. Homer's commission prescribed the Bahamas as a therapeutic cure for the nation's problems.

On December 4, 1884, the artist and his father, Charles Savage Homer, left Maine and made their way to New York City, where they boarded the Ward Line's "first class passenger steamship" the *Cienfuegos* en route to the Bahamas. Capable of ferrying passengers from New York to Nassau in just four days, the ship had been launched the year before from the John and Roach Sons Shipyard in Chester, Pennsylvania. With her iron hull, six watertight cargo compartments, and commodious accommodations, the *Cienfuegos* had been heavily promoted as the best choice for passage to the Islands. After a brief stop in Savannah, Georgia, the steamship continued to Nassau, the port city of the main island, New Providence (fig. 1). As the *Cienfuegos* steamed into the harbor, Homer and his elderly father would have been able to see the contours of the three forts and water battery that defended the town. As the passengers were discharged from the steamship, they were likely dazzled by New Providence; in four days they had traveled from the snows and cold of winter to the floral abundance and balmy atmosphere of the Bahamas. These travelers hoped to enjoy the "peculiar natural advantages" of the winter resort, which included "a dry, rarified atmosphere" to ease the symptoms of visitors with pulmonary disease. The Homers reached the islands at the start of the season and joined about

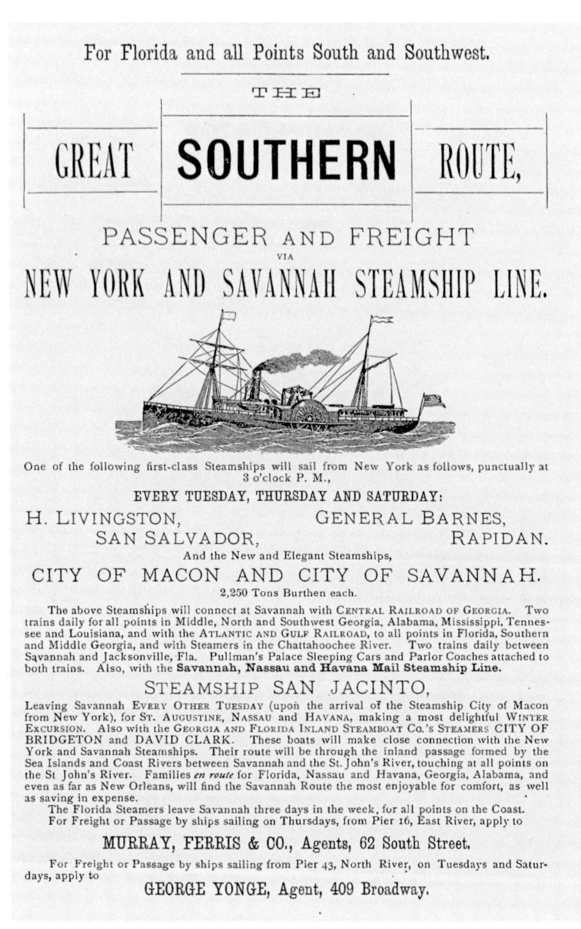

FIG. 1. *Guide to Nassau, Island of New Providence, Bahamas, West Indies: With Illustrations from Photographs; The Royal Victoria Hotel and the New York, Nassau & Savannah Mail Steamship Line; With Meteorological Tables and Other Statistics of Interest to Invalids and Travelers*, 1876. Advertisement, Murray, Ferris & Company, 1876 (detail, p. 35). Library of Congress, Washington, D.C.

150 other white visitors vacationing in the "natural resort."[12]

Winslow and his father lodged at the Royal Victoria Hotel, the first luxury accommodations in the Bahamas and the center of tourist activity on New Providence (fig. 2). In 1870, the proprietors of the hotel and the colonial government had partnered to lure wealthy vacationers to "the great sanitarium of the western hemisphere." The resulting guide is lavishly illustrated with prints adapted from photographs, accompanied by florid prose encouraging visits to the island. From en-suite bathrooms with running water to the large, elegant hotel dining room, the Royal Victoria was a modern establishment targeted at wealthy, and sometimes infirm, white travelers and their companions. The guide places emphasis on the two most celebrated aspects of the hotel's building and grounds: the depiction of the building, featuring the latest in modern architecture, and the beautiful and bountiful formal gardens encircling the structure. Sited near the colonial governmental complex at the top of Parliament Street, the four-story hotel was constructed of limestone, with three of the stories surrounded by ten-foot-wide piazzas. Ailing hotel guests could promenade along these piazzas and avail themselves of the refreshing breezes and fine views of land and sea, without exerting themselves too much by leaving the building. Hardier visitors could stroll along the wide paths of the hotel's elaborate tropical garden, or walk to the nearby colonial governmental complex to interact with Conchs, Bahamian residents of European descent. Hotel staff offered excursions to the markets to revel in the local color, whether sampling the tropical island bounty, in the form of tropical fruits including "pine-apple, sappadilla, cashews, sweet sop, sour sop, papaw, sweet and sour orange, lemon, lime, star apple, coco plum," or gazing at the picturesque black Bahamian market folk as they moved through their daily lives.

Homer and his father likely took in the gardens during their stay at the Royal Victoria. Representations of the garden space, in word and image, touted the Royal Victoria's position as the preeminent Bahamian hotel.

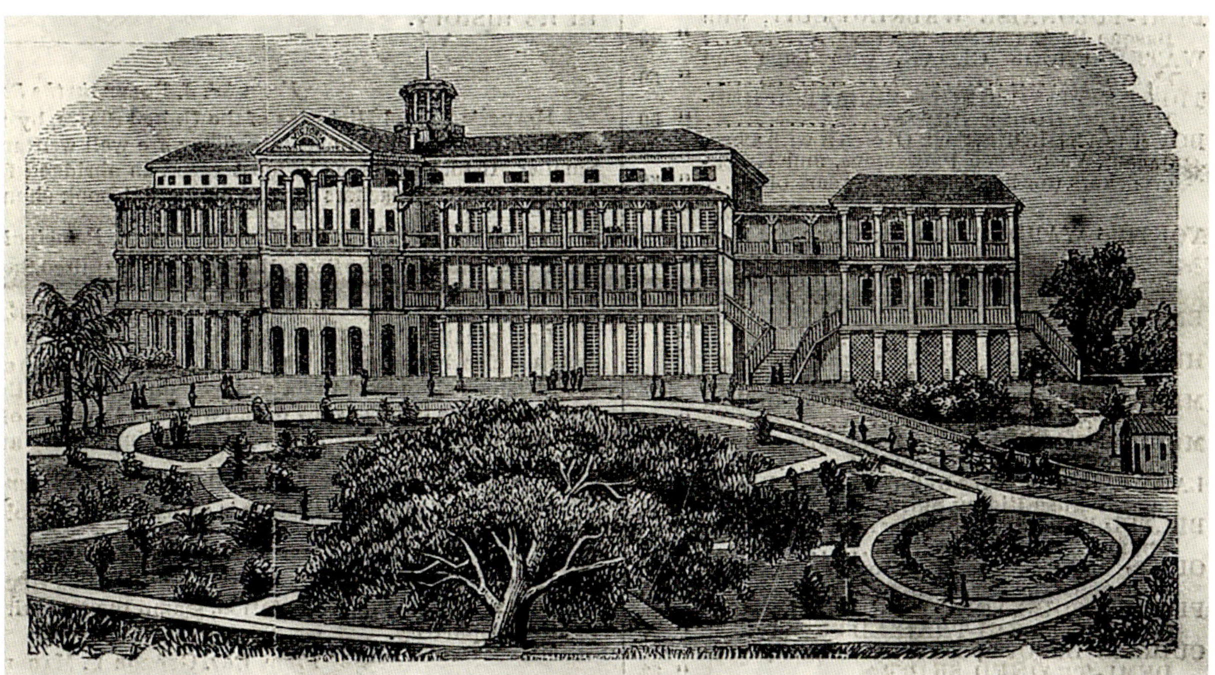

FIG. 2. Unidentified artist, *Winter Resort, Royal Victoria Hotel*, published in *Harper's Weekly*, September 1875. Wood engraving. Private collection.

The *Guide to Nassau*'s print of the hotel and gardens featured its exotic plants and flowers as well as guests moving safely along the well-maintained paths. Here the eye could feast on two hundred varieties of exotic plants, shrubs, and trees, their focal point being the huge cotton tree, or ceiba, at the center of the garden, and the palm trees, those ubiquitous symbols of the tropics, at the far left. The print naturalizes the appearance of a variety of plants and flowers; however, it is unlikely that the varieties of plants and shrubs touted in the guidebooks, some of which were non-native but tropical, would have grown naturally in that location. The uprooting and replanting of them in the hotel soil, by unseen and unnamed black Bahamian laborers, brought the tropical wilds to the tourists in the safest way possible.[13] The Royal Victoria's garden at once fulfilled Western aesthetic expectations for a picturesque garden and displayed how nature could be tamed into a semblance of ordered civilization. This effort to promote the Bahamas' exotic flora and fauna as a respite from the United States was moderately successful, with numbers of tourists climbing through the end of the nineteenth century.[14]

The Royal Victoria's success at creating a controlled environment for its visitors was not limited to carefully cultivated gardens, as hotel management also facilitated white visitors' interactions with black natives. Homer did take advantage of the regular sightseeing tours around New Providence, which allowed him to come into close proximity to black Bahamians, albeit in a regulated fashion. These guided excursions included visits to the Revolutionary War–era fortifications Fort Charlotte and Fort

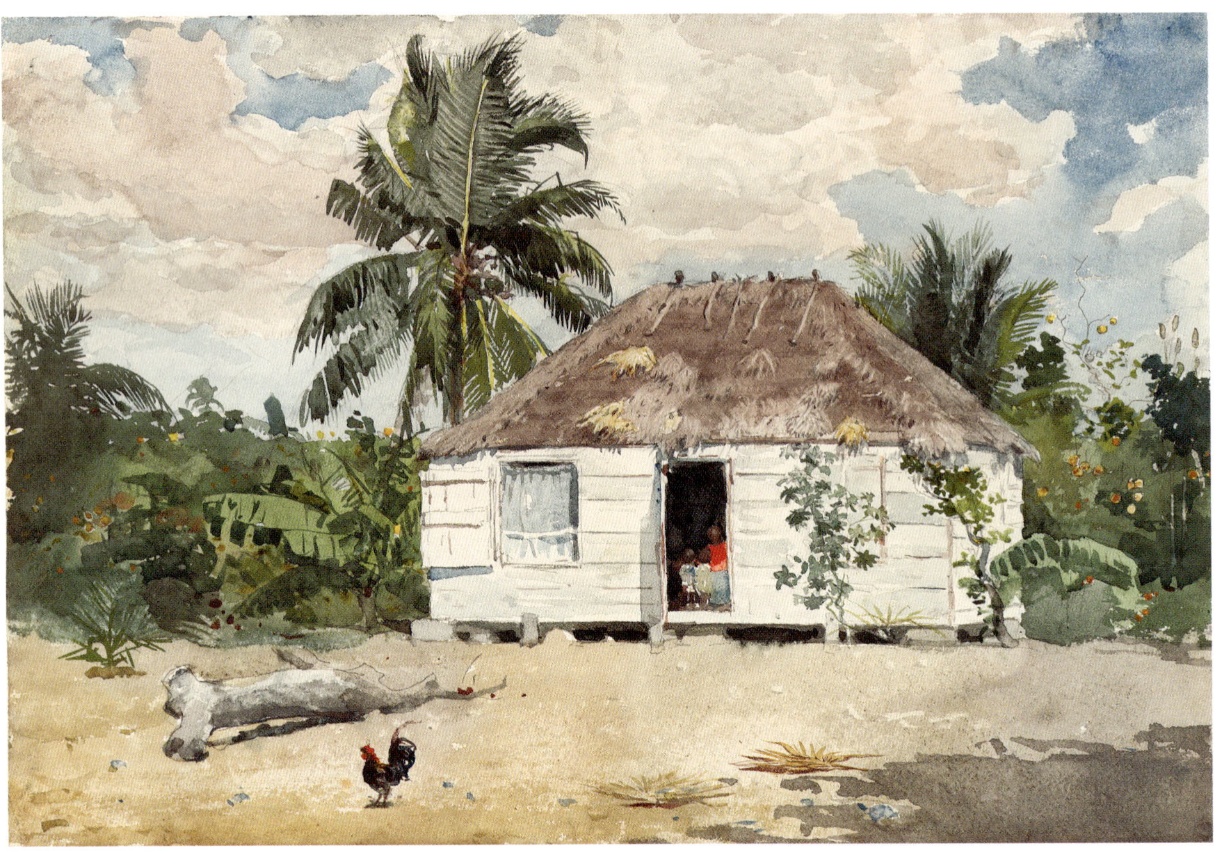

FIG. 3. Winslow Homer, *Native Hut, Nassau*, 1885. Watercolor and graphite with scraping and blotting on wove paper, 14½ × 20¹⁵⁄₁₆ in. (36.8 × 53.2 cm). National Gallery of Art, Washington, D.C. Collection of Mr. and Mrs. Paul Mellon. [1994.59.20]

Fincastle, the local outdoor market, and Foxhill, a nearby black community settled by freedmen. As invalid visitors and their attendant relatives moved from the modern architecture of the Royal Victoria and were conveyed along the macadamized streets past the wealthy Conchs' walled estates to the thatched "huts" of the black locals, a guide would have offered an account of the island's history. Among notable historical information included in this tour would have been the British "discovery" of the island in the seventeenth century, the creating of an economy based upon sugar cane and rum production executed by enslaved workers, and the peaceful transition from the slave economy to one based in part on tourism. The Foxhill neighborhood would have been held up as an exemplar: the African roots of the community visible in the design and siting of houses, and the ability of residents to choose agricultural work in the cane fields, fishing, or the creation of tourist goods. And, as the writer identified only by the initials I.L.G. concluded in the *Guide to Nassau*, "The colored people here seem to have a good chance, in many respects. There is next to no prejudice against them."[15] Assured that these communities were happy and their relations with white Conchs were

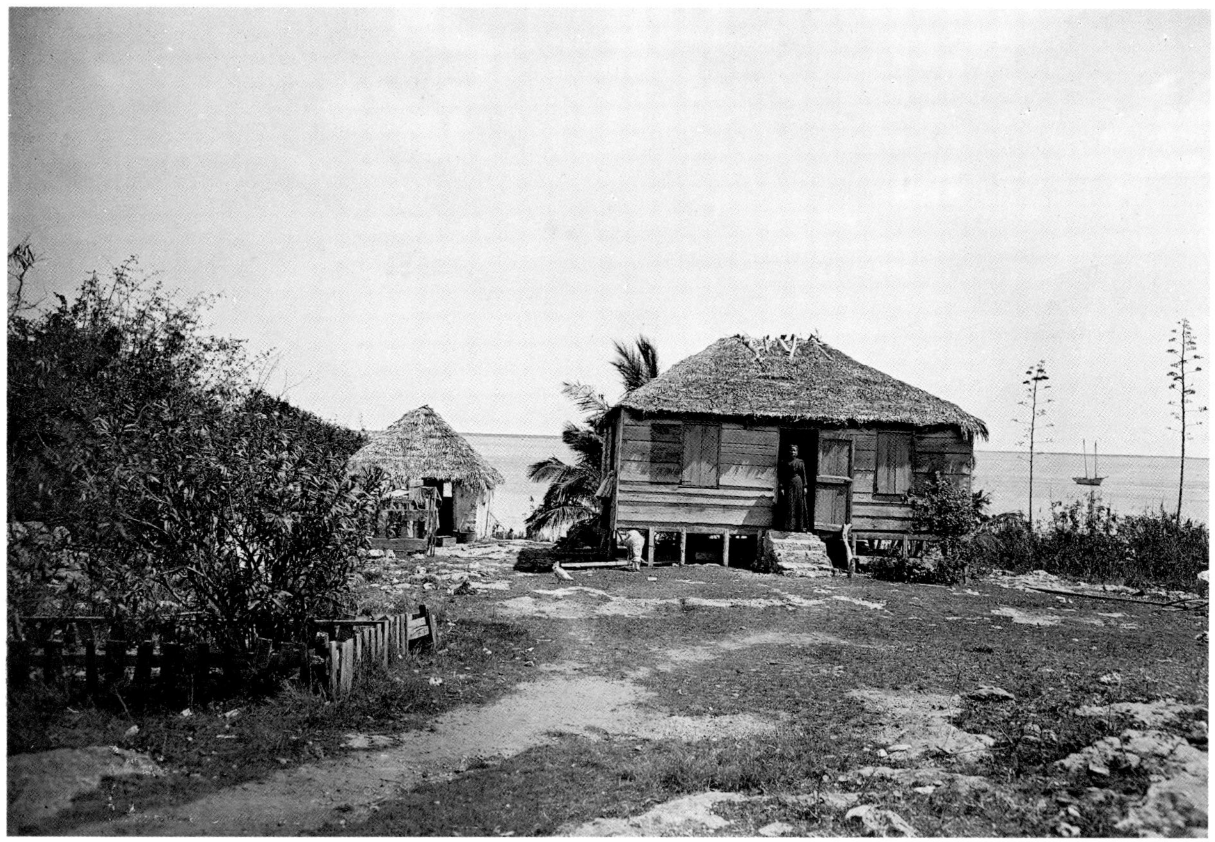

FIG. 4. William Henry Jackson, *Negro Cabin, Foxhill, Nassau, Bahama Islands*, c. 1901. Glass plate negative, 8 × 10 in. (20.3 × 25.4 cm). Library of Congress, Prints and Photographs Division, Washington, D.C.

uncomplicated, American visitors could participate in unfettered and sustained looking and interactions with black communities, something that was more difficult to do in their own communities.[16]

Homer likely encountered the subject of his *Native Hut, Nassau*, a rendering of traditional black Bahamian housing, on such a guided outing (fig. 3). The brilliant blue of the sky and the coconut palm communicate the tropical locale, while the paper showing through against the brilliant green of the palm tree creates visually compelling passages of high contrast. *Native Hut* shares the same composition and subject matter as several images created for tourists, including William Henry Jackson's *Negro Cabin, Foxhill, Nassau, Bahama Islands*. Both the title and inclusion of the photograph in Jackson's portfolio of tourist images signal that the home was of visual interest, and worthy of preservation in a scrapbook as part of the resort experience (fig. 4). In addition to the huts' ability to be shuttered in the event of heavy rain or strong wind, they were described as a transplanted African form. The relationship to the continent, plus what was viewed as a rudimentary construction, encouraged viewers to see black Bahamian culture and its relationship to Africa as comprising an unbroken, unchanged lineage. Although Homer's work shares similarities with Jackson's photograph, close observation reveals that he amplified the everyday scene through the inclusion of several details such as the open door, partially occupied by a small boy in red; along with the lone cock patrolling the yard, this element animates the scene, transforming it from a mere documentary depiction of Bahamian housing. Elevating what might be mundane to a mini-domestic drama through such additions was central to Homer's practice. In this regard, we might briefly consider the way the artist translated Mathew Brady's photograph of Lincoln's inauguration into a print by the addition of the black figure, an inclusion that grounds the scene in an immediate and American reality (plate 4).

If the number of pictures of a single subject is a gauge of interest, Homer was enamored with black Bahamians, with more than half the artist's 1884 paintings of the islands including depictions of black locals. These selections hew closely to what were understood to be the unique elements of the Bahamas experience. In addition to the fishermen, sponge divers, and turtle harvesters working the sea, market women recur with some frequency in the artist's oeuvre. In tourist images as well as in Homer's work, these individuals function as markers of the tropical locale, depicted as not especially hardworking, but simply picturesque; absent are the aspects of their lives that remained particularly difficult. The market woman was so closely associated with this aspect of Bahamian culture that she was the only such black figure photographed or pictured on the Royal Victoria's grounds.

On the Way to Market, Bahamas is one of six scenes of local market women on Nassau streets Homer made during his visit (fig. 5). Silhouetted against a low, bright wall home to a garden of overgrown tropical plants and flowers, lush palm and orange trees, a black Bahamian woman holding a chicken or rooster strides confidently down the coral street in the hot sun. Although this image eschews the gloomy palette of the North Sea, Homer's market woman has much in common with his depictions of Cullercoats fisherwomen such as *Fisher Girls on Shore, Tynemouth* (plate 40). The artist's Bahamas market woman and Cullercoats fisherwomen are represented as one half of the laboring culture; the Cullercoats women knit garments, and repair nets in support of their husbands, while the market woman brings the bounty from the market home to her family. Homer essentially traps women in this complex, liminal shoreline, while giving men free rein of the sea. In contrast, the Bahamian woman is excluded from the largely white world contained behind the wall. Miles Unger has described the "element of racial tension" in these walled watercolors as paradoxical, as the woman labors while being "excluded from the best these tropical islands offered."[17]

The art historian Krista Thompson has identified the process through which the experience of the Bahamas and other warm climates was tightly circumscribed, and ultimately changed, as "tropicalization"—comprising "the complex visual systems through which the islands were imaged for tourist consumption."[18] Homer joined the promoters of the Bahamas in this project, which included studiously avoiding any hint of Bahamian modernity. Late nineteenth-century photo postcards from the Bahamas were likewise

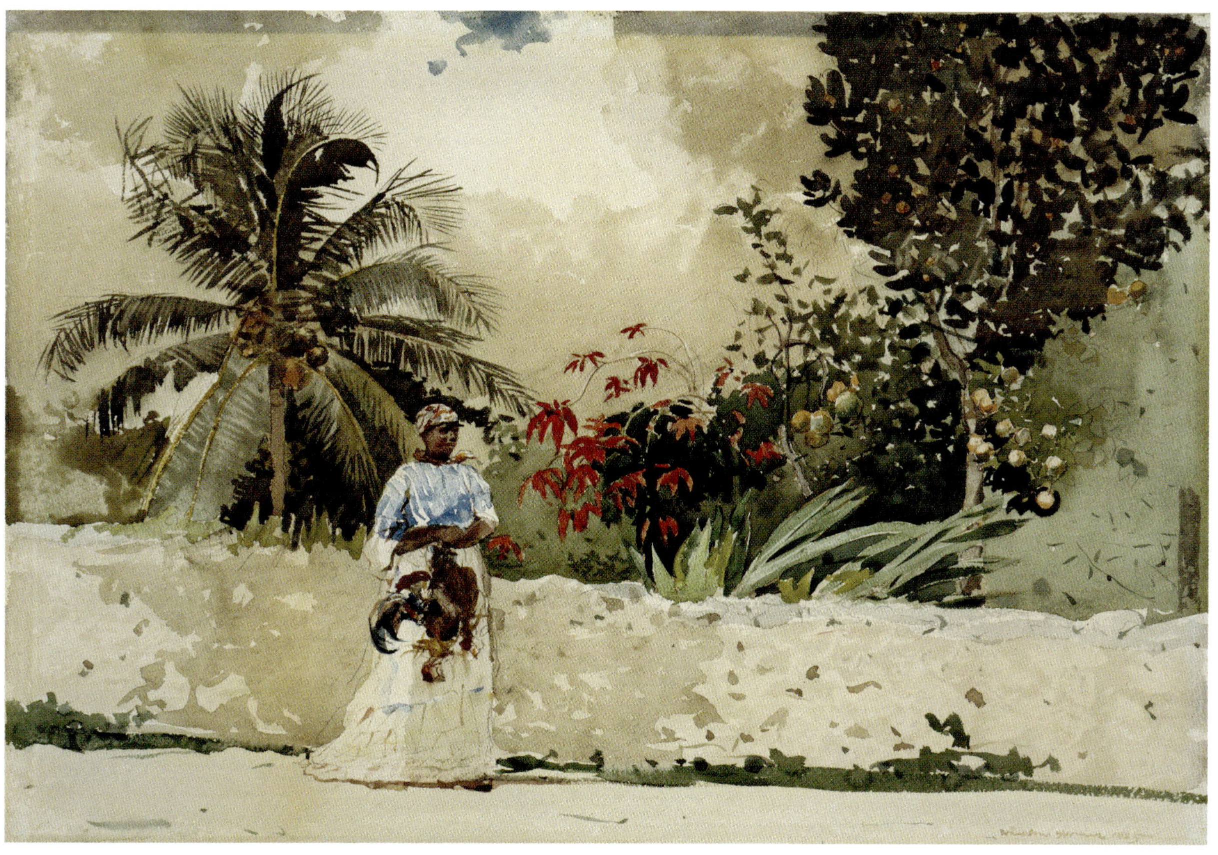

FIG. 5. Winslow Homer, *On the Way to Market, Bahamas*, 1885. Watercolor over pencil, $13^{15}/_{16} \times 20^{1}/_{16}$ in. (35.4 × 51 cm). Brooklyn Museum. Gift of Gunnar Maske in memory of Elizabeth Treadway White Maske. [69.50]

careful to emphasize the exotic locale without revealing any attempts to modernize. Promotional campaigns carefully modulated their representations of black Bahamians, aiming to present them as picturesque and harmless. Bahamian locals, the laundress, market woman, fisherman, and guides, were highlighted as figures in service to whites, both locals and tourists. At the same time, the segments of Nassau that served tourists upgraded their facilities with the latest in telegraph, electric, and sanitation improvements and infrastructure. The marketing of these upgrades required a delicate balancing act; the lodging and main tourist enclaves had to be modern and ensure comfort, yet the overall landscape of the islands needed to stay sufficiently pristine and untouched. These visual elisions concealed or downplayed the major modernization projects then underway in favor of promoting the Bahamas as undeveloped and pure, while potential visitors were reassured by the textual description of modern facilities to be found at the hotels.

The foreign money that poured into the islands to fund these improvements was focused on the white tourist experience—improvements from which the black

Bahamian residents did not benefit. Although away from the tourist and colonial center black Bahamians in New Providence and the outlying islands outnumbered the Conchs four to one, the Bahamas were segregated spatially, politically, and economically. Political representation was limited to landowners, who were primarily white, while the growing black middle classes were disenfranchised. Through law and custom, black Bahamians were barred from enjoying tourist sites, including beaches and landmarks. Access to these sites was restricted by race, as segregation was a key element of the tourism development "plan" enforced by elites and development investors. The historian Peter Wood has likened the deep racial divide of the Bahamas to the conditions of the bitterly segregated Reconstruction South.[19] In a practice that continued until the 1940s, white staff at Nassau hotels were brought to work in publicly visible service positions.[20] Hotel guests were able to interact with black Bahamians in the capacity of servants, minstrels, and the occasional "locals" conducting their everyday business, but nonwhite Bahamians were unable to access the resorts without performing these roles. Locals who attempted to sell items or interact with white visitors were driven from the premises by an armed hotel manager.[21] Krista Thompson has suggested that the segregation worked both ways, so that, in addition to keeping blacks out, custom prevented Homer from traveling freely across the Bahamas.[22]

At the same time that Homer pursued his interest in representing black Bahamians, he participated in events held at the nearby Government House, attended by the highest echelons of white Bahamian society, the crown-appointed government officials and their families. Favoring formal dress more appropriate for England than the sultry Bahamas climate, Conch social life revolved around elaborate dinners featuring turtle baked in its own shell and covered with a light crust, followed by dances and balls. Of particular note was Homer's attendance at a costume ball held by Lady Edith Blake, the wife of the Bahamian colonial governor Sir Henry Arthur Blake (fig. 6).[23] Like Homer's mother, Henrietta Benson Homer, Lady Blake was a watercolorist with a deep interest in nature, and like Winslow, Blake had learned how to paint from her mother, Catherine Osborne. Blake's interest in Bahamian nature constituted an engagement with the world of science that was different from Homer's engagement with the temperate islands' idyllic sights.[24]

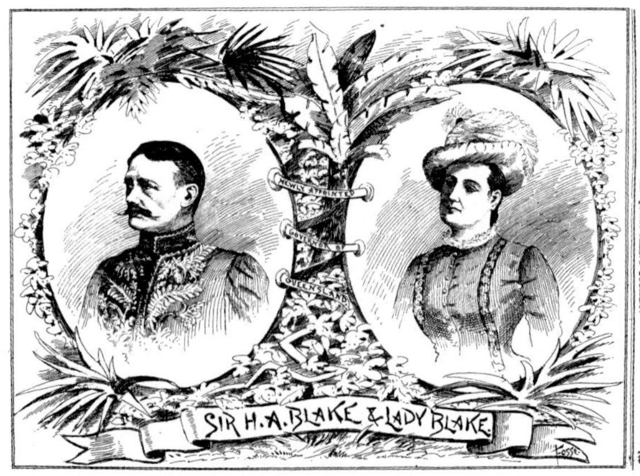

FIG. 6. Unidentified artist, *Sir Henry Arthur Blake and Lady Edith Blake*, published in *The Queensland Figaro*, November 17, 1888. Woodcut engraving. Private collection.

Children Under a Palm Tree (1885, private collection), which resulted from the social interaction between the two artists, is a visual outlier among Homer's Bahamas production. Its muted and dark palette features neither the jewel-like brilliance of his tropical palette, nor black subjects occupied in the tasks of everyday

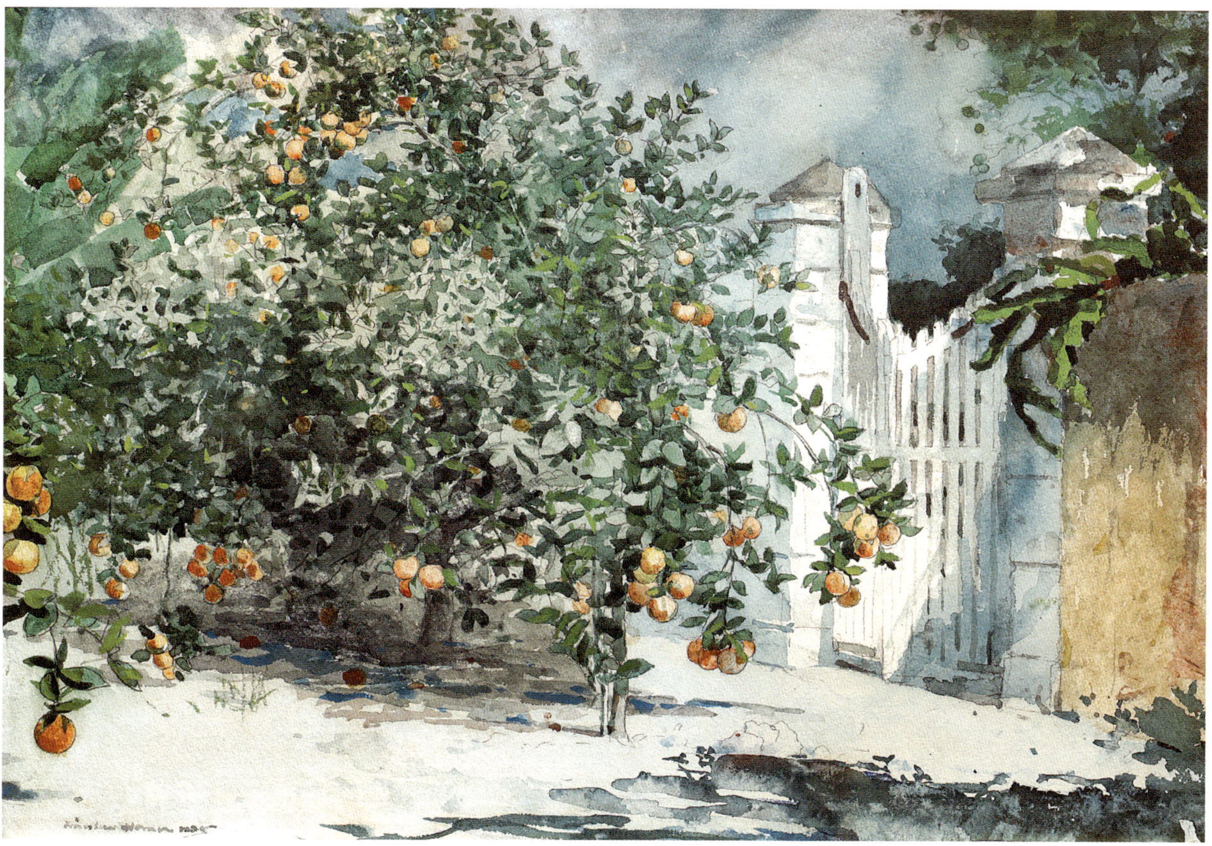

FIG. 7. Winslow Homer, *Orange Trees and Gate*, 1885. Watercolor, 14 1/2 × 20 3/4 in. (36.8 × 52.7 cm). Private collection.

life. Archival evidence suggests that Homer painted the children at a costume ball hosted by the Blakes at the colonial overseer's Government House; however, it does not feature any hint of architecture as a means of organizing the page or offering more specific locational detail. Rather, we see the children of the colonial governor, clad in Orientalized garb against a backdrop flecked with palms. The Blakes' daughter, Olive, the young girl in the center, holds a peacock feather fan and is dressed in elaborate Ottoman-style clothing with a scarlet headdress and broad cummerbund tied around her yellow dress. Her younger brothers, Maurice and Arthur, are dressed as young princes with colored vests, flowing white trousers, and the *taqiyah*, or skullcap. Homer's only Bahamian picture of Conchs highlights the inequities of the colonial system which governed the administration of the island.[25]

Orange Trees and Gate is one of a series of watercolors of verdant flora emerging from behind the high walls of different Bahamian estates, and is an example of how Homer found ways to trouble his representations of the Bahamas beyond the use of a muddy palette (fig. 7). Homer's image was made from inside one of these estates, taking up a subject of interest to visitors (oranges and conch shells), while presenting the orange-tree

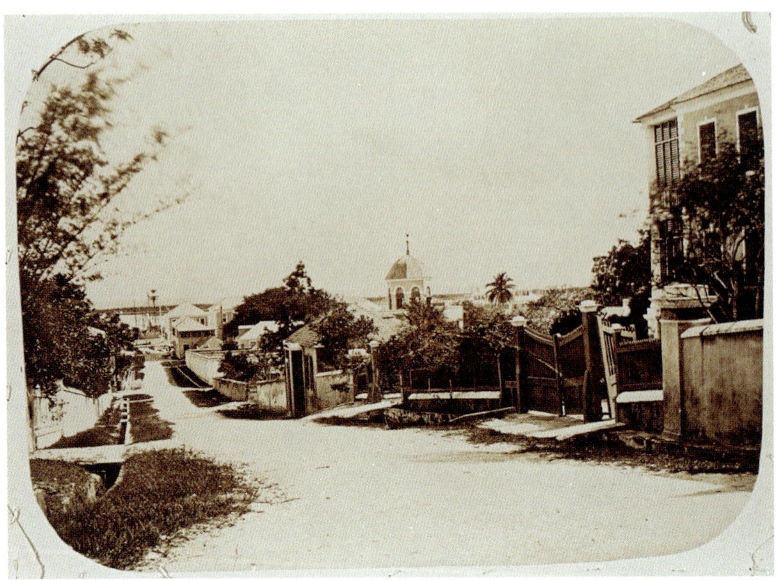

FIG. 8. Mary Gardiner Davis, *Street in Nassau*, ca. 1861–62. Albumen silver print, 6 × 8⅛ in. (15.2 × 20.6 cm). Schlesinger Library on the History of Women in America, Radcliffe Institute. [A70-v.2-1]

bounty as part of a larger landscape. Homer's painting does not provide a classic picture-postcard view, such as the commercially produced photograph of a Bahamian street included by Mary Gardiner Davis in her scrapbook (fig. 8). Davis braved the Atlantic blockade shortly after the bombing of Fort Sumter, with her husband, William Nye Davis, a well-to-do Boston gentleman, in order to recuperate in Nassau's Great Sanitarium. The couple had consulted early guides to the islands in preparation for their journey. And once there, Mary kept an extensive scrapbook filled with drawings, watercolors, engravings, botanical specimens, and purchased photographs documenting their travels to the Bahamas.[26] The photographs in Davis's scrapbook reveal how photographers were already creating pictures of the island for sale. Taken from the top of a hill that slopes gently away from the viewer toward the oceanfront, this representation offers a commanding prospect of Nassau. In its ordering of the space, it carefully delineates Nassau's public byway, separated by ditches, walls, and gates from the private estates. Far from creating a typical scenic panorama, Homer blocked off half the composition with the thick and lush green leaves and oranges of the fruit tree, which are a distraction. In other words, the orange, one of the reoccurring emblems of subtropical locales, is the very object that prevents us from fully seeing the tropics. Additionally, in contrast to the airlessness of the Davis-owned photograph, Homer's watercolor is infused with a camera-like observational power, which the critic Henry James once hailed as the artist's ability to see "everything at one with its envelope of light and air."[27] To be sure, the scene is filled with warm tropical colors and striking Caribbean light, but Homer treated a subject that many Americans may have read about but had not actually seen, and used it to mark the space as tropical, neatly encapsulating the notion of paradise that Nassau evoked in the minds of a white American audience, while also troubling it.

Homer's selection of subjects, from orange trees to sparkling waters and picturesque life, suggests that he had engaged with tourist photography and travel writing of the period. His use of a light palette and focus on black Bahamians are emblematic of the variety and complexity of the tourist imagery of the period that rendered the Bahamas as a safe, tropical locale, with a salubrious climate and exotic sights. Homer found a way to hint at the stratification within Bahamian society to expose a disquieting element of life in paradise, complicating the Bahamas as more than a place "where the invalid . . . may enjoy the finest and most equable climate in the world, during the winter months, absolutely free from all danger of epidemic disease."[28] It is intriguing that the only image he made that directly engaged the colonial status of the Bahamas, *Children Under a Palm Tree*, adhered to a set of representational norms he used for illustrating the tenuous political situation in Cuba. In the section that follows, I argue that in Cuba, Homer continued to use tourist photography as a starting point for his complex subtropical oeuvre, which celebrated and troubled that vacation paradise.

Cuba, "Our American 'South'"

> Our American "South" is rich in flowery vines. In some districts almost every tree is crowned with them, aiding each other in grace and beauty. . . . Yet in no section of the South are there such complicated and such gorgeously flowered vine-tangles as flourish in armed safety in the hot and humid wild gardens of Cuba.
>
> —John Muir, *A Thousand Mile Walk to the Gulf*, 1916

> But such you are! You can cry and howl at bull fights and cock-fights and in the pits of operas and theaters, and drive bulls and horses distracted, and urge gallant game-cocks to the death, and applaud opera singers into patriotic sounds, and leave them to imprisonment and fines.
>
> —Richard Henry Dana, Jr., *To Cuba and Back*, 1859

Trading a British colonial outpost for a Spanish one, in February 1885, Winslow Homer traveled via the USS *Santiago* for his first trip to Cuba, a popular tourist destination in the North Caribbean Sea. In images and prose, guidebooks celebrated Cuba's warm weather and lush subtropical landscapes, while differentiating the province from other tourist locales, such as the Bahamas and Florida, by emphasizing its cosmopolitan cities and citizens. Homer's specific destination, Santiago de Cuba, was founded in 1515 and had been the colony's capital for much of the sixteenth century, and with its regular influx of captives from the African continent, and immigrants fleeing the Haitian slave revolt of 1791, the city featured an eclectic mix of cultures. This intriguing mix of Spanish, African, and indigenous influences, visible in architecture, customs, and landscape, often surfaces as the defining feature of the island for the American visitor. After three centuries of Spanish colonization, Cuba and its status as a haven for refined travelers was roiled by a series of independence movements and armed rebellions that were harshly suppressed by the Provincial Governor and his army.

Artists and writers who brought Cuba into the American imagination grappled with the tension of representing Cuba's role as an untroubled tropical paradise. Naturalist John Muir, who traveled to Cuba as part of his one-thousand-mile hike along the coast of the Gulf of Mexico in 1867, wrote a popular account of his experience framed solely in terms of the island's tropical features. Muir described Cuba as "Our American 'South'" that was "full of exceedingly showy and interesting plants . . . flourish[ing] in armed safety in the hot and humid wild gardens." Muir famously even described the sights and sounds of urban Santiago in a tropical mode, marveling about the botanical life to be found there: "Wandered about the narrow streets, stunned with the babel of strange sounds and sights; went gazing, also, among the gorgeously flowered garden squares." He spent hours at the city's Botanical Gardens, taking in their "magnificent flowery arbors" and walking around their "shady fountains." Muir's descriptions of Cuba's cultivated spaces rival his characterizations of the bounty of Bahamian ecology, rendering the former as lush and visually appealing as Nassau's gardens. They elide the troubling presence of Old World Spain in the American hemisphere.[29]

Homer family friend, the politician and writer Richard Henry Dana, Jr., penned an 1859 travel account, *To Cuba and Back*, which painted a more complex picture of colonial life. He was well aware that nineteenth-century American ideas about the Spanish toggled between two divergent notions: on the one hand, that the Spanish were a foul and immoral people, marked by "dirt, noise and smell," and, on the other, that their culture as translated in Cuba was decadent, beautiful, and to be indulged in. Readers of Dana's account may have delighted in his captivating tales of masked balls, street spectacles, and bullfights; however, he also forced them to grapple with a Cuba that was organized by and in service of Spanish interests. Chief among Dana's concerns in crafting the text was the use of language to aptly describe Cuba's identity as a colony in the New World, under the control of Old World powers. He mused: "I must guard myself, by the way, while here, against using the words America and American, when I mean the United States and the people of our Republic; for this is America also; and they here use the word America as including the entire continent and islands, and distinguish between Spanish and English America, these islands and the main."[30] Dana's struggle to properly define the island reveals the tension between a desire to see the Spanish grip on Cuba—one of the few remaining colonial strongholds in the Western hemisphere—broken, and the celebration of the very elements that contributed to making the Cuban culture so different, exotic even, from that of its Anglo-American neighbors. Homer had been personally acquainted with Dana since the artist's teenage years, and one wonders whether his attention to Cuba's political situation was heightened because of his relationship to the author.

From Homer's base in one of Santiago de Cuba's modest rooming houses, the artist acclaimed the availability of picture-worthy subjects in a letter to his brother Charles: "Here I am fixed for a month. . . . I expect some fine things, it is certainly the richest field for an artist that I have seen."[31] As Homer's Cuba pictures engage with colonial architecture more fully than the Bahamas works, "the richest field" likely referred to the built environment. Remarking on this tendency, art historian Helen Cooper notes, "unusual in these watercolors is Homer's focus on man-made sites, a subject that had never before interested him: views of the characteristic Spanish architecture . . . and Morro Castle. . . . Architecture was indeed the great feature of Santiago."[32] Like its population, the city's historic architecture was made up of different European styles, including a sixteenth-century late Baroque cathedral, Nuestra Señora de la Asunción, the neoclassical

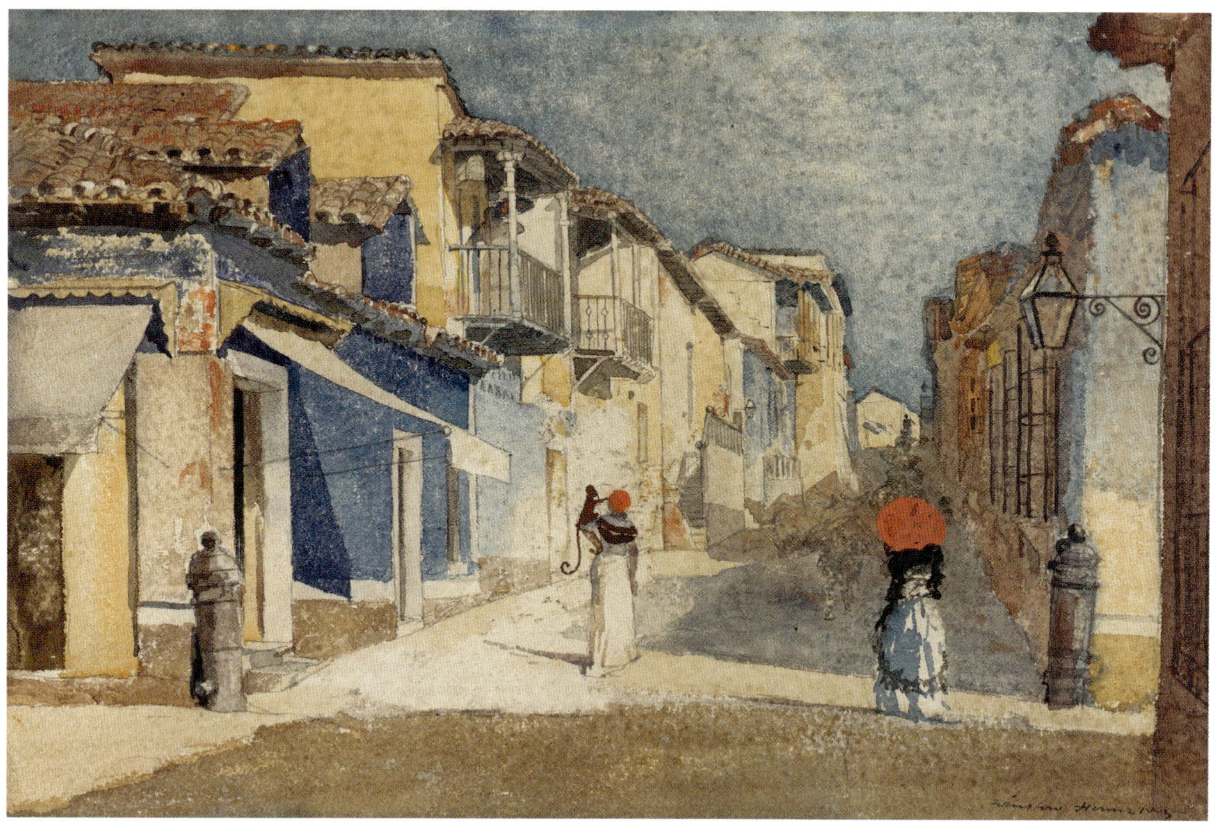

FIG. 9. Winslow Homer, *Street Scene, Santiago de Cuba*, 1885. Watercolor, opaque watercolor, and graphite, with scraping, on wove paper, 12 × 17$^{11}/_{16}$ in. (30.5 × 44.9 cm). Philadelphia Museum of Art. Gift of Dr. and Mrs. George Woodward, 1939. [1939-7-15]

Ayuntamiento, or Town Hall, and the Spanish colonial—a fusion of Old and New World—*aduana*, or customs house, and elite houses with rippling red-tiled roofs, large windows, and tiny balconies. Homer focused on Spanish colonial architecture to the exclusion of the other styles.

Homer's *Street Scene, Santiago de Cuba* presents one of the most frequently photographed architectural scenes, a view of a street lined with colonial buildings (fig. 9). Homer offers us the street from the perspective of a visitor standing at its foot and looking upward along the lane. Adopting a muted palette that is markedly different from the colors used to depict picturesque Bahamian life, Homer painted the wide expanse of the street in a neutral tone, with the occasional brown roof tile highlighted against the blue sky. Wearing long dresses that skim the ground, two women bearing accoutrements, a pet monkey and a red parasol, stroll along the avenue. On one of the second-floor balconies, a characteristic Spanish colonial architectural feature, a fluttering fan flashes ever so briefly. Although this scene appears to be somewhat generalized, those who were well versed in the nuances of Cuban society would have recognized the subject of the painting. Here, Homer is referencing the elaborate public courtship rituals between men and women in Cuba. In the late afternoon, chaperoned women walked the streets and used fans to signal interest in potential suitors. Those whose movement was restricted gestured to men from balconies or from behind iron gates. This creolized ritual courtship may have seemed exotic to Homer, but he resorted to a traditional, Renaissance perspective to depict it on a street. This compositional choice, coupled with tile-roofed buildings topped with radiating muted colors, emphasizes the picturesque nature of the scene.

Architecture may have been a great and attractive feature of the city, but Homer seems to have invoked it for reasons beyond the pure delight of sketching; architecture often operates as a proxy for Cuban society. Homer's *Customs House, Santiago de Cuba* (1885, location unknown) takes as its subject the governmental building dedicated to facilitating maritime commerce. When encountered in person, the structure's grandeur attests to the power of the Spanish Navy and the robustness of the economy. Its high ceilings, sweeping staircase, and beautifully carved woodwork all contribute to a feeling of strength and stability. However, the extent of the grand building is not visible in Homer's picture. Instead, he uses the corner view to render the building symbolizing Spanish colonial influence and economic power, allowing the viewer to look through the first-floor arcade to a gathering of soldiers depicted in a series of quick, pale gray strokes. Homer makes visible the political situation that he described to his brother in February 1885: "This is a redhot place full of soldiers."[33] By framing the scene through a less conventional vantage point, the artist weakens the appearance of the grand edifice, rendering its dominance over the landscape impotent. By the mid-nineteenth century, the United States had become Cuba's most important trading partner. Or as the writer Anthony Trollope, who visited the island in 1859, noted, "The trade of the country is falling into the hands of the Americans from the States, Havana will soon become as much American as New Orleans."[34] As Cuba moved closer and closer to Trollope's vision of an American influence, Spain's control over the island weakened. American merchant ships brought not only commodities but also culture, as baseball replaced bullfighting as the primary sport. The rust-red flag of *Customs House* hangs limply at the corner of the building, testifying to waning Spanish cultural influence, while offering the viewer a reminder of the revolutionaries' bloody attempts to wrest control of the country from the Spanish.[35] Homer was always reticent when it came to explaining meaning in his pictures, and even years after his 1885 watercolors, he offered no direct explanation of the work. But, as Elizabeth Broun has argued, the tenor of the times in late nineteenth-century Cuba made an artist's decision about if and how to picture Spain's presence in Cuba politically significant.[36]

In his Cuba works, Homer focused on the features of the country's landscape that spoke to the ongoing insurgency against the Spanish colonial forces. Castillo de San Pedro de la Roca, known as Morro Castle, a military fortress in the city built by the Spanish in the seventeenth century, was still in use as a prison in Homer's time. Author and artist Samuel Hazard described the paradox represented by the sight of Morro; the structure he glimpsed from the boat on which he was traveling picturesquely revealed itself as "the

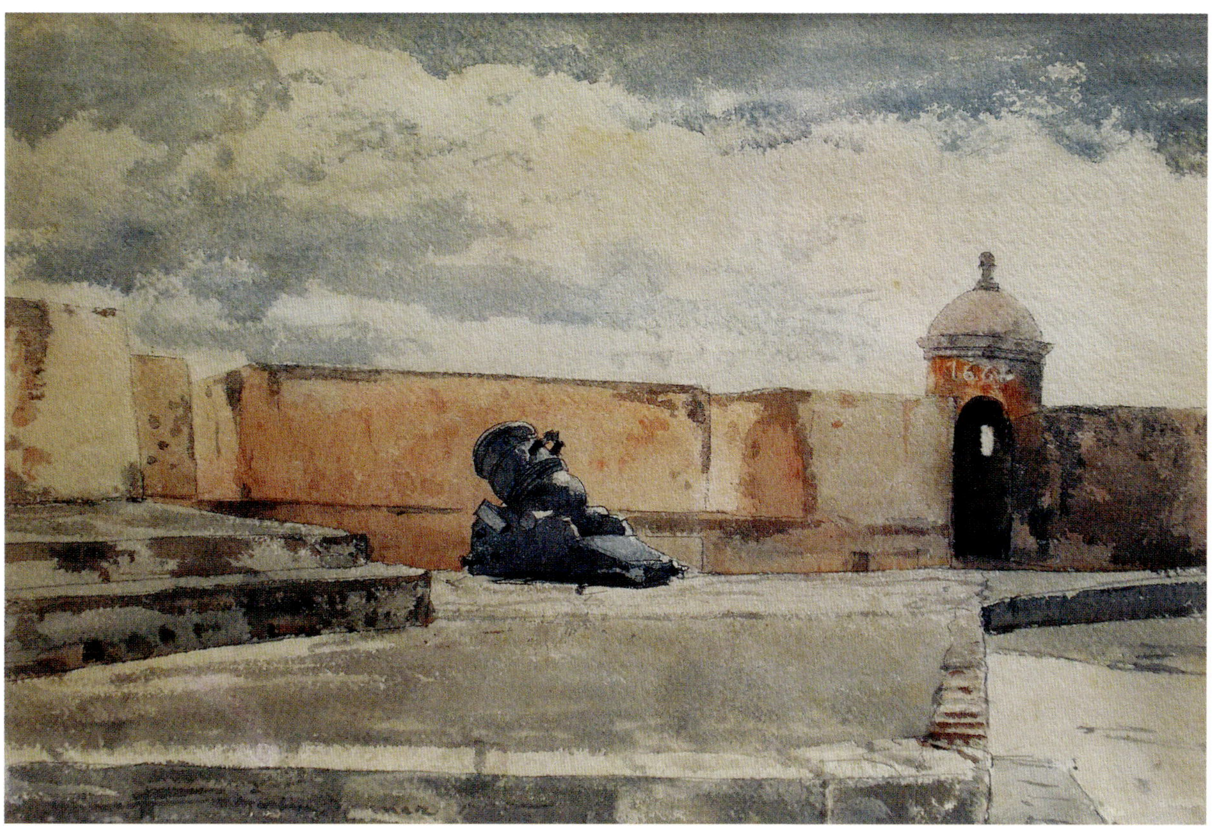

FIG. 10. Winslow Homer, *Morro Castle*, 1885. Watercolor on paper, $13^1/_4 \times 19^1/_8$ in. (33.6 × 48.6 cm). Courtesy of West Point Museum Collection, United States Military Academy. [18764]

indistinct outlines of the Morro Castle—looking as I see them through my window, like some beautiful painting to which the oval of the dead-eye forms a frame," but the excitement of his arrival was tempered by the sight of the watchtower of the "grim" fortress.[37] Used to house political prisoners prior to their execution, this tower was a visible reminder for Hazard of the brutality of the colonial regime. As he did in the Bahamas views, Homer deploys the same subject matter as that featured in representations made for tourists, while heightening the narrative and dramatic tension of the scene by adopting unusual vantage points.

Homer's vision of Morro Castle is rendered looking down on its battlements from above, as if he were imprisoned in its tower with the rebel insurgents (fig. 10). In contrast, the Detroit Photographic Company photograph of around 1898 made for the tourist trade presents the fortress as it could be seen from ships steaming into the harbor (fig. 11). The power of this photograph stems from the vantage point that emphasizes the massive size and strength of the seemingly impenetrable fortress. Rather than painting the scene from the sea as Hazard had described it, or as the Detroit Photographic Company had captured it, Homer offers us a conflicted view.

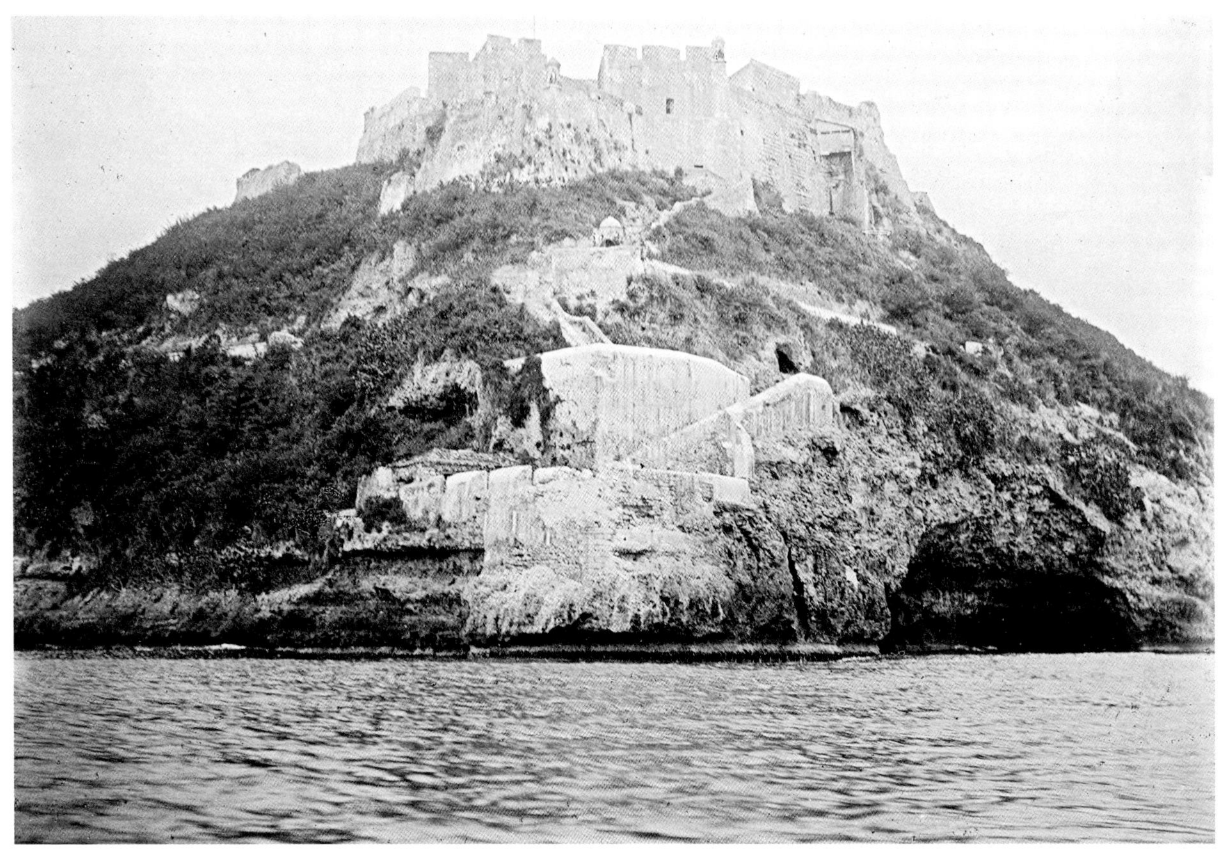

FIG. 11. Detroit Photographic Company, *Morro Castle, Santiago de Cuba*, c. 1898. Glass plate negative, 8 × 10 in. (20.3 × 25.4 cm). Library of Congress, Prints and Photographs Division, Washington, D.C.

With the exception of a cannon, the interior of the castle appears abandoned and empty. In the context of his oeuvre, this work shares an ambivalence with another Homer painting about war, *Sharpshooter* (plate 6). This Civil War image compels the viewer to reflect on the issue of a soldier being executed by an unseen army, in the same way that *Morro Castle* forces us to take in the Spanish stronghold and execution site before choosing sides in the impending conflict. He offers us none of what is presumably a dazzling view past "the frowning battlements," nor does he offer us visual pleasure in the form of vibrant color. Art historian Martha Tedeschi has acknowledged the difference between Homer's images of the Bahamas and Cuba, writing: "In contrast to the free confident brushwork of his Nassau watercolors, these [Cuban] works are finicky in handling and more neutral in color. Brick reds, gray blues, and mustard yellows make up the artist's Cuban palette, and heavy gray skies often hang over the scenes."[38] In *Morro Castle*, the sky is not one of the oppressive heat and humidity of the tropics, but rather of a foreboding that something more is to come.

In addition to adjusting his palette and subject matter to add complexity to his Cuba pictures, Homer also relied on the expressive

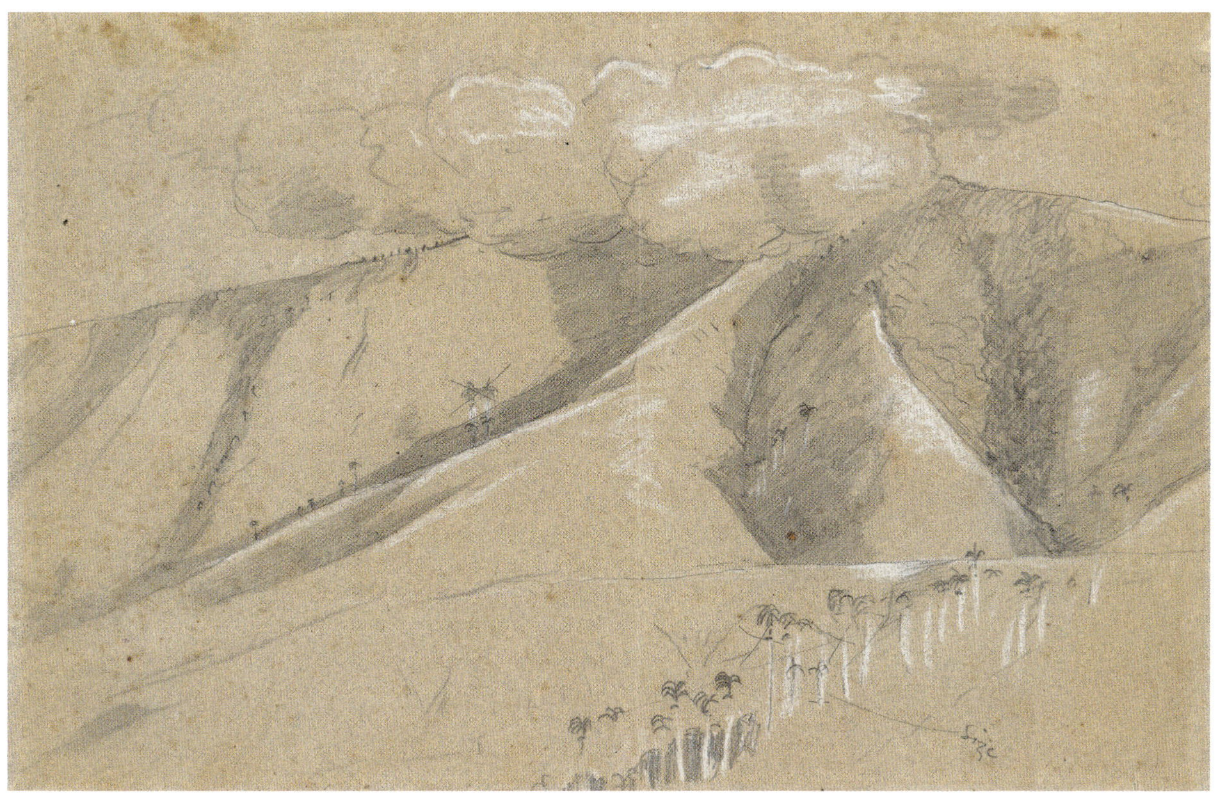

FIG. 12. Winslow Homer, *Royal Palms, Santiago de Cuba*, 1885. Graphite and white chalk on paper, 11 13/16 × 18 1/4 in. (30 × 46.4 cm). Bowdoin College Museum of Art, Brunswick. Museum Purchase. [1969.24]

power of atmospherics. The drawing *Royal Palms, Santiago de Cuba* combines atmosphere and a vast wild landscape to offer a distressing view of the Cuban countryside (fig. 12). Using the brown paper as a ground, Homer deploys quick, sweeping strokes in black with white highlights to render an impossibly steep mountain whose sides are studded with royal palm, a variety of the ubiquitous tropical tree. A stubborn white cloud, signaling a rising storm, cloaks the peak of the mountain, quashing any hope of a successful summit. The population of palm trees is threatened by the rising storm's forceful and violent wind. Eleanor Harvey has theorized that American artists used various aspects of the landscape—terrain, weather, and meteorology—to grapple with the destabilizing effects of conflict. By depicting the storm at the top of an already impassable mountain, Homer explores the use of atmosphere to create and sustain mood.

In *Volante, Mountain Road, Cuba* (1885, location unknown), Homer expanded the repertoire of atmospheric elements he originated in *Royal Palms* as a proxy for state of mind and tone. For this work, Homer chose a subject that had long drawn the attention of tourists and boosters. A volante is a small, two-passenger, horse-pulled carriage with two wheels and

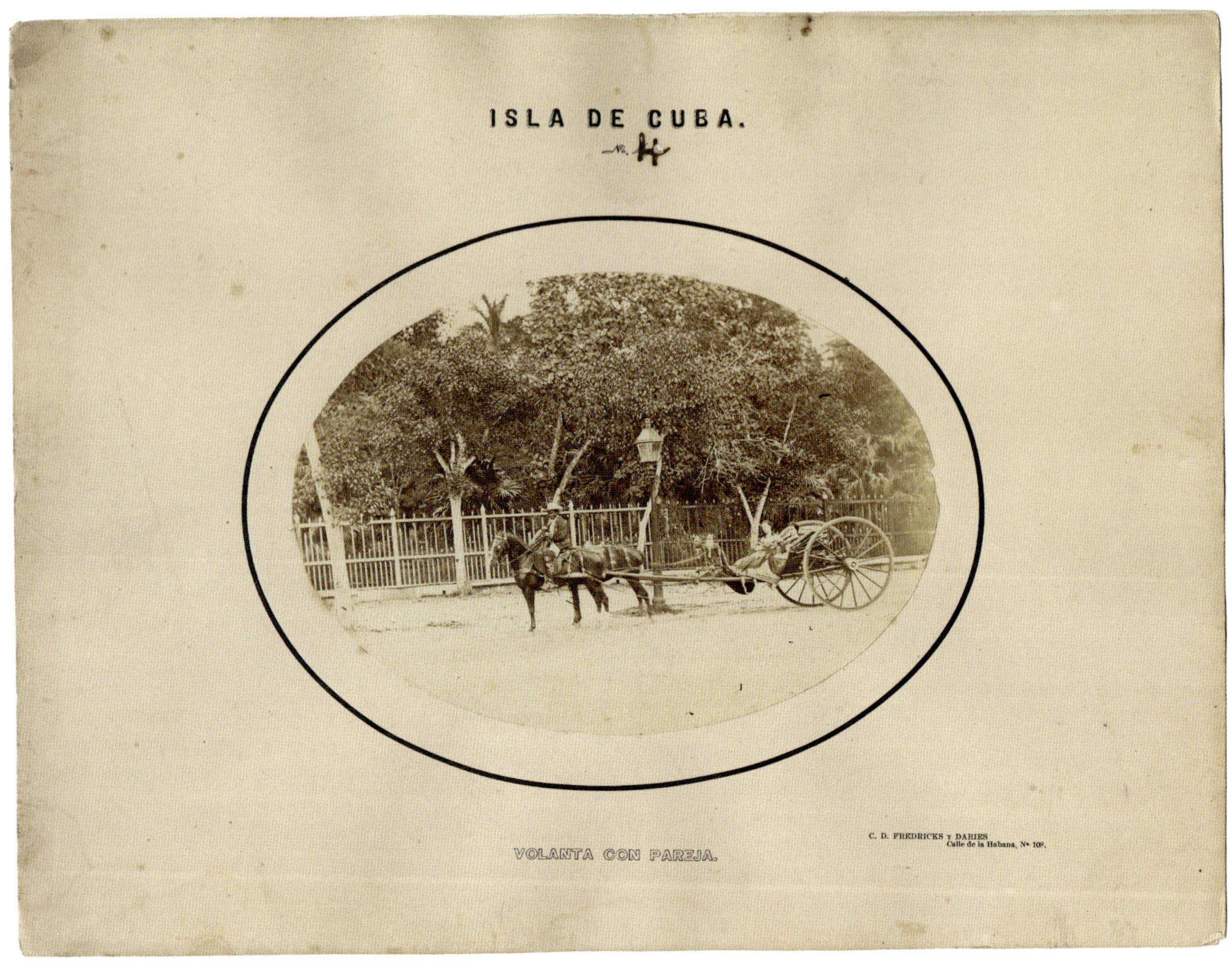

FIG. 13. Charles D. Fredericks y Daries, *Isla de Cuba, No. 14 Volanta con pareja*, c. 1880. Albumen silver print, $10\frac{3}{4} \times 13\frac{15}{16}$ in. (27.4 × 35.4 cm). University of Miami Library, Cuban Heritage Collection, Tom Porht Photograph Collection. [CHC5252]

an open, hooded body that was popular in Cuba, Mexico, Spain, and Louisiana in the late nineteenth century. Samuel Hazard remarked on the visual appeal of these carriages, drawing attention to the way "their curious shapes, drivers, livery, harness, etc. attract the eye." Hazard describes the volante as a sign of privilege, noting that wealthy women preferred to shop from volantes; they were often driven "among the stores," and "articles [were] brought to them at the side-walk."[39] The volante appears in several guidebooks and was also a popular subject in nineteenth-century Cuban genre scenes. Photographic depictions of the volante, such as *Volanta con pareja*, include stylish white women pulled by a horse and a black liveried driver (fig. 13). Yet, Homer's painting features neither the pomp of the volante nor any apparent destination. He depicts the vehicle with equal measures of detail and rapid brushwork, which suggests all the elements of the carriage while also instilling a sense of movement. The heavy gray skies cited by Tedeschi as evidence of Homer's changing practice reappear in this work. Ominously, the horse and figures struggle against unseen forces. Homer's moody painting resists popular and pleasing representations of the volante for the suggestion of a brewing uncertainty over Cuba's political fate. Viewed in the context of Homer's other Cuban images, the landscape in *Volante* and *Royal Palms* forecasts the growing political tension on the island.[40]

This representational facility is reminiscent of Homer's prior depictions of the South during the Civil War, such as *Skirmish in the Wilderness*, which is based on sketches Homer made at the actual site of the Battle of the Wilderness (plate 13). As in *Volante*, Homer kept the human figures small and faceless and allowed nature to dominate the picture, enveloping the soldiers. Perhaps because of his Civil War experience, Homer is able to evoke the confusion and fear produced by armed conflict. In his Cuban landscapes, Homer once again conveyed a comparable level of impending doom, even hinting at the coming crisis through the dramatic use of atmospherics.

The artist's engagement with the freedom struggle infused his work and inspired him to elevate his representations of picturesque elements of Cuban culture beyond the conventions of the visual culture of tourism. Since the eighteenth century, *peleas de gallos* (cock fights) had been a popular pastime for thrill seekers and gamblers in Cuba. The fights were a recurrent feature of tourist literature, such as *Valla de Gallos* from Pierre Toussaint Frédéric (Federico) Miahle's *Album Pintoresco de la Isla de Cuba*.[41] Compositionally, these popular nineteenth-century illustrations encircled the fighting birds with a ring of spectators in a seedy, shadowy arena. The crowd, made up of men and boys who gleefully "urge gallant games-cocks to the death," is implicated in the bloody aggression of the fight as much as the birds themselves, and the cock fight is naturalized as a part of Cuban culture.[42] In *The Cock Fight*, a watercolor of 1885, Homer pared down the event to its barest essence, fighters against a neutral background (fig. 14). This scene might be read as an allegory of the struggles between the revolutionaries and the colonial government. A young and small yet beautifully colored rooster stands over its older, larger, and wildly plumed foe whom it has just conquered. The fight is so recently concluded that the dust speckles the ray of light illuminating the victor, while the feathers that have become dislodged from its foe are gently floating to the ground. Homer's neutral background reinforces the notion that we are witnessing the end of a battle in which the young (colonized) has defeated the established (colonizer).

Homer departed Santiago de Cuba and rejoined his father with a portfolio filled with sketches, drawings, and watercolors, and with the cries of gamblers at cock fights and the whistle of the wind through the fronds of royal palms still echoing in his ears. He would never return to Cuba, but the province and its struggles had made a lasting impression on him. Freed from the concerns of the mainland United States, Homer engaged in the delicate act of representing the tropics by creating work that was vibrant and playful, as well as dull and foreboding. His Bahamas pictures are sharp, incisive, and fluidly rendered in brilliant color, while in Cuba, he darkly embedded painted landscapes with political tension. Full of apprehension and drama, Homer's watercolors of Cuba offer a more nuanced view of

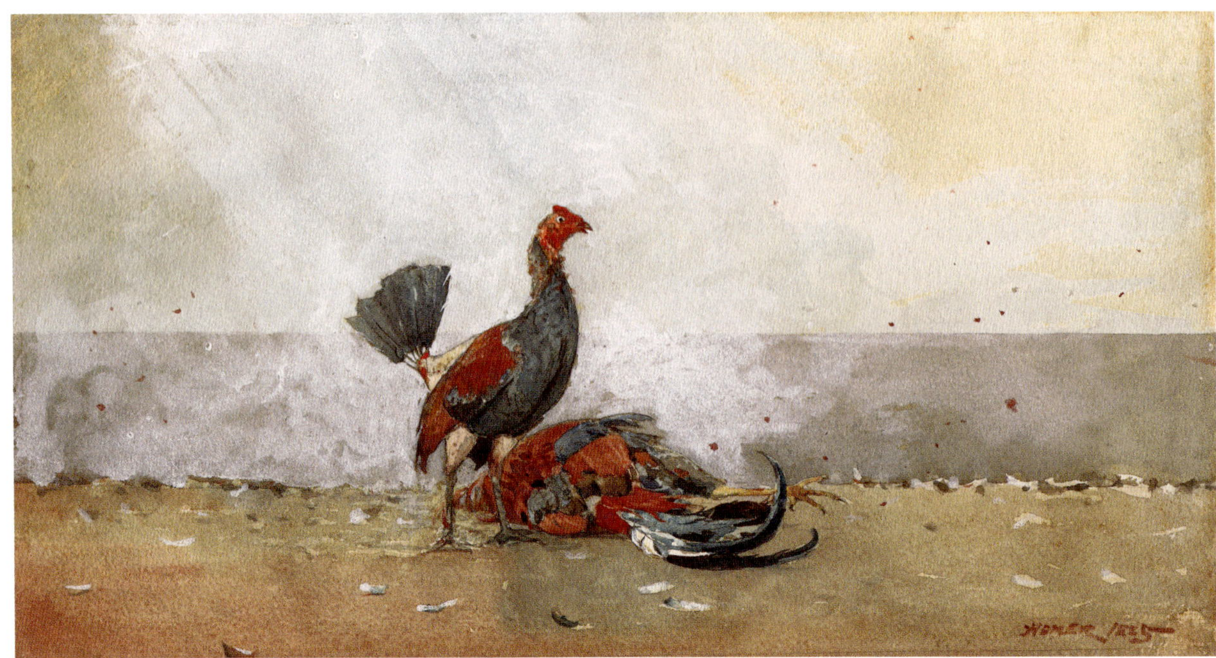

FIG. 14. Winslow Homer, *The Cock Fight*, 1885. Transparent and opaque watercolor, with traces of scraping, over graphite, on thick, moderately textured, cream wove paper (top and lower edges trimmed), $10^{3}/_{8} \times 19$ in. (26.5×48.4 cm). The Art Institute of Chicago. George F. Harding Collection. [1982.1579]

their subject, which prompted him to return to earlier practices, from the time of the Civil War and his apprenticeship days. This stark contrast suggests that Homer conceptualized the two islands differently, envisioning the Bahamas as a carefree midwinter resort while conceiving of Cuba as the site of contention between the Old World and the New.

Florida, "for Tourists, Invalids and Emigrants"

> Right here, close by where I now write, from among the beautiful palmettos, and under the grand old oaks, one still hears the whispers of wild and terrible tragedy.
>
> —Harriet Beecher Stowe, *Letters from Florida*, 1879

Homer's next visit to the subtropics was a fishing trip in Florida. Signaling that the trip was intended as leisure rather than labor, Homer brought his Eastman Kodak #1 camera with him.[43] As has been well documented, the Eastman Kodak #1 possessed an allure for amateur photographers, as it came preloaded with film and was lightweight, thus easily portable. The George Eastman Company proudly advertised, "You Press the Button, We Do the Rest," thus assuring amateur photographers that they were not required to develop the film, but just had to frame the scene. Apparently, Homer took the slogan's challenge to heart as he used the camera in Florida, on this and subsequent visits, to take a series of photographs both from and of watercraft. Homer seems to appear in at least one of these images, indicating that the camera was used on at least one occasion by another, unknown photographer.

In 1513, explorer Juan Ponce De León set sail from Santiago de Cuba in search of the fountain of youth; he found *La Florida*, the "land of flowers" instead, and quickly secured it, over the objections of the Seminole tribe, for the Spanish empire. Over the course of the next three hundred years, the territory was traded back and forth between the English, French, and Spanish, ensuring that Florida developed a creolized culture, reflecting a mix of Seminole, African, and European influences. Florida's long coastline was treacherous and the cause of shipwrecks, while its many inlets, lagoons, and keys served as a safe refuge for marauding pirates and buccaneers. By 1845, Florida had been accepted into the Union as a slave state. Following the American Civil War, the state's entrepreneurs developed a tourism infrastructure to lure travelers to Florida's many rich offerings. Wealthy visitors could take in the eclectic architecture, explore the rich biodiversity, savor the unusual cuisine, or seek respite from the cold.

As with his trips to the Bahamas and Cuba, Homer, with father Charles in tow once again, likely traveled to Florida via one of the numerous steamship lines catering to tourists journeying from New York City to Jacksonville. Once in the state, the artist followed an itinerary that took him from Jacksonville overland to Tampa, onto Key West and the St. Johns River basin, before returning to Prout's Neck, Maine, via New York City.[44] Fishing was indeed Homer's primary goal on the 1886 trip, and although the experience was different from ocean fishing at Prout's Neck, or freshwater fishing in the Adirondacks, the Florida waters did not disappoint. Similarly, the work produced on this trip follows Homer's now familiar pattern of confirming the importance of tourist sites through the sheer act of representing them, while interpreting them anew. As such, read alongside other widely circulated depictions of the Florida tropics, these images may yield insights into the artist's creative process and outlook on Florida.

By 1885, the nearly 150-year-long American tradition of representing the state as a site of bounty and potential was threatened by development. Flora, specifically palm and orange trees, and fauna, especially vibrantly colored birds and reptiles, figured largely in depictions of the state. Notably, John Bartram, a Philadelphia Quaker and respected naturalist, traveled to Florida in 1765–66 at the behest of King George III, in order to explore England's latest territorial acquisition. Bartram collected soil, plant, and animal specimens, while his son William Bartram filled sketchpads of floral and faunal observations, and mapped the region's savannahs, wetlands, rivers, and creeks. The pair's findings were popular in the colonies and in England; William Bartram's journal remains in publication to this day.[45] John James Audubon, an enterprising artist whose renderings of Floridian wildlife were later included in *The Birds of America* (1827–38), depicted the wild abundance of many of the same locations visited and explored by Homer, among them the St. Johns River. Bartram's and Audubon's publications stoked an interest in Florida's ecological diversity that encouraged people to travel to the region. Homer's trip, nearly fifty years after Audubon roamed the state, coincided with a period of rapid development meant to support tourism. One result of this growth was the eradication of most vestiges of Florida's unique Old South past. Witness this description of Florida from Edward King's account of the post–Civil War South: "The romance of the place is now gradually departing. The merry processions of the carnival, with mask, violin and guitar, are no longer kept up with the old taste; the rotund figure of the padre, the delicate form of the Spanish lady, clad in mantilla and basquina, and the tall, erect, brilliantly uniformed cavaliers are gone; the 'posy dance,' with its arbors and garlands, is forgotten; and the romantic suburbs are undergoing a complete transformation."[46] King bemoans the rapidly disappearing exotic customs and the state's changing landscape. Homer, and his contemporaries Martin Johnson Heade, George Inness, and Thomas Moran, traveled to the state in order to paint and experience its wild landscapes and customs before they were transformed by tourist development. Meanwhile, photographers, including William Henry Jackson, created rapidly circulating photographs that boosted Florida's prominence as a desirable tourist destination.

At Tampa, Florida speaks to Homer's desire and ability to picture the landscape as a both beautiful and quiescent place (fig. 15). This watercolor draws on the compositional strategies of the Kodak photographs and watercolors made earlier in the trip, while celebrating the bounty and splendor of Florida's ecosystem. Homer has again used the vantage point of a boater to paint land, but in a nod to photographic convention, he has framed the scene more tightly in order to represent the activity on the shore. As in a photograph with a short focal length, Homer presents the characters in tight focus against a vague and fluid background. The viewer seems to have stumbled onto an Edenic paradise, with a snowy egret on the left and a roseate spoonbill on the right populating the richly rendered jungle. The swaying gray-green moss, live oaks, and palms produce a cooling shade and protective shelter from the hot Florida sun and from the dangerous creatures that inhabit Homer's other Florida views. Here, the artist has achieved a contemplative mood, celebrating the best of his Florida experience.

Driven by tourist growth and agricultural development, photographs of Florida circulated broadly and reified certain elements as key visual components of the narrative of any visit to the state: nature, wildlife, steamboat cruises, and leisure activities. In 1892, William Henry Jackson, famed landscape photographer of the West (discussed earlier here in relation to his portfolio on the Bahamas), began photographing northeastern Florida for a Detroit postcard company. Many of these photographs were produced using a Swiss photographic process that made it possible to mass-produce color postcards, prints, and albums for sale to the American market.[47] The infrastructure of tourism, ever elided in Homer's visions, is evoked in Jackson's photograph *Deep Creek* (fig. 16). The vision of placid, unspoiled nature in a thickly forested mangrove is appreciated by a solitary angler, whose fishing hole is soon to be exposed and threatened by the noisy paddle and smoky emissions of the steamboat laden with tourists and bearing down upon him. It shares with Homer's stunning watercolor *At Tampa* an interest in representing the biodiversity of the southern jungle, converging with popular visions of tourist photography.

Homer did not limit his Florida activities to art making; he took advantage of Florida's

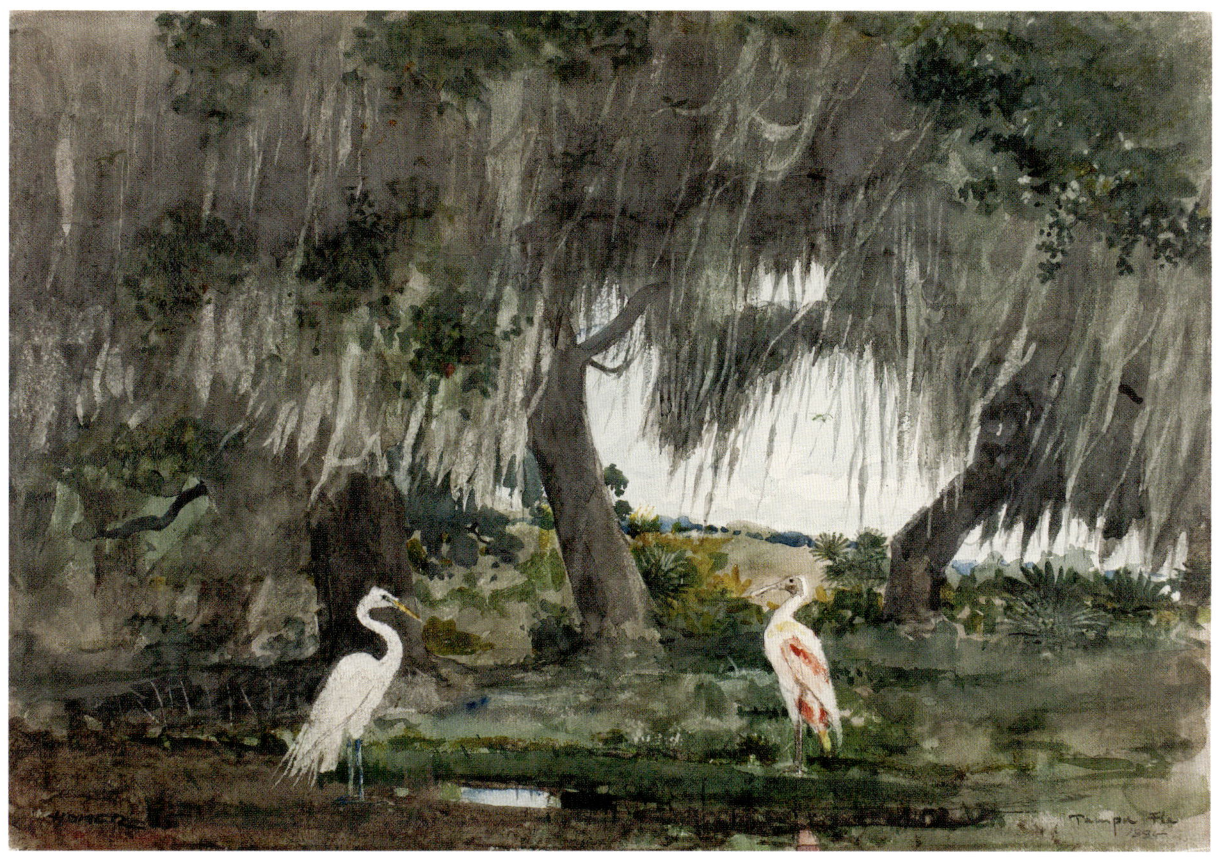

FIG. 15. Winslow Homer, *At Tampa, Florida*, 1885. Watercolor on graphite on wove paper, 14 × 19 15/16 in. (35.6 × 50.6 cm). Arkell Museum at Canajoharie. Gift of Bartlett Arkell. [1941,31799]

legendary fishing offerings. He chose the Brock House in the town of Enterprise, a popular fishing destination, as his base of operations for fishing in the St. Johns River, a wide and long tributary that flows northward throughout the state for four hundred miles. The river was well stocked with wide-mouthed bass, bluegill, redear sunfish, and channel catfish, species not available to him in Maine. Homer wrote to his younger brother, Arthur, that the "fishing [here] is the best in America as far as I can find."[48] In order to locate these fish, however, anglers in small watercraft targeted the edges of vegetation along banks, sharp bends, and drop-offs near shallow bars along the St. Johns. Trawling for fish likely propelled Homer to the Thornhill Bar, a popular late nineteenth-century fishing spot, less than ten miles southeast of Enterprise, where he found fish and picture-worthy sights.

Homer frequently painted, photographed, and fished from a canoe. The images produced from his vessel often feature a wide expanse of water in the foreground with an element—a bar, small island, or vegetation—occupying the background (plates 60B–F). The resulting pictures, including eleven watercolors from

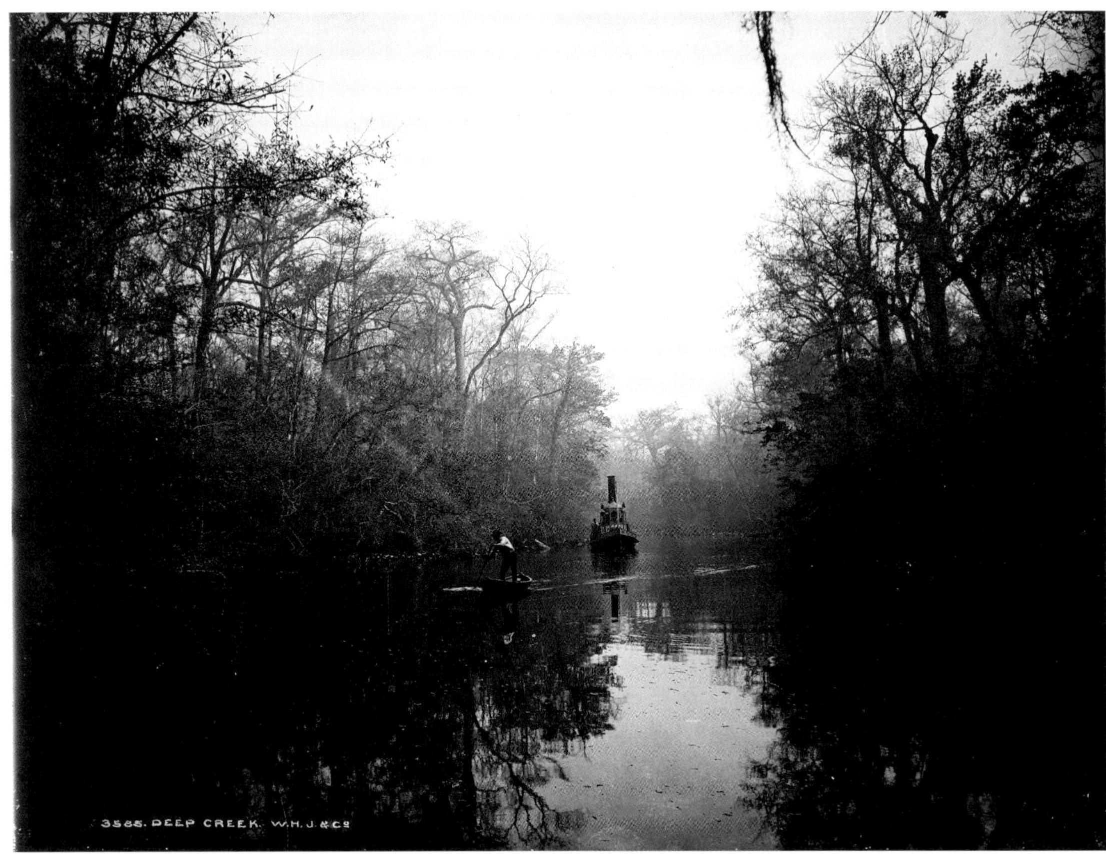

FIG. 16. William Henry Jackson, *Deep Creek*, c. 1897. Glass plate negative, 8 × 10 in. (20.3 × 25.4 cm). Library of Congress, Prints and Photographs Division, Washington, D.C.

his 1885–86 Florida trip, are compositionally similar. In its depiction of the shoal, the watercolor *Thornhill Bar* embraces the same sort of sensibility as the photographs, but in color (fig. 17). Several different species of palm trees rise above the shoal toward the sky as the water below reflects their mirror image. From the right half of the painting, a small canoe with one or two occupants nudges closer and closer to the shore, leaving a trail of disturbed vegetation in its wake. As Homer has represented it, the bar is not particularly inviting; if the occupants of the boat were to proceed to the shore, they would be impeded by the palm trees at the center of the composition. The only access to the bar seems to be in the left third of the watercolor, adjacent to the fallen live oak tree dripping with moss, and even that point of access is fraught, as a sea creature lumbers along the only viable path onto the shoal. Although the photographs created using the Kodak #1 and the painting share the same basic subject matter, using pigment, Homer heightens the drama through the contrast of the light piercing the moody, muddy clouds. The undercurrent of drama is palpable but ambivalent, leaving the viewer to wonder if the danger is imagined, emerging from

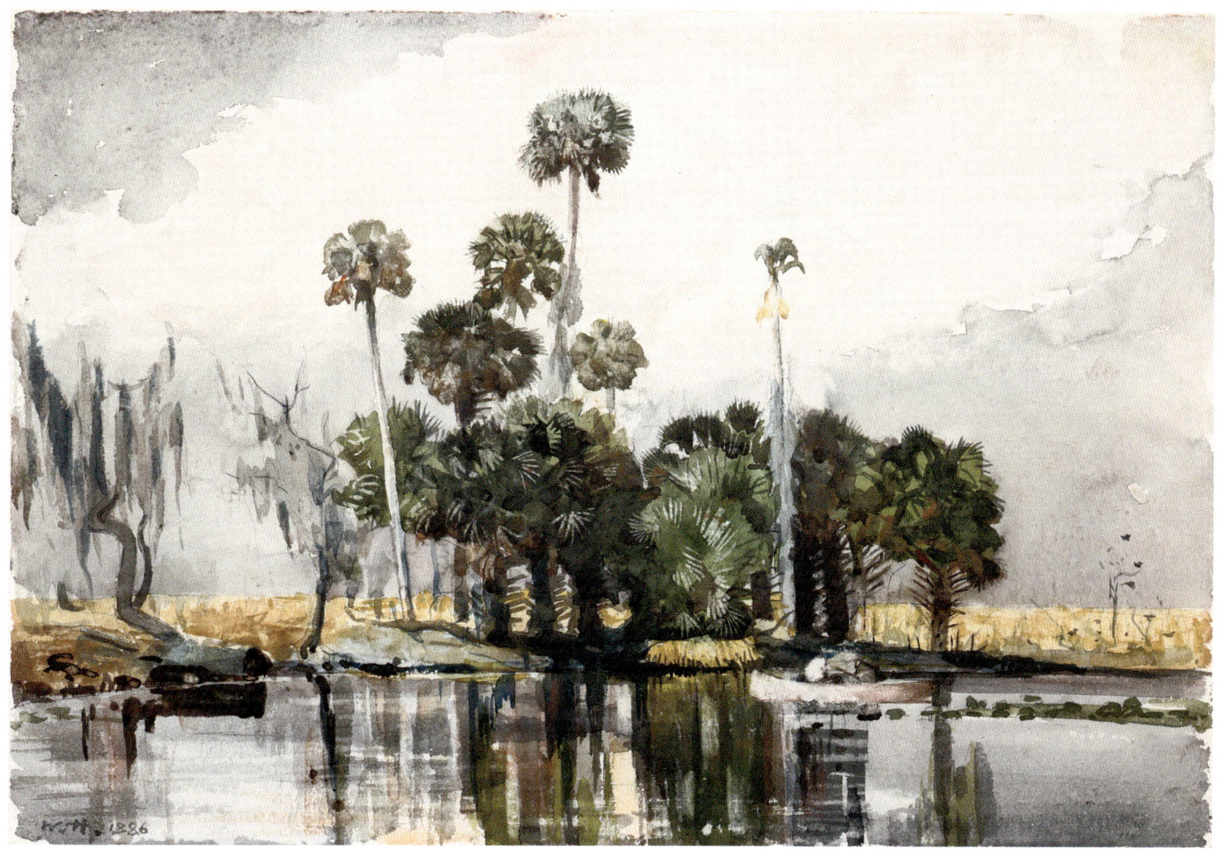

FIG. 17. Winslow Homer, *Thornhill Bar (Florida)*, 1886. Watercolor over graphite pencil on paper, 14 × 20 in. (35.56 × 50.8 cm). Museum of Fine Arts, Boston. Gift of Mrs. Robert B. Osgood. [39.620]

the wild landscape, or directed at the Florida landscape from encroaching civilization.

In his magnificent and inventive scenes of Florida, the artist Thomas Moran avoided the question of danger, but instead imagined the region as existing in the past, not the present. Before taking up the tropics as his subject, Moran had been best known for his grand composite landscape paintings of the American West. Like Homer in the Bahamas, Moran was commissioned to represent a tropical region for a popular periodical, in this case to produce illustrations from sketches for a *Scribner's* article. "An Island of the Sea," penned by Julia E. Dodge, was intended to draw tourist traffic to Fort George Island, fifteen miles away from Jacksonville, at the mouth of the St. Johns River.[49] Moran, and his wife, Mary Nimmo, spent two weeks exploring and sketching the island's ancient Indian hummocks, abandoned and decaying plantation structures, and wild vegetation. Like travel leaflets, Moran's views portrayed the state as a tropical paradise. With its exotic architecture and ancient sailing vessels, Moran's *Morning on the St. Johns, Florida* dreamily renders the body of water as if it were Venice's Great Lagoon, rather

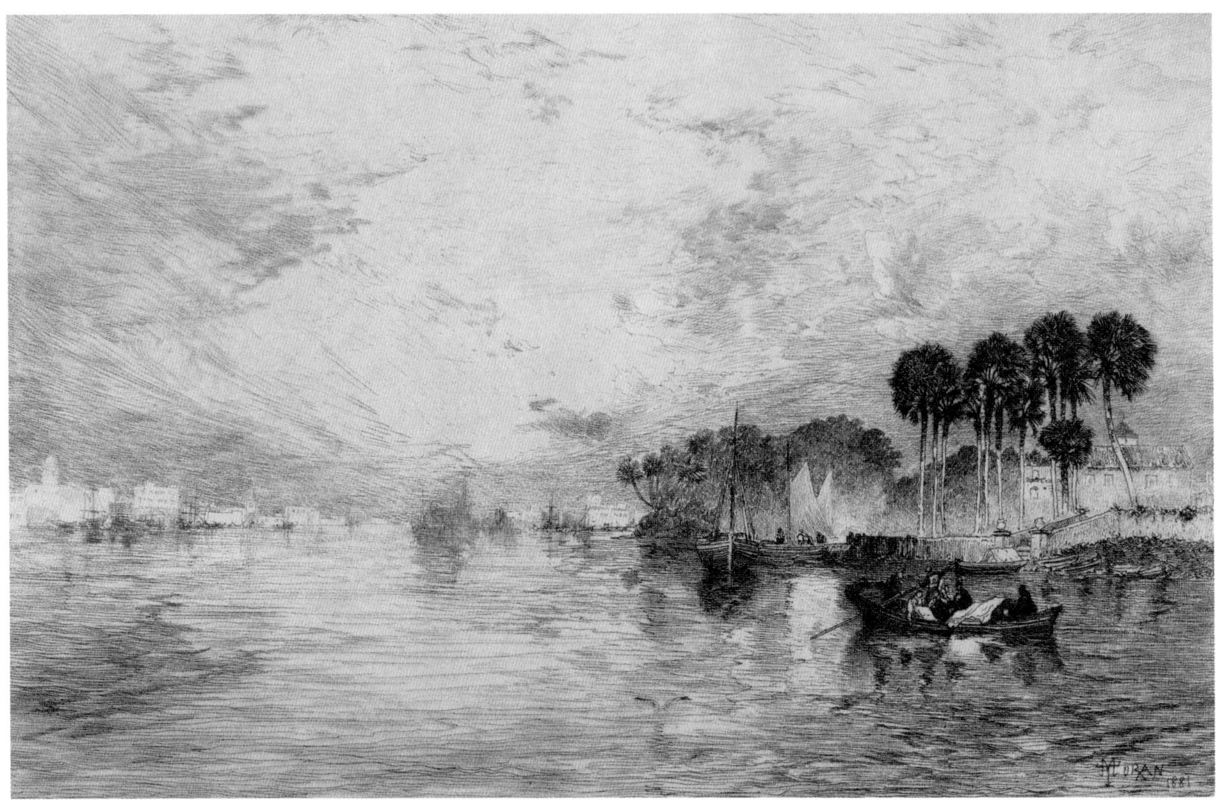

FIG. 18. Thomas Moran, *Morning on the St. Johns, Florida*, 1886. Etching and drypoint, 11 × 14 3/8 in. (28 × 36.6 cm). National Gallery of Art, Washington, D.C. Reba and Dave Williams Collection, Gift of Reba and Dave Williams. [2008.115.3590]

than an American waterway (fig. 18). In the artist's figuring, Florida's tropical landscape transformed into an American inheritor of the Renaissance's cultural legacy, echoing the writer Edward King's description of the state as "our American Italy."[50] Moran's gilded and otherworldly vision of the St. Johns River set firmly in the past and Homer's representation of a wild, untamed, and potentially dangerous landscape represent two very different but contemporaneous visions of Florida.

The contradiction between the beauty and palpable perils of the Florida landscape is a leitmotif in writing on the region. Harriet Beecher Stowe built a winter home in the state after the Civil War. And, from a cottage on a bend in the St. Johns, she wrote two books describing her journey to the state, highlighting nearby towns and resorts, and outlining the opportunities for invalids, tourists, and entrepreneurs. Her popularity remained high, and even as she touted the benefits of Florida in print, her tiny cottage became a tourist destination in its own right. In her writing, Stowe described the beautiful and fearsome nature of the landscape: "Right here, close by where I now write, from among the beautiful palmettos, and under the grand old oaks, one still hears the whispers of wild and terrible tragedy."[51] Here, Stowe likely gestures

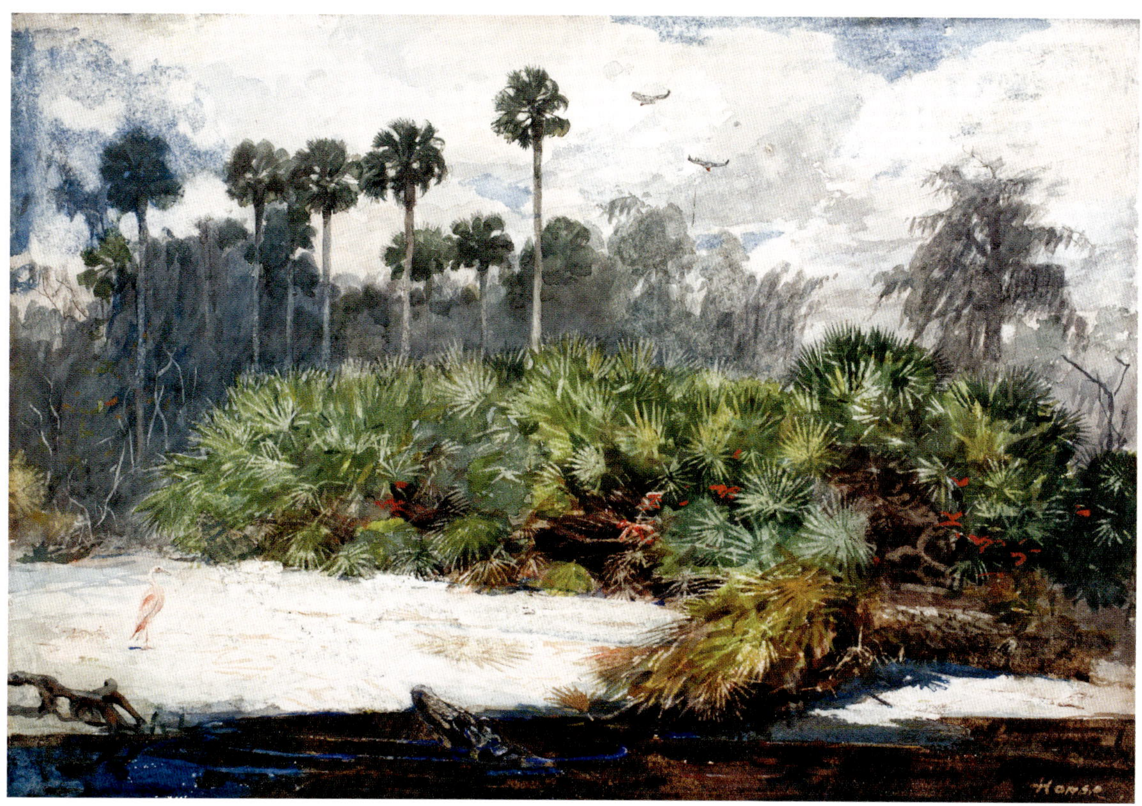

FIG. 19. Winslow Homer, *In a Florida Jungle*, 1885–86. Watercolor over graphite on moderately thick, smooth off-white wove paper, 14 1/8 × 20 1/16 in. (35.8 × 51 cm). Worcester Art Museum. Museum Purchase. [1911.19]

toward the lasting stain of the state's troubled history, including the near-extermination of the indigenous population and its support of chattel slavery.

Responding to this defect of the landscape, Homer often showed it as a primeval territory where strange flora and fauna abounded. With the vantage point of a viewer safely ensconced in a boat, whose ability to glimpse land across a glassy expanse of water offers some respite, *In a Florida Jungle* shares a great deal with *Thornhill Bar* (fig. 19). However, in a return to the muddy, somber palette of the Cuban works, *Florida Jungle* pictures nature as a beautiful yet powerful and dangerous force. Conservator Judith Walsh argues that there is ample technical evidence that Homer reworked several passages of the scene in order to intensify its charged narrative. Two key narrative features, the spoonbill and the snout of the alligator prey and predator, were moved closer together to lend the picture "a new dramatic tension."[52] Subtle changes such as these served to elevate Homer's watercolors from tourist views to commentaries on the hazards, and the troubled history, of the Florida landscape.

Even while traveling for leisure and engaged more with fishing than with other pursuits, Homer found the landscape so enticing that he could not resist making work using both a camera and his watercolors. Jewel-like in their brilliant palette, but rife with an often-unseen danger, the Florida pictures are a synthesis of elements seen in the Bahamas and Cuba watercolors. Homer reused, rather than abandoned, his visual vocabulary of the subtropics developed during his 1884–85 travel. In subsequent years, he would continue to reflect on and redeploy this nuanced representational language to communicate what he had seen and experienced in the three different destinations.[53]

Exhibiting the Tropics

Homer's "winter work" achieved visibility through numerous venues, exhibitions, and publications, ensuring that multiple audiences were able to assess his Bahamas, Cuba, and Florida watercolors. On April 19, 1885, the *New York Times* noted and celebrated the availability of Homer's new works on paper: "Mr. Winslow Homer has been a diligent student this Winter to the effects of color in the Bahamas. . . . He brings back a big portfolio of watercolor sketches, in which his well-known boldness in painting things as they are appears to great advantage. Most artists do not dare to paint the subtropics at their most brilliant moments."[54] Rather than parsing the differences between the representations of the various locales, critics' reception of the 1885 and subsequent shows varied according to the reviewer's stance on the overall artistic merit of the tropics as subject matter. Homer's ability to discern and pictorially define the difference between southern locales was not acknowledged, as geographic commonalities blinded exhibition-goers from delving more deeply into his carefully expressed nuance. No reviewer recognized the difference, or commented on the disparities between Homer's views of the most popular Bahamas tourist sights and his moody and dramatic representations of the remnants of Spanish colonial occupation in Cuba, nor did they acknowledge the primal representations of Florida's beautiful yet dangerous biodiversity.

The article "A Midwinter Resort"—the magazine commission that had brought Homer to the Bahamas in 1884—was finally published in *Century Magazine* in 1887, including text by William Conant Church and illustrated with prints based on Homer's watercolors from his visit. From their participation in documenting the Civil War, to their engagement with popular periodicals and American art, Church and Homer traveled in the same circles. Although the precise nature of the *Century* collaboration remains murky, it is possible to speculate based on the contemporaneous outlook of the periodical. Founded in 1881 as the successor to *Scribner's*, *Century* was a conservative history- and literary-based magazine, whose contents ranged from poetry to open letters, short stories, and lavishly illustrated feature articles. If *Atlantic Monthly* was the magazine of New England, *Century* strove to be a national periodical with a unifying impact, which, under the editorship of the conservative Richard Watson Gilder, published a three-year-long series of articles on the Civil War, offering Northern and Southern accounts equal weight within the magazine, even publishing a eulogy for Robert E. Lee. The reunification of the country following the horrors of the Civil War remained an unstated goal of the journal, and it was an outlet that was read widely by Americans across the country.

Nine engravings of Homer's Nassau watercolors (not including the present work) were reproduced in "A Midwinter Resort." The mediated picturesque of the Bahamas pictures was lost in translation, with the flat, smudgy lines of the wood engravings replacing the loose handling and brilliant color of the watercolors. Combined with Church's text, the illustrated article is unusually cheerless, and the Bahamas are described as anything but a splendid midwinter resort. In keeping with the "serious" tone of the journal, the author took a distinctly and somewhat amusing yet curmudgeonly tone. Directing his comments at potential visitors, Church first warned of the perils to be found in a trip to Nassau, before grudgingly allowing that "for those not compelled to live there, the Bahamas have their charms."[55] He even summoned a list of political, maritime, and climactic disasters that had punctuated the area's history and intimated that the region was in decline, writing, "it is evident that the empire of the Bahamas was not one to be coveted then, and is not much to be desired now." Church's Caribbean contradicts received wisdom about the Bahamas. The islands, in word and image, are written off as a locale marked by poorly managed black Bahamians who pose a danger to whites. Presaging Homer's great painting *The Gulf Stream*, Church represents the sea as a terrifying environment where monsters lurk in the deep. Five men who go out to sea meet a disastrous end; their skeletons are found in a shark, "neatly arranged in a row." Rather than offering a description of "the gentlest[,] most caressing mood" of the sea, Church offers a fantastic account of treacherous waters that conflates white peril with the failure of the British colonial regime.

Homer's acceptance of the *Century* commission proved to be important to his career, as he kept on engaging with the tropics through travel and art. In subject matter and palette, he continued to differentiate between tropical places. He returned to the Bahamas in December 1898, and in the winter of 1899, he expanded his itinerary of British colonies to include Bermuda, where he fished and painted. He ventured back to Florida for fishing on six more occasions, producing both photographs and watercolors. And, although he never physically returned to Cuba, the island, its people and its politics, continued to fascinate him.

The eruption of Cuba's War of Independence in 1895 set in motion a series of political events, including the sinking of the USS *Maine* and the eruption of the Spanish-American War in 1898, which again put Cuba on the artist's radar. An 1898 drawing from his sketchbook reveals his continued preoccupation with the island and its politics (fig. 20). In it, a woman leans out of a window over a cannon labeled "U.S. Battery" and announces, "I protest!" as a ship steams by on the horizon. Below the scene, Homer has written, "The Portland papers say there will be a battery put on Prout's Neck, ME." The sketch indicates that developments in Cuban affairs had made their way to Maine. The artist's father, Charles Savage Homer, who stayed in the Bahamas when Homer traveled to Cuba, was nevertheless engaged with geopolitics. Art historian and Homer expert Philip C. Beam writes that in 1898 Homer's father and a neighbor "telegraphed daily to the War Department that the Spanish fleet had just been sighted off

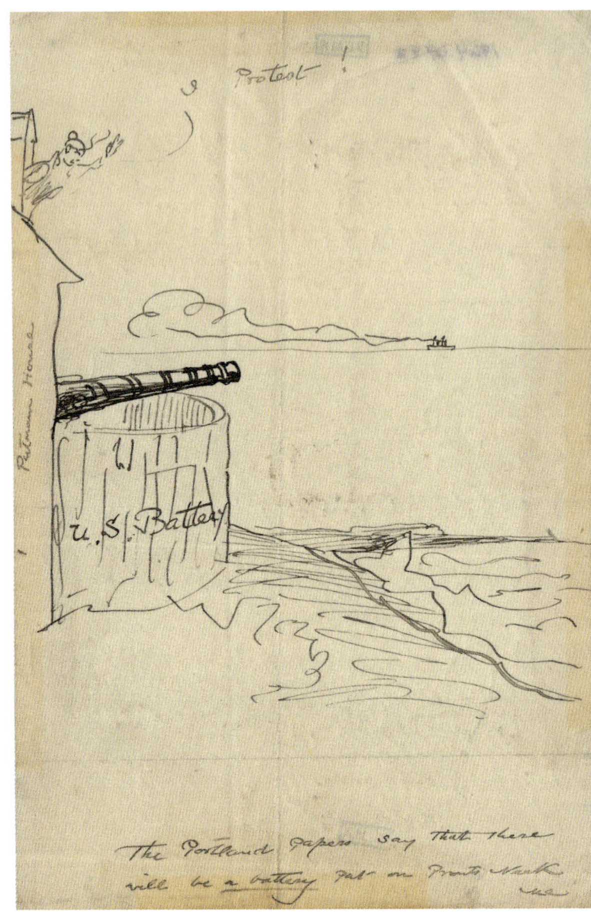

FIG. 20. Winslow Homer, *I Protest!*, 1898. Ink, 8 7/8 × 5 9/16 in. (22.5 × 14.1 cm). Bowdoin College Museum of Art, Brunswick. Gift of the Homer Family. [1964.69.82]

the coast of Maine."[56] These actions may have been premature but nonetheless predictive, as Homer amassed sketches, watercolors, and newspaper photographs along with accounts of the Spanish-American War in his windowless Prout's Neck studio (plate 57). Once again deploying a dark, moody palette, he conflated his Cuban experience and current events in his 1901 painting *Searchlight on Harbor Entrance, Santiago de Cuba* (Metropolitan Museum of Art). In this work, a powerfully liberating bolt of light slices through the dark to illuminate the fort and the harbor, which is finally and irretrievably free of colonial interference.

Homer did not limit the deployment of elements of his tropical experiences to the 1901 painting. From the brilliance of the Bahamas to the danger of Florida, Homer returned to these tropical watercolors as source material for his larger paintings. We are reminded of that practice when we turn to one of the last photographs of Homer taken in the final decades of his life in the Prout's Neck studio. Taken at an oblique angle, the photograph captures Homer with palette in hand standing in front of his great 1899 painting, *The Gulf Stream* (see Goodyear, fig. 36). That warm and swift Atlantic Ocean current, the Gulf Stream originates in Mexico before encircling first the Bahamas, then Cuba, and eventually grazing against Florida's shores. Homer's assembling of source material for the painting from his earlier watercolors represented a return to the past, while his reconfiguration of this material in 1899 in the pastiche that is *The Gulf Stream* represents the distillation of experiences of each locale into a single work. The bright, lush coloring of the Bahamas works surfaces in the middle- and background to merge with the concern for atmospheric threats rendered in a muddy palette in the foreground from the Cuban works; these features combine with the Florida images' insistence on the threat of imminent disaster to be found in nature represented by a looming waterspout to arrive at a powerful work that, like his watercolors, was at once celebrated for its truthfulness while critiqued for being an unworthy painting subject. From the word pictures of florid guidebook prose to photographs of popular subtropical destinations, Homer's consumption of tourist media reminds us that neat translations do not surface in his work, but instead flowed in and out of his art until the very end. More than a century later, it is evident that Homer's tropical images helped concretize conceptions of the Bahamas as a tourist destination rooted in the past, Cuba as a "red-hot" locale doomed to being constantly in flux, and Florida as an untamed tropical wilderness where danger lurked. Mired in the past and part of our contemporary present, they suggest the trouble of paradise.

NOTES

1. See, for example, Randall Griffin, *Winslow Homer: An American Vision* (London: Phaidon, 2006); Abigail Booth Gerdts and Lloyd Goodrich, *Record of Works by Winslow Homer*, 6 vols. (New York: Spanierman Gallery, 2005–14); Elizabeth Johns, *Winslow Homer: The Nature of Observation* (Berkeley: University of California Press, 2002); Nicolai Cikovsky, Jr., and Franklin Kelly, *Winslow Homer* (New Haven, Conn.: Yale University Press, 1995); and Philip Beam, *Winslow Homer at Prout's Neck* (Boston: Little, Brown, 1966).
2. As my colleague Frank Goodyear writes in this volume, the Academy camera survives, but none of the photographs produced by it is extant.
3. John Hannavy, "Camera Design: General," *Encyclopedia of Nineteenth-Century Photography* (New York: Routledge, 2013), 254; Warwick Brookes, Twin-lens camera, shutter, and changing mechanism, British Patent 4320, filed 1881.
4. Mike Robinson and David Picard, "Moments, Magic, and Memories: Photographing Tourists, Tourist Photographs, and Making Worlds," in *The Framed World: Tourism, Tourists, and Photography*, ed. Mike Robinson and David Picard (London: Ashgate, 2009), 2; Eric J. Leed, *The Mind of the Traveler: From Gilgamesh to Global Tourism* (New York: Basic Books, 1991).
5. Critic William Dean Howells described these guidebooks as "chatty and sociable." Howells, "Reviews and Literary Notices: Harper's Hand-Book for Travellers in Europe and the East; Fifth Year," *Atlantic Monthly* 19 (1867): 380–83.
6. David Tatham notes that the photograph is labeled with the inscription "Sept 1882 Cullercoats Newcastle-on-Tyne." David Tatham, "Winslow Homer's Library," *American Art Journal* 9, no. 1 (May 1977): 93–94.
7. On his return to the United States in 1885, Homer opted to abandon the hustle and bustle of New York City life, relocating to Prout's Neck, Maine, a peninsula situated ten miles south of Portland. During the spring, summer, and fall, Homer and his family collaborated to develop the region for tourism. During the winter, Homer sought out a series of warmer climes, as both a tourist and a practicing artist.
8. See, for example, Kathleen Foster, *American Watercolor in the Age of Homer and Sargent* (New Haven, Conn.: Yale University Press, 2017); Nicolai Cikovsky, Jr., *Winslow Homer Watercolors* (New York: Universe, 2009); Miles Unger, *The Watercolors of Winslow Homer* (New York: W. W. Norton, 2001); Patti Hannaway, *Winslow Homer in the Tropics* (Richmond, Va.: Westover, 1973); and *Winslow Homer's Sub-Tropical America*, exh. cat. (Coral Gables, Fla.: Lowe Art Museum, University of Miami, 1968).
9. *Guide to Nassau, Island of New Providence, Bahamas, West Indies: With Illustrations from Photographs; The Royal Victoria Hotel and the New York, Nassau & Savannah Mail Steamship Line; With Meteorological Tables and Other Statistics of Interest to Invalids and Travelers* (New York: Murray, Ferris, 1876), 13.
10. Howard Johnson, *The Bahamas in Slavery and Freedom* (Kingston, Jamaica: Ian Randle, 1991), 33; Helen A. Cooper, *Winslow Homer Watercolors* (New Haven, Conn.: Yale University Press, 1986), 130.
11. *General Description of the City of Nassau and Island of New Providence, Bahamas, West Indies with Metereological Tables and other Statistics of Interest to Invalids and Travelers* (New York: George Edward Sears, 1870), 4.
12. *Guide to Nassau*, 17.
13. Henry S. Villard, *The Royal Victoria Hotel* (Nassau, Bahamas: Henry S. Villard, 1976), 14; Krista A. Thompson, *An Eye for the Tropics: Tourism, Photography, and Framing the Caribbean Picturesque* (Durham, N.C.: Duke University Press, 2006), 5.

14. William Drysdale, "The Voyage to the Indies," *New York Times*, Saturday, August 10, 1884; Royal Victoria Hotel (Nassau, Bahamas), Nassau and Savannah Mail Steamship Line New York, *Nassau, N.P. Bahamas: With Illustrations from Photographs* (New York, 1876), 2; Villard, *Royal Victoria Hotel*, 16.
15. *Guide to Nassau*, 19.
16. Reconstruction complicated this in the United States.
17. Unger, *Watercolors of Winslow Homer*, 127.
18. Thompson, *Eye for the Tropics*, 10.
19. Peter Wood, *Weathering the Storm: Inside Winslow Homer's "Gulf Stream"* (Athens: University of Georgia Press, 2004), 86.
20. Britain granted self-government to the Bahamas in 1964; the islands claimed independence on July 10, 1973. Michael Craton, *Islanders in the Stream* (Athens: University of Georgia Press, 1992).
21. Thompson, *Eye for the Tropics*, 120.
22. Ibid., 126.
23. Louis D. Powles, *The Land of the Pink Pearl, or Recollections of Life in the Bahamas* (London: Sampson Low, Marston, Searle and Rivington, 1888), 115, 128.
24. Frances Clarke, "Blake, Lady Edith," in *Dictionary of Irish Biography*, ed. James McGuire and James Quinn (Cambridge: Cambridge University Press, 2009), unpaginated. Lady Blake published her first book, *Twelve Months in Southern Europe* (1876), which was based on the time she spent in Austria, Germany, Italy, Sicily, Greece, and Turkey, before she married. Driven by an interest in the ecological landscape of the Bahamas (and, during later colonial appointments, those of Newfoundland, Jamaica, Hong Kong, and Ceylon, respectively), she observed, collected, and depicted an array of flora and fauna. Her interest was also cultural; she collected indigenous materials, including several pieces of native material culture.
25. The painting was featured on the June 26, 2011, episode of the BBC television program *Fake or Fortune?*, where it was valued at over $100,000. Since the painting's appearance on the show, the ownership of the work has been disputed, with several claimants attempting to take possession. As of the publication of this essay, the contested ownership has not been resolved. *Fake or Fortune?* series 1, episode 2, June 26, 2011; Sotheby's New York, May 21, 2009, American Paintings, Drawing and Sculpture, lot 16; Barbara Ross and Dareh Gregorian, "Winslow Homer's *Children Under a Palm Tree* at the Center of International Court Battle," *New York Daily News*, November 25, 2013. Octavian Dalvimart, *The Costume of Turkey* (London: Howlett & Brimmer, 1802); Onur Inal, "Women's Fashions in Transition: Ottoman Borderlands and the Anglo-Ottoman Exchange of Costumes," *Journal of World History* 22, no. 2 (2011): 234; Jennifer Harrison, "'Pitchforking Irish Coercionists into Colonial Vacancies': The Case of Sir Henry Blake and the Queensland Governorship," *Queensland Review* 20, no. 2 (2013): 138. The Bahamas was Sir Arthur's first post, but within a few years he was appointed colonial administrator of Queensland, Australia, before relocating to Newfoundland, Jamaica, Hong Kong, and then Ceylon.
26. They later traveled to Cuba and Europe in search of a climate more conducive to William's fragile health. William Howard Gardiner to [William Nye Davis and Mary Gardiner Davis], December 7, 1862, letter in the Schlesinger Library on the History of Women in America, Radcliffe Institute.
27. Henry James, "On Some Pictures Lately Exhibited," *Galaxy* 20 (July 1875): 94.
28. *General Description of the City of Nassau and Island of New Providence*, 4.
29. John Muir, *A Thousand Mile Walk to the Gulf*, ed. William Frederic Badè (Boston and New York: Houghton Mifflin, 1916), 25.
30. Richard Henry Dana, Jr., *To Cuba and Back: A Vacation Voyage* (London: Smith, Elder, 1859), 55.
31. As quoted in Gordon Hendricks, *The Life and Work of Winslow Homer* (New York: Harry N. Abrams, 1979), 180.
32. Cooper, *Winslow Homer Watercolors*, 144–45.
33. Winslow Homer to Charles Homer, 1885, as cited in Cikovsky and Kelly, *Winslow Homer*, 397.
34. Anthony Trollope, "Cuba," *New England Review* 31, no. 3 (2010): 180. Http://www.jstor.org/stable/27920388.
35. Trumbull White, *Pictorial History of Our War with Spain for Cuba's Freedom: A Thrilling Account of the Land and Naval Operations of American Soldiers and Sailors in Our War with Spain, and the Heroic Struggles of Cuban Patriots Against Spanish Tyranny, Including a Description and History of Cuba, Spain, Philippine Islands, Our Army and Navy, Fighting Strength, Coast Defenses, and Our Relations with*

Other Nations, Etc., Etc. (New York: Freedom Press, 1898): 146; Louis Pérez, Jr., *Cuba and the United States: Ties of Singular Intimacy* (Athens: University of Georgia Press, 1998), 71; Abigail Booth Gerdts and Lloyd Goodrich, *Record of Works by Winslow Homer*, vol. 4, *1883 to 1889* (New York: Spanierman Gallery, 2012), 369, no. 1306, illustrated; also illustrated in color on 547.

36. Elizabeth Broun, "Childe Hassam's America," *American Art* 13, no. 3 (Fall 1999): 41–42.
37. Samuel Hazard, *Cuba with Pen and Pencil* (Hartford, Conn.: Hartford Publishing, 1871), 31.
38. Ibid., 31; Martha Tedeschi, "Memoranda of Travel: The Tropics," in *Watercolors by Winslow Homer: The Color of Light*, by Martha Tedeschi and Kristi Dahm (New Haven, Conn.: Yale University Press, 2008), 172.
39. Hazard, *Cuba with Pen*, 70, 157.
40. See Eleanor Harvey, *The Civil War and American Art* (New Haven, Conn.: Yale University Press, 2012).
41. Winslow Homer to Charles Savage Homer, February 1885, letter in the Winslow Homer Collection, Bowdoin College Museum of Art; Pierre Toussaint Frédéric (Federico) Miahle (after), Storch & Kramer, Berlin (lithographer), *Album Pintoresco de la Isla de Cuba [Picturesque Album of the Island of Cuba]* (Havana: B. May y Ca., 1855). Miahle's album includes scenes drawn from everyday Cuban life, such as Afro-Cuban street vendors, sugar and tobacco cultivation, and dancing, as well as topographical views.
42. Dana, *To Cuba and Back*, 179.
43. This visit represented the first of seven trips to the state until 1909, shortly before his death the following year. On Homer's second trip to Florida, he visited Lake Monroe and stayed at the Brock House hotel in Enterprise.
44. Scholars continue to debate Homer's precise itinerary. Here, I rely on Patricia Junker's account of his Florida tour. Patricia Junker, "Fishing on the St. John's and Homosassa Rivers: Winslow Homer's Florida," in *Winslow Homer, Artist and Angler*, ed. Patricia Junker (Fort Worth: Amon Carter Museum; San Francisco: Fine Arts Museums of San Francisco, 2002), 165–66. The challenges of reconstructing the Florida timeline are discussed in Abigail Booth Gerdts, "Summary Biography 1883–1889," in Gerdts and Goodrich, *Record of Works by Winslow Homer*, 4:189–90.
45. Dr. William Stork, *A Description of East-Florida, with a Journal Kept by John Bartram of Philadelphia, Botanist to His Majesty for the Floridas; upon A Journey from St. Augustine up the River to St. John's as far as the Lakes* (London: Board of Trade and Plantations, 1766); William Bartram, *Travels through North and South Carolina, Georgia, East and West Florida, the Cherokee Country, the Extensive Territories of the Muscogulges, or Creek Confederacy, and the Country of the Chactaws* (Philadelphia, 1791); Thomas P. Slaughter, *The Natures of John and William Bartram* (New York: Alfred A. Knopf, 1996).
46. Edward King, *The Great South* (repr.; Baton Rouge: Louisiana State University Press, 1972), 393.
47. Jackson was employed by the Detroit Photographic Company, a photographic publishing firm established in the late 1890s. The founders, Detroit businessman and publisher William A. Livingston, Jr., and photographer and photo-publisher Edwin H. Husher, obtained the exclusive rights to use the Swiss color photolithography "Photochrom" process. This process permitted the mass production of color postcards, prints, and albums for sale to the American market. In 1897, Jackson became a partner in the firm, adding thousands of negatives to the inventory, some taken as early as the 1870s. In 1905, the company changed its name to the Detroit Publishing Company. For more on the firm, see Thomas W. Southall, "In the Colors of Nature: Detroit Publishing Company Photochroms," in *Intersections: Lithography, Photography, and the Traditions of Printmaking*, ed. Kathleen Stewart Howe (Albuquerque: University of New Mexico Press, 1998), 67–75.
48. Winslow Homer to Arthur Savage Homer, 1904, letter in the Winslow Homer Collection, Bowdoin College Museum of Art.
49. Thomas Moran and Anne Morand, *The Field Sketches, 1856–1923* (Norman: University of Oklahoma Press, for the Thomas Gilcrease Institute of American History and Art, Tulsa, 1996), 44–45; Julia E. Dodge, "An Island of the Sea," *Scribner's Monthly* 14, no. 5 (September 1877): 652–61.
50. King, *Great South*, 179.
51. Harriet Beecher Stowe, *Letters from Florida* (New York: D. Appleton, 1879), 8.
52. Judith C. Walsh, "Observations on the Watercolor Techniques of Homer and Sargent," in *American*

Traditions in Watercolor: The Worcester Art Museum Collection (New York: Abbeville, 1987), 50.

53. Robert Schlageter, "Introduction," *Winslow Homer's Florida, 1886–1909* (Jacksonville, Fla.: The Gallery, 1977), 3.
54. *New York Times*, April 19, 1885, as cited in Cikovsky, *Winslow Homer Watercolors*, 116.
55. William C. Church, "A Midwinter Resort," *Century Magazine* 55 (February 1887), 499, 500, 502. Church was well steeped in the world of journalism; in 1855, at the ripe age of twenty-four, he was appointed editor of the New York *Sun*, before volunteering to fight in the Civil War under General W. T. Sherman. Church and Homer likely first encountered each other during the Battle of Fair Oaks, before Church left the service to launch the *Army and Navy Journal*. Later, Church was the founding editor of the literary magazine *The Galaxy*, overseeing the publication of Henry James's intriguing 1875 interview with Homer. He was also a founding member of the Metropolitan Museum of Art, and he and Homer likely traveled in the same circles. *Guide to Nassau*, 18.
56. Philip Beam, *Winslow Homer at Prout's Neck* (repr.; Portland, Maine: Downeast Books, 2014), 44.

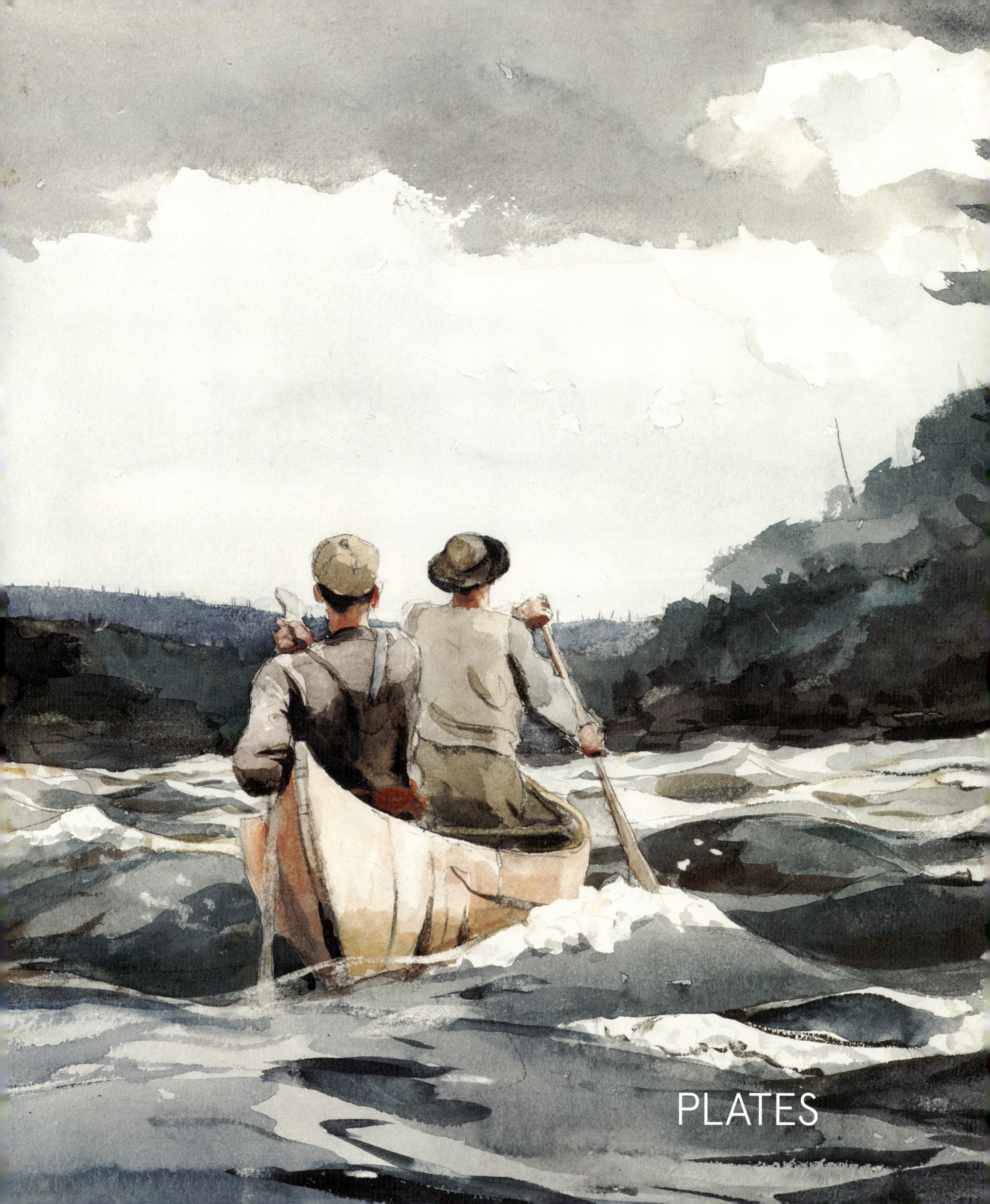

PLATES

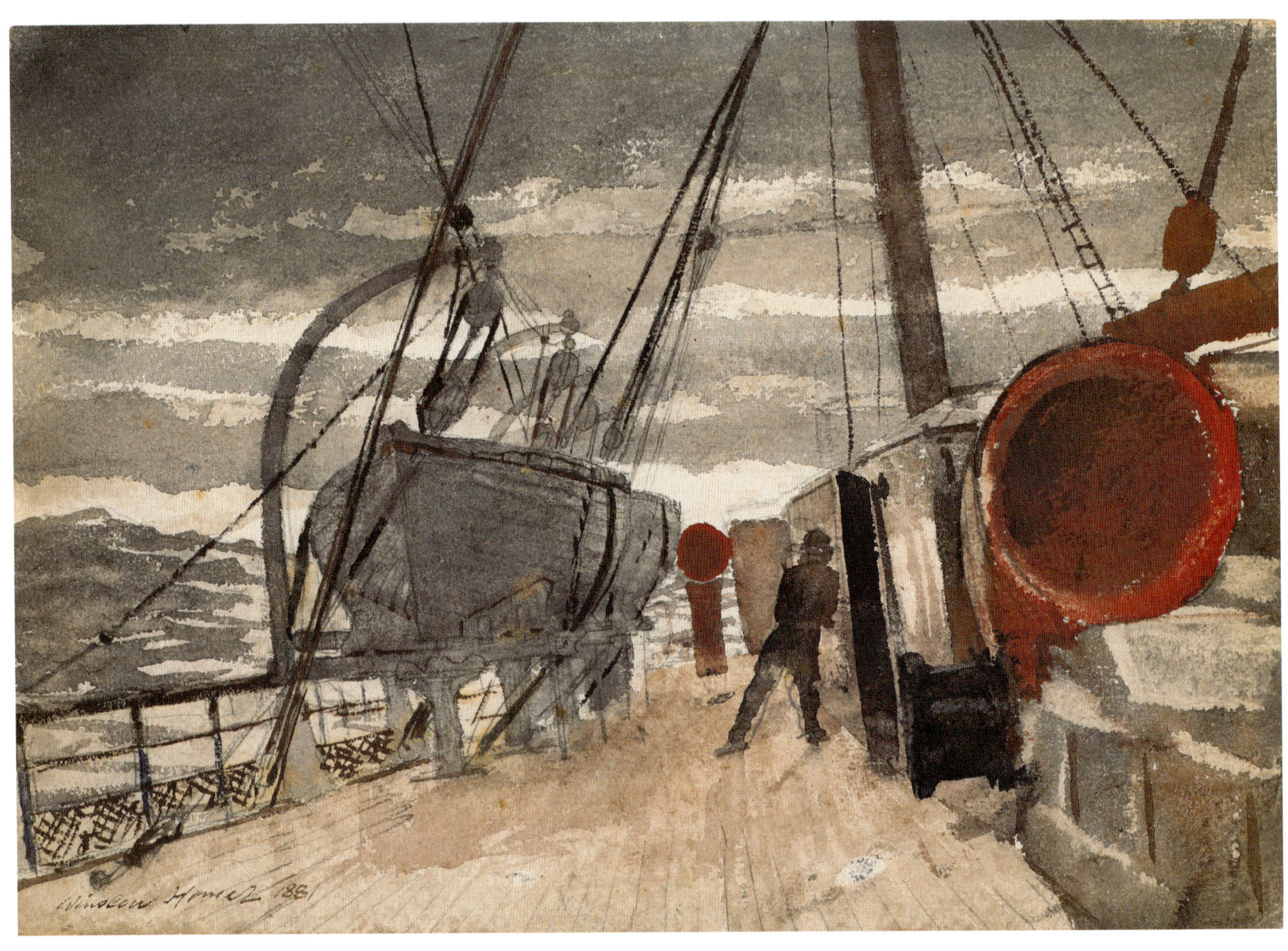

PLATE 33. Winslow Homer, *Marine*, 1881. Watercolor, $9\frac{3}{4} \times 13\frac{1}{2}$ in. (24.8 × 34.3 cm). Bowdoin College Museum of Art, Brunswick. Bequest of the Honorable Augustus F. Moulton, Class of 1873, A.M. 1876, L.L.D. 1928. [1933.1]

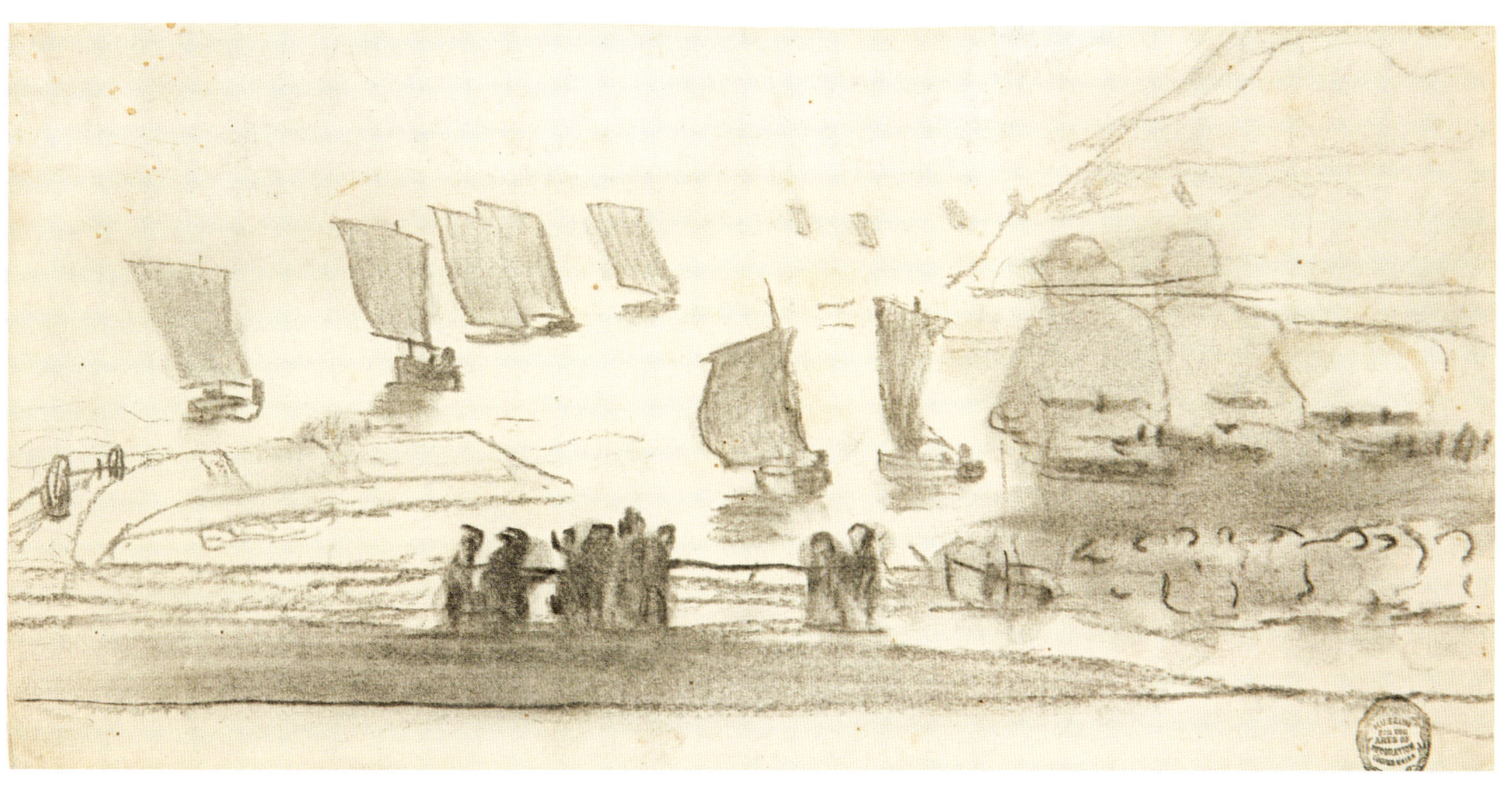

PLATE 34. Winslow Homer, *Beach Scene with People and Fishing Boats, Cullercoats*, c. 1881–82. Charcoal, 6 × 11¾ in. (15.3 × 29.9 cm). Cooper-Hewitt, National Design Museum, Smithsonian Institution, New York. Gift of Charles Savage Homer, Jr. [1912-12-26]

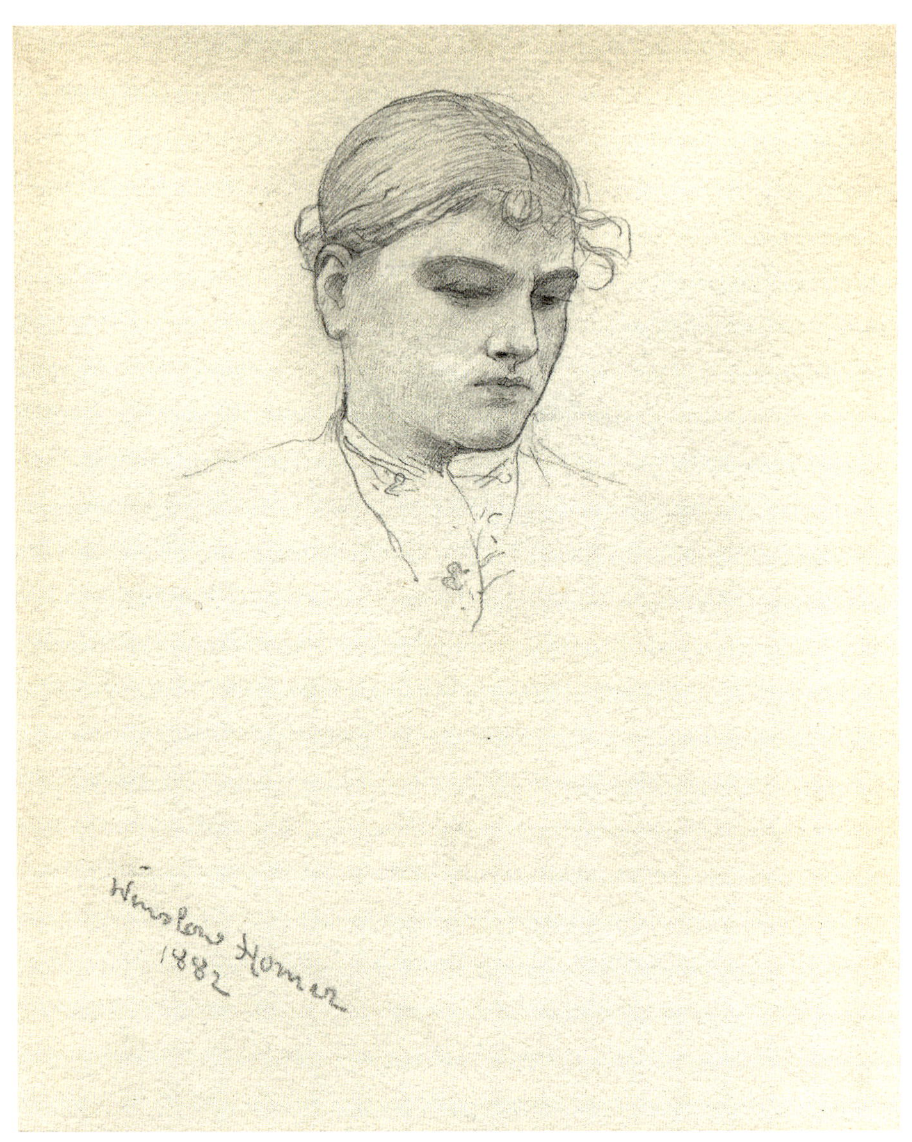

PLATE 35. Winslow Homer, *Head of a Woman*, 1882. Graphite, 9 3/8 × 9 9/16 in. (23.8 × 24.3 cm), sheet. The Columbus Museum, Georgia. Museum purchase made possible by a generous donation from Mr. and Mrs. Stephen T. Butler, in memory of Sarah Smith Hart. [2008.34.38]

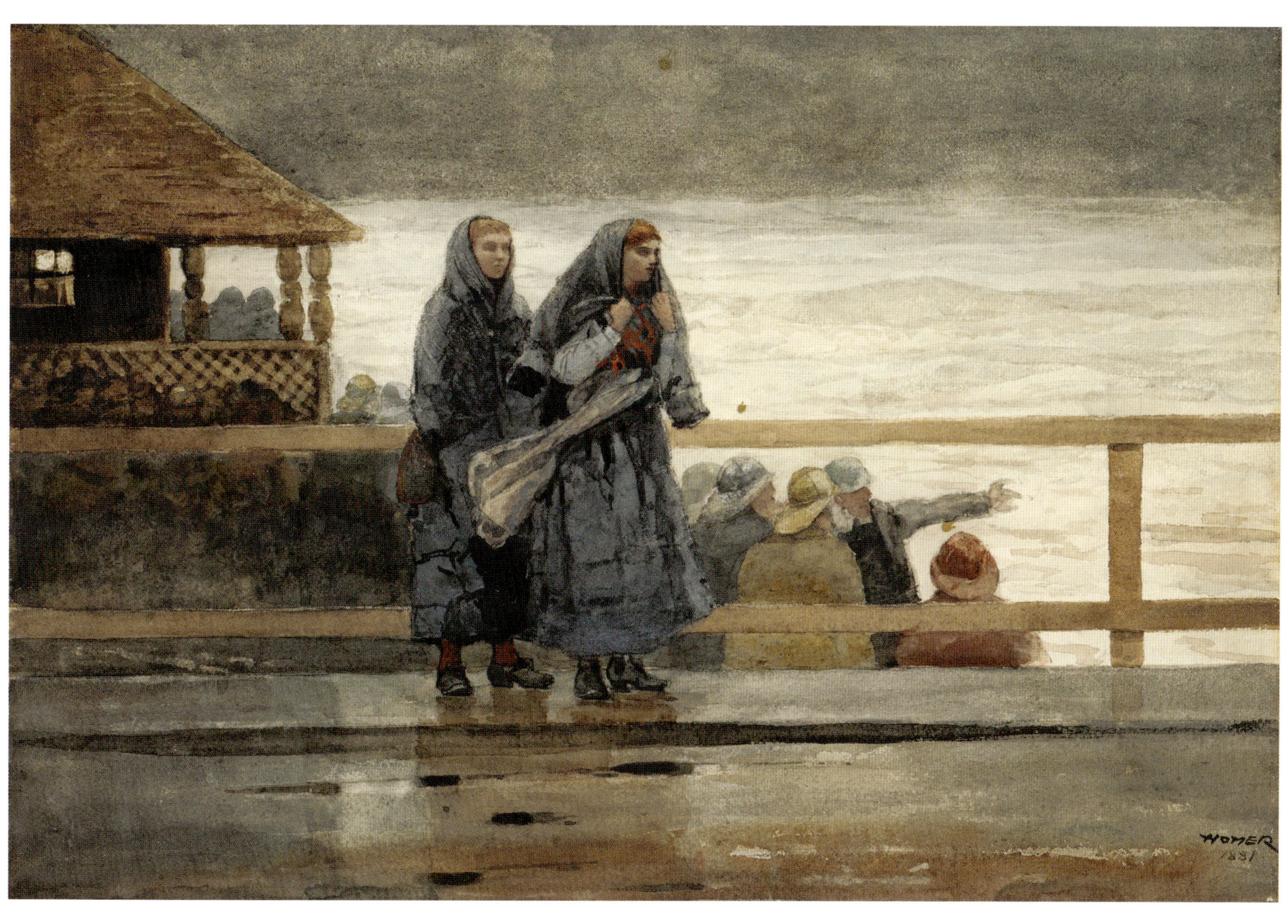

PLATE 36. Winslow Homer, *Perils of the Sea*, 1881. Watercolor over graphite on cream wove paper, 14⅝ × 20¹⁵⁄₁₆ in. (37.1 × 53.2 cm). Sterling and Francine Clark Art Institute, Williamstown. [1955.774]

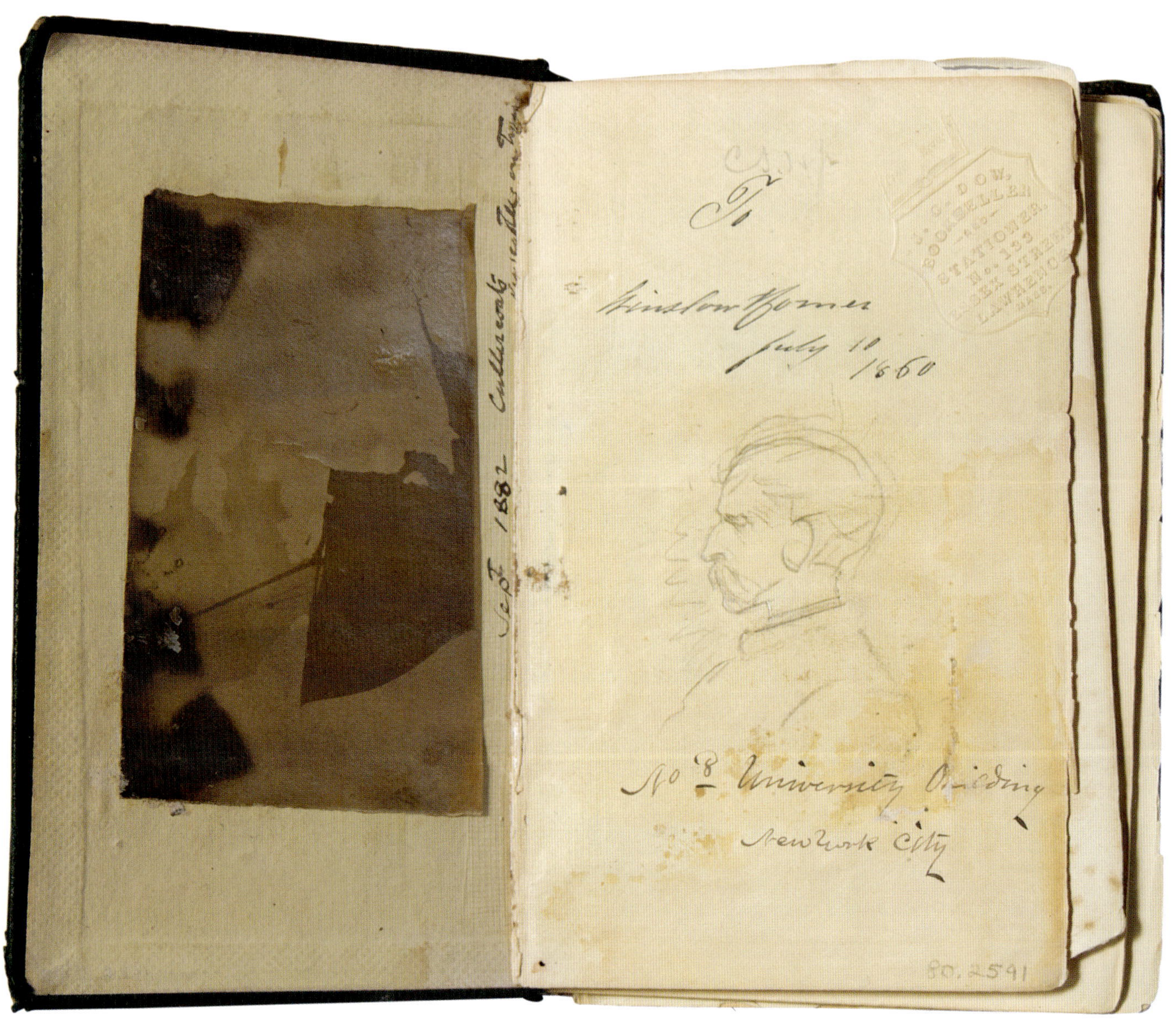

PLATE 37. Winslow Homer, *Cullercoats Coble*, 1882. Albumen silver print, 6½ × 4 in. (16.5 × 10.2 cm). Private collection, courtesy of The Strong Museum, Rochester, New York.

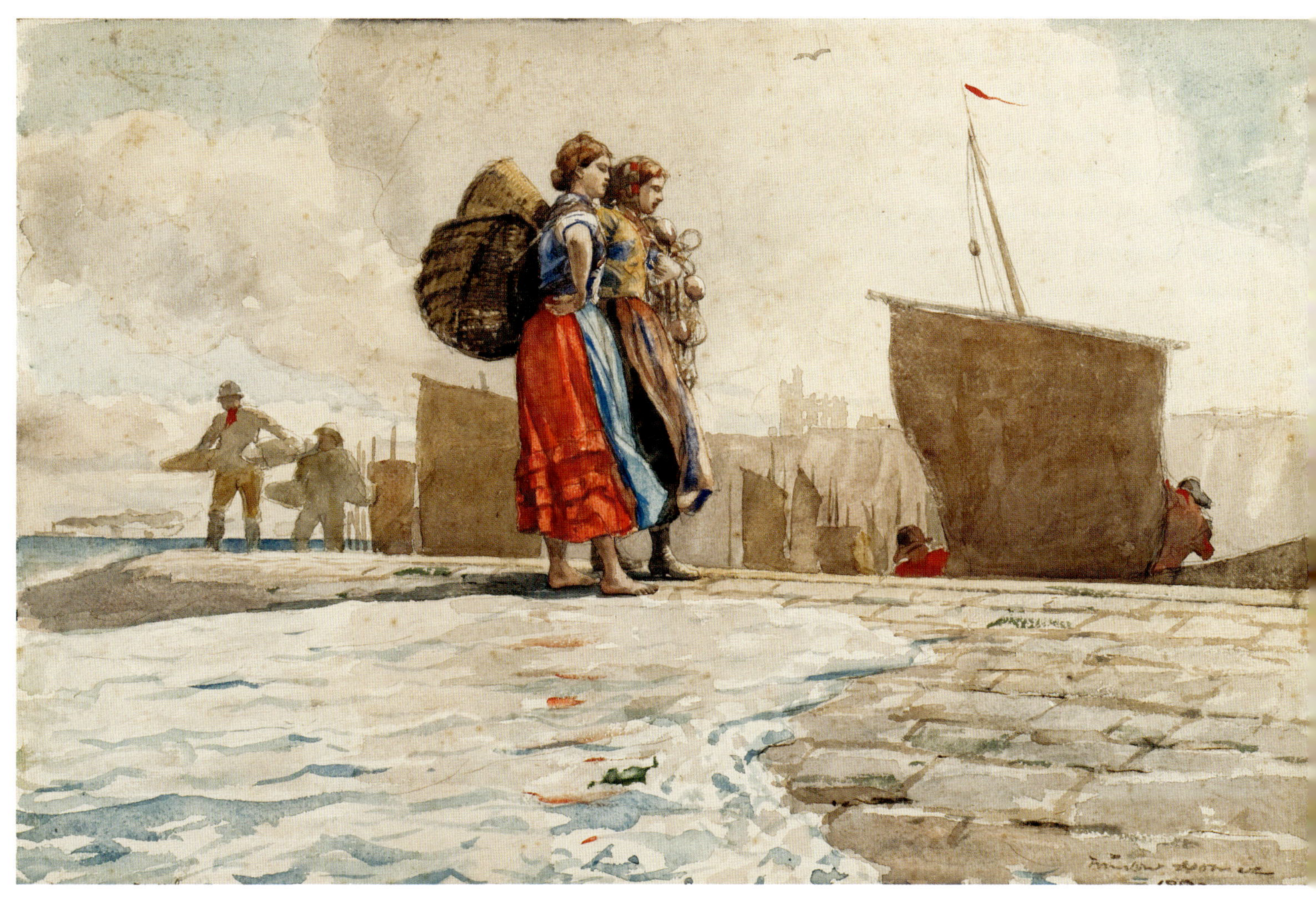

PLATE 38. Winslow Homer, *The Breakwater, Cullercoats*, 1882. Watercolor on ivory wove paper, 13¼ × 19¾ in. (33.6 × 50.2 cm). Portland Museum of Art, Maine. Bequest of Charles Shipman Payson. [1988.55.16]

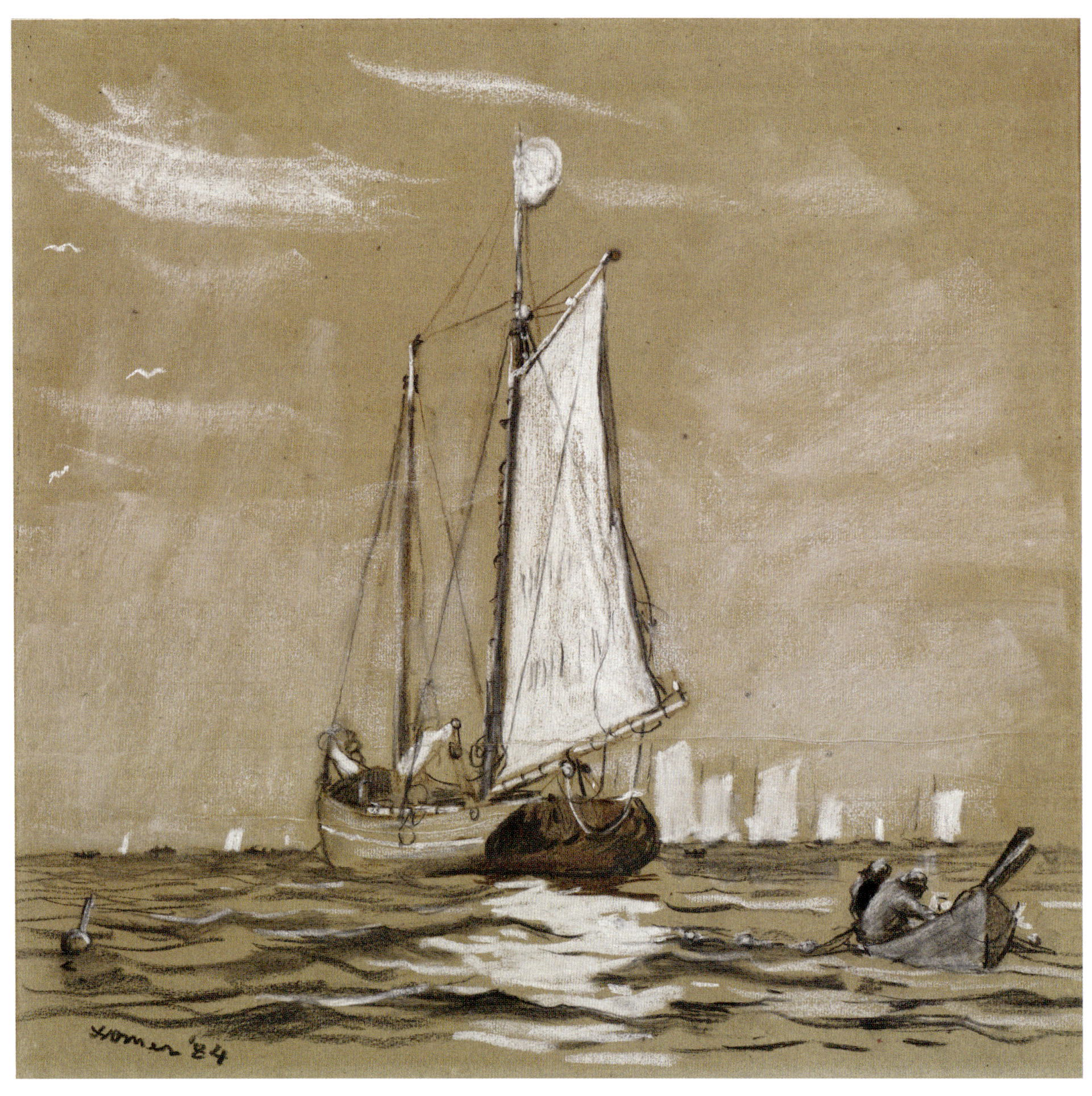

PLATE 39. Winslow Homer, *A Fishing Schooner*, 1884. Charcoal and white chalk, 17½ × 17½ in. (44.4 × 44.4 cm). Colby College Museum of Art, Waterville. The Lunder Collection. [2013.142]

PLATE 40. Winslow Homer, *Fisher Girls on Shore, Tynemouth*, 1884. Charcoal and white chalk, 22½ × 17¼ in. (57.2 × 43.9 cm). Wadsworth Atheneum Museum of Art, Hartford. Gift of Mrs. James Lippincott Goodman. [1986.260]

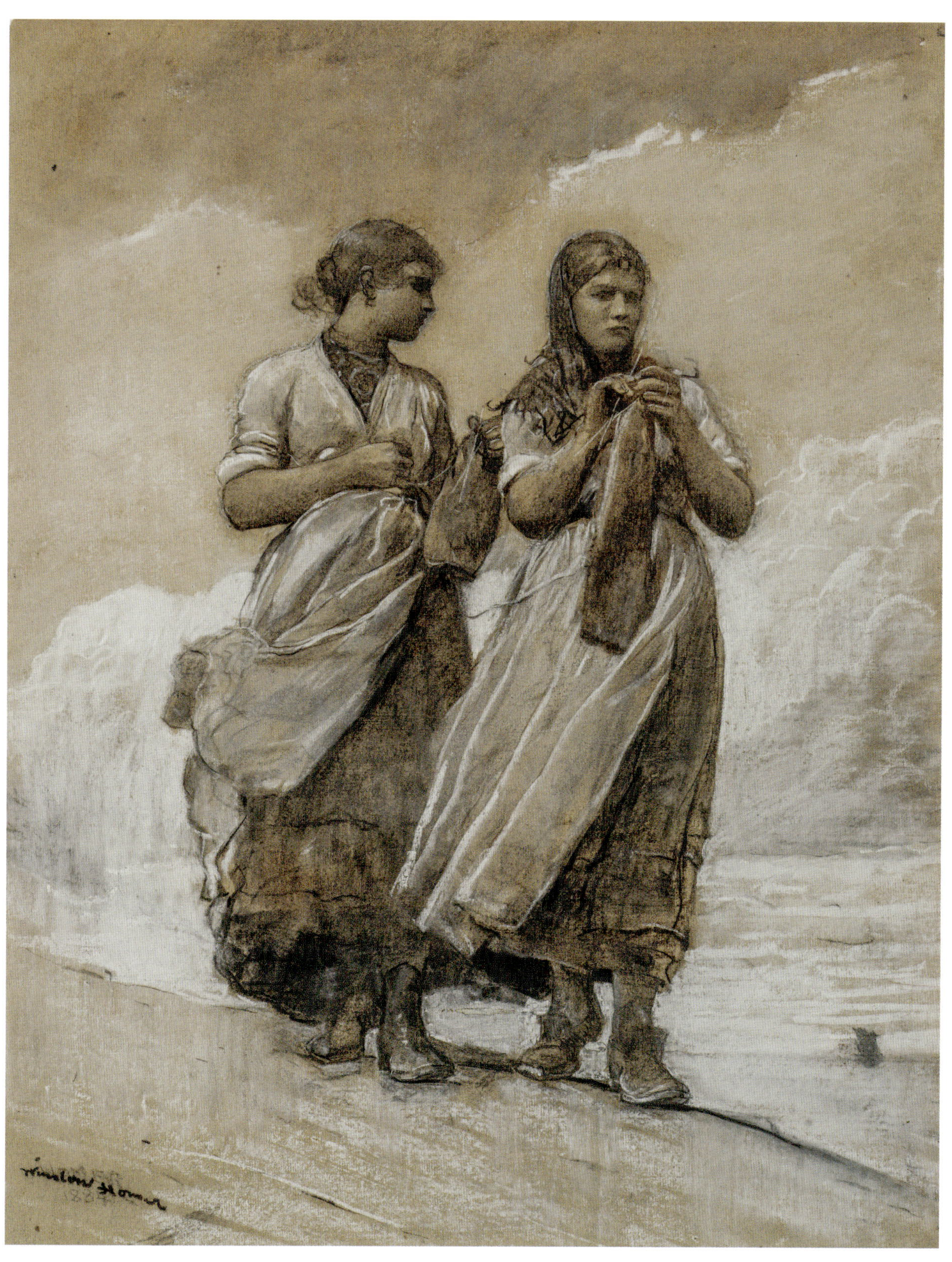

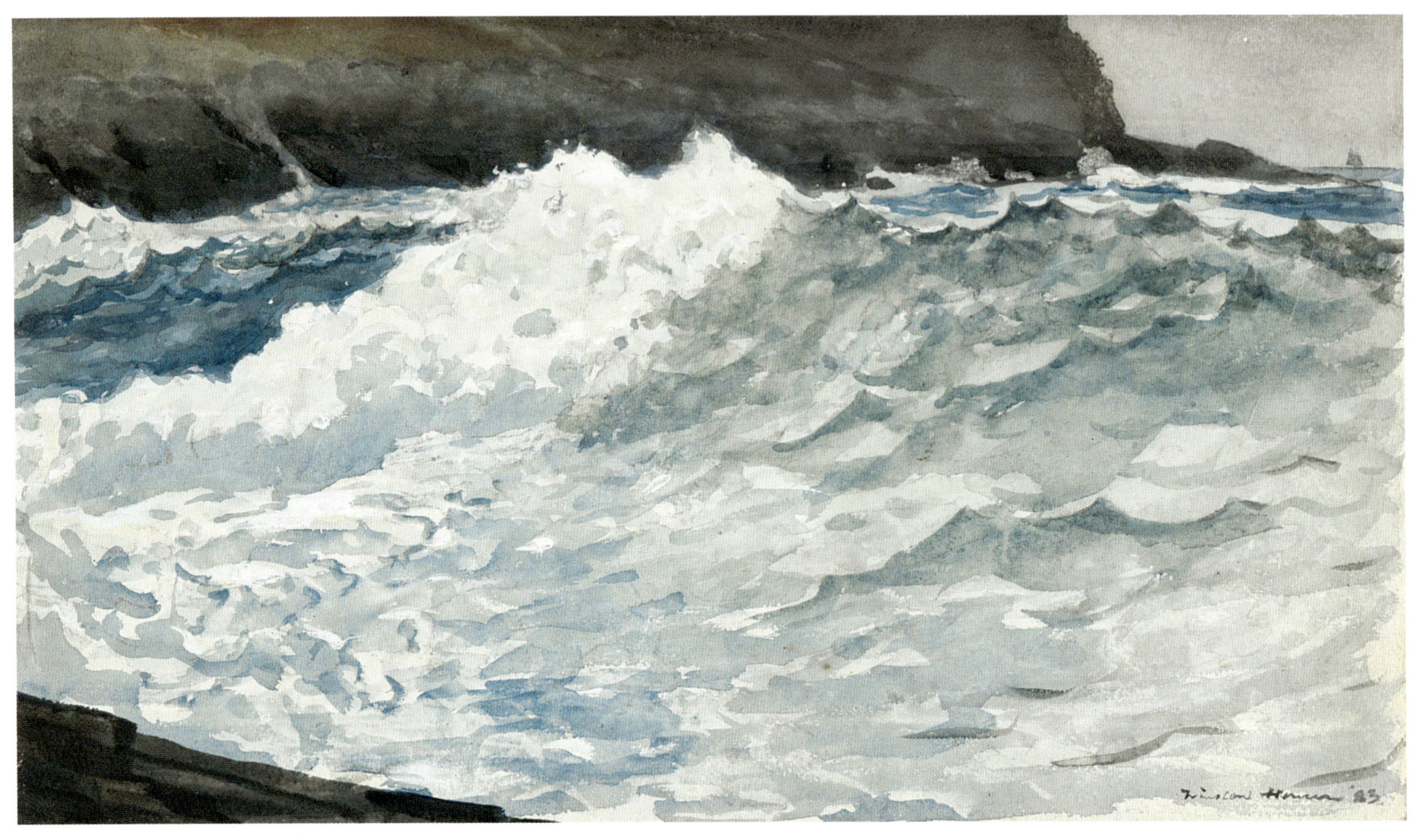

PLATE 41. Winslow Homer, *Surf at Prout's Neck*, 1883. Watercolor, $11\frac{7}{16} \times 19\frac{7}{16}$ in. (29 × 49.4 cm). Yale University Art Gallery, New Haven. Bequest of Doris M. Brixey. [1984.32.15]

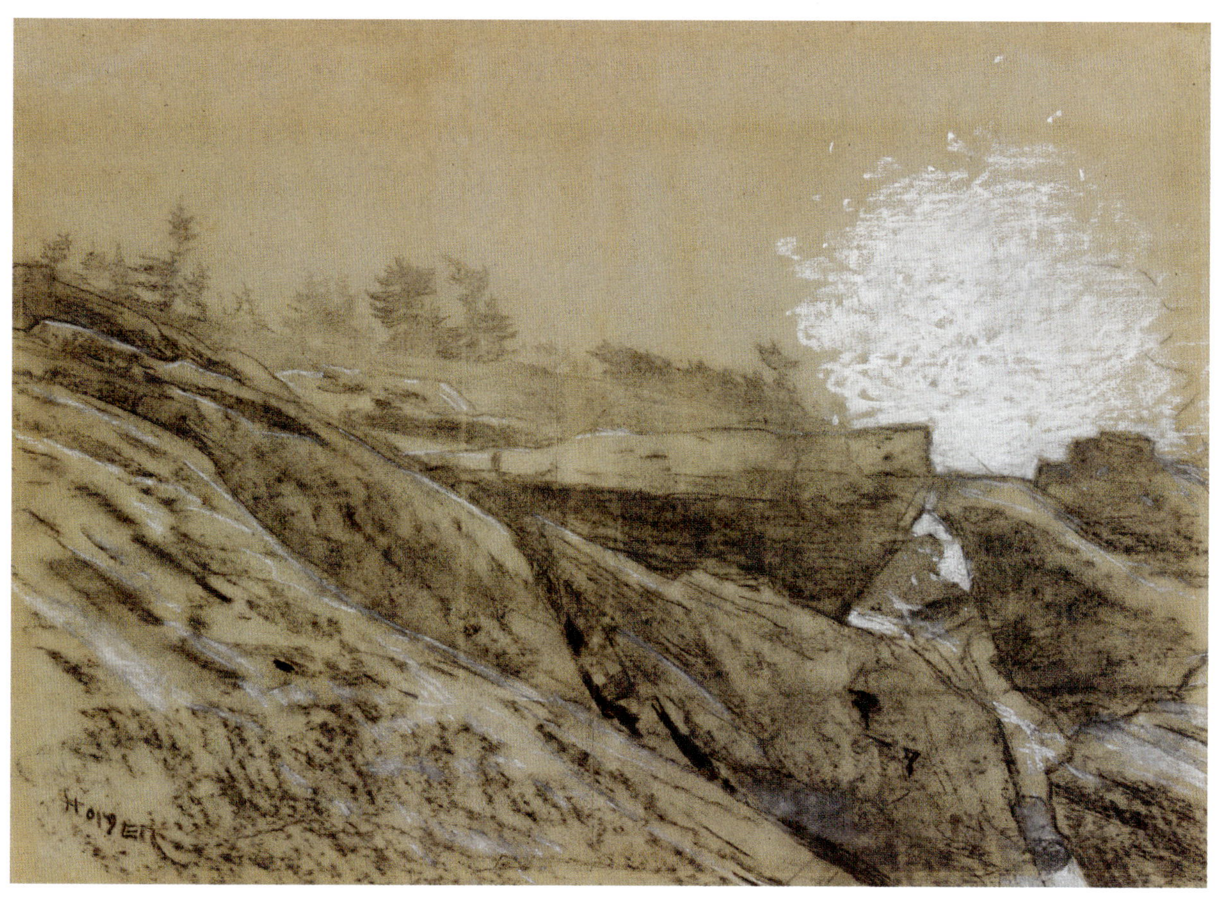

PLATE 42. Winslow Homer, *Surf and Rock near Cannon Rock, Prout's Neck*, 1884. Charcoal and white chalk, 17¼ × 23⅜ in. (43.8 × 59.4 cm). Bowdoin College Museum of Art, Brunswick. Museum Purchase, Hamlin Fund. [1967.40]

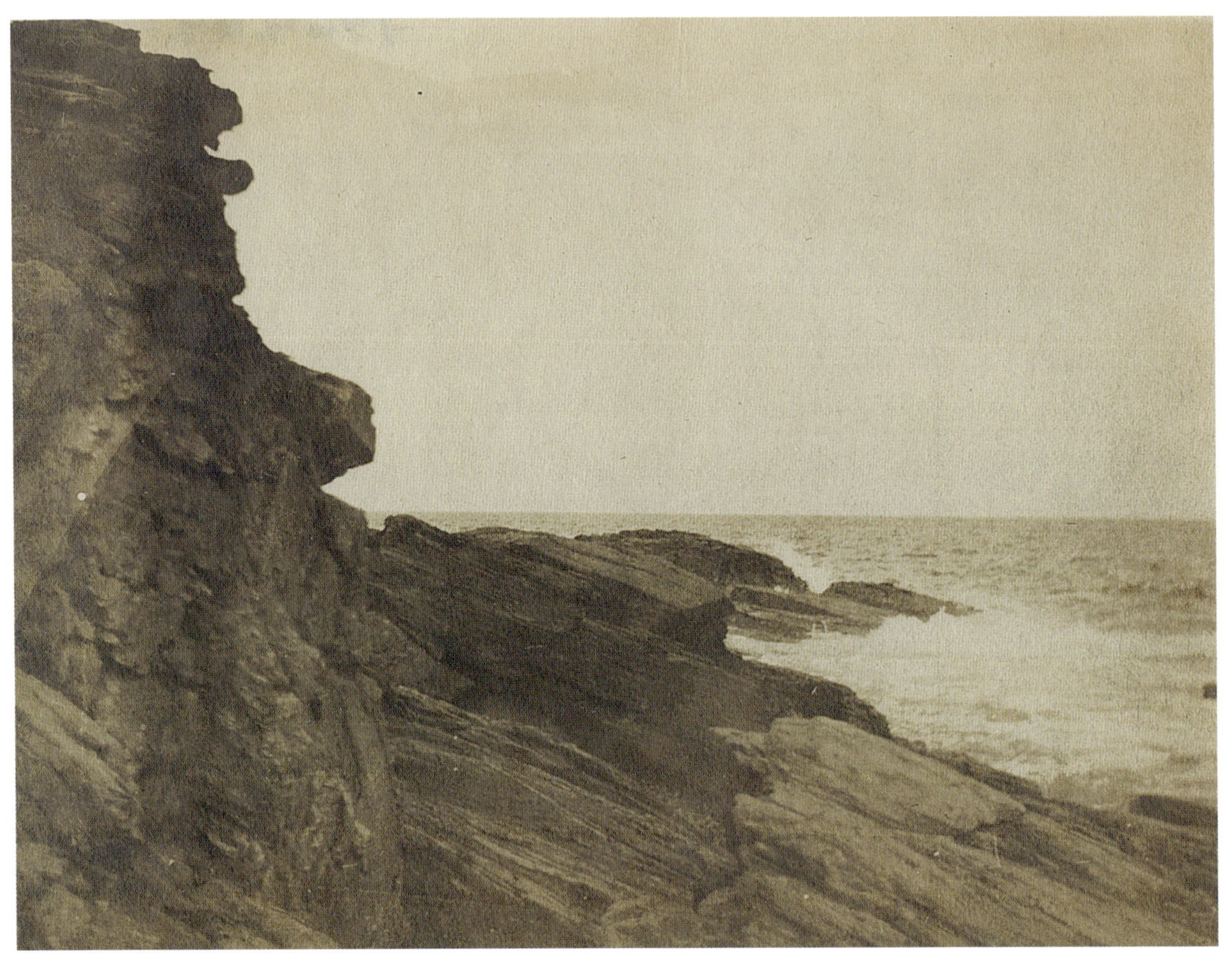

PLATE 43. Winslow Homer, *Cliff at Prout's Neck*, c. 1883–87. Albumen silver print, 3⅝ × 4½ in. (9.2 × 11.4 cm). Bowdoin College Museum of Art, Brunswick. Gift of the Homer Family. [1964.69.177.10]

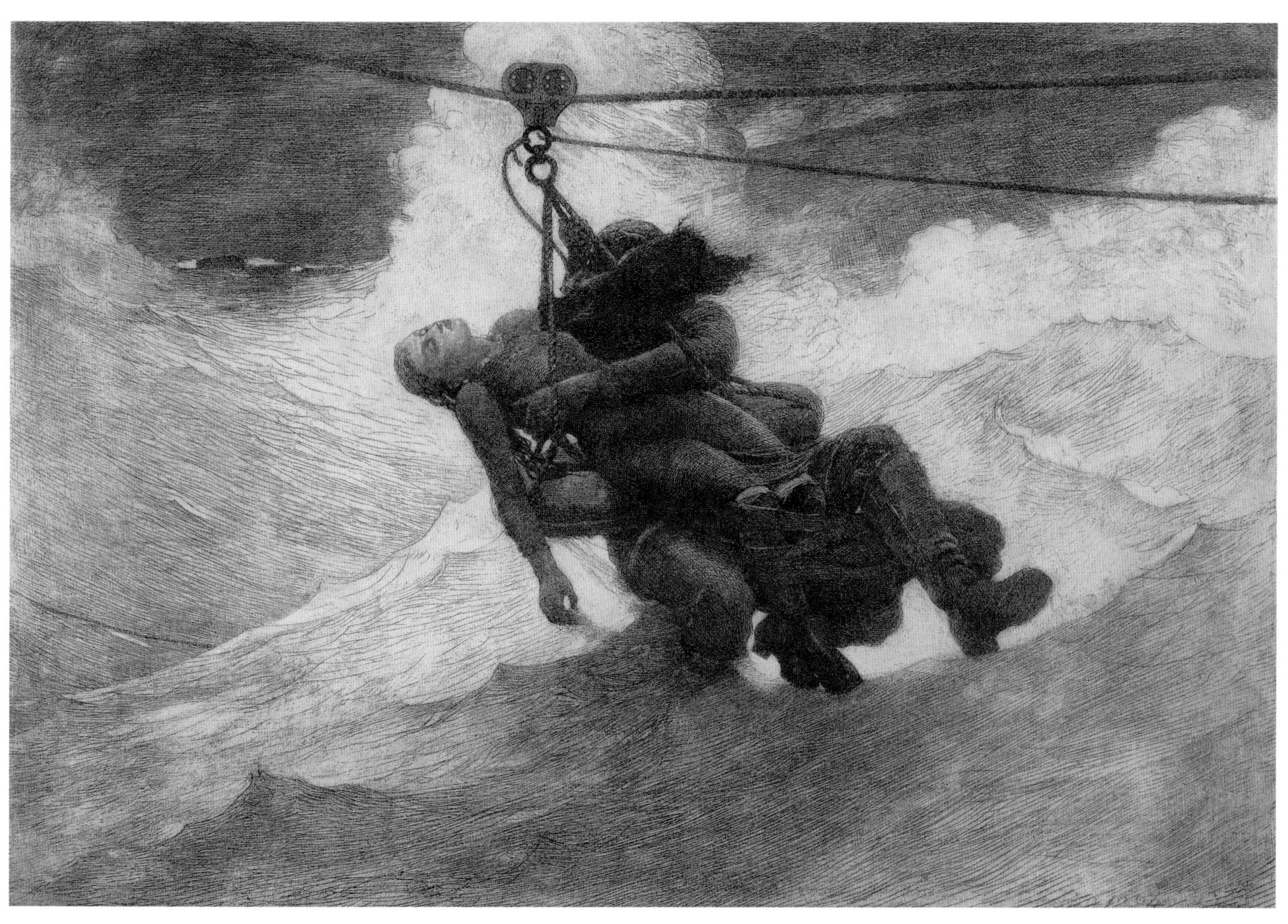

PLATE 44. Winslow Homer, *The Life Line*, 1884. Etching in green ink with aquatint and drypoint on beige, moderately thick, moderately textured wove paper, 17½ × 23 in. (44.5 × 58.4 cm). Brooklyn Museum. Museum Purchase, Carll H. de Silver Fund. [35.1062]

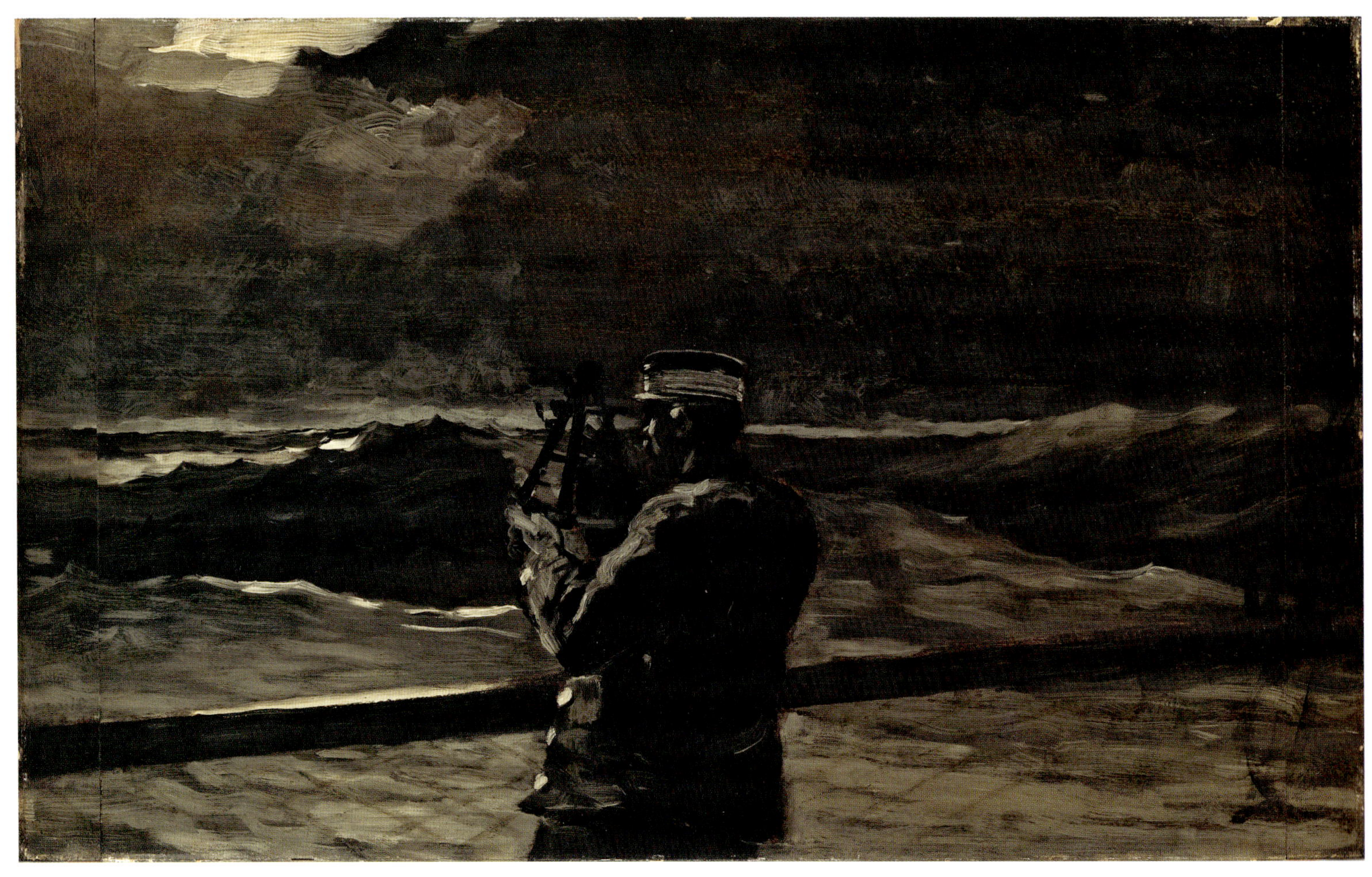

PLATE 45. Winslow Homer, *Taking an Observation*, 1884. Oil on panel, 15¼ × 24 in. (38.7 × 60.9 cm). Portland Museum of Art, Maine. Bequest of Charles Shipman Payson. [1988.55.3]

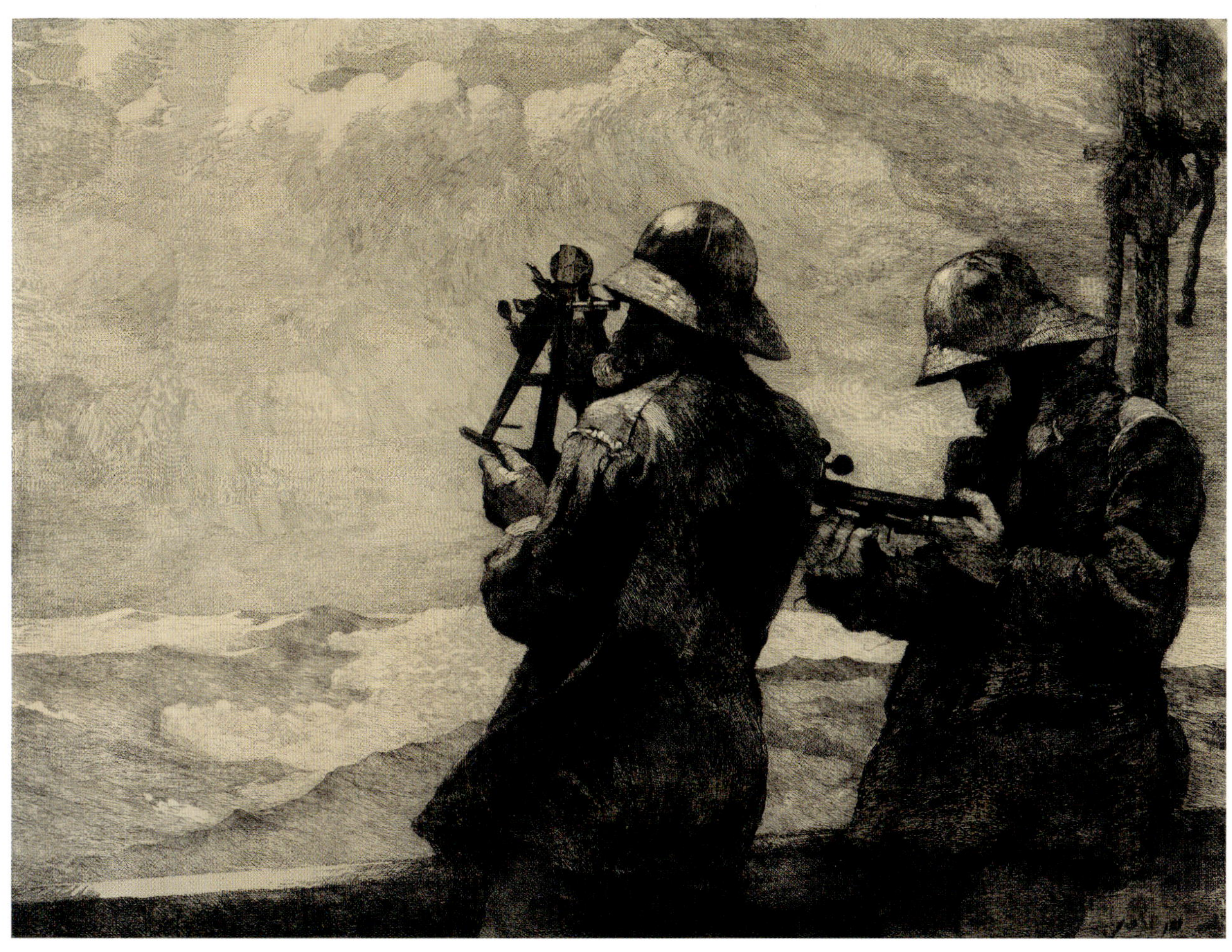

PLATE 46. Winslow Homer, *Eight Bells*, 1887. Etching, 19 7/16 × 25 in. (49.4 × 63.5 cm). Bowdoin College Museum of Art, Brunswick. Gift of Charles Shipman Payson. [1967.67]

PLATE 47. Winslow Homer, *Eight Bells*, 1886. Oil on canvas, 25 3/16 × 30 3/16 in. (64 × 76.7 cm). Addison Gallery of American Art, Andover. Gift of an anonymous donor. [1930.379]

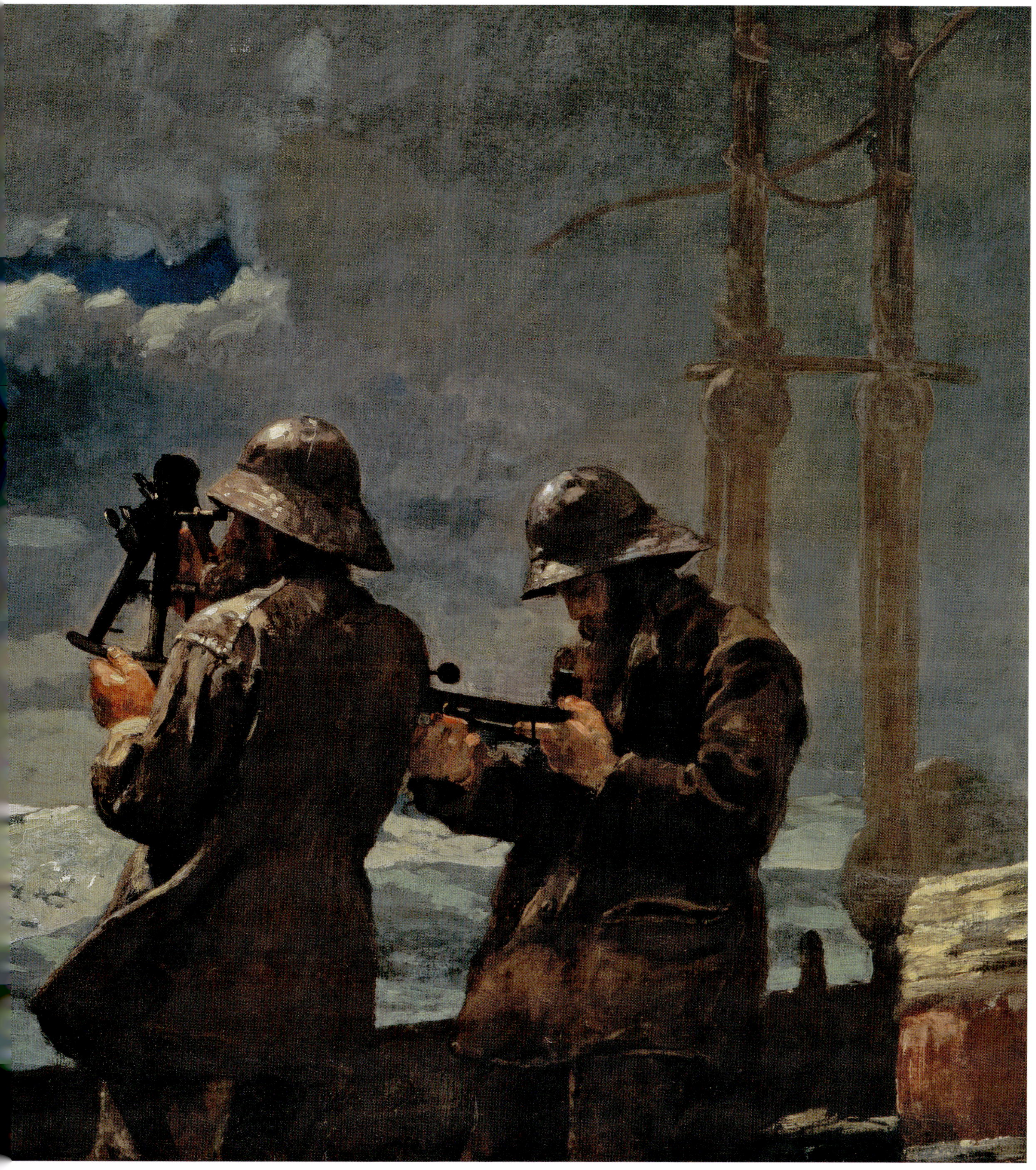

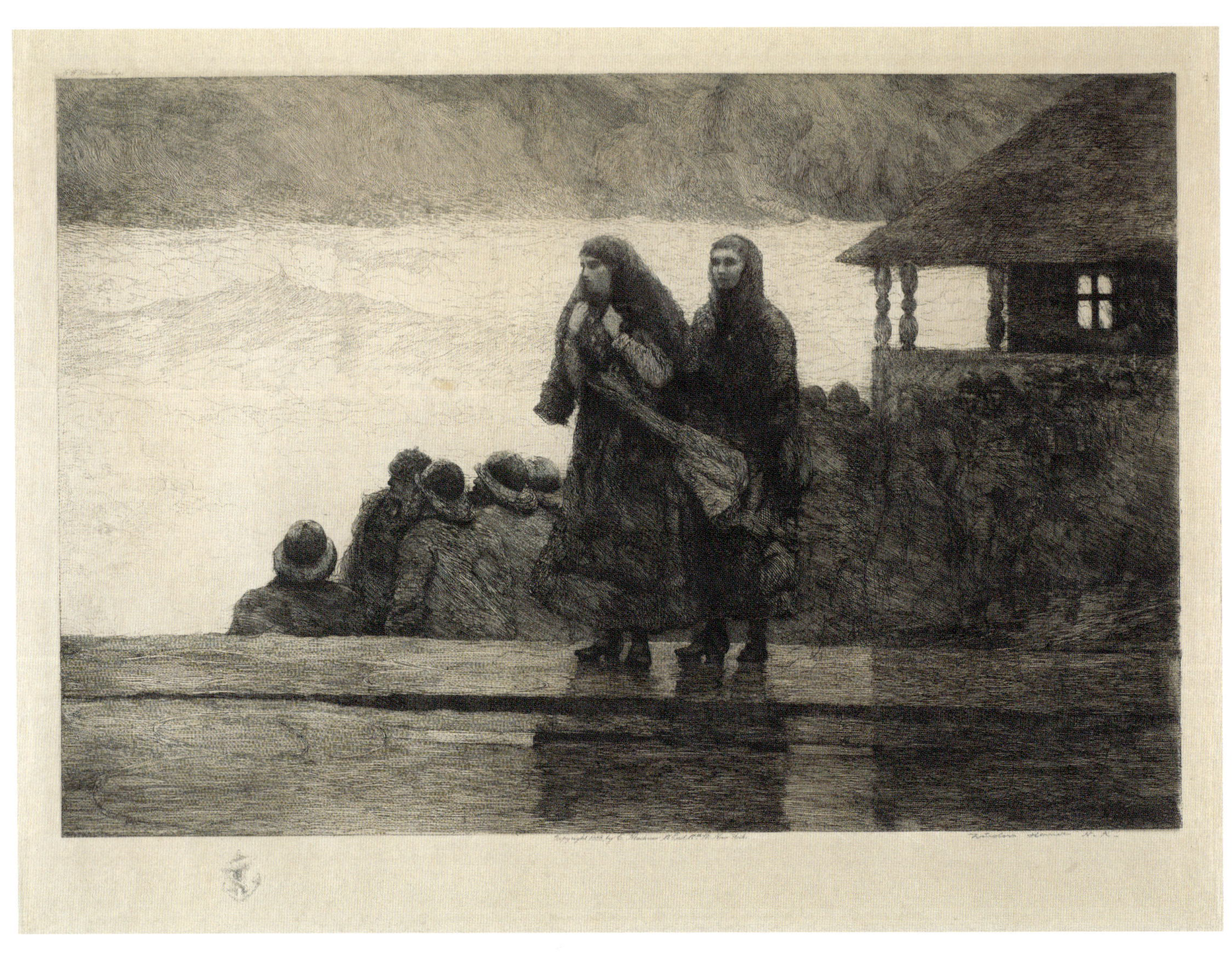

PLATE 48. Winslow Homer, *Perils of the Sea*, 1888. Etching, 16 × 21¼ in. (40.6 × 54 cm). Bowdoin College Museum of Art, Brunswick. Gift of Fred A. Neuren. [1969.1]

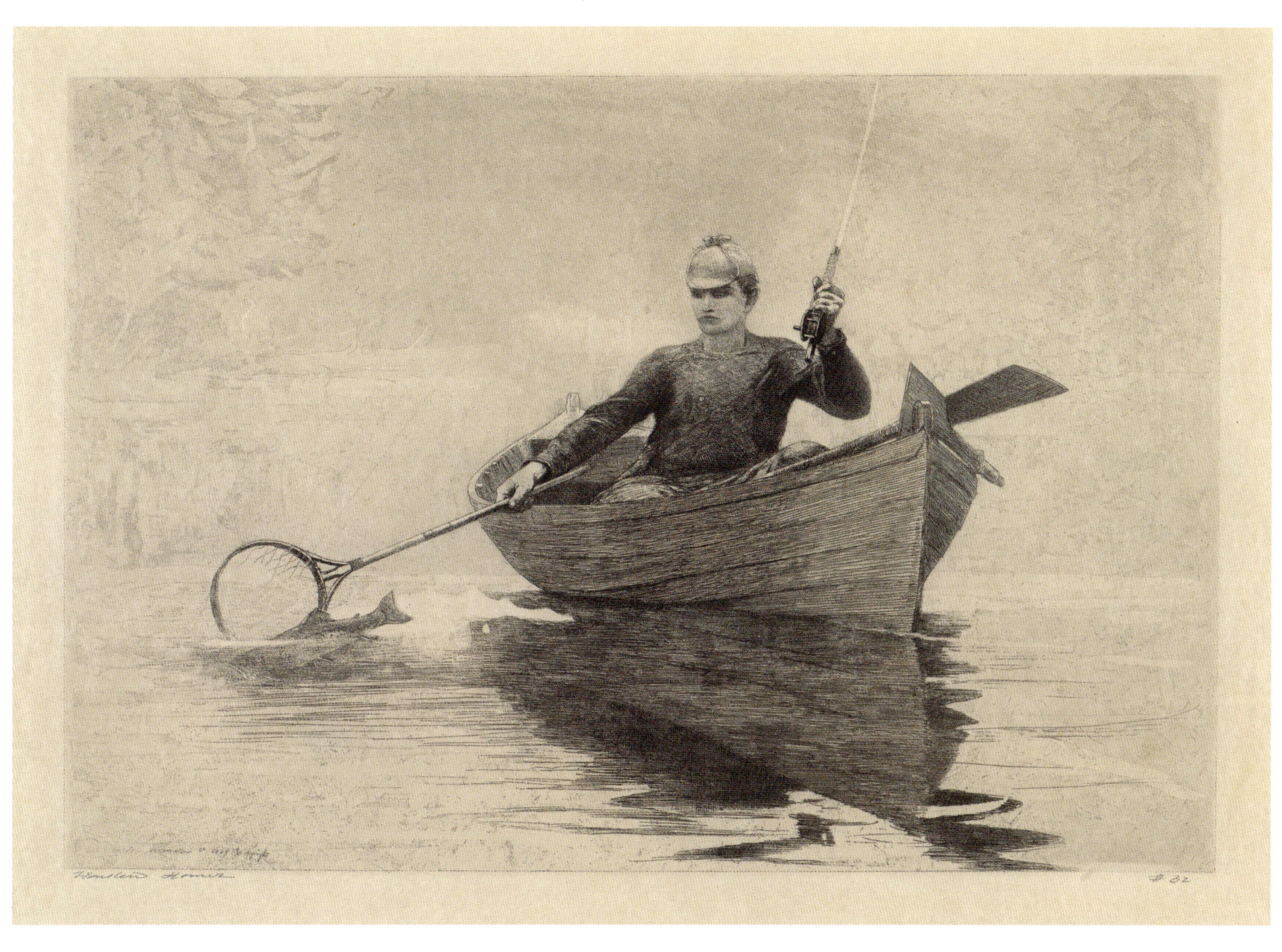

PLATE 49. Winslow Homer, *Fly Fishing, Saranac Lake,* 1889. Etching, 17½ × 22¹¹⁄₁₆ in. (44.5 × 57.6 cm). Bowdoin College Museum of Art, Brunswick. Gift of the Homer Family. [1964.69.203]

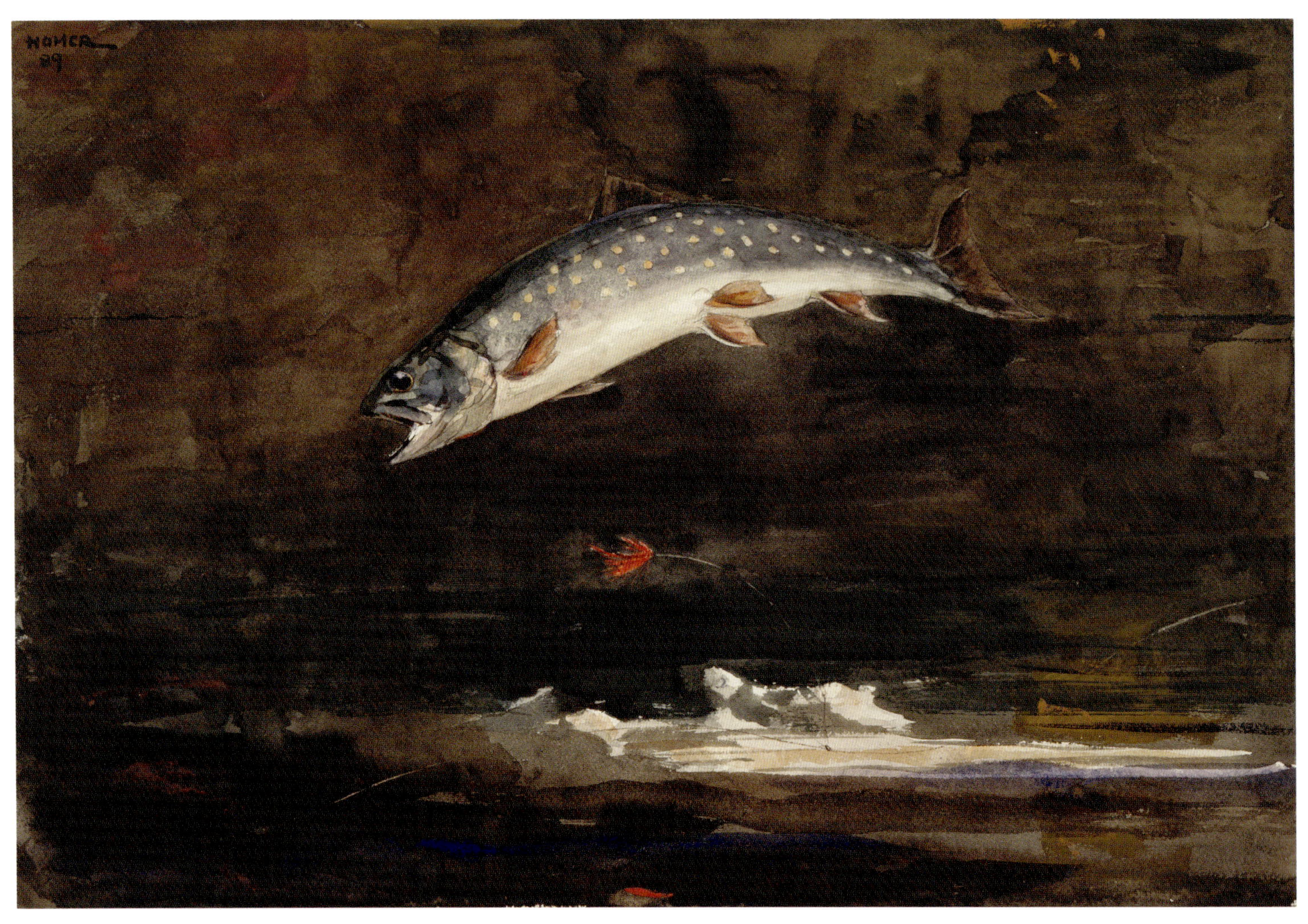

PLATE 50. Winslow Homer, *Jumping Trout*, 1889. Watercolor over graphite on cream, medium-weight, moderately textured wove paper, $13\frac{15}{16} \times 19\frac{15}{16}$ in. (35.4 × 50.6 cm). Brooklyn Museum. Museum Purchase, Dick S. Ramsay Fund. [41.220]

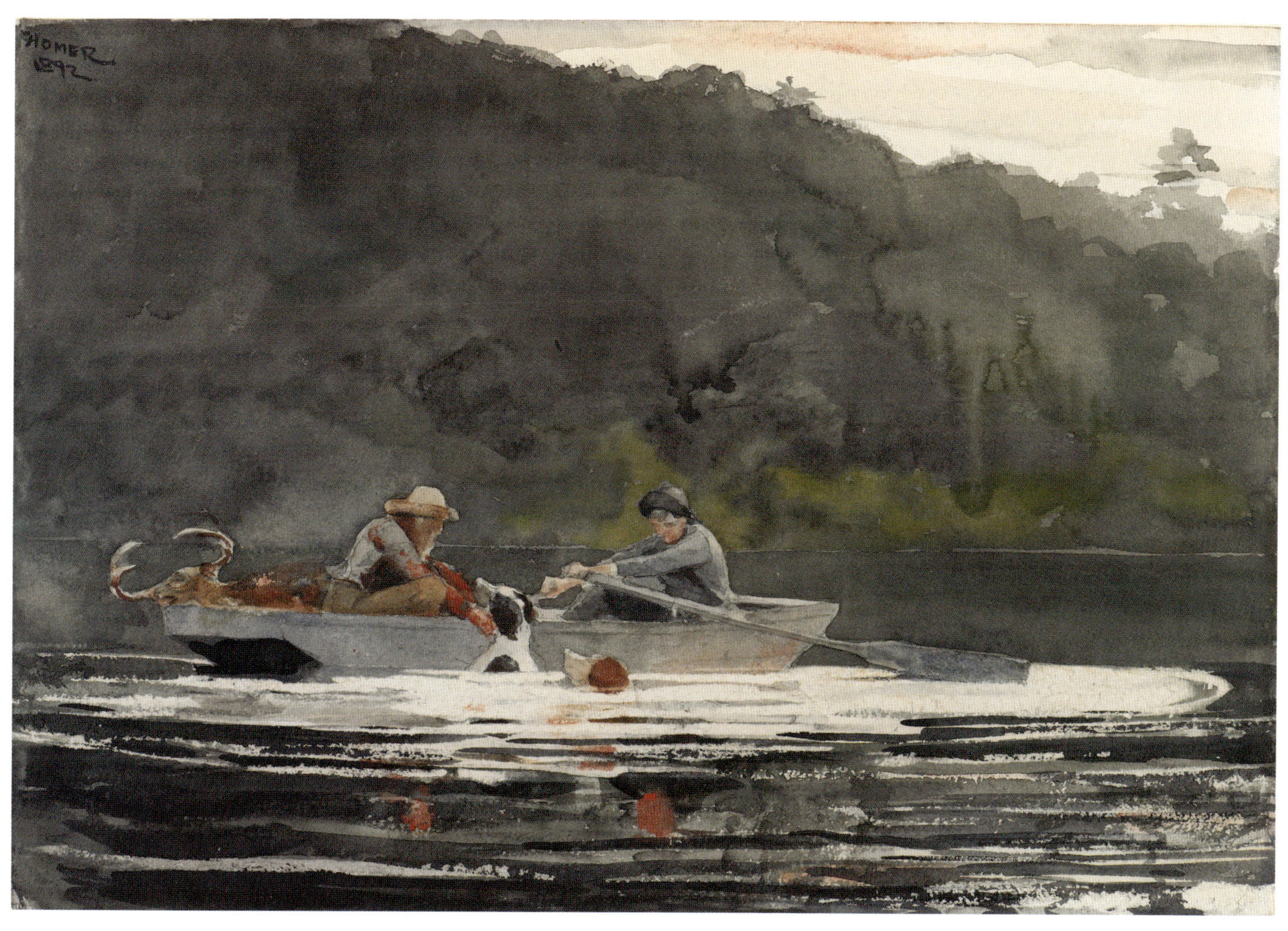

PLATE 51. Winslow Homer, *The End of the Hunt*, 1892. Watercolor over graphite, 15⅛ × 21⅜ in. (38.4 × 54.3 cm). Bowdoin College Museum of Art, Brunswick. Gift of Misses Harriet Sarah and Mary Sophia Walker. [1894.11]

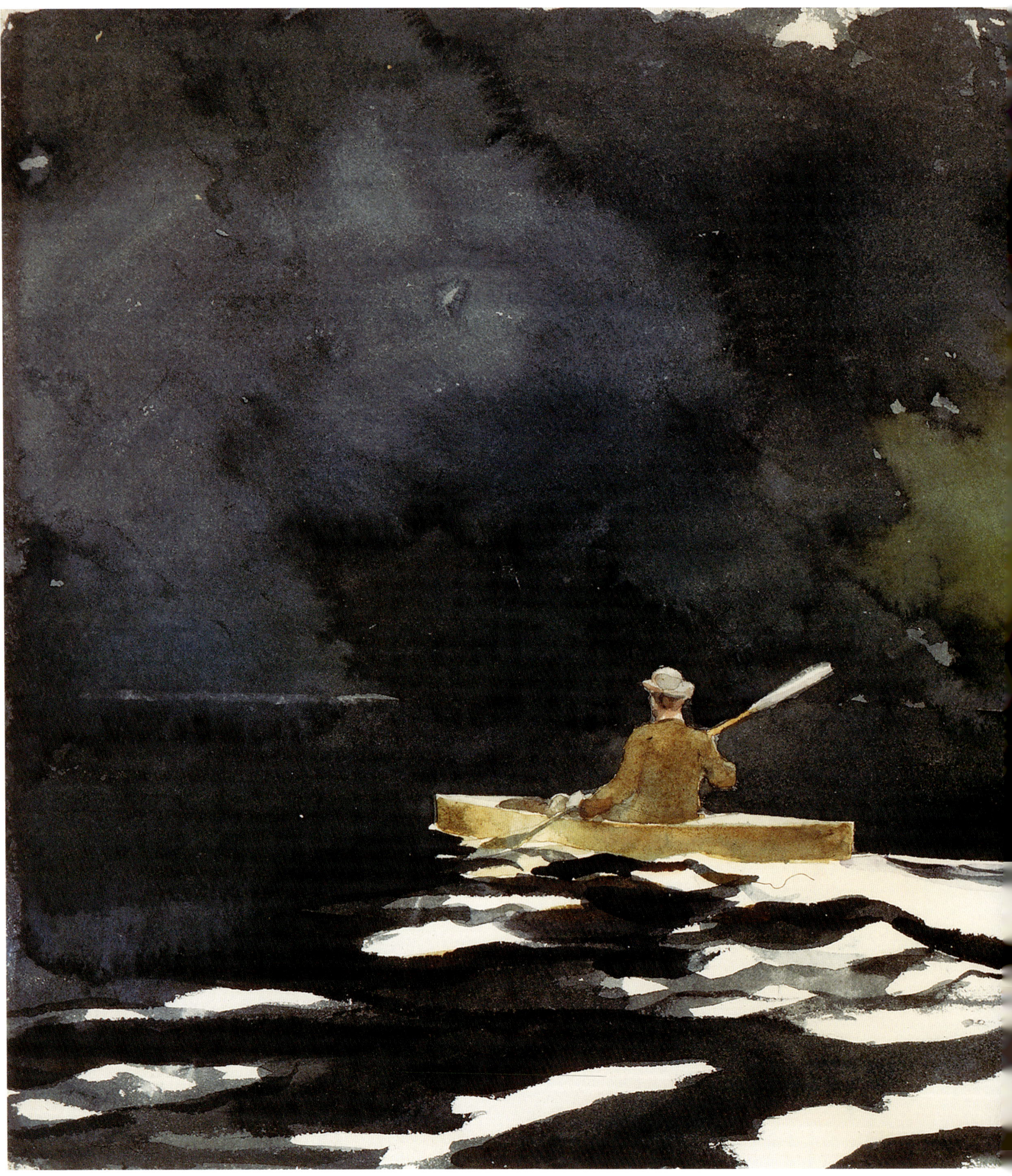

PLATE 52. Winslow Homer, *Paddling at Dusk*, 1892. Watercolor over graphite on wove paper, 15⅛ × 21⁷⁄₁₆ in. (38.4 × 54.5 cm). Memorial Art Gallery, University of Rochester. Gift of Dr. and Mrs. James H. Lockhart, Jr. [84.51]

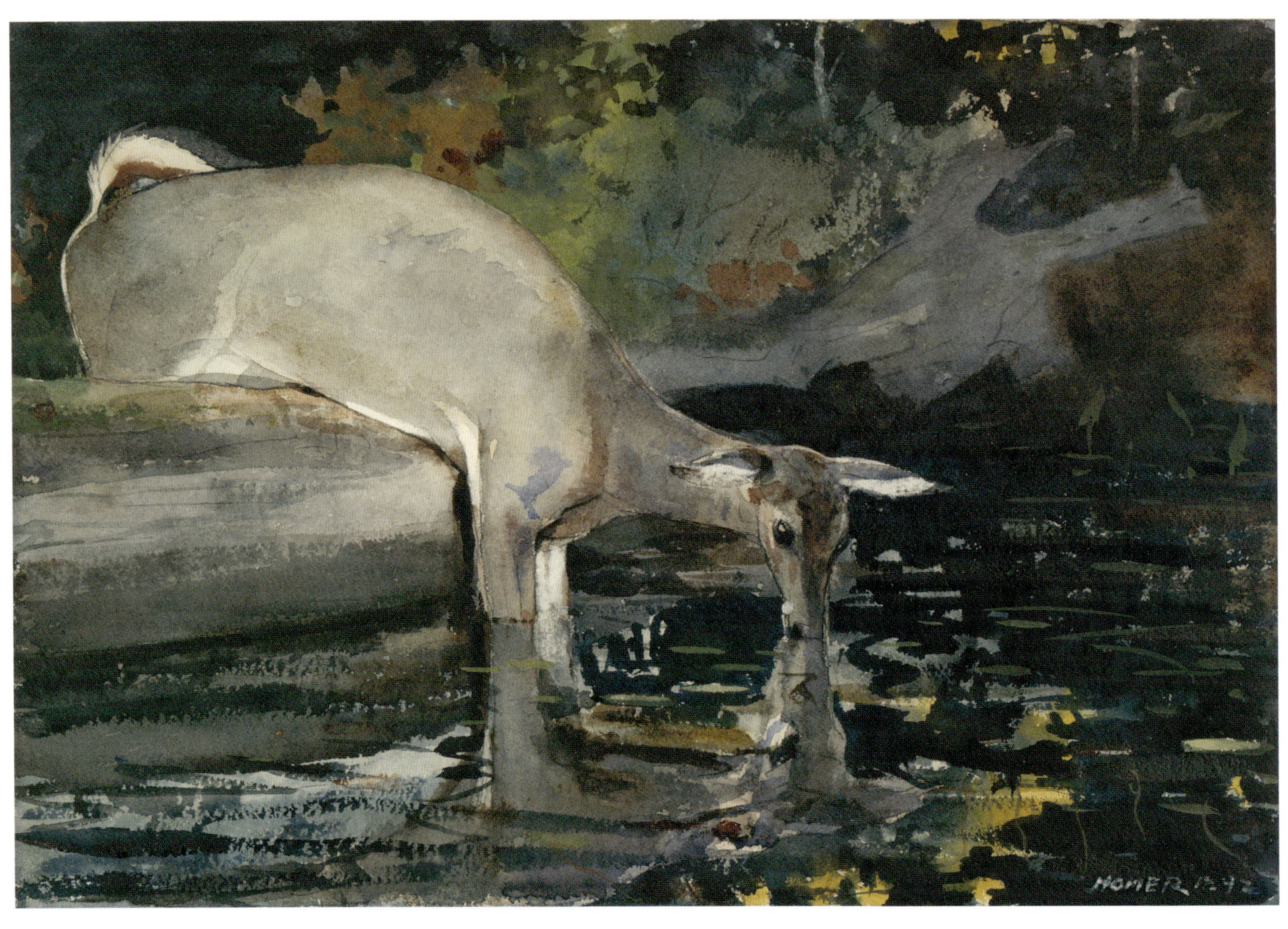

PLATE 53. Winslow Homer, *Deer Drinking*, 1892. Watercolor, $14\frac{1}{16} \times 20\frac{1}{16}$ in. (35.7 × 51 cm). Yale University Art Gallery, New Haven. Museum Purchase, The Robert W. Carle, B.A. 1897, Fund. [1976.36]

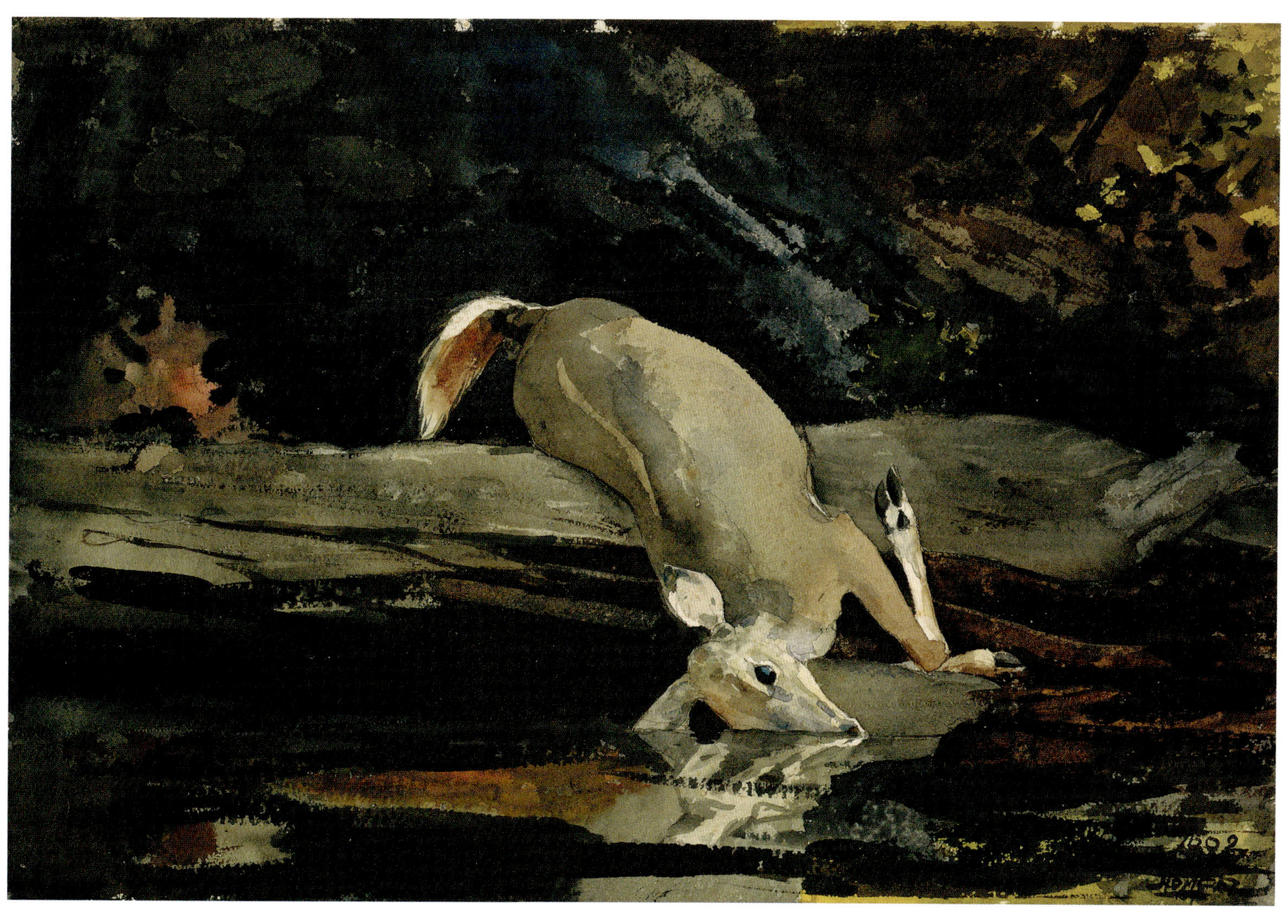

PLATE 54. Winslow Homer, *The Fallen Deer*, 1892. Watercolor over graphite pencil, 13⅞ × 19$\frac{13}{16}$ in. (35.2 × 50.3 cm). Museum of Fine Arts, Boston. Museum Purchase, Charles Henry Hayden Fund. [23.443]

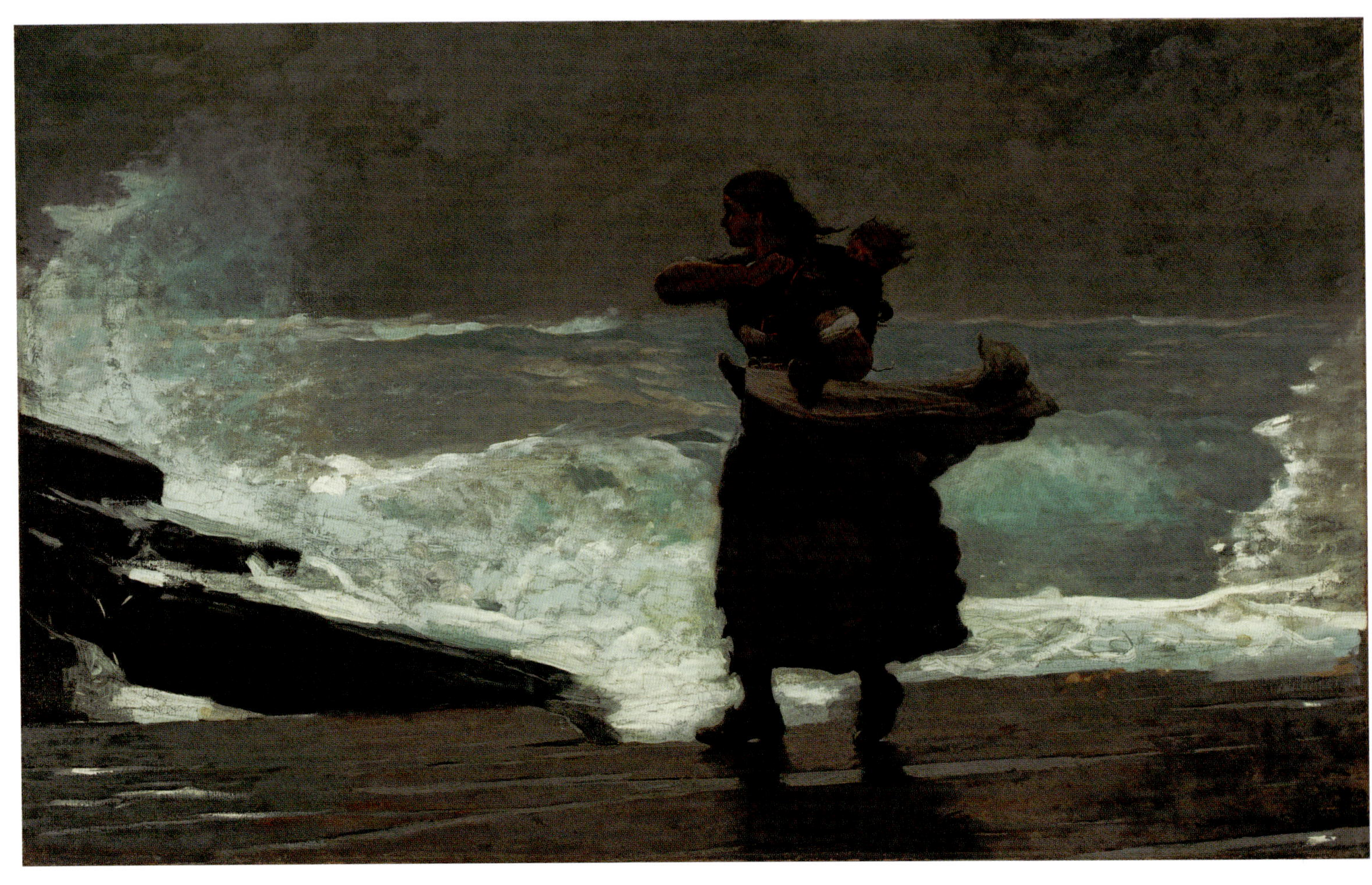

PLATE 55. Winslow Homer, *The Gale*, 1883–93. Oil on canvas, 30¼ × 48$\frac{5}{16}$ in. (76.8 × 122.7 cm). Worcester Art Museum. Museum Purchase. [1916.48]

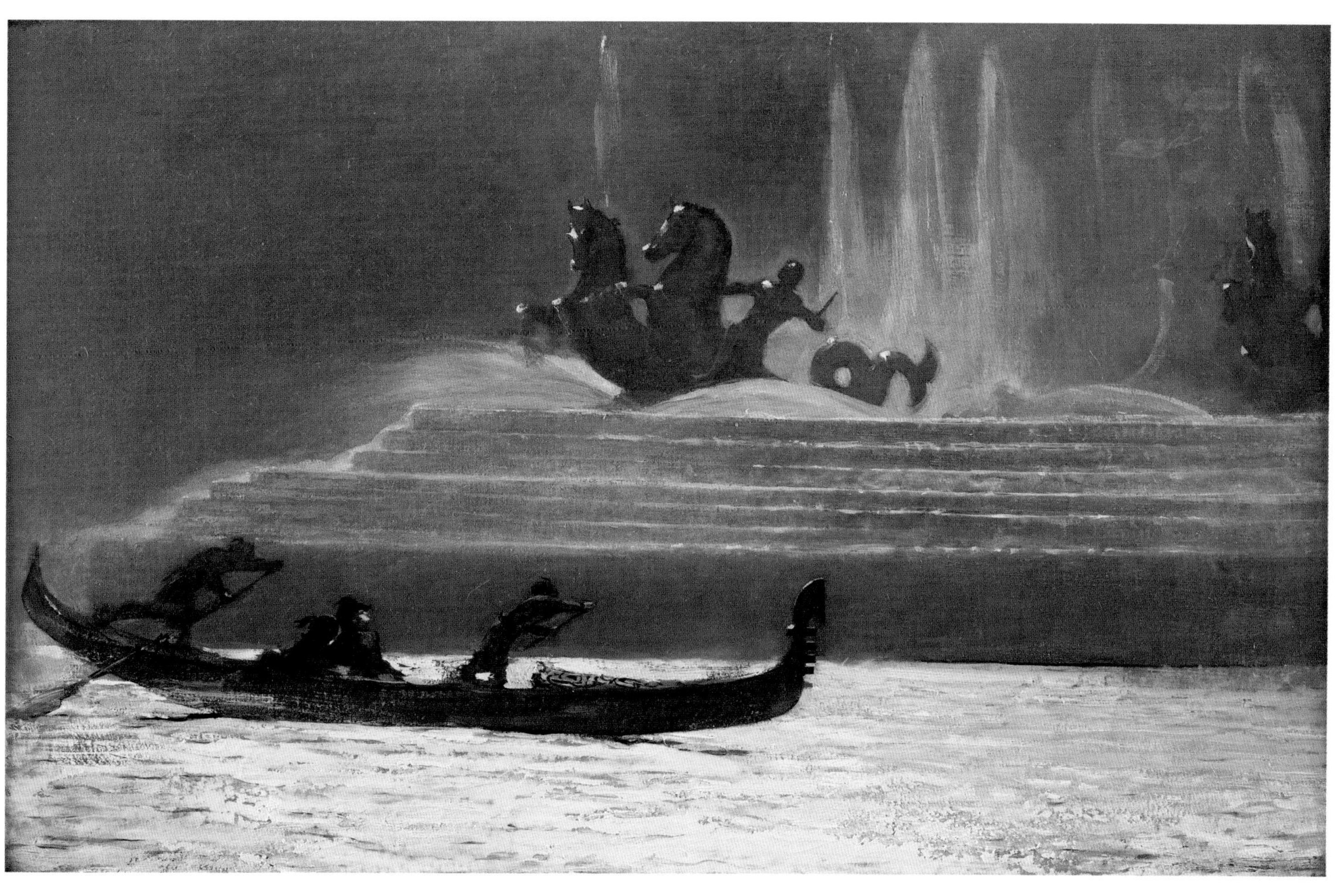

PLATE 56. Winslow Homer, *The Fountains at Night, World's Columbian Exposition,* 1893. Oil on canvas, 16⅜ × 25⅛ in. (41.6 × 63.8 cm). Bowdoin College Museum of Art, Brunswick. Bequest of Mrs. Charles Savage Homer, Jr. [1938.2]

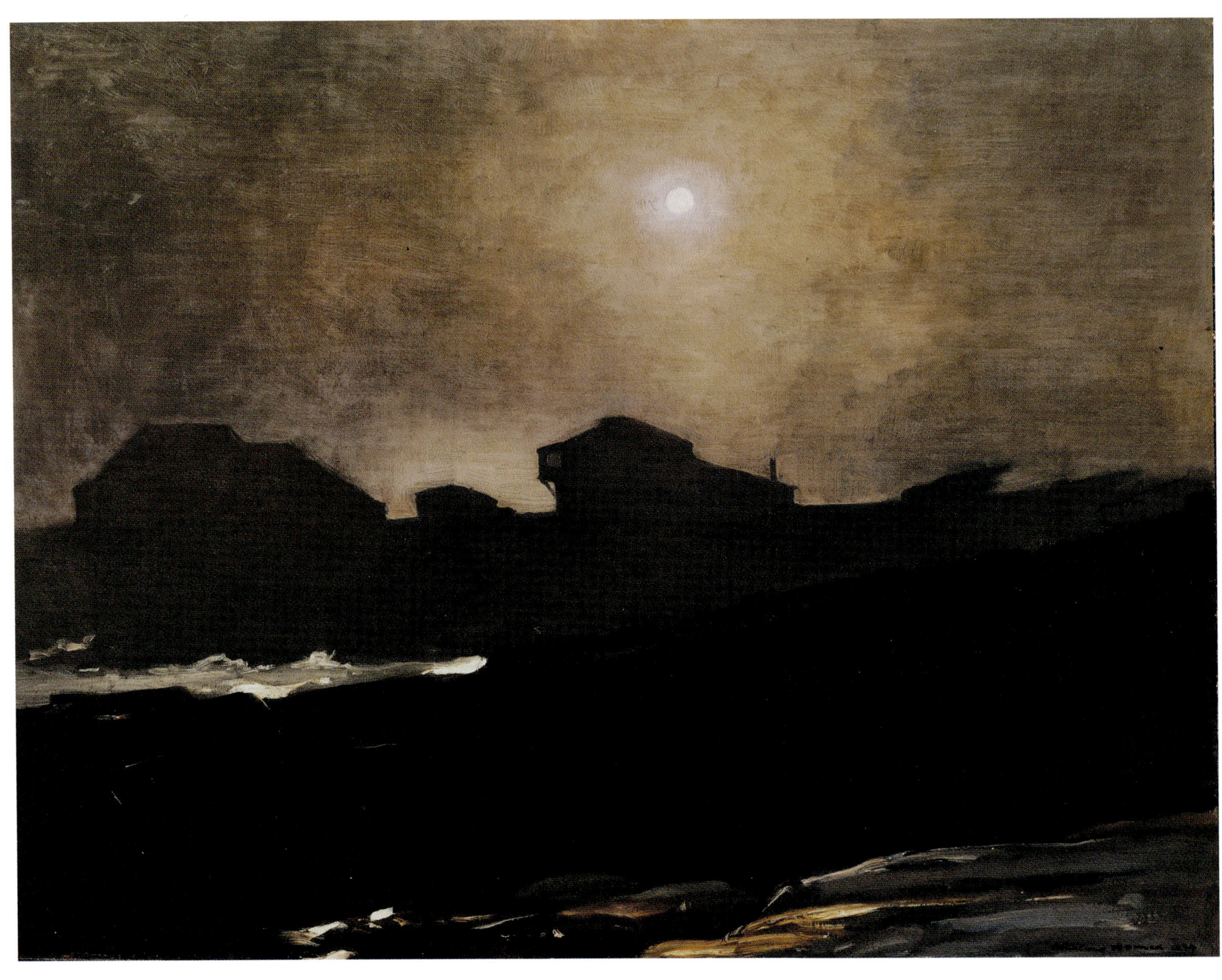

PLATE 57. Winslow Homer, *The Artist's Studio in an Afternoon Fog*, 1894. Oil on canvas, 24 × 30¼ in. (60.9 × 76.8 cm). Memorial Art Gallery, University of Rochester. Museum Purchase, R. T. Miller Fund. [41.32]

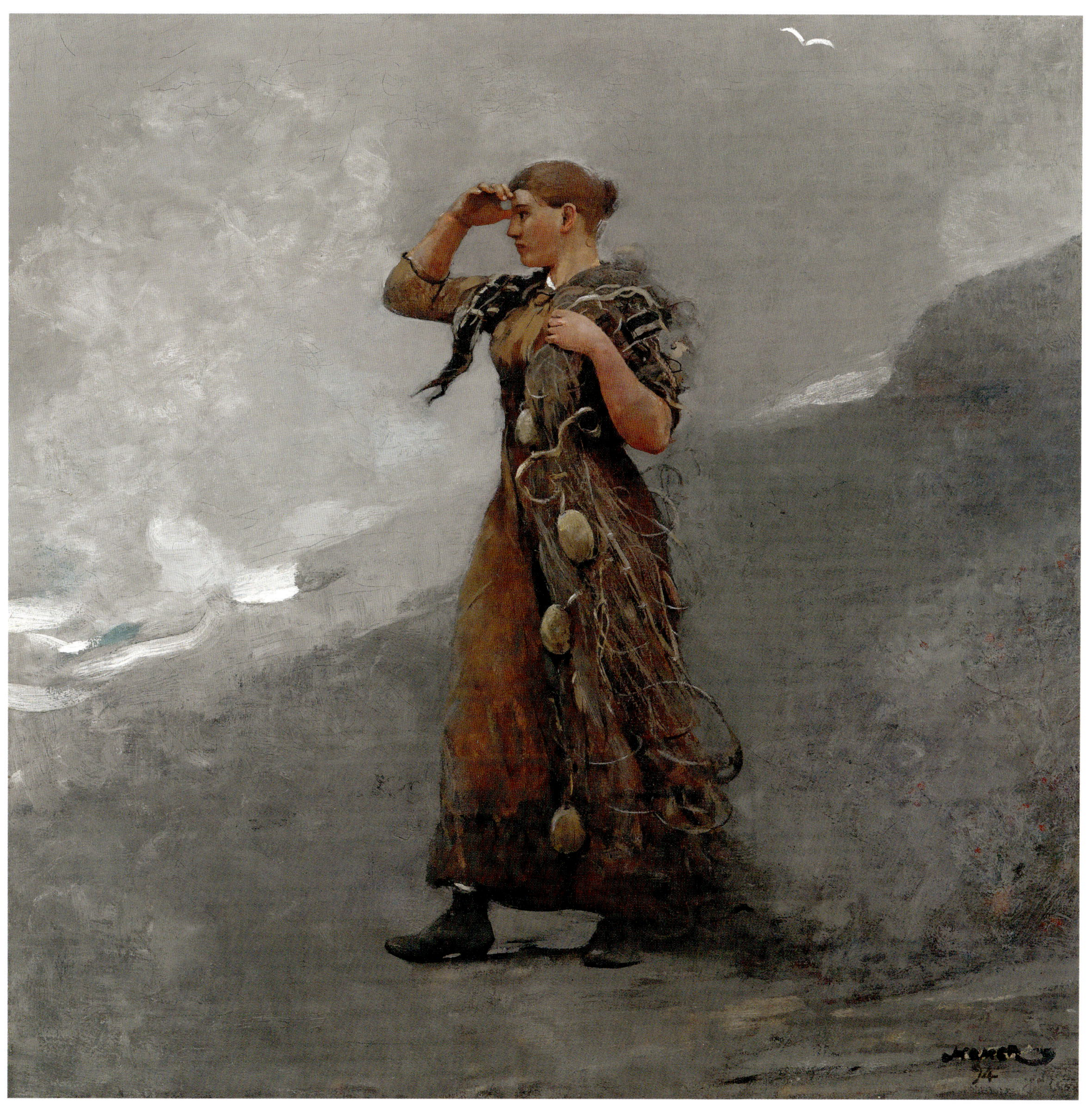

PLATE 58. Winslow Homer, *The Fisher Girl*, 1894. Oil on canvas, 28¼ × 28¼ in. (71.8 × 71.8 cm). Mead Art Museum, Amherst College. Gift of George D. Pratt, Class of 1893. [1933.7]

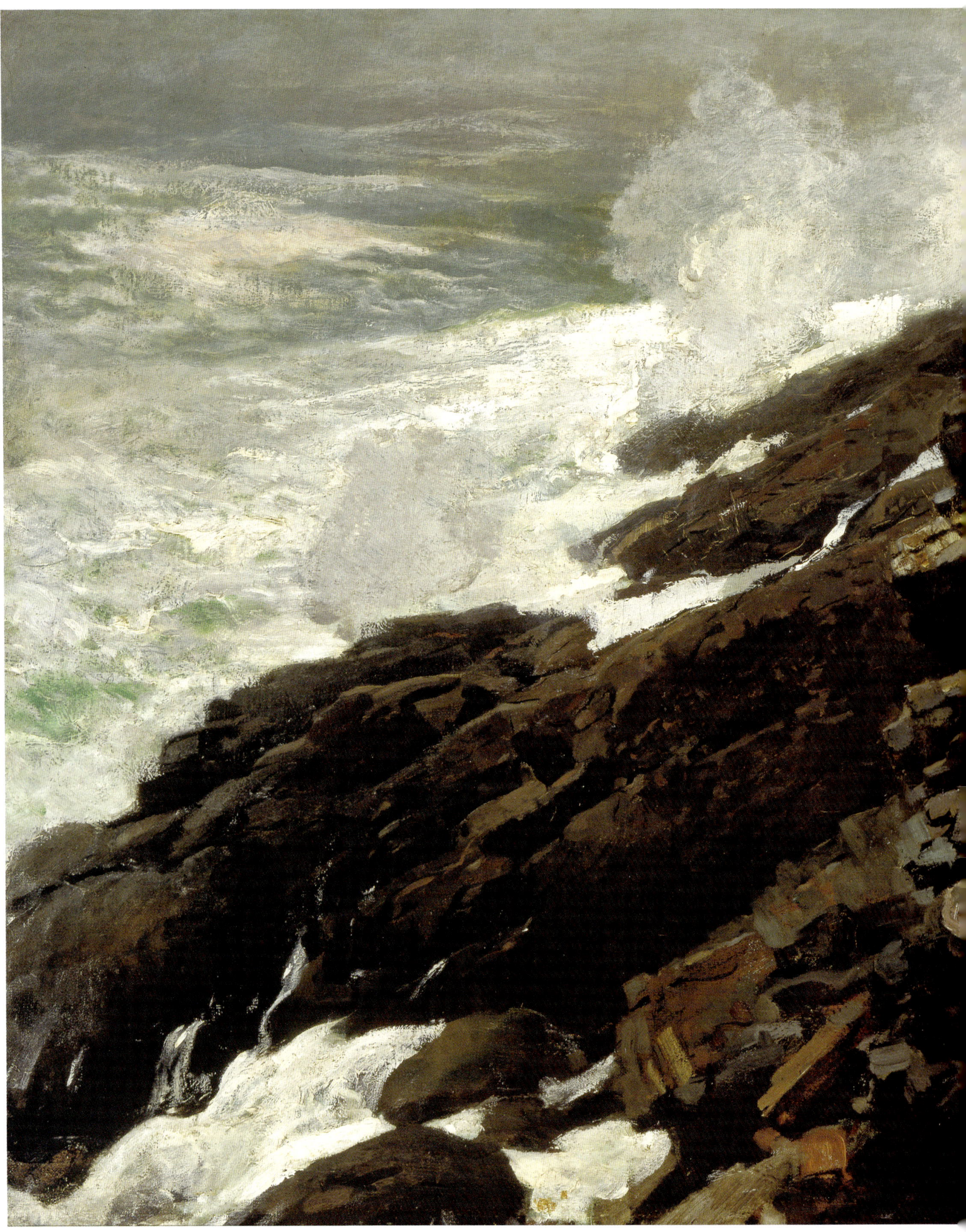

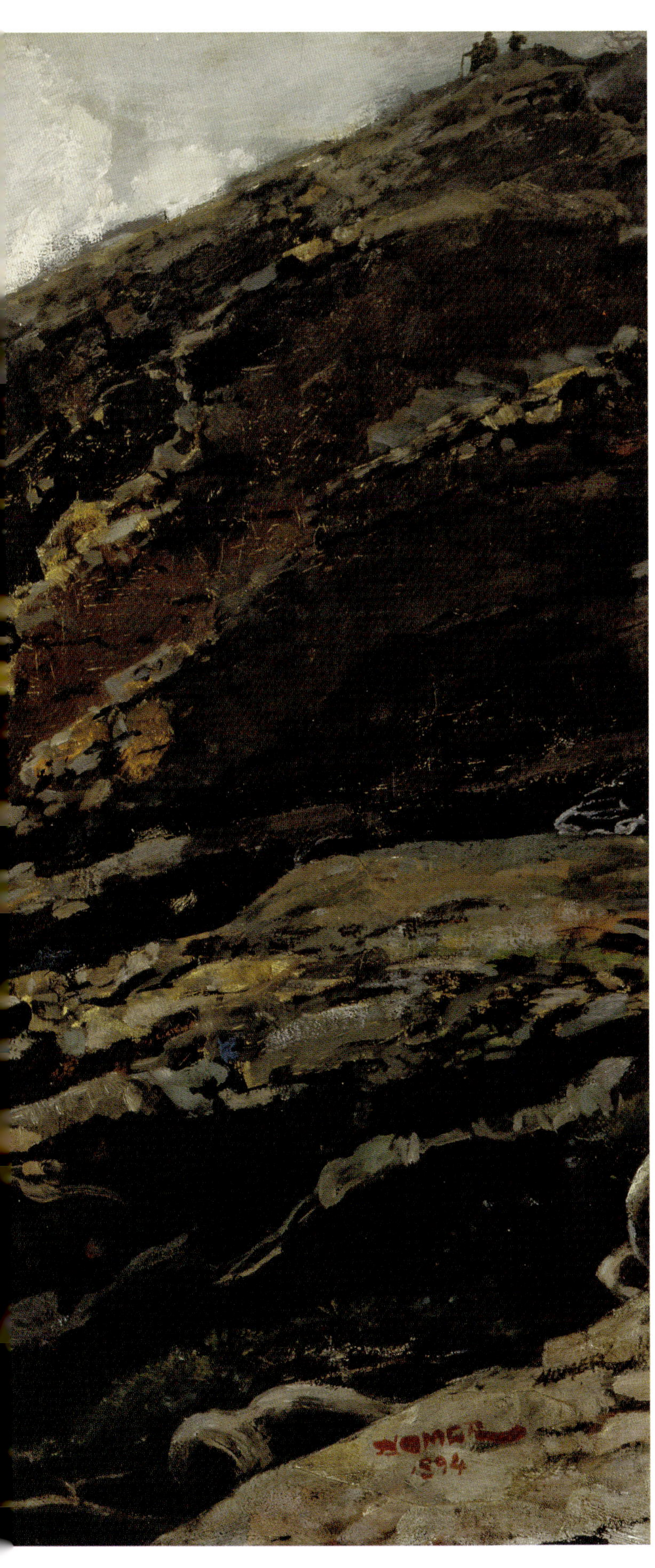

PLATE 59. Winslow Homer, *High Cliff, Coast of Maine,* 1894. Oil on canvas, 30¼ × 38¼ in. (76.8 × 97.2 cm). Smithsonian American Art Museum, Washington. Gift of William T. Evans. [1909.7.29]

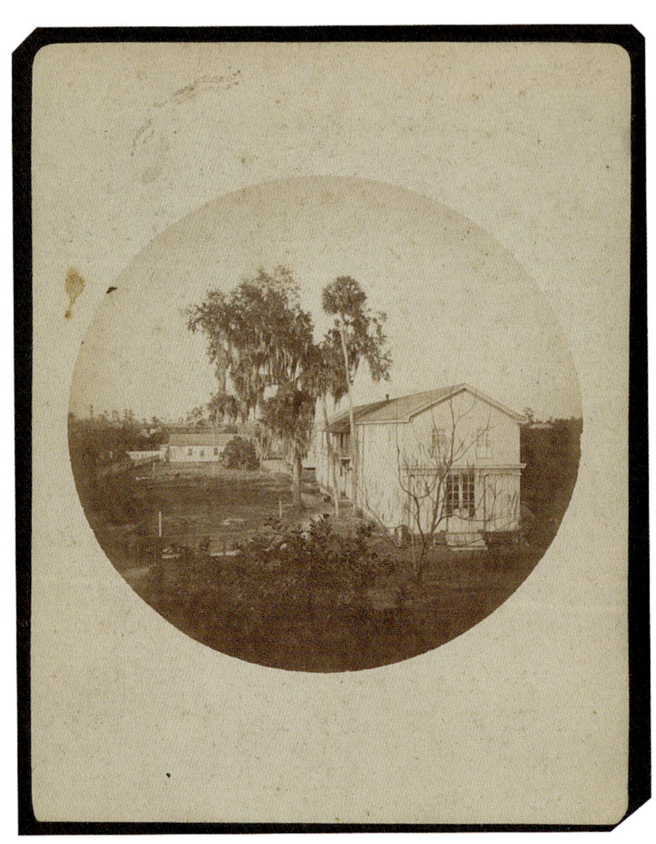

PLATE 60A. Winslow Homer, *Tropical Scene*, c. 1895. Gelatin silver print, 2⅝ × 2⅝ in. (6.7 × 6.7 cm), image. Bowdoin College Museum of Art, Brunswick. Gift of the Homer Family. [1964.69.180]

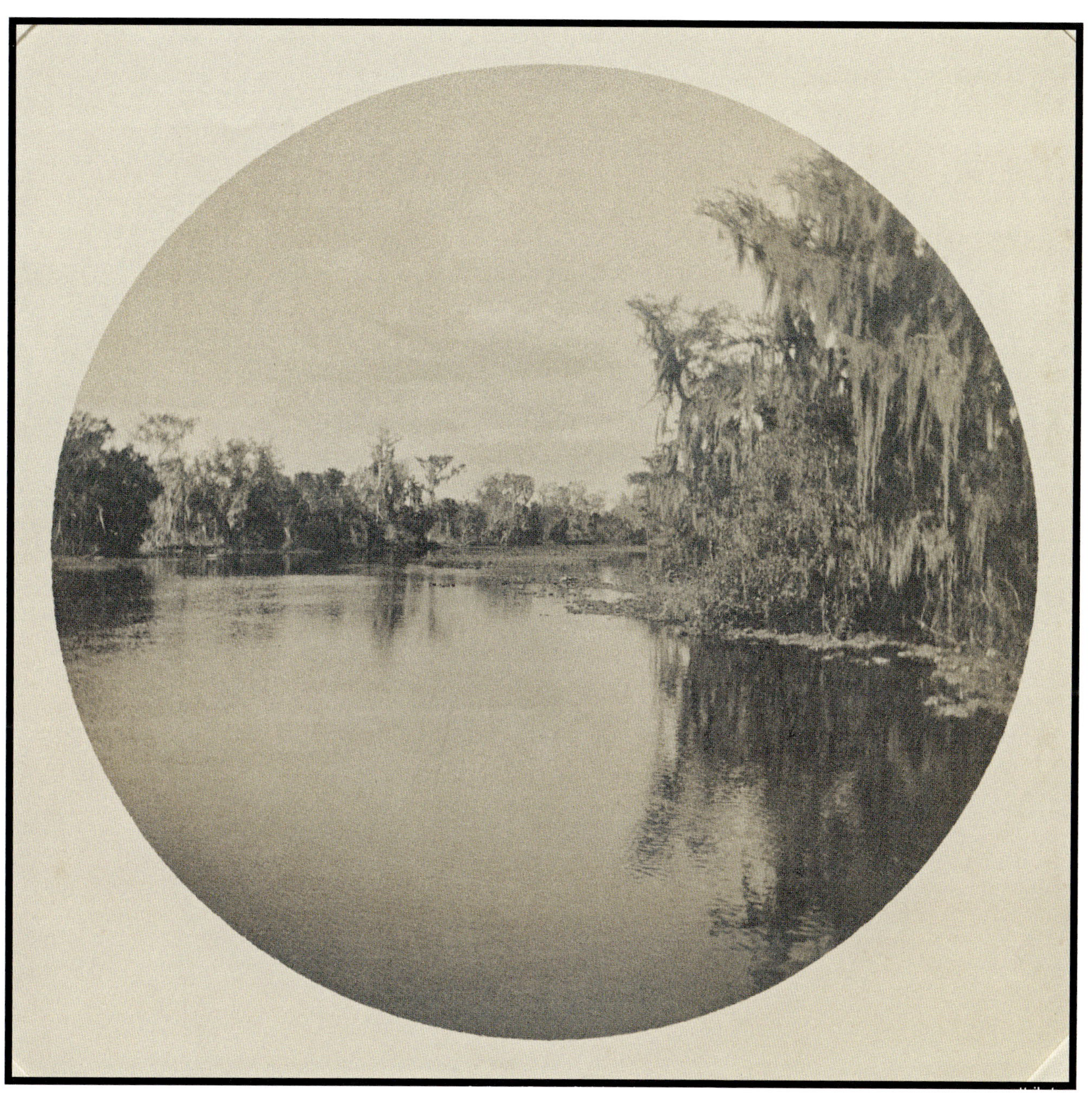

PLATE 60B. Attributed to Winslow Homer, *River Scene, Florida*, c. 1904–5. Gelatin silver print, enlargement from original "Kodak" sheet: 17 × 13½ in. (43.2 × 34.3 cm). Sterling and Francine Clark Art Institute, Williamstown, Massachusetts, acquired with funds donated by the Fitzpatrick Family. [1999.12]

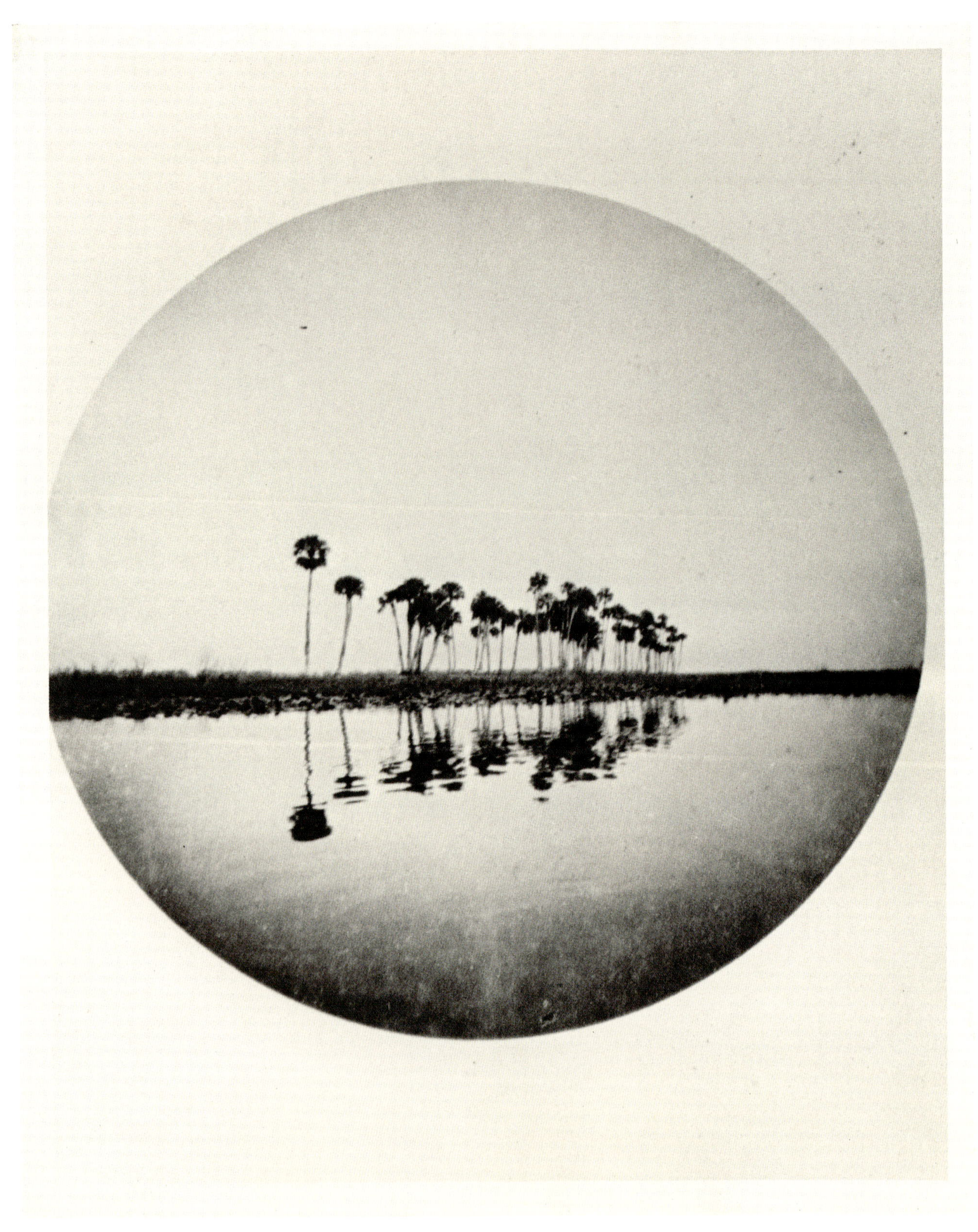

PLATE 60C. Winslow Homer, *Palm Trees*, c. 1904. Gelatin silver copy print, 10 × 8 in. (25.4 × 20.3 cm). The Museum of Fine Arts, Houston. Museum Purchase. [72.17]

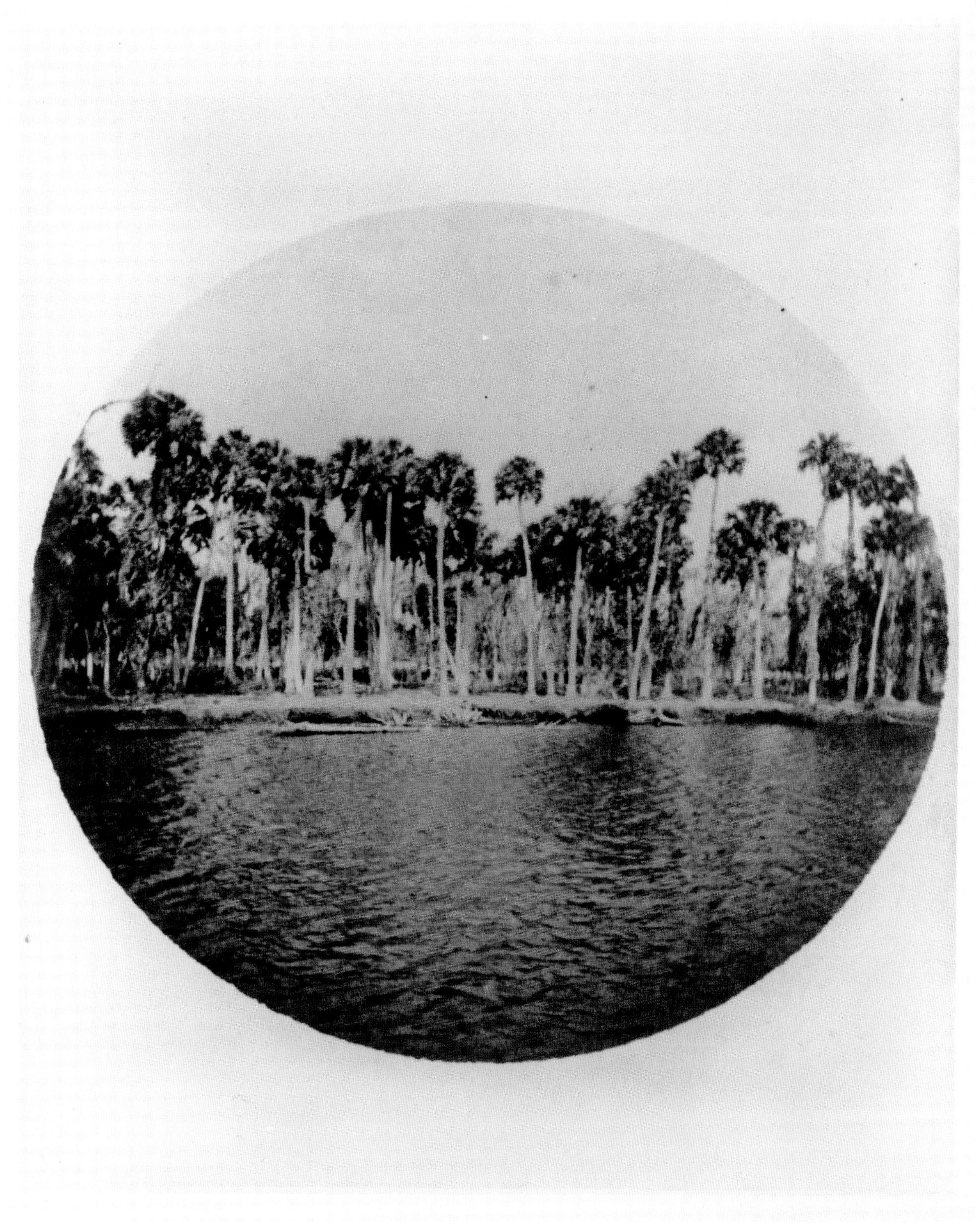

PLATE 60D. Winslow Homer, *St. Johns River, Florida*, c. 1895. Gelatin silver print. Location unknown. Image courtesy of Bowdoin College Museum of Art, Brunswick. Gift of the Homer Family. [HomerMemorabilia38.5]

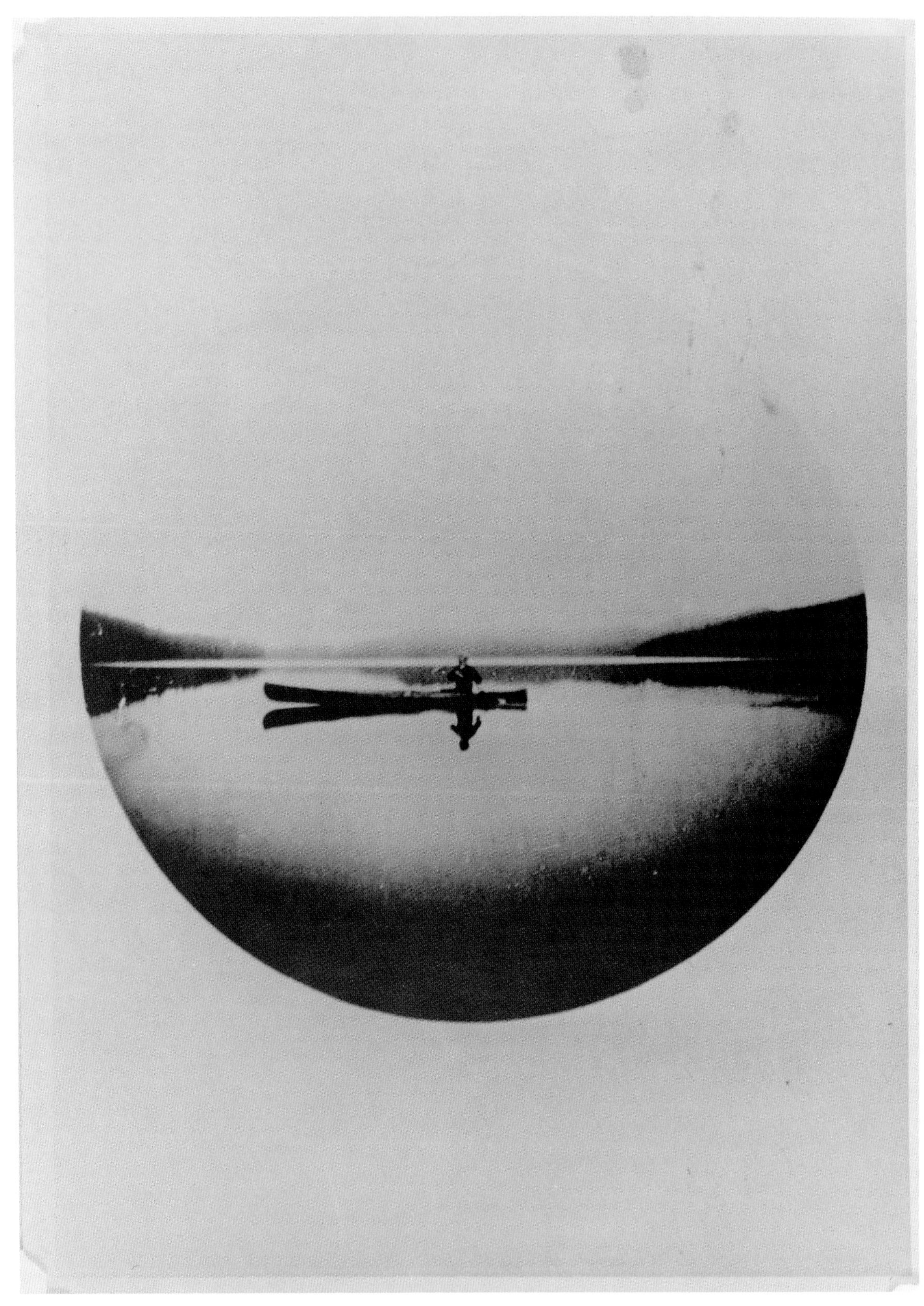

PLATE 60E. Winslow Homer, *Winslow Homer in a Canoe*, c. 1895. Gelatin silver print. Location unknown. Image courtesy of Bowdoin College Museum of Art, Brunswick. Gift of the Homer Family. [HomerMemorabilia38.1]

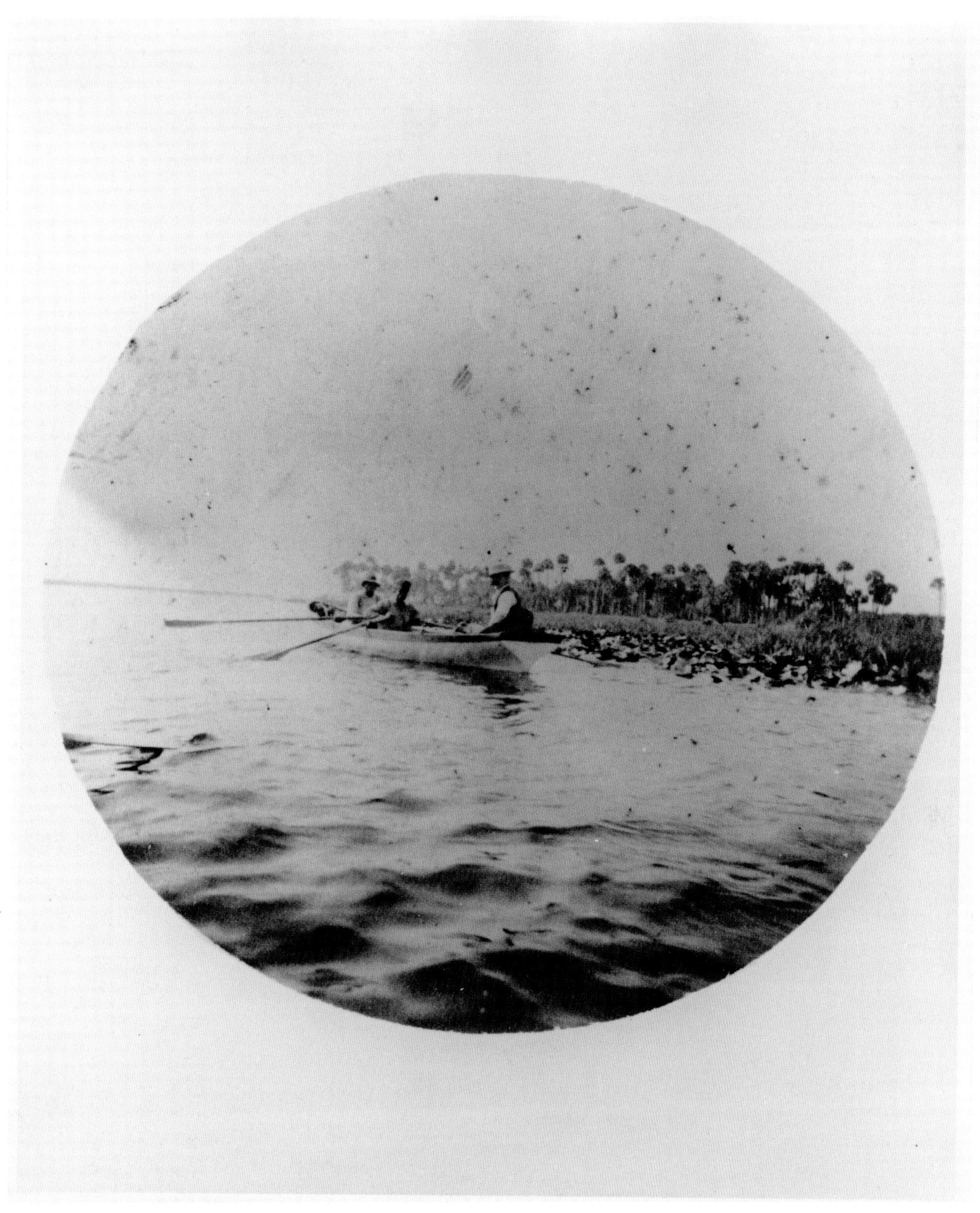

PLATE 60F. Unidentified photographer, *Winslow Homer and Guides, Homosassa River, Florida*, c. 1895. Gelatin silver print. Location unknown. Image courtesy of Bowdoin College Museum of Art, Brunswick. Gift of the Homer Family. [HomerMemorabilia38.2]

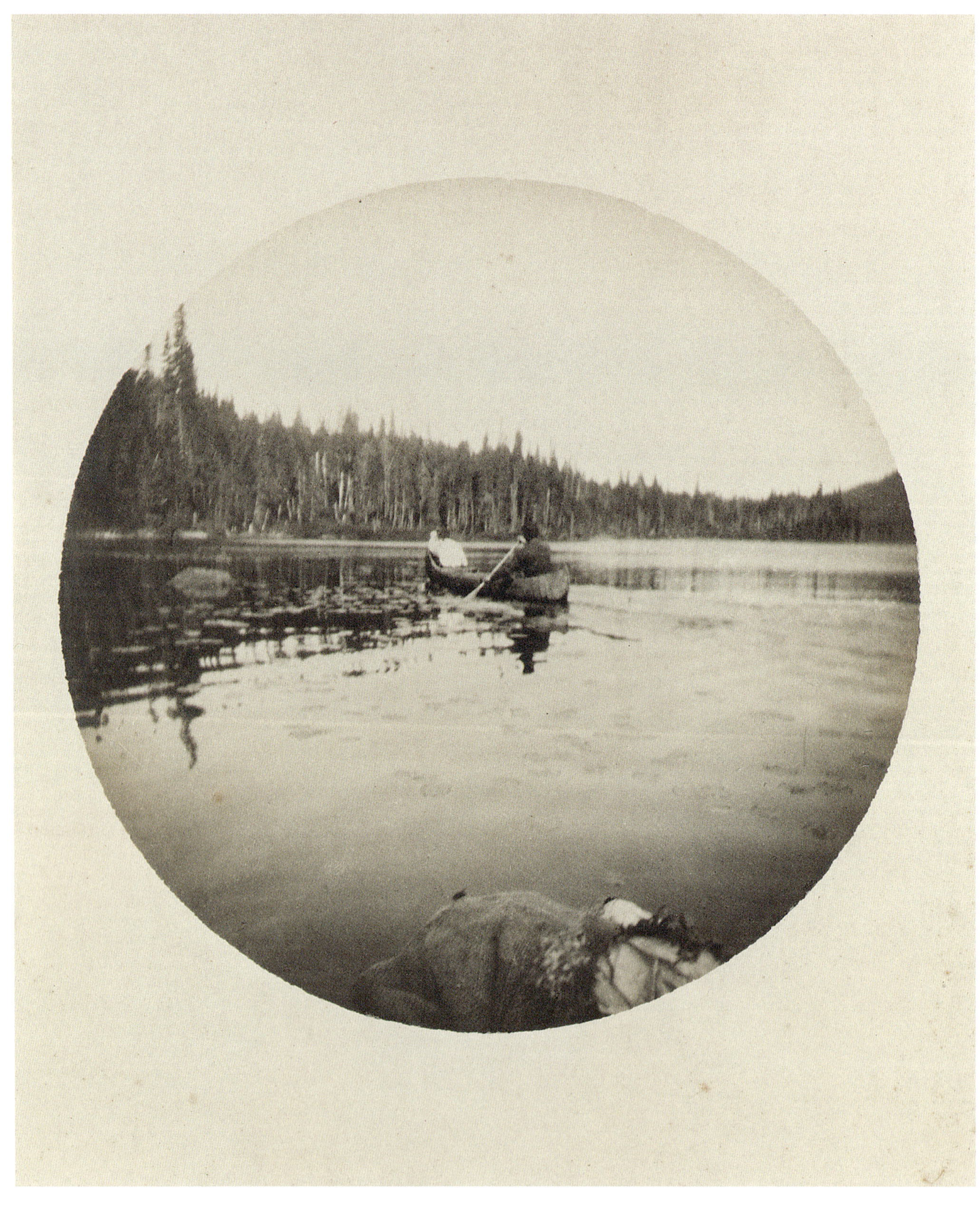

PLATE 60G. Winslow Homer, *Two Canoeists, Lake St. John, Province of Quebec,* c. 1895. Gelatin silver print. Location unknown. Image courtesy of Christie's Images Limited © 1999.

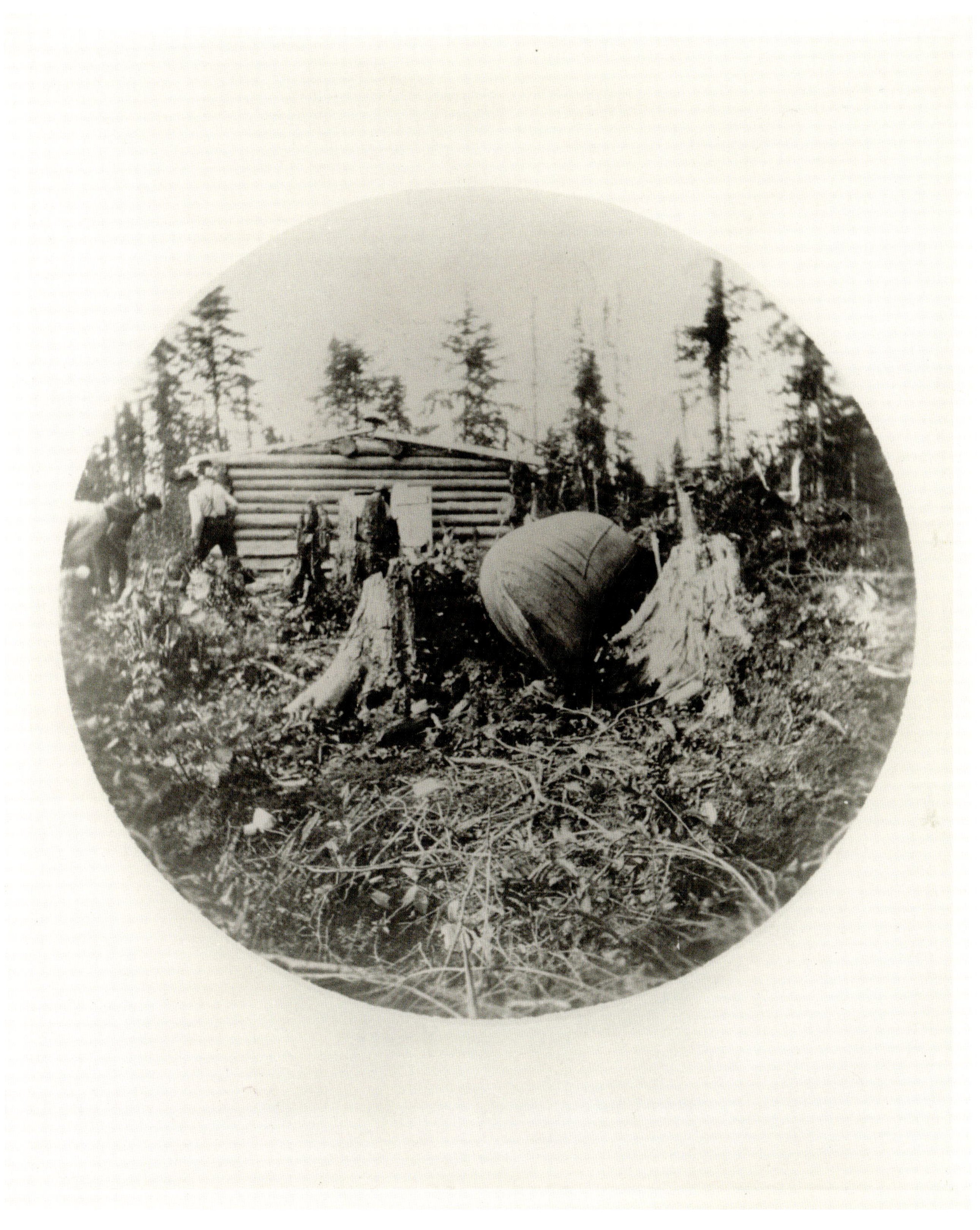

PLATE 60H. Winslow Homer, *Cabin at the Tourilli Club, Province of Quebec*, c. 1895. Gelatin silver print. Location unknown. Image courtesy of Bowdoin College Museum of Art, Brunswick. Gift of the Homer Family. [HomerMemorabilia38.6]

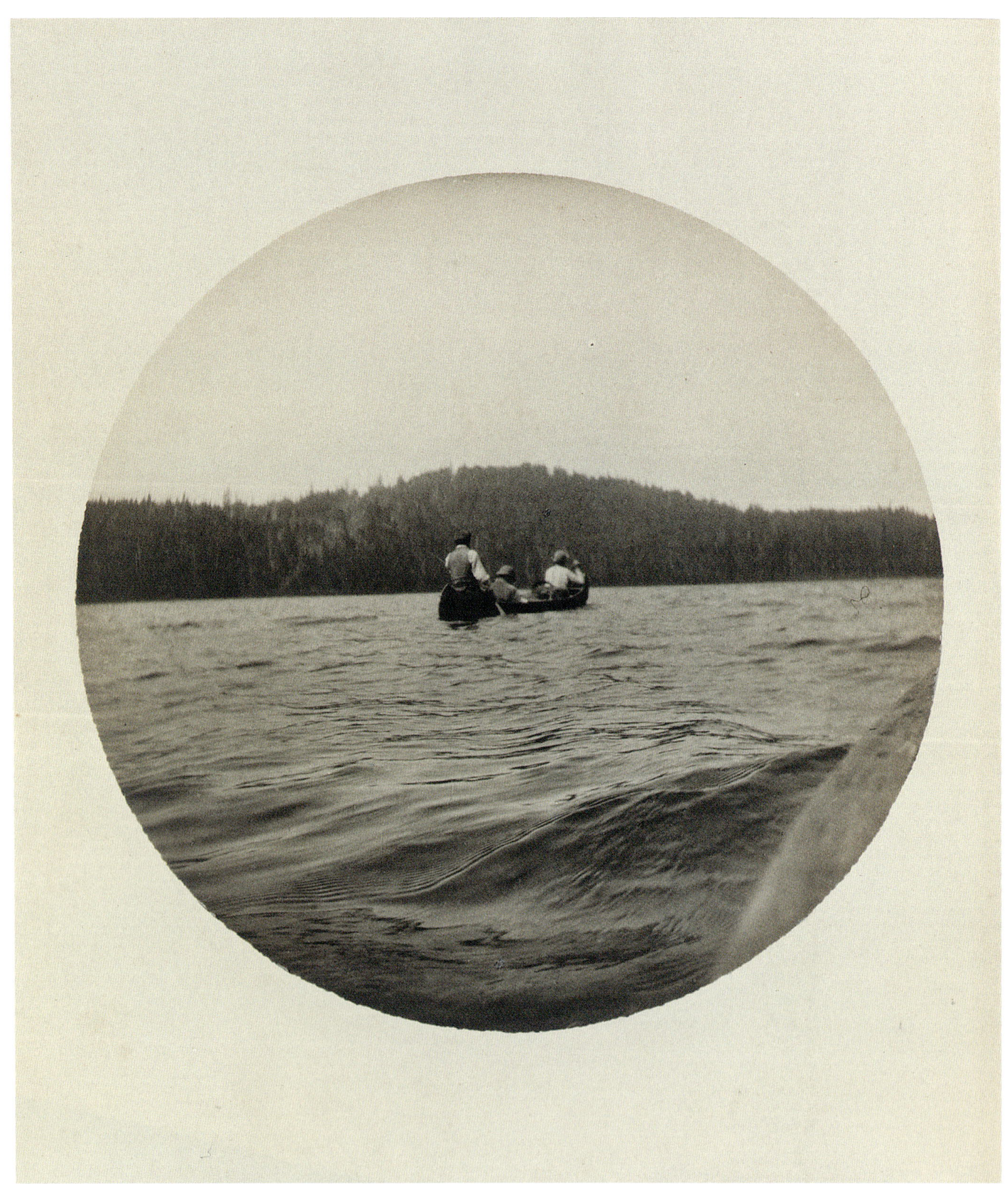

PLATE 601. Winslow Homer, *Three Canoeists, Lake St. John, Province of Quebec,* c. 1895. Gelatin silver print. Location unknown. Image courtesy of Christie's Images Limited © 1999.

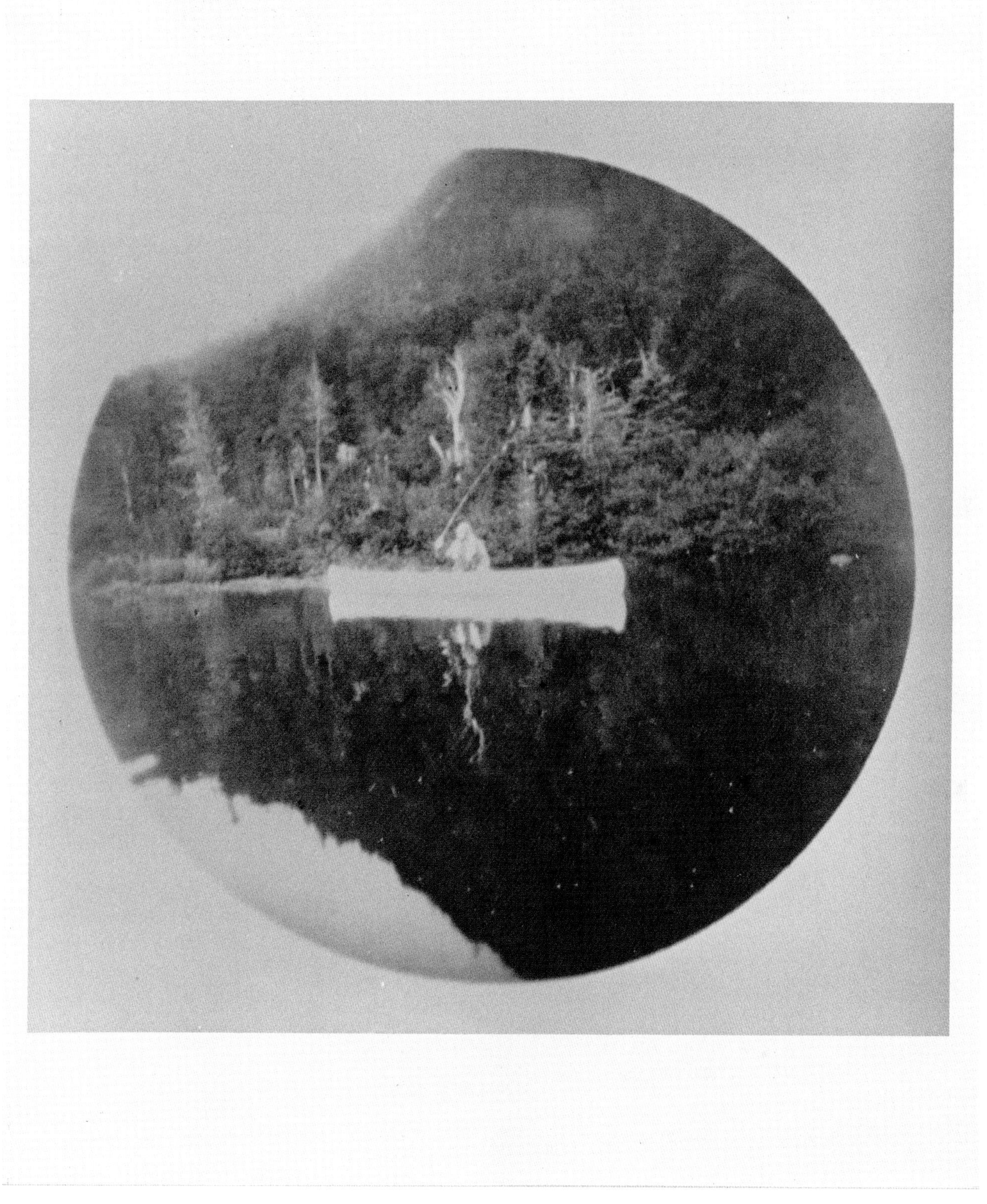

PLATE 60J. Winslow Homer, *Fisherman, Adirondacks*, c. 1894. Gelatin silver copy print, 10 × 8 in. (25.4 × 20.3 cm). The Museum of Fine Arts, Houston. Museum Purchase. [72.16]

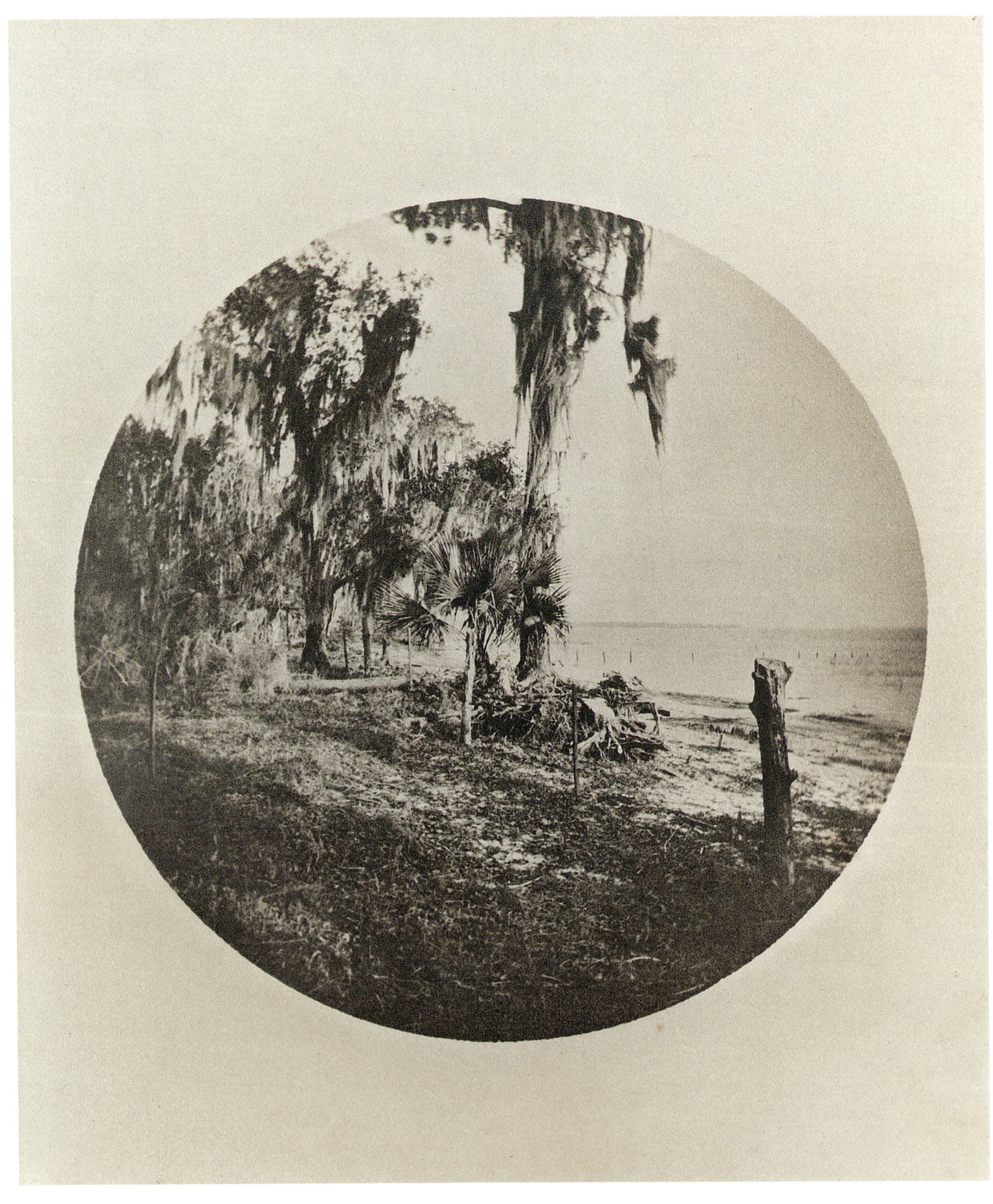

PLATE 60K. Winslow Homer, *Palm Tree and Beach Scene, Florida Coast*, c. 1895. Gelatin silver print. Location unknown. Image courtesy of Christie's Images Limited © 1999.

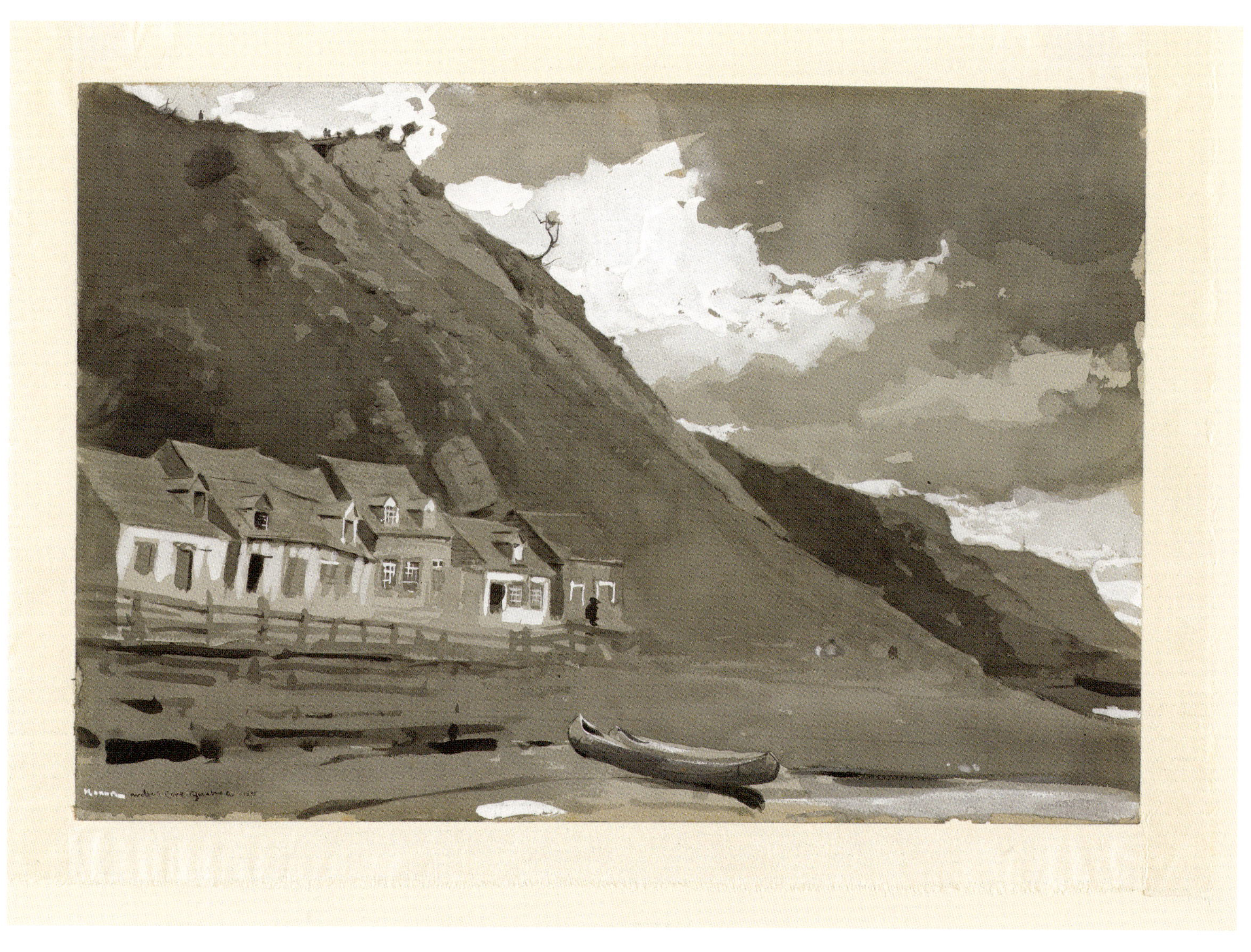

PLATE 61. Winslow Homer, *Wolfe's Cove, Quebec*, 1895. Watercolor and gouache over graphite, 13⅞ × 20 in. (35.2 × 50.8 cm). Bowdoin College Museum of Art, Brunswick. Museum Purchase, with donations from Neal W. Allen, Class of 1907, John F. Dana, Class of 1898, John H. Halford, Class of 1907, William W. Lawrence, Class of 1898, and Benjamin R. Shute, Class of 1931. [1955.2]

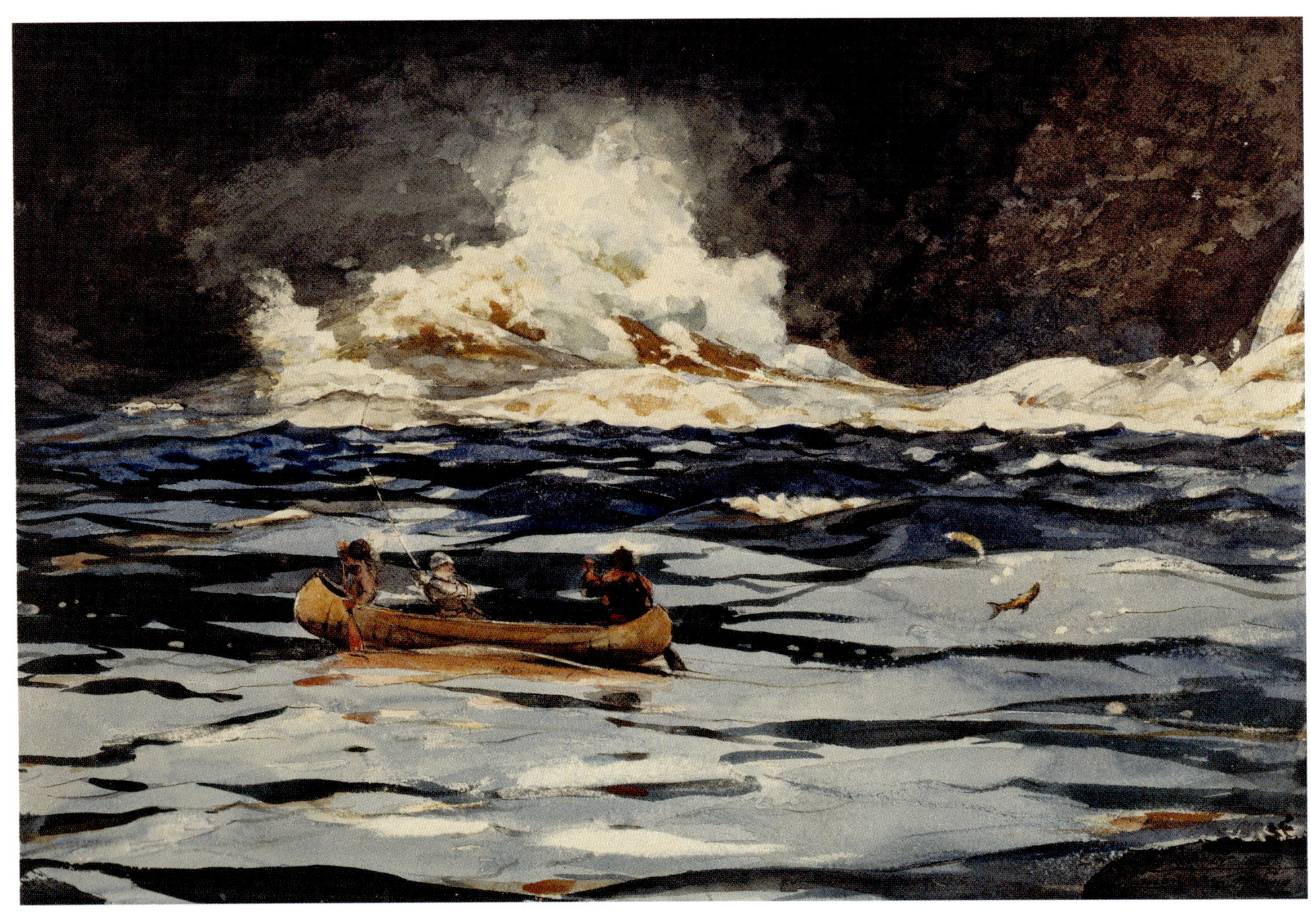

PLATE 62. Winslow Homer, *Under the Falls, the Grand Discharge*, 1895. Transparent watercolor over graphite with touches of opaque watercolor and gold leaf, and possibly brown ink, on cream, moderately thick, slightly textured wove paper, 12⅞ × 19⅞ in. (32.7 × 50.5 cm). Brooklyn Museum. Bequest of Helen Babbott Sanders. [78.151.2]

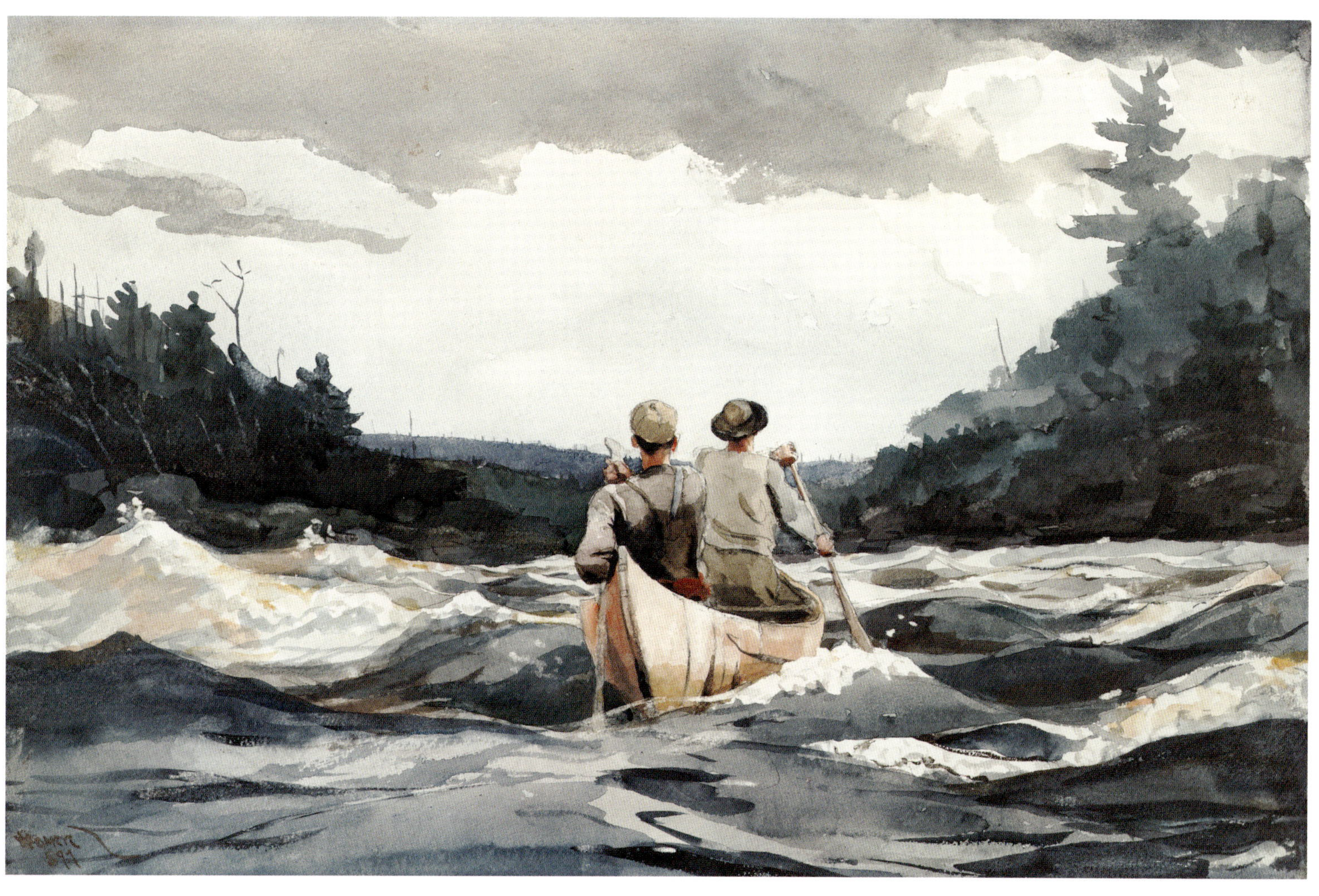

PLATE 63. Winslow Homer, *Canoe in Rapids*, 1897. Watercolor over graphite, 13 15/16 × 21 in. (35.4 × 53.3 cm). Harvard Art Museums/Fogg Museum, Cambridge. Museum Purchase, Louise E. Bettens Fund. [1924.30]

PLATE 64. Winslow Homer, *The Turkey Buzzard*, 1904. Watercolor over graphite, 13 15/16 × 19 3/4 in. (35.4 × 50.1 cm). Worcester Art Museum. Museum Purchase. [1917.6]

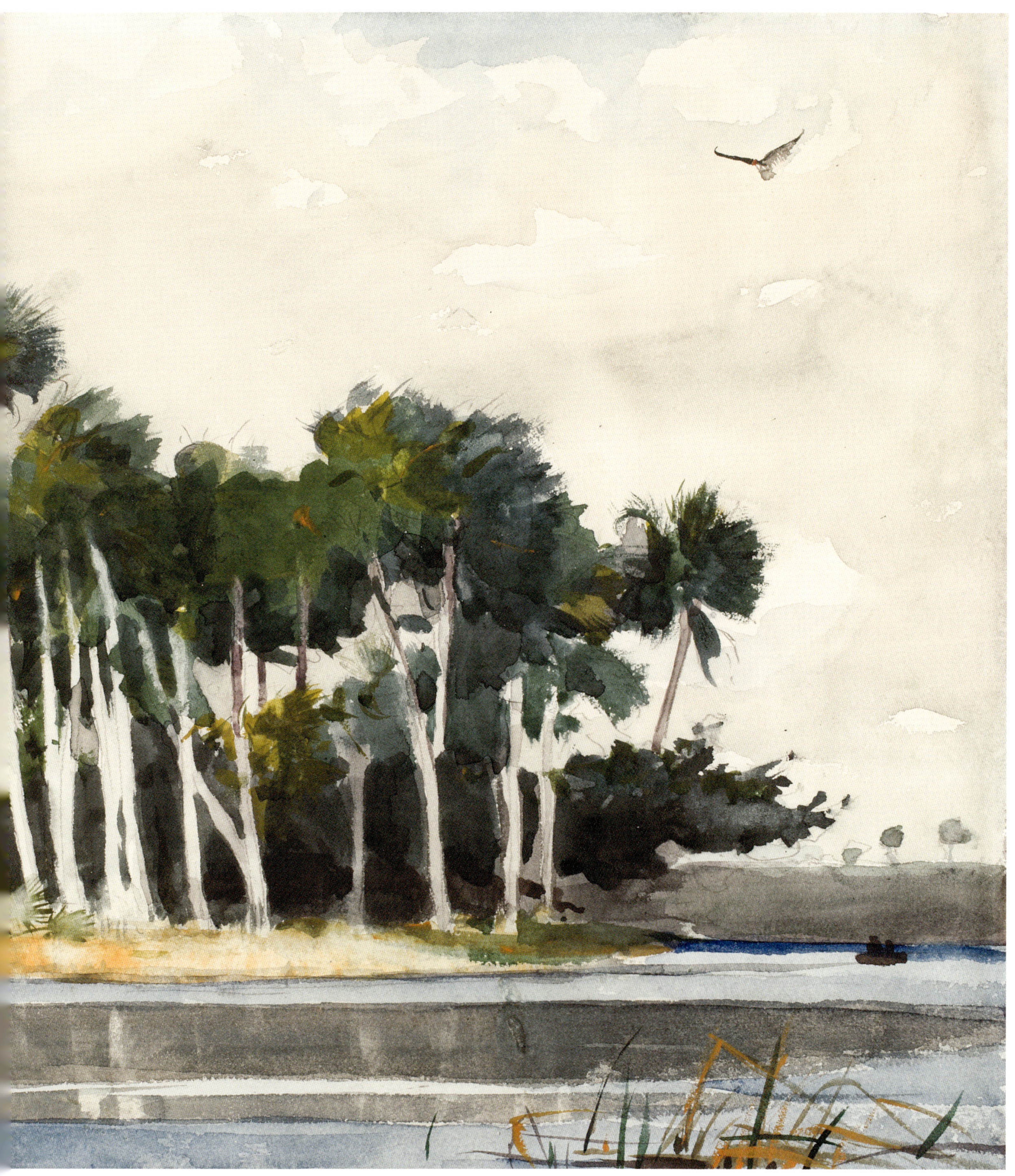

SELECTED BIBLIOGRAPHY

Adams, Henry. "Mortal Themes: Winslow Homer." *Art in America* 71 (February 1983): 112–26.

Aldrich, Thomas. "Among the Studios." *Our Young Folks* 2, no. 7 (July 1866): 393–98.

Athens, Elizabeth, et al. *Coming Away: Winslow Homer and England*. New Haven, Conn.: Yale University Press, 2017.

Beam, Philip. *Winslow Homer at Prout's Neck*. New York: Little, Brown, 1966.

———. *Winslow Homer's Magazine Engravings*. New York: Harper & Row, 1979.

Beaux, Cecilia. *Background with Figures*. Boston: Houghton Mifflin, 1930.

Boylan, Alexis. "From Gilded Age to Gone with the Wind: The Plantation in Early Twentieth-Century Art." In *Landscape of Slavery: The Plantation in American Art*, edited by Angela D. Mack and Stephen G. Hoffius, 115–39. Columbia: University of South Carolina Press, 2008.

Burnham, Patricia, and Lucretia Giese, eds. *Redefining American History Painting*. Cambridge: Cambridge University Press, 1995.

Burns, Sarah. "Barefoot Boys and Other Country Children: Sentiment and Ideology in Nineteenth-Century American Art." *American Art Journal* 20, no. 1 (1988): 24–50.

———. *Inventing the Modern Artist: Art and Culture in Gilded Age America*. New Haven, Conn.: Yale University Press, 1996.

———. "Revitalizing the 'Painted-Out' North: Winslow Homer, Manly Health, and New England Regionalism in Turn-of-the-Century America." *American Art* 9, no. 2 (Summer 1995): 20–37.

———. "Winslow Homer and the Natural Woman." In *American Victorians and Virgin Nature*, edited by T. J. Jackson Lears, 16–38. Boston: Isabella Stewart Gardner Museum, 2002.

Calo, Mary Ann. "Winslow Homer's Visits to Virginia During Reconstruction." *American Art Journal* 12 (Winter 1980): 4–27.

Chase, J. Eastman. "Some Recollections of Winslow Homer." *Harper's Weekly* 54 (October 22, 1910): 13.

Cikovsky, Nicolai, Jr., ed. *Winslow Homer: A Symposium*. Studies in the History of Art. Vol. 26. Washington, D.C.: National Gallery of Art, 1990.

———. "Winslow Homer's *School Time*: A Picture Thoroughly National." In *Essays in Honor of Paul Mellon, Collector and Benefactor*, edited by John Wilmerding, 47–69. Washington, D.C.: National Gallery of Art, 1986.

Cikovsky, Nicolai, Jr., and Franklin Kelly. *Winslow Homer*. New Haven, Conn.: Yale University Press, 1995.

Coke, Van Deren. *The Painter and the Photograph: From Delacroix to Warhol*. Albuquerque: University of New Mexico Press, 1964.

Conrads, Margaret. *Winslow Homer and His Critics: Forging a National Art in the 1870s*. Princeton, N.J.: Princeton University Press, 2001.

Cooper, Helen. *Winslow Homer Watercolors*. New Haven, Conn.: Yale University Art Gallery, 1986.

Cox, Kenyon. "The Art of Winslow Homer." *Scribner's Magazine* 56, no. 3 (September 1914): 377–88.

Danly, Susan, and Cheryl Leibold, eds. *Eakins and the Photograph: Works by Thomas Eakins and His Circle in the Collection of the Pennsylvania Academy of the Fine Arts*. Washington, D.C.: Smithsonian Institution Press, 1994.

Davidson, Gail, et al. *Frederic Church, Winslow Homer, and Thomas Moran: Tourism and the American Landscape*. New York: Bulfinch, 2006.

Denenberg, Thomas A., ed. *Weatherbeaten: Winslow Homer and Maine*. New Haven, Conn.: Yale University Press, 2012.

Docherty, Linda J. "A Problem of Perspective: Winslow Homer, John H. Sherwood, and *Weaning the Calf*." *North Carolina Museum of Art Bulletin* 16 (1993): 32–48.

Downes, William H. *The Life and Works of Winslow Homer*. Boston: Houghton Mifflin, 1911.

Ferber, Linda, and William Gerdts. *The New Path: Ruskin and the American Pre-Raphaelites*. New York: Schocken, 1985.

Foster, Kathleen. *Shipwreck! Winslow Homer and "The Life Line."* Philadelphia: Philadelphia Museum of Art, 2012.

Foster, Kathleen, et al. *Thomas Eakins Rediscovered: Charles Bregler's Thomas Eakins Collection at the Pennsylvania Academy of the Fine Arts*. New Haven, Conn.: Yale University Press, 1998.

Gardner, Albert Ten Eyck. *Winslow Homer: American Artist*. New York: C. N. Potter, 1961.

Gardner, Alexander. *Gardner's Photographic Sketch Book of the Civil War*. New York: Dover, 1959.

Gelman, Barbara. *The Wood Engravings of Winslow Homer*. New York: Crown, 1969.

Gerdts, Abigail Booth, and Lloyd Goodrich. *Record of Works by Winslow Homer*. 6 vols. New York: Spanierman Gallery, 2005–14.

Goodrich, Lloyd. *The Graphic Art of Winslow Homer*. New York: Museum of Graphic Art, 1968.

———. *Winslow Homer*. New York: Macmillan, 1944.

———. *Winslow Homer*. New York: Whitney Museum of American Art, 1973.

Griffin, Randall C. *Homer, Eakins, and Anshutz: The Search for American Identity in the Gilded Age*. University Park: Pennsylvania State University Press, 2004.

———. *Winslow Homer: An American Vision*. New York: Phaidon, 2006.

Hannaway, Patti. *Winslow Homer in the Tropics*. New York: Westover, 1973.

Harrison, Tony. *Winslow Homer in England*. Ocean Park, Maine: Hornby Editions, 2004.

Harvey, Eleanor. *The Civil War and American Art*. New Haven, Conn.: Yale University Press, 2012.

Hendricks, Gordon. *The Life and Work of Winslow Homer*. New York: Harry N. Abrams, 1979.

Hiley, Michael. *Frank Sutcliffe: Photographer of Whitby*. Boston: D. R. Godine, 1974.

Jacobson, Ken, and Jenny Jacobson. *Carrying off the Palaces: John Ruskin's Lost Daguerreotypes*. London: Quaritch, 2015.

James, Henry. "On Some Pictures Lately Exhibited." *Galaxy* 20 (July 1875): 89–97.

Johns, Elizabeth. *Winslow Homer: The Nature of Observation*. Berkeley: University of California Press, 2002.

Jones, Kimberly, et al. *In the Forest of Fontainebleau: Painters and Photographers from Corot to Monet*. New Haven, Conn.: Yale University Press, 2008.

Junker, Patricia. *Winslow Homer in the 1890s: Prout's Neck Observed*. New York: Hudson Hills, 1990.

———, ed. *Winslow Homer: Artist and Angler*. New York: Thames & Hudson, 2003.

Kelsey, Robin. *Photography and the Art of Chance*. Cambridge, Mass.: Harvard University Press, 2015.

Kimball, Roger. "Modernizing Winslow Homer." In *The Rape of the Masters*, 115–28. San Francisco: Encounter Books, 2004.

Kushner, Marilyn, et al. *Winslow Homer: Illustrating America*. New York: George Braziller, 2000.

Leja, Michael. *Looking Askance: Skepticism and American Art from Eakins to Duchamp*. Berkeley: University of California Press, 2007.

Lynes, Barbara Buhler, and Jonathan Weinberg, eds. *Shared Intelligence: American Painting and the Photograph*. Berkeley: University of California Press, 2011.

Mayer, Lance, and Gay Myers. *American Painters on Technique, 1860–1945*. Los Angeles: Getty Publications, 2013.

Prown, Jules. "Winslow Homer in His Art." In *Reading American Art*, edited by Marianne Doezema and Elizabeth Milroy, 264–79. New Haven, Conn.: Yale University Press, 1998.

Rensselaer, Mariana G. Van. *Six Portraits: Della Robbia, Correggio, Blake, Corot, George Fuller, Winslow Homer*. Boston: Houghton Mifflin, 1889.

Robertson, Bruce. *Reckoning with Winslow Homer: His Late Paintings and Their Influence*. Cleveland: Cleveland Museum of Art, 1990.

Robinson, Mike, and David Picard, eds. *The Framed World: Tourism, Tourists, and Photography*. London: Ashgate, 2009.

Sheldon, George. "American Painters—Winslow Homer and F. A. Bridgman." *Art Journal* 4 (August 1878): 225–29.

———. *Hours with Art and Artists*. New York: D. Appleton, 1882.

Simpson, Marc. *Winslow Homer: The Clark Collection*. New Haven, Conn.: Yale University Press, 2013.

Simpson, Marc, et al. *Winslow Homer: Paintings of the Civil War*. San Francisco: Fine Arts Museums of San Francisco, 1988.

Staiti, Paul. "Winslow Homer and the Drama of Thermodynamics." *American Art* 15, no. 1 (Spring 2001): 10–33.

Stonehouse, Augustus. "Winslow Homer." *Art Review* (February 1887): 84–86.

Strauss, David. "Towards a Consumer Culture: 'Adirondack Murray' and the Wilderness Vacation." *American Quarterly* 39, no. 2 (Summer 1987): 270–86.

Tatham, David. "Trapper, Hunter, and Woodsman: Winslow Homer's Adirondack Figures." *American Art Journal* 22, no. 4 (Winter 1990): 41–67.

———. *Winslow Homer and the Illustrated Book*. Syracuse, N.Y.: Syracuse University Press, 1992.

———. *Winslow Homer and the Pictorial Press*. Syracuse, N.Y.: Syracuse University Press, 2003.

———. *Winslow Homer in London: A New York Artist Abroad*. Syracuse, N.Y.: Syracuse University Press, 2010.

———. *Winslow Homer in the Adirondacks*. Syracuse, N.Y.: Syracuse University Press, 2004.

———. "Winslow Homer's Library." *American Art Journal* 9, no. 1 (May 1977): 92–98.

Tedeschi, Martha, and Kristi Dahm. *Watercolors by Winslow Homer: The Color of Light*. New Haven, Conn.: Yale University Press, 2008.

Thompson, Krista A. *An Eye for the Tropics: Tourism, Photography, and Framing the Caribbean Picturesque*. Durham, N.C.: Duke University Press, 2006.

Unger, Miles. *The Watercolors of Winslow Homer*. New York: W. W. Norton, 2001.

Updike, John. *Still Looking: Essays on American Art*. New York: Alfred A. Knopf, 2005.

Waggoner, Diane, et al. *East of the Mississippi: Nineteenth-Century American Landscape Photography*. New Haven, Conn.: Yale University Press, 2017.

———. *The Pre-Raphaelite Lens: British Photography and Painting, 1848–1875*. London: Ashgate, 2010.

Walsh, Judith C. "Observations on the Watercolor Techniques of Homer and Sargent." In *American Traditions in Watercolor: The Worcester Art Museum Collection*, 45–65. New York: Abbeville, 1987.

Wilmerding, John, ed. *Essays in Honor of Paul Mellon, Collector and Benefactor*. Washington, D.C.: National Gallery of Art, 1986.

———. *Winslow Homer*. New York: Praeger, 1972.

———. "Winslow Homer's English Period." *American Art Journal* 7, no. 2 (November 1975): 60–69.

Wilson, Christopher Kent. "Winslow Homer's *The Veteran in a New Field*: A Study of the Harvest Metaphor and Popular Culture." *American Art Journal* 17, no. 4 (Autumn 1985): 2–27.

Wolf, Bryan J. "The Labor of Seeing: Pragmatism, Ideology, and Gender in Winslow Homer's *The Morning Bell*." *Prospects* 17 (1992): 273–318.

Wood, Peter. *Near Andersonville: Winslow Homer's Civil War*. Cambridge, Mass.: Harvard University Press, 2010.

———. "Waiting in Limbo: A Reconsideration of Winslow Homer's *The Gulf Stream*." In *The Southern Enigma: Essays in Race, Class and Folk Culture*, edited by Walter J. Fraser and Winifred B. Moore, Jr., 76–95. Westport, Conn.: Greenwood Press, 1983.

———. *Weathering the Storm: Inside Winslow Homer's "Gulf Stream."* Athens: University of Georgia Press, 2004.

Wood, Peter, and Karen Dalton. *Winslow Homer's Images of Blacks: The Civil War and Reconstruction Years*. Austin: University of Texas Press, 1988.

INDEX

Page references in *italics* refer to illustrations.

ILLUSTRATION CREDITS

Addison Gallery of American Art, Phillips Academy, Andover, MA / Art Resource, NY: plate 47

The Art Institute of Chicago / Art Resource, NY: Byrd fig. 9

Photo: Brooklyn Museum: plates 44, 50, 62; Byrd fig. 7

© 1999 Christie's Images Limited: plates 60G, 60I, 60K

Image © The Columbus Museum: plate 35

Thomas Colville Fine Art, LLC: Byrd fig. 3

Cooper-Hewitt, National Design Museum, Smithsonian Institution / Art Resource, NY: plate 34, Photo: Matt Flynn: plate 15

Photography by Luc Demers: plates 1–4, 7, 17, 21, 32, 42; Goodyear figs. 7, 23

Detroit Institute of Arts, USA / Founders Society purchase and Dexter M. Ferry Jr. fund / Bridgeman Images: plate 8

Image courtesy de Young Museum, San Francisco: plate 25

Photography by Dennis Griggs: frontispiece; Goodyear fig. 2

Photo: Imaging Department © President and Fellows of Harvard College: plate 63

© President and Fellows of Harvard College: Goodyear fig. 3

Photography by: Mitro Hood: plate 23

Mead Art Museum, Amherst College, Massachusetts, Gift of George D. Pratt (Class of 1893) / Bridgeman Images: plate 58

Photograph © 2018 Museum of Fine Arts, Boston: plate 54; Goodyear fig. 6; Byrd fig. 15

Photography by Pixel Acuity: Byrd fig. 14

Schlesinger Library, Radcliffe Institute, Harvard University: Byrd fig. 4

Digital photography by Peter Siegel: plates 28, 29, 32, 33, 48, 49, 51, 61; Goodyear figs. 1, 24

© Smith College Museum of Art, Petegorsky / Gipe photo: plate 18

Smithsonian American Art Museum, Washington, D.C. / Art Resource, NY: plate 59

Image © Sterling and Francine Clark Art Institute, Williamstown, Massachusetts, USA (photo by Michael Agee): plates 36, 60B

Image Courtesy of The Strong, Rochester, New York: plate 37

© The Sutcliffe Gallery: Goodyear fig. 22

Terra Foundation for American Art, Chicago / Art Resource, NY: plate 12

Allen Phillips/Wadsworth Atheneum: plates 22, 40

Image Courtesy of the Worcester Art Museum (MA): plates 55, 64; Goodyear fig. 21; Byrd fig. 16

Yale University Art Gallery: plates 41, 53

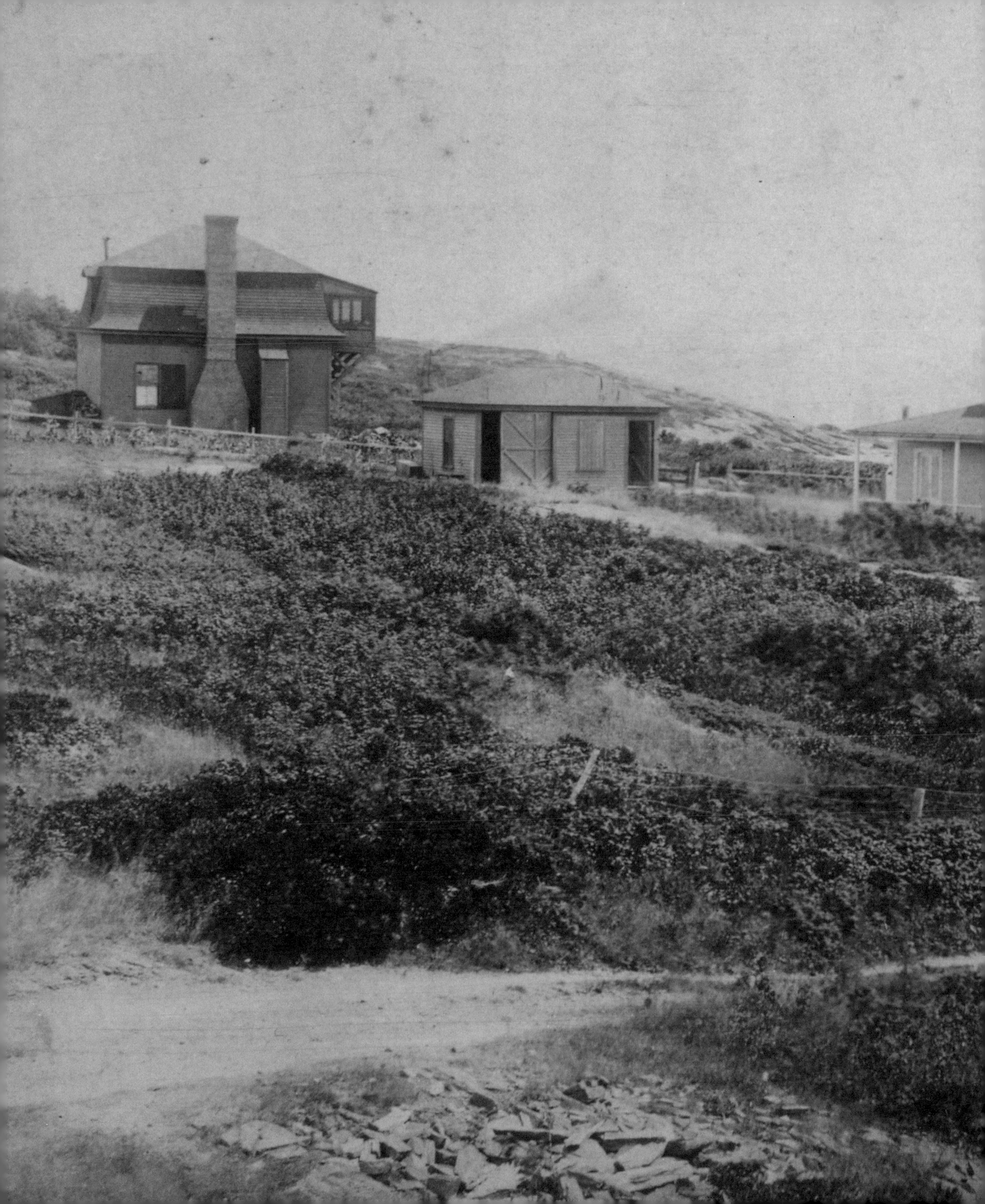